Internetworking Technologies Handbook, Fourth Edition

Cisco Systems, et. al.

Cisco Press

800 East 96th Street, 3rd Floor
Indianapolis, IN 46240 USA

Internetworking Technologies Handbook, Fourth Edition

Cisco Systems et al.

Copyright © 2004 Cisco Systems, Inc.

Cisco Press logo is a trademark of Cisco Systems, Inc.

Published by:
Cisco Press
800 East 96th Street, 3rd Floor
Indianapolis, IN 46240 USA

Printed in the United States of America 1 2 3 4 5 6 7 8 9 0

First Printing September 2003

Library of Congress Cataloging-in-Publication Number: 619472051191

ISBN: 1-58705-119-2

Warning and Disclaimer

This book is designed to provide information about internetworking technologies. Every effort has been made to make this book as complete and accurate as possible, but no warranty or fitness is implied.

The information is provided on an "as is" basis. The authors, Cisco Press, and Cisco Systems, Inc. shall have neither liability nor responsibility to any person or entity with respect to any loss or damages arising from the information contained in this book or from the use of the discs or programs that may accompany it.

The opinions expressed in this book belong to the authors and are not necessarily those of Cisco Systems, Inc.

Trademark Acknowledgments

All terms mentioned in this book that are known to be trademarks or service marks have been appropriately capitalized. Cisco Press or Cisco Systems, Inc. cannot attest to the accuracy of this information. Use of a term in this book should not be regarded as affecting the validity of any trademark or service mark.

Feedback Information

At Cisco Press, our goal is to create in-depth technical books of the highest quality and value. Each book is crafted with care and precision, undergoing rigorous development that involves the unique expertise of members of the professional technical community.

Reader feedback is a natural continuation of this process. If you have any comments regarding how we could improve the quality of this book, or otherwise alter it to better suit your needs, you can contact us through e-mail at feedback@ciscopress.com. Please make sure to include the book title and ISBN in your message.

We greatly appreciate your assistance.

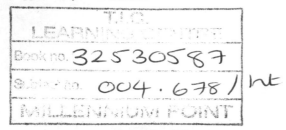

Publisher	John Wait
Editor-In-Chief	John Kane
Cisco Representative	Anthony Wolfenden
Cisco Press Program Manager	Sonia Torres Chavez
Cisco Marketing Communications Manager	Scott Miller
Cisco Marketing Program Manager	Edie Quiroz
Executive Editor	Jim Schachterle
Managing Editor	Patrick Kanouse
Development Editor	Jill Batistick
Project Editor	Marc Fowler
Copy Editor	Gayle Johnson
Author Contributors	Tony Allen, Matt Carling, Bradley Dunsmore, Sachin Gupta, Wayne Hickey, Qiang Huang, Marcelo Nobrega, Tom Nosella, Ivan Pepelnjak, Danny Rodriguez, Marcus Sitzman, Srinivas Vegesna
Technical Editors	Bruce Alexander, Tony Allen, Jeff Apcar, Brad Dunsmore, Venkat Kankipati, Saeed Sardar
Team Coordinator	Tammi Barnett
Book Designer	Gina Rexrode
Cover Designer	Louisa Adair
Production Team	Octal Publishing
Indexer	Tim Wright

CISCO SYSTEMS

Corporate Headquarters
Cisco Systems, Inc.
170 West Tasman Drive
San Jose, CA 95134-1706
USA
www.cisco.com
Tel: 408 526-4000
    800 553-NETS (6387)
Fax: 408 526-4100

European Headquarters
Cisco Systems International BV
Haarlerbergpark
Haarlerbergweg 13-19
1101 CH Amsterdam
The Netherlands
www-europe.cisco.com
Tel: 31 0 20 357 1000
Fax: 31 0 20 357 1100

Americas Headquarters
Cisco Systems, Inc.
170 West Tasman Drive
San Jose, CA 95134-1706
USA
www.cisco.com
Tel: 408 526-7660
Fax: 408 527-0883

Asia Pacific Headquarters
Cisco Systems, Inc.
Capital Tower
168 Robinson Road
#22-01 to #29-01
Singapore 068912
www.cisco.com
Tel: +65 6317 7777
Fax: +65 6317 7799

Cisco Systems has more than 200 offices in the following countries and regions. Addresses, phone numbers, and fax numbers are listed on the **Cisco.com Web site at www.cisco.com/go/offices.**

Argentina • Australia • Austria • Belgium • Brazil • Bulgaria • Canada • Chile • China PRC • Colombia • Costa Rica • Croatia • Czech Republic
Denmark • Dubai, UAE • Finland • France • Germany • Greece • Hong Kong SAR • Hungary • India • Indonesia • Ireland • Israel • Italy
Japan • Korea • Luxembourg • Malaysia • Mexico • The Netherlands • New Zealand • Norway • Peru • Philippines • Poland • Portugal
Puerto Rico • Romania • Russia • Saudi Arabia • Scotland • Singapore • Slovakia • Slovenia • South Africa • Spain • Sweden
Switzerland • Taiwan • Thailand • Turkey • Ukraine • United Kingdom • United States • Venezuela • Vietnam • Zimbabwe

Contents at a Glance

Table of Contents

Icons Used in This Book

Cisco uses the following standard icons to represent different networking devices.
You will encounter several of these icons within this book.

 Router

 Multilayer Switch

 Switch

 PIX Firewall

 ATM Switch

 Content Switch

 Route/Switch Processor

 Cisco 7500 Series Router

 ISDN/Frame Relay switch

 Hub

 Bridge

 NetRanger Intrusion Detection System

 Local Director

 Access Server

 CiscoSecure Scanner

 IP/TV Broadcast Server

 Cisco CallManager

 Cisco Directory Server

 PC

 Laptop

 Cisco Works Workstation

 Web Browser

 Web Server

 Network Cloud

 Concentrator

 Phone

 Gateway

 Fax

 File Server

 Printer

 VPN Concentrator

Command Syntax Conventions

The conventions used to present command syntax in this book are the same conventions used in the IOS Command Reference. The Command Reference describes these conventions as follows:

- Vertical bars (|) separate alternative, mutually exclusive elements.

- Square brackets ([ ]) indicate an optional element.

- Braces ({ }) indicate a required choice.

- Braces within brackets ([{ }]) indicate a required choice within an optional element.

- **Bold** indicates commands and keywords that are entered literally as shown. In configuration examples and output (not general command syntax), bold indicates commands that are manually input by the user (such as a show command).

- *Italic* indicates arguments for which you supply actual values.

Introduction

Networking and the Internet have become one of the most influential forces in our lives today. They continue to change the way we work, live, play, and learn. In less than ten years, the entire world has become connected, making it easy and inexpensive to communicate around the globe instantly. Few would argue that the Internet has changed every aspect of our lives. It's improved education and made the world's information available to any student anywhere, anytime; it's how we communicate with our relatives; it's how we plan our vacations. We now have the world and its information at our fingertips—creating new opportunities for every business, government, educational institution, and individual.

This book seeks to give you a fundamental understanding of the different concepts and technologies used in the field of networking. This book is a comprehensive reference that surveys a number of different networking technologies, protocols, and paradigms; legacy technologies are included as well as the most current technologies. It is our hope at Cisco Press that you will find the fourth edition of this book current, relevant, and useful, whether you are a networking engineer or other networking professional or a business decision-maker. This book is also helpful if you simply want to understand more about the Internet and the technologies on which it runs.

Objectives

This book provides basic technical information about the various technologies used in the field of networking. It is designed for use with other Cisco Press books and as a standalone reference tool.

This book is not intended to provide all possible information on the technologies covered; rather, it seeks to provide a general overview highlighting the most relevant and important details of each technology.

Updates to the Fourth Edition

For the publication of the fourth edition of this book, we have added new chapters on optical networking, Voice over IP (VoIP), DPT/SRT, EAP, storage networking, QoS, and IOS. There are also many updates to existing chapters, and the most relevant and current information has been included where appropriate.

Audience

The Internetworking Technologies Handbook is written for anyone who wants to understand internetworking. We anticipate that the information in this book will help you assess the applicability of specific technologies in your networking environments and give you a basic understanding of the many internetworking technologies.

Organization

This book is organized into the following nine sections:

- **Part I: Introduction to Internetworking**—Provides introductory information about the basic concepts and technologies of networking, including LAN and WAN technologies, Cisco IOS software, bridging and switching technologies, routing protocols, and network management.

- **Part II: LAN Protocols**—Covers LAN protocols and their technologies.

- **Part III: WAN Technologies**—Discusses WAN technologies, including Frame Relay, HSSI, ISDN, PPP, SMDS, dialup, SDLC, X.25, and VPNs.

- **Part IV: Multiservice Access Technologies**—Provides overview information on access networking technologies, including voice/data integration, wireless, DSL, cable, optical, VoIP, DPT/SRT, and EAP.

- **Part V: Bridging and Switching**—Discusses bridging and switching technologies, including transparent bridging, mixed-media bridging, source-route bridging, LAN switching and VLANs, ATM, MPLS, and data link switching.

- **Part VI: Network Protocols**—Covers networking protocols, including OSIP, IP, IPv6, NetWare, AppleTalk, IBM SNA, and DECnet.

- **Part VII: Routing Protocols**—Provides overview information on routing protocols, including BGP, Enhanced IGRP, IBM SNA, IGRP, Internet Protocol Multicast, NetWare Link-Services, OSPF, OSIRP, routing information, resource reservation, and SMRP.

- **Part VIII: Network Management**—Discusses security technologies, directory-enabled networking, network caching technologies, and storage networking.

- **Appendixes:**—These Appendixes provide answers to review questions and discussion of early technologies.

Acknowledgments and Contributors

Cisco Press would like to express its deepest gratitude to the talented people who contributed to the fourth edition of this book. Without their help and expertise, we would not have been able to publish this edition. Thank you to all who helped write and edit the chapters in this new edition. In alphabetical order, the contributors are as follows:

Bruce Alexander is the technical marketing manager for the Cisco Systems Wireless Networking Business Unit. He joined Cisco as a result of Cisco's acquisition of Aironet Wireless Communications, where he was the director of technical support. He has worked in the RF technology area for more than 27 years, and he has worked with RF WAN technology for 17 years. Alexander has worked extensively with the RF engineering group at Texlon, in both hardware and software, where he was the senior instructor for national education centers. Additionally, he has held an amateur radio license since 1978. He is a cofounder of Ameritron Amateur Radio Company. Alexander attended Akron University, where he majored in computer programming and business administration.

Tony Allen, CD (Canadian Decoration), is a network consulting engineer working for Cisco Systems on the Americas International Advanced Services Team in Toronto, Canada. For the last four years, he has helped service provider customers plan, design, implement, and operate their network solutions. Before joining Cisco, he spent 17 years with the Canadian Military, working in a variety of telecommunications engineering and maintenance positions. He currently specializes in the design, engineering, and testing of VoIP, optical wireless technologies, and broadband networks. He has a wife, Deborah, and two children: Sara, 5, and Alexander, 3. His hobbies include keeping abreast of the latest technology, gardening, physical fitness, and spending quality time with his family.

Matt Carling is a network consulting engineer in the Advanced Services Group at Cisco Systems. During the past three years at Cisco, he has worked closely with many service provider customers to provide networking optimization solutions, technology and services deployment, and implementation of Cisco best practices networking techniques. He has more than 12 years of experience in networking. He has a bachelor of engineering degree in computer engineering and a graduate diploma in management sciences, both from the University of Canberra, Australia.

Bradley Dunsmore is a new product instructor for the Advanced Services Group at Cisco Systems in Research Triangle Park, N.C. He holds the Cisco CCNP, CCDP, CCSI, and CSS-1 certifications, as well as an MCSE+Internet from Microsoft. In his current position, he designs network topologies for new courses in his group and trains instructors to teach the courses. Additionally, he designs networks that allow the remote and secure downloading of these courses. He specializes in SS7 Interconnect solutions, WAN communications, and Cisco security products.

Sachin Gupta is a product manager for the Cisco Catalyst 6500. He holds a CCIE certification in Routing and Switching. Before his current position, he worked for Cisco as a technical marketing engineer in the Internet Technologies division, where he focused on Cisco IOS software technologies. Before that, Gupta was a customer support engineer at Cisco. He has a master's degree in electrical engineering from Stanford University.

Wayne Hickey has more than 20 years of telecommunications and computer data experience, including SONET, SDH, DWDM, IP, ATM, Frame, HFC, voice, video, and SSEM. He is a product manager for the Optical Technical Business Unit at Cisco Systems. Previously, he spent 19 years working for Aliant Telecom (NBTel), the third-largest telecommunications provider in Canada, where he focused on transmission network design and the evaluation of emerging access and transmission technologies. Hickey has coauthored and authored several papers on Polarization Mode Dispersion (PMD) and long-haul transmission systems. He has applied for several patents on primary and secondary projects for hybrid fiber coaxial (HFC).

Qiang Huang, CCIE No. 4937, is a customer support engineer in the Cisco VPN and Network Security Groups. He has extensive knowledge in many security products and technologies, and he has served as the technical lead for his group for the past several years. Huang has multiple CCIE certifications, including ISP Dial, Routing and Switching, and Security. He has a master's degree in electrical and computer engineering from Colorado State University.

Venkat Kankipati has been a software development manager at Cisco Systems for six years. His expertise spans a wide range of technologies, including SNA protocols and security and network performance. Before joining Cisco, he worked for Bay Networks. Kankipati has a master's degree in computer science from the University of Massachusetts, a master's degree in computer applications from the University of Madras, and a bachelor of science degree from the University of Bombay, India.

Marcelo Nobrega, CCIE No. 8069, is a senior network consulting engineer at Cisco Systems in the Advanced Services Group, which supports Americas International Theater. He has worked with design deployment, administration, and troubleshooting of large service provider networks since 1994. He has been with Cisco Systems since 2000. His focus has been on core IP and routing protocols, network management, IP Telephony, and, most recently, IP call centers. Nobrega has a bachelor of science degree in electronic engineering and a master's degree in computer science from Pontificia Universidade Catolica University in Rio de Janeiro, Brazil.

Tom Nosella, CCIE No. 1395, is senior manager of technical marketing in the Storage Technology Group at Cisco Systems. He and his team create, validate, and promote Cisco storage networking designs and solutions for Cisco's enterprise and service provider customers. Before joining Cisco, he was director of engineering at Bell Canada in Residential and Commercial Internet Services, where he led a team of senior engineers. He has a bachelor of engineering and management degree from McMaster University in Ontario, Canada.

Ivan Pepelnjak, CCIE No. 1354, has more than ten years of experience in designing, installing, troubleshooting, and operating large service provider and enterprise WAN and LAN networks. He is chief technologies advisor at NIL Data Communications. He is the architect of NIL's Service Provider Academy program, he is one of the architects of the Service Provider curriculum at Cisco Systems, and he is the lead developer of several service provider courses that cover MPLS, BGP, and IP QoS. Pepelnjak is one of the Cisco routing authorities in Europe. He wrote the Cisco Press book EIGRP Network Design Solutions and cowrote the Cisco Press book MPLS and VPN Architectures.

Danny Rodriguez is a network security engineer in the Security Consulting Services organization at Cisco Systems, where he performs security posture assessments and security design reviews for Fortune 500 companies. He is also responsible for the training and development of the other security engineers in his group. During his tenure with Cisco, he has been an education specialist in the Security Training department in the Cisco Internet Learning and Solutions Group (ILSG). He authored the Cisco Intrusion Detection courses and contributed to lab exercises for Cisco's core security courses. He also has taught courses on security to Cisco engineers, Cisco learning and Channel Partners, and end users. Rodriguez was also a key contributor to the CCSP certification program. He holds certifications as a CCDA and a CSS-1.

Saeed Sardar has worked as a development engineer in the High-Speed Switching Group at Cisco Systems for more than two years. He has worked extensively with testing and resolving control and data plane issues for Cisco IOS on the Cisco Catalyst 6000 series relating to IPv4, IPv6, MPLS, QoS, and multicast routing and hardware forwarding on a variety of LAN and WAN modules.

Marcus Sitzman, CCIE No. 9004, is a network security engineer with Cisco Systems. He has more than six years of experience in the networking field. Since joining Cisco in 2000, he has continued to focus on security technologies and products. He currently provides security posture assessments and security consulting to Cisco customers. He has trained other Cisco engineers in the area of security and was the technical speaker at Cisco's Networkers Convention.

Alan Troup is a technical writer for the Cisco MDS 9000 family of storage switches. He was previously a technical publications manager in one of Cisco's optical switch divisions. He has a bachelor of arts degree in English from San Jose State University.

Srinivas Vegesna, CCIE No. 1399, is manager of software development in Core IP Engineering at Cisco Systems. Before his current position, he was a consulting engineer and manager of Cisco's Service Provider Consulting Services. His expertise is in general IP networking, with a special focus on IP and IP QoS. In his more than eight years at Cisco, Vegesna has worked with a large number of service provider and enterprise customers, helping them design, implement, and troubleshoot large-scale IP networks. He has a master of science degree from Arizona State University and an MBA from Santa Clara University.

Third Edition Contributors

Contributors to the Third Edition (in alphabetical order) are Marc Bresniker, Gerry Burgess, Dave Buster, Kevin Hamilton, Brian Junnila, Andrew Kessler, William Lane, Kevin Mahler, Erick Mar, Kevin Mousseau, Jim O'Shea, William Parkhurst, Edie Quiroz, Neil Reid, Frank Rivest, Mark Sportack, John Strassner, and Natalie Timms.

First Edition Contributors

Principal authors of the first edition of this book were Merilee Ford, H. Kim Lew, Steve Spanier, and Tim Stevenson.

Introduction to Internetworking

Objectives

- Learn what makes up an internetwork.
- Learn the basics of the OSI model.
- Learn the differences between connection-oriented and connectionless services.
- Learn about the different types of addresses used in an internetwork.
- Learn about flow control and error-checking basics.

CHAPTER 1

Internetworking Basics

This chapter works with the next six chapters to act as a foundation for the technology discussions that follow. In this chapter, some fundamental concepts and terms used in the evolving language of internetworking are addressed. In the same way that this book provides a foundation for understanding modern networking, this chapter summarizes some common themes presented throughout the remainder of this book. Topics include flow control, error checking, and multiplexing, but this chapter focuses mainly on mapping the Open System Interconnection (OSI) model to networking/internetworking functions, and also summarizing the general nature of addressing schemes within the context of the OSI model. The OSI model represents the building blocks for internetworks. Understanding the conceptual model helps you understand the complex pieces that make up an internetwork.

What Is an Internetwork?

An *internetwork* is a collection of individual networks, connected by intermediate networking devices, that functions as a single large network. Internetworking refers to the industry, products, and procedures that meet the challenge of creating and administering internetworks. Figure 1-1 illustrates some different kinds of network technologies that can be interconnected by routers and other networking devices to create an internetwork.

Figure 1-1 *Different Network Technologies Can Be Connected to Create an Internetwork*

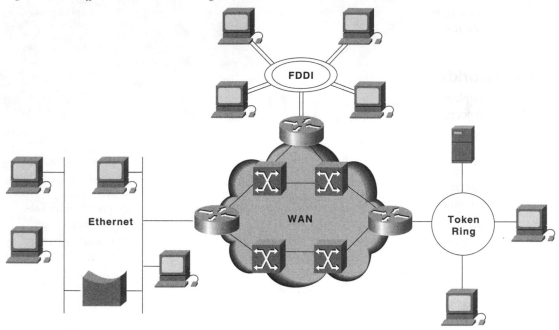

History of Internetworking

The first networks were time-sharing networks that used mainframes and attached terminals. Such environments were implemented by both IBM's Systems Network Architecture (SNA) and Digital's network architecture.

Local-area networks (LANs) evolved around the PC revolution. LANs enabled multiple users in a relatively small geographical area to exchange files and messages, as well as access shared resources such as file servers and printers.

Wide-area networks (WANs) interconnect LANs with geographically dispersed users to create connectivity. Some of the technologies used for connecting LANs include T1, T3, ATM, ISDN, ADSL, Frame Relay, radio links, and others. New methods of connecting dispersed LANs are appearing everyday.

Today, high-speed LANs and switched internetworks are becoming widely used, largely because they operate at very high speeds and support such high-bandwidth applications as multimedia and videoconferencing.

Internetworking evolved as a solution to three key problems: isolated LANs, duplication of resources, and a lack of network management. Isolated LANs made electronic communication between different offices or departments impossible. Duplication of resources meant that the same hardware and software had to be supplied to each office or department, as did separate support staff. This lack of network management meant that no centralized method of managing and troubleshooting networks existed.

Internetworking Challenges

Implementing a functional internetwork is no simple task. Many challenges must be faced, especially in the areas of connectivity, reliability, network management, and flexibility. Each area is key in establishing an efficient and effective internetwork.

The challenge when connecting various systems is to support communication among disparate technologies. Different sites, for example, may use different types of media operating at varying speeds, or may even include different types of systems that need to communicate.

Because companies rely heavily on data communication, internetworks must provide a certain level of reliability. This is an unpredictable world, so many large internetworks include redundancy to allow for communication even when problems occur.

Furthermore, network management must provide centralized support and troubleshooting capabilities in an internetwork. Configuration, security, performance, and other issues must be adequately addressed for the internetwork to function smoothly. Security within an internetwork is essential. Many people think of network security from the perspective of protecting the private network from outside attacks. However, it is just as important to protect the network from internal attacks, especially because most security breaches come from inside. Networks must also be secured so that the internal network cannot be used as a tool to attack other external sites.

Early in the year 2000, many major web sites were the victims of distributed denial of service (DDOS) attacks. These attacks were possible because a great number of private networks currently connected with the Internet were not properly secured. These private networks were used as tools for the attackers.

Because nothing in this world is stagnant, internetworks must be flexible enough to change with new demands.

Open System Interconnection Reference Model

The *Open System Interconnection (OSI) reference model* describes how information from a software application in one computer moves through a network medium to a software application in another computer. The OSI reference model is a conceptual model composed of seven layers, each specifying particular network functions. The model was developed by the International Organization for Standardization (ISO) in 1984, and it is now considered the primary architectural model for intercomputer communications. The OSI model divides the tasks involved with moving information between networked computers into seven smaller, more manageable task groups. A task or group of tasks is then assigned to each of the seven OSI layers. Each layer is reasonably self-contained so that the tasks assigned to each layer can be implemented independently. This enables the solutions offered by one layer to be updated without adversely affecting the other layers. The following list details the seven layers of the Open System Interconnection (OSI) reference model:

- Layer 7—Application
- Layer 6—Presentation
- Layer 5—Session
- Layer 4—Transport
- Layer 3—Network
- Layer 2—Data link
- Layer 1—Physical

NOTE   A handy way to remember the seven layers is the sentence "All people seem to need data processing." The beginning letter of each word corresponds to a layer.

- All—Application layer
- People—Presentation layer
- Seem—Session layer
- To—Transport layer
- Need—Network layer
- Data—Data link layer
- Processing—Physical layer

Figure 1-2 illustrates the seven-layer OSI reference model.

Figure 1-2   *The OSI Reference Model Contains Seven Independent Layers*

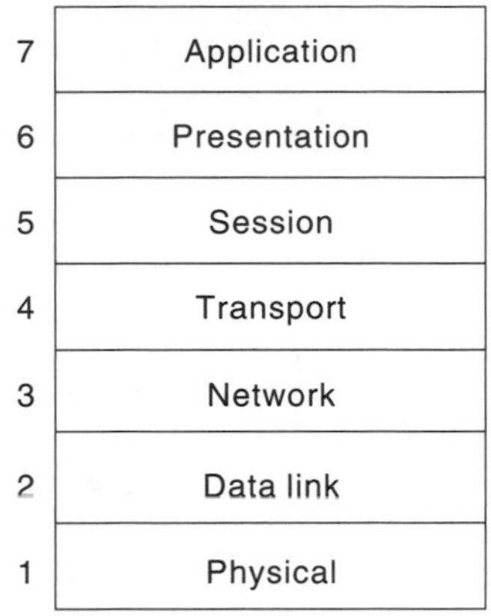

7	Application
6	Presentation
5	Session
4	Transport
3	Network
2	Data link
1	Physical

Characteristics of the OSI Layers

The seven layers of the OSI reference model can be divided into two categories: upper layers and lower layers.

The *upper layers* of the OSI model deal with application issues and generally are implemented only in software. The highest layer, the application layer, is closest to the end user. Both users and application layer processes interact with software applications that contain a communications component. The term upper layer is sometimes used to refer to any layer above another layer in the OSI model.

The *lower layers* of the OSI model handle data transport issues. The physical layer and the data link layer are implemented in hardware and software. The lowest layer, the physical layer, is closest to the physical network medium (the network cabling, for example) and is responsible for actually placing information on the medium.

Figure 1-3 illustrates the division between the upper and lower OSI layers.

Figure 1-3   *Two Sets of Layers Make Up the OSI Layers*

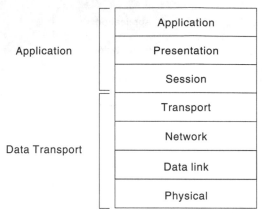

Protocols

The OSI model provides a conceptual framework for communication between computers, but the model itself is not a method of communication. Actual communication is made possible by using communication protocols. In the context of data networking, a *protocol* is a formal set of rules and conventions that governs how computers exchange information over a network medium. A protocol implements the functions of one or more of the OSI layers.

A wide variety of communication protocols exist. Some of these protocols include LAN protocols, WAN protocols, network protocols, and routing protocols. *LAN protocols* operate at the physical and data link layers of the OSI model and define communication over the various LAN media. *WAN protocols* operate at the lowest three layers of the OSI model and define communication over the various wide-area media. *Routing protocols* are network layer protocols that are responsible for exchanging information between routers so that the routers can select the proper path for network traffic. Finally, *network protocols* are the various upper-layer protocols that exist in a given protocol suite. Many protocols rely on others for operation. For example, many routing protocols use network protocols to exchange information between routers. This concept of building upon the layers already in existence is the foundation of the OSI model.

OSI Model and Communication Between Systems

Information being transferred from a software application in one computer system to a software application in another must pass through the OSI layers. For example, if a software application in System A has information to transmit to a software application in System B, the application program in System A will pass its information to the application layer (Layer 7) of System A. The application layer then passes the information to the presentation layer (Layer 6), which relays the data to the session layer (Layer 5), and so on down to the physical layer (Layer 1). At the physical layer, the information is placed on the physical network medium and is sent across the medium to System B. The physical layer of System B removes the information from the physical medium, and then its physical layer passes the information up to the data link layer (Layer 2), which passes it to the network layer (Layer 3), and so on, until it reaches the application layer (Layer 7) of System B. Finally, the application layer of System B passes the information to the recipient application program to complete the communication process.

Interaction Between OSI Model Layers

A given layer in the OSI model generally communicates with three other OSI layers: the layer directly above it, the layer directly below it, and its peer layer in other networked computer systems. The data link layer in System A, for example, communicates with the network layer of System A, the physical layer of System A, and the data link layer in System B. Figure 1-4 illustrates this example.

Figure 1-4   *OSI Model Layers Communicate with Other Layers*

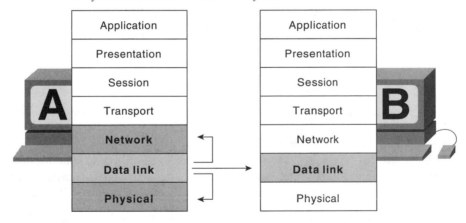

OSI Layer Services

One OSI layer communicates with another layer to make use of the services provided by the second layer. The services provided by adjacent layers help a given OSI layer communicate with its peer layer in other computer systems. Three basic elements are involved in layer services: the service user, the service provider, and the service access point (SAP).

In this context, the *service user* is the OSI layer that requests services from an adjacent OSI layer. The *service provider* is the OSI layer that provides services to service users. OSI layers can provide services to multiple service users. The SAP is a conceptual location at which one OSI layer can request the services of another OSI layer.

Figure 1-5 illustrates how these three elements interact at the network and data link layers.

Figure 1-5   *Service Users, Providers, and SAPs Interact at the Network and Data Link Layers*

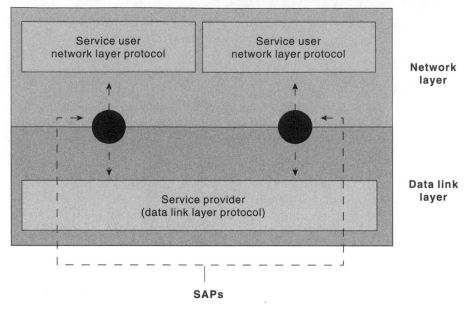

OSI Model Layers and Information Exchange

The seven OSI layers use various forms of control information to communicate with their peer layers in other computer systems. This *control information* consists of specific requests and instructions that are exchanged between peer OSI layers.

Control information typically takes one of two forms: headers and trailers. *Headers* are prepended to data that has been passed down from upper layers. *Trailers* are appended to data that has been passed down from upper layers. An OSI layer is not required to attach a header or a trailer to data from upper layers.

Headers, trailers, and data are relative concepts, depending on the layer that analyzes the information unit. At the network layer, for example, an information unit consists of a Layer 3 header and data. At the data link layer, however, all the information passed down by the network layer (the Layer 3 header and the data) is treated as data.

In other words, the data portion of an information unit at a given OSI layer potentially can contain headers, trailers, and data from all the higher layers. This is known as *encapsulation.* Figure 1-6 shows how the header and data from one layer are encapsulated into the header of the next lowest layer.

Figure 1-6   *Headers and Data Can Be Encapsulated During Information Exchange*

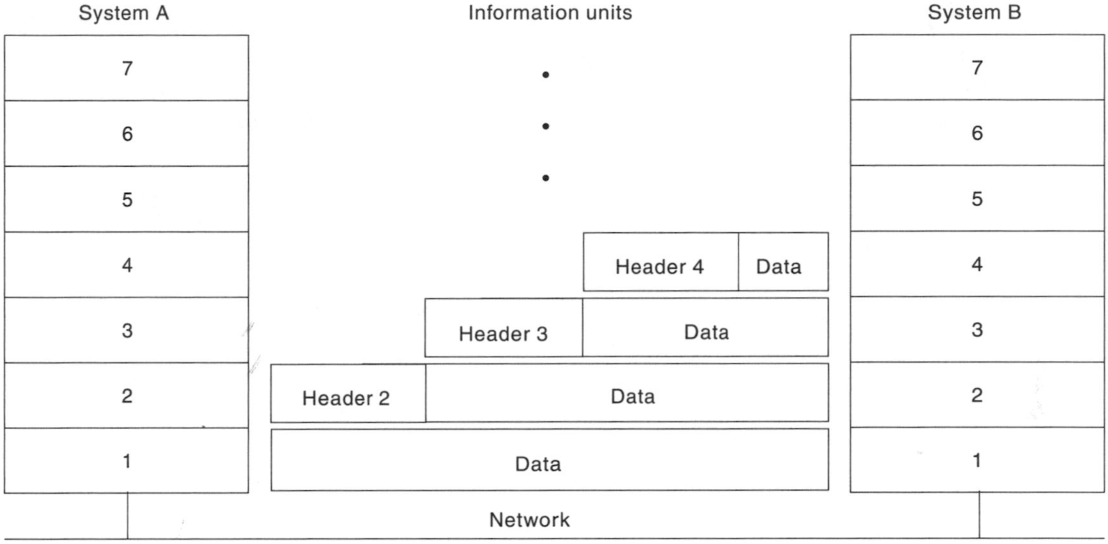

Information Exchange Process

The information exchange process occurs between peer OSI layers. Each layer in the source system adds control information to data, and each layer in the destination system analyzes and removes the control information from that data.

If System A has data from a software application to send to System B, the data is passed to the application layer. The application layer in System A then communicates any control information required by the application layer in System B by prepending a header to the data. The resulting information unit (a header and the data) is passed to the presentation layer, which prepends its own header containing control information intended for the presentation layer in System B. The information unit grows in size as each layer prepends its own header (and, in some cases, a trailer) that contains control information to be used by its peer layer in System B. At the physical layer, the entire information unit is placed onto the network medium.

The physical layer in System B receives the information unit and passes it to the data link layer. The data link layer in System B then reads the control information contained in the header prepended by the data link layer in System A. The header is then removed, and the remainder of the information unit is passed to the network layer. Each layer performs the same actions: The layer reads the header from its peer layer, strips it off, and passes the remaining information unit to the next highest layer. After the application layer performs these actions, the data is passed to the recipient software application in System B, in exactly the form in which it was transmitted by the application in System A.

OSI Model Physical Layer

The physical layer defines the electrical, mechanical, procedural, and functional specifications for activating, maintaining, and deactivating the physical link between communicating network systems. Physical layer specifications define characteristics such as voltage levels, timing of voltage changes, physical data rates, maximum transmission distances, and physical connectors. Physical layer implementations can be categorized as either LAN or WAN specifications. Figure 1-7 illustrates some common LAN and WAN physical layer implementations.

Figure 1-7   *Physical Layer Implementations Can Be LAN or WAN Specifications*

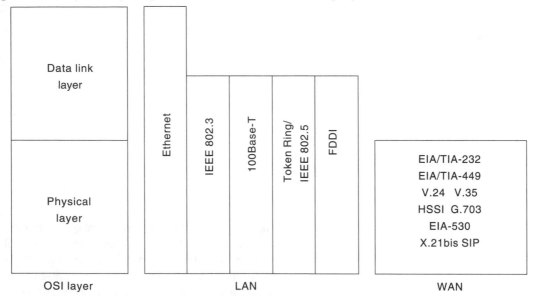

Physical layer implementations

OSI Model Data Link Layer

The data link layer provides reliable transit of data across a physical network link. Different data link layer specifications define different network and protocol characteristics, including physical addressing, network topology, error notification, sequencing of frames, and flow control. Physical addressing (as opposed to network addressing) defines how devices are addressed at the data link layer. Network topology consists of the data link layer specifications that often define how devices are to be physically connected, such as in a bus or a ring topology. Error notification alerts upper-layer protocols that a transmission error has occurred, and the sequencing of data frames reorders frames that are transmitted out of sequence. Finally, flow control moderates the transmission of data so that the receiving device is not overwhelmed with more traffic than it can handle at one time.

The Institute of Electrical and Electronics Engineers (IEEE) has subdivided the data link layer into two sublayers: Logical Link Control (LLC) and Media Access Control (MAC). Figure 1-8 illustrates the IEEE sublayers of the data link layer.

Figure 1-8   *The Data Link Layer Contains Two Sublayers*

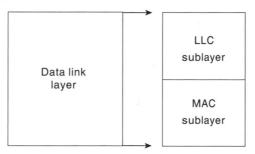

The *Logical Link Control (LLC)* sublayer of the data link layer manages communications between devices over a single link of a network. LLC is defined in the IEEE 802.2 specification and supports both connectionless and connection-oriented services used by higher-layer protocols. IEEE 802.2 defines a number of fields in data link layer frames that enable multiple higher-layer protocols to share a single physical data link. The *Media Access Control (MAC)* sublayer of the data link layer manages protocol access to the physical network medium. The IEEE MAC specification defines MAC addresses, which enable multiple devices to uniquely identify one another at the data link layer.

OSI Model Network Layer

The network layer defines the network address, which differs from the MAC address. Some network layer implementations, such as the Internet Protocol (IP), define network addresses in a way that route selection can be determined systematically by comparing the source network address with the destination network address and applying the subnet mask. Because this layer defines the logical network layout, routers can use this layer to determine how to forward packets. Because of this, much of the design and configuration work for internetworks happens at Layer 3, the network layer.

OSI Model Transport Layer

The transport layer accepts data from the session layer and segments the data for transport across the network. Generally, the transport layer is responsible for making sure that the data is delivered error-free and in the proper sequence. Flow control generally occurs at the transport layer.

Flow control manages data transmission between devices so that the transmitting device does not send more data than the receiving device can process. Multiplexing enables data from several applications to be transmitted onto a single physical link. Virtual circuits are established, maintained, and terminated by the transport layer. Error checking involves creating various mechanisms for detecting transmission errors, while error recovery involves acting, such as requesting that data be retransmitted, to resolve any errors that occur.

The transport protocols used on the Internet are TCP and UDP.

OSI Model Session Layer

The session layer establishes, manages, and terminates communication sessions. Communication sessions consist of service requests and service responses that occur between applications located in different network devices. These requests and responses are coordinated by protocols implemented at the session layer. Some examples of session-layer implementations include Zone Information Protocol (ZIP), the AppleTalk protocol that coordinates the name binding process; and Session Control Protocol (SCP), the DECnet Phase IV session layer protocol.

OSI Model Presentation Layer

The presentation layer provides a variety of coding and conversion functions that are applied to application layer data. These functions ensure that information sent from the application layer of one system would be readable by the application layer of another system. Some examples of presentation layer coding and conversion schemes include common data representation formats, conversion of character representation formats, common data compression schemes, and common data encryption schemes.

Common data representation formats, or the use of standard image, sound, and video formats, enable the interchange of application data between different types of computer systems. Conversion schemes are used to exchange information with systems by using different text and data representations, such as EBCDIC and ASCII. Standard data compression schemes enable data that is compressed at the source device to be properly decompressed at the destination. Standard data encryption schemes enable data encrypted at the source device to be properly deciphered at the destination.

Presentation layer implementations are not typically associated with a particular protocol stack. Some well-known standards for video include QuickTime and Motion Picture Experts Group (MPEG). QuickTime is an Apple Computer specification for video and audio, and MPEG is a standard for video compression and coding.

Among the well-known graphic image formats are Graphics Interchange Format (GIF), Joint Photographic Experts Group (JPEG), and Tagged Image File Format (TIFF). GIF is a standard for compressing and coding graphic images. JPEG is another compression and coding standard for graphic images, and TIFF is a standard coding format for graphic images.

OSI Model Application Layer

The application layer is the OSI layer closest to the end user, which means that both the OSI application layer and the user interact directly with the software application.

This layer interacts with software applications that implement a communicating component. Such application programs fall outside the scope of the OSI model. Application layer functions typically include identifying communication partners, determining resource availability, and synchronizing communication.

When identifying communication partners, the application layer determines the identity and availability of communication partners for an application with data to transmit. When determining resource availability, the application layer must decide whether sufficient network resources for the requested communication exist. In synchronizing communication, all communication between applications requires cooperation that is managed by the application layer.

Some examples of application layer implementations include Telnet, File Transfer Protocol (FTP), and Simple Mail Transfer Protocol (SMTP).

Information Formats

The data and control information that is transmitted through internetworks takes a variety of forms. The terms used to refer to these information formats are not used consistently in the internetworking industry but sometimes are used interchangeably. Common information formats include frames, packets, datagrams, segments, messages, cells, and data units.

A frame is an information unit whose source and destination are data link layer entities. A frame is composed of the data link layer header (and possibly a trailer) and upper-layer data. The header and trailer contain control information intended for the data link layer entity in the destination system. Data from upper-layer entities is encapsulated in the data link layer header and trailer. Figure 1-9 illustrates the basic components of a data link layer frame.

Figure 1-9 *Data from Upper-Layer Entities Makes Up the Data Link Layer Frame*

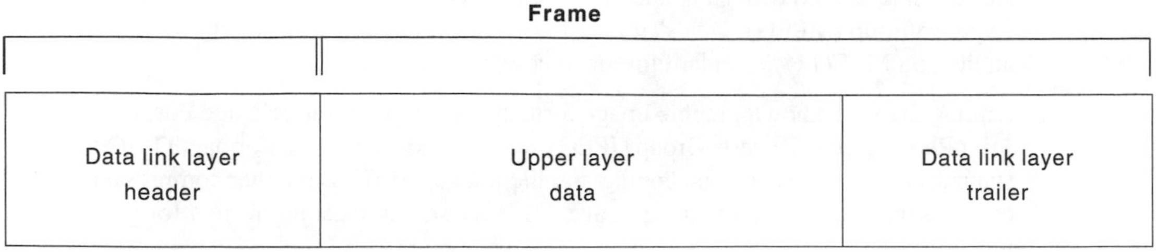

Frame

Data link layer header	Upper layer data	Data link layer trailer

A *packet* is an information unit whose source and destination are network layer entities. A packet is composed of the network layer header (and possibly a trailer) and upper-layer data. The header and trailer contain control information intended for the network layer entity in the destination system. Data from upper-layer entities is encapsulated in the network layer header and trailer. Figure 1-10 illustrates the basic components of a network layer packet.

Figure 1-10 *Three Basic Components Make Up a Network Layer Packet*

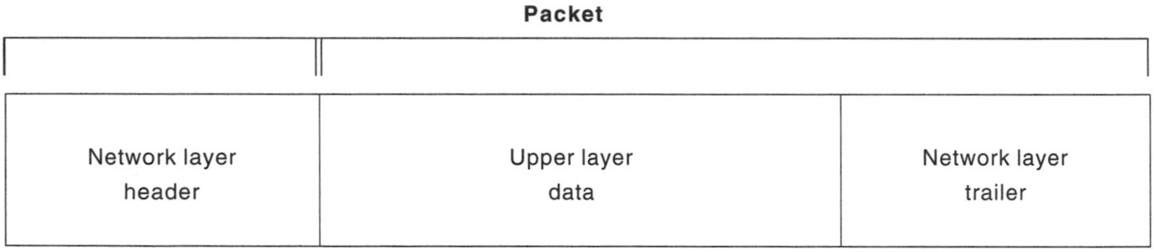

Packet

Network layer header	Upper layer data	Network layer trailer

The term *datagram* usually refers to an information unit whose source and destination are network layer entities that use connectionless network service.

The term *segment* usually refers to an information unit whose source and destination are transport layer entities.

A *message* is an information unit whose source and destination entities exist above the network layer (often at the application layer).

A *cell* is an information unit of a fixed size whose source and destination are data link layer entitics. Cells are used in switched environments, such as Asynchronous Transfer Mode (ATM) and Switched Multimegabit Data Service (SMDS) networks. A cell is composed of the header and payload. The header contains control information intended for the destination data link layer entity and is typically 5 bytes long. The payload contains upper-layer data that is encapsulated in the cell header and is typically 48 bytes long.

The length of the header and the payload fields always are the same for each cell. Figure 1-11 depicts the components of a typical cell.

Figure 1-11 *Two Components Make Up a Typical Cell*

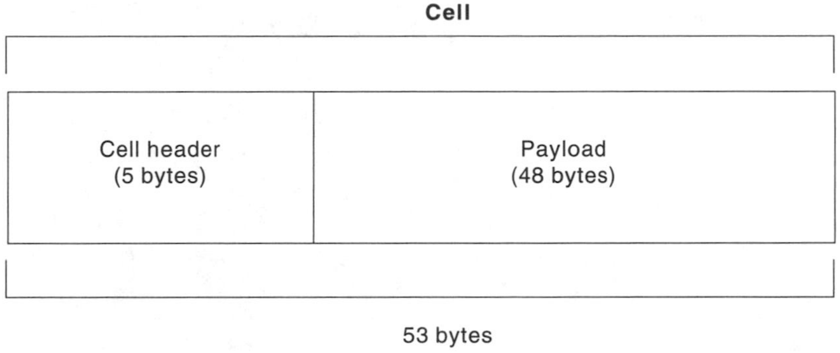

Cell

Cell header (5 bytes)	Payload (48 bytes)

53 bytes

Data unit is a generic term that refers to a variety of information units. Some common data units are service data units (SDUs), protocol data units, and bridge protocol data units (BPDUs). SDUs are information units from upper-layer protocols that define a service request to a lower-layer protocol. PDU is OSI terminology for a packet. BPDUs are used by the spanning-tree algorithm as hello messages.

ISO Hierarchy of Networks

Large networks typically are organized as hierarchies. A hierarchical organization provides such advantages as ease of management, flexibility, and a reduction in unnecessary traffic. Thus, the International Organization for Standardization (ISO) has adopted a number of terminology conventions for addressing network entities. Key terms defined in this section include end system (ES), intermediate system (IS), area, and autonomous system (AS).

An *ES* is a network device that does not perform routing or other traffic forwarding functions. Typical ESs include such devices as terminals, personal computers, and printers. An *IS* is a network device that performs routing or other traffic-forwarding functions. Typical ISs include such devices as routers, switches, and bridges. Two types of IS networks exist: intradomain IS and interdomain IS. An intradomain IS communicates within a single autonomous system, while an interdomain IS communicates within and between autonomous systems. An *area* is a logical group of network segments and their attached devices. Areas are subdivisions of autonomous systems (AS's). An AS is a collection of networks under a common administration that share a common routing strategy. Autonomous systems are subdivided into areas, and an AS is sometimes called a domain. Figure 1-12 illustrates a hierarchical network and its components.

Figure 1-12 *A Hierarchical Network Contains Numerous Components*

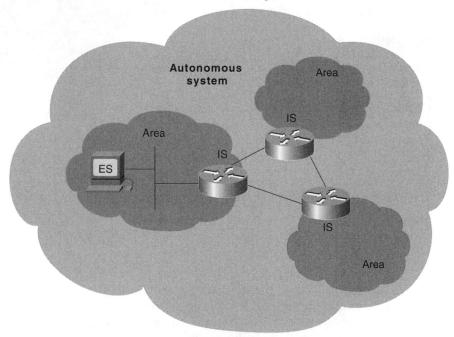

Connection-Oriented and Connectionless Network Services

In general, transport protocols can be characterized as being either connection-oriented or connectionless. Connection-oriented services must first establish a connection with the desired service before passing any data. A connectionless service can send the data without any need to establish a connection first. In general, connection-oriented services provide some level of delivery guarantee, whereas connectionless services do not.

Connection-oriented service involves three phases: connection establishment, data transfer, and connection termination.

During connection establishment, the end nodes may reserve resources for the connection. The end nodes also may negotiate and establish certain criteria for the transfer, such as a window size used in TCP connections. This resource reservation is one of the things exploited in some denial of service (DOS) attacks. An attacking system will send many requests for establishing a connection but then will never complete the connection. The attacked computer is then left with resources allocated for many never-completed connections. Then, when an end node tries to complete an actual connection, there are not enough resources for the valid connection.

The data transfer phase occurs when the actual data is transmitted over the connection. During data transfer, most connection-oriented services will monitor for lost packets and handle resending them. The protocol is generally also responsible for putting the packets in the right sequence before passing the data up the protocol stack.

When the transfer of data is complete, the end nodes terminate the connection and release resources reserved for the connection.

Connection-oriented network services have more overhead than connectionless ones. Connection-oriented services must negotiate a connection, transfer data, and tear down the connection, whereas a connectionless transfer can simply send the data without the added overhead of creating and tearing down a connection. Each has its place in internetworks.

Internetwork Addressing

Internetwork addresses identify devices separately or as members of a group. Addressing schemes vary depending on the protocol family and the OSI layer. Three types of internetwork addresses are commonly used: data link layer addresses, Media Access Control (MAC) addresses, and network layer addresses.

Data Link Layer Addresses

A *data link layer address* uniquely identifies each physical network connection of a network device. Data-link addresses sometimes are referred to as *physical* or *hardware addresses*. Data-link addresses usually exist within a flat address space and have a pre-established and typically fixed relationship to a specific device.

End systems generally have only one physical network connection and thus have only one data-link address. Routers and other internetworking devices typically have multiple physical network connections and therefore have multiple data-link addresses. Figure 1-13 illustrates how each interface on a device is uniquely identified by a data-link address.

Figure 1-13 *Each Interface on a Device Is Uniquely Identified by a Data-Link Address.*

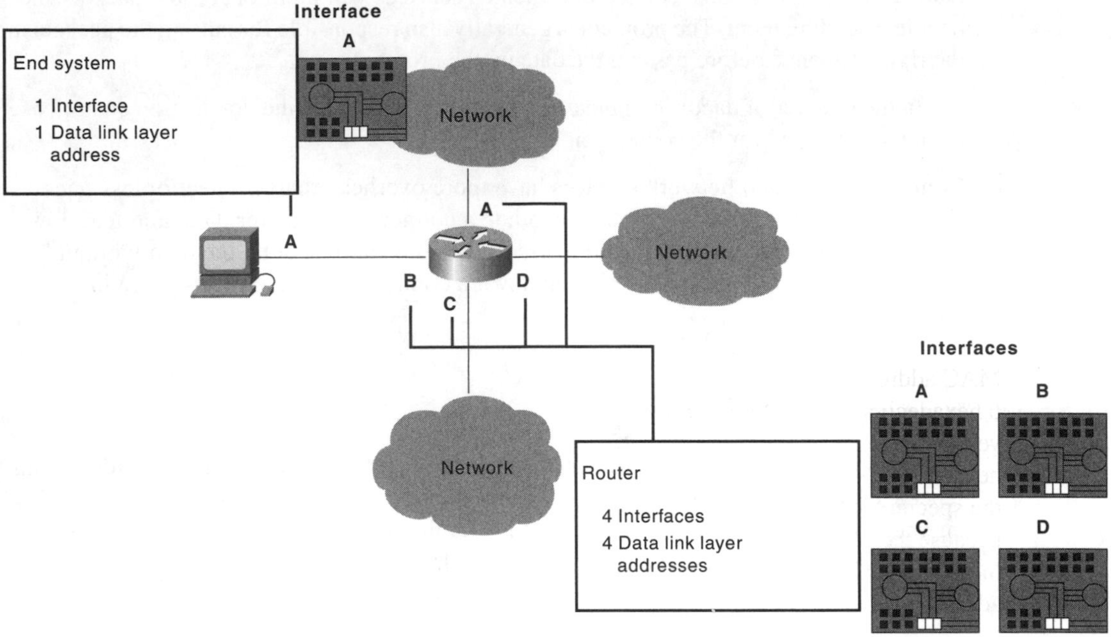

MAC Addresses

Media Access Control (MAC) addresses consist of a subset of data link layer addresses. MAC addresses identify network entities in LANs that implement the IEEE MAC addresses of the data link layer. As with most data-link addresses, MAC addresses are unique for each LAN interface. Figure 1-14 illustrates the relationship between MAC addresses, data-link addresses, and the IEEE sublayers of the data link layer.

Figure 1-14 *MAC Addresses, Data-Link Addresses, and the IEEE Sublayers of the Data Link Layer Are All Related*

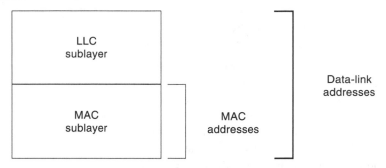

MAC addresses are 48 bits in length and are expressed as 12 hexadecimal digits. The first 6 hexadecimal digits, which are administered by the IEEE, identify the manufacturer or vendor and thus comprise the Organizationally Unique Identifier (OUI). The last 6 hexadecimal digits comprise the interface serial number, or another value administered by the specific vendor. MAC addresses sometimes are called *burned-in addresses (BIAs)* because they are burned into read-only memory (ROM) and are copied into random-access memory (RAM) when the interface card initializes. Figure 1-15 illustrates the MAC address format.

Figure 1-15 *The MAC Address Contains a Unique Format of Hexadecimal Digits*

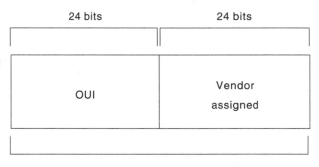

Mapping Addresses

Because internetworks generally use network addresses to route traffic around the network, there is a need to map network addresses to MAC addresses. When the network layer has determined the destination station's network address, it must forward the information over a physical network using a MAC address. Different protocol suites use different methods to perform this mapping, but the most popular is Address Resolution Protocol (ARP).

Different protocol suites use different methods for determining the MAC address of a device. The following three methods are used most often. Address Resolution Protocol (ARP) maps network addresses to MAC addresses. The Hello protocol enables network devices to learn the MAC addresses of other network devices. MAC addresses either are embedded in the network layer address or are generated by an algorithm.

Address Resolution Protocol (ARP) is the method used in the TCP/IP suite. When a network device needs to send data to another device on the same network, it knows the source and destination network addresses for the data transfer. It must somehow map the destination address to a MAC address before forwarding the data. First, the sending station will check its ARP table to see if it has already discovered this destination station's MAC address. If it has not, it will send a broadcast on the network with the destination station's IP address contained in the broadcast. Every station on the network receives the broadcast and compares the embedded IP address to its own. Only the station with the matching IP address replies to the sending station with a packet containing the MAC address for the station. The first station then adds this information to its ARP table for future reference and proceeds to transfer the data.

When the destination device lies on a remote network, one beyond a router, the process is the same except that the sending station sends the ARP request for the MAC address of its default gateway. It then forwards the information to that device. The default gateway will then forward the information over whatever networks necessary to deliver the packet to the network on which the destination device resides. The router on the destination device's network then uses ARP to obtain the MAC of the actual destination device and delivers the packet.

The Hello protocol is a network layer protocol that enables network devices to identify one another and indicate that they are still functional. When a new end system powers up, for example, it broadcasts hello messages onto the network. Devices on the network then return hello replies, and hello messages are also sent at specific intervals to indicate that they are still functional. Network devices can learn the MAC addresses of other devices by examining Hello protocol packets.

Three protocols use predictable MAC addresses. In these protocol suites, MAC addresses are predictable because the network layer either embeds the MAC address in the network layer address or uses an algorithm to determine the MAC address. The three protocols are Xerox Network Systems (XNS), Novell Internetwork Packet Exchange (IPX), and DECnet Phase IV.

Network Layer Addresses

A *network layer address* identifies an entity at the network layer of the OSI layers. Network addresses usually exist within a hierarchical address space and sometimes are called *virtual* or *logical addresses*.

The relationship between a network address and a device is logical and unfixed; it typically is based either on physical network characteristics (the device is on a particular network segment) or on groupings that have no physical basis (the device is part of an AppleTalk zone). End systems require one network layer address for each network layer protocol that they support. (This assumes that the device has only one physical network connection.) Routers and other internetworking devices require one network layer address per physical network connection for each network layer protocol supported. For example, a router with three interfaces each running AppleTalk, TCP/IP, and OSI must have three network layer addresses for each interface. The router therefore has nine network layer addresses. Figure 1-16 illustrates how each network interface must be assigned a network address for each protocol supported.

Figure 1-16 *Each Network Interface Must Be Assigned a Network Address for Each Protocol Supported*

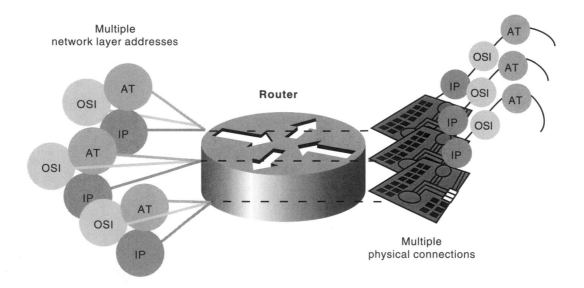

Hierarchical Versus Flat Address Space

Internetwork address space typically takes one of two forms: hierarchical address space or flat address space. A *hierarchical address space* is organized into numerous subgroups, each successively narrowing an address until it points to a single device (in a manner similar to street addresses). A *flat address space* is organized into a single group (in a manner similar to U.S. Social Security numbers).

Hierarchical addressing offers certain advantages over flat-addressing schemes. Address sorting and recall is simplified using comparison operations. For example, "Ireland" in a street address eliminates any other country as a possible location. Figure 1-17 illustrates the difference between hierarchical and flat address spaces.

Figure 1-17 *Hierarchical and Flat Address Spaces Differ in Comparison Operations*

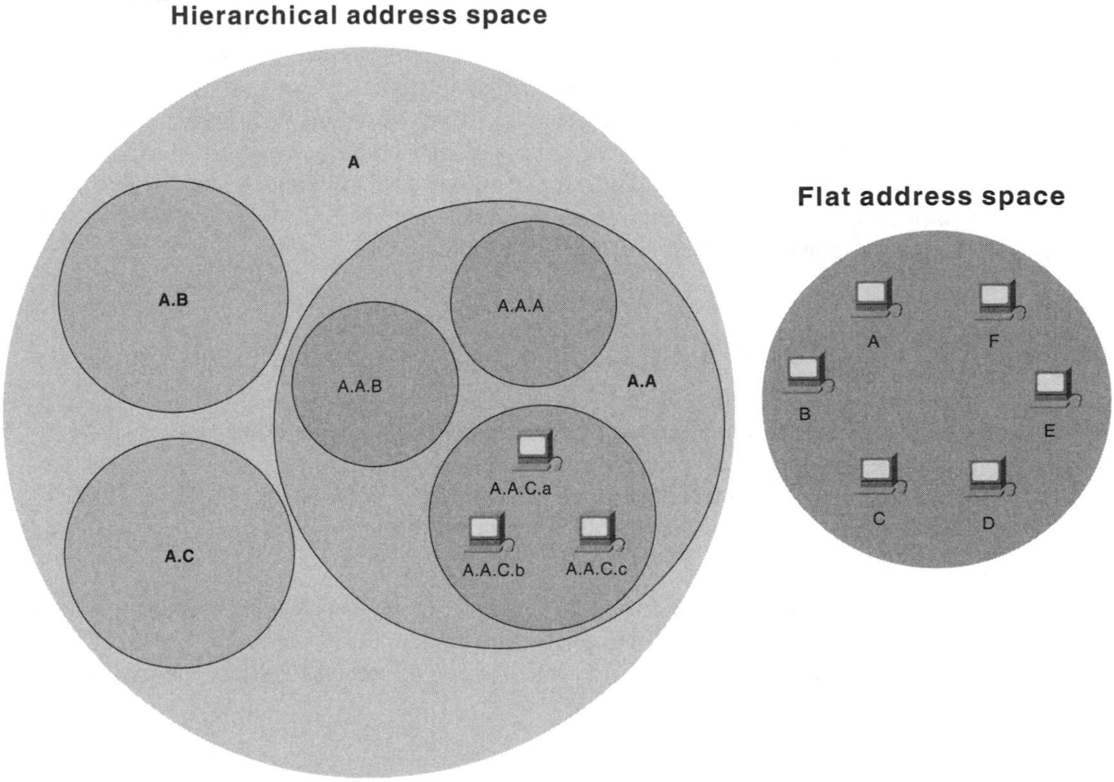

Address Assignments

Addresses are assigned to devices as one of two types: static and dynamic. *Static addresses* are assigned by a network administrator according to a preconceived internetwork addressing plan. A static address does not change until the network administrator manually changes it. *Dynamic addresses* are obtained by devices when they attach to a network, by means of some protocol-specific process. A device using a dynamic address often has a different address each time that it connects to the network. Some networks use a server to assign addresses. Server-assigned addresses are recycled for reuse as devices disconnect. A device is therefore likely to have a different address each time that it connects to the network.

Addresses Versus Names

Internetwork devices usually have both a name and an address associated with them. Internetwork names typically are location-independent and remain associated with a device wherever that device moves (for example, from one building to another). Internetwork addresses usually are location-dependent and change when a device is moved (although MAC addresses are an exception to this rule). As with network addresses being mapped to MAC addresses, names are usually mapped to network addresses through some protocol. The Internet uses Domain Name System (DNS) to map the name of a device to its IP address. For example, it's easier for you to remember www.cisco.com instead of some IP address. Therefore, you type www.cisco.com into your browser when you want to access Cisco's web site. Your computer performs a DNS lookup of the IP address for Cisco's web server and then communicates with it using the network address.

Flow Control Basics

Flow control is a function that prevents network congestion by ensuring that transmitting devices do not overwhelm receiving devices with data. A high-speed computer, for example, may generate traffic faster than the network can transfer it, or faster than the destination device can receive and process it. The three commonly used methods for handling network congestion are buffering, transmitting source-quench messages, and windowing.

Buffering is used by network devices to temporarily store bursts of excess data in memory until they can be processed. Occasional data bursts are easily handled by buffering. Excess data bursts can exhaust memory, however, forcing the device to discard any additional datagrams that arrive.

Source-quench messages are used by receiving devices to help prevent their buffers from overflowing. The receiving device sends source-quench messages to request that the source reduce its current rate of data transmission. First, the receiving device begins discarding received data due to overflowing buffers. Second, the receiving device begins sending source-quench messages to the transmitting device at the rate of one message for each packet dropped. The source device receives the source-quench messages and lowers the data rate until it stops receiving the messages. Finally, the source device then gradually increases the data rate as long as no further source-quench requests are received.

Windowing is a flow-control scheme in which the source device requires an acknowledgment from the destination after a certain number of packets have been transmitted. With a window size of 3, the source requires an acknowledgment after sending three packets, as follows. First, the source device sends three packets to the destination device. Then, after receiving the three packets, the destination device sends an acknowledgment to the source. The source receives the acknowledgment and sends three more packets. If the destination does not receive one or more of the packets for some reason, such as overflowing buffers, it does not receive enough packets to send an acknowledgment. The source then retransmits the packets at a reduced transmission rate.

Error-Checking Basics

Error-checking schemes determine whether transmitted data has become corrupt or otherwise damaged while traveling from the source to the destination. Error checking is implemented at several of the OSI layers.

One common error-checking scheme is the cyclic redundancy check (CRC), which detects and discards corrupted data. Error-correction functions (such as data retransmission) are left to higher-layer protocols. A CRC value is generated by a calculation that is performed at the source device. The destination device compares this value to its own calculation to determine whether errors occurred during transmission. First, the source device performs a predetermined set of calculations over the contents of the packet to be sent. Then, the source places the calculated value in the packet and sends the packet to the destination. The destination performs the same predetermined set of calculations over the contents of the packet and then compares its computed value with that contained in the packet. If the values are equal, the packet is considered valid. If the values are unequal, the packet contains errors and is discarded.

Multiplexing Basics

Multiplexing is a process in which multiple data channels are combined into a single data or physical channel at the source. Multiplexing can be implemented at any of the OSI layers. Conversely, *demultiplexing* is the process of separating multiplexed data channels at the destination. One example of multiplexing is when data from multiple applications is multiplexed into a single lower-layer data packet. Figure 1-18 illustrates this example.

Figure 1-18 *Multiple Applications Can Be Multiplexed into a Single Lower-Layer Data Packet*

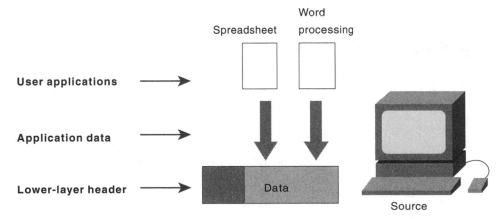

Another example of multiplexing is when data from multiple devices is combined into a single physical channel (using a device called a multiplexer). Figure 1-19 illustrates this example.

Figure 1-19 *Multiple Devices Can Be Multiplexed into a Single Physical Channel*

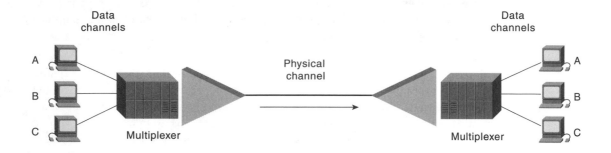

A *multiplexer* is a physical layer device that combines multiple data streams into one or more output channels at the source. Multiplexers demultiplex the channels into multiple data streams at the remote end and thus maximize the use of the bandwidth of the physical medium by enabling it to be shared by multiple traffic sources.

Some methods used for multiplexing data are time-division multiplexing (TDM), asynchronous time-division multiplexing (ATDM), frequency-division multiplexing (FDM), and statistical multiplexing.

In TDM, information from each data channel is allocated bandwidth based on preassigned time slots, regardless of whether there is data to transmit. In ATDM, information from data channels is allocated bandwidth as needed by using dynamically assigned time slots. In FDM, information from each data channel is allocated bandwidth based on the signal frequency of the traffic. In statistical multiplexing, bandwidth is dynamically allocated to any data channels that have information to transmit.

Standards Organizations

A wide variety of organizations contribute to internetworking standards by providing forums for discussion, turning informal discussion into formal specifications, and proliferating specifications after they are standardized.

Most standards organizations create formal standards by using specific processes: organizing ideas, discussing the approach, developing draft standards, voting on all or certain aspects of the standards, and then formally releasing the completed standard to the public.

Some of the best-known standards organizations that contribute to internetworking standards include these:

- **International Organization for Standardization (ISO)**—ISO is an international standards organization responsible for a wide range of standards, including many that are relevant to networking. Its best-known contribution is the development of the OSI reference model and the OSI protocol suite.

- **American National Standards Institute (ANSI)**—ANSI, which is also a member of the ISO, is the coordinating body for voluntary standards groups within the United States. ANSI developed the Fiber Distributed Data Interface (FDDI) and other communications standards.

- **Electronic Industries Association (EIA)**—EIA specifies electrical transmission standards, including those used in networking. The EIA developed the widely used EIA/TIA-232 standard (formerly known as RS-232).

- **Institute of Electrical and Electronic Engineers (IEEE)**—IEEE is a professional organization that defines networking and other standards. The IEEE developed the widely used LAN standards IEEE 802.3 and IEEE 802.5.

- **International Telecommunication Union Telecommunication Standardization Sector (ITU-T)**—Formerly called the Committee for International Telegraph and Telephone (CCITT), ITU-T is now an international organization that develops communication standards. The ITU-T developed X.25 and other communications standards.

- **Internet Activities Board (IAB)**—IAB is a group of internetwork researchers who discuss issues pertinent to the Internet and set Internet policies through decisions and task forces. The IAB designates some Request For Comments (RFC) documents as Internet standards, including Transmission Control Protocol/Internet Protocol (TCP/IP) and the Simple Network Management Protocol (SNMP).

Summary

This chapter introduced the building blocks on which internetworks are built. Understanding where complex pieces of internetworks fit into the OSI model will help you understand the concepts better. Internetworks are complex systems that, when viewed as a whole, are too much to understand. Only by breaking the network down into the conceptual pieces can it be easily understood. As you read and experience internetworks, try to think of them in terms of OSI layers and conceptual pieces.

Understanding the interaction between various layers and protocols makes designing, configuring, and diagnosing internetworks possible. Without understanding of the building blocks, you cannot understand the interaction between them.

Review Questions

1 What are the layers of the OSI model?

2 Which layer determines path selection in an internetwork?

3 What types of things are defined at the physical layer?

4 What is one method of mapping network addresses to MAC addresses?

5 Which includes more overhead, connection-oriented or connectionless services?

For More Information

- Cisco's web site (www.cisco.com) is a wonderful source for more information about these topics. The Documentation section includes in-depth discussions on many of the topics covered in this chapter.

- Teare, Diane. *Designing Cisco Networks*. Indianapolis: Cisco Press, July 1999.

Objectives

- Learn about different LAN protocols.
- Understand the different methods used to deal with media contention.
- Learn about different LAN topologies.

CHAPTER 2

Introduction to LAN Protocols

This chapter introduces the various media-access methods, transmission methods, topologies, and devices used in a local-area network (LAN). Topics addressed focus on the methods and devices used in Ethernet/IEEE 802.3, Token Ring/IEEE 802.5, and Fiber Distributed Data Interface (FDDI). Subsequent chapters in Part II, "LAN Protocols," address specific protocols in more detail. Figure 2-1 illustrates the basic layout of these three implementations.

Figure 2-1 *Three LAN Implementations Are Used Most Commonly*

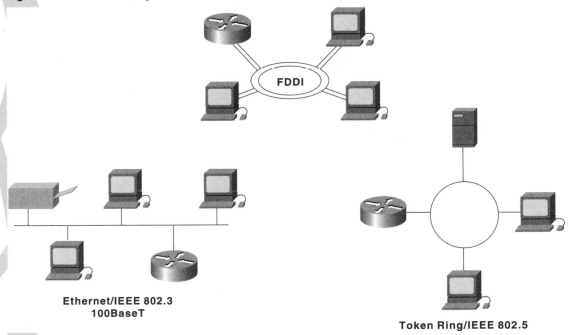

FDDI

Ethernet/IEEE 802.3
100BaseT

Token Ring/IEEE 802.5

What Is a LAN?

A *LAN* is a high-speed data network that covers a relatively small geographic area. It typically connects workstations, personal computers, printers, servers, and other devices. LANs offer computer users many advantages, including shared access to devices and applications, file exchange between connected users, and communication between users via electronic mail and other applications.

LAN Protocols and the OSI Reference Model

LAN protocols function at the lowest two layers of the OSI reference model, as discussed in Chapter 1, "Internetworking Basics," between the physical layer and the data link layer. Figure 2-2 illustrates how several popular LAN protocols map to the OSI reference model.

Figure 2-2 *Popular LAN Protocols Mapped to the OSI Reference Model*

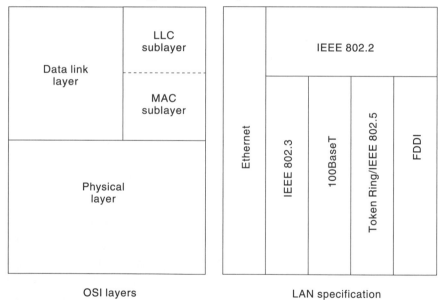

LAN Media-Access Methods

Media contention occurs when two or more network devices have data to send at the same time. Because multiple devices cannot talk on the network simultaneously, some type of method must be used to allow one device access to the network media at a time. This is done in two main ways: carrier sense multiple access collision detect (CSMA/CD) and token passing.

In networks using *CSMA/CD* technology such as Ethernet, network devices contend for the network media. When a device has data to send, it first listens to see if any other device is currently using the network. If not, it starts sending its data. After finishing its transmission, it listens again to see if a collision occurred. A collision occurs when two devices send data simultaneously. When a collision happens, each device waits a random length of time before resending its data. In most cases, a collision will not occur again between the two devices. Because of this type of network contention, the busier a network becomes, the more collisions occur. This is why performance of Ethernet degrades rapidly as the number of devices on a single network increases.

In *token-passing* networks such as Token Ring and FDDI, a special network packet called a token is passed around the network from device to device. When a device has data to send, it must wait until it has the token and then sends its data. When the data transmission is complete, the token is released so that other devices may use the network media. The main advantage of token-passing networks is that they are deterministic. In other words, it is easy to calculate the maximum time that will pass before a device has the opportunity to send data. This explains the popularity of token-passing networks in some real-time environments such as factories, where machinery must be capable of communicating at a determinable interval.

For CSMA/CD networks, switches segment the network into multiple collision domains. This reduces the number of devices per network segment that must contend for the media. By creating smaller collision domains, the performance of a network can be increased significantly without requiring addressing changes.

Normally CSMA/CD networks are half-duplex, meaning that while a device sends information, it cannot receive at the time. While that device is talking, it is incapable of also listening for other traffic. This is much like a walkie-talkie. When one person wants to talk, he presses the transmit button and begins speaking. While he is talking, no one else on the same frequency can talk. When the sending person is finished, he releases the transmit button and the frequency is available to others.

When switches are introduced, full-duplex operation is possible. Full-duplex works much like a telephone—you can listen as well as talk at the same time. When a network device is attached directly to the port of a network switch, the two devices may be capable of operating in full-duplex mode. In full-duplex mode, performance can be increased, but not quite as much as some like to claim. A 100-Mbps Ethernet segment is capable of transmitting 200 Mbps of data, but only 100 Mbps can travel in one direction at a time. Because most data connections are asymmetric (with more data traveling in one direction than the other), the gain is not as great as many claim. However, full-duplex operation does increase the throughput of most applications because the network media is no longer shared. Two devices on a full-duplex connection can send data as soon as it is ready.

Token-passing networks such as Token Ring can also benefit from network switches. In large networks, the delay between turns to transmit may be significant because the token is passed around the network.

LAN Transmission Methods

LAN data transmissions fall into three classifications: unicast, multicast, and broadcast. In each type of transmission, a single packet is sent to one or more nodes.

In a *unicast transmission*, a single packet is sent from the source to a destination on a network. First, the source node addresses the packet by using the address of the destination node. The package is then sent onto the network, and finally, the network passes the packet to its destination.

A *multicast transmission* consists of a single data packet that is copied and sent to a specific subset of nodes on the network. First, the source node addresses the packet by using a multicast address. The packet is then sent into the network, which makes copies of the packet and sends a copy to each node that is part of the multicast address.

A *broadcast transmission* consists of a single data packet that is copied and sent to all nodes on the network. In these types of transmissions, the source node addresses the packet by using the broadcast address. The packet is then sent on to the network, which makes copies of the packet and sends a copy to every node on the network.

LAN Topologies

LAN topologies define the manner in which network devices are organized. Four common LAN topologies exist: bus, ring, star, and tree. These topologies are logical architectures, but the actual devices need not be physically organized in these configurations. Logical bus and ring topologies, for example, are commonly organized physically as a star. A *bus topology* is a linear LAN architecture in which transmissions from network stations propagate the length of the medium and are received by all other stations. Of the three most widely used LAN implementations, Ethernet/IEEE 802.3 networks—including 100BaseT—implement a bus topology, which is illustrated in Figure 2-3.

Figure 2-3   *Some Networks Implement a Local Bus Topology*

A *ring topology* is a LAN architecture that consists of a series of devices connected to one another by unidirectional transmission links to form a single closed loop. Both Token Ring/IEEE 802.5 and FDDI networks implement a ring topology. Figure 2-4 depicts a logical ring topology.

Figure 2-4   *Some Networks Implement a Logical Ring Topology*

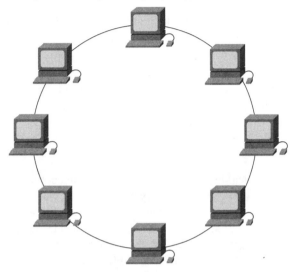

A *star topology* is a LAN architecture in which the endpoints on a network are connected to a common central hub, or switch, by dedicated links. Logical bus and ring topologies are often implemented physically in a star topology, which is illustrated in Figure 2-5.

A *tree topology* is a LAN architecture that is identical to the bus topology, except that branches with multiple nodes are possible in this case. Figure 2-5 illustrates a logical tree topology.

Figure 2-5   *A Logical Tree Topology Can Contain Multiple Nodes*

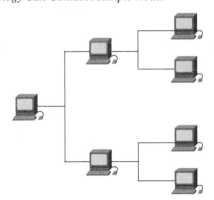

LAN Devices

Devices commonly used in LANs include repeaters, hubs, LAN extenders, bridges, LAN switches, and routers.

NOTE   Repeaters, hubs, and LAN extenders are discussed briefly in this section. The function and operation of bridges, switches, and routers are discussed generally in Chapter 4, "Introduction to Cisco IOS Software," and Chapter 5, "Bridging and Switching Basics."

A *repeater* is a physical layer device used to interconnect the media segments of an extended network. A repeater essentially enables a series of cable segments to be treated as a single cable. Repeaters receive signals from one network segment and amplify, retime, and retransmit those signals to another network segment. These actions prevent signal deterioration caused by long cable lengths and large numbers of connected devices. Repeaters are incapable of performing complex filtering and other traffic processing. In addition, all electrical signals, including electrical disturbances and other errors, are repeated and amplified. The total number of repeaters and network segments that can be connected is limited due to timing and other issues. Figure 2-6 illustrates a repeater connecting two network segments.

Figure 2-6   *A Repeater Connects Two Network Segments*

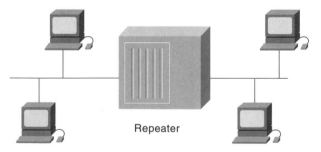

A *hub* is a physical layer device that connects multiple user stations, each via a dedicated cable. Electrical interconnections are established inside the hub. Hubs are used to create a physical star network while maintaining the logical bus or ring configuration of the LAN. In some respects, a hub functions as a multiport repeater.

A *LAN extender* is a remote-access multilayer switch that connects to a host router. LAN extenders forward traffic from all the standard network layer protocols (such as IP, IPX, and AppleTalk) and filter traffic based on the MAC address or network layer protocol type. LAN extenders scale well because the host router filters out unwanted broadcasts and multicasts. However, LAN extenders are not capable of segmenting traffic or creating security firewalls. Figure 2–7 illustrates multiple LAN extenders connected to the host router through a WAN.

Figure 2-7   *Multiple LAN Extenders Can Connect to the Host Router Through a WAN*

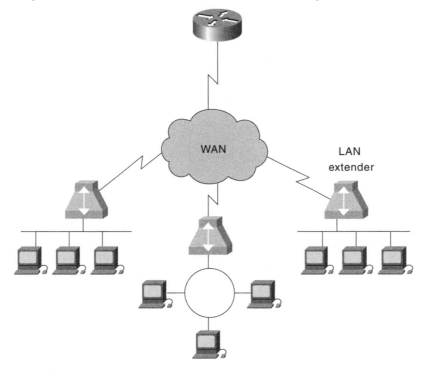

Review Questions

1 Describe the type of media access used by Ethernet.

2 Describe the type of media access used by Token Ring.

3 Describe unicast, multicast, and broadcast transmissions.

For More Information

- Cisco's web site (www.cisco.com) is a wonderful source for more information about these topics. The Documentation section includes in-depth discussions on many of the topics covered in this chapter.

- Teare, Diane. *Designing Cisco Networks*. Indianapolis: Cisco Press, July 1999.

Objectives

- Become familiar with WAN terminology.
- Learn about different types of WAN connections.
- Become familiar with different types of WAN equipment.

CHAPTER 3

Introduction to WAN Technologies

This chapter introduces the various protocols and technologies used in wide-area network (WAN) environments. Topics summarized here include point-to-point links, circuit switching, packet switching, virtual circuits, dialup services, and WAN devices. Chapters in Part III, "WAN Protocols," address specific technologies in more detail.

What Is a WAN?

A *WAN* is a data communications network that covers a relatively broad geographic area and that often uses transmission facilities provided by common carriers, such as telephone companies. WAN technologies generally function at the lower three layers of the OSI reference model: the physical layer, the data link layer, and the network layer. Figure 3-1 illustrates the relationship between the common WAN technologies and the OSI model.

Figure 3-1 *WAN Technologies Operate at the Lowest Levels of the OSI Model*

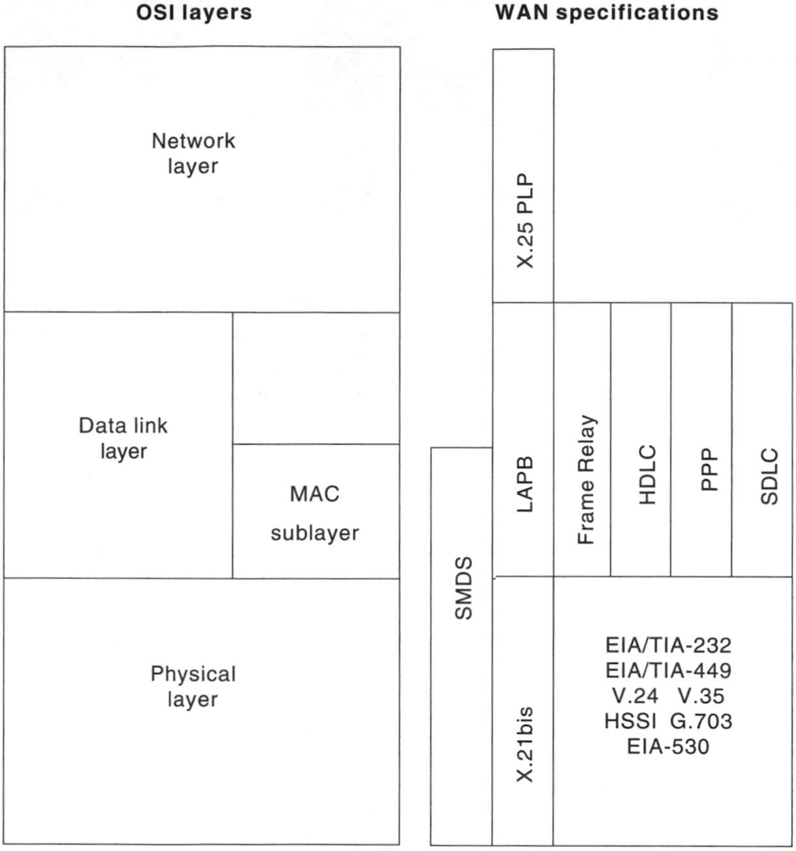

Point-to-Point Links

A *point-to-point link* provides a single, pre-established WAN communications path from the customer premises through a carrier network, such as a telephone company, to a remote network. Point-to-point lines are usually leased from a carrier and thus are often called leased lines. For a point-to-point line, the carrier allocates pairs of wire and facility hardware to your line only. These circuits are generally priced based on bandwidth required and distance between the two connected points. Point-to-point links are generally more expensive than shared services such as Frame Relay. Figure 3-2 illustrates a typical point-to-point link through a WAN.

Figure 3-2   *A Typical Point-to-Point Link Operates Through a WAN to a Remote Network*

Circuit Switching

Switched circuits allow data connections that can be initiated when needed and terminated when communication is complete. This works much like a normal telephone line works for voice communication. Integrated Services Digital Network (ISDN) is a good example of circuit switching. When a router has data for a remote site, the switched circuit is initiated with the circuit number of the remote network. In the case of ISDN circuits, the device actually places a call to the telephone number of the remote ISDN circuit. When the two networks are connected and authenticated, they can transfer data. When the data transmission is complete, the call can be terminated. Figure 3-3 illustrates an example of this type of circuit.

Figure 3-3   *A Circuit-Switched WAN Undergoes a Process Similar to That Used for a Telephone Call*

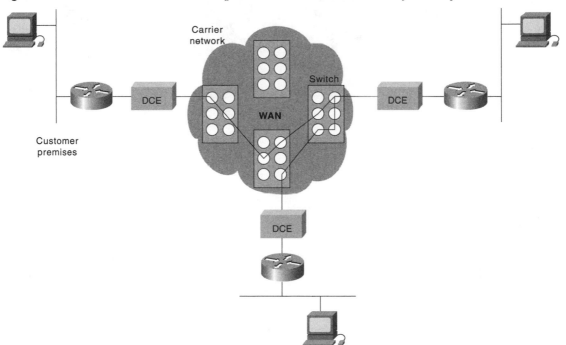

Packet Switching

Packet switching is a WAN technology in which users share common carrier resources. Because this allows the carrier to make more efficient use of its infrastructure, the cost to the customer is generally much better than with point-to-point lines. In a packet switching setup, networks have connections into the carrier's network, and many customers share the carrier's network. The carrier can then create virtual circuits between customers' sites by which packets of data are delivered from one to the other through the network. The section of the carrier's network that is shared is often referred to as a cloud.

Some examples of packet-switching networks include Asynchronous Transfer Mode (ATM), Frame Relay, Switched Multimegabit Data Services (SMDS), and X.25. Figure 3-4 shows an example packet-switched circuit.

The virtual connections between customer sites are often referred to as a virtual circuit.

Figure 3-4   *Packet Switching Transfers Packets Across a Carrier Network*

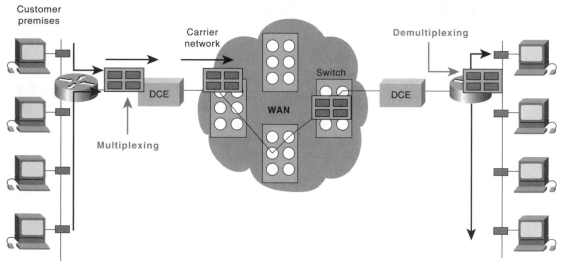

WAN Virtual Circuits

A *virtual circuit* is a logical circuit created within a shared network between two network devices. Two types of virtual circuits exist: switched virtual circuits (SVCs) and permanent virtual circuits (PVCs).

SVCs are virtual circuits that are dynamically established on demand and terminated when transmission is complete. Communication over an SVC consists of three phases: circuit establishment, data transfer, and circuit termination. The establishment phase involves creating the virtual circuit between the source and destination devices. Data transfer involves transmitting data between the devices over the virtual circuit, and the circuit termination phase involves tearing down the virtual circuit between the source and destination devices. SVCs are used in situations in which data transmission between devices is sporadic, largely because SVCs increase bandwidth used due to the circuit establishment and termination phases, but they decrease the cost associated with constant virtual circuit availability.

PVC is a permanently established virtual circuit that consists of one mode: data transfer. PVCs are used in situations in which data transfer between devices is constant. PVCs decrease the bandwidth use associated with the establishment and termination of virtual circuits, but they increase costs due to constant virtual circuit availability. PVCs are generally configured by the service provider when an order is placed for service.

WAN Dialup Services

Dialup services offer cost-effective methods for connectivity across WANs. Two popular dialup implementations are dial-on-demand routing (DDR) and dial backup.

DDR is a technique whereby a router can dynamically initiate a call on a switched circuit when it needs to send data. In a DDR setup, the router is configured to initiate the call when certain criteria are met, such as a particular type of network traffic needing to be transmitted. When the connection is made, traffic passes over the line. The router configuration specifies an idle timer that tells the router to drop the connection when the circuit has remained idle for a certain period.

Dial backup is another way of configuring DDR. However, in dial backup, the switched circuit is used to provide backup service for another type of circuit, such as point-to-point or packet switching. The router is configured so that when a failure is detected on the primary circuit, the dial backup line is initiated. The dial backup line then supports the WAN connection until the primary circuit is restored. When this occurs, the dial backup connection is terminated.

WAN Devices

WANs use numerous types of devices that are specific to WAN environments. WAN switches, access servers, modems, CSU/DSUs, and ISDN terminal adapters are discussed in the following sections. Other devices found in WAN environments that are used in WAN implementations include routers, ATM switches, and multiplexers.

WAN Switch

A *WAN switch* is a multiport internetworking device used in carrier networks. These devices typically switch such traffic as Frame Relay, X.25, and SMDS, and operate at the data link layer of the OSI reference model. Figure 3-5 illustrates two routers at remote ends of a WAN that are connected by WAN switches.

Figure 3-5   *Two Routers at Remote Ends of a WAN Can Be Connected by WAN Switches*

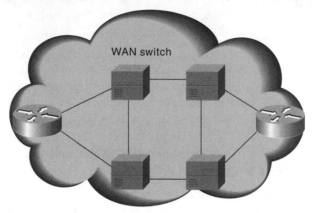

Access Server

An *access server* acts as a concentration point for dial-in and dial-out connections. Figure 3–6 illustrates an access server concentrating dial-out connections into a WAN.

Figure 3-6   *An Access Server Concentrates Dial-Out Connections into a WAN*

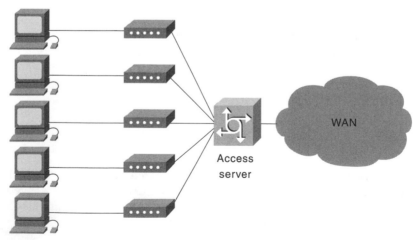

Modem

A *modem* is a device that interprets digital and analog signals, enabling data to be transmitted over voice-grade telephone lines. At the source, digital signals are converted to a form suitable for transmission over analog communication facilities. At the destination, these analog signals are returned to their digital form. Figure 3-7 illustrates a simple modem-to-modem connection through a WAN.

Figure 3-7   *A Modem Connection Through a WAN Handles Analog and Digital Signals*

CSU/DSU

A *channel service unit/digital service unit (CSU/DSU)* is a digital-interface device used to connect a router to a digital circuit like a T1. The CSU/DSU also provides signal timing for communication between these devices. Figure 3–8 illustrates the placement of the CSU/DSU in a WAN implementation.

Figure 3-8   *The CSU/DSU Stands Between the Switch and the Terminal*

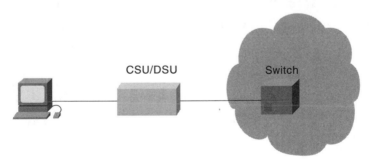

ISDN Terminal Adapter

An *ISDN terminal adapter* is a device used to connect ISDN Basic Rate Interface (BRI) connections to other interfaces, such as EIA/TIA-232 on a router. A terminal adapter is essentially an ISDN modem, although it is called a terminal adapter because it does not actually convert analog to digital signals. Figure 3-9 illustrates the placement of the terminal adapter in an ISDN environment.

Figure 3-9   *The Terminal Adapter Connects the ISDN Terminal Adapter to Other Interfaces*

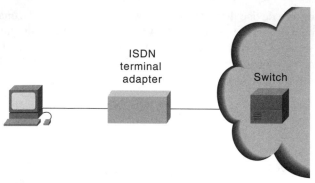

Review Questions

1 What are some types of WAN circuits?

2 What is DDR, and how is it different from dial backup?

3 What is a CSU/DSU used for?

4 What is the difference between a modem and an ISDN terminal adapter?

For More Information

- Mahler, Kevin. *CCNA Training Guide*. Indianapolis: New Riders, 1999.
- *Cisco IOS Dial Solutions*. Indianapolis: Cisco Press, 1998.
- *Cisco IOS Wide Area Networking Solutions*. Indianapolis: Cisco Press, 1999.

Objectives

- Understand Cisco IOS system architecture components.

- Work with the Cisco IOS Command Line Interface (CLI) and common commands.

- Learn about Cisco IOS troubleshooting techniques.

- Understand upgrading and release information.

CHAPTER 4

Introduction to Cisco IOS Software

The Cisco IOS software is network system software that runs on Cisco routers and switches. It is used to configure, monitor, and troubleshoot the system.

System Architecture

Like a computer, a router has a CPU that varies in performance and capabilities depending on the router platform. Two examples of processors that Cisco uses are the Motorola 68030 and the Orion/R4600. The Cisco IOS software running in the router requires the CPU or processor to make routing and bridging decisions, maintain routing tables, and other system management functions. The CPU must have access to data in memory to make decisions or to get instructions.

There are usually four types of memory on a Cisco router:

- **ROM**—ROM is generally the memory on a chip or multiple chips. It is available on a router's processor board. It is read-only, which means that data cannot be written to it. The initial software that runs on a Cisco router is called the *bootstrap software* and is usually stored in ROM. The bootstrap software is invoked when the router boots up.

- **Flash**—Flash memory is located on a processor board SIMM but can be expanded using PCMCIA (removable) cards. Flash memory is most commonly used to store one or more Cisco IOS software images. Configuration files or system information can also be copied to Flash. On some high-end systems, Flash memory is also used to hold bootstrap software.

- **RAM**—RAM is very fast memory that loses its information when the system is restarted. It is used in PCs to store running applications and data. On a router, RAM is used to hold IOS system tables and buffers. RAM memory is basically used for all system operational storage requirements.

- **NVRAM**—On the router, NVRAM is used to store the startup configuration. This is the configuration file that IOS reads when the router boots up. It is extremely fast memory and is persistent across reboots.

Although CPU and memory are required components to run IOS, a router must also have various interfaces to allow packet forwarding. Interfaces are input and output connections to the router that carries data that needs to be routed or switched. The most common types of interfaces are Ethernet and serial. Similar to the driver software on a computer with parallel ports and USB ports, IOS has device drivers to support these various interface types.

All Cisco routers have a console port that provides an EIA/TIA-232 asynchronous serial connection. The console port can be connected to a computer's serial connection to gain terminal access to the router. Most routers also have an auxiliary port that is very similar to the console port, but is typically used for modem connection for remote router management.

Example 4-1 shows the console output of a new Cisco 3640 router that has just been started. Notice the processor, interface, and memory information that is listed.

Example 4-1 *Cisco 3640 Router Console Output at Startup*

```
System Bootstrap, Version 11.1(20)AA2, EARLY DEPLOYMENT RELEASE SOFTWARE (fc1)
Copyright (c) 1999 by Cisco Systems, Inc.
C3600 processor with 98304 Kbytes of main memory
Main memory is configured to 64 bit mode with parity disabled

program load complete, entry point: 0x80008000, size: 0xa8d168
Self decompressing the image : ################################################
################################################################ [OK]

                    Restricted Rights Legend

Use, duplication, or disclosure by the Government is
subject to restrictions as set forth in subparagraph
(c) of the Commercial Computer Software - Restricted
Rights clause at FAR sec. 52.227-19 and subparagraph
(c) (1) (ii) of the Rights in Technical Data and Computer
Software clause at DFARS sec. 252.227-7013.

            Cisco Systems, Inc.
            170 West Tasman Drive
            San Jose, California 95134-1706

Cisco Internetwork Operating System Software
IOS (tm) 3600 Software (C3640-IS-M), Version 12.2(10), RELEASE SOFTWARE (fc2)
Copyright (c) 1986-2002 by Cisco Systems, Inc.
Compiled Mon 06-May-02 23:23 by pwade
Image text-base: 0x60008930, data-base: 0x610D2000

cisco 3640 (R4700) processor (revision 0x00) with 94208K/4096K bytes of memory.
Processor board ID 17746964
R4700 CPU at 100Mhz, Implementation 33, Rev 1.0
Bridging software.
X.25 software, Version 3.0.0.
SuperLAT software (copyright 1990 by Meridian Technology Corp).
5 Ethernet/IEEE 802.3 interface(s)
```

Example 4-1 *Cisco 3640 Router Console Output at Startup (Continued)*

```
1 Serial network interface(s)
DRAM configuration is 64 bits wide with parity disabled.
125K bytes of non-volatile configuration memory.
8192K bytes of processor board System flash (Read/Write)
16384K bytes of processor board PCMCIA Slot0 flash (Read/Write)

         --- System Configuration Dialog ---

Would you like to enter the initial configuration dialog? [yes/no]:
```

When a new router is first started, IOS runs an autoinstall process wherein the user is prompted to answer a few questions. IOS then configures the system based on the input provided. After initial setup, the configuration is most commonly modified using the command-line interface (CLI). Other ways of configuring the router include HTTP and network management applications.

Cisco IOS CLI

Cisco IOS has three command modes, each with access to different command sets:

- **User mode**—This is the first mode a user has access to after logging into the router. The user mode can be identified by the > prompt following the router name. This mode allows the user to execute only the basic commands, such as those that show the system's status. The system cannot be configured or restarted from this mode.

- **Privileged mode**—This mode allows users to view the system configuration, restart the system, and enter configuration mode. It also allows all the commands that are available in user mode. Privileged mode can be identified by the # prompt following the router name. The user mode **enable** command tells IOS that the user wants to enter privileged mode. If an enable password or enable secret password has been set, the user needs to enter the correct password or secret to be granted access to privileged mode. An enable secret password uses stronger encryption when it is stored in the configuration and, therefore, is safer. Privileged mode allows the user to do anything on the router, so it should be used with caution. To exit privileged mode, the user executes the **disable** command.

- **Configuration mode**—This mode allows users to modify the running system configuration. To enter configuration mode, enter the command **configure terminal** from privileged mode. Configuration mode has various submodes, starting with global configuration mode, which can be identified by the (config)# prompt following the router name. As the configuration mode submodes change depending on what is being configured, the words inside the parentheses change. For example, when you enter interface configuration submode, the prompt changes to (config-if)# following the router name. To exit configuration mode, the user can enter **end** or press Ctrl-Z.

Note that in these modes, entering the context-sensitive command **?** at any point shows the available commands at that level. The **?** can also be used in the middle of a command to show possible completion options. Example 4-2 shows the use of the **?** command to display the commands available within a given command mode.

Example 4-2 *Using Context-Sensitive Help*

```
Router>?
Exec commands:
  access-enable    Create a temporary Access-List entry
  access-profile   Apply user-profile to interface
  clear            Reset functions
...
```

The following steps introduce you to the commands used to change command mode, view system information, and configure a password. Real CLI output from a Cisco 3640 router running Cisco IOS software is shown.

Step 1 Enter enabled mode by entering **enable** and pressing **Enter**:

```
Router> enable
Router#
```

Step 2 To see which version of IOS is running on the system, enter the **show version** command:

```
Router# show version
Cisco Internetwork Operating System Software
IOS (tm) 3600 Software (C3640-IS-M), Version 12.2(10), RELEASE SOFTWARE
(fc2)
Copyright (c) 1986-2002 by Cisco Systems, Inc.
Compiled Mon 06-May-02 23:23 by pwade
Image text-base: 0x60008930, data-base: 0x610D2000

ROM: System Bootstrap, Version 11.1(20)AA2, EARLY DEPLOYMENT RELEASE
SOFTWARE
  (fc1)

Router uptime is 47 minutes
System returned to ROM by reload
System image file is "slot0:c3640-is-mz.122-10.bin"

cisco 3640 (R4700) processor (revision 0x00) with 94208K/4096K bytes of
memory.
Processor board ID 17746964
R4700 CPU at 100Mhz, Implementation 33, Rev 1.0
Bridging software.
X.25 software, Version 3.0.0.
SuperLAT software (copyright 1990 by Meridian Technology Corp).
5 Ethernet/IEEE 802.3 interface(s)
1 Serial network interface(s)
DRAM configuration is 64 bits wide with parity disabled.
125K bytes of non-volatile configuration memory.
8192K bytes of processor board System flash (Read/Write)
16384K bytes of processor board PCMCIA Slot0 flash (Read/Write)

Configuration register is 0x2002
```

From the output, you can see that this is a Cisco 3640 router running
Cisco IOS software, Version 12.2(10) and the software image is located
on the PCMCIA Flash card in slot 0.

Step 3   Next, configure the router name to be "IOS." To enter configuration
mode, use the command **configure terminal**:

```
Router# configure terminal
Enter configuration commands, one per line.  End with CNTL/Z.
Router(config)# hostname IOS
IOS(config)#
```

Notice that the prompt changes to "IOS" immediately after you enter the
hostname command. All configuration changes in Cisco IOS take place
immediately.

Step 4   Next, you need to set the enable password and the enable secret password. The enable secret password is stored using stronger encryption and
overrides the enable password if it is configured. To set both passwords,
you enter the following:

```
IOS(config)# enable password cisco
IOS(config)# enable secret san-fran
IOS(config)# exit
IOS#
```

To get into enabled mode, you need to enter the password **san-fran**. The
exit command takes you up one level in the configuration, or out of the
current submode.

Step 5   After configuring the router name and setting the enable and enable
secret passwords, you can examine the running configuration:

```
IOS# show running-config
Building configuration...

Current configuration : 743 bytes
!
version 12.2
service timestamps debug uptime
service timestamps log uptime
no service password-encryption
!
hostname IOS
!
enable secret 5 $1$IP7a$HClNetI.hpRdox84d.FYU.
enable password cisco
!
ip subnet-zero
!
call rsvp-sync
!
interface Ethernet0/0
 no ip address
 shutdown
 half-duplex
```

```
!
interface Serial0/0
 no ip address
 shutdown
 no fair-queue
!
interface Ethernet2/0
 no ip address
 shutdown
 half-duplex
!
interface Ethernet2/1
 no ip address
 shutdown
 half-duplex
!
interface Ethernet2/2
 no ip address
 shutdown
 half-duplex
!
interface Ethernet2/3
 no ip address
 shutdown
 half-duplex
!
ip classless
ip http server
ip pim bidir-enable
!
dial-peer cor custom
!
line con 0
line aux 0
line vty 0 4
!
end
```

Step 6   The **show running-config** output shows the configuration that is
currently active in the system; however, this configuration is lost if the
system is restarted. To save this configuration to NVRAM, you must
issue the following command:

```
IOS# copy running-config startup-config
Destination filename [startup-config]?
Building configuration...
[OK]
```

Step 7   To view the startup configuration saved in NVRAM, use the command
show startup-config.

In the preceding step sequence, notice the Ethernet and serial interfaces that show up in the
configuration file. Each interface requires that certain parameters such as encapsulation and
address be set before the interface can be used properly. In addition, IP routing or bridging
might need to be configured. Refer to the Cisco IOS installation and configuration guides
available at www.cisco.com for your version of software to learn about all possible
configuration options and recommended guidelines.

Table 4-1 describes some of the more common commands used to monitor the system.

Table 4-1   *Commands Used to Monitor Cisco IOS Devices*

Cisco IOS Command	Description
show interface	Displays current status and configuration details for all interfaces in the system
show processes cpu	Displays CPU utilization and the current processes running in the system
show buffers	Shows how system buffers are currently allocated and functioning for packet forwarding
show memory	Shows how memory is allocated to various system functions and memory utilization
show diag	Displays details on hardware cards in the system
show ip route	Displays the current active IP routing table
show arp	Displays the current active IP address-to-MAC address mapping in the ARP table

Debugging and Logging

Cisco IOS software allows for detailed debugging for all protocols and processes running in the system for troubleshooting purposes. More information on debugging can be obtained in the Cisco IOS Debug Command Reference, available on www.cisco.com.

CAUTION   Only Cisco IOS experts should enable and disable **debug** commands, because they can have a severe performance impact and should be used with care. Improper use might leave the system inaccessible and in a frozen state in which no packet forwarding takes place.

System messages are shown on the console and can be enabled for any session into the router. Different levels of severity can be configured for different access methods into the router. The eight message severity levels are as follows:

- **Emergency (severity 0)**—The system is unusable

- **Alert (severity 1)**—Immediate action is needed

- **Critical (severity 2)**—Critical condition

- **Error (severity 3)**—Error condition

- **Warning (severity 4)**—Warning condition

- **Notification (severity 5)**—Normal but significant condition

- **Informational (severity 6)**—Informational message

- **Debugging (severity 7)**—Debugging message

The **logging** command directs the output to various terminals attached to the system or virtually connected, such as Telnet sessions. Example 4-3 shows how the **logging** command can be used to determine the severity level of the messages shown.

Example 4-3 **logging** *Command*

```
IOS(config)# logging ?
  Hostname or A.B.C.D     IP address of the logging host
  buffered                Set buffered logging parameters
  console                 Set console logging level
  exception               Limit size of exception flush output
  facility                Facility parameter for syslog messages
  history                 Configure syslog history table
  host     Set syslog server host name or IP address
monitor                   Set terminal line (monitor) logging level
on                        Enable logging to all supported destinations
  rate-limit              Set messages per second limit
  source-interface        Specify interface for source address in logging
    transactions
  trap                    Set syslog server logging level

IOS(config)# logging console ?
  <0-7>          Logging severity level
  alerts         Immediate action needed          (severity=1)
  critical       Critical conditions              (severity=2)
  debugging      Debugging messages               (severity=7)
  emergencies    System is unusable               (severity=0)
  errors          Error conditions                 (severity=3)
  guaranteed     Guarantee console messages
  informational Informational messages            (severity=6)
  notifications Normal but significant conditions (severity=5)
  warnings       Warning conditions               (severity=4)
  <cr>
```

Enabling a higher level of messages shows all lower-level messages as well. The debugging level, or level 7, shows all messages. System messages may also be buffered and seen using the **show logging** command in privileged mode. A user may also send logging messages to a syslog server using the **logging host** command in configuration mode. A syslog server can be configured on a UNIX device or PC to accept these messages from a router and place them in a file. This allows for large files containing system messages to be maintained, because you are not restricted by the amount of memory on the router.

Reloading and Upgrading

A system restart on Cisco routers is called a *reload*. If the router needs to be reloaded for any reason, the **reload** command needs to be entered from privileged mode, as shown in Example 4-4. The **reload** command also allows a time to be set so that the system restarts after the specified time expires.

Example 4-4 *System Reload Options*

```
IOS# reload ?
  LINE    Reason for reload
  at      Reload at a specific time/date
  cancel  Cancel pending reload
  in      Reload after a time interval
<cr>
```

The system can also be reloaded by switching it off and then back on again.

The configuration register is used to specify the router's behavior during the reloading process. It determines whether the IOS image should be loaded, determines whether terminal access parameters are provided, and enables or disables the Esc key. The configuration register can be modified in configuration mode using the **config-register** command.

CAUTION   Use the **config-register** command only if you completely understand its effects. Incorrect use of this command can make the system inaccessible.

By default, the router first tries to boot from the first image in the onboard system Flash, if available, and then it tries the PCMCIA Flash cards. The user may also specify which images or locations to attempt booting from and the order using the **boot system** command in configuration mode:

```
IOS(config)# boot system slot0
```

This causes the system to attempt booting from an image in the Flash memory in PCMCIA slot 0 before going to the onboard system Flash.

To upgrade the Cisco IOS software version running on a router, you must first determine the right image to upgrade to using the upgrade planners available on www.cisco.com.

CAUTION   Attempting to load an incorrect image for your system might leave the system inaccessible. Ensure that you have the correct software image and meet the RAM and Flash memory requirements to run and store the image before installing.

The **copy** command copies an image into Flash memory. There are many ways to do this, as demonstrated in Example 4-5.

Example 4-5 *Options for Copying an IOS Image into Flash Memory*

```
IOS# copy ?
  /erase          Erase destination file system.
  flash:          Copy from flash: file system
  ftp:            Copy from ftp: file system
  null:           Copy from null: file system
  nvram:          Copy from nvram: file system
  pram:           Copy from pram: file system
  rcp:            Copy from rcp: file system
  running-config  Copy from current system configuration
  slot0:          Copy from slot0: file system
  slot1:          Copy from slot1: file system
  startup-config  Copy from startup configuration
  system:         Copy from system: file system
  tftp:           Copy from tftp: file system
  xmodem:         Copy from xmodem: file system
  ymodem:         Copy from ymodem: file system
```

The most common methods are TFTP and FTP. After the file has been placed on your TFTP or FTP server, enter the **copy** command from privileged mode and answer the questions on server IP address and source and destination filenames. After you specify which image the system should load using the **boot system** command, a **reload** is required for the new version of IOS to be booted.

Summary

This chapter introduced the fundamentals of Cisco IOS software, the operating system that runs on Cisco routers and switches. Cisco IOS software runs on a CPU and requires several types of memory to store the image, configuration, running applications, and data. The CLI is the most common method used to configure, monitor, and troubleshoot a system running Cisco IOS software. The software provides comprehensive debugging and logging capabilities. You can upgrade the software image by downloading it using one of many options and then following a series of simple steps.

Review Questions

1 What are the four main memory types in a router?

2 What are the three Cisco IOS command modes?

3 What is the process of restarting a Cisco IOS system called?

For More Information

- Cisco IOS software Release 12.2 documentation: www.cisco.com/pcgi-bin/Support/browse/psp_view.pl?p=Software:IOS:12.2&s=Documentation.

- *Cisco IOS Configuration Fundamentals,* Cisco Press, 1997, ISBN 0641049129.

- *Cisco IOS in a Nutshell,* O'Reilly & Associates, Inc., 2001, ISBN 156592942X.

- *Inside Cisco IOS Software Architecture,* Pearson Education, 2000, ISBN 1578701813.

Objectives

- Learn about different LAN protocols.
- Learn about the different methods used to deal with media contention.
- Learn about different LAN topologies.

CHAPTER 5

Bridging and Switching Basics

This chapter introduces the technologies employed in devices loosely referred to as bridges and switches. Topics summarized here include general link layer device operations, local and remote bridging, ATM switching, and LAN switching. Chapters in Part V, "Bridging and Switching," address specific technologies in more detail.

What Are Bridges and Switches?

Bridges and *switches* are data communications devices that operate principally at Layer 2 of the OSI reference model. As such, they are widely referred to as data link layer devices.

Bridges became commercially available in the early 1980s. At the time of their introduction, bridges connected and enabled packet forwarding between homogeneous networks. More recently, bridging between different networks has also been defined and standardized.

Several kinds of bridging have proven important as internetworking devices. *Transparent bridging* is found primarily in Ethernet environments, while *source-route bridging* occurs primarily in Token Ring environments. *Translational bridging* provides translation between the formats and transit principles of different media types (usually Ethernet and Token Ring). Finally, *source-route transparent bridging* combines the algorithms of transparent bridging and source-route bridging to enable communication in mixed Ethernet/Token Ring environments.

Today, switching technology has emerged as the evolutionary heir to bridging-based internetworking solutions. Switching implementations now dominate applications in which bridging technologies were implemented in prior network designs. Superior throughput performance, higher port density, lower per-port cost, and greater flexibility have contributed to the emergence of switches as replacement technology for bridges and as complements to routing technology.

Link Layer Device Overview

Bridging and switching occur at the link layer, which controls data flow, handles transmission errors, provides physical (as opposed to logical) addressing, and manages access to the physical medium. Bridges provide these functions by using various link layer protocols that dictate specific flow control, error handling, addressing, and media-access algorithms. Examples of popular link layer protocols include Ethernet, Token Ring, and FDDI.

Bridges and switches are not complicated devices. They analyze incoming frames, make forwarding decisions based on information contained in the frames, and forward the frames toward the destination. In some cases, such as source-route bridging, the entire path to the destination is contained in each frame. In other cases, such as transparent bridging, frames are forwarded one hop at a time toward the destination.

Upper-layer protocol transparency is a primary advantage of both bridging and switching. Because both device types operate at the link layer, they are not required to examine upper-layer information. This means that they can rapidly forward traffic representing any network layer protocol. It is not uncommon for a bridge to move AppleTalk, DECnet, TCP/IP, XNS, and other traffic between two or more networks.

Bridges are capable of filtering frames based on any Layer 2 fields. For example, a bridge can be programmed to reject (not forward) all frames sourced from a particular network. Because link layer information often includes a reference to an upper-layer protocol, bridges usually can filter on this parameter. Furthermore, filters can be helpful in dealing with unnecessary broadcast and multicast packets.

By dividing large networks into self-contained units, bridges and switches provide several advantages. Because only a certain percentage of traffic is forwarded, a bridge or switch diminishes the traffic experienced by devices on all connected segments. The bridge or switch will act as a firewall for some potentially damaging network errors and will accommodate communication between a larger number of devices than would be supported on any single LAN connected to the bridge. Bridges and switches extend the effective length of a LAN, permitting the attachment of distant stations that was not previously permitted.

Although bridges and switches share most relevant attributes, several distinctions differentiate these technologies. Bridges are generally used to segment a LAN into a couple of smaller segments. Switches are generally used to segment a large LAN into many smaller segments. Bridges generally have only a few ports for LAN connectivity, whereas switches generally have many. Small switches such as the Cisco Catalyst 2924XL have 24 ports capable of creating 24 different network segments for a LAN. Larger switches such as the Cisco Catalyst 6500 can have hundreds of ports. Switches can also be used to connect LANs with different media—for example, a 10-Mbps Ethernet LAN and a 100-Mbps Ethernet LAN can be connected using a switch. Some switches support cut-through switching, which reduces latency and delays in the network, while bridges support only store-and-forward traffic switching. Finally, switches reduce collisions on network segments because they provide dedicated bandwidth to each network segment.

Types of Bridges

Bridges can be grouped into categories based on various product characteristics. Using one popular classification scheme, bridges are either local or remote. *Local bridges* provide a direct connection between multiple LAN segments in the same area. *Remote bridges* connect multiple LAN segments in different areas, usually over telecommunications lines. Figure 5-1 illustrates these two configurations.

Figure 5-1   *Local and Remote Bridges Connect LAN Segments in Specific Areas*

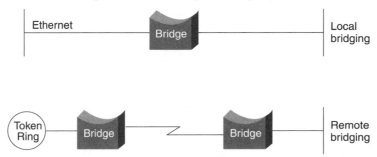

Remote bridging presents several unique internetworking challenges, one of which is the difference between LAN and WAN speeds. Although several fast WAN technologies now are establishing a presence in geographically dispersed internetworks, LAN speeds are often much faster than WAN speeds. Vast differences in LAN and WAN speeds can prevent users from running delay-sensitive LAN applications over the WAN.

Remote bridges cannot improve WAN speeds, but they can compensate for speed discrepancies through a sufficient buffering capability. If a LAN device capable of a 3-Mbps transmission rate wants to communicate with a device on a remote LAN, the local bridge must regulate the 3-Mbps data stream so that it does not overwhelm the 64-kbps serial link. This is done by storing the incoming data in onboard buffers and sending it over the serial link at a rate that the serial link can accommodate. This buffering can be achieved only for short bursts of data that do not overwhelm the bridge's buffering capability.

The Institute of Electrical and Electronic Engineers (IEEE) differentiates the OSI link layer into two separate sublayers: the *Media Access Control (MAC)* sublayer and the *Logical Link Control (LLC)* sublayer. The MAC sublayer permits and orchestrates media access, such as contention and token passing, while the LLC sublayer deals with framing, flow control, error control, and MAC sublayer addressing.

Some bridges are *MAC-layer bridges*, which bridge between homogeneous networks (for example, IEEE 802.3 and IEEE 802.3), while other bridges can translate between different link layer protocols (for example, IEEE 802.3 and IEEE 802.5). The basic mechanics of such a translation are shown in Figure 5-2.

Figure 5-2   *A MAC-Layer Bridge Connects the IEEE 802.3 and IEEE 802.5 Networks*

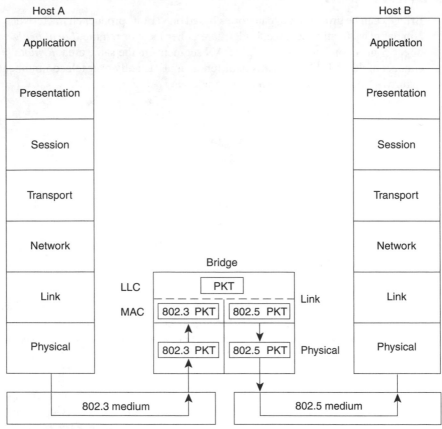

Figure 5-2 illustrates an IEEE 802.3 host (Host A) formulating a packet that contains application information and encapsulating the packet in an IEEE 802.3-compatible frame for transit over the IEEE 802.3 medium to the bridge. At the bridge, the frame is stripped of its IEEE 802.3 header at the MAC sublayer of the link layer and is subsequently passed up to the LLC sublayer for further processing. After this processing, the packet is passed back down to an IEEE 802.5 implementation, which encapsulates the packet in an IEEE 802.5 header for transmission on the IEEE 802.5 network to the IEEE 802.5 host (Host B).

A bridge's translation between networks of different types is never perfect because one network likely will support certain frame fields and protocol functions not supported by the other network.

Types of Switches

Switches are data link layer devices that, like bridges, enable multiple physical LAN segments to be interconnected into a single larger network. Similar to bridges, switches forward and flood traffic based on MAC addresses. Any network device will create some latency. Switches can use different forwarding techniques—two of these are store-and-forward switching and cut-through switching.

In *store-and-forward switching*, an entire frame must be received before it is forwarded. This means that the latency through the switch is relative to the frame size—the larger the frame size, the longer the delay through the switch. *Cut-through switching* allows the switch to begin forwarding the frame when enough of the frame is received to make a forwarding decision. This reduces the latency through the switch. Store-and-forward switching gives the switch the opportunity to evaluate the frame for errors before forwarding it. This capability to not forward frames containing errors is one of the advantages of switches over hubs. Cut-through switching does not offer this advantage, so the switch might forward frames containing errors. Many types of switches exist, including ATM switches, LAN switches, and various types of WAN switches.

ATM Switch

Asynchronous Transfer Mode (ATM) switches provide high-speed switching and scalable bandwidths in the workgroup, the enterprise network backbone, and the wide area. ATM switches support voice, video, and data applications, and are designed to switch fixed-size information units called cells, which are used in ATM communications. Figure 5-3 illustrates an enterprise network comprised of multiple LANs interconnected across an ATM backbone.

Figure 5-3   *Multi-LAN Networks Can Use an ATM-Based Backbone When Switching Cells*

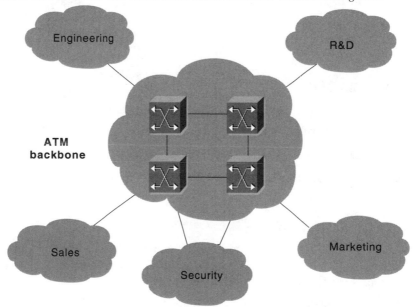

LAN Switch

LAN switches are used to interconnect multiple LAN segments. LAN switching provides dedicated, collision-free communication between network devices, with support for multiple simultaneous conversations. LAN switches are designed to switch data frames at high speeds. Figure 5-4 illustrates a simple network in which a LAN switch interconnects a 10-Mbps and a 100-Mbps Ethernet LAN.

Figure 5-4   *A LAN Switch Can Link 10-Mbps and 100-Mbps Ethernet Segments*

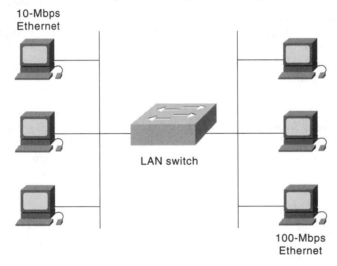

Review Questions

1   What layer of the OSI reference model to bridges and switches operate.

2   What is controlled at the link layer?

3   Under one popular classification scheme what are bridges classified as?

4   What is a switch?

For More Information

- Cisco's web site (www.cisco.com) is a wonderful source for more information about these topics. The Documentation section includes in-depth discussions on many of the topics covered in this chapter.

- Clark, Kennedy, and Kevin Hamilton. *Cisco LAN Switching*. Indianapolis: Cisco Press, August 1999.

- Cisco Systems, Inc. *Cisco IOS Bridging and IBM Network Solutions*. Indianapolis: Cisco Press, June 1998.

Objectives

- Learn the basics of routing protocols.
- Learn the differences between link-state and distance vector routing protocols.
- Learn about the metrics used by routing protocols to determine path selection.
- Learn the basics of how data travels from end stations through intermediate stations and on to the destination end station.
- Understand the difference between routed protocols and routing protocols.

CHAPTER 6

Routing Basics

This chapter introduces the underlying concepts widely used in routing protocols. Topics summarized here include routing protocol components and algorithms. In addition, the role of routing protocols is briefly contrasted with the role of routed or network protocols. Subsequent chapters in Part VII, "Routing Protocols," address specific routing protocols in more detail, while the network protocols that use routing protocols are discussed in Part VI, "Network Protocols."

What Is Routing?

Routing is the act of moving information across an internetwork from a source to a destination. Along the way, at least one intermediate node typically is encountered. Routing is often contrasted with bridging, which might seem to accomplish precisely the same thing to the casual observer. The primary difference between the two is that bridging occurs at Layer 2 (the link layer) of the OSI reference model, whereas routing occurs at Layer 3 (the network layer). This distinction provides routing and bridging with different information to use in the process of moving information from source to destination, so the two functions accomplish their tasks in different ways.

The topic of routing has been covered in computer science literature for more than two decades, but routing achieved commercial popularity as late as the mid-1980s. The primary reason for this time lag is that networks in the 1970s were simple, homogeneous environments. Only relatively recently has large-scale internetworking become popular.

Routing Components

Routing involves two basic activities: determining optimal routing paths and transporting information groups (typically called packets) through an internetwork. In the context of the routing process, the latter of these is referred to as packet switching. Although packet switching is relatively straightforward, path determination can be very complex.

Path Determination

Routing protocols use metrics to evaluate what path will be the best for a packet to travel. A metric is a standard of measurement, such as path bandwidth, that is used by routing algorithms to determine the optimal path to a destination. To aid the process of path determination, routing algorithms initialize and maintain routing tables, which contain route information. Route information varies depending on the routing algorithm used.

Routing algorithms fill routing tables with a variety of information. Destination/next hop associations tell a router that a particular destination can be reached optimally by sending the packet to a particular router representing the "next hop" on the way to the final destination. When a router receives an incoming packet, it checks the destination address and attempts to associate this address with a next hop. Figure 6-1 depicts a sample destination/next hop routing table.

Figure 6-1 *Destination/Next Hop Associations Determine the Data's Optimal Path*

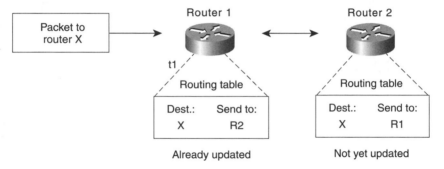

Routing tables also can contain other information, such as data about the desirability of a path. Routers compare metrics to determine optimal routes, and these metrics differ depending on the design of the routing algorithm used. A variety of common metrics will be introduced and described later in this chapter.

Routers communicate with one another and maintain their routing tables through the transmission of a variety of messages. The routing update message is one such message that generally consists of all or a portion of a routing table. By analyzing routing updates from all other routers, a router can build a detailed picture of network topology. A link-state advertisement, another example of a message sent between routers, informs other routers of the state of the sender's links. Link information also can be used to build a complete picture of network topology to enable routers to determine optimal routes to network destinations.

Switching

Switching algorithms is relatively simple; it is the same for most routing protocols. In most cases, a host determines that it must send a packet to another host. Having acquired a router's address by some means, the source host sends a packet addressed specifically to a router's physical (Media Access Control [MAC]-layer) address, this time with the protocol (network layer) address of the destination host.

As it examines the packet's destination protocol address, the router determines that it either knows or does not know how to forward the packet to the next hop. If the router does not know how to forward the packet, it typically drops the packet. If the router knows how to forward the packet, however, it changes the destination physical address to that of the next hop and transmits the packet.

The next hop may be the ultimate destination host. If not, the next hop is usually another router, which executes the same switching decision process. As the packet moves through the internetwork, its physical address changes, but its protocol address remains constant, as illustrated in Figure 6-2.

The preceding discussion describes switching between a source and a destination end system. The International Organization for Standardization (ISO) has developed a hierarchical terminology that is useful in describing this process. Using this terminology, network devices without the capability to forward packets between subnetworks are called *end systems (ESs)*, whereas network devices with these capabilities are called *intermediate systems (ISs)*. ISs are further divided into those that can communicate within routing domains (*intradomain ISs*) and those that communicate both within and between routing domains (*interdomain ISs*). A routing domain generally is considered a portion of an internetwork under common administrative authority that is regulated by a particular set of administrative guidelines. Routing domains are also called autonomous systems. With certain protocols, routing domains can be divided into routing areas, but intradomain routing protocols are still used for switching both within and between areas.

Figure 6-2   *Numerous Routers May Come into Play During the Switching Process*

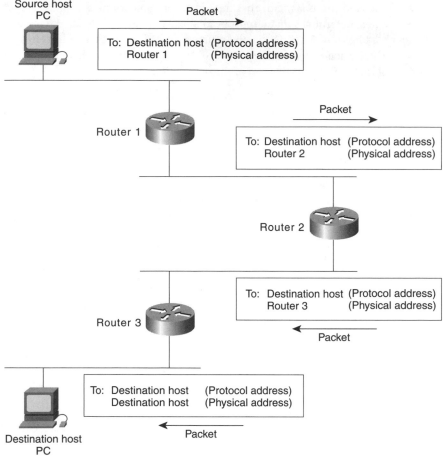

Routing Algorithms

Routing algorithms can be differentiated based on several key characteristics. First, the particular goals of the algorithm designer affect the operation of the resulting routing protocol. Second, various types of routing algorithms exist, and each algorithm has a different impact on network and router resources. Finally, routing algorithms use a variety of metrics that affect calculation of optimal routes. The following sections analyze these routing algorithm attributes.

Design Goals

Routing algorithms often have one or more of the following design goals:

- Optimality
- Simplicity and low overhead
- Robustness and stability
- Rapid convergence
- Flexibility

Optimality refers to the capability of the routing algorithm to select the best route, which depends on the metrics and metric weightings used to make the calculation. For example, one routing algorithm may use a number of hops and delays, but it may weigh delay more heavily in the calculation. Naturally, routing protocols must define their metric calculation algorithms strictly.

Routing algorithms also are designed to be as simple as possible. In other words, the routing algorithm must offer its functionality efficiently, with a minimum of software and utilization overhead. Efficiency is particularly important when the software implementing the routing algorithm must run on a computer with limited physical resources.

Routing algorithms must be *robust*, which means that they should perform correctly in the face of unusual or unforeseen circumstances, such as hardware failures, high load conditions, and incorrect implementations. Because routers are located at network junction points, they can cause considerable problems when they fail. The best routing algorithms are often those that have withstood the test of time and that have proven stable under a variety of network conditions.

In addition, routing algorithms must converge rapidly. *Convergence* is the process of agreement, by all routers, on optimal routes. When a network event causes routes to either go down or become available, routers distribute routing update messages that permeate networks, stimulating recalculation of optimal routes and eventually causing all routers to agree on these routes. Routing algorithms that converge slowly can cause routing loops or network outages.

In the routing loop displayed in Figure 6-3, a packet arrives at Router 1 at time t1. Router 1 already has been updated and thus knows that the optimal route to the destination calls for Router 2 to be the next stop. Router 1 therefore forwards the packet to Router 2, but because this router has not yet been updated, it believes that the optimal next hop is Router 1. Router 2 therefore forwards the packet back to Router 1, and the packet continues to bounce back and forth between the two routers until Router 2 receives its routing update or until the packet has been switched the maximum number of times allowed.

Figure 6-3   *Slow Convergence and Routing Loops Can Hinder Progress*

To reach network: Send to:

27	Node A
57	Node B
17	Node C
24	Node A
52	Node A
16	Node B
26	Node A
.	.
.	.
.	.

Routing algorithms should also be flexible, which means that they should quickly and accurately adapt to a variety of network circumstances. Assume, for example, that a network segment has gone down. As many routing algorithms become aware of the problem, they will quickly select the next-best path for all routes normally using that segment. Routing algorithms can be programmed to adapt to changes in network bandwidth, router queue size, and network delay, among other variables.

Algorithm Types

Routing algorithms can be classified by type. Key differentiators include these:

- Static versus dynamic
- Single-path versus multipath
- Flat versus hierarchical
- Host-intelligent versus router-intelligent
- Intradomain versus interdomain
- Link-state versus distance vector

Static Versus Dynamic

Static routing algorithms are hardly algorithms at all, but are table mappings established by the network administrator before the beginning of routing. These mappings do not change unless the network administrator alters them. Algorithms that use static routes are simple to design and work well in environments where network traffic is relatively predictable and where network design is relatively simple.

Because static routing systems cannot react to network changes, they generally are considered unsuitable for today's large, constantly changing networks. Most of the dominant routing algorithms today are *dynamic routing algorithms*, which adjust to changing network circumstances by analyzing incoming routing update messages. If the message indicates that a network change has occurred, the routing software recalculates routes and sends out new routing update messages. These messages permeate the network, stimulating routers to rerun their algorithms and change their routing tables accordingly.

Dynamic routing algorithms can be supplemented with static routes where appropriate. A router of last resort (a router to which all unroutable packets are sent), for example, can be designated to act as a repository for all unroutable packets, ensuring that all messages are at least handled in some way.

Single-Path Versus Multipath

Some sophisticated routing protocols support multiple paths to the same destination. Unlike single-path algorithms, these multipath algorithms permit traffic multiplexing over multiple lines. The advantages of multipath algorithms are obvious: They can provide substantially better throughput and reliability. This is generally called load sharing.

Flat Versus Hierarchical

Some routing algorithms operate in a flat space, while others use routing hierarchies. In a *flat routing system*, the routers are peers of all others. In a hierarchical routing system, some routers form what amounts to a routing backbone. Packets from nonbackbone routers travel to the backbone routers, where they are sent through the backbone until they reach the general area of the destination. At this point, they travel from the last backbone router through one or more nonbackbone routers to the final destination.

Routing systems often designate logical groups of nodes, called domains, autonomous systems, or areas. In *hierarchical systems*, some routers in a domain can communicate with routers in other domains, while others can communicate only with routers within their domain. In very large networks, additional hierarchical levels may exist, with routers at the highest hierarchical level forming the routing backbone.

The primary advantage of hierarchical routing is that it mimics the organization of most companies and therefore supports their traffic patterns well. Most network communication occurs within small company groups (domains). Because intradomain routers need to know only about other routers within their domain, their routing algorithms can be simplified, and, depending on the routing algorithm being used, routing update traffic can be reduced accordingly.

Host-Intelligent Versus Router-Intelligent

Some routing algorithms assume that the source end node will determine the entire route. This is usually referred to as *source routing*. In source-routing systems, routers merely act as store-and-forward devices, mindlessly sending the packet to the next stop.

Other algorithms assume that hosts know nothing about routes. In these algorithms, routers determine the path through the internetwork based on their own calculations. In the first system, the hosts have the routing intelligence. In the latter system, routers have the routing intelligence.

Intradomain Versus Interdomain

Some routing algorithms work only within domains; others work within and between domains. The nature of these two algorithm types is different. It stands to reason, therefore, that an optimal intradomain-routing algorithm would not necessarily be an optimal interdomain-routing algorithm.

Link-State Versus Distance Vector

Link-state algorithms (also known as shortest path first algorithms) flood routing information to all nodes in the internetwork. Each router, however, sends only the portion of the routing table that describes the state of its own links. In link-state algorithms, each router builds a picture of the entire network in its routing tables. Distance vector algorithms (also known as Bellman-Ford algorithms) call for each router to send all or some portion of its routing table, but only to its neighbors. In essence, link-state algorithms send small updates everywhere, while distance vector algorithms send larger updates only to neighboring routers. *Distance vector* algorithms know only about their neighbors.

Because they converge more quickly, link-state algorithms are somewhat less prone to routing loops than distance vector algorithms. On the other hand, link-state algorithms require more CPU power and memory than distance vector algorithms. Link-state algorithms, therefore, can be more expensive to implement and support. Link-state protocols are generally more scalable than distance vector protocols.

Routing Metrics

Routing tables contain information used by switching software to select the best route. But how, specifically, are routing tables built? What is the specific nature of the information that they contain? How do routing algorithms determine that one route is preferable to others?

Routing algorithms have used many different metrics to determine the best route. Sophisticated routing algorithms can base route selection on multiple metrics, combining them in a single (hybrid) metric. All the following metrics have been used:

- Path length
- Reliability
- Delay
- Bandwidth
- Load
- Communication cost

Path length is the most common routing metric. Some routing protocols allow network administrators to assign arbitrary costs to each network link. In this case, path length is the sum of the costs associated with each link traversed. Other routing protocols define hop count, a metric that specifies the number of passes through internetworking products, such as routers, that a packet must take en route from a source to a destination.

Reliability, in the context of routing algorithms, refers to the dependability (usually described in terms of the bit-error rate) of each network link. Some network links might go down more often than others. After a network fails, certain network links might be repaired more easily or more quickly than other links. Any reliability factors can be taken into account in the assignment of the reliability ratings, which are arbitrary numeric values usually assigned to network links by network administrators.

Routing delay refers to the length of time required to move a packet from source to destination through the internetwork. Delay depends on many factors, including the bandwidth of intermediate network links, the port queues at each router along the way, network congestion on all intermediate network links, and the physical distance to be traveled. Because delay is a conglomeration of several important variables, it is a common and useful metric.

Bandwidth refers to the available traffic capacity of a link. All other things being equal, a 10-Mbps Ethernet link would be preferable to a 64-kbps leased line. Although bandwidth is a rating of the maximum attainable throughput on a link, routes through links with greater bandwidth do not necessarily provide better routes than routes through slower links. For example, if a faster link is busier, the actual time required to send a packet to the destination could be greater.

Load refers to the degree to which a network resource, such as a router, is busy. Load can be calculated in a variety of ways, including CPU utilization and packets processed per second. Monitoring these parameters on a continual basis can be resource-intensive itself.

Communication cost is another important metric, especially because some companies may not care about performance as much as they care about operating expenditures. Although line delay may be longer, they will send packets over their own lines rather than through the public lines that cost money for usage time.

Network Protocols

Routed protocols are transported by routing protocols across an internetwork. In general, routed protocols in this context also are referred to as network protocols. These network protocols perform a variety of functions required for communication between user applications in source and destination devices, and these functions can differ widely among protocol suites. Network protocols occur at the upper five layers of the OSI reference model: the network layer, the transport layer, the session layer, the presentation layer, and the application layer.

Confusion about the terms *routed protocol* and *routing protocol* is common. Routed protocols are protocols that are routed over an internetwork. Examples of such protocols are the Internet Protocol (IP), DECnet, AppleTalk, Novell NetWare, OSI, Banyan VINES, and Xerox Network System (XNS). Routing protocols, on the other hand, are protocols that implement routing algorithms. Put simply, routing protocols are used by intermediate systems to build tables used in determining path selection of routed protocols. Examples of these protocols include Interior Gateway Routing Protocol (IGRP), Enhanced Interior Gateway Routing Protocol (Enhanced IGRP), Open Shortest Path First (OSPF), Exterior Gateway Protocol (EGP), Border Gateway Protocol (BGP), Intermediate System-to-Intermediate System (IS-IS), and Routing Information Protocol (RIP). Routed and routing protocols are discussed in detail later in this book.

Review Questions

1 Describe the process of routing packets.

2 What are some routing algorithm types?

3 Describe the difference between static and dynamic routing.

4 What are some of the metrics used by routing protocols?

Objective

- Become familiar with the basic functions of a network management system.

CHAPTER 7

Network Management Basics

Introduction

This chapter describes functions common to most network-management architectures and protocols. It also presents the five conceptual areas of management as defined by the International Organization for Standardization (ISO). Subsequent chapters in Part VIII, "Network Management," address specific network management technologies, protocols, and platforms in more detail.

What Is Network Management?

Network management means different things to different people. In some cases, it involves a solitary network consultant monitoring network activity with an outdated protocol analyzer. In other cases, network management involves a distributed database, autopolling of network devices, and high-end workstations generating real-time graphical views of network topology changes and traffic. In general, network management is a service that employs a variety of tools, applications, and devices to assist human network managers in monitoring and maintaining networks.

A Historical Perspective

The early 1980s saw tremendous expansion in the area of network deployment. As companies realized the cost benefits and productivity gains created by network technology, they began to add networks and expand existing networks almost as rapidly as new network technologies and products were introduced. By the mid-1980s, certain companies were experiencing growing pains from deploying many different (and sometimes incompatible) network technologies.

The problems associated with network expansion affect both day-to-day network operation management and strategic network growth planning. Each new network technology requires its own set of experts. In the early 1980s, the staffing requirements alone for managing large, heterogeneous networks created a crisis for many organizations. An urgent need arose for automated network management (including what is typically called network capacity planning) integrated across diverse environments.

Network Management Architecture

Most network management architectures use the same basic structure and set of relationships. End stations (managed devices), such as computer systems and other network devices, run software that enables them to send alerts when they recognize problems (for example, when one or more user-determined thresholds are exceeded). Upon receiving these alerts, management entities are programmed to react by executing one, several, or a group of actions, including operator notification, event logging, system shutdown, and automatic attempts at system repair.

Management entities also can poll end stations to check the values of certain variables. Polling can be automatic or user-initiated, but agents in the managed devices respond to all polls. Agents are software modules that first compile information about the managed devices in which they reside, then store this information in a management database, and finally provide it (proactively or reactively) to management entities within network management systems (NMSs) via a network management protocol. Well-known network management protocols include the Simple Network Management Protocol (SNMP) and Common Management Information Protocol (CMIP). Management proxies are entities that provide management information on behalf of other entities. Figure 7-1 depicts a typical network management architecture.

Figure 7-1   *A Typical Network Management Architecture Maintains Many Relationships*

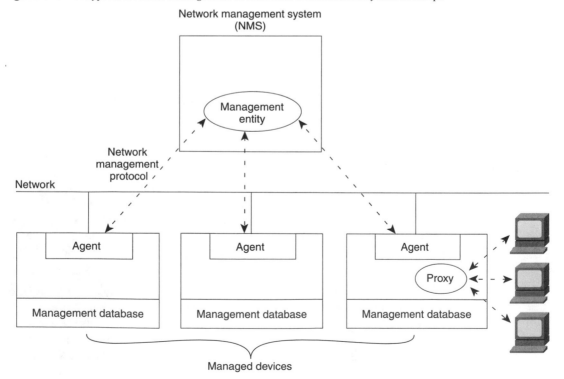

ISO Network Management Model

The ISO has contributed a great deal to network standardization. Its network management model is the primary means for understanding the major functions of network management systems. This model consists of five conceptual areas, as discussed in the next sections.

Performance Management

The goal of *performance management* is to measure and make available various aspects of network performance so that internetwork performance can be maintained at an acceptable level. Examples of performance variables that might be provided include network throughput, user response times, and line utilization.

Performance management involves three main steps. First, performance data is gathered on variables of interest to network administrators. Second, the data is analyzed to determine normal (baseline) levels. Finally, appropriate performance thresholds are determined for each important variable so that exceeding these thresholds indicates a network problem worthy of attention.

Management entities continually monitor performance variables. When a performance threshold is exceeded, an alert is generated and sent to the network management system.

Each of the steps just described is part of the process to set up a reactive system. When performance becomes unacceptable because of an exceeded user-defined threshold, the system reacts by sending a message. Performance management also permits proactive methods: For example, network simulation can be used to project how network growth will affect performance metrics. Such simulation can alert administrators to impending problems so that counteractive measures can be taken.

Configuration Management

The goal of *configuration management* is to monitor network and system configuration information so that the effects on network operation of various versions of hardware and software elements can be tracked and managed.

Each network device has a variety of version information associated with it. An engineering workstation, for example, may be configured as follows:

- Operating system, Version 3.2
- Ethernet interface, Version 5.4
- TCP/IP software, Version 2.0
- NetWare software, Version 4.1
- NFS software, Version 5.1

- Serial communications controller, Version 1.1
- X.25 software, Version 1.0
- SNMP software, Version 3.1

Configuration management subsystems store this information in a database for easy access. When a problem occurs, this database can be searched for clues that may help solve the problem.

Accounting Management

The goal of *accounting management* is to measure network utilization parameters so that individual or group uses on the network can be regulated appropriately. Such regulation minimizes network problems (because network resources can be apportioned based on resource capacities) and maximizes the fairness of network access across all users.

As with performance management, the first step toward appropriate accounting management is to measure utilization of all important network resources. Analysis of the results provides insight into current usage patterns, and usage quotas can be set at this point. Some correction, of course, will be required to reach optimal access practices. From this point, ongoing measurement of resource use can yield billing information as well as information used to assess continued fair and optimal resource utilization.

Fault Management

The goal of *fault management* is to detect, log, notify users of, and (to the extent possible) automatically fix network problems to keep the network running effectively. Because faults can cause downtime or unacceptable network degradation, fault management is perhaps the most widely implemented of the ISO network management elements.

Fault management involves first determining symptoms and isolating the problem. Then the problem is fixed and the solution is tested on all-important subsystems. Finally, the detection and resolution of the problem is recorded.

Security Management

The goal of *security management* is to control access to network resources according to local guidelines so that the network cannot be sabotaged (intentionally or unintentionally) and sensitive information cannot be accessed by those without appropriate authorization. A security management subsystem, for example, can monitor users logging on to a network resource and can refuse access to those who enter inappropriate access codes.

Security management subsystems work by partitioning network resources into authorized and unauthorized areas. For some users, access to any network resource is inappropriate, mostly because such users are usually company outsiders. For other (internal) network users, access to information originating from a particular department is inappropriate. Access to Human Resource files, for example, is inappropriate for most users outside the Human Resources department.

Security management subsystems perform several functions. They identify sensitive network resources (including systems, files, and other entities) and determine mappings between sensitive network resources and user sets. They also monitor access points to sensitive network resources and log inappropriate access to sensitive network resources.

Review Questions

1 Name the different areas of network management.

2 What are the goals of performance management?

3 What are the goals of configuration management?

4 What are the goals of accounting management?

5 What are the goals of fault management?

6 What are the goals of security management?

Objectives

- Understand the required and optional MAC frame formats, their purposes, and their compatibility requirements.

- List the various Ethernet physical layers, signaling procedures, and link media requirements/limitations.

- Describe the trade-offs associated with implementing or upgrading Ethernet LANs—choosing data rates, operational modes, and network equipment.

CHAPTER 8

Ethernet Technologies

Background

The term *Ethernet* refers to the family of local-area network (LAN) products covered by the IEEE 802.3 standard that defines what is commonly known as the CSMA/CD protocol. Three data rates are currently defined for operation over optical fiber and twisted-pair cables:

- 10 Mbps—10Base-T Ethernet
- 100 Mbps—Fast Ethernet
- 1000 Mbps—Gigabit Ethernet

10-Gigabit Ethernet is under development and will likely be published as the IEEE 802.3ae supplement to the IEEE 802.3 base standard in late 2001 or early 2002.

Other technologies and protocols have been touted as likely replacements, but the market has spoken. Ethernet has survived as the major LAN technology (it is currently used for approximately 85 percent of the world's LAN-connected PCs and workstations) because its protocol has the following characteristics:

- Is easy to understand, implement, manage, and maintain
- Allows low-cost network implementations
- Provides extensive topological flexibility for network installation
- Guarantees successful interconnection and operation of standards-compliant products, regardless of manufacturer

Ethernet—A Brief History

The original Ethernet was developed as an experimental coaxial cable network in the 1970s by Xerox Corporation to operate with a data rate of 3 Mbps using a carrier sense multiple access collision detect (CSMA/CD) protocol for LANs with sporadic but occasionally heavy traffic requirements. Success with that project attracted early attention and led to the 1980 joint development of the 10-Mbps Ethernet Version 1.0 specification by the three-company consortium: Digital Equipment Corporation, Intel Corporation, and Xerox Corporation.

The original IEEE 802.3 standard was based on, and was very similar to, the Ethernet Version 1.0 specification. The draft standard was approved by the 802.3 working group in 1983 and was subsequently published as an official standard in 1985 (ANSI/IEEE Std. 802.3-1985). Since then, a number of supplements to the standard have been defined to take advantage of improvements in the technologies and to support additional network media and higher data rate capabilities, plus several new optional network access control features.

Throughout the rest of this chapter, the terms *Ethernet* and *802.3* will refer exclusively to network implementations compatible with the IEEE 802.3 standard.

Ethernet Network Elements

Ethernet LANs consist of network nodes and interconnecting media. The network nodes fall into two major classes:

- **Data terminal equipment (DTE)**—Devices that are either the source or the destination of data frames. DTEs are typically devices such as PCs, workstations, file servers, or print servers that, as a group, are all often referred to as end stations.

- **Data communication equipment (DCE)**—Intermediate network devices that receive and forward frames across the network. DCEs may be either standalone devices such as repeaters, network switches, and routers, or communications interface units such as interface cards and modems.

Throughout this chapter, standalone intermediate network devices will be referred to as either *intermediate nodes* or *DCEs*. Network interface cards will be referred to as *NICs*.

The current Ethernet media options include two general types of copper cable: unshielded twisted-pair (UTP) and shielded twisted-pair (STP), plus several types of optical fiber cable.

Ethernet Network Topologies and Structures

LANs take on many topological configurations, but regardless of their size or complexity, all will be a combination of only three basic interconnection structures or network building blocks.

The simplest structure is the point-to-point interconnection, shown in Figure 8-1. Only two network units are involved, and the connection may be DTE-to-DTE, DTE-to-DCE, or DCE-to-DCE. The cable in point-to-point interconnections is known as a network link. The maximum allowable length of the link depends on the type of cable and the transmission method that is used.

Figure 8-1   *Example Point-to-Point Interconnection*

The original Ethernet networks were implemented with a coaxial bus structure, as shown in Figure 8-2. Segment lengths were limited to 500 meters, and up to 100 stations could be connected to a single segment. Individual segments could be interconnected with repeaters, as long as multiple paths did not exist between any two stations on the network and the number of DTEs did not exceed 1024. The total path distance between the most-distant pair of stations was also not allowed to exceed a maximum prescribed value.

Figure 8-2   *Example Coaxial Bus Topology*

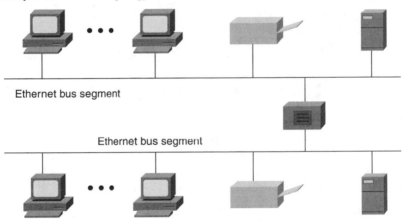

Although new networks are no longer connected in a bus configuration, some older bus-connected networks do still exist and are still useful.

Since the early 1990s, the network configuration of choice has been the star-connected topology, shown in Figure 8-3. The central network unit is either a multiport repeater (also known as a hub) or a network switch. All connections in a star network are point-to-point links implemented with either twisted-pair or optical fiber cable.

Figure 8-3 *Example Star-Connected Topology*

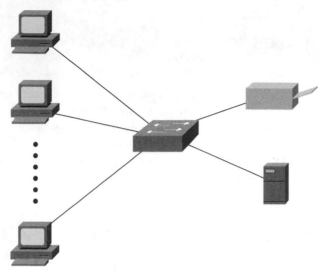

The IEEE 802.3 Logical Relationship to the ISO Reference Model

Figure 8-4 shows the IEEE 802.3 logical layers and their relationship to the OSI reference model. As with all IEEE 802 protocols, the ISO data link layer is divided into two IEEE 802 sublayers, the Media Access Control (MAC) sublayer and the MAC-client sublayer. The IEEE 802.3 physical layer corresponds to the ISO physical layer.

Figure 8-4 *Ethernet's Logical Relationship to the ISO Reference Model*

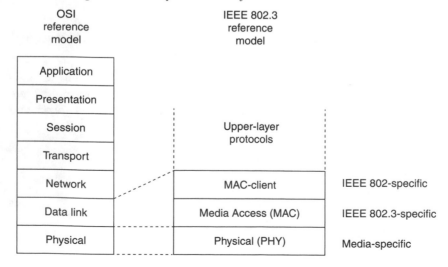

The MAC-client sublayer may be one of the following:

- Logical Link Control (LLC), if the unit is a DTE. This sublayer provides the interface between the Ethernet MAC and the upper layers in the protocol stack of the end station. The LLC sublayer is defined by IEEE 802.2 standards.

- Bridge entity, if the unit is a DCE. Bridge entities provide LAN-to-LAN interfaces between LANs that use the same protocol (for example, Ethernet to Ethernet) and also between different protocols (for example, Ethernet to Token Ring). Bridge entities are defined by IEEE 802.1 standards.

Because specifications for LLC and bridge entities are common for all IEEE 802 LAN protocols, network compatibility becomes the primary responsibility of the particular network protocol. Figure 8-5 shows different compatibility requirements imposed by the MAC and physical levels for basic data communication over an Ethernet link.

Figure 8-5   *MAC and Physical Layer Compatibility Requirements for Basic Data Communication*

MII = Medium-independent interface
MDI = Medium-dependent interface - the link connector

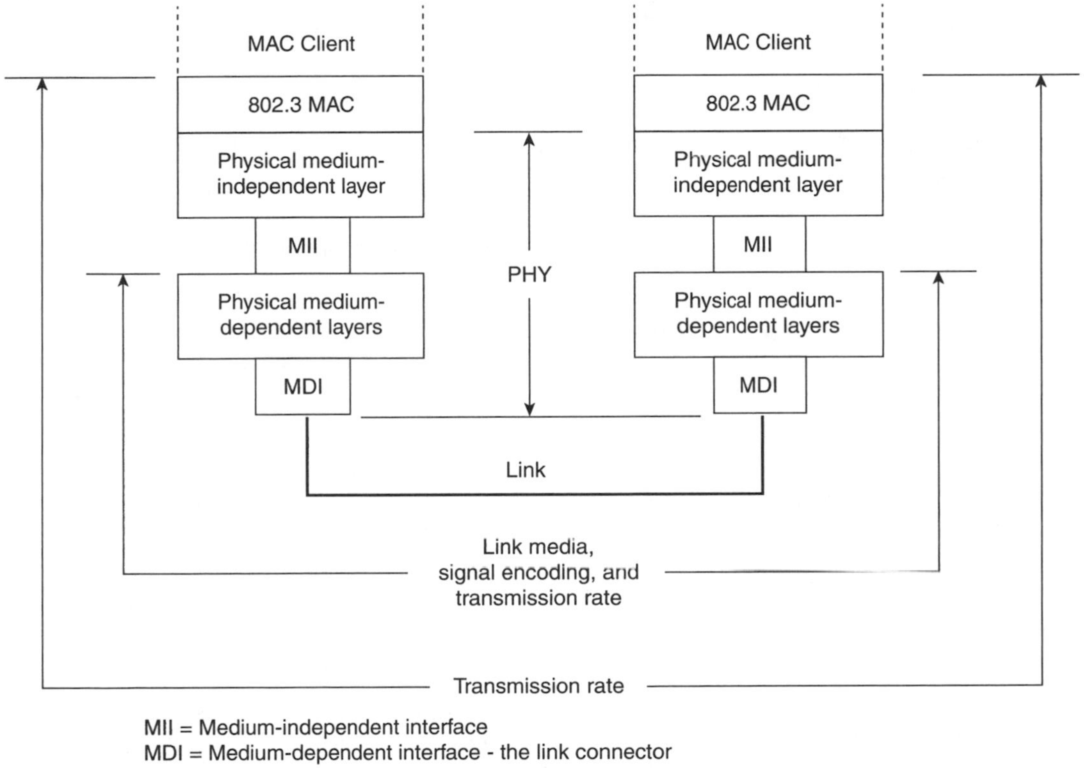

The MAC layer controls the node's access to the network media and is specific to the individual protocol. All IEEE 802.3 MACs must meet the same basic set of logical requirements, regardless of whether they include one or more of the defined optional protocol extensions. The only requirement for basic communication (communication that does not require optional protocol extensions) between two network nodes is that both MACs must support the same transmission rate.

The 802.3 physical layer is specific to the transmission data rate, the signal encoding, and the type of media interconnecting the two nodes. Gigabit Ethernet, for example, is defined to operate over either twisted-pair or optical fiber cable, but each specific type of cable or signal-encoding procedure requires a different physical layer implementation.

The Ethernet MAC Sublayer

The MAC sublayer has two primary responsibilities:

- Data encapsulation, including frame assembly before transmission, and frame parsing/error detection during and after reception

- Media access control, including initiation of frame transmission and recovery from transmission failure

The Basic Ethernet Frame Format

The IEEE 802.3 standard defines a basic data frame format that is required for all MAC implementations, plus several additional optional formats that are used to extend the protocol's basic capability. The basic data frame format contains the seven fields shown in Figure 8-6.

- **Preamble (PRE)**—Consists of 7 bytes. The PRE is an alternating pattern of ones and zeros that tells receiving stations that a frame is coming, and that provides a means to synchronize the frame-reception portions of receiving physical layers with the incoming bit stream.

- **Start-of-frame delimiter (SOF)**—Consists of 1 byte. The SOF is an alternating pattern of ones and zeros, ending with two consecutive 1-bits indicating that the next bit is the left-most bit in the left-most byte of the destination address.

- **Destination address (DA)**—Consists of 6 bytes. The DA field identifies which station(s) should receive the frame. The left-most bit in the DA field indicates whether the address is an individual address (indicated by a 0) or a group address (indicated by a 1). The second bit from the left indicates whether the DA is globally administered (indicated by a 0) or locally administered (indicated by a 1). The remaining 46 bits are a uniquely assigned value that identifies a single station, a defined group of stations, or all stations on the network.

- **Source addresses (SA)**—Consists of 6 bytes. The SA field identifies the sending station. The SA is always an individual address and the left-most bit in the SA field is always 0.

- **Length/Type**—Consists of 4 bytes. This field indicates either the number of MAC-client data bytes that are contained in the data field of the frame, or the frame type ID if the frame is assembled using an optional format. If the Length/Type field value is less than or equal to 1500, the number of LLC bytes in the Data field is equal to the Length/Type field value. If the Length/Type field value is greater than 1536, the frame is an optional type frame, and the Length/Type field value identifies the particular type of frame being sent or received.

- **Data**—Is a sequence of *n* bytes of any value, where *n* is less than or equal to 1500. If the length of the Data field is less than 46, the Data field must be extended by adding a filler (a pad) sufficient to bring the Data field length to 46 bytes.

- **Frame check sequence (FCS)**—Consists of 4 bytes. This sequence contains a 32-bit cyclic redundancy check (CRC) value, which is created by the sending MAC and is recalculated by the receiving MAC to check for damaged frames. The FCS is generated over the DA, SA, Length/Type, and Data fields.

Figure 8-6   *The Basic IEEE 802.3 MAC Data Frame Format*

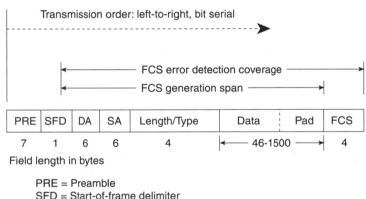

NOTE   Individual addresses are also known as unicast addresses because they refer to a single MAC and are assigned by the NIC manufacturer from a block of addresses allocated by the IEEE. Group addresses (a.k.a. multicast addresses) identify the end stations in a workgroup and are assigned by the network manager. A special group address (all 1s—the broadcast address) indicates all stations on the network.

Frame Transmission

Whenever an end station MAC receives a transmit-frame request with the accompanying address and data information from the LLC sublayer, the MAC begins the transmission sequence by transferring the LLC information into the MAC frame buffer.

- The preamble and start-of-frame delimiter are inserted in the PRE and SOF fields.

- The destination and source addresses are inserted into the address fields.

- The LLC data bytes are counted, and the number of bytes is inserted into the Length/Type field.

- The LLC data bytes are inserted into the Data field. If the number of LLC data bytes is less than 46, a pad is added to bring the Data field length up to 46.

- An FCS value is generated over the DA, SA, Length/Type, and Data fields and is appended to the end of the Data field.

After the frame is assembled, actual frame transmission will depend on whether the MAC is operating in half-duplex or full-duplex mode.

The IEEE 802.3 standard currently requires that all Ethernet MACs support half-duplex operation, in which the MAC can be either transmitting or receiving a frame, but it cannot be doing both simultaneously. Full-duplex operation is an optional MAC capability that allows the MAC to transmit and receive frames simultaneously.

Half-Duplex Transmission—The CSMA/CD Access Method

The CSMA/CD protocol was originally developed as a means by which two or more stations could share a common media in a switch-less environment when the protocol does not require central arbitration, access tokens, or assigned time slots to indicate when a station will be allowed to transmit. Each Ethernet MAC determines for itself when it will be allowed to send a frame.

The CSMA/CD access rules are summarized by the protocol's acronym:

- **Carrier sense**—Each station continuously listens for traffic on the medium to determine when gaps between frame transmissions occur.

- **Multiple access**—Stations may begin transmitting any time they detect that the network is quiet (there is no traffic).

- **Collision detect**—If two or more stations in the same CSMA/CD network (collision domain) begin transmitting at approximately the same time, the bit streams from the transmitting stations will interfere (collide) with each other, and both transmissions will be unreadable. If that happens, each transmitting station must be capable of detecting that a collision has occurred before it has finished sending its frame.

Each must stop transmitting as soon as it has detected the collision and then must wait a quasirandom length of time (determined by a back-off algorithm) before attempting to retransmit the frame.

The worst-case situation occurs when the two most-distant stations on the network both need to send a frame and when the second station does not begin transmitting until just before the frame from the first station arrives. The collision will be detected almost immediately by the second station, but it will not be detected by the first station until the corrupted signal has propagated all the way back to that station. The maximum time that is required to detect a collision (the collision window, or "slot time") is approximately equal to twice the signal propagation time between the two most-distant stations on the network.

This means that both the minimum frame length and the maximum collision diameter are directly related to the slot time. Longer minimum frame lengths translate to longer slot times and larger collision diameters; shorter minimum frame lengths correspond to shorter slot times and smaller collision diameters.

The trade-off was between the need to reduce the impact of collision recovery and the need for network diameters to be large enough to accommodate reasonable network sizes. The compromise was to choose a maximum network diameter (about 2500 meters) and then to set the minimum frame length long enough to ensure detection of all worst-case collisions.

The compromise worked well for 10 Mbps, but it was a problem for higher data-rate Ethernet developers. Fast Ethernet was required to provide backward compatibility with earlier Ethernet networks, including the existing IEEE 802.3 frame format and error-detection procedures, plus all applications and networking software running on the 10-Mbps networks.

Although signal propagation velocity is essentially constant for all transmission rates, the time required to transmit a frame is inversely related to the transmission rate. At 100 Mbps, a minimum-length frame can be transmitted in approximately one-tenth of the defined slot time, and any collision that occurred during the transmission would not likely be detected by the transmitting stations. This, in turn, meant that the maximum network diameters specified for 10-Mbps networks could not be used for 100-Mbps networks. The solution for Fast Ethernet was to reduce the maximum network diameter by approximately a factor of 10 (to a little more than 200 meters).

The same problem also arose during specification development for Gigabit Ethernet, but decreasing network diameters by another factor of 10 (to approximately 20 meters) for 1000-Mbps operation was simply not practical. This time, the developers elected to maintain approximately the same maximum collision domain diameters as 100-Mbps networks and to increase the apparent minimum frame size by adding a variable-length nondata extension field to frames that are shorter than the minimum length (the extension field is removed during frame reception).

Figure 8-7 shows the MAC frame format with the gigabit extension field, and Table 8-1 shows the effect of the trade-off between the transmission data rate and the minimum frame size for 10-Mbps, 100-Mbps, and 1000-Mbps Ethernet.

Figure 8-7 *MAC Frame with Gigabit Carrier Extension*

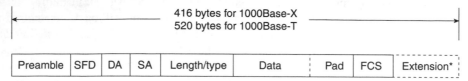

* The extension field is automatically
 removed during frame reception

Table 8-1 *Limits for Half-Duplex Operation*

Parameter	10 Mbps	100 Mbps	1000 Mbps
Minimum frame size	64 bytes	64 bytes	520 bytes[1] (with extension field added)
Maximum collision diameter, DTE to DTE	100 meters UTP	100 meters UTP 412 meters fiber	100 meters UTP 316 meters fiber
Maximum collision diameter with repeaters	2500 meters	205 meters	200 meters
Maximum number of repeaters in network path	5	2	1

[1] 520 bytes applies to 1000Base-T implementations. The minimum frame size with extension field for 1000Base-X is reduced to 416 bytes because 1000Base-X encodes and transmits 10 bits for each byte.

Another change to the Ethernet CSMA/CD transmit specification was the addition of frame bursting for gigabit operation. Burst mode is a feature that allows a MAC to send a short sequence (a burst) of frames equal to approximately 5.4 maximum-length frames without having to relinquish control of the medium. The transmitting MAC fills each interframe interval with extension bits, as shown in Figure 8-8, so that other stations on the network will see that the network is busy and will not attempt transmission until after the burst is complete.

Figure 8-8   *A Gigabit Frame-Burst Sequence*

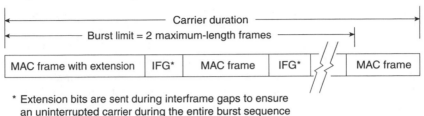

* Extension bits are sent during interframe gaps to ensure
an uninterrupted carrier during the entire burst sequence

If the length of the first frame is less than the minimum frame length, an extension field is
added to extend the frame length to the value indicated in Table 8-1. Subsequent frames
in a frame-burst sequence do not need extension fields, and a frame burst may continue as
long as the burst limit has not been reached. If the burst limit is reached after a frame
transmission has begun, transmission is allowed to continue until that entire frame has been
sent.

Frame extension fields are not defined, and burst mode is not allowed for 10 Mbps and 100
Mbps transmission rates.

Full-Duplex Transmission—An Optional Approach to Higher Network Efficiency

Full-duplex operation is an optional MAC capability that allows simultaneous two-way
transmission over point-to-point links. Full duplex transmission is functionally much
simpler than half-duplex transmission because it involves no media contention, no
collisions, no need to schedule retransmissions, and no need for extension bits on the end
of short frames. The result is not only more time available for transmission, but also an
effective doubling of the link bandwidth because each link can now support full-rate,
simultaneous, two-way transmission.

Transmission can usually begin as soon as frames are ready to send. The only restriction is
that there must be a minimum-length interframe gap between successive frames, as shown
in Figure 8-9, and each frame must conform to Ethernet frame format standards.

Figure 8-9   *Full Duplex Operation Allows Simultaneous Two-Way Transmission on the Same Link*

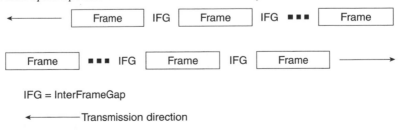

IFG = InterFrameGap

Transmission direction

Flow Control

Full-duplex operation requires concurrent implementation of the optional flow-control capability that allows a receiving node (such as a network switch port) that is becoming congested to request the sending node (such as a file server) to stop sending frames for a selected short period of time. Control is MAC-to-MAC through the use of a pause frame that is automatically generated by the receiving MAC. If the congestion is relieved before the requested wait has expired, a second pause frame with a zero time-to-wait value can be sent to request resumption of transmission. An overview of the flow control operation is shown in Figure 8-10.

Figure 8-10 *An Overview of the IEEE 802.3 Flow Control Sequence*

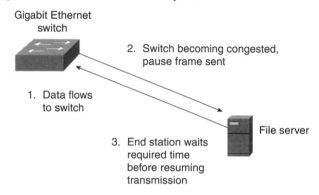

The full-duplex operation and its companion flow control capability are both options for all Ethernet MACs and all transmission rates. Both options are enabled on a link-by-link basis, assuming that the associated physical layers are also capable of supporting full-duplex operation.

Pause frames are identified as MAC control frames by an exclusive assigned (reserved) length/type value. They are also assigned a reserved destination address value to ensure that an incoming pause frame is never forwarded to upper protocol layers or to other ports in a switch.

Frame Reception

Frame reception is essentially the same for both half-duplex and full-duplex operations, except that full-duplex MACs must have separate frame buffers and data paths to allow for simultaneous frame transmission and reception.

Frame reception is the reverse of frame transmission. The destination address of the received frame is checked and matched against the station's address list (its MAC address, its group addresses, and the broadcast address) to determine whether the frame is destined for that station. If an address match is found, the frame length is checked and the received FCS is compared to the FCS that was generated during frame reception. If the frame length is okay and there is an FCS match, the frame type is determined by the contents of the Length/Type field. The frame is then parsed and forwarded to the appropriate upper layer.

The VLAN Tagging Option

VLAN tagging is a MAC option that provides three important capabilities not previously available to Ethernet network users and network managers:

- Provides a means to expedite time-critical network traffic by setting transmission priorities for outgoing frames.

- Allows stations to be assigned to logical groups, to communicate across multiple LANs as though they were on a single LAN. Bridges and switches filter destination addresses and forward VLAN frames only to ports that serve the VLAN to which the traffic belongs.

- Simplifies network management and makes adds, moves, and changes easier to administer.

A VLAN-tagged frame is simply a basic MAC data frame that has had a 4-byte VLAN header inserted between the SA and Length/Type fields, as shown in Figure 8-11.

Figure 8-11 *VLAN-Tagged Frames Are Identified When the MAC Finds the LAN Type Value in the Normal Length/ Type Field Location*

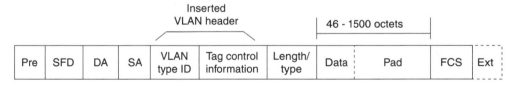

* Indicates fields of the basic frame format

The VLAN header consists of two fields:

- A reserved 2-byte type value, indicating that the frame is a VLAN frame

- A two-byte Tag-Control field that contains both the transmission priority (0 to 7, where 7 is the highest) and a VLAN ID that identifies the particular VLAN over which the frame is to be sent

The receiving MAC reads the reserved type value, which is located in the normal Length/Type field position, and interprets the received frame as a VLAN frame. Then the following occurs:

- If the MAC is installed in a switch port, the frame is forwarded according to its priority level to all ports that are associated with the indicated VLAN identifier.
- If the MAC is installed in an end station, it removes the 4-byte VLAN header and processes the frame in the same manner as a basic data frame.

VLAN tagging requires that all network nodes involved with a VLAN group be equipped with the VLAN option.

The Ethernet Physical Layers

Because Ethernet devices implement only the bottom two layers of the OSI protocol stack, they are typically implemented as network interface cards (NICs) that plug into the host device's motherboard. The different NICs are identified by a three-part product name that is based on the physical layer attributes.

The naming convention is a concatenation of three terms indicating the transmission rate, the transmission method, and the media type/signal encoding. For example, consider this:

- 10Base-T = 10 Mbps, baseband, over two twisted-pair cables
- 100Base-T2 = 100 Mbps, baseband, over two twisted-pair cables
- 100Base-T4 = 100 Mbps, baseband, over four-twisted pair cables
- 1000Base-LX = 100 Mbps, baseband, long wavelength over optical fiber cable

A question sometimes arises as to why the middle term always seems to be "Base." Early versions of the protocol also allowed for broadband transmission (for example, 10Broad), but broadband implementations were not successful in the marketplace. All current Ethernet implementations use baseband transmission.

Encoding for Signal Transmission

In baseband transmission, the frame information is directly impressed upon the link as a sequence of pulses or data symbols that are typically attenuated (reduced in size) and distorted (changed in shape) before they reach the other end of the link. The receiver's task is to detect each pulse as it arrives and then to extract its correct value before transferring the reconstructed information to the receiving MAC.

Filters and pulse-shaping circuits can help restore the size and shape of the received waveforms, but additional measures must be taken to ensure that the received signals are sampled at the correct time in the pulse period and at same rate as the transmit clock:

- The receive clock must be recovered from the incoming data stream to allow the receiving physical layer to synchronize with the incoming pulses.

- Compensating measures must be taken for a transmission effect known as baseline wander.

Clock recovery requires level transitions in the incoming signal to identify and synchronize on pulse boundaries. The alternating 1s and 0s of the frame preamble were designed both to indicate that a frame was arriving and to aid in clock recovery. However, recovered clocks can drift and possibly lose synchronization if pulse levels remain constant and there are no transitions to detect (for example, during long strings of 0s).

Baseline wander results because Ethernet links are AC-coupled to the transceivers and because AC coupling is incapable of maintaining voltage levels for more than a short time. As a result, transmitted pulses are distorted by a droop effect similar to the exaggerated example shown in Figure 8-12. In long strings of either 1s or 0s, the droop can become so severe that the voltage level passes through the decision threshold, resulting in erroneous sampled values for the affected pulses.

Figure 8-12 *A Concept Example of Baseline Wander*

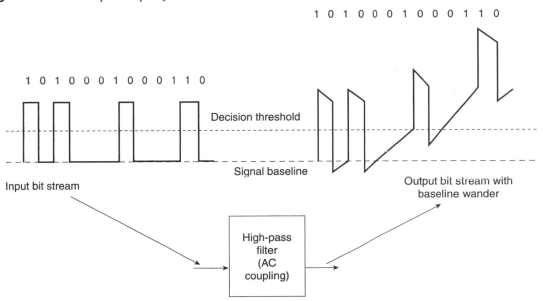

Fortunately, encoding the outgoing signal before transmission can significantly reduce the effect of both these problems, as well as reduce the possibility of transmission errors. Early

Ethernet implementations, up to and including 10Base-T, all used the Manchester encoding method, shown in Figure 8-13. Each pulse is clearly identified by the direction of the midpulse transition rather than by its sampled level value.

Figure 8-13 *Transition-Based Manchester Binary Encoding*

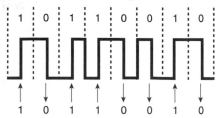

Unfortunately, Manchester encoding introduces some difficult frequency-related problems that make it unsuitable for use at higher data rates. Ethernet versions subsequent to 10Base-T all use different encoding procedures that include some or all of the following techniques:

- **Using data scrambling**—A procedure that scrambles the bits in each byte in an orderly (and recoverable) manner. Some 0s are changed to 1s, some 1s are changed to 0s, and some bits are left the same. The result is reduced run-length of same-value bits, increased transition density, and easier clock recovery.

- **Expanding the code space**—A technique that allows assignment of separate codes for data and control symbols (such as start-of-stream and end-of-stream delimiters, extension bits, and so on) and that assists in transmission error detection.

- **Using forward error-correcting codes**—An encoding in which redundant information is added to the transmitted data stream so that some types of transmission errors can be corrected during frame reception.

NOTE   Forward error-correcting codes are used in 1000Base-T to achieve an effective reduction in the bit error rate. Ethernet protocol limits error handling to detection of bit errors in the received frame. Recovery of frames received with uncorrectable errors or missing frames is the responsibility of higher layers in the protocol stack.

The 802.3 Physical Layer Relationship to the ISO Reference Model

Although the specific logical model of the physical layer may vary from version to version, all Ethernet NICs generally conform to the generic model shown in Figure 8-14.

Figure 8-14 *The Generic Ethernet Physical Layer Reference Model*

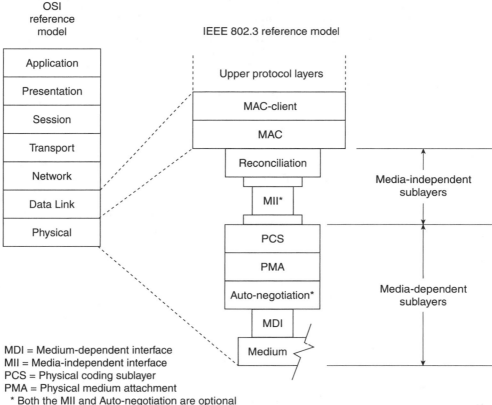

The physical layer for each transmission rate is divided into sublayers that are independent of the particular media type and sublayers that are specific to the media type or signal encoding.

- The reconciliation sublayer and the optional media-independent interface (MII in 10-Mbps and 100-Mbps Ethernet, GMII in Gigabit Ethernet) provide the logical connection between the MAC and the different sets of media-dependent layers. The MII and GMII are defined with separate transmit and receive data paths that are bit-serial for 10-Mbps implementations, nibble-serial (4 bits wide) for 100-Mbps implementations, and byte-serial (8 bits wide) for 1000-Mbps implementations. The media-independent interfaces and the reconciliation sublayer are common for their respective transmission rates and are configured for full-duplex operation in 10Base-T and all subsequent Ethernet versions.

- The media-dependent physical coding sublayer (PCS) provides the logic for encoding, multiplexing, and synchronization of the outgoing symbol streams as well symbol code alignment, demultiplexing, and decoding of the incoming data.

- The physical medium attachment (PMA) sublayer contains the signal transmitters and receivers (transceivers), as well as the clock recovery logic for the received data streams.

- The medium-dependent interface (MDI) is the cable connector between the signal transceivers and the link.

- The Auto-negotiation sublayer allows the NICs at each end of the link to exchange information about their individual capabilities, and then to negotiate and select the most favorable operational mode that they both are capable of supporting. Auto-negotiation is optional in early Ethernet implementations and is mandatory in later versions.

Depending on which type of signal encoding is used and how the links are configured, the PCS and PMA may or may not be capable of supporting full-duplex operation.

10-Mbps Ethernet—10Base-T

10Base-T provides Manchester-encoded 10-Mbps bit-serial communication over two unshielded twisted-pair cables. Although the standard was designed to support transmission over common telephone cable, the more typical link configuration is to use two pair of a four-pair Category 3 or 5 cable, terminated at each NIC with an 8-pin RJ-45 connector (the MDI), as shown in Figure 8-15. Because each active pair is configured as a simplex link where transmission is in one direction only, the 10Base-T physical layers can support either half-duplex or full-duplex operation.

Figure 8-15 *The Typical 10Base-T Link Is a Four-Pair UTP Cable in Which Two Pairs Are Not Used*

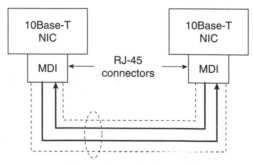

Four-pair category 3 or 5 UTP cable

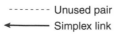

-------- Unused pair
←———— Simplex link

Although 10Base-T may be considered essentially obsolete in some circles, it is included here because there are still many 10Base-T Ethernet networks, and because full-duplex operation has given 10BaseT an extended life.

10Base-T was also the first Ethernet version to include a link integrity test to determine the health of the link. Immediately after powerup, the PMA transmits a normal link pulse (NLP) to tell the NIC at the other end of the link that this NIC wants to establish an active link connection:

- If the NIC at the other end of the link is also powered up, it responds with its own NLP.
- If the NIC at the other end of the link is not powered up, this NIC continues sending an NLP about once every 16 ms until it receives a response.

The link is activated only after both NICs are capable of exchanging valid NLPs.

100 Mbps—Fast Ethernet

Increasing the Ethernet transmission rate by a factor of ten over 10Base-T was not a simple task, and the effort resulted in the development of three separate physical layer standards for 100 Mbps over UTP cable: 100Base-TX and 100Base-T4 in 1995, and 100Base-T2 in 1997. Each was defined with different encoding requirements and a different set of media-dependent sublayers, even though there is some overlap in the link cabling. Table 8-2 compares the physical layer characteristics of 10Base-T to the various 100Base versions.

Table 8-2   *Summary of 100Base-T Physical Layer Characteristics*

Ethernet Version	Transmit Symbol Rate[1]	Encoding	Cabling	Full-Duplex Operation
10Base-T	10 MBd	Manchester	Two pairs of UTP Category –3 or better	Supported
100Base-TX	125 MBd	4B/5B	Two pairs of UTP Category –5 or Type 1 STP	Supported
100Base-T4	33 MBd	8B/6T	Four pairs of UTP Category –3 or better	Not supported
100Base-T2	25 MBd	PAM5x5	Two pairs of UTP Category –3 or better	Supported

[1] One baud = one transmitted symbol per second, where the transmitted symbol may contain the equivalent value of 1 or more binary bits.

Although not all three 100-Mbps versions were successful in the marketplace, all three have been discussed in the literature, and all three did impact future designs. As such, all three are important to consider here.

100Base-X

100Base-X was designed to support transmission over either two pairs of Category 5 UTP copper wire or two strands of optical fiber. Although the encoding, decoding, and clock recovery procedures are the same for both media, the signal transmission is different— electrical pulses in copper and light pulses in optical fiber. The signal transceivers that were included as part of the PMA function in the generic logical model of Figure 8-14 were redefined as the separate physical media-dependent (PMD) sublayers shown in Figure 8-16.

Figure 8-16   *The 100Base-X Logical Model*

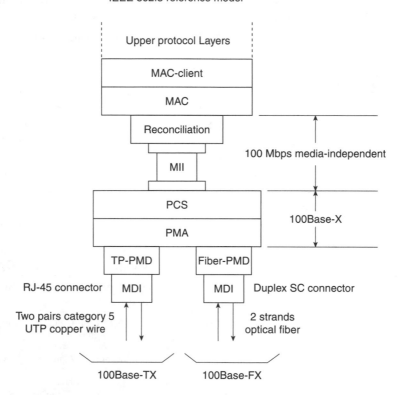

The 100Base-X encoding procedure is based on the earlier FDDI optical fiber physical media-dependent and FDDI/CDDI copper twisted-pair physical media-dependent signaling standards developed by ISO and ANSI. The 100Base-TX physical media-dependent sublayer (TP-PMD) was implemented with CDDI semiconductor transceivers and RJ-45 connectors; the fiber PMD was implemented with FDDI optical transceivers and the Low Cost Fibre Interface Connector (commonly called the duplex SC connector).

The 4B/5B encoding procedure is the same as the encoding procedure used by FDDI, with only minor adaptations to accommodate Ethernet frame control. Each 4-bit data nibble (representing half of a data byte) is mapped into a 5-bit binary code-group that is transmitted bit-serial over the link. The expanded code space provided by the 32 5-bit code-groups allow separate assignment for the following:

- The 16 possible values in a 4-bit data nibble (16 code-groups).

- Four control code-groups that are transmitted as code-group pairs to indicate the start-of-stream delimiter (SSD) and the end-of-stream delimiter (ESD). Each MAC frame is "encapsulated" to mark both the beginning and end of the frame. The first byte of preamble is replaced with SSD code-group pair that precisely identifies the frame's code-group boundaries. The ESD code-group pair is appended after the frame's FCS field.

- A special IDLE code-group that is continuously sent during interframe gaps to maintain continuous synchronization between the NICs at each end of the link. The receipt of IDLE is interpreted to mean that the link is quiet.

- Eleven invalid code-groups that are not intentionally transmitted by a NIC (although one is used by a repeater to propagate receive errors). Receipt of any invalid code-group will cause the incoming frame to be treated as an invalid frame.

Figure 8-17 shows how a MAC frame is encapsulated before being transmitted as a 100Base-X code-group stream.

Figure 8-17 *The 100Base-X Code-Group Stream with Frame Encapsulation*

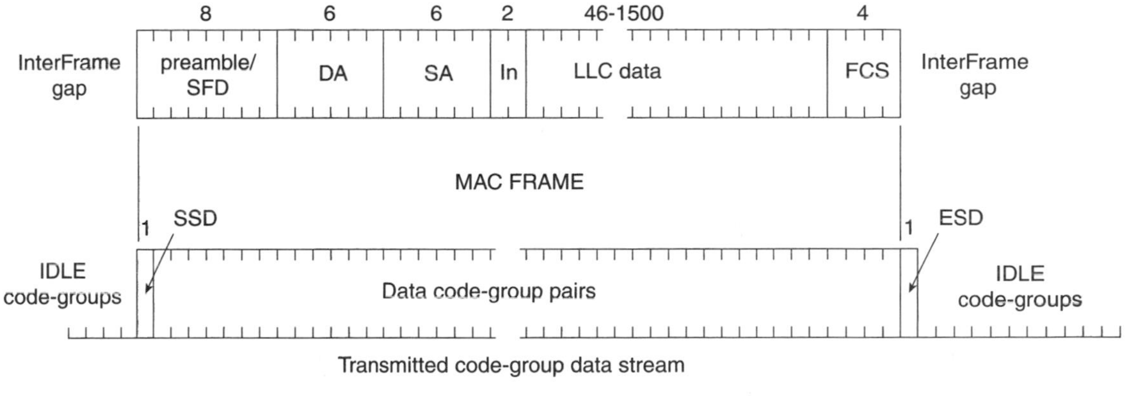

Transmitted code-group data stream

100Base-TX transmits and receives on the same link pairs and uses the same pin assignments on the MDI as 10Base-T. 100Base-TX and 100Base-FX both support half-duplex and full-duplex transmission.

100Base-T4

100Base-T4 was developed to allow 10BaseT networks to be upgraded to 100-Mbps
operation without requiring existing four-pair Category 3 UTP cables to be replaced with
the newer Category 5 cables. Two of the four pairs are configured for half-duplex operation
and can support transmission in either direction, but only in one direction at a time. The
other two pairs are configured as simplex pairs dedicated to transmission in one direction
only. Frame transmission uses both half-duplex pairs, plus the simplex pair that is
appropriate for the transmission direction, as shown in Figure 8-18. The simplex pair for
the opposite direction provides carrier sense and collision detection. Full-duplex operation
cannot be supported on 100Base-T4.

Figure 8-18 *The 100Base-T4 Wire-Pair Usage During Frame Transmission*

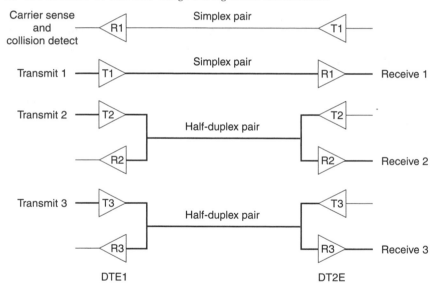

Transmission paths for DTE1 shown in bold

100Base-T4 uses an 8B6T encoding scheme in which each 8-bit binary byte is mapped into
a pattern of six ternary (three-level: $+1, 0, -1$) symbols known as 6T code-groups. Separate
6T code-groups are used for IDLE and for the control code-groups that are necessary for
frame transmission. IDLE received on the dedicated receive pair indicates that the link is
quiet.

During frame transmission, 6T data code-groups are transmitted in a delayed round-robin
sequence over the three transmit wire–pairs, as shown in Figure 8-19. Each frame is
encapsulated with start-of-stream and end-of-packet 6T code-groups that mark both the
beginning and end of the frame, and the beginning and end of the 6T code-group stream on

each wire pair. Receipt of a non-IDLE code-group over the dedicated receive-pair any time before the collision window expires indicates that a collision has occurred.

Figure 8-19 *The 100Base-T4 Frame Transmission Sequence*

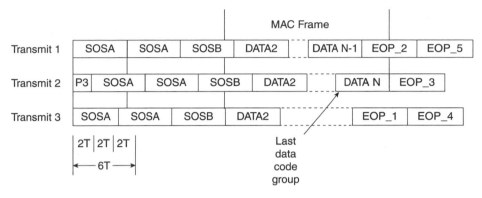

6T=1 temporary code group

100Base-T2

The 100Base-T2 specification was developed as a better alternative for upgrading networks with installed Category 3 cabling than was being provided by 100Base-T4. Two important new goals were defined:

- To provide communication over two pairs of Category 3 or better cable
- To support both half-duplex and full-duplex operation

100Base-T2 uses a different signal transmission procedure than any previous twisted-pair Ethernet implementations. Instead of using two simplex links to form one full-duplex link, the 100Base-T2 dual-duplex baseband transmission method sends encoded symbols simultaneously in both directions on both wire pairs, as shown in Figure 8-20. The term "TDX<3:2>" indicates the 2 most significant bits in the nibble before encoding and transmission. "RDX<3:2>" indicates the same 2 bits after receipt and decoding.

Figure 8-20 *The 100Base-T2 Link Topology*

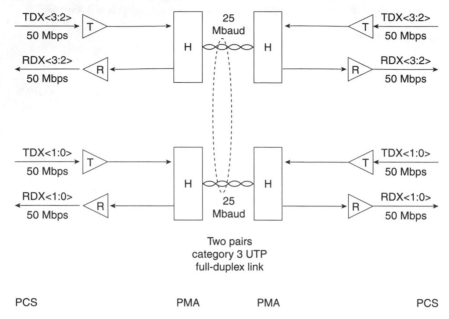

H = Hybrid canceller transceiver
T = Transmit encoder
R = Receive decoder
Two PAM5 code symbols = One nibble

Dual-duplex baseband transmission requires the NICs at each end of the link to be operated in a master/slave loop-timing mode. Which NIC will be master and which will be slave is determined by autonegotiation during link initiation. When the link is operational, synchronization is based on the master NIC's internal transmit clock. The slave NIC uses the recovered clock for both transmit and receive operations, as shown in Figure 8-21. Each transmitted frame is encapsulated, and link synchronization is maintained with a continuous stream of IDLE symbols during interframe gaps.

Figure 8-21 *The 100Base-T2 Loop Timing Configuration*

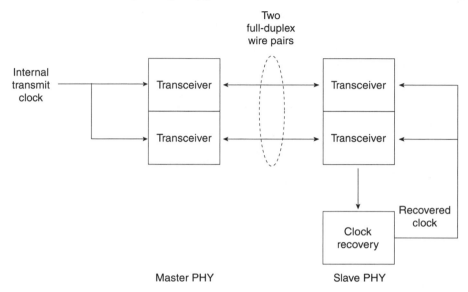

The 100Base-T2 encoding process first scrambles the data frame nibbles to randomize the bit sequence. It then maps the two upper bits and the two lower bits of each nibble into two five-level $(+2, +1, 0, -1, -2)$ pulse amplitude-modulated (PAM5) symbols that are simultaneously transmitted over the two wire pairs (PAM5x5). Different scrambling procedures for master and slave transmissions ensure that the data streams traveling in opposite directions on the same wire pair are uncoordinated.

Signal reception is essentially the reverse of signal transmission. Because the signal on each wire pair at the MDI is the sum of the transmitted signal and the received signal, each receiver subtracts the transmitted symbols from the signal received at the MDI to recover the symbols in the incoming data stream. The incoming symbol pair is then decoded, unscrambled, and reconstituted as a data nibble for transfer to the MAC.

1000 Mbps—Gigabit Ethernet

The Gigabit Ethernet standards development resulted in two primary specifications: 1000Base-T for UTP copper cable and 1000Base-X STP copper cable, as well as single and multimode optical fiber (see Figure 8-22).

Figure 8-22 *Gigabit Ethernet Variations*

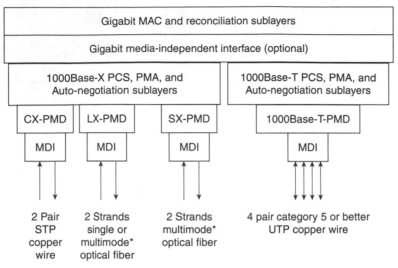

1000Base-T

1000Base-T Ethernet provides full-duplex transmission over four-pair Category 5 or better UTP cable. 1000Base-T is based largely on the findings and design approaches that led to the development of the Fast Ethernet physical layer implementations:

- 100Base-TX proved that binary symbol streams could be successfully transmitted over Category 5 UTP cable at 125 MBd.

- 100Base-T4 provided a basic understanding of the problems related to sending multilevel signals over four wire pairs.

- 100Base-T2 proved that PAM5 encoding, coupled with digital signal processing, could handle both simultaneous two-way data streams and potential crosstalk problems resulting from alien signals on adjacent wire pairs.

1000Base-T scrambles each byte in the MAC frame to randomize the bit sequence before it is encoded using a 4-D, 8-State Trellis Forward Error Correction (FEC) coding in which four PAM5 symbols are sent at the same time over four wire pairs. Four of the five levels in each PAM5 symbol represent 2 bits in the data byte. The fifth level is used for FEC coding, which enhances symbol recovery in the presence of noise and crosstalk. Separate scramblers for the master and slave PHYs create essentially uncorrelated data streams between the two opposite-travelling symbol streams on each wire pair.

The 1000Base-T link topology is shown in Figure 8-23. The term "TDX<7:6>" indicates the 2 most significant bits in the data byte before encoding and transmission. "RDX<7:6>" indicates the same 2 bits after receipt and decoding.

Figure 8-23 *The 1000Base-T Link Topology*

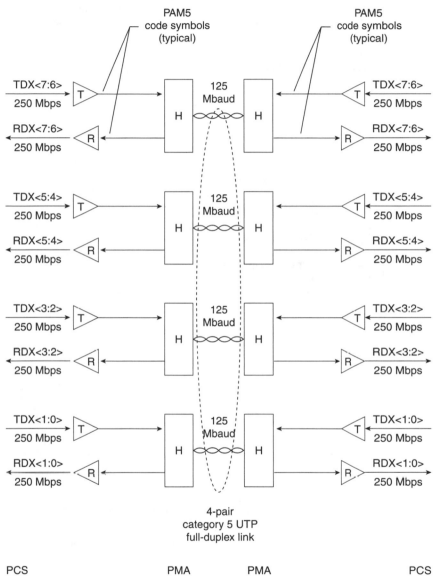

PCS   PMA   PMA   PCS

H = Hybrid canceller transceiver
T = Transmit encoder
R = Receive decoder
Four PAM5 code symbols = One 4D-PAM5 code group

The clock recovery and master/slave loop timing procedures are essentially the same as those used in 100Base-T2 (see Figure 8-24). Which NIC will be master (typically the NIC in a multiport intermediate network node) and which will be slave is determined during autonegotiation.

Figure 8-24 *1000Base-T Master/Slave Loop Timing Configuration*

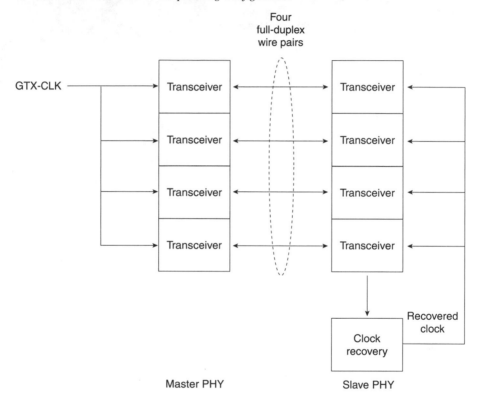

Each transmitted frame is encapsulated with start-of-stream and end-of-stream delimiters, and loop timing is maintained by continuous streams of IDLE symbols sent on each wire pair during interframe gaps. 1000Base-T supports both half-duplex and full-duplex operation.

1000Base-X

All three 1000Base-X versions support full-duplex binary transmission at 1250 Mbps over two strands of optical fiber or two STP copper wire–pairs, as shown in Figure 8-25. Transmission coding is based on the ANSI Fibre Channel 8B/10B encoding scheme. Each 8-bit data byte is mapped into a 10-bit code-group for bit-serial transmission. Like earlier

Ethernet versions, each data frame is encapsulated at the physical layer before transmission, and link synchronization is maintained by sending a continuous stream of IDLE code-groups during interframe gaps. All 1000Base-X physical layers support both half-duplex and full-duplex operation.

Figure 8-25 *1000Base-X Link Configuration*

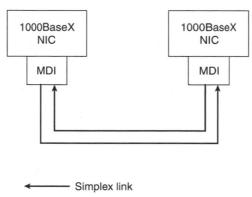

The principal differences among the 1000Base-X versions are the link media and connectors that the particular versions will support and, in the case of optical media, the wavelength of the optical signal (see Table 8-3).

Table 8-3   *1000Base-X Link Configuration Support*

Link Configuration	1000Base-CX	1000Base-SX (850 nm Wavelength)	1000Base-LX (1300 nm Wavelength)
150 Ω STP copper	Supported	Not supported	Not supported
125/62.5 μm multimode optical fiber[1]	Not supported	Supported	Supported
125/50 μm multimode optical fiber	Not supported	Supported	Supported
125/10 μm single mode optical fiber	Not supported	Not supported	Supported
Allowed connectors	IEC style 1 or Fibre Channel style 2	SFF MT-RJ or Duplex SC	SFF MT-RJ or Duplex SC

[1] The 125/62.5 μm specification refers to the cladding and core diameters of the optical fiber.

Network Cabling—Link Crossover Requirements

Link compatibility requires that the transmitters at each end of the link be connected to the receivers at the other end of the link. However, because cable connectors at both ends of the link are keyed the same, the conductors must cross over at some point to ensure that transmitter outputs are always connected to receiver inputs.

Unfortunately, when this requirement first came up in the development of 10Base-T, IEEE 802.3 chose not to make a hard rule as to whether the crossover should be implemented in the cable as shown in Figure 8-26a or whether it should be implemented internally as shown in Figure 8-26b.

Figure 8-26   *Alternative Ways for Implementing the Link Crossover Requirement*

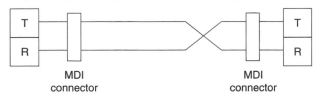

(a) Cable-based crossover

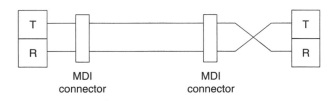

(b) Internal crossover

Instead, IEEE 802.3 defined two rules and made two recommendations:

- There must be an odd number of crossovers in all multiconductor links.

- If a PMD is equipped with an internal crossover, its MDI must be clearly labeled with the graphical X symbol.

- Implementation of an internal crossover function is optional.

- When a DTE is connected to a repeater or switch (DCE) port, it is recommended that the crossover be implemented within the DCE port.

The eventual result was that ports in most DCEs were equipped with PMDs that contained internal crossover circuitry and that DTEs had PMDs without internal crossovers. This led to the following oft-quoted de facto "installation rule":

- Use a straight-through cable when connecting DTE to DCE. Use a crossover cable when connecting DTE to DTE or DCE to DCE.

Unfortunately, the de facto rule does not apply to all Ethernet versions that have been developed subsequent to 10Base-T. As things now stand, the following is true:

- All fiber-based systems use cables that have the crossover implemented within the cable.

- All 100Base systems using twisted-pair links use the same rules and recommendations as 10Base-T.

- 1000Base-T NICs may implement a selectable internal crossover option that can be negotiated and enabled during autonegotiation. When the selectable crossover option is not implemented, 10Base-T rules and recommendations apply.

System Considerations

Given all the choices discussed previously, it might seem that it would be no problem to upgrade an existing network or to plan a new network. The problem is twofold. Not all the choices are reasonable for all networks, and not all Ethernet versions and options are available in the market, even though they may have been specified in the standard.

Choosing UTP-Based Components and Media Category

By now, it should be obvious that UTP-based NICs are available for 10-Mbps, 100-Mbps, and 1000-Mbps implementations. The choice is relatively simple for both 10-Mbps and 1000-Mbps operation: 10Base-T and 1000Base-T. From the previous discussions, however, it would not seem to be that simple for 100-Mbps implementations.

Although three UTP-based NICs are defined for 100 Mbps, the market has effectively narrowed the choice to just 100Base-TX, which became widely available during the first half of 1995:

- By the time 100Base-T4 products first appeared on the market, 100Base-TX was well entrenched, and development of the full-duplex option, which 100Base-T4 could not support, was well underway.

- The 100Base-T2 standard was not approved until spring 1997, too late to interest the marketplace. As a result, 100Base-T2 products were not even manufactured.

Several choices have also been specified for UTP media: Category 3, 4, 5, or 5E. The differences are cable cost and transmission rate capability, both of which increase with the category numbers. However, current transmission rate requirements and cable cost should not be the deciding factors in choosing which cable category to install. To allow for future transmission rate needs, cables lower than Category 5 should not even be considered, and if gigabit rates are a possible future need, Category 5E should be seriously considered:

- Installation labor costs are essentially constant for all types of UTP four-pair cable.

- Labor costs for upgrading installed cable (removing the existing and installing new) are typically greater than the cost of the original installation.

- UTP cable is backward-compatible. Higher-category cable will support lower-category NICs, but not vice versa.

- The physical life of UTP cable (decades) is much longer than the useable life of the connected equipment.

Auto-negotiation—An Optional Method for Automatically Configuring Link Operational Modes

The purpose of autonegotiation is to find a way for two NICs that share a UTP link to communicate with each other, regardless of whether they both implemented the same Ethernet version or option set.

Autonegotiation is performed totally within the physical layers during link initiation, without any additional overhead either to the MAC or to higher protocol layers. Autonegotiation allows UTP-based NICs to do the following:

- Advertise their Ethernet version and any optional capabilities to the NIC at the other end of the link

- Acknowledge receipt and understanding of the operational modes that both NICs share

- Reject any operational modes that are not shared

- Configure each NIC for highest-level operational mode that both NICs can support

Autonegotiation is specified as an option for 10Base-T, 100Base-TX, and 100Base-T4, but it is required for 100Base-T2 and 1000Base-T implementations. Table 8-4 lists the defined selection priority levels (highest level = top priority) for UTP-based Ethernet NICs.

Table 8-4   *The Defined Autonegotiation Selection Levels for UTP NICs*

Selection Level	Operational Mode	Maximum Total Data Transfer Rate (Mbps)[1]
9	1000Base-T full-duplex	2000
8	1000Base-T half-duplex	1000
7	100Base-T2 full-duplex	200
6	100Base-TX full-duplex	200
5	100Base-T2 half-duplex	100
4	100Base-T4 half-duplex	100
3	100Base-TX half-duplex	100
2	10Base-T full-duplex	20
1	10Base-T half-duplex	10

1 Because full-duplex operation allows simultaneous two-way transmission, the maximum total transfer rate for full-duplex operation is double the half-duplex transmission rate.

The autonegotiation function in UTP-based NICs uses a modified 10Base-T link integrity pulse sequence in which the NLPs are replaced by bursts of fast link pulses (FLPs), as

shown in Figure 8-27. Each FLP burst is an alternating clock/data sequence in which the
data bits in the burst identify the operational modes supported by the transmitting NIC and
also provide information used by the autonegotiation handshake mechanism. If the NIC at
the other end of the link is a compatible NIC but does not have autonegotiation capability,
a parallel detection function still allows it to be recognized. A NIC that fails to respond to
FLP bursts and returns only NLPs is treated as a 10Base-T half-duplex NIC.

Figure 8-27 *Autonegotiation FLP Bursts Replace NLPs During Link Initiation*

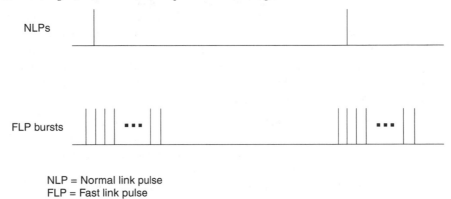

NLPs

FLP bursts

NLP = Normal link pulse
FLP = Fast link pulse

At first glance, it may appear that the autonegotiation process would always select the mode
supported by the NIC with the lessor capability, which would be the case if both NICs use
the same encoding procedures and link configuration. For example, if both NICs are
100Base-TX but only one supports full-duplex operation, the negotiated operational mode
will be half-duplex 100Base-TX. Unfortunately, the different 100Base versions are not
compatible with each other at 100 Mbps, and a 100Base-TX full-duplex NIC would
autonegotiate with a 100Base-T4 NIC to operate in 10Base-T half-duplex mode.

Autonegotiation in 1000Base-X NICs is similar to autonegotiation in UTP-based systems,
except that it currently applies only to compatible 1000Base-X devices and is currently
constrained to negotiate only half-duplex or full-duplex operation and flow control
direction.

Network Switches Provide a Second, and Often Better, Alternative to Higher Link Speeds in CSMA/CD Network Upgrades

Competitively priced network switches became available on the market shortly after the
mid-1990s and essentially made network repeaters obsolete for large networks. Although

repeaters can accept only one frame at a time and then send it to all active ports (except the port on which it is being received), switches are equipped with the following:

- MAC-based ports with I/O frame buffers that effectively isolate the port from traffic being sent at the same time to or from other ports on the switch
- Multiple internal data paths that allow several frames to be transferred between different ports at the same time

These may seem like small differences, but they produce a major effect in network operation. Because each port provides access to a high-speed network bridge (the switch), the collision domain in the network is reduced to a series of small domains in which the number of participants is reduced to two—the switch port and the connected NIC (see Figure 8-28). Furthermore, because each participant is now in a private collision domain, his or her available bandwidth has not only been markedly increased, it was also done without having to change the link speed.

Consider, for example, a 48-station workgroup with a couple of large file servers and several network printers on a 100-Mbps CSMA/CD network. The average available bandwidth, not counting interframe gaps and collision recovery, would be $100 \div 50 = 2$ Mbps (network print servers do not generate network traffic). On the other hand, if the same workgroup were still on a 10Base-T network in which the repeaters had been replaced with network switches, the bandwidth available to each user would be 10 Mbps.

Clearly, network configuration is as important as raw link speed.

NOTE   To ensure that each end station will be capable of communicating at full rate, the network switches should be nonsaturating (be capable of accepting and transferring data at the full rate from each port simultaneously).

Multispeed NICs

Auto-negotiation opened the door to the development of low-cost, multispeed NICs that, for example, support both half- and full-duplex operation under either 100Base-TX or 10Base-T signaling procedures. Multispeed NICs allow staged network upgrades in which the 10Base-T half-duplex end stations can be connected to 100Base-TX full-duplex switch ports without requiring the NIC in the PC to be changed. Then, as more bandwidth is needed for individual PCs, the NICs in those PCs can be upgraded to 100Base-TX full-duplex mode.

Figure 8-28 *Replacing the Network Repeaters with Switches Reduces the Collision Domains to Two NICs Each*

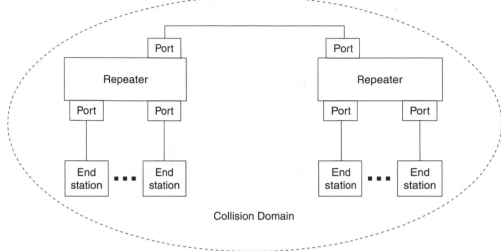

(a) Repeater-based CSMA/CD network

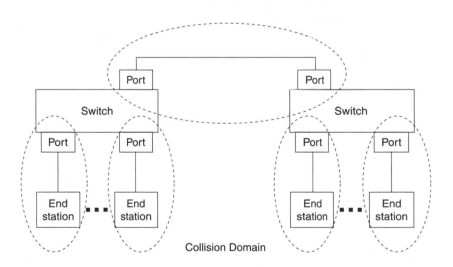

(b) Switch-based CSMA/CD network

Choosing 1000Base-X Components and Media

Although Table 8-3 shows that there is considerable flexibility of choice in the 1000Base-X link media, there is not total flexibility. Some choices are preferred over others:

- NICs at both ends of the link must be the same 1000Base-X version (CX, LX, or SX), and the link connectors must match the NIC connectors.

- The 1000Base-CX specification allows either style 1 or style 2 connectors, but style 2 is preferred because some style 1 connectors are not suitable for operation at 1250 Mbps. 1000Base-CX links are intended for patch-cord use within a communications closet and are limited to 25 meters.

- The 1000Base-LX and 1000Base-SX specifications allow either the small form factor SFF MT-RJ or the larger duplex SC connectors. Because SFF MT-RJ connectors are only about half as large as duplex SC connectors, and because space is a premium, it follows that SFF MT-RJ connectors may become the predominant connector.

- 1000Base-LX transceivers generally cost more than 1000Base-SX transceivers.

- The maximum operating range for optical fibers depends on both the transmission wavelength and the modal bandwidth (MHz.km) rating of the fiber. See Table 8-5.

Table 8-5   *Maximum Operating Ranges for Common Optical Fibers*

Fiber Core Diameter/ Modal Bandwidth	1000Base-SX (850 nm Wavelength)	1000Base-LX (1300 nm Wavelength)
62.5 µm multimode fiber (200/ 500) MHz.km	275 meters	550 meters[1]
50 µm multimode fiber (400/ 400) MHz.km	500 meters	550 meters[1]
50 µm multimode fiber (500/ 500) MHz.km	550 meters	550 meters[1]
10 µm single-mode fiber	Not supported	5000 meters

[1] 1000Base-LX transceivers may also require use of an offset-launch, mode-conditioning patch cord when coupling to some existing multimode fibers.

The operating ranges shown in Table 8-5 are those specified in the IEEE 802.3 standard. In practice, however, the maximum operating range for LX transceivers over 62.5 µm multimode fiber is approximately 700 meters, and some LX transceivers have been qualified to support a 10,000-meter operating range over single-mode fiber.

Multiple-Rate Ethernet Networks

Given the opportunities shown by the example in the previous sections, it is not surprising that most large Ethernet networks are now implemented with a mix of transmission rates and link media, as shown in the cable model in Figure 8-29.

Figure 8-29 *An Example Multirate Network Topology—the ISO/IEC 11801 Cable Model*

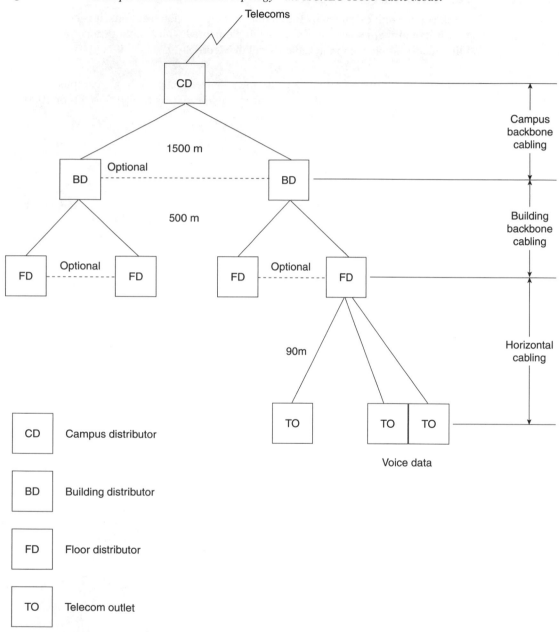

The ISO/IEC 11801 cable model is the network model on which the IEEE 802.3 standards are based:

- **Campus distributor**—The term *campus* refers to a facility with two or more buildings in a relatively small area. This is the central point of the campus backbone and the telecom connection point with the outside world. In Ethernet LANs, the campus distributor would typically be a gigabit switch with telecom interface capability.

- **Building distributor**—This is the building's connection point to the campus backbone. An Ethernet building distributor would typically be a 1000/100- or 1000/100/10-Mbps switch.

- **Floor distributor**—This is the floor's connection point to the building distributor. ISO/IEC 11801 recommends at least one floor distributor for every 1000 m^2 of floor space in office environments, and, if possible, a separate distributor for each floor in the building. An Ethernet floor distributor would typically be a 1000/100/10- or 100/10-Mbps switch.

- **Telecom outlet**—This is the network connection point for PCs, workstations, and print servers. File servers are typically colocated with and directly connected to the campus, building, or floor distributors, as appropriate for their intended use.

- **Campus backbone cabling**—This is typically single- or multimode cable that interconnects the central campus distributor with each of the building distributors.

- **Building backbone cabling**—This is typically Category 5 or better UTP or multimode fiber cable that interconnects the building distributor with each of the floor distributors in the building.

- **Horizontal cabling**—This is predominantly Category 5 or better UTP cable, although a few installations are using multimode fiber.

As with UTP cable selection, the choice of link media and intermediate network nodes should always be made with an eye to future transmission rate needs and the life expectancy of the network elements, unpredictable though they may be. In the 1990s, LAN transmission rates increased 100 times and, by 2002, will increase yet another 10 times.

This does not mean that all—or even some—end stations and their interconnecting links will require gigabit capability. It does mean, however, that more central network nodes (such as most campus distributors and many building distributors) should be equipped with gigabit capability, and that all floor distributors should have at least 100 Mbps capability. It also means that all network switches should be nonblocking and that all ports should have full-duplex capability, and that any new campus backbone links should be installed with single-mode fiber.

Link Aggregation—Establishing Higher-Speed Network Trunks

Link aggregation is a recent optional MAC capability that allows several physical links to be combined into one logical higher-speed trunk. It provides the means to increase the effective data rate between two network nodes in unit multiples of the individual link transmission rate rather than in an order-of-magnitude step.

Link aggregation can be a cost-effective way to provide higher-speed connections in Ethernet LANs that are reaching saturation with 100 Mbps transmission rates but that won't require gigabit capability, at least in the short term. For example, the maximum length for 62.5 μm multimode fiber links is 2000 meters at 100 Mbps, and multimode fiber has been often used for campus backbone links. The logical upgrade would seem to be to reuse these links for 1000 Mbps operation, but the maximum supportable length for multimode fiber is only 700 meters and only with 1000Base-LX. If the existing links are longer than 700 meters, aggregating n existing links will support an effective transmission rate of $(100\ n)$ Mbps.

Link aggregation should be viewed as a network configuration option that is primarily used in the few interconnections that require higher data rates than can be provided by single links, such as switch-to-switch and in switch-to-file server. It can also be used to increase the reliability of critical links. Aggregated links can be rapidly reconfigured (typically in about 1 second or less) in case of link failure, with low risk of duplicated or reordered frames.

Link aggregation does not affect either the IEEE 802.3 data frame format(s) or any higher layers in the protocol stack. It is backward-compatible with "aggregation-unaware" devices and can be used with any Ethernet data rate (although it does not make sense for 10 Mbps because it would likely cost less to procure a pair of 100-Mbps NICs). Link aggregation can be enabled only on parallel point-to-point links and those that support full-duplex same-speed operation.

Network Management

All higher-speed Ethernet specifications include definitions for managed objects and control agents that are compatible with Simple Network Management Protocol (SNMP) and that can be used to gather statistics about the operation of the network nodes and to assist in network management. Because user information is anecdotal at best and usually comes long after the fact, all larger networks should at least be configured with managed switches and network servers to ensure that potential problems and bottlenecks can be identified before they cause serious network deterioration.

Migrating to Higher-Speed Networks

By now, it should be apparent that upgrading existing networks typically does not require wholesale equipment or media changes, but it does require knowledge of the current network configuration and the network location of potential problems. This means that a network management system should be in place and that a cable plant database should be both available and accurate. It is time-consuming and often difficult to determine link type and availability after the cables have been pulled through conduit, buried in walls, and layered in cable trays.

Links are often the limiting factors in network upgrades. Existing Category 5 links should support all current Ethernet rates from 10 Mbps to 1000 Mbps, although they should be tested to ensure their capability to support gigabit rates. If the network is equipped with only Category 3 cable, some links will have to be replaced before upgrading to 1000 Mbps. A similar situation exists with single- and multimode fiber. Multimode fiber cannot be used for all backbone installations. Single-mode fiber, on the other hand, not only can support all backbone lengths up to 10,000 meters at 1000 Mbps, but it also will be capable of supporting backbone use at 10-gigabit data rates in the future.

Switch replacement can begin as soon as the necessary links are available. Existing switches at the campus and building distributor levels can often be reused at the building or floor distributor level. NICs can generally be replaced to extend the useful life of end stations. And so on.

Summary

The chapter began with an overview of the Ethernet technology, the network building blocks, and Ethernet's relationship to the ISO seven-layer reference model. The requirements for MAC and PHY compatibility also were introduced.

The basic MAC responsibilities were defined:

- **Data encapsulation**—Assembling the frame into the defined format before transmission begins, and disassembling the frame after it has been received and checked for transmission errors.
- **Media access control**—In the required CSMA/CD half-duplex mode, and in the optional full-duplex mode.

Two optional MAC capability extensions and their associated frame formats were discussed. The VLAN tagging option allows network nodes to be defined with logical as well as physical addresses, and provides a means to assign transmission priorities on a frame-by-frame basis. A specific format for the pause frame, which is used for short-term link flow control, is defined in the standard but was not covered here because it is automatic MAC capability that is invoked as needed to prevent input buffer overrun.

The PHY layer discussions included descriptions of the signaling procedures and media requirements/limitations for the following:

- 10Base-T
- 100Base-TX, 100Base-T4, and 100Base-T2
- 1000Base-T, 1000Base-CX, 1000Base-LX, and 1000Base-SX

Although 100Base-FX was not specifically discussed, it uses the same signaling procedure as 100Base-TX, but over optical fiber media rather than UTP copper.

The remaining sections of the chapter were devoted to systems considerations for both twisted-pair and optical fiber LAN implementations:

- Link crossover requirements in UTP networks
- Matching of PMDs and network media to ensure desired data rates
- Use of link aggregation to create higher-speed logical trunks
- Implementation of multispeed networks

After essentially finishing the chapter, you should have a reasonable working knowledge of the Ethernet protocol and network technology. The next section should help determine whether you need to go back and reread the chapter.

Review Questions

1. Shouldn't all 10Base-T networks just be upgraded to 100 Mbps? Why or why not?

2. Which 100Base version(s) are recommended? Why?

3. Which 1000Base version(s) are recommended? Where would they be used?

4. What cable types should be used for new networks? For upgrading existing networks? Why?

5. How do you know when a network needs to be upgraded? Where do you start?

Objectives

- Provide background information about FDDI technology.

- Explain how FDDI works.

- Describe the differences between FDDI and Copper Distributed Data Interface (CDDI).

- Describe how CDDI works.

CHAPTER 9

Fiber Distributed Data Interface

Introduction

The *Fiber Distributed Data Interface (FDDI)* specifies a 100-Mbps token-passing, dual-ring LAN using fiber-optic cable. FDDI is frequently used as high-speed backbone technology because of its support for high bandwidth and greater distances than copper. It should be noted that relatively recently, a related copper specification, called Copper Distributed Data Interface (CDDI), has emerged to provide 100-Mbps service over copper. CDDI is the implementation of FDDI protocols over twisted-pair copper wire. This chapter focuses mainly on FDDI specifications and operations, but it also provides a high-level overview of CDDI.

FDDI uses dual-ring architecture with traffic on each ring flowing in opposite directions (called counter-rotating). The dual rings consist of a primary and a secondary ring. During normal operation, the primary ring is used for data transmission, and the secondary ring remains idle. As will be discussed in detail later in this chapter, the primary purpose of the dual rings is to provide superior reliability and robustness. Figure 9-1 shows the counter-rotating primary and secondary FDDI rings.

Figure 9-1 *FDDI Uses Counter-Rotating Primary and Secondary Rings*

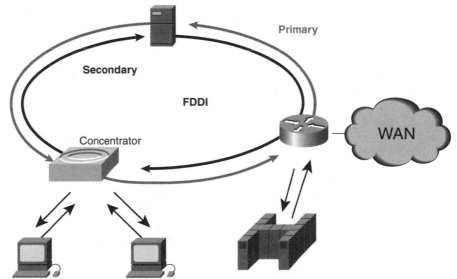

Standards

FDDI was developed by the American National Standards Institute (ANSI) X3T9.5 standards committee in the mid-1980s. At the time, high-speed engineering workstations were beginning to tax the bandwidth of existing local-area networks (LANs) based on Ethernet and Token Ring. A new LAN media was needed that could easily support these workstations and their new distributed applications. At the same time, network reliability had become an increasingly important issue as system managers migrated mission-critical applications from large computers to networks. FDDI was developed to fill these needs. After completing the FDDI specification, ANSI submitted FDDI to the International Organization for Standardization (ISO), which created an international version of FDDI that is completely compatible with the ANSI standard version.

FDDI Transmission Media

FDDI uses optical fiber as the primary transmission medium, but it also can run over copper cabling. As mentioned earlier, FDDI over copper is referred to as *Copper-Distributed Data Interface (CDDI)*. Optical fiber has several advantages over copper media. In particular, security, reliability, and performance all are enhanced with optical fiber media because fiber does not emit electrical signals. A physical medium that does emit electrical signals (copper) can be tapped and therefore would permit unauthorized access to the data that is transiting the medium. In addition, fiber is immune to electrical interference from radio frequency interference (RFI) and electromagnetic interference (EMI). Fiber historically has supported much higher bandwidth (throughput potential) than copper, although recent technological advances have made copper capable of transmitting at 100 Mbps. Finally, FDDI allows 2 km between stations using multimode fiber, and even longer distances using a single mode.

FDDI defines two types of optical fiber: single-mode and multimode. A *mode* is a ray of light that enters the fiber at a particular angle. *Multimode* fiber uses LED as the light-generating device, while *single-mode* fiber generally uses lasers.

Multimode fiber allows multiple modes of light to propagate through the fiber. Because these modes of light enter the fiber at different angles, they will arrive at the end of the fiber at different times. This characteristic is known as *modal dispersion*. Modal dispersion limits the bandwidth and distances that can be accomplished using multimode fibers. For this reason, multimode fiber is generally used for connectivity within a building or a relatively geographically contained environment.

Single-mode fiber allows only one mode of light to propagate through the fiber. Because only a single mode of light is used, modal dispersion is not present with single-mode fiber. Therefore, single-mode fiber is capable of delivering considerably higher performance connectivity over much larger distances, which is why it generally is used for connectivity between buildings and within environments that are more geographically dispersed.

Figure 9-2 depicts single-mode fiber using a laser light source and multimode fiber using a light emitting diode (LED) light source.

Figure 9-2   *Light Sources Differ for Single-Mode and Multimode Fibers*

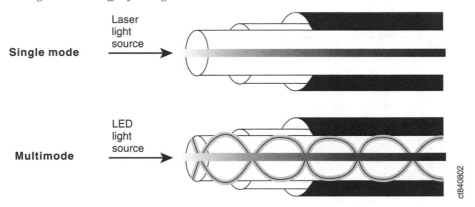

FDDI Specifications

FDDI specifies the physical and media-access portions of the OSI reference model. FDDI is not actually a single specification, but it is a collection of four separate specifications, each with a specific function. Combined, these specifications have the capability to provide high-speed connectivity between upper-layer protocols such as TCP/IP and IPX, and media such as fiber-optic cabling.

FDDI's four specifications are the Media Access Control (MAC), Physical Layer Protocol (PHY), Physical-Medium Dependent (PMD), and Station Management (SMT) specifications. The *MAC* specification defines how the medium is accessed, including frame format, token handling, addressing, algorithms for calculating cyclic redundancy check (CRC) value, and error-recovery mechanisms. The *PHY* specification defines data encoding/decoding procedures, clocking requirements, and framing, among other functions. The *PMD* specification defines the characteristics of the transmission medium, including fiber-optic links, power levels, bit-error rates, optical components, and connectors. The *SMT* specification defines FDDI station configuration, ring configuration, and ring control features, including station insertion and removal, initialization, fault isolation and recovery, scheduling, and statistics collection.

FDDI is similar to IEEE 802.3 Ethernet and IEEE 802.5 Token Ring in its relationship with the OSI model. Its primary purpose is to provide connectivity between upper OSI layers of common protocols and the media used to connect network devices. Figure 9-3 illustrates the four FDDI specifications and their relationship to each other and to the IEEE-defined Logical Link Control (LLC) sublayer. The LLC sublayer is a component of Layer 2, the MAC layer, of the OSI reference model.

Figure 9-3 *FDDI Specifications Map to the OSI Hierarchical Model*

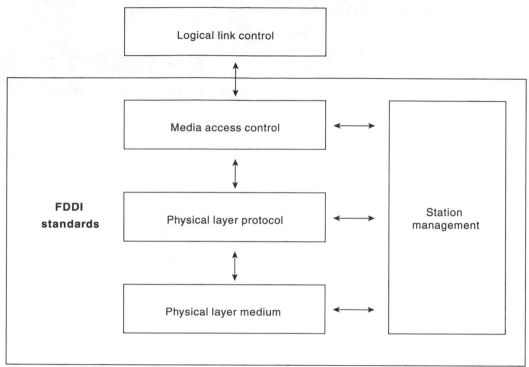

FDDI Station-Attachment Types

One of the unique characteristics of FDDI is that multiple ways actually exist by which to connect FDDI devices. FDDI defines four types of devices: single-attachment station (SAS), dual-attachment station (DAS), single-attached concentrator (SAC), and dual-attached concentrator (DAC).

An SAS attaches to only one ring (the primary) through a concentrator. One of the primary advantages of connecting devices with SAS attachments is that the devices will not have any effect on the FDDI ring if they are disconnected or powered off. Concentrators will be covered in more detail in the following discussion.

Each FDDI DAS has two ports, designated A and B. These ports connect the DAS to the dual FDDI ring. Therefore, each port provides a connection for both the primary and the secondary rings. As you will see in the next section, devices using DAS connections will affect the rings if they are disconnected or powered off. Figure 9-4 shows FDDI DAS A and B ports with attachments to the primary and secondary rings.

Figure 9-4   *FDDI DAS Ports Attach to the Primary and Secondary Rings*

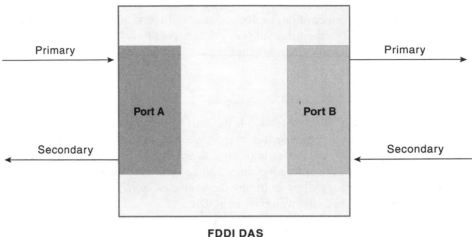

An *FDDI concentrator* (also called a *dual-attachment concentrator [DAC]*) is the building block of an FDDI network. It attaches directly to both the primary and secondary rings and ensures that the failure or power-down of any SAS does not bring down the ring. This is particularly useful when PCs, or similar devices that are frequently powered on and off, connect to the ring. Figure 9-5 shows the ring attachments of an FDDI SAS, DAS, and concentrator.

Figure 9-5   *A Concentrator Attaches to Both the Primary and Secondary Rings*

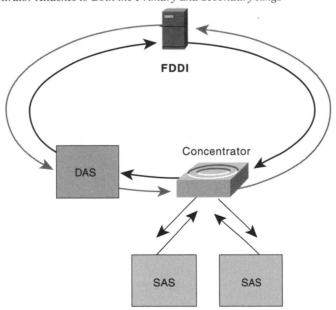

FDDI Fault Tolerance

FDDI provides a number of fault-tolerant features. In particular, FDDI's dual-ring environment, the implementation of the optical bypass switch, and dual-homing support make FDDI a resilient media technology.

Dual Ring

FDDI's primary fault-tolerant feature is the *dual ring*. If a station on the dual ring fails or is powered down, or if the cable is damaged, the dual ring is automatically wrapped (doubled back onto itself) into a single ring. When the ring is wrapped, the dual-ring topology becomes a single-ring topology. Data continues to be transmitted on the FDDI ring without performance impact during the wrap condition. Figure 9-6 and Figure 9-7 illustrate the effect of a ring wrapping in FDDI.

Figure 9-6   *A Ring Recovers from a Station Failure by Wrapping*

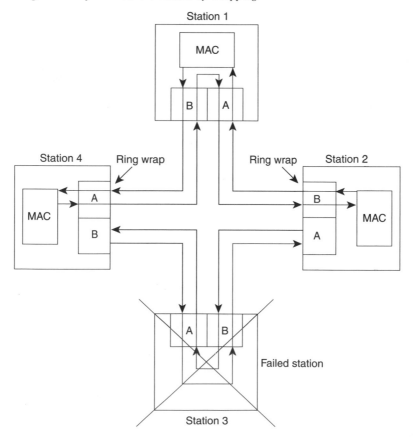

Figure 9-7   *A Ring also Wraps to Withstand a Cable Failure*

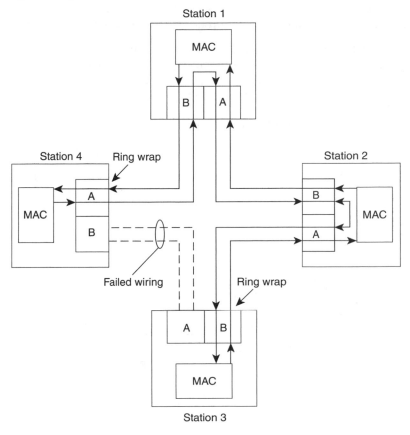

When a single station fails, as shown in Figure 9-6, devices on either side of the failed (or powered-down) station wrap, forming a single ring. Network operation continues for the remaining stations on the ring. When a cable failure occurs, as shown in Figure 9-7, devices on either side of the cable fault wrap. Network operation continues for all stations.

It should be noted that FDDI truly provides fault tolerance against a single failure only. When two or more failures occur, the FDDI ring segments into two or more independent rings that are incapable of communicating with each other.

Optical Bypass Switch

An *optical bypass switch* provides continuous dual-ring operation if a device on the dual ring fails. This is used both to prevent ring segmentation and to eliminate failed stations from the ring. The optical bypass switch performs this function using optical mirrors that pass light from the ring directly to the DAS device during normal operation. If a failure of the DAS device occurs, such as a power-off, the optical bypass switch will pass the light through itself by using internal mirrors and thereby will maintain the ring's integrity.

The benefit of this capability is that the ring will not enter a wrapped condition in case of a device failure. Figure 9-8 shows the functionality of an optical bypass switch in an FDDI network. When using the OB, you will notice a tremendous digression of your network as the packets are sent through the OB unit.

Figure 9-8   *The Optical Bypass Switch Uses Internal Mirrors to Maintain a Network*

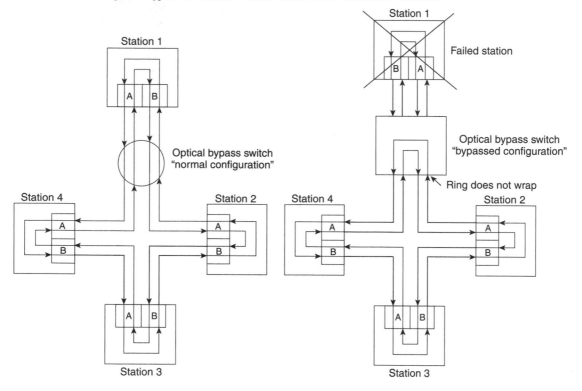

Dual Homing

Critical devices, such as routers or mainframe hosts, can use a fault-tolerant technique called *dual homing* to provide additional redundancy and to help guarantee operation. In dual-homing situations, the critical device is attached to two concentrators. Figure 9-9 shows a dual-homed configuration for devices such as file servers and routers.

Figure 9-9   *A Dual-Homed Configuration Guarantees Operation*

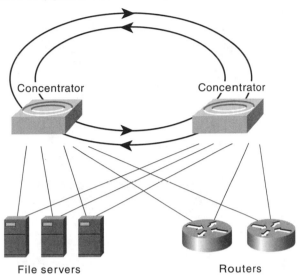

One pair of concentrator links is declared the active link; the other pair is declared passive. The passive link stays in backup mode until the primary link (or the concentrator to which it is attached) is determined to have failed. When this occurs, the passive link automatically activates.

FDDI Frame Format

The FDDI frame format is similar to the format of a Token Ring frame. This is one of the areas in which FDDI borrows heavily from earlier LAN technologies, such as Token Ring. FDDI frames can be as large as 4,500 bytes. Figure 9-10 shows the frame format of an FDDI data frame and token.

Figure 9-10 *The FDDI Frame Is Similar to That of a Token Ring Frame*

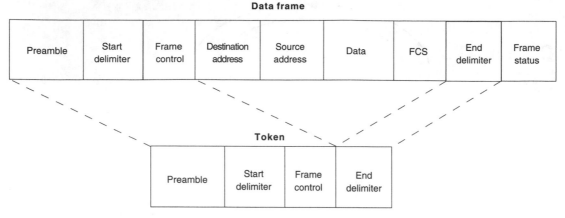

FDDI Frame Fields

The following descriptions summarize the FDDI data frame and token fields illustrated in Figure 9-10.

- **Preamble**—Gives a unique sequence that prepares each station for an upcoming frame.

- **Start delimiter**—Indicates the beginning of a frame by employing a signaling pattern that differentiates it from the rest of the frame.

- **Frame control**—Indicates the size of the address fields and whether the frame contains asynchronous or synchronous data, among other control information.

- **Destination address**—Contains a unicast (singular), multicast (group), or broadcast (every station) address. As with Ethernet and Token Ring addresses, FDDI destination addresses are 6 bytes long.

- **Source address**—Identifies the single station that sent the frame. As with Ethernet and Token Ring addresses, FDDI source addresses are 6 bytes long.

- **Data**—Contains either information destined for an upper-layer protocol or control information.

- **Frame check sequence (FCS)**—Is filed by the source station with a calculated cyclic redundancy check value dependent on frame contents (as with Token Ring and Ethernet). The destination address recalculates the value to determine whether the frame was damaged in transit. If so, the frame is discarded.

- **End delimiter**—Contains unique symbols; cannot be data symbols that indicate the end of the frame.

- **Frame status**—Allows the source station to determine whether an error occurred; identifies whether the frame was recognized and copied by a receiving station.

Copper Distributed Data Interface

Copper Distributed Data Interface (CDDI) is the implementation of FDDI protocols over twisted-pair copper wire. Like FDDI, CDDI provides data rates of 100 Mbps and uses dual-ring architecture to provide redundancy. CDDI supports distances of about 100 meters from desktop to concentrator.

CDDI is defined by the ANSI X3T9.5 Committee. The CDDI standard is officially named the Twisted-Pair Physical Medium-Dependent (TP-PMD) standard. It is also referred to as the Twisted-Pair Distributed Data Interface (TP-DDI), consistent with the term Fiber Distributed Data Interface (FDDI). CDDI is consistent with the physical and media-access control layers defined by the ANSI standard.

The ANSI standard recognizes only two types of cables for CDDI: shielded twisted pair (STP) and unshielded twisted pair (UTP). STP cabling has 150-ohm impedance and adheres to EIA/TIA 568 (IBM Type 1) specifications. UTP is data-grade cabling (Category 5) consisting of four unshielded pairs using tight-pair twists and specially developed insulating polymers in plastic jackets adhering to EIA/TIA 568B specifications.

Figure 9-11 illustrates the CDDI TP-PMD specification in relation to the remaining FDDI specifications.

Figure 9-11 *CDDI TP-PMD and FDDI Specifications Adhere to Different Standards*

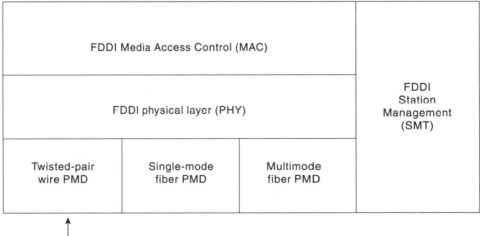

Summary

The Fiber Distributed Data Interface (FDDI) specifies a 100-Mbps token-passing, dual-ring LAN architecture using fiber-optic cable. FDDI is frequently implemented as a high-speed backbone technology because of its support for high bandwidth and greater distances than copper.

Review Questions

1 What are the benefits of using FDDI instead of CDDI?

2 What role does the DAC play in the FDDI network?

WAN Technologies

Objectives

- Describe the history of Frame Relay.
- Describe how Frame Relay works.
- Describe the primary functionality traits of Frame Relay.
- Describe Frame Relay network implementation.
- Describe the format of Frame Relay frames.

CHAPTER **10**

Frame Relay

Introduction

Frame Relay is a high-performance WAN protocol that operates at the physical and data link layers of the OSI reference model. Frame Relay originally was designed for use across Integrated Services Digital Network (ISDN) interfaces. Today, it is used over a variety of other network interfaces as well. This chapter focuses on Frame Relay's specifications and applications in the context of WAN services.

Frame Relay is an example of a packet-switched technology. Packet-switched networks enable end stations to dynamically share the network medium and the available bandwidth. The following two techniques are used in packet-switching technology:

- Variable-length packets
- Statistical multiplexing

Variable-length packets are used for more efficient and flexible data transfers. These packets are switched between the various segments in the network until the destination is reached.

Statistical multiplexing techniques control network access in a packet-switched network. The advantage of this technique is that it accommodates more flexibility and more efficient use of bandwidth. Most of today's popular LANs, such as Ethernet and Token Ring, are packet-switched networks.

Frame Relay often is described as a streamlined version of X.25, offering fewer of the robust capabilities, such as windowing and retransmission of last data that are offered in X.25. This is because Frame Relay typically operates over WAN facilities that offer more reliable connection services and a higher degree of reliability than the facilities available during the late 1970s and early 1980s that served as the common platforms for X.25 WANs. As mentioned earlier, Frame Relay is strictly a Layer 2 protocol suite, whereas X.25 provides services at Layer 3 (the network layer) as well. This enables Frame Relay to offer higher performance and greater transmission efficiency than X.25, and makes Frame Relay suitable for current WAN applications, such as LAN interconnection.

Frame Relay Standardization

Initial proposals for the standardization of Frame Relay were presented to the Consultative Committee on International Telephone and Telegraph (CCITT) in 1984. Because of lack of interoperability and lack of complete standardization, however, Frame Relay did not experience significant deployment during the late 1980s.

A major development in Frame Relay's history occurred in 1990 when Cisco, Digital Equipment Corporation (DEC), Northern Telecom, and StrataCom formed a consortium to focus on Frame Relay technology development. This consortium developed a specification that conformed to the basic Frame Relay protocol that was being discussed in CCITT, but it extended the protocol with features that provide additional capabilities for complex internetworking environments. These Frame Relay extensions are referred to collectively as the Local Management Interface (LMI).

Since the consortium's specification was developed and published, many vendors have announced their support of this extended Frame Relay definition. ANSI and CCITT have subsequently standardized their own variations of the original LMI specification, and these standardized specifications now are more commonly used than the original version.

Internationally, Frame Relay was standardized by the International Telecommunication Union—Telecommunications Standards Section (ITU-T). In the United States, Frame Relay is an American National Standards Institute (ANSI) standard.

Frame Relay Devices

Devices attached to a Frame Relay WAN fall into the following two general categories:

- Data terminal equipment (DTE)
- Data circuit-terminating equipment (DCE)

DTEs generally are considered to be terminating equipment for a specific network and typically are located on the premises of a customer. In fact, they may be owned by the customer. Examples of DTE devices are terminals, personal computers, routers, and bridges.

DCEs are carrier-owned internetworking devices. The purpose of DCE equipment is to provide clocking and switching services in a network, which are the devices that actually transmit data through the WAN. In most cases, these are packet switches. Figure 10-1 shows the relationship between the two categories of devices.

Figure 10-1 *DCEs Generally Reside Within Carrier-Operated WANs*

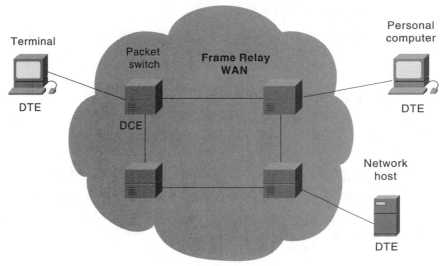

The connection between a DTE device and a DCE device consists of both a physical layer component and a link layer component. The physical component defines the mechanical, electrical, functional, and procedural specifications for the connection between the devices. One of the most commonly used physical layer interface specifications is the recommended standard (RS)-232 specification. The link layer component defines the protocol that establishes the connection between the DTE device, such as a router, and the DCE device, such as a switch. This chapter examines a commonly utilized protocol specification used in WAN networking: the Frame Relay protocol.

Frame Relay Virtual Circuits

Frame Relay provides connection-oriented data link layer communication. This means that a defined communication exists between each pair of devices and that these connections are associated with a connection identifier. This service is implemented by using a Frame Relay virtual circuit, which is a logical connection created between two data terminal equipment (DTE) devices across a Frame Relay packet-switched network (PSN).

Virtual circuits provide a bidirectional communication path from one DTE device to another and are uniquely identified by a data-link connection identifier (DLCI). A number of virtual circuits can be multiplexed into a single physical circuit for transmission across the network. This capability often can reduce the equipment and network complexity required to connect multiple DTE devices.

A virtual circuit can pass through any number of intermediate DCE devices (switches) located within the Frame Relay PSN.

Frame Relay virtual circuits fall into two categories: switched virtual circuits (SVCs) and permanent virtual circuits (PVCs).

Switched Virtual Circuits

Switched virtual circuits (SVCs) are temporary connections used in situations requiring only sporadic data transfer between DTE devices across the Frame Relay network. A communication session across an SVC consists of the following four operational states:

- **Call setup**—The virtual circuit between two Frame Relay DTE devices is established.
- **Data transfer**—Data is transmitted between the DTE devices over the virtual circuit.
- **Idle**—The connection between DTE devices is still active, but no data is transferred. If an SVC remains in an idle state for a defined period of time, the call can be terminated.
- **Call termination**—The virtual circuit between DTE devices is terminated.

After the virtual circuit is terminated, the DTE devices must establish a new SVC if there is additional data to be exchanged. It is expected that SVCs will be established, maintained, and terminated using the same signaling protocols used in ISDN.

Few manufacturers of Frame Relay DCE equipment support switched virtual circuit connections. Therefore, their actual deployment is minimal in today's Frame Relay networks.

Previously not widely supported by Frame Relay equipment, SVCs are now the norm. Companies have found that SVCs save money in the end because the circuit is not open all the time.

Permanent Virtual Circuits

Permanent virtual circuits (PVCs) are permanently established connections that are used for frequent and consistent data transfers between DTE devices across the Frame Relay network. Communication across a PVC does not require the call setup and termination states that are used with SVCs. PVCs always operate in one of the following two operational states:

- **Data transfer**—Data is transmitted between the DTE devices over the virtual circuit.
- **Idle**—The connection between DTE devices is active, but no data is transferred. Unlike SVCs, PVCs will not be terminated under any circumstances when in an idle state.

DTE devices can begin transferring data whenever they are ready because the circuit is permanently established.

Data-Link Connection Identifier

Frame Relay virtual circuits are identified by *data-link connection identifiers (DLCIs)*. DLCI values typically are assigned by the Frame Relay service provider (for example, the telephone company).

Frame Relay DLCIs have local significance, which means that their values are unique in the LAN, but not necessarily in the Frame Relay WAN.

Figure 10-2 illustrates how two different DTE devices can be assigned the same DLCI value within one Frame Relay WAN.

Figure 10-2 *A Single Frame Relay Virtual Circuit Can Be Assigned Different DLCIs on Each End of a VC*

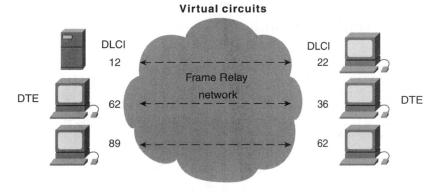

Congestion-Control Mechanisms

Frame Relay reduces network overhead by implementing simple congestion-notification mechanisms rather than explicit, per-virtual-circuit flow control. Frame Relay typically is implemented on reliable network media, so data integrity is not sacrificed because flow control can be left to higher-layer protocols. Frame Relay implements two congestion-notification mechanisms:

- Forward-explicit congestion notification (FECN)
- Backward-explicit congestion notification (BECN)

FECN and BECN each is controlled by a single bit contained in the Frame Relay frame header. The Frame Relay frame header also contains a Discard Eligibility (DE) bit, which is used to identify less important traffic that can be dropped during periods of congestion.

The *FECN bit* is part of the Address field in the Frame Relay frame header. The FECN mechanism is initiated when a DTE device sends Frame Relay frames into the network. If the network is congested, DCE devices (switches) set the value of the frames' FECN bit to 1. When the frames reach the destination DTE device, the Address field (with the FECN bit set) indicates that the frame experienced congestion in the path from source to destination. The DTE device can relay this information to a higher-layer protocol for processing. Depending on the implementation, flow control may be initiated, or the indication may be ignored.

The *BECN bit* is part of the Address field in the Frame Relay frame header. DCE devices set the value of the BECN bit to 1 in frames traveling in the opposite direction of frames with their FECN bit set. This informs the receiving DTE device that a particular path through the network is congested. The DTE device then can relay this information to a higher-layer protocol for processing. Depending on the implementation, flow-control may be initiated, or the indication may be ignored.

Frame Relay Discard Eligibility

The *Discard Eligibility (DE) bit* is used to indicate that a frame has lower importance than other frames. The DE bit is part of the Address field in the Frame Relay frame header.

DTE devices can set the value of the DE bit of a frame to 1 to indicate that the frame has lower importance than other frames. When the network becomes congested, DCE devices will discard frames with the DE bit set before discarding those that do not. This reduces the likelihood of critical data being dropped by Frame Relay DCE devices during periods of congestion.

Frame Relay Error Checking

Frame Relay uses a common error-checking mechanism known as the *cyclic redundancy check (CRC)*. The CRC compares two calculated values to determine whether errors occurred during the transmission from source to destination. Frame Relay reduces network overhead by implementing error checking rather than error correction. Frame Relay typically is implemented on reliable network media, so data integrity is not sacrificed because error correction can be left to higher-layer protocols running on top of Frame Relay.

Frame Relay Local Management Interface

The *Local Management Interface (LMI)* is a set of enhancements to the basic Frame Relay specification. The LMI was developed in 1990 by Cisco Systems, StrataCom, Northern Telecom, and Digital Equipment Corporation. It offers a number of features (called extensions) for managing complex internetworks. Key Frame Relay LMI extensions include global addressing, virtual circuit status messages, and multicasting.

The LMI global addressing extension gives Frame Relay data-link connection identifier (DLCI) values global rather than local significance. DLCI values become DTE addresses that are unique in the Frame Relay WAN. The global addressing extension adds functionality and manageability to Frame Relay internetworks. Individual network interfaces and the end nodes attached to them, for example, can be identified by using standard address-resolution and discovery techniques. In addition, the entire Frame Relay network appears to be a typical LAN to routers on its periphery.

LMI virtual circuit status messages provide communication and synchronization between Frame Relay DTE and DCE devices. These messages are used to periodically report on the status of PVCs, which prevents data from being sent into black holes (that is, over PVCs that no longer exist).

The LMI multicasting extension allows multicast groups to be assigned. Multicasting saves bandwidth by allowing routing updates and address-resolution messages to be sent only to specific groups of routers. The extension also transmits reports on the status of multicast groups in update messages.

Frame Relay Network Implementation

A common private Frame Relay network implementation is to equip a T1 multiplexer with both Frame Relay and non-Frame Relay interfaces. Frame Relay traffic is forwarded out the Frame Relay interface and onto the data network. Non-Frame Relay traffic is forwarded to the appropriate application or service, such as a private branch exchange (PBX) for telephone service or to a video-teleconferencing application.

A typical Frame Relay network consists of a number of DTE devices, such as routers, connected to remote ports on multiplexer equipment via traditional point-to-point services such as T1, fractional T1, or 56-Kb circuits. An example of a simple Frame Relay network is shown in Figure 10-3.

Figure 10-3 *A Simple Frame Relay Network Connects Various Devices to Different Services over a WAN*

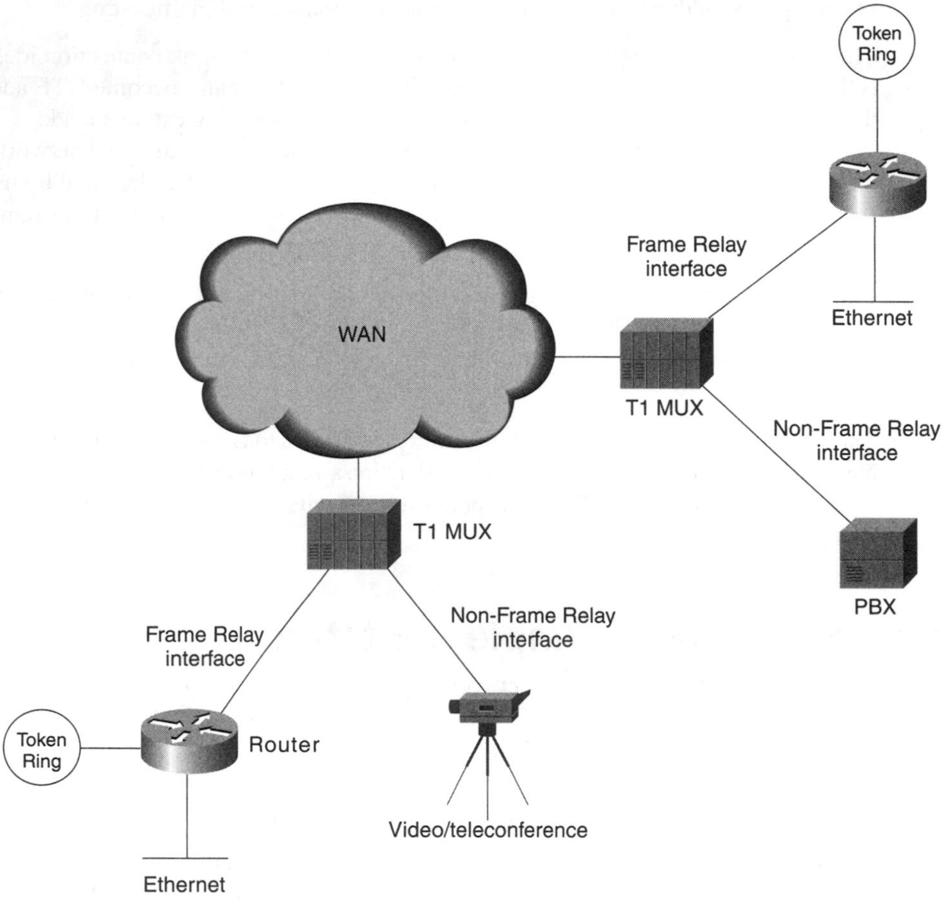

The majority of Frame Relay networks deployed today are provisioned by service providers that intend to offer transmission services to customers. This is often referred to as a public Frame Relay service. Frame Relay is implemented in both public carrier-provided networks and in private enterprise networks. The following section examines the two methodologies for deploying Frame Relay.

Public Carrier-Provided Networks

In public carrier-provided Frame Relay networks, the Frame Relay switching equipment is located in the central offices of a telecommunications carrier. Subscribers are charged based on their network use but are relieved from administering and maintaining the Frame Relay network equipment and service.

Generally, the DCE equipment also is owned by the telecommunications provider. DCE equipment either will be customer-owned or perhaps will be owned by the telecommunications provider as a service to the customer.

The majority of today's Frame Relay networks are public carrier-provided networks.

Private Enterprise Networks

More frequently, organizations worldwide are deploying private Frame Relay networks. In private Frame Relay networks, the administration and maintenance of the network are the responsibilities of the enterprise (a private company). All the equipment, including the switching equipment, is owned by the customer.

Frame Relay Frame Formats

To understand much of the functionality of Frame Relay, it is helpful to understand the structure of the Frame Relay frame. Figure 10-4 depicts the basic format of the Frame Relay frame, and Figure 10-5 illustrates the LMI version of the Frame Relay frame.

Flags indicate the beginning and end of the frame. Three primary components make up the Frame Relay frame: the header and address area, the user-data portion, and the frame check sequence (FCS). The address area, which is 2 bytes in length, is comprised of 10 bits representing the actual circuit identifier and 6 bits of fields related to congestion management. This identifier commonly is referred to as the data-link connection identifier (DLCI). Each of these is discussed in the descriptions that follow.

Standard Frame Relay Frame

Standard Frame Relay frames consist of the fields illustrated in Figure 10-4.

Figure 10-4 *Five Fields Comprise the Frame Relay Frame*

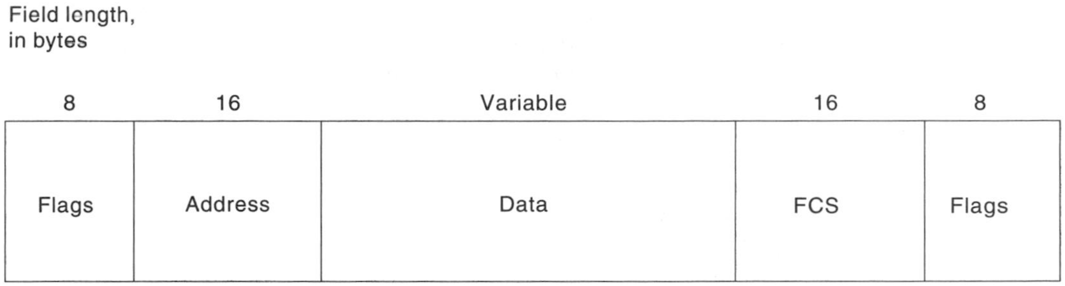

Field length,
in bytes

8	16	Variable	16	8
Flags	Address	Data	FCS	Flags

The following descriptions summarize the basic Frame Relay frame fields illustrated in Figure 10-4.

- **Flags**—Delimits the beginning and end of the frame. The value of this field is always the same and is represented either as the hexadecimal number 7E or as the binary number 01111110.

- **Address**—Contains the following information:

  - **DLCI**—The 10-bit DLCI is the essence of the Frame Relay header. This value represents the virtual connection between the DTE device and the switch. Each virtual connection that is multiplexed onto the physical channel will be represented by a unique DLCI. The DLCI values have local significance only, which means that they are unique only to the physical channel on which they reside. Therefore, devices at opposite ends of a connection can use different DLCI values to refer to the same virtual connection.

  - **Extended Address (EA)**—The EA is used to indicate whether the byte in which the EA value is 1 is the last addressing field. If the value is 1, then the current byte is determined to be the last DLCI octet. Although current Frame Relay implementations all use a two-octet DLCI, this capability does allow longer DLCIs to be used in the future. The eighth bit of each byte of the Address field is used to indicate the EA.

  - **C/R**—The C/R is the bit that follows the most significant DLCI byte in the Address field. The C/R bit is not currently defined.

  - **Congestion Control**—This consists of the 3 bits that control the Frame Relay congestion-notification mechanisms. These are the FECN, BECN, and DE bits, which are the last 3 bits in the Address field.

    Forward-explicit congestion notification (FECN) is a single-bit field that can be set to a value of 1 by a switch to indicate to an end DTE device, such as a router, that congestion was experienced in the direction of the frame transmission from source to destination. The primary benefit of the use of the FECN and BECN fields is the capability of higher-layer protocols to react intelligently to these congestion indicators. Today, DECnet and OSI are the only higher-layer protocols that implement these capabilities.

    Backward-explicit congestion notification (BECN) is a single-bit field that, when set to a value of 1 by a switch, indicates that congestion was experienced in the network in the direction opposite of the frame transmission from source to destination.

Discard eligibility (DE) is set by the DTE device, such as a router, to indicate that the marked frame is of lesser importance relative to other frames being transmitted. Frames that are marked as "discard eligible" should be discarded before other frames in a congested network. This allows for a basic prioritization mechanism in Frame Relay networks.

- **Data**—Contains encapsulated upper-layer data. Each frame in this variable-length field includes a user data or payload field that will vary in length up to 16,000 octets. This field serves to transport the higher-layer protocol packet (PDU) through a Frame Relay network.

- **Frame Check Sequence**—Ensures the integrity of transmitted data. This value is computed by the source device and verified by the receiver to ensure integrity of transmission.

LMI Frame Format

Frame Relay frames that conform to the LMI specifications consist of the fields illustrated in Figure 10-5.

Figure 10-5 *Nine Fields Comprise the Frame Relay That Conforms to the LMI Format*

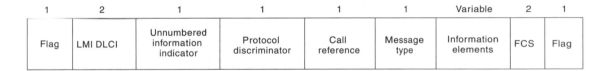

The following descriptions summarize the fields illustrated in Figure 10-5.

- **Flag**—Delimits the beginning and end of the frame.

- **LMI DLCI**—Identifies the frame as an LMI frame instead of a basic Frame Relay frame. The LMI-specific DLCI value defined in the LMI consortium specification is DLCI = 1023.

- **Unnumbered Information Indicator**—Sets the poll/final bit to zero.

- **Protocol Discriminator**—Always contains a value indicating that the frame is an LMI frame.

- **Call Reference**—Always contains zeros. This field currently is not used for any purpose.

- **Message Type**—Labels the frame as one of the following message types:
    - **Status-inquiry message**—Allows a user device to inquire about the status of the network.

- **Status message**—Responds to status-inquiry messages. Status messages include keepalives and PVC status messages.
- **Information Elements**—Contains a variable number of individual information elements (IEs). IEs consist of the following fields:
    - **IE Identifier**—Uniquely identifies the IE.
    - **IE Length**—Indicates the length of the IE.
    - **Data**—Consists of 1 or more bytes containing encapsulated upper-layer data.
- **Frame Check Sequence (FCS)**—Ensures the integrity of transmitted data.

Summary

Frame Relay is a networking protocol that works at the bottom two levels of the OSI reference model: the physical and data link layers. It is an example of packet-switching technology, which enables end stations to dynamically share network resources.

Frame Relay devices fall into the following two general categories:

- Data terminal equipment (DTEs), which include terminals, personal computers, routers, and bridges
- Data circuit-terminating equipment (DCEs), which transmit the data through the network and are often carrier-owned devices (although, increasingly, enterprises are buying their own DCEs and implementing them in their networks)

Frame Relay networks transfer data using one of the following two connection types:

- Switched virtual circuits (SVCs), which are temporary connections that are created for each data transfer and then are terminated when the data transfer is complete (not a widely used connection)
- Permanent virtual circuits (PVCs), which are permanent connections

The DLCI is a value assigned to each virtual circuit and DTE device connection point in the Frame Relay WAN. Two different connections can be assigned the same value within the same Frame Relay WAN—one on each side of the virtual connection.

In 1990, Cisco Systems, StrataCom, Northern Telecom, and Digital Equipment Corporation developed a set of Frame Relay enhancements called the Local Management Interface (LMI). The LMI enhancements offer a number of features (referred to as extensions) for managing complex internetworks, including the following:

- Global addressing
- Virtual circuit status messages
- Multicasting

Review Questions

1 What kind of technology is Frame Relay?

2 Name the two kinds of packet-switching techniques discussed in this chapter, and briefly describe each.

3 Describe the difference between SVCs and PVCs.

4 What is the data-link connection identifier (DLCI)?

5 Describe how LMI Frame Relay differs from basic Frame Relay.

Objectives

- Discuss the history and standards of HSSI.
- Explain the technical specifications of HSSI.
- Describe the benefits of employing HSSI technology.
- Discuss how HSSI operates.

CHAPTER 11

High-Speed Serial Interface

Introduction

The *High-Speed Serial Interface (HSSI)* is a DTE/DCE interface that was developed by Cisco Systems and T3plus Networking to address the need for high-speed communication over WAN links. The HSSI specification is available to any organization wanting to implement HSSI.

HSSI Interface Basics

HSSI defines both electrical and physical interfaces on DTE and DCE devices. It operates at the physical layer of the OSI reference model.

HSSI technical characteristics are summarized in Table 11-1.

Table 11-1 *HSSI Technical Characteristics*

Characteristic	Value
Maximum signaling rate	52 Mbps
Maximum cable length	50 feet
Number of connector points	50
Interface	DTE-DCE
Electrical technology	Differential ECL
Typical power consumption	610 mW
Topology	Point-to-point
Cable type	Shielded twisted-pair wire

The maximum signaling rate of HSSI is 52 Mbps. At this rate, HSSI can handle the T3 speeds (45 Mbps) of many of today's fast WAN technologies, as well as the Office Channel-1 (OC-1) speeds (52 Mbps) of the synchronous digital hierarchy (SDH). In addition, HSSI easily can provide high-speed connectivity between LANs, such as Token Ring and Ethernet.

The use of differential emitter-coupled logic (ECL) helps HSSI achieve high data rates and low noise levels. ECL has been used in Cray computer system interfaces for years and is specified by the ANSI High-Performance Parallel Interface (HIPPI) communications standard for supercomputer LAN communications. ECL is an off-the-shelf technology that permits excellent retiming on the receiver, resulting in reliable timing margins.

HSSI uses a subminiature, FCC-approved 50-pin connector that is smaller than its V.35 counterpart. To reduce the need for male-male and female-female adapters, HSSI cable connectors are specified as male. The HSSI cable uses the same number of pins and wires as the Small Computer Systems Interface 2 (SCSI-2) cable, but the HSSI electrical specification is more concise.

HSSI Operation

The flexibility of the HSSI clock and data-signaling protocol makes user (or vendor) bandwidth allocation possible. The DCE controls the clock by changing its speed or by deleting clock pulses. In this way, the DCE can allocate bandwidth between applications. For example, a PBX may require a particular amount of bandwidth, a router another amount, and a channel extender a third amount. Bandwidth allocation is key to making T3 and other broadband services affordable and popular.

HSSI assumes a peer-to-peer intelligence in the DCE and DTE. The control protocol is simplified, with just two control signals required ("DTE available" and "DCE available"). Both signals must be asserted before the data circuit can become valid. The DCE and DTE are expected to be capable of managing the networks behind their interfaces. Reducing the number of control signals improves circuit reliability by reducing the number of circuits that can fail.

Loopback Tests

HSSI provides four loopback tests, which are illustrated in Figure 11-1. The first provides a local cable test as the signal loops back after it reaches the DTE port. The second test reaches the line port of the local DCE. The third test reaches the line port of the remote DCE. Finally, the fourth test is a DCE-initiated test of the DTE's DCE port.

Figure 11-1 *HSSI Supports Four Loopback Tests*

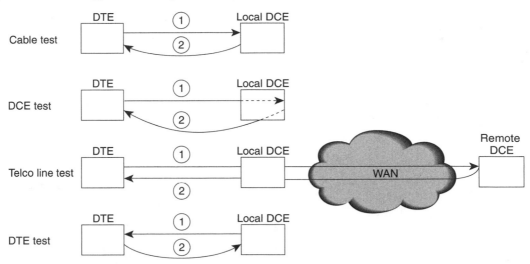

Summary

HSSI is an interface technology that was developed by Cisco Systems and T3plus
Networking in the late 1990s to fill the need for a high-speed data communication solution
over WAN links. It uses differential emitter-coupled logic (ECL), which provides high-
speed data transfer with low noise levels. HSSI pin connectors are significantly smaller than
pin connectors for competing technologies. The HSSI cable uses the same number of pins
and wires as the Small Computer Systems Interface 2 (SCSI-2) cable, but its electrical
specification is more concise. HSSI makes bandwidth resources easy to allocate, making
T3 and other broadband services available and affordable. HSSI requires the presence of
only two control signals, making it highly reliable because there are fewer circuits that can
fail. HSSI performs four loopback tests for reliability.

Review Questions

   1 Name at least three benefits of implementing HSSI technology in a network.

   2 Name the four loopback tests that HSSI performs.

Objectives

- Explain what ISDN is.
- Describe ISDN devices and how they operate.
- Describe the specifications for ISDN data transmittal for the three layers at which ISDN transmits.

CHAPTER **12**

Integrated Services Digital Network

Introduction

Integrated Services Digital Network (ISDN) is comprised of digital telephony and data-transport services offered by regional telephone carriers. ISDN involves the digitization of the telephone network, which permits voice, data, text, graphics, music, video, and other source material to be transmitted over existing telephone wires. The emergence of ISDN represents an effort to standardize subscriber services, user/network interfaces, and network and internetwork capabilities. ISDN applications include high-speed image applications (such as Group IV facsimile), additional telephone lines in homes to serve the telecommuting industry, high-speed file transfer, and videoconferencing. Voice service is also an application for ISDN. This chapter summarizes the underlying technologies and services associated with ISDN.

ISDN Devices

ISDN devices include terminals, terminal adapters (TAs), network-termination devices, line-termination equipment, and exchange-termination equipment. ISDN terminals come in two types. Specialized ISDN terminals are referred to as terminal equipment type 1 (TE1). Non-ISDN terminals, such as DTE, that predate the ISDN standards are referred to as terminal equipment type 2 (TE2). TE1s connect to the ISDN network through a four-wire, twisted-pair digital link. TE2s connect to the ISDN network through a TA. The ISDN TA can be either a standalone device or a board inside the TE2. If the TE2 is implemented as a standalone device, it connects to the TA via a standard physical-layer interface. Examples include EIA/TIA-232-C (formerly RS-232-C), V.24, and V.35.

Beyond the TE1 and TE2 devices, the next connection point in the ISDN network is the network termination type 1 (NT1) or network termination type 2 (NT2) device. These are network-termination devices that connect the four-wire subscriber wiring to the conventional two-wire local loop. In North America, the NT1 is a customer premises equipment (CPE) device. In most other parts of the world, the NT1 is part of the network provided by the carrier. The NT2 is a more complicated device that typically is found in digital private branch exchanges (PBXs) and that performs Layer 2 and 3 protocol functions and concentration services. An NT1/2 device also exists as a single device that combines the functions of an NT1 and an NT2.

ISDN specifies a number of reference points that define logical interfaces between functional groups, such as TAs and NT1s. ISDN reference points include the following:

- **R**—The reference point between non-ISDN equipment and a TA.
- **S**—The reference point between user terminals and the NT2.
- **T**—The reference point between NT1 and NT2 devices.
- **U**—The reference point between NT1 devices and line-termination equipment in the carrier network. The U reference point is relevant only in North America, where the NT1 function is not provided by the carrier network.

Figure 12-1 illustrates a sample ISDN configuration and shows three devices attached to an ISDN switch at the central office. Two of these devices are ISDN-compatible, so they can be attached through an S reference point to NT2 devices. The third device (a standard, non-ISDN telephone) attaches through the reference point to a TA. Any of these devices also could attach to an NT1/2 device, which would replace both the NT1 and the NT2. In addition, although they are not shown, similar user stations are attached to the far-right ISDN switch.

Figure 12-1 *Sample ISDN Configuration Illustrates Relationships Between Devices and Reference Points*

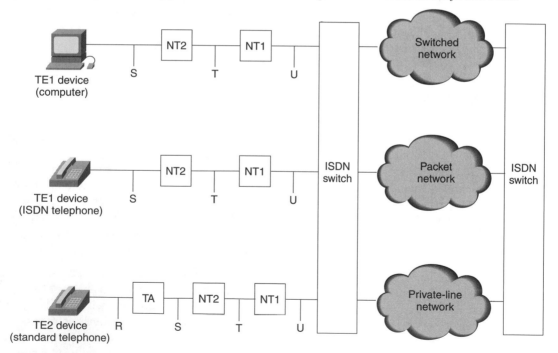

Services

There are two types of services associated with ISDN:

- BRI
- PRI

ISDN BRI Service

The ISDN Basic Rate Interface (BRI) service offers two B channels and one D channel (2B+D). BRI B-channel service operates at 64 kbps and is meant to carry user data; BRI D-channel service operates at 16 kbps and is meant to carry control and signaling information, although it can support user data transmission under certain circumstances. The D channel signaling protocol comprises Layers 1 through 3 of the OSI reference model. BRI also provides for framing control and other overhead, bringing its total bit rate to 192 kbps. The BRI physical layer specification is International Telecommunication Union–Telecommunications Standards Section (ITU-T) (formerly the Consultative Committee for International Telegraph and Telephone [CCITT]) I.430.

ISDN PRI Service

ISDN Primary Rate Interface (PRI) service offers 23 B channels and 1 D channel in North America and Japan, yielding a total bit rate of 1.544 Mbps (the PRI D channel runs at 64 kbps). ISDN PRI in Europe, Australia, and other parts of the world provides 30 B channels plus one 64-kbps D channel and a total interface rate of 2.048 Mbps. The PRI physical layer specification is ITU-T I.431.

ISDN Specifications

This section describes the various ISDN specifications for Layer 1, Layer 2, and Layer 3.

Layer 1

ISDN physical layer (Layer 1) frame formats differ depending on whether the frame is outbound (from terminal to network) or inbound (from network to terminal). Both physical layer interfaces are shown in Figure 12-2.

The frames are 48 bits long, of which 36 bits represent data. The bits of an ISDN physical layer frame are used as follows:

- **F**—Provides synchronization
- **L**—Adjusts the average bit value
- **E**—Ensures contention resolution when several terminals on a passive bus contend for a channel

- **A**—Activates devices
- **S**—Is unassigned
- **B1**, **B2**, and **D**—Handle user data

Figure 12-2 *ISDN Physical Layer Frame Formats Differ Depending on Their Direction*

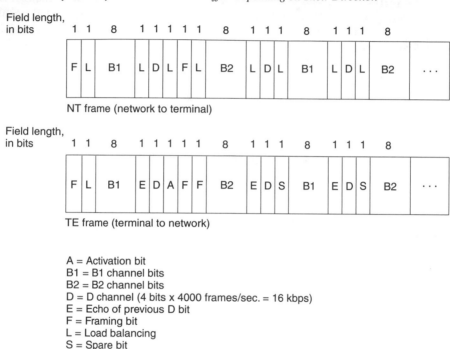

A = Activation bit
B1 = B1 channel bits
B2 = B2 channel bits
D = D channel (4 bits x 4000 frames/sec. = 16 kbps)
E = Echo of previous D bit
F = Framing bit
L = Load balancing
S = Spare bit

Multiple ISDN user devices can be physically attached to one circuit. In this configuration, collisions can result if two terminals transmit simultaneously. Therefore, ISDN provides features to determine link contention. When an NT receives a D bit from the TE, it echoes back the bit in the next E-bit position. The TE expects the next E bit to be the same as its last transmitted D bit.

Terminals cannot transmit into the D channel unless they first detect a specific number of ones (indicating "no signal") corresponding to a pre-established priority. If the TE detects a bit in the echo (E) channel that is different from its D bits, it must stop transmitting immediately. This simple technique ensures that only one terminal can transmit its D message at one time. After successful D-message transmission, the terminal has its priority reduced by requiring it to detect more continuous ones before transmitting. Terminals cannot raise their priority until all other devices on the same line have had an opportunity to send a D message. Telephone connections have higher priority than all other services, and signaling information has a higher priority than nonsignaling information.

Layer 2

Layer 2 of the ISDN signaling protocol is Link Access Procedure, D channel (LAPD). LAPD is similar to High-Level Data Link Control (HDLC) and Link Access Procedure, Balanced (LAPB) (see Chapter 16, "Synchronous Data Link Control and Derivatives," and Chapter 17, "X.25," for more information on these protocols). As the expansion of the LAPD acronym indicates, this layer is used across the D channel to ensure that control and signaling information flows and is received properly. The LAPD frame format (see Figure 12-3) is very similar to that of HDLC; like HDLC, LAPD uses supervisory, information, and unnumbered frames. The LAPD protocol is formally specified in ITU-T Q.920 and ITU-T Q.921.

Figure 12-3 *LAPD Frame Format Is Similar to That of HDLC and LAPB*

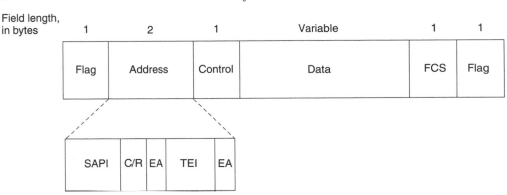

SAPI = Service access point identifier (6 bits)
C/R = Command/response bit
EA = Extended addressing bits
TEI = Terminal endpoint identifier

The LAPD Flag and Control fields are identical to those of HDLC. The LAPD Address field can be either 1 or 2 bytes long. If the extended address bit of the first byte is set, the address is 1 byte; if it is not set, the address is 2 bytes. The first Address-field byte contains the service access point identifier (SAPI), which identifies the portal at which LAPD services are provided to Layer 3. The C/R bit indicates whether the frame contains a command or a response. The Terminal Endpoint Identifier (TEI) field identifies either a single terminal or multiple terminals. A TEI of all ones indicates a broadcast.

Layer 3

Two Layer 3 specifications are used for ISDN signaling: ITU-T (formerly CCITT) I.450 (also known as ITU-T Q.930) and ITU-T I.451 (also known as ITU-T Q.931). Together, these protocols support user-to-user, circuit-switched, and packet-switched connections. A variety of call-establishment, call-termination, information, and miscellaneous messages are specified, including SETUP, CONNECT, RELEASE, USER INFORMATION, CANCEL, STATUS, and DISCONNECT. These messages are functionally similar to those provided by the X.25 protocol (see Chapter 17 for more information). Figure 12-4, from ITU-T I.451, shows the typical stages of an ISDN circuit-switched call.

Figure 12-4 *An ISDN Circuit-Switched Call Moves Through Various Stages to Its Destination*

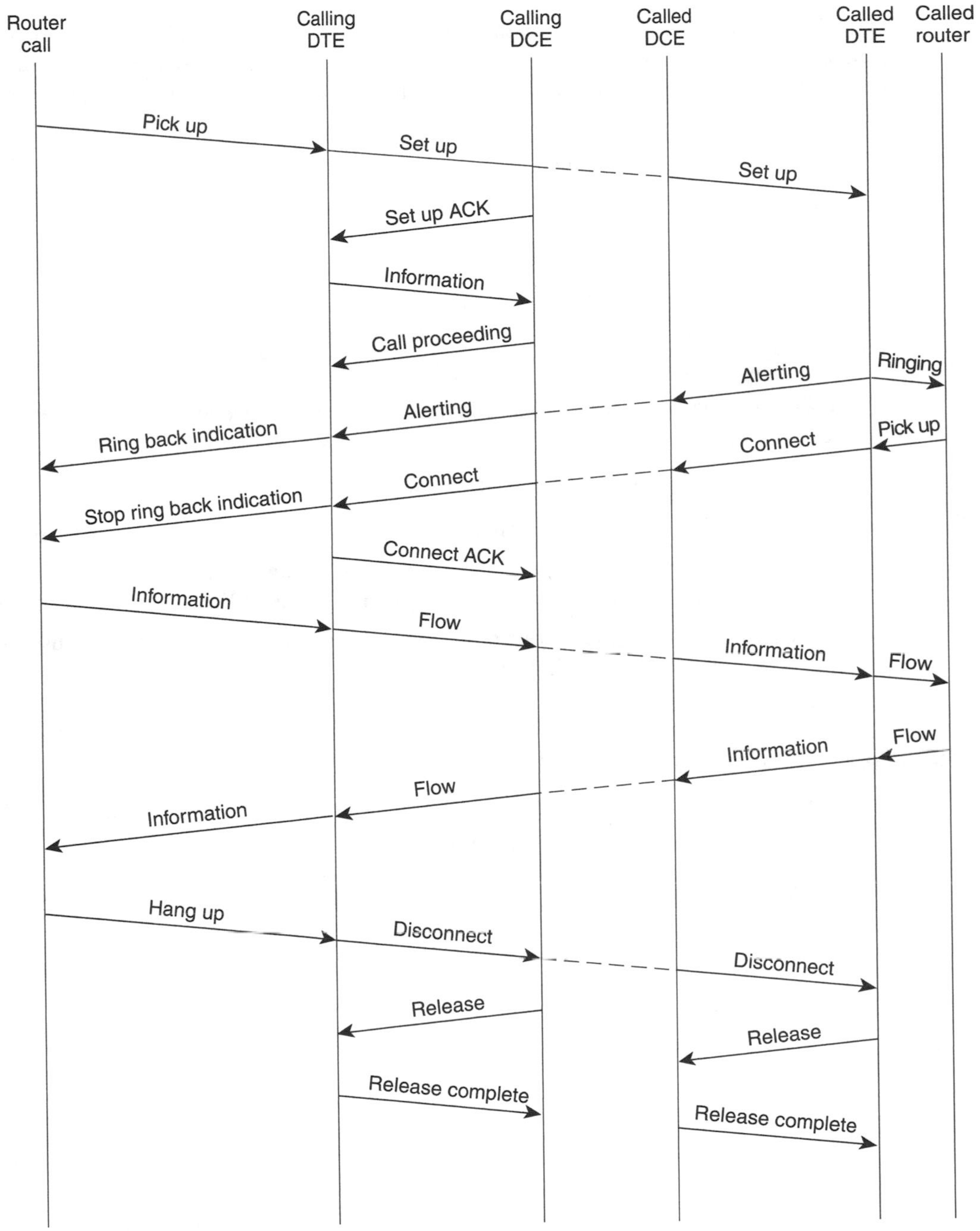

Summary

ISDN is comprised of digital telephony and data-transport services offered by regional telephone carriers. ISDN involves the digitization of the telephone network to transmit voice, data, text, graphics, music, video, and other source material over existing telephone wires.

ISDN devices include the following:

- Terminals
- Terminal adapters (TAs)
- Network-termination devices
- Line-termination equipment
- Exchange-termination equipment

The ISDN specification references specific connection points that define logical interfaces between devices.

ISDN uses the following two types of services:

- Basic Rate Interface (BRI, which offers two B channels and one D channel (2B+D)
- Primary Rate Interface (PRI), which offers 23 B channels and 1 D channel in North America and Japan, and 30 B channels and 1 D channel in Europe and Australia

ISDN runs on the bottom three layers of the OSI reference model, and each layer uses a different specification to transmit data.

Review Questions

1 Which reference point for ISDN logical devices is relevant only in North America?

2 What are the two speeds of ISDN PRI services?

3 Of the 48 bits in the ISDN physical layer frame formats, how many bits represent data?

Objectives

- Describe the development of PPP.
- Describe the components of PPP and how they operate.
- Provide a summary of the basic protocol elements and operations of PPP.

CHAPTER 13

Point-to-Point Protocol

Introduction

The *Point-to-Point Protocol (PPP)* originally emerged as an encapsulation protocol for transporting IP traffic over point-to-point links. PPP also established a standard for the assignment and management of IP addresses, asynchronous (start/stop) and bit-oriented synchronous encapsulation, network protocol multiplexing, link configuration, link quality testing, error detection, and option negotiation for such capabilities as network layer address negotiation and data-compression negotiation. PPP supports these functions by providing an extensible Link Control Protocol (LCP) and a family of Network Control Protocols (NCPs) to negotiate optional configuration parameters and facilities. In addition to IP, PPP supports other protocols, including Novell's Internetwork Packet Exchange (IPX) and DECnet.

PPP Components

PPP provides a method for transmitting datagrams over serial point-to-point links. PPP contains three main components:

*   A method for encapsulating datagrams over serial links. PPP uses the High-Level Data Link Control (HDLC) protocol as a basis for encapsulating datagrams over point-to-point links. (See Chapter 16, "Synchronous Data Link Control and Derivatives," for more information on HDLC.)

*   An extensible LCP to establish, configure, and test the data link connection.

*   A family of NCPs for establishing and configuring different network layer protocols. PPP is designed to allow the simultaneous use of multiple network layer protocols.

General Operation

To establish communications over a point-to-point link, the originating PPP first sends LCP frames to configure and (optionally) test the data link. After the link has been established and optional facilities have been negotiated as needed by the LCP, the originating PPP sends NCP frames to choose and configure one or more network layer protocols. When each of the chosen network layer protocols has been configured, packets from each network layer protocol can be sent over the link. The link will remain configured for communications until explicit LCP or NCP frames close the link, or until some external event occurs (for example, an inactivity timer expires or a user intervenes).

Physical Layer Requirements

PPP is capable of operating across any DTE/DCE interface. Examples include EIA/TIA-232-C (formerly RS-232-C), EIA/TIA-422 (formerly RS-422), EIA/TIA-423 (formerly RS-423), and International Telecommunication Union Telecommunication Standardization Sector (ITU-T) (formerly CCITT) V.35. The only absolute requirement imposed by PPP is the provision of a duplex circuit, either dedicated or switched, that can operate in either an asynchronous or synchronous bit-serial mode, transparent to PPP link layer frames. PPP does not impose any restrictions regarding transmission rate other than those imposed by the particular DTE/DCE interface in use.

PPP Link Layer

PPP uses the principles, terminology, and frame structure of the International Organization for Standardization (ISO) HDLC procedures (ISO 3309-1979), as modified by ISO 3309:1984/PDAD1 "Addendum 1: Start/Stop Transmission." ISO 3309-1979 specifies the HDLC frame structure for use in synchronous environments. ISO 3309:1984/PDAD1 specifies proposed modifications to ISO 3309-1979 to allow its use in asynchronous environments. The PPP control procedures use the definitions and control field encodings standardized in ISO 4335-1979 and ISO 4335-1979/Addendum 1-1979. The PPP frame format appears in Figure 13-1.

Figure 13-1 *Six Fields Make Up the PPP Frame*

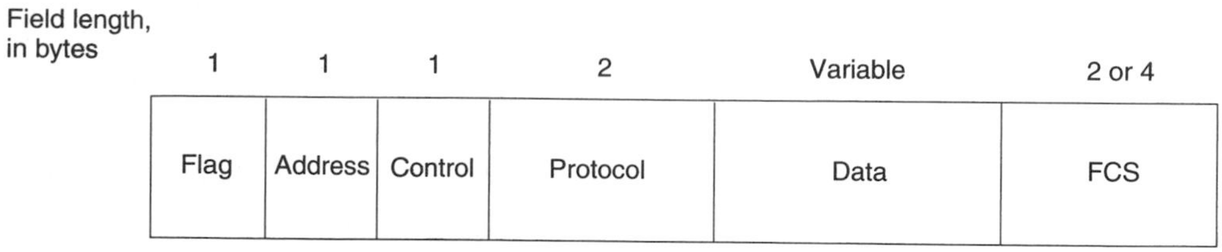

The following descriptions summarize the PPP frame fields illustrated in Figure 13-1:

- **Flag**—A single byte that indicates the beginning or end of a frame. The flag field consists of the binary sequence 01111110.

- **Address**—A single byte that contains the binary sequence 11111111, the standard broadcast address. PPP does not assign individual station addresses.

- **Control**—A single byte that contains the binary sequence 00000011, which calls for transmission of user data in an unsequenced frame. A connectionless link service similar to that of Logical Link Control (LLC) Type 1 is provided. (For more information about LLC types and frame types, refer to Chapter 16.)

- **Protocol**—Two bytes that identify the protocol encapsulated in the information field of the frame. The most up-to-date values of the protocol field are specified in the most recent Assigned Numbers Request For Comments (RFC).

- **Data**—Zero or more bytes that contain the datagram for the protocol specified in the protocol field. The end of the information field is found by locating the closing flag sequence and allowing 2 bytes for the FCS field. The default maximum length of the information field is 1,500 bytes. By prior agreement, consenting PPP implementations can use other values for the maximum information field length.

- **Frame check sequence (FCS)**—Normally 16 bits (2 bytes). By prior agreement, consenting PPP implementations can use a 32-bit (4-byte) FCS for improved error detection.

The LCP can negotiate modifications to the standard PPP frame structure. Modified frames, however, always will be clearly distinguishable from standard frames.

PPP Link-Control Protocol

The PPP LCP provides a method of establishing, configuring, maintaining, and terminating the point-to-point connection. LCP goes through four distinct phases.

First, link establishment and configuration negotiation occur. Before any network layer datagrams (for example, IP) can be exchanged, LCP first must open the connection and negotiate configuration parameters. This phase is complete when a configuration-acknowledgment frame has been both sent and received.

This is followed by link quality determination. LCP allows an optional link quality determination phase following the link-establishment and configuration-negotiation phase. In this phase, the link is tested to determine whether the link quality is sufficient to bring up network layer protocols. This phase is optional. LCP can delay transmission of network layer protocol information until this phase is complete.

At this point, network layer protocol configuration negotiation occurs. After LCP has finished the link quality determination phase, network layer protocols can be configured separately by the appropriate NCP and can be brought up and taken down at any time. If LCP closes the link, it informs the network layer protocols so that they can take appropriate action.

Finally, link termination occurs. LCP can terminate the link at any time. This usually is done at the request of a user but can happen because of a physical event, such as the loss of carrier or the expiration of an idle-period timer.

Three classes of LCP frames exist. Link-establishment frames are used to establish and configure a link. Link-termination frames are used to terminate a link, and link-maintenance frames are used to manage and debug a link.

These frames are used to accomplish the work of each of the LCP phases.

Summary

The Point-to-Point Protocol (PPP) originally emerged as an encapsulation protocol for transporting IP traffic over point-to-point links. PPP also established a standard for assigning and managing IP addresses, asynchronous and bit-oriented synchronous encapsulation, network protocol multiplexing, link configuration, link quality testing, error detection, and option negotiation for added networking capabilities.

PPP provides a method for transmitting datagrams over serial point-to-point links, which include the following three components:

- A method for encapsulating datagrams over serial links
- An extensible LCP to establish, configure, and test the connection
- A family of NCPs for establishing and configuring different network layer protocols

PPP is capable of operating across any DTE/DCE interface. PPP does not impose any restriction regarding transmission rate other than those imposed by the particular DTE/DCE interface in use.

Six fields make up the PPP frame. The PPP LCP provides a method of establishing, configuring, maintaining, and terminating the point-to-point connection.

Review Questions

1 What are the main components of PPP?

2 What is the only absolute physical layer requirement imposed by PPP?

3 How many fields make up the PPP frame, and what are they?

4 How many phases does the PPP LCP go through, and what are they?

Objectives

- Tell how SMDS works, and describe its components.
- Describe the operational elements of the SMDS environment, and outline its underlying protocol.
- Discuss related technologies.
- Discuss SMDS access classes and cell formats.

CHAPTER **14**

Switched Multimegabit Data Service

Introduction

Switched Multimegabit Data Service (SMDS) is a high-speed, packet-switched, datagram-based WAN networking technology used for communication over public data networks (PDNs). SMDS can use fiber- or copper-based media; it supports speeds of 1.544 Mbps over Digital Signal level 1 (DS-1) transmission facilities, or 44.736 Mbps over Digital Signal level 3 (DS-3) transmission facilities. In addition, SMDS data units are large enough to encapsulate entire IEEE 802.3, IEEE 802.5, and Fiber Distributed Data Interface (FDDI) frames. This chapter summarizes the operational elements of the SMDS environment and outlines the underlying protocol. A discussion of related technologies, such as Distributed Queue Dual Bus (DQDB) is also provided. The chapter closes with discussions of SMDS access classes and cell formats.

SMDS Network Components

SMDS networks consist of several underlying devices to provide high-speed data service. These include customer premises equipment (CPE), carrier equipment, and the subscriber network interface (SNI). CPE is terminal equipment typically owned and maintained by the customer. CPE includes end devices, such as terminals and personal computers, and intermediate nodes, such as routers, modems, and multiplexers. Intermediate nodes, however, sometimes are provided by the SMDS carrier. Carrier equipment generally consists of high-speed WAN switches that must conform to certain network equipment specifications, such as those outlined by Bell Communications Research (Bellcore). These specifications define network operations, the interface between a local carrier network and a long-distance carrier network, and the interface between two switches inside a single carrier network.

The SNI is the interface between CPE and carrier equipment. This interface is the point at which the customer network ends and the carrier network begins. The function of the SNI is to render the technology and operation of the carrier SMDS network transparent to the customer. Figure 14-1 illustrates the relationships among these three components of an SMDS network.

Figure 14-1 *The SNI Provides an Interface Between the CPE and the Carrier Equipment in SMDS*

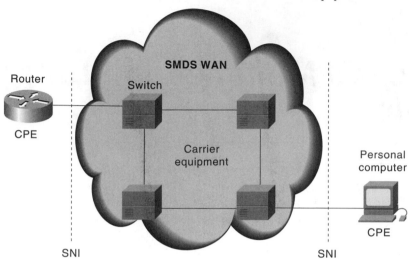

SMDS Interface Protocol

The *SMDS Interface Protocol (SIP)* is used for communications between CPE and SMDS carrier equipment. SIP provides connectionless service across the subscriber network interface (SNI), allowing the CPE to access the SMDS network. SIP is based on the IEEE 802.6 Distributed Queue Dual Bus (DQDB) standard for cell relay across metropolitan-area networks (MANs). The DQDB was chosen as the basis for SIP because it is an open standard that supports all the SMDS service features. In addition, DQDB was designed for compatibility with current carrier transmission standards, and it is aligned with emerging standards for Broadband ISDN (BISDN), which will allow it to interoperate with broadband video and voice services. Figure 14-2 illustrates where SIP is used in an SMDS network.

SIP Levels

SIP consists of three levels. SIP Level 3 operates at the Media Access Control (MAC) sublayer of the data link layer of the OSI reference model. SIP Level 2 operates at the MAC sublayer of the data link layer. SIP Level 1 operates at the physical layer of the OSI reference model. Figure 14-3 illustrates how SIP maps to the OSI reference model, including the IEEE data link sublayers.

Figure 14-2 *SIP Provides Connectionless Service Between the CPE and Carrier Equipment*

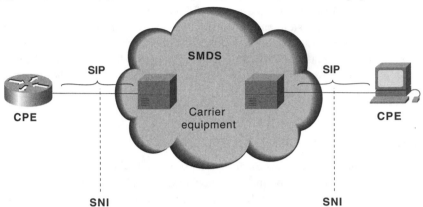

Figure 14-3 *SIP Provides Services Associated with the Physical and Data Link Layers of the OSI Model*

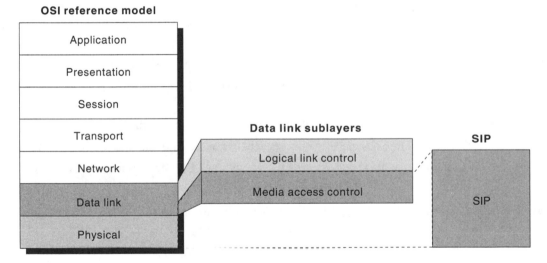

SIP Level 3 begins operation when user information is passed to it in the form of SMDS service data units (SDUs). SMDS SDUs then are encapsulated in a SIP Level 3 header and trailer. The resulting frame is called a Level 3 protocol data unit (PDU). SIP Level 3 PDUs then are passed to SIP Level 2.

SIP Level 2, which operates at the Media Access Control (MAC) sublayer of the data link layer, begins operating when it receives SIP Level 3 PDUs. The PDUs then are segmented into uniformly sized (53-octet) Level 2 PDUs, called cells. The cells are passed to SIP Level 1 for placement on the physical medium.

SIP Level 1 operates at the physical layer and provides the physical-link protocol that operates at DS-1 or DS-3 rates between CPE devices and the network. SIP Level 1 consists of the transmission system and Physical Layer Convergency Protocol (PLCP) sublayers. The transmission system sublayer defines the characteristics and method of attachment to a DS-1 or DS-3 transmission link. The PLCP specifies how SIP Level 2 cells are to be arranged relative to the DS-1 or DS-3 frame. PLCP also defines other management information.

Distributed Queue Dual Bus

The *Distributed Queue Dual Bus (DQDB)* is a data link layer communication protocol designed for use in metropolitan-area networks (MANs). DQDB specifies a network topology composed of two unidirectional logical buses that interconnect multiple systems. It is defined in the IEEE 802.6 DQDB standard.

An access DQDB describes just the operation of the DQDB protocol (in SMDS, SIP) across a user-network interface (in SMDS, across the SNI). Such operation is distinguished from the operation of a DQDB protocol in any other environment (for example, between carrier equipment within the SMDS PDN).

The access DQDB is composed of the basic SMDS network components:

- **Carrier equipment**—A switch in the SMDS network operates as one station on the bus.
- **CPE**—One or more CPE devices operate as stations on the bus.
- **SNI**—The SNI acts as the interface between the CPE and the carrier equipment.

Figure 14-4 depicts a basic access DQDB, with two CPE devices and one switch (carrier equipment) attached to the dual bus.

Figure 14-4 *A Basic Access DQDB May Consist of an End Node, a Router, and a Switch*

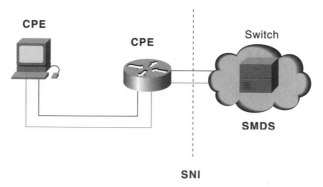

An SMDS access DQDB typically is arranged in a single-CPE configuration or a multi-CPE configuration.

A single-CPE access DQDB configuration consists of one switch in the carrier SMDS network and one CPE station at the subscriber site. Single-CPE DQDB configurations create a two-node DQDB subnetwork. Communication occurs only between the switch and the one CPE device across the SNI. No contention is on the bus because no other CPE devices attempt to access it.

A multi-CPE configuration consists of one switch in the carrier SMDS network and a number of interconnected CPE devices at the subscriber site (all belonging to the same subscriber). In multi-CPE configurations, local communication between CPE devices is possible. Some local communication will be visible to the switch serving the SNI, and some will not.

Contention for the bus by multiple devices requires the use of the DQDB distributed queuing algorithm, which makes implementing a multi-CPE configuration more complicated than implementing a single-CPE configuration.

SMDS Access Classes

SMDS access classes enable SMDS networks to accommodate a broad range of traffic requirements and equipment capabilities. Access classes constrain CPE devices to a sustained or average rate of data transfer by establishing a maximum sustained information transfer rate and a maximum allowed degree of traffic burstiness. (Burstiness, in this context, is the propensity of a network to experience sudden increases in bandwidth demand.) SMDS access classes sometimes are implemented using a credit-management scheme. In this case, a credit-management algorithm creates and tracks a credit balance for each customer interface. As packets are sent into the network, the credit balance is decremented. New credits are allocated periodically, up to an established maximum. Credit management is used only on DS-3-rate SMDS interfaces, not on DS-1-rate interfaces.

Five access classes are supported for DS-3-rate access (corresponding to sustained information rates). Data rates supported are 4, 10, 16, 25, and 34 Mbps.

SMDS Addressing Overview

SMDS *protocol data units (PDUs)* carry both a source and a destination address. SMDS addresses are 10-digit values resembling conventional telephone numbers.

The SMDS addressing implementation offers group addressing and security features.

SMDS group addresses allow a single address to refer to multiple CPE stations, which specify the group address in the Destination Address field of the PDU. The network makes multiple copies of the PDU, which are delivered to all members of the group. Group addresses reduce the amount of network resources required for distributing routing information, resolving addresses, and dynamically discovering network resources. SMDS group addressing is analogous to multicasting on LANs.

SMDS implements two security features: source address validation and address screening. *Source address validation* ensures that the PDU source address is legitimately assigned to the SNI from which it originated. Source address validation prevents address spoofing, in which illegal traffic assumes the source address of a legitimate device. *Address screening* allows a subscriber to establish a private virtual network that excludes unwanted traffic. If an address is disallowed, the data unit is not delivered.

SMDS Reference: SIP Level 3 PDU Format

Figure 14-5 illustrates the format of the SMDS Interface Protocol (SIP) Level 3 protocol data unit (PDU).

The following descriptions briefly summarize the function of the SIP Level 3 PDU fields illustrated in Figure 14-5.

Figure 14-5 *A SIP Level 3 Protocol Data Unit Consists of 15 Fields*

Field length,
in bytes

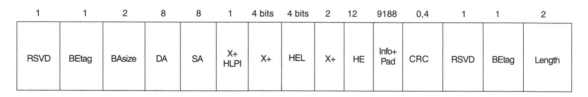

1	1	2	8	8	1	4 bits	4 bits	2	12	9188	0,4	1	1	2
RSVD	BEtag	BAsize	DA	SA	X+ HLPI	X+	HEL	X+	HE	Info+ Pad	CRC	RSVD	BEtag	Length

RSVD	=	Reserved
BEtag	=	Beginning-end tag
BAsize	=	Buffer allocation size
DA	=	Destination address
SA	=	Source address
HLPI	=	Higher-layer protocol identifier
X+	=	Carried across network unchanged
HEL	=	Header extension length
HE	=	Header extension
Info+Pad	=	Information + padding
		(to ensure that this field ends on a 32-bit boundary)
CRC	=	Cyclic redundancy check

- **X+**—Ensures that the SIP PDU format aligns with the DQDB protocol format. SMDS does not process or change the values in these fields, which may be used by systems connected to the SMDS network.

- **RSVD**—Consists of zeros.

- **BEtag**—Forms an association between the first and last segments of a segmented SIP Level 3 PDU. Both fields contain identical values and are used to detect a condition in which the last segment of one PDU and the first segment of the next PDU are both lost, which results in the receipt of an invalid Level 3 PDU.

- **BAsize**—Contains the buffer allocation size.

- **Destination address (DA)**—Consists of two parts:
  - **Address type**—Occupies the 4 most significant bits of the field. The Address Type can be either 1100 or 1110. The former indicates a 60-bit individual address, while the latter indicates a 60-bit group address.
  - **Address**—Gives the individual or group SMDS address for the destination. SMDS address formats are consistent with the North American Numbering Plan (NANP).

  The 4 most significant bits of the Destination Address subfield contain the value 0001 (the internationally defined country code for North America). The next 40 bits contain the binary-encoded value of the 10-digit SMDS address. The final 16 (least significant) bits are populated with ones for padding.

- **Source address (SA)**—Consists of two parts:
  - **Address type**—Occupies the 4 most significant bits of the field. The Source Address Type field can indicate only an individual address.
  - **Address**—Occupies the individual SMDS address of the source. This field follows the same format as the Address subfield of the Destination Address field.

- **Higher layer protocol identifier (HLPI)**—Indicates the type of protocol encapsulated in the Information field. The value is not important to SMDS, but it can be used by certain systems connected to the network.

- **Header extension length (HEL)**—Indicates the number of 32-bit words in the Header Extension (HE) field. Currently, the field size for SMDS is fixed at 12 bytes. (Thus, the HEL value is always 0011.)

- **Header extension (HE)**—Contains the SMDS version number. This field also conveys the carrier-selection value, which is used to select the particular interexchange carrier to carry SMDS traffic from one local carrier network to another.

- **Information and Padding (Info + Pad)**—Contains an encapsulated SMDS service data unit (SDU) and padding that ensures that the field ends on a 32-bit boundary.

- **Cyclic redundancy check (CRC)**—Contains a value used for error checking.

- **Length**—Indicates the length of the PDU.

SMDS Reference: SIP Level 2 Cell Format

Figure 14-6 illustrates the format of the SMDS Interface Protocol (SIP) Level 2 cell format.

Figure 14-6 *Seven Fields Comprise the SMDS SIP Level 2 Cell*

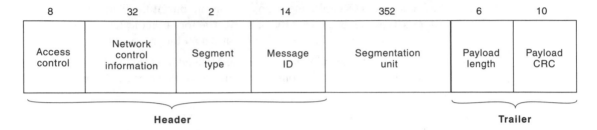

The following descriptions briefly summarize the functions of the SIP Level 2 PDU fields illustrated in Figure 14-6:

- **Access control**—Contains different values, depending on the direction of information flow. If the cell was sent from a switch to a CPE device, only the indication of whether the Level 3 protocol data unit (PDU) contains information is important. If the cell was sent from a CPE device to a switch, and if the CPE configuration is multi-CPE, this field can carry request bits that indicate bids for cells on the bus going from the switch to the CPE device.

- **Network control information**—Contains a value indicating whether the PDU contains information.

- **Segment type**—Indicates whether the cell is the first, the last, or a middle cell from a segmented Level 3 PDU. Four possible segment type values exist:
    - **00**—Continuation of message
    - **01**—End of message
    - **10**—Beginning of message
    - **11**—Single-segment message

- **Message ID**—Associates Level 2 cells with a Level 3 PDU. The message ID is the same for all the segments of a given Level 3 PDU. In a multi-CPE configuration, Level 3 PDUs originating from different CPE devices must have a different message ID. This allows the SMDS network receiving interleaved cells from different Level 3 PDUs to associate each Level 2 cell with the correct Level 3 PDU.

- **Segmentation unit**—Contains the data portion of the cell. If the Level 2 cell is empty, this field is populated with zeros.

- **Payload length**—Indicates how many bytes of a Level 3 PDU actually are contained in the Segmentation Unit field. If the Level 2 cell is empty, this field is populated with zeros.

- **Payload cyclic redundancy check (CRC)**—Contains a CRC value used to detect errors in the following fields:
    - Segment Type
    - Message ID
    - Segmentation Unit
    - Payload Length
    - Payload CRC

    The Payload CRC value does not cover the Access Control or the Network Control Information fields.

Summary

SMDS is a high-speed, packet-switched, datagram-based WAN networking technology used for communication over public data networks (PDNs). SMDS can use fiber- or copper-based media. It supports speeds of 1.544 Mbps over DS-1 transmission facilities, or 44.736 Mbps over DS-3 transmission facilities.

The following devices comprise SMDS networks:

- Customer premises equipment (CPE)
- Carrier equipment
- Subscriber network interface (SNI)

The SNI is the interface between the CPE and carrier equipment; it transparently enables data transmission between the two networks.

- SMDS uses SIP to communicate between CPE and the carrier site using the DQDB standard for cell relay across MANs.

- SIP consist of the following three levels:
    - SIP Level 3, which operates at the MAC sublayer of the data link layer of the OSI reference model
    - SIP Level 2, which also operates at the MAC sublayer of the data link layer of the OSI reference model
    - SIP Level 1, which operates at the physical layer of the OSI reference model

- SMDS PDUs carry both a source and a destination address, and offer both group addressing and security features.

Review Questions

1   Where does the SNI interface exist?

2   What does SIP stand for?

3   At which layers of the OSI reference model do each of the three SIP levels operate?

4   How do multiple devices reconcile usage of a DQDB?

5   A credit-management scheme is sometimes used to implement SMDS access classes on which SMDS interfaces only?

Objectives

- Describe the history of dialup technology.
- Describe dialup connectivity technology.
- Describe the different types of dialup methods.
- Discuss the benefits (and drawbacks) of different dialup technologies.

CHAPTER 15

Dialup Technology

Introduction

Dialup is simply the application of the Public Switched Telephone Network (PSTN) to carry data on behalf of the end user. It involves a customer premises equipment (CPE) device sending the telephone switch a phone number to direct a connection to. The AS3600, AS5200, AS5300, and AS5800 are all examples of routers that have the capability to run a PRI along with banks of digital modems. The AS2511, on the other hand, is an example of a router that communicates with external modems.

Since the time of *Internetworking Technologies Handbook,* 2nd edition, the carrier market has continued to grow, and there have been demands for higher modem densities. The answer to this need was a higher degree of interoperation with the telco equipment and the refinement of the digital modem: a modem capable of direct digital access to the PSTN. This has allowed the development of faster CPE modems that take advantage of the clarity of signal that the digital modems enjoy. The fact that the digital modems connecting into the PSTN through a PRI or a BRI can transmit data at more than 53 K using the V.90 communication standard attests to the success of the idea.

A Short Dialup Technology Background

Dialup technology traces its origins back to the days of the telegraph. Simple signals being sent across an extended circuit were created manually by tapping contacts together to turn the circuit either on or off. In an effort to improve the service, Alexander Graham Bell invented the telephone in 1875 and changed communication forever. Having the capability to send a voice across the line made the technology more accessible and attractive to consumers. By 1915, the Bell system stretched from New York to San Francisco. Demand for the service drove technological innovations, which led to the first transatlantic phone service in 1927 via radio signal. Other innovations along the way included microwave stations that started connecting American cities in 1948, integrated digital networks to improve the quality of service, and communication satellites, which went into service in 1962 with the launch of Telstar 1. By 1970, more than 90 percent of American homes had telephone service.

In 1979 the modulator-demodulator (modem) was introduced, and dialup networking was born. The early modems were slower and subject to proprietary communication schemes. Early uses of modems were for intermittent point-to-point WAN connections. Often, the call would come into a regular phone at a data center. An operator would hear modem tones and place the handset onto a special cradle that was the modem.

In the late 1980s, the ITU-T began setting up V-series recommendations to standardize communications between both data communications equipment (DCE) and data terminal equipment (DTE). Early standards included these:

- **V.8**—Standardized the method that modems use to initially determine the V-series modulation at which they will communicate. Note that this standard applies only to the communication session between the two DCE devices. This was later updated with V.8bis, which also specified some of the communication standards between the DTE devices going over the DCE's connection.

- **V.21, V.23, V.27ter, V.29**—Defined 300, 600/1200, 2400/4800, and 9600 baud communications, respectively.

- **V.25, V.25bis, V.25ter**—Served as a series of standards for automated dialing, answering, and control.

Modems increased greatly in sophistication in the late 1980s. This was due in part to the breakup of the Bell system in 1984. With the client premises equipment in the hands of free enterprise, competition spurred on the development of speedier connections. More recent standards include these:

- **V.32bis, V.34, V.90**—Standardized 14400, 33600, and up to 56000 baud communication speeds.

- **V.110**—Allowed an asynchronous DTE device to use an ISDN DCE (terminal adapter).

The first access servers were the AS2509 and the AS2511. The AS2509 could support 8 incoming connections using external modems, while the AS2511 could support 16. The AS5200 was introduced with 2 PRIs and could support 48 users using digital modems—this represented a major leap forward in technology. Modem densities have increased steadily, with the AS5300 supporting four and then eight PRIs. The AS5800 was later introduced to fill the needs of carrier class installations needing to handle dozens of incoming T1s and hundreds of user connections

A couple of outdated technologies bear mentioning in a historical discussion of dialer technology. 56 Kflex is an older (pre-V.90) 56 K modem standard that was proposed by Rockwell. Cisco supports version 1.1 of the 56 Kflex standard on its internal modems, but it recommends migrating the CPE modems to V.90 as soon as possible. Another outdated technology is the AS5100. The AS5100 was a joint venture between Cisco and a modem manufacturer. The AS5100 was created as a way to increase modem density through the use of quad modem cards. It involved a group of AS2511s built as cards that were inserted into a backplane shared by quad modem cards, and a dual T1 card.

Today dialup is still used as an economical alternative (depending on the connection requirements) to dedicated connectivity. It has important uses as backup connectivity, in case the primary lines go down. Dialup also offers the flexibility to create dynamic connections as needed.

Dialup Connectivity Technology

This section provides information from various dialup options. Also included are advanced options for dialup connectivity and various dialup methods.

Plain Old Telephone Service

The regular phone lines used in voice calls are referred to as Plain old telephone service (POTS). They are ubiquitous, familiar, and easy to obtain; local calls are normally free of charge. This is the kind of service that the phone network was built on. Sounds carried over this service are sampled at a rate of 8000 times per second (using 8 bits per sample) in their conversion to digital signals so that sound can be carried on a 64 kbps channel at acceptable levels.

NOTE	So what's an acceptable level? Studies have shown the voice range to be 300 Hz to 3400 Hz. 4000 Hz covers the range, but according to Nyquist's theorem, sound must be sampled at twice that rate to capture both the high and the low of the sound waves.

The encoding and decoding of voice is done by a piece of telco gear called a CODEC. The CODEC was needed to allow backward-compatibility with the old analog phones that were already in widespread use when the digital network was introduced. Thus, most phones found in the home are simple analog devices.

Dialup connectivity across POTS lines has historically been limited to about 33,600 bps via modem—often referred to as V.34 speeds. Recent improvements have increased the speed at which data can be sent from a digital source to a modem on a POTS line, but using POTS lines on both ends of the connection still results in V.34 connectivity in both directions.

Basic Rate Interface

Intended for home use, this application of ISDN uses the same copper as a POTS line, but it offers direct digital connectivity to the telephone network. A special piece of equipment known as a terminal adapter is required (although, depending on the country, it may be integrated into the router or DCE device). Always make sure to check—the plug used to connect to the wall socket looks the same whether it's the S/T or U demarcation point.

Normally, a Basic rate interface (BRI) interface has two B (bearer) channels to carry data, and one D (delta) channel to carry control and signaling information. Local telephone carriers may have different plans to suit local needs. Each B channel is a 64 K line. The individual 64 K channels of the telephone network are commonly referred to as digital service 0 (DS0). This is a common denominator regardless of the types of services offered, as will be shown later in this chapter.

The BRI interface is a dedicated connection to the switch and will remain up even if no calls are placed.

NOTE   So how do three channels get across a single pair of copper wires? It's a process called time division multiplexing (TDM). The signals on the cable are divided into time slots. This means that both ends of the line must synchronize their timing when the line is initialized. Having the line up shows a state of MULTIPLE_FRAME_ESTABLISHED, which, among other things, means the clocking is synchronized and the two devices communicating are now sending TDM frames back and forth.

T1/E1

The T1/E1 line is designed for use in businesses. T1 boasts 24 TDM channels run across a cable with 2 copper pairs. E1 offers 32 channels, although 1 is dedicated to frame synchronization. As is the case with the BRI, the T1/E1 connection goes directly into the telco switch. The connection is dedicated, so like a BRI, the T1/E1 remains connected and communicating to the switch all the time—even if there are no active calls. Each of the channels in the T1/E1 is just a B channel, which is to say that it's a 64-K DS0. The T1/E1 is also referred to as digital service 1 (DS1).

The North American T1 uses frames to define the timing between individual channels. For T1s, each frame has 24 9-bit channels (8 bits of data, 1 bit for framing). That adds up to 193 bits per frame. So, at 8000 of those per second, the T1 is carrying 1.544 Mbps between the switch and the customer premises equipment (CPE).

The E1 similarly uses frames for timing, but the E1 uses 32 8-bit channels for a 256-bit frame. Again at the 8000 Hz rate, the channel yields 2.048 Mbps of traffic between the switch and the CPE. Most of the world uses the E1.

Depending on the region, various line code and framing schemes will have to be used for the CPE and the switch to understand each other. For example, in North America, the encoding scheme most often seen is called binary 8 zero substitution (B8ZS), and the most common framing done is extended super frame (ESF). The telco through which the T1/E1 service is purchased must indicate which line code and framing should be used.

For dialup purposes, there are two types of T1/E1: Primary Rate Interface (PRI) and channel associated signaling (CAS). PRI and CAS T1/E1s are normally seen in central locations that receive calls from remote sites or customers.

Primary Rate Interface

T1 Primary rate interface (PRI) service offers 23 B channels at 64 kbps at the cost of one D-channel (the 24th channel) for call signaling. Using NFAS to allow multiple PRIs to use a single D channel can minimize this disadvantage. E1 PRI service allows 30 channels, but it uses the 16th channel for ISDN signaling. The PRI service is an ISDN connection. It allows either voice-grade (modem) or true ISDN calls to be made and received through the T1/E1. This is the type of service most often seen in access servers because it fosters higher connection speeds.

Channel Associated Signaling

T1 Channel associated signaling (CAS) lines have 24 56K channels—part of each channel is borrowed for call signaling. This type of service is also called robbed-bit signaling. The E1 CAS still uses only the 16th channel for call signaling, but it uses the R2 international standard for analog call signals.

CAS is not an ISDN interface; it allows only analog calls to come into the access server. This is often done to allow an access server to work with a channel bank, and this scenario is seen more commonly in South America, Europe, and Asia.

NOTE   So what kind of signals need a call signaling channel? Each end of a call must indicate to the other end what is going on with a message such as caller ID information, on-hook or off-hook status, and call setup. If a message is sent from the switch indicating that a new call is coming in, the CPE must tell the switch which channels are available. If the switch sends a call into a channel that isn't expecting it, the switch will get back a message indicating that the channel isn't available. An access server must maintain state information on its lines and be prepared to coordinate inward and outward calls with the switch.

Modems

From a terminology standpoint, a modem is considered data communication equipment (DCE), and the device using the modem is called data terminal equipment (DTE). As indicated earlier, modems must adhere to a number of communication standards to work with other modems: Bell103, Bell212A, V.21, V.22, V.22bis, V.23, V.32, V.32bis, V.FC, and V.34, to name a few. These standards reflect a dual analog conversion model, which is shown in Figure 15-1.

Figure 15-1 *Communication Standards Reflect a Dual Analog Conversion Model*

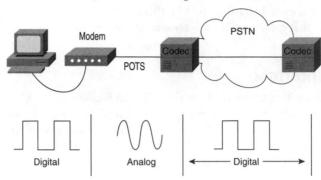

Advances in access server technology have allowed the development of new standards to take advantage of better connectivity at the server end. These standards are X2, 56 Kflex, and V.90. X2 and 56 Kflex represent earlier proprietary standards that were made obsolete by V.90. The assumption made by all these standards is that the access server has digital connectivity to the telephone network. The new model is shown in Figure 15-2.

Figure 15-2 *New Standards Model*

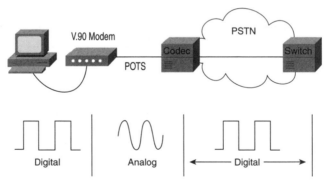

Notice that the signal goes through only one analog conversion. Because the conversion is done on the client's side, traffic generated by the client modem is limited to V.34 speeds. The traffic coming from the access server is not subject to the noise problems that an analog conversion would introduce, so it can be sent at much higher speeds. Thus, the client can receive data at v.90 speeds but can send data at only V.34 speeds.

So how does it really work? Here's the overall flow of the data as it goes through a modem as shown in Figure 15-3.

Figure 15-3 *Overall Flow of Data as it Goes Through a Modem*

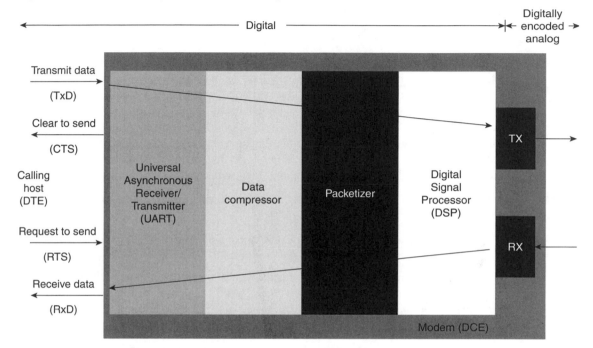

Going from the DTE device, the data is sent through the UART, which handles buffering and flow control with the host. The data compressor passes the data to the packetizer, which puts a checksum on it and sends it on to the DSP. The packetizer also handles retransmits if the data doesn't get through to the other DCE. The data travels onward to the digital to analog processor, which pushes the data out the RJ11 jack to the phone line. Receiving data goes in the reverse process.

In theory, V.90 modems could send data at 56 kbps, but because of limits placed on the phone lines by government agencies, 53 kbps is all that is currently possible.

PPP

PPP bears mentioning because it is so vital to the operation of dialup technologies. Until PPP came along in 1989 (RFC 1134—currently up to RFC 1661), dialup protocols were specific to the protocol being used. To use multiple protocols, it was necessary to encapsulate any other protocols within packets of whatever protocol the dialup link was running. Many of the proprietary link methods (such as SLIP) didn't even have the capability to negotiate addressing. Fortunately, PPP does this and many more things with flexibility and extensibility. PPP connection establishment happens in three phases: Link

Control Protocol (LCP), authentication, and Network Control Protocol (NCP). (See Chapter 13, "Point-to-Point Protocol," for more information.)

LCP

LCP is the lowest layer of PPP. Because PPP does not follow a client/server model, both ends of the point-to-point connection must agree on the negotiated protocols. When negotiation begins, each of the peers wanting to establish a PPP connection must send a configure request (CONFREQ). Included in the CONFREQ are any options that are not the link default. These often include maximum receive unit, async control character map, authentication protocol, and the magic number. At this stage, the peers negotiate their authentication method and indicate whether they will support PPP multilink.

In the general flow of LCP negotiations, there are three possible responses to any CONFREQ:

1   A configure-acknowledge (CONFACK) must be issued if the peer recognizes the options and agrees to the values seen in the CONFREQ.

2   A configure-reject (CONFREJ) must be sent if any of the options in the CONFREQ are not recognized (such as some vendor-specific options) or if the values for any of the options have been explicitly disallowed in the configuration of the peer.

3   A configure-negative-acknowledge (CONFNAK) must be sent if all the options in the CONFREQ are recognized, but the values are not acceptable to the peer.

The two peers continue to exchange CONFREQs, CONFREJs, and CONFNAKs until each sends a CONFACK, until the dial connection is broken, or until one or both of the peers indicates that the negotiation cannot be completed.

Authentication

Authentication is an optional phase, but it is *highly* recommended on all dial connections. In some instances, it is a requirement for proper operation—dialer profiles, being a case in point.

The two principal types of authentication in PPP are the Password Authentication Protocol (PAP) and the Challenge Handshake Authentication Protocol (CHAP), defined by RFC 1334 and updated by RFC 1994.

When discussing authentication, it is helpful to use the terms *requester* and *authenticator* to distinguish the roles played by the devices at either end of the connection, although either peer can act in either role.

Requester describes the device that requests network access and supplies authentication information; the *authenticator* verifies the validity of the authentication information and either allows or disallows the connection. It is common for both peers to act in both roles when a DDR connection is being made between routers.

PAP is fairly simple. After successful completion of the LCP negotiation, the requester repeatedly sends its username/password combination across the link until the authenticator responds with an acknowledgment or until the link is broken. The authenticator may disconnect the link if it determines that the username/password combination is not valid.

CHAP is somewhat more complicated. The authenticator sends a challenge to the requester, which then responds with a value. This value is calculated by using a "one-way hash" function to hash the challenge and the CHAP password together. The resulting value is sent to the authenticator along with the requester's CHAP host name (which may be different from its actual host name) in a response message.

The authenticator reads the host name in the response message, looks up the expected password for that host name, and then calculates the value that it expects the requester to send in its response by performing the same hash function the requester performed. If the resulting values match, the authentication is successful. Failure should lead to a disconnection. By RFC standards, the authenticator can request another authentication at any time during the connection.

NCP

NCP negotiation is conducted in much the same manner as LCP negotiation with CONFREQs, CONFREJs, CONFNAKs, and CONFACKs. However, in this phase of negotiation, the elements being negotiated have to do with higher-layer protocols—IP, IPX, bridging, CDP, and so on. One or more of these protocols may be negotiated. Refer to the following RFCs for more detail on their associated protocols:

- RFC 1332 "IP Control Protocol"
- RFC 1552 "IPX Control Protocol"
- RFC 1378 "AppleTalk Control Protocol"
- RFC 1638 "Bridging Control Protocol"
- RFC 1762 "DECnet Control Protocol"
- RFC 1763 "VINES Control Protocol"

A Couple of Advanced Considerations

The Multilink Point-to-Point Protocol (MLP, RFC 1990) feature provides a load-balanced method for splitting and recombining packets to a single end system across a logical pipe (also called a bundle) formed by multiple links. Multilink PPP provides bandwidth on demand and reduces transmission latency across WAN connections. At the same time, it provides multivendor interoperability, packet fragmentation with proper sequencing, and load calculation on both inbound and outbound traffic. The Cisco implementation of multilink PPP supports the fragmentation and packet sequencing specifications in RFC1717.

Multilink PPP works over the following interface types (single or multiple):

- Asynchronous serial interfaces
- BRIs
- PRIs

Multichassis multilink PPP (MMP), on the other hand, provides the additional capability for links to terminate at multiple routers with different remote addresses. MMP can also handle both analog and digital traffic.

This functionality is intended for situations in which there is a large pool of dial-in users, and a single access server cannot provide enough dial-in ports. MMP allows companies to provide a single dialup number to their users and to apply the same solution to analog and digital calls. This feature allows Internet service providers, for example, to allocate a single ISDN rotary number to several ISDN PRIs and not have to worry about whether a user's second link is on the same router.

MMP does not require reconfiguration of telephone company switches.

AAA

Another technology that should be mentioned because of its importance is Authentication, Authorization, and Accounting (AAA). The protocols used in AAA can be either TACACS or RADIUS. These two protocols were developed in support of a centralized method to keep track of users and accesses made on a network. AAA is employed by setting up a server (or group of servers) to centrally administer the user database. Information such as the user's password, what address should be assigned to the user, and what protocols the user is allowed to run can be controlled and monitored from a single workstation. AAA also has powerful auditing capabilities that can be used to follow administratively important trends such as connection speeds and disconnect reasons. Any medium or large dialup installation should be using AAA, and it's not a bad idea for small shops, either.

Dialup Methods

Most routers support automated methods for dynamic links to be connected when traffic that needs to get to the other end arrives. Cisco's implementation is called dial-on-demand routing (DDR). It provides WAN connectivity on an economical, as-needed basis, either as a primary link or as backup for a nondial serial link.

At its heart, DDR is just an extension of routing. Interesting packets are routed to a dialer interface that triggers a dial attempt. Each of the concept's *dialer interface* and *interesting traffic* bear explanation.

What's a Dialer?

The term *dialer* has a few meanings, depending on the specifics of the configuration, but in general, it refers to the interface where the routing is actually happening. This is the interface that knows the address and phone number where the traffic is supposed to go. When looking at the routing table, the dialer interface should be the interface referenced for the next hop to reach the network on the other side. The dialer interface does not have to be the physical interface that is doing the dialing, but it can be made so by placing the configuration command **dialer in-band** in a physical interface. Thereafter, the interface becomes a dialer. For example, an async interface is not a dialer by default, but placing the configuration command **dialer in-band** in the async interface causes dialer behavior on that interface. For example, calls received by that async interface after applying the command will have an idle timeout applied to the connection from then on. An example of a physical interface that is also a dialer by default would be the BRI interface.

NOTE   An idle timer is used by Cisco IOS to track how long a connection has gone without interesting traffic. By default, it's set to 2 minutes; after 2 minutes of inactivity, the call is hung up.

Beyond making physical interfaces into dialers, there are interfaces called dialer interfaces. These are logical interfaces that call upon real interfaces to place calls. The advantage of using a dialer interface is flexibility. A group of potential DDR links can share a handful of BRI interfaces. Dialer interface configuration comes in two flavors: dialer map-based (sometimes referred to as legacy DDR) and dialer profiles. Which method you use depends on the circumstances under which you need dial connectivity. Dialer map-based DDR was first introduced in IOS Version 9.0; dialer profiles were introduced in IOS Version 11.2.

Interesting Traffic

The term *interesting* is used to describe packets or traffic that will either trigger a dial attempt or, if a dial link is already active, reset the idle timer on the dialer interface. For a packet to be considered interesting, it must have these characteristics:

- The packet must meet the "permit" criteria defined by an access list.
- The access list must be referenced by the dialer–list, or the packet must be of a protocol that is universally permitted by the dialer–list.

- The dialer-list must be associated with a dialer interface by use of a dialer group.

Packets are never automatically considered to be interesting (by default). Interesting packet definitions must be explicitly declared in a router or access server configuration.

Benefits and Drawbacks

The benefits of dialup are flexibility and cost savings. First, let's look at why flexibility is important. Intermittent connectivity is most often needed in mobile situations. A mobile workforce needs to be capable of connecting from wherever they are. Phone lines are normally available from wherever business is transacted, so a modem connection is the only reasonable choice for mobile users.

In long-distance situations, a user often dials into a local ISP and uses an IPSec-encrypted tunnel going back to a home gateway system that allows access to the rest of the corporate network. In this example, the phone call itself costs nothing, and an account with the local ISP could be significantly less expensive than the long-distance charges that would otherwise be incurred. As another example, a BRI attached at a central office located in an area that offers inexpensive rates on ISDN could have database servers configured to call out to other sites and exchange data periodically. Each site needs only one BRI line, which is significantly less expensive than dedicated links to each of the remote locations. Finally, in the case of a backup link, the savings are seen when the primary link goes down but business continues, albeit slower than normal.

Cost savings is a two-edged sword where dialup is concerned, however. The downside of a dialup line is that connection costs for a heavily used line are higher than the price of dedicated connectivity. Going over long distance raises the price even higher.

There's also speed to consider. Dialup connectivity has a strong high-end bandwidth, particularly with the capability to tie channels together using PPP multilink, but dedicated connectivity through a serial port can outperform dialup connections.

Another consideration is security. Certainly, any PPP connection should be authenticated, but this presents anyone with the dialup number an opportunity to break into the system. A significant part of any dialup system's configuration concerns the capability to keep out unwanted guests. The good news is that it can be done, and AAA goes a long way toward dealing with this problem. However, it is a disadvantage to have potential intruders coming in through dialup lines.

Summary

Dialup technology has been around for a long time, but only in the last 20 years or so have the phone lines been available for dialup networking. In that time, a number of standards have been created to make sure that modems can communicate properly with each other and with the systems that employ them. Cisco moved into the access market with the AS2509 and AS2511, which used external analog modems, but Cisco currently produces access servers with cutting edge digital modem technology.

Current dialup technologies include the venerable POTS line as a low-cost and ubiquitous means of connecting via modem. To do this, it uses a single channel, or DS0. A step up from the POTS line is the ISDN BRI line, with two DS0 channels and a D channel used for signaling. Getting up to industrial-strength lines is the T1/E1. The T1 has 24 channels, and the E1 has 32, although the E1 uses slot 0 for framing and slot 16 for call signaling. PRI service is geared to allow ISDN clients to connect, while CAS will allow only asynchronous calls in.

Modems themselves have advanced considerably in recent years to take advantage of the direct digital connection that the access server modems have to the PSTN. This results in V.90 connections that can transfer data from the server to the client at speeds up to 53 kbps. Because of the analog conversion on the analog line, transmissions from the client modem are still capable of only 33.6 kbps.

After a connection is established, it's important to have a robust transport to use the link. PPP fills that need. With its three-phase startup—LCP, authentication, and NCP—PPP adapts to its environment and can learn its connection information while supporting a strong authentication scheme. PPP can extend a connection into a bundle across multiple connections by using PPP multilink. A step beyond that is extending the PPP multilink capability across multiple chassis. For large installations, this is invaluable because users get their PPP multilink sessions wherever the vacant DS0s are.

Dial-on-demand routing (DDR) uses two important concepts: the dialer and interesting traffic. The dialer is simply the interface that is handling the routing and controlling whether a call is placed. Interesting traffic is the traffic that has been defined as worth bringing up the link or keeping it up for.

When to use dialup technology is a question of usage pattern. In some circumstances, such as with a mobile endpoint, dialup is the only solution that will work. Also, in cases where intermittent connectivity is needed, it can be more cost-effective. However, if connectivity is needed most of the time, dialup may become the more costly alternative. Speed is another concern: Dialup connections are not typically as fast as a dedicated network connection. Security can be a concern for dialup sites as well.

Obviously, dialup technology has a place today at the outer edge of the network, providing access to those who need it from unfamiliar locations or from locations where better technologies are simply not available. Whenever the need calls for flexibility or low utilization in a connection, dialup technologies should be looked at as a viable solution.

Review Questions

1   How many years did it take the telephone to reach 90 percent of the homes in the United States?

2   Which V series recommendations pertain to bits per second?

3   How many DS 0s are in a BRI, T1, and E1m respectively?

4   What is the flow of data going through a modem from the RJ 11 to the DTE?

5   What are the three phases of PPP negotiation? Why is the order significant?

6   How does interesting traffic relate to the idle timer?

7   Is a BRI interface a dialer? How would an async interface become a dialer?

8   When is dialup connectivity appropriate to use? When isn't it appropriate?

For More Information

- Cisco Systems. *Cisco IOS Dial Solutions.* Indianapolis: Cisco Press, 1998.

- ftp://ftp.cisco.com/pub/rfc/RFC/

- http://hea-www.harvard.edu/~fine/ISDN/overview.html

- http://isds.bus.lsu/edu/cvoc/projects/TechLibrary/CableIS/history.html

- http://www.att.com/history/

- http://www.cisco.com/tac/

- http://www.digitalcentury.com/encyclo/update/cmodem.html http://www.itu.int/itudoc/itu-t/rec/v/

Objectives

- Describe the history of SDLC.
- Describe the types and topologies of SDLC.
- Describe the frame format of SDLC.
- Describe derivative protocols of SDLC.

CHAPTER 16

Synchronous Data Link Control and Derivatives

Introduction

IBM developed the *Synchronous Data Link Control (SDLC)* protocol in the mid-1970s for use in Systems Network Architecture (SNA) environments. SDLC was the first link layer protocol based on synchronous, bit-oriented operation. This chapter provides a summary of SDLC's basic operational characteristics and outlines several derivative protocols.

After developing SDLC, IBM submitted it to various standards committees. The International Organization for Standardization (ISO) modified SDLC to create the High-Level Data Link Control (HDLC) protocol. The International Telecommunication Union–Telecommunication Standardization Sector (ITU-T; formerly CCITT) subsequently modified HDLC to create Link Access Procedure (LAP) and then Link Access Procedure, Balanced (LAPB). The Institute of Electrical and Electronic Engineers (IEEE) modified HDLC to create IEEE 802.2. Each of these protocols has become important in its domain, but SDLC remains the primary SNA link layer protocol for WAN links.

SDLC Types and Topologies

SDLC supports a variety of link types and topologies. It can be used with point-to-point and multipoint links, bounded and unbounded media, half-duplex and full-duplex transmission facilities, and circuit-switched and packet-switched networks.

SDLC identifies two types of network nodes: primary and secondary. *Primary nodes* control the operation of other stations, called secondaries. The primary polls the secondaries in a predetermined order, and secondaries can then transmit if they have outgoing data. The primary also sets up and tears down links and manages the link while it is operational. *Secondary nodes* are controlled by a primary, which means that secondaries can send information to the primary only if the primary grants permission.

SDLC primaries and secondaries can be connected in four basic configurations:

- **Point-to-point**—Involves only two nodes, one primary and one secondary.
- **Multipoint**—Involves one primary and multiple secondaries.

- **Loop**—Involves a loop topology, with the primary connected to the first and last secondaries. Intermediate secondaries pass messages through one another as they respond to the requests of the primary.

- **Hub go-ahead**—Involves an inbound and an outbound channel. The primary uses the outbound channel to communicate with the secondaries. The secondaries use the inbound channel to communicate with the primary. The inbound channel is daisy-chained back to the primary through each secondary.

SDLC Frame Format

The SDLC frame is shown in Figure 16-1.

Figure 16-1 *Six Fields Comprise the SDLC Frame*

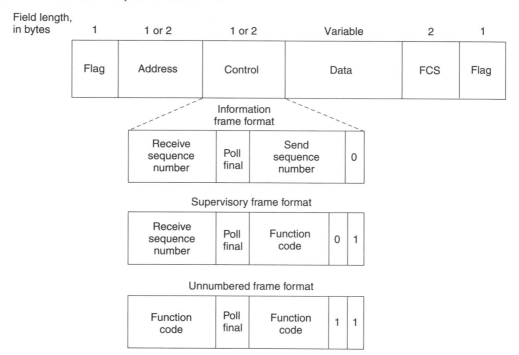

The following descriptions summarize the fields illustrated in Figure 16-1:

- **Flag**—Initiates and terminates error checking.

- **Address**—Contains the SDLC address of the secondary station, which indicates whether the frame comes from the primary or secondary. This address can contain a specific address, a group address, or a broadcast address. A primary is either a communication source or a destination, which eliminates the need to include the address of the primary.

- **Control**—Employs three different formats, depending on the type of SDLC frame used:

  - **Information (I) frame**—Carries upper-layer information and some control information. This frame sends and receives sequence numbers, and the poll final (P/F) bit performs flow and error control. The send sequence number refers to the number of the frame to be sent next. The receive sequence number provides the number of the frame to be received next. Both sender and receiver maintain send and receive sequence numbers.

    A primary station uses the P/F bit to tell the secondary whether it requires an immediate response. A secondary station uses the P/F bit to tell the primary whether the current frame is the last in its current response.

  - **Supervisory (S) frame**—Provides control information. An S frame can request and suspend transmission, report on status, and acknowledge receipt of I frames. S frames do not have an information field.

  - **Unnumbered (U) frame**—Supports control purposes and is not sequenced. A U frame can be used to initialize secondaries. Depending on the function of the U frame, its control field is 1 or 2 bytes. Some U frames have an information field.

- **Data**—Contains a path information unit (PIU) or exchange identification (XID) information.

- **Frame check sequence (FCS)**—Precedes the ending flag delimiter and is usually a cyclic redundancy check (CRC) calculation remainder. The CRC calculation is redone in the receiver. If the result differs from the value in the original frame, an error is assumed.

A typical SDLC-based network configuration is shown in Figure 16-2. As illustrated, an IBM establishment controller (formerly called a cluster controller) in a remote site connects to dumb terminals and to a Token Ring network. In a local site, an IBM host connects (via channel-attached techniques) to an IBM front-end processor (FEP), which also can have links to local Token Ring LANs and an SNA backbone. The two sites are connected through an SDLC-based 56-kbps leased line.

Figure 16-2 *An SDLC Line Links Local and Remote Sites over a Serial Line*

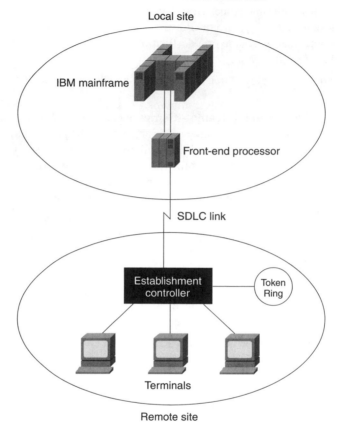

Derivative Protocols

Despite the fact that it omits several features used in SDLC, HDLC is generally considered to be a compatible superset of SDLC. LAP is a subset of HDLC and was created to ensure ongoing compatibility with HDLC, which had been modified in the early 1980s. IEEE 802.2 is a modification of HDLC for LAN environments. *Qualified Logical Link Control (QLLC)* is a link layer protocol defined by IBM that enables SNA data to be transported across X.25 networks.

High-Level Data Link Control

HDLC shares the frame format of SDLC, and HDLC fields provide the same functionality as those in SDLC. Also, as in SDLC, HDLC supports synchronous, full-duplex operation.

HDLC differs from SDLC in several minor ways, however. First, HDLC has an option for a 32-bit checksum. Also, unlike SDLC, HDLC does not support the loop or hub go-ahead configurations.

The major difference between HDLC and SDLC is that SDLC supports only one transfer mode, whereas HDLC supports three:

- **Normal response mode (NRM)**—This transfer mode is also used by SDLC. In this mode, secondaries cannot communicate with a primary until the primary has given permission.

- **Asynchronous response mode (ARM)**—This transfer mode enables secondaries to initiate communication with a primary without receiving permission.

- **Asynchronous balanced mode (ABM)**—ABM introduces the combined node, which can act as a primary or a secondary, depending on the situation. All ABM communication occurs between multiple combined nodes. In ABM environments, any combined station can initiate data transmission without permission from any other station.

Link-Access Procedure, Balanced

LAPB is best known for its presence in the X.25 protocol stack. LAPB shares the same frame format, frame types, and field functions as SDLC and HDLC. Unlike either of these, however, LAPB is restricted to the ABM transfer mode and is appropriate only for combined stations. Also, LAPB circuits can be established by either the data terminal equipment (DTE) or the data circuit-terminating equipment (DCE). The station initiating the call is determined to be the primary, and the responding station is the secondary. Finally, LAPB use of the P/F bit is somewhat different from that of the other protocols. For details on LAPB, see Chapter 17, "X.25."

IEEE 802.2

IEEE 802.2 is often referred to as the Logical Link Control (LLC). It is extremely popular in LAN environments, where it interoperates with protocols such as IEEE 802.3, IEEE 802.4, and IEEE 802.5. IEEE 802.2 offers three types of service.

Type 1 provides unacknowledged connectionless service, which means that LLC Type 1 does not confirm data transfers. Because many upper-layer protocols, such as Transmission Control Protocol/Internet Protocol (TCP/IP), offer reliable data transfer that can compensate for unreliable lower-layer protocols, Type 1 is a commonly used service.

Type 2 provides connection-oriented service. LLC Type 2 (often called LLC2) service establishes logical connections between sender and receiver and is therefore connection-oriented. LLC2 acknowledges data upon receipt and is used in IBM communication systems.

Type 3 provides acknowledged connectionless service. Although LLC Type 3 service supports acknowledged data transfer, it does not establish logical connections. As a compromise between the other two LLC services, LLC Type 3 is useful in factory-automation environments where error detection is important but context storage space (for virtual circuits) is extremely limited.

End stations can support multiple LLC service types. A Class I device supports only Type 1 service. A Class II device supports both Type 1 and Type 2 services. Class III devices support both Type 1 and Type 3 services, and Class IV devices support all three types of service.

Upper-layer processes use IEEE 802.2 services through service access points (SAPs). The IEEE 802.2 header begins with a destination service access point (DSAP) field, which identifies the receiving upper-layer process. In other words, after the receiving node's IEEE 802.2 implementation completes its processing, the upper-layer process identified in the DSAP field receives the remaining data. Following the DSAP address is the source service access point (SSAP) address, which identifies the sending upper-layer process.

Qualified Logical Link Control

QLLC provides the data-link control capabilities that are required to transport SNA data across X.25 networks. Together, QLLC and X.25 replace SDLC in the SNA protocol stack. QLLC uses the packet-level layer (Layer 3) of the X.25 protocol stack. To indicate that a Layer 3 X.25 packet must be handled by QLLC, a special bit called the qualifier bit, in the general format identifier (GFI) of the Layer 3 X.25 packet-level header, is set to 1. The SNA data is carried as user data in Layer 3 X.25 packets. For more information about the X.25 protocol stack, see Chapter 17.

Summary

The SDLC protocol was developed by IBM in the mid-1970s for use in SNA environments. SDLC was the first link-layer protocol based on synchronous, bit-oriented operation, and it remains the primary SNA link layer protocol for WAN links.

SDLC supports a variety of link types and topologies. It can be used with point-to-point and multipoint links, bounded and unbounded media, half-duplex and full-duplex transmission facilities, and circuit-switched and packet-switched networks.

SDLC identifies two types of network nodes: primary and secondary. Primary nodes control the operation of other stations, called secondaries.

SDLC primaries and secondaries can be connected in four basic configurations: point-to-point, multipoint, loop, and hub go-ahead.

The following protocols are derivatives of SDLC:

- HDLC, which supports three transfer modes, while SDLC supports only one
- LAPB, which is restricted to the ABM transfer mode and is appropriate only for combined stations
- IEEE 802.2, which is often referred to as LLC and has three types
- QLLC, which provides the data-link control capabilities that are required to transport SNA data across X.25 networks

Review Questions

1 Name two of the link types that SDLC supports.

2 Name the four basic SDLC connection configurations.

3 How many fields does the SDLC frame have, and what are they?

4 List the derivative protocols of SDLC, and describe their primary difference(s) from SDLC.

Objectives

- Discuss the history and development of the X.25 protocol.
- Describe the basic functions and components of X.25.
- Describe the frame formats of X.25.

CHAPTER 17

X.25

Introduction

X.25 is an International Telecommunication Union–Telecommunication Standardization Sector (ITU-T) protocol standard for WAN communications that defines how connections between user devices and network devices are established and maintained. X.25 is designed to operate effectively regardless of the type of systems connected to the network. It is typically used in the packet-switched networks (PSNs) of common carriers, such as the telephone companies. Subscribers are charged based on their use of the network. The development of the X.25 standard was initiated by the common carriers in the 1970s. At that time, there was a need for WAN protocols capable of providing connectivity across public data networks (PDNs). X.25 is now administered as an international standard by the ITU-T.

X.25 Devices and Protocol Operation

X.25 network devices fall into three general categories: data terminal equipment (DTE), data circuit-terminating equipment (DCE), and packet-switching exchange (PSE). Data terminal equipment devices are end systems that communicate across the X.25 network. They are usually terminals, personal computers, or network hosts, and are located on the premises of individual subscribers. DCE devices are communications devices, such as modems and packet switches, that provide the interface between DTE devices and a PSE, and are generally located in the carrier's facilities. PSEs are switches that compose the bulk of the carrier's network. They transfer data from one DTE device to another through the X.25 PSN. Figure 17-1 illustrates the relationships among the three types of X.25 network devices.

Figure 17-1 *DTEs, DCEs, and PSEs Make Up an X.25 Network*

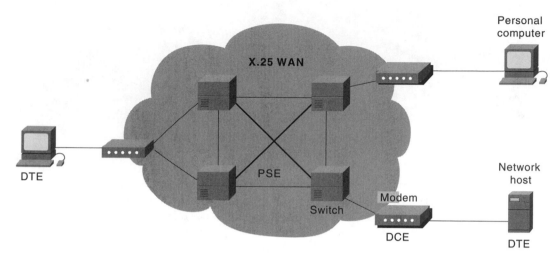

Packet Assembler/Disassembler

The *packet assembler/disassembler (PAD)* is a device commonly found in X.25 networks. PADs are used when a DTE device, such as a character-mode terminal, is too simple to implement the full X.25 functionality. The PAD is located between a DTE device and a DCE device, and it performs three primary functions: buffering (storing data until a device is ready to process it), packet assembly, and packet disassembly. The PAD buffers data sent to or from the DTE device. It also assembles outgoing data into packets and forwards them to the DCE device. (This includes adding an X.25 header.) Finally, the PAD disassembles incoming packets before forwarding the data to the DTE. (This includes removing the X.25 header.) Figure 17-2 illustrates the basic operation of the PAD when receiving packets from the X.25 WAN.

Figure 17-2 *The PAD Buffers, Assembles, and Disassembles Data Packets*

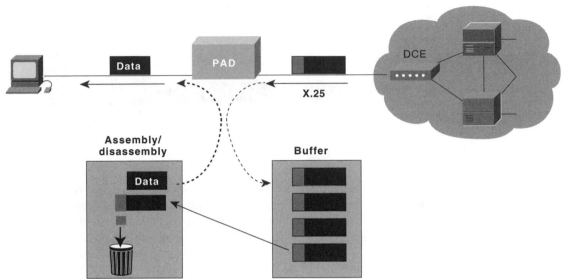

X.25 Session Establishment

X.25 sessions are established when one DTE device contacts another to request a communication session. The DTE device that receives the request can either accept or refuse the connection. If the request is accepted, the two systems begin full-duplex information transfer. Either DTE device can terminate the connection. After the session is terminated, any further communication requires the establishment of a new session.

X.25 Virtual Circuits

A *virtual circuit* is a logical connection created to ensure reliable communication between two network devices. A virtual circuit denotes the existence of a logical, bidirectional path from one DTE device to another across an X.25 network. Physically, the connection can pass through any number of intermediate nodes, such as DCE devices and PSEs. Multiple virtual circuits (logical connections) can be multiplexed onto a single physical circuit (a physical connection). Virtual circuits are demultiplexed at the remote end, and data is sent to the appropriate destinations. Figure 17-3 illustrates four separate virtual circuits being multiplexed onto a single physical circuit.

Figure 17-3 *Virtual Circuits Can Be Multiplexed onto a Single Physical Circuit*

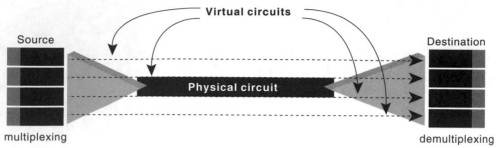

Two types of X.25 virtual circuits exist: switched and permanent. *Switched virtual circuits (SVCs)* are temporary connections used for sporadic data transfers. They require that two DTE devices establish, maintain, and terminate a session each time the devices need to communicate. *Permanent virtual circuits (PVCs)* are permanently established connections used for frequent and consistent data transfers. PVCs do not require that sessions be established and terminated. Therefore, DTEs can begin transferring data whenever necessary because the session is always active.

The basic operation of an X.25 virtual circuit begins when the source DTE device specifies the virtual circuit to be used (in the packet headers) and then sends the packets to a locally connected DCE device. At this point, the local DCE device examines the packet headers to determine which virtual circuit to use and then sends the packets to the closest PSE in the path of that virtual circuit. PSEs (switches) pass the traffic to the next intermediate node in the path, which may be another switch or the remote DCE device.

When the traffic arrives at the remote DCE device, the packet headers are examined and the destination address is determined. The packets are then sent to the destination DTE device. If communication occurs over an SVC and neither device has additional data to transfer, the virtual circuit is terminated.

The X.25 Protocol Suite

The X.25 protocol suite maps to the lowest three layers of the OSI reference model. The following protocols are typically used in X.25 implementations: Packet-Layer Protocol (PLP), Link Access Procedure, Balanced (LAPB), and those among other physical-layer serial interfaces (such as EIA/TIA-232, EIA/TIA-449, EIA-530, and G.703). Figure 17-4 maps the key X.25 protocols to the layers of the OSI reference model.

Figure 17-4 *Key X.25 Protocols Map to the Three Lower Layers of the OSI Reference Model*

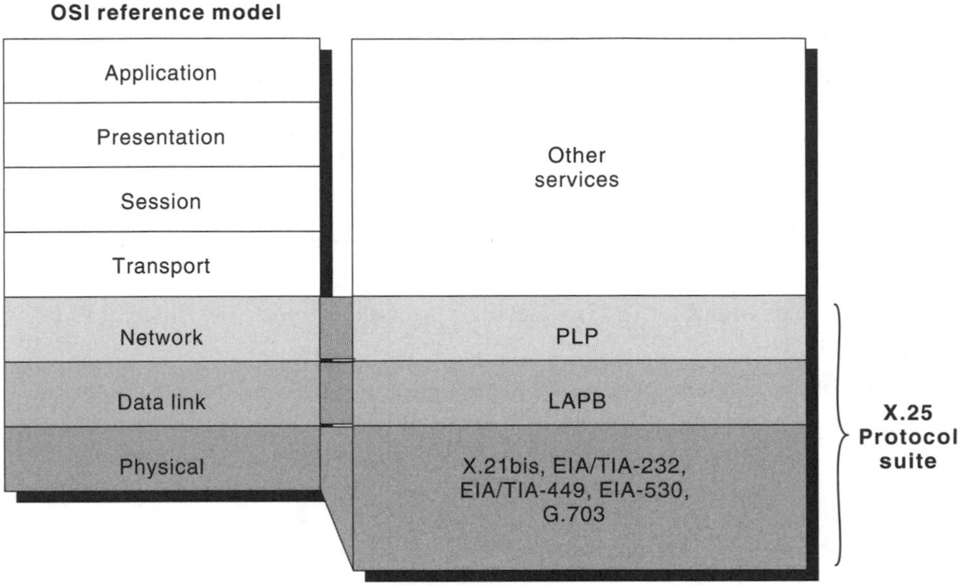

OSI reference model

Packet-Layer Protocol

PLP is the X.25 network layer protocol. PLP manages packet exchanges between DTE devices across virtual circuits. PLPs also can run over Logical Link Control 2 (LLC2) implementations on LANs and over Integrated Services Digital Network (ISDN) interfaces running Link Access Procedure on the D channel (LAPD).

The PLP operates in five distinct modes: call setup, data transfer, idle, call clearing, and restarting.

Call setup mode is used to establish SVCs between DTE devices. A PLP uses the X.121 addressing scheme to set up the virtual circuit. The call setup mode is executed on a per-virtual-circuit basis, which means that one virtual circuit can be in call setup mode while another is in data transfer mode. This mode is used only with SVCs, not with PVCs.

Data transfer mode is used for transferring data between two DTE devices across a virtual circuit. In this mode, PLP handles segmentation and reassembly, bit padding, and error and flow control. This mode is executed on a per-virtual-circuit basis and is used with both PVCs and SVCs.

Idle mode is used when a virtual circuit is established but data transfer is not occurring. It is executed on a per-virtual-circuit basis and is used only with SVCs.

Call clearing mode is used to end communication sessions between DTE devices and to terminate SVCs. This mode is executed on a per-virtual-circuit basis and is used only with SVCs.

Restarting mode is used to synchronize transmission between a DTE device and a locally connected DCE device. This mode is not executed on a per-virtual-circuit basis. It affects all the DTE device's established virtual circuits.

Four types of PLP packet fields exist:

- **General Format Identifier (GFI)**—Identifies packet parameters, such as whether the packet carries user data or control information, what kind of windowing is being used, and whether delivery confirmation is required.

- **Logical Channel Identifier (LCI)**—Identifies the virtual circuit across the local DTE/DCE interface.

- **Packet Type Identifier (PTI)**—Identifies the packet as one of 17 different PLP packet types.

- **User Data**—Contains encapsulated upper-layer information. This field is present only in data packets. Otherwise, additional fields containing control information are added.

Link Access Procedure, Balanced

LAPB is a data link layer protocol that manages communication and packet framing between DTE and DCE devices. LAPB is a bit-oriented protocol that ensures that frames are correctly ordered and error-free.

Three types of LAPB frames exist: information, supervisory, and unnumbered. The information frame (I-frame) carries upper-layer information and some control information. I-frame functions include sequencing, flow control, and error detection and recovery. I-frames carry send- and receive-sequence numbers. The supervisory frame (S-frame) carries control information. S-frame functions include requesting and suspending transmissions, reporting on status, and acknowledging the receipt of I-frames. S-frames carry only receive-sequence numbers. The unnumbered frame (U frame) carries control information. U-frame functions include link setup and disconnection, as well as error reporting. U frames carry no sequence numbers.

The X.21bis Protocol

X.21bis is a physical layer protocol used in X.25 that defines the electrical and mechanical procedures for using the physical medium. X.21bis handles the activation and deactivation of the physical medium connecting DTE and DCE devices. It supports point-to-point connections, speeds up to 19.2 kbps, and synchronous, full-duplex transmission over four-wire media. Figure 17-5 shows the format of the PLP packet and its relationship to the LAPB frame and the X.21bis frame.

Figure 17-5 *The PLP Packet Is Encapsulated Within the LAPB Frame and the X.21bis Frame*

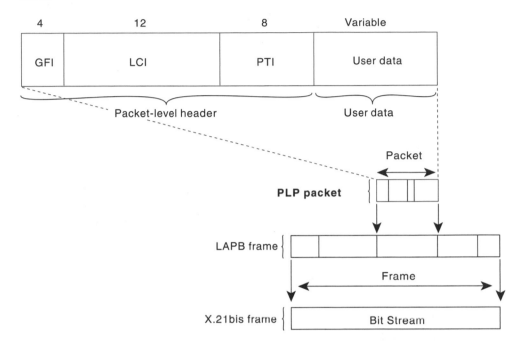

LAPB Frame Format

LAPB frames include a header, encapsulated data, and a trailer. Figure 17-6 illustrates the format of the LAPB frame and its relationship to the PLP packet and the X.21bis frame.

The following descriptions summarize the fields illustrated in Figure 17-6:

- **Flag**—Delimits the beginning and end of the LAPB frame. Bit stuffing is used to ensure that the flag pattern does not occur within the body of the frame.

- **Address**—Indicates whether the frame carries a command or a response.

- **Control**—Qualifies command and response frames and indicates whether the frame is an I-frame, an S-frame, or a U-frame. In addition, this field contains the frame's sequence number and its function (for example, whether receiver-ready or disconnect). Control frames vary in length depending on the frame type.

- **Data**—Contains upper-layer data in the form of an encapsulated PLP packet.

- **FCS**—Handles error checking and ensures the integrity of the transmitted data.

Figure 17-6 *An LAPB Frame Includes a Header, a Trailer, and Encapsulated Data*

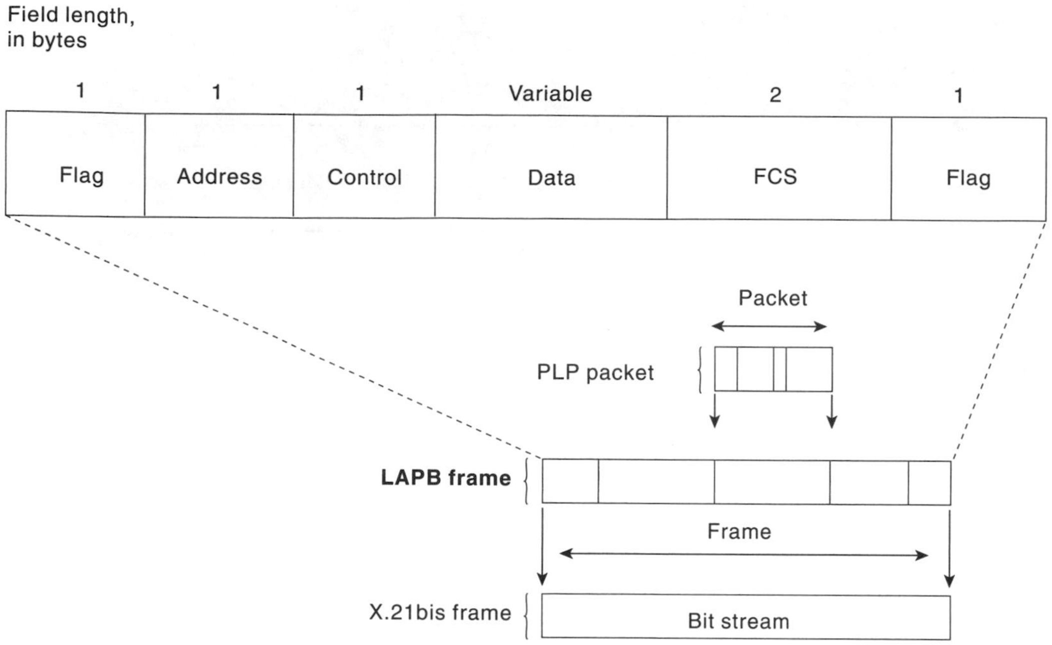

Field length,
in bytes

X.121 Address Format

X.121 addresses are used by the X.25 PLP in call setup mode to establish SVCs. Figure 17-7 illustrates the format of an X.121 address.

The X.121 Address field includes the International Data Number (IDN), which consists of two fields: the Data Network Identification Code (DNIC) and the National Terminal Number (NTN).

DNIC is an optional field that identifies the exact PSN in which the destination DTE device is located. This field is sometimes omitted in calls within the same PSN. The DNIC has two subfields: Country and PSN. The Country subfield specifies the country in which the destination PSN is located. The PSN field specifies the exact PSN in which the destination DTE device is located.

The NTN identifies the exact DTE device in the PSN for which a packet is destined. This field varies in length.

Figure 17-7 *The X.121 Address Includes an IDN Field*

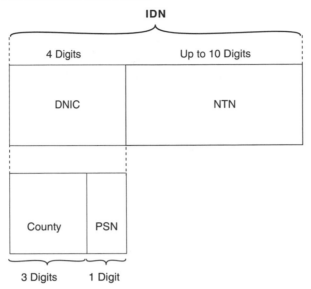

Summary

X.25 is an ITU-T standard protocol that defines how connections between user devices and network devices are established and maintained, and that operates effectively regardless of the type of systems connected to the network. X.25 devices include DTEs, DCEs, and PSNs. X.25 connections contain both SVCs and PVCs within the physical circuit. X.25 uses the following three protocols, which map to the bottom three layers of the OSI reference model:

- PLP, which maps to the network layer
- LAPB, which maps to the data link layer
- X.21bis, EIA/TIA-232, EIA/TIA-449, EIA-530, and G.703, which map to the physical layer

Review Questions

1 In what kind of networks does X.25 generally operate?

2 Name the three general categories into which X.25 devices fall.

3 What are the three main functions of the PAD?

4 Name the X.25 protocol suite and the layers in the OSI reference model to which they map.

Objectives

- Understand the definition of VPN and the categorization of VPNs based on the underlying technologies, applications, and provided services.

- Understand the basics of IPSec protocols and the IKE protocol.

- Understand the basics of L2TP.

- Understand the basics of MPLS-based VPN.

CHAPTER 18

Virtual Private Networks (VPNs)

As more companies have started to rely on the Internet for their communications, the market of virtual private networks (VPNs) has grown significantly in recent years. VPN technologies continue to evolve as new standards, products, and services emerge. This has caused companies that want to deploy VPNs some confusion over what is a VPN, what types of services certain types of VPNs provide, and what is the right type of VPN for them.

Trying to clearly define and categorize VPN is an ongoing task. This chapter is not an attempt to provide a clear-cut definition of VPNs. Instead, it's an introduction to and overview of different types of VPN technologies.

VPN Definition

A *VPN* is a logic network that operates on top of a shared physical infrastructure. Compared to the traditional ways of using dedicated leased circuits to interconnect offices at different geographic locations to build a private network, the current VPN is virtual in the sense that the network facilities used to build it (such as the Internet) are shared by other companies as well. VPNs provide privacy, just as legacy private networks do. The circuits are dedicated to the customers, who can have their own IP addressing, routing schemes, and security policies.

The "private" in VPN terminology can also be interpreted from a security perspective. What secure services a VPN can provide has become a more common question asked by companies when they consider implementing VPNs.

Let's first consider the example of VPNs using dedicated circuits, such as Frame Relay. They are sometimes called *trusted VPNs,* because customers trust that the network facilities operated by the service providers will not be compromised. So no real secure services are provided by this type of VPN.

As more companies use the Internet as the backbone of their VPNs, our presumption is no longer true. Furthermore, the data traversing the Internet is more subject to attacks, such as loss of privacy, loss of integrity, and identity spoofing. So it becomes critical for VPNs to provide secure services, such as confidentiality, integrity, and authentication, to protect the data from possible attacks. To provide such secure services, tunneling technologies and cryptographic algorithms are often used to secure communications across the Internet. This type of VPN is called a *secure VPN*.

Based on this definition, we can put current VPN technologies into two categories:

- **Trusted VPN technologies**—The most promising technologies are the MPLS-based technologies: MPLS VPNs using BGP and MPLS-based L2VPNs.

- **Secure VPN technologies**—The most popular technologies are IPSec, L2TP or L2TP protected by IPSec, and PPTP. IPSec has become the de facto standard for secure VPN in recent years.

VPN Applications

VPN technologies are applied in the following scenarios:

- **Intranets**—With VPN technologies, companies can use the Internet as a backbone to link their geographically dispersed sites via VPNs.

- **Extranets**—VPN technologies can also be used to create instant, on-demand links between companies and their business partners.

- **Remote-access**—VPNs let remote users access corporate networks through VPNs after logging on to a local Internet service provider (ISP). This is much more cost-effective than the traditional way of companies maintaining a large modem bank themselves.

IPSec

An international group organized under the Internet Engineering Task Force (IETF) has developed the IP security (IPSec) protocol suite to secure IP traffic at the network layer. IPSec is a set of protocols defined in several RFCs. It uses cryptographic technologies to provide key security services against common security threats on the Internet. These security services are as follows:

- Authentication guarantees that the VPN device communicates with the intended entity.

- Confidentiality ensures the data's privacy by encrypting the data.

- Integrity guarantees that the data's content has not been modified during transmission.

The following are some of the key cryptographic technologies used by the IPSec protocol suite to achieve these security services:

- Content encryption algorithms are usually symmetrical encryption algorithms that are used to encrypt data. The most commonly used algorithms are DES, 3DES, and AES.

- The hard-to-invert and strong collision-free characters of certain hash algorithms are used to generate a digital fingerprint that provides authentication and integrity for a specific message. IPSec uses a keyed hash function to generate a keyed hash-based message authentication code (HMAC) to provide data origin authentication and data integrity. The hash algorithms used by IPSec are MD5 and SHA-1.

- The Diffie-Hellman (DH) key exchange protocol allows two VPN devices to securely generate a common shared secret over an insecure channel without any prior shared secrets. With an authenticated DH exchange, the two VPN peers can establish a secure channel that protects the messages between them during the negotiation of the IPSec security association.

- The Public Key Infrastructure (PKI) consists of protocols, standards, and services that support the application of public key algorithms. Compared to content encryption algorithms, public key algorithms are asymmetric. Each entity generates a pair of mathematically associated keys. The public key is published to the public domain, and the corresponding private key is kept private. Given the public key, it is mathematically infeasible to find out the private key. This characteristic makes public key algorithms useful for both encryption and digital certification. RSA is the most famous example of a public key algorithm. Via a trusted certificate authority (CA), each VPN entity in a PKI system can bind its public key and its identity, such as IP address and fully qualified domain name, using a certificate issued by a CA. When used in an IPSec VPN, PKI provides security services, such as authentication and nonrepudiation.

The IPSec VPN architecture has the following components:

- An authentication header (AH) is added to an IP packet to provide data origin authentication and data integrity checking.

- An encapsulating security payload (ESP) for IP provides encryption, data origin authentication, and data integrity checking.

- Internet Security Association and Key Management Protocol (ISAKMP) and Internet Key Exchange (IKE) allow VPN devices to securely negotiate and manage IPSec security associations (SAs) and generate, exchange, and manage the keys that are used by the cryptographic algorithms employed by IPSec.

In the following sections, the discussion is divided into the following topics:

- Authentication header

- Encapsulating Security Payload

- IPSec transport mode and tunnel mode

- Security Association

- Internet Key Exchange protocol

Authentication Header (AH)

Defined in RFC 2402, AH is a header that IPSec adds to an IP datagram. It resides between the IP header and the Layer 4 protocol header. The header is basically a keyed HMAC calculated based on the IP payload and the IP header except for the mutable fields that change during the transmission, such as the TTL field. Verification of the AH header by the recipient provides data origin authentication and data integrity. Figure 18-1 shows the format of the AH.

Figure 18-1 *Authentication Header*

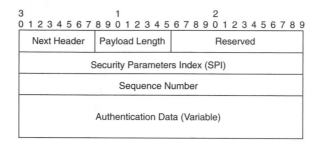

The fields are as follows:

- Next Header (1 byte) indicates the higher-level AH protocol, such as UDP or TCP.

- Payload Length (1 byte) specifies the length of the AH.

- Reserved (2 bytes) is reserved for future use. It is currently set to 0.

- Security Parameters Index (SPI) (4 bytes) specifies the set of security parameters known as the security association for the IPSec connection.

- Sequence Number (4 bytes) tracks the order of IPSec packets for anti-replay purposes.

- Authentication Data (variable size) contains the IP packet's integrity check value (ICV).

AH packets are IP packets with protocol type 51.

Encapsulating Security Payload (ESP)

ESP is defined in RFC 2406. Compared to AH, ESP provides data confidentiality by encrypting the IP packets. The authentication provided by ESP does not cover the IP header, as does AH.

Figure 18-2 illustrates the format of the ESP.

Figure 18-2 *Encapsulating Security Payload*

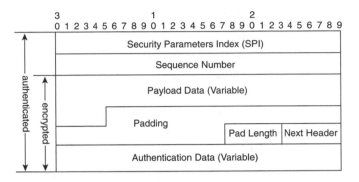

The fields are as follows:

- Security Parameters Index (SPI) (4 bytes) specifies the set of security parameters known as the security association for the IPSec connection.

- Sequence Number (4 bytes) tracks the order of IPSec packets for anti-replay purposes.

The following fields are encrypted:

- Payload Data contains the actual data carried in the IP packets.

- Padding (0 to 255 bytes) allows the length of plain text to be a multiple of a certain number of bytes to satisfy the requirement of some encryption algorithms that operate on blocks of data or the requirement of data alignment.

- Pad Length (1 byte) specifies the length of the padding.

- Next Header (1 byte) defines the protocol type of the data carried in the Payload Data field.

- Authentication Data (variable length) contains the integrity check value (ICV). Unlike the AH, the IP header of the ESP packet is not covered by integrity checking.

IPSec Transport Mode and Tunnel Mode

Both AH and ESP have two encapsulation modes—transport mode and tunnel mode (see Figure 18-3).

In transport mode, the IP header of the original IP packet is used as the IP header of the IPSec packet, and the IPSec header is inserted between the IP header and the IP payload. In tunnel mode, IPSec encapsulates the complete original IP packet, and a new IP header is added as the IP header of the IPSec packet.

Tunnel mode provides limited traffic flow confidentiality by hiding the original IP address information.

Figure 18-3 *IPSec Transport Mode and Tunnel Mode*

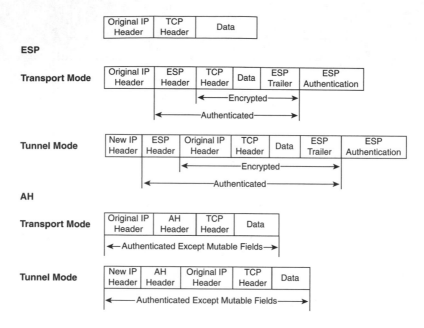

Security Association (SA)

From the preceding section, you can see that an IPSec entity can have different choices of encryption algorithms, hash algorithms, IPSec modes, and so on. These parameters and other information required to establish an IPSec connection are maintained by the IPSec SAs. In general, an SA is a relation between two identities that applies security services to the traffic they carry. For an IPSec connection, two unidirectional SAs are maintained on each IPSec peer—one for inbound traffic and one for outbound traffic.

An IPSec SA is uniquely identified by three parameters: usage of AH or ESP, SPI, and the destination IP address.

Internet Key Exchange (IKE) Protocol

Although IPSec supports manual configuration of its security associations, it becomes obvious that you need an automatic mechanism to achieve scalability and flexibility. This mechanism should allow VPN devices to negotiate and manage IPSec SAs and generate and distribute keys without human intervention. IKE, defined in RFC 2409, is the protocol designed for this purpose.

IKE is a hybrid protocol that integrates ISAKMP and Oakley Key Exchange. ISAKMP, defined in RFC 2408, is an open framework that defines the procedure and packet format to establish, negotiate, modify, and delete security associations. In conjunction with IPSec Domain of Interpretation, defined in RFC 2407, IKE defines a detailed implementation to manage IPSec security associations under the ISAKMP framework.

IKE is a two-phase protocol. In an IKE phase I exchange, the two VPN entities attempt to establish an authenticated, secure channel that is used to protect subsequent communications between the two entities. This is accomplished in three steps:

Step 1   The two VPN entities negotiate the cryptographic algorithms that will be used in the phase I exchange to establish the phase I security association, also known as *ISAKMP SA* or *IKE SA*.

Step 2   The two VPN entities go through a DH exchange. This exchange allows them to securely generate a common secret over the insecure channel without any prior shared secret. Together with other information in the negotiation, this common secret is used to generate several keys, one of which is used to protect subsequent communications between the two VPN entities.

Step 3   Each VPN entity authenticates the other by sending its identity, such as IP address, FQDN, and a keyed hash payload, for the other side to verify. There are three IKE authentication methods:

— Authentication with a preshared key. A preshared key is a shared secret preinstalled on each VPN entity via an out-of-band mechanism. This preshared key is one of the input parameters for the keyed hash payload. So without matching the preshared key, the hash verification in IKE authentication will not succeed.

— Authentication with public key encryption. Each IPSec peer first generates a pseudo-random number called a nonce. The nonce is then encrypted using the other party's public key. The other party's ability to decrypt the nonce using its private key and reconstruct the hash payload authenticates the IKE exchange. The IPSec peers might need to use an out-of-band mechanism to exchange their public keys in advance.

— Authentication with digital signatures. The hash payload used for IKE authentication is signed by the IPSec entity's private key. During IKE authentication, each party performs the hash verification after decrypting the hash payload using the peer's public key, which is obtained from the peer's digital certificate. The use of digital certificates provides nonrepudiation.

The IKE phase I exchange can be accomplished in either main mode or aggressive mode. Main mode uses a minimum of six packets, and aggressive modes uses a minimum of three packets. Main mode is more secure than aggressive mode but less efficient.

In IKE phase II exchange, also known as *quick mode*, the two VPN entities negotiate and establish IPSec SAs. This exchange is protected by the phase I SA, and all the exchanges are authenticated. The data encryption keys used by IPSec are also derived in this phase. An extra DH exchange can be performed to generate new shared secrets that are used to derive IPSec data encryption keys. The newer key generated by this DH exchange is independent from the older keys generated in phase I. This extra security is called Perfect Forward Secrecy (PFS).

After a quick mode exchange, two unidirectional IPSec SAs are established. IPSec uses them to protect the data traffic.

Layer 2 Tunneling Protocol (L2TP)

The IETF was faced with competing proposals from Microsoft and Cisco Systems for a protocol specification that would secure the transmission of IP datagrams through uncontrolled and untrusted network domains. Microsoft's proposal was an attempt to standardize the Point-to-Point Tunneling Protocol (PPTP), which it had championed. Cisco also had a protocol designed to perform a similar function. The IETF combined the best elements of each proposal and specified the open standard L2TP.

PPP establishes a Layer 2 point-to-point link on which PPP connections encapsulate and transport multiprotocol packets. A network access server (NAS) terminates the Layer 2 point-to-point link established by users via various technologies, such as dialup POTS, ISDN, and ADSL. The NAS is the termination point of both Layer 2 point-to-point links and PPP sessions.

With L2TP, the termination points of the Layer 2 circuit and PPP session can be separated by different devices interconnected by IP networks. In other words, users can dial in to a local NAS, and the PPP session is extended by an L2TP connection across a shared infrastructure, such as the Internet or a Frame Relay network, to a home gateway that processes and manages the PPP session. As far as the users are concerned, they get the same functionality but pay only local phone charges.

L2TP simulates a point-to-point connection by encapsulating PPP datagrams for transportation through routed networks or internetworks. When the PPP datagrams arrive at their intended destination, the encapsulation is removed, and the datagrams are restored to their original format. Thus, a point-to-point communications session can be supported through disparate networks. This technique is called tunneling.

The followings are the key components in an L2TP connection:

- **Network Access Server (NAS)**—A device provides on-demand local network access to users. It is the termination point of Layer 2 point-to-point links established by end users typically using PSTN or ISDN lines.

- **L2TP Access Concentrator (LAC)**—A node usually acts as the initiator of the L2TP tunnel to the L2TP Network Server (LNS). LAC forwards packets between end users and LNS.

- **L2TP Network Server (LNS)**—A node acts as the termination point of the PPP sessions that travel through the L2TP tunnel initiated by LAC.

LAC and LNS only define the logic functions of an L2TP connection. Their physical locations depend on different implementation topologies and requirements, as discussed in the following sections.

Implementation Topologies

L2TP can be implemented in two distinct topologies:

- Compulsory tunneling or client-transparent tunneling
- Voluntary tunneling or client-aware tunneling

The distinction between these two topologies is whether the client machine that is using L2TP to access a remote network is aware that its connection is being tunneled. LAC's physical location varies in these two topologies.

Compulsory Tunneling

Compulsory tunneling features LACs distributed geographically close to the remote users. Such geographic dispersion is intended to reduce the long-distance telephone charges that would otherwise be incurred by remote users dialing into a centrally located LAC.

Remote users need not support L2TP directly, as shown in Figure 18-4. They merely establish a point-to-point communication session with the NAS, which is also the LAC, using PPP. Ostensibly, the user encapsulates IP datagrams in PPP frames. The LAC exchanges PPP messages with the remote user and establishes an L2TP tunnel with the LNS through which the remote user's PPP messages are passed. The LAC can also authenticate the end users and use the users' information, such as domain name, to direct the end users to the matching LNS.

Figure 18-4 *Compulsory L2TP Tunnels*

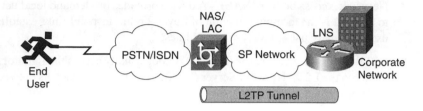

The LNS is the remote user's gateway to his home network. It is the terminus of the tunnel; it strips off all L2TP encapsulation and serves up network access for the remote user.

As can be seen in this scenario, the end users don't have any choice, and the L2TP tunnel established by L2TP-supported NAS is transparent to the end users.

Voluntary Tunneling

As shown in Figure 18-5, the LAC function resides on the client machine, and the end user is responsible for initiating the L2TP connection. The client first gets IP connectivity by either establishing a PPP connection to a NAS at the local ISP or connecting to a local LAN segment. Then it initiates the L2TP connection to the LNS, which terminates the L2TP tunnel and the extended PPP session.

Figure 18-5 *Voluntary L2TP Tunnels*

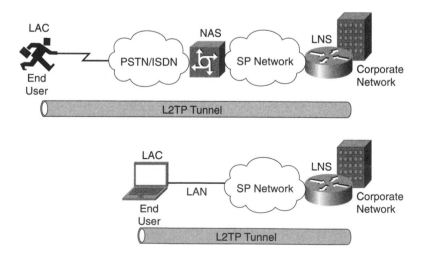

L2TP Protected by IPSec

As useful as L2TP is, it is important to recognize that it is not a panacea. It enables flexibility in delivering remote access, but it does not afford a high degree of security for data in transit. This is due in large part to PPP's relatively insecure nature. In fairness, PPP was designed explicitly for point-to-point communications, so securing the connection should not have been a high priority.

An additional cause of concern stems from the fact that L2TP's tunnels are not cryptographic. Their data payloads are transmitted in the clear, wrapped only by L2TP and PPP framing. However, additional security may be afforded by implementing the IPSec protocols in conjunction with L2TP. As described in the "IPSec" section, the IPSec protocols support strong authentication technologies as well as encryption.

MPLS VPNs

The IPSec and L2TP VPNs described in the previous sections are often provisioned and operated by enterprise customers. They are often called CPE-based VPNs. In recent years, service providers have been trying to leverage their existing IP infrastructure to provide new services, such as provider-provisioned VPNs (PPVPNs), to enterprise customers. A few multiprotocol label switching- (MPLS) based VPNs are offered by service providers:

- BGP/MPLS VPNs
- MPLS-based Layer 2 VPNs

BGP/MPLS VPN

The BGP/MPLS VPN, described in IETF draft-ietf-ppvpn-rfc2547bis, is a Layer 3 VPN. In this case, enterprise customers completely outsource their VPN to service providers who manage the IP VPN as well as the customer's routing across the VPN. Service providers that offer the BGP/MPLS VPN already have an MPLS-enabled core IP network that forwards traffic from one customer site to another. BGP is used to distribute the VPN route information across the provider's core network.

As illustrated in Figure 18-6, an MPLS VPN contains the following key components:

- The service provider network has MPLS-enabled provider (P) routers. The P routers forward the VPN traffic between provider edge (PE) routers.

- As its name implies, a PE router is on the edge of the provider network. It connects to customer sites to exchange routing information with customer edge (CE) routers. As shown in Figure 18-6, a PE router can involve multiple customer VPNs, which have their own IP addressing and routing schemes. This traffic separation is achieved by maintaining a Virtual Routing and Forwarding (VRF) table for each customer's VPN. A VRF contains the VPN routing information for a particular customer VPN. The VPN routing information is exchanged between the PE routers using BGP.

- CE routers provide customer access to the service provider network. A CE router can exchange customer routing information with the PE router using various routing protocols.

Figure 18-6 *BGP/MPLS VPN Components*

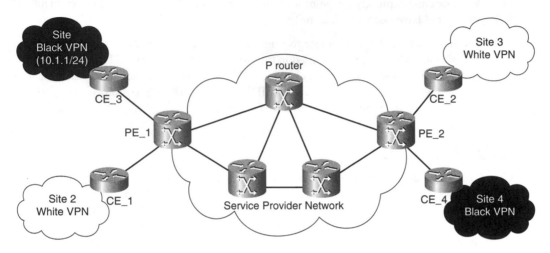

Through the service provider MPLS cloud, VPN data traffic is forwarded between PE routers. The forwarding decision is made based on two sources of information: a label forwarding table maintained by the P router (also called a *Label Switch Router [LSR]*), and a label carried in the data packets.

The MPLS labels used to make forwarding decisions are headers created by LSR. The format of the labels depends on the link layer technologies. For example, ATM and Frame Relay can carry a label as part of their link layer headers—the VCI or VPI field of the ATM cell header, and the DLCI field of the Frame Relay header, respectively. For link layer technologies that cannot carry a label in their link layer headers, such as Ethernet, FDDI, PPP, and Token Ring, a "shim" label header is inserted between the link layer and network layer headers. The MPLS labels are distributed via a Label Distribution Protocol (LDP).

A data packet can carry multiple labels in the form of a last-in-first-out (LIFO) label stack. In the case of BGP/MPLS VPN, the data packets have two labels. The inner label identifies the remote PE router that advertises the customer route, and the outer label forwards the data packet through the MPLS cloud to the PE router.

In Figure 18-6, assume that router CE_1 at White VPN Site 2 advertises a route 10.1.1/24 to router PE_1. PE_1 adds this route to its White VPN VRF table and assigns a label to this route. This VPN route and the label are distributed to PE_2 at the other end of the White VPN via BGP. When hosts at White VPN Site 3 want to communicate with 10.1.1/24, its

CE_2 router forwards the packet to PE_2 based on the VPN route it learns from PE_2. Upon receiving the packet, PE_2 looks up its VRF table. The lookup indicates that 10.1.1/24 can be reached via PE_1. So PE_2 inserts the corresponding label it learned from PE_1 for 10.1.1/24 and attempts to send the data packet to PE_1.

Continuing the discussion, note that to reach PE_1, another lookup is performed to find out the label associated with the route to PE_1 within the MPLS core. Finally, PE_2 sends the data packet with two labels. The P routers in the MPLS cloud swap the outer label to forward the packets from PE_2 to PE_1. When PE_1 gets the packet, it looks at the inner label to make the forwarding decision to the right CE router, such as CE_1.

Because VPN customers can use RFC 1918 private IP addresses, it is very possible that one PE router might manage two customer VPNs that have overlapping address spaces. This is an issue for BGP, which assumes the global uniqueness of the IPv4 address it carries. To solve this problem, BGP/MPLS VPN combines the following two mechanisms:

- Introducing the VPN-IPv4 address that converts the nonunique IPv4 address to a globally unique address family. A VPN-IPv4 address contains an 8-byte route distinguisher (RD) followed by a 4-byte IPv4 address.

- Deployment of multiprotocol BGP extensions to support the distribution of the VPN-IPv4 address.

As shown in Figure 18-6, in the MPLS VPN, the CE routers directly peer with the PE routers. This model is called the peer model. Compared to the overlay model used by IPSec VPN, in which customer routers peer only with other customer routers to form point-to-point tunnels that create a "virtual backbone," the peer model scales much better in a large-scale deployment.

The other advantage of MPLS VPN is in the area of quality of service (QoS). MPLS supports classification of packets into different classes of services (CoS) and handling of packets via appropriate QoS characteristics.

MPLS-Based Layer 2 VPN

The IETF PPVPN group and the PWE3 group are working to define a framework and standards for provider-provisioned Layer 2 VPN. The L2VPN lets the service provider provide Layer 2 transport for Layer 2 services, such as Ethernet, Frame Relay, and ATM, to customers over an IP/MPLS backbone. This keeps the service provider from having to maintain IP, Frame Relay, and ATM networks. It also gives service providers a feasible migration path from Frame Relay and ATM infrastructures to an MPLS-based IP infrastructure without interrupting existing services.

In contrast to the BGP/MPLS VPN described in the previous section, customers who use L2VPN need to manage their own routing.

The L2VPN framework defined by IETF PPVPN group has two models:

- Virtual Private Wire Service (VPWS) implements a point-to-point topology in which the PE routers at each end of the provider core are connected by a "pseudo wire" (PW). The Layer 2 protocol payloads, such as Frame Relay and ATM, are encapsulated at the ingress PE router and are forwarded between PE routers as pseudo-wire PDUs. This model has two promising technologies:

  — Any Transport Over MPLS (AToM) supports the transport of any protocol, such as Frame Relay, ATM, Ethernet, PPP, or HDLC, over the MPLS core network. The encapsulation and label distribution mechanisms are defined under two groups of IETF drafts: Martini drafts and Kompella drafts.

  — L2TP version 3 is used for the same purpose over IP core networks.

- Virtual Private LAN Service (VPLS) implements an emulated LAN bridge where all the VPLS PE routers are connected.

Summary

Over the past few years, VPN technologies have grown dramatically. New VPN technologies let enterprise customers save money by using VPN to transfer data securely over the Internet and let service providers offer new provider-provisioned VPN services to enterprise customers. The underlying technologies provide different characteristics for various types of VPNs that suit various customer requirements. IPSec L2TP-based VPNs offer strong security services and often are managed by enterprise customers. MPLS-based Layer 2 and Layer 3 VPNs provisioned by service providers offer large-scale deployment and strong QoS management.

Review Questions

1 What is a VPN?

2 What key security services does IPSec provide?

3 What is the function of the IKE protocol?

4 IKE is a two-phase protocol. What does each phase accomplish?

5 What are L2TP's operation modes?

6 How does MPLS support hierarchical routing in BGP/MPLS VPN?

For More Information

- Davie, Bruce and Yakov Rekhter. *MPLS Technology and Applications.*
- Schneier, Bruce. *Applied Cryptography.*
- RFC 2401, *Security Architecture for the Internet Protocol.*
- RFC 2402, *IP Authentication Header.*
- RFC 2406, *IP Encapsulating Security Payload (ESP).*
- RFC 2407, *The Internet IP Security Domain of Interpretation for ISAKMP.*
- RFC 2408, *Internet Security Association and Key Management Protocol (ISAKMP).*
- RFC 2409, *The Internet Key Exchange (IKE).*
- RFC 2661, *Layer Two Tunneling Protocol "L2TP".*
- RFC 3193, *Securing L2TP using IPSec.*
- IETF Draft: draft-ietf-ppvpn-rfc2547bis-02, *BGP/MPLS VPN.*
- IETF Draft: draft-ietf-ppvpn-l2-framework, *L2VPN Framework.*
- Virtual Private Network Consortium, http://vpnc.org.

PART IV

Multiservice Access Technologies

Objectives

- Provide an overview of technologies and applications of integrated voice/data networking.

- Outline the differences between the various voice/data integration technologies, and tell when each should be used.

- Understand the specific protocols involved in voice/data networking.

- List specific network engineering challenges and solutions associated with the integration of voice and data.

19

Voice/Data Integration Technologies

Introduction

Voice/data integration is important to network designers of both service providers and enterprise. Service providers are attracted by the lower-cost model—the cost of packet voice is currently estimated to be only 20 to 50 percent of the cost of a traditional circuit-based voice network. Likewise, enterprise network designers are interested in direct cost savings associated with toll-bypass and tandem switching. Both are also interested in so-called "soft savings" associated with reduced maintenance costs and more efficient network control and management. Finally, packet-based voice systems offer access to newly enhanced services, such as Unified Messaging and application control. These, in turn, promise to increase the productivity of users and differentiate services.

Integration of voice and data technologies has accelerated rapidly in recent years because of both supply- and demand-side interactions. On the demand side, customers are leveraging investment in network infrastructure to take advantage of integrated applications, such as voice applications. On the supply side, vendors have been able to take advantage of breakthroughs in many areas, including standards, technology, and network performance.

Standards

Many standards for interoperability for voice signaling have finally been ratified and matured to the point of reasonable interoperability. This reduces the risk and costs faced by vendors offering components of a voice/data system, and it also reduces the risk to consumers. Standards, such as H.323 (approved by the International Telecommunications Union [ITU] in June 1996), are now evolving through their third and fourth iterations, while products based on initial standards still enjoy strong capabilities and interoperability. The general maturity of standards has, in turn, generated robust protocol stacks that can be purchased "off the shelf" by vendors, further ensuring interoperability.

Technology

Recent advances in technology have also enabled voice integration with data. For example, new Digital Signal Processor (DSP) technology has allowed analog signals to be processed in the digital domain, which was difficult or impossible only a few years earlier. These powerful new chips offer tremendous processing speeds, allowing voice to be sampled, digitized, and compressed in real time. Further breakthroughs in the technology allow as many as four voice conversations to be managed at the same time on a single chip, with even greater performance in development. These technologies greatly reduce the cost and complexity of developing products and deploying voice over data solutions.

In other areas, the industry has also enjoyed breakthroughs in voice codec (coder/decoder) technology. Previously, it was assumed that voice quality would suffer as bandwidth was decreased in a relatively linear fashion. However, new, sophisticated algorithms employed in new codecs have changed that view. It is now possible to obtain reasonably good-sounding voice at a fraction of the bandwidth once required. More importantly, these new algorithms have been incorporated into the standards to allow interoperability of highly compressed voice.

Network Performance

Finally, data-networking technology has improved to the point that voice can be carried reliably. Over the last few years, growth in voice traffic has been relatively small, while data traffic has grown exponentially. The result is that data traffic is now greater than voice traffic in many networks. In addition, the relative importance of data traffic has grown, as businesses and organizations come to base more business practices and policies on the ubiquity of data networks. This increase in importance of data networks has forced a fundamental change in the way data networks are engineered, built, and managed. Typical "best-effort" data modeling has given way to advanced policy-based networking with managed quality of service to support an even greater range of applications. Voice traffic, as an application on a data network, has benefited greatly from these technologies. For example, support of delay-sensitive SNA traffic over IP networks resulted in breakthroughs in latency management and queuing prioritization, which were then applied to voice traffic.

As stated previously, deployment of new technologies and applications must also be driven by greater demand from users. Breakthroughs in technology don't necessarily result in increased deployment unless they fill a real user need at a reasonable cost. For example, digital audio tape (DAT) technologies never enjoyed widespread use outside the audiophile community because of the high cost and only marginally better perceived performance than analog tapes. Voice/data integration, however, provides users with very real benefits, both now and in the future. Most users of voice/data integration technologies gain in two ways: Packet voice technologies are less expensive, and, in the future, they will offer much greater capabilities compared to today's circuit-based voice systems.

Economic Advantages

It has been estimated that packet voice networking costs only 20 to 30 percent of an equivalent circuit-based voice network. This is true for both carriers (service providers) and enterprise (private) users. Logically, this implies that enterprise users can operate long-distance voice services between facilities at less cost than purchasing long-distance voice services from a carrier, and it's often true. For example, many enterprise users have deployed integrated voice/data technologies to transport voice-over-data wide-area networks (WANs) between traditional PBXs across different geographical locations. The resulting savings in long-distance toll charges often provide payback in as little as six months (especially if international calls are avoided). Using data systems to carry voice as "virtual tie lines" between switches is also useful to service providers. In fact, many carriers have started to embrace packet-based voice technologies as their primary network infrastructure strategy going forward.

However, savings associated with packet voice technologies don't stop with simple transport. It is also possible to switch voice calls in the data domain more economically than traditional circuit-based voice switches. For large, multisite enterprises, the savings result from using the data network to act as a "tandem switch" to route voice calls between PBXs on a call-by-call basis. The resulting voice network structure is simpler to administer and uses a robust, nonblocking switching fabric made up of data systems at its core.

Advances in Applications

Real cost savings are sufficient for deployment of voice/data integration technologies. However, there are added benefits, which will become more evident in the future. As applications evolve, organizations will gain increased user productivity from the integration of voice and computer applications. Computer telephony integration (CTI) was begun by private branch exchange (PBX) vendors in the 1980s to integrate computers with PBXs to provide applications, such as advanced call center features (for example, "screen pops" for agents).

However, as voice/data integration continues, the line between voice and data applications will continue to blur. For example, Unified Messaging systems are now available that combine voice mail, e-mail, and fax messaging into a single, convenient system. With these advanced systems, users can have e-mail read to them over the phone or can add document attachments to voice mail. At the enterprise level, new applications, such as virtual call centers, allow call center agents to be distributed anywhere within reach of the data network, while still receiving the full suite of call center functions and features. They can even receive calls over their computers rather than using a traditional telephone instrument, and they can provide "blended contact center" support to answer Web user questions with electronic chat capability and e-mail between voice calls. These capabilities go far beyond simple cost savings and will ultimately make organizations much more effective and profitable.

The strong pressures driving the integration of voice and data networks have resulted in various solutions to the problem, each with its own strengths and weaknesses. Three general approaches exist:

- Voice over ATM

- Voice over Frame Relay

- Voice over IP

There are also mixed solutions, including voice over IP, over Frame Relay, and so on. These are illustrated in Figure 19-1. The figure shows that voice over ATM and voice over Frame Relay are primarily transport mechanisms between PBXs, while voice over IP can connect all the way to the desktop. More details are available later in this chapter.

Figure 19-1 *Mixed Solutions Including Voice over IP, Voice over Frame Relay, and so on.*

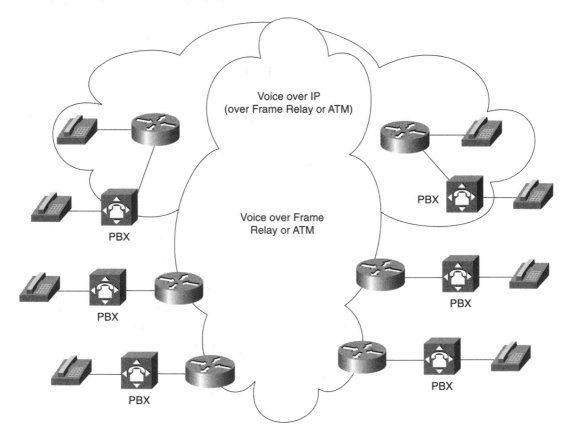

New World Voice Technologies

Voice over ATM (VoATM) can be supported as standard pulse code modulated (PCM) voice via circuit emulation (AAL1, described later) or as variable bit rate voice in ATM cells as AAL2 (also described later). ATM offers many advantages for transport and switching of voice. First, quality of service (QoS) guarantees can be specified by service provisioning or on a per-call basis. In addition, call setup signaling for ATM switched virtual circuits (SVCs), Q.2931, is based on call setup signaling for voice ISDN, Q.931. Administration is similar to circuit-based voice networks.

However, VoATM suffers from the burden of additional complexity and incomplete support and interoperability among vendors. It also tends to be more expensive because it is oriented toward all optical networks. Most importantly, ATM is typically deployed as a WAN Layer 2 protocol and, therefore, does not extend all the way to the desktop. Nevertheless, ATM is quite effective for providing trunking and tandem-switching services between existing voice switches and PBXs.

Voice over Frame Relay (VoFR) has become widely deployed across many networks. Like VoATM, it is typically employed as a tie trunk or tandem-switching function between remote PBXs. It benefits from much simpler administration and relatively lower cost than VoATM, especially when deployed over a private WAN network. It also scales more economically than VoATM, supporting links from T1 down to 56 Kbps. When deployed over a carefully engineered Frame Relay network, VoFR works very well and provides good quality. However, voice quality over Frame Relay can suffer depending on network latency and jitter. Although minimal bandwidth and burstiness are routinely contracted, latency and jitter are often not included in service level agreements (SLAs) with service providers. As a result, voice performance can vary. Even if quality is good at first, voice quality can degrade over time as a service provider's network becomes saturated with more traffic. For this reason, many large enterprise customers are beginning to specify latency and jitter, as well as overall packet throughput from carriers. In these situations, VoFR can provide excellent service.

Voice over IP (VoIP) has begun to be deployed in recent years as well. Unlike voice over Frame Relay and Voice over ATM, Voice over IP is a Layer 3 solution, and it offers much more value and utility because IP goes all the way to the desktop. This means that in addition to providing basic tie trunk and tandem-switching functions to PBXs, VoIP can actually begin to replace those PBXs as an application. As a Layer 3 solution, VoIP is routable and can be carried transparently over any type of network infrastructure, including both Frame Relay and ATM. Of all the packet voice technologies, VoIP has perhaps the most difficult time supporting voice quality because QoS cannot be guaranteed. Normal applications, such as TCP running on IP, are insensitive to latency, but must retransmit lost packets due to collisions or congestion. Voice is much more sensitive to packet delay than packet loss. In addition to normal traffic congestion, QoS for VoIP is often dependent on lower layers that are ignorant of the voice traffic mingled with the data traffic.

Voice Networking

Basic voice technology has been available for more than 100 years. During that time, the technology has matured to the point at which it has become ubiquitous and largely invisible to most users. This legacy of slow evolution continues to affect today's advanced voice networks in many ways, so it is important to understand the fundamentals of traditional voice technology before emulating it on data networks.

Traditional analog telephone instruments used for plain old telephone service (POTS) use a simple two-wire interface to the network. They rely on an internal two-wire/four-wire hybrid circuit to combine both transmit and receive signals. This economical approach has been effective but requires special engineering regarding echo. Note that the cost and cabling required rule out the idea of running a four-wire circuit to the subscriber's premises from the local exchange; therefore, the final mile to the subscriber is via hybrid filter circuits, which permit unique full-duplex signals in each direction to share the same two-wire local loop.

Hybrid echo is the primary source of echo generated from the public switched telephone network (PSTN). This electrically generated echo is created as voice signals are transmitted across the network via the hybrid connection at the two-wire/four-wire PSTN conversion points reflecting electrical energy to the speaker from the four-wire circuit. The signal path between two telephones, involving a call other than a local one, requires amplification using a four-wire circuit in the PSTN.

Basic Telephony

Three types of signaling are required for traditional telephony: supervision, alerting, and addressing. Supervision monitors the state of the instrument—for example, allowing the central office or PBX (a digital or analog telephone switchboard located on the subscriber premises and used to connect private and public telephone networks) to know when the receiver has been picked up to make a call, or when a call is terminated. Alerting concerns the notification of a user that a call is present (ringing) or simple call progress tones during a call (such as busy, ringback, and so on). Finally, addressing enables the user to dial a specific extension.

In addition to signaling, telephony services also provide media transport for the voice itself, analog-to-digital conversion, bonding and grounding for safety, power, and a variety of other functions when needed.

Analog voice interfaces have evolved over the years to provide for these basic functions while addressing specific applications. Because basic POTS two-wire analog interfaces operate in a master/slave model, two basic types of analog interfaces are necessary for data equipment to emulate: the user side and the network side. The user side (telephone) expects to receive power from the network as well as supervision.

A foreign exchange service (FXS) interface is used to connect an analog telephone, fax machine, modem, or any other device that would be connected to a phone line. It outputs 48 vdc power, ringing, and so on, and it accepts dialed digits. The opposite of an FXS interface is a foreign exchange office (FXO) interface. It is used to connect to a switching system providing services and supervision, and it expects the switch to provide supervision and other elements. (Why "foreign"? The terms *FXS* and *FXO* were originally used within telephone company networks to describe provision of telephone service from a central office other than normally assigned.)

Within FXS and FXO interfaces, it is also necessary to emulate variants in supervision. Typical telephones operate in a loop-start mode. The telephone normally presents a high impedance between the two wires. When the receiver goes off-hook, a low-impedance closed circuit is created between the two wires. The switch, sensing current flow, then knows that the receiver is off-hook and applies a dial tone. The switch also checks to be sure that the receiver is on-hook before sending a ringing signal. This system works well for simple telephones, but it can cause problems on trunks between PBXs and COs with high activity. In that situation, the remote end and the CO switch can both try to seize the line at the same time. This situation, called *glare*, can freeze the trunk until one side releases it. The solution is to short tip or ring to ground as a signal for line seizure rather than looping it. This is called *ground start*.

After the line is seized, it is necessary to dial the number. Normal human fingers cannot outrun the dial receivers in a modern switch, but digits dialed by a PBX can. In that case, many analog trunks use a delay start or wink start method to notify the calling device when the switch is ready to accept digits.

Another analog interface often used for trunking is E&M. This is a four- or six-wire interface that includes separate wires for supervision in addition to the voice pair. *E&M* stands for "ear and mouth" or "Earth and magneto" and is derived from the early telephony days. The E&M leads are used to signal on-hook and off-hook states.

Analog voice works well for basic trunk connections between switches or PBXs, but it is uneconomical when the number of connections exceeds six to eight circuits. At that point, it is usually more efficient to use digital trunks. In North America, the T1 (1.544 Mbps) trunk speed is used, consisting of 24 digitized analog voice conversations. In other parts of the world, E1 (2.048 Mbps) is used to carry 30 voice channels. (Engineers refer to the adoption of E1 and T1 internationally as "the baseball rule"—there is a strong correlation of countries that play baseball to the use of T1. Therefore, the United States, Canada, and Japan have the largest T1 networks, while other countries use E1.)

The first step in conversion to digital is sampling. The Nyquist theorem states that the sampling frequency should be twice the rate of the highest desired frequency. Early telephony engineers decided that a range of 4000 hertz would be sufficient to capture human voices (which matches the performance of long analog loops). Therefore, voice channels are sampled at a rate of 8000 times per second, or once every 125 μ. Each of these samples consists of an 8-bit measurement, for a total of 64,000 bps to be transmitted. As a final step, companding is used to provide greater accuracy of low-amplitude components. In North America, this is µ-law (Mu-law), while elsewhere it is typically A-law. For international internetworking purposes, it is agreed that the North American side will make the conversion.

To construct a T1, 24 channels are assembled for a total of 1.536 Mbps, and an additional 8 bits are added every 125 μ for framing, resulting in a rate of 1.544 Mbps. Often, T1 frames are combined into larger structures called SuperFrames (12 frames) and Extended-SuperFrames (24 frames). Additional signaling can then be transmitted by "robbing bits" from the interior frames.

Basic T1 and E1 interfaces emulate a collection of analog voice trunks and use robbed bit signaling to transfer supervisory information similar to the E&M analog model. As such, each channel carries its own signaling, and the interface is called channel associated

signaling (CAS). A more efficient method uses a common signaling channel for all the voice channels. Primary Rate Interface (PRI) for ISDN is the most common example of this common channel signaling (CCS).

If voice/data integration is to be successful, all of these voice interfaces must be supported to provide the widest possible range of applications. Over the years, users have grown to expect a certain level of performance, reliability, and behavior of a telecommunications system, which must be supported going forward. All these issues have been solved by various packet voice systems today so that users can enjoy the same level of support to which they have become accustomed.

Voice over ATM

The ATM Forum and the ITU have specified different classes of services to represent different possible traffic types for VoATM.

Designed primarily for voice communications, constant bit rate (CBR) and variable bit rate (VBR) classes have provisions for passing real-time traffic and are suitable for guaranteeing a certain level of service. CBR, in particular, allows the amount of bandwidth, end-to-end delay, and delay variation to be specified during the call setup.

Designed principally for bursty traffic, unspecified bit rate (UBR) and available bit rate (ABR) are more suitable for data applications. UBR, in particular, makes no guarantees about the delivery of the data traffic.

The method of transporting voice channels through an ATM network depends on the nature of the traffic. Different ATM adaptation types have been developed for different traffic types, each with its benefits and detriments. ATM adaptation layer 1 (AAL1) is the most common adaptation layer used with CBR services.

Unstructured AAL1 takes a continuous bit stream and places it within ATM cells. This is a common method of supporting a full E1 byte stream from end to end. The problem with this approach is that a full E1 may be sent, regardless of the actual number of voice channels in use. (An EI is a wide-area digital transmission scheme used predominantly in Europe that carries data at a rate of 2.048 Mbps.)

Structured AAL1 contains a pointer in the payload that allows the digital signal level 0 (DS0) structure to be maintained in subsequent cells. This allows network efficiencies to be gained by not using bandwidth for unused DS0s. (A DS0 is a framing specification used in transmitting digital signals over a single channel at 64 Kbps on a T1 facility.)

The remapping option allows the ATM network to terminate structured AAL1 cells and remap DS0s to the proper destinations. This eliminates the need for permanent virtual circuits (PVCs) between every possible source/destination combination. The major difference from the previous approach is that a PVC is not built across the network from edge to edge.

VoATM Signaling

Figure 19-2 describes the transport method, in which voice signaling is carried through the network transparently. PVCs are created for both signaling and voice transport. First, a signaling message is carried transparently over the signaling PVC from end station to end station. Second, coordination between the end systems allows the selection of a PVC to carry the voice communication between end stations.

Figure 19-2 *The VoATM Signaling Transport Model Describes the Transport Method, in Which Voice Signaling Is Carried Through the Network Transparently*

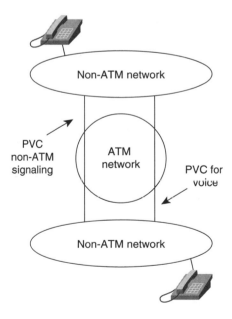

At no time is the ATM network participating in the interpretation of the signaling that takes place between end stations. However, as a value-added feature, some products are capable of understanding CAS and can prevent the sending of empty voice cells when the end stations are on-hook.

Figure 19-3 shows the translate model. In this model, the ATM network interprets the signaling from both non-ATM and ATM network devices. PVCs are created between the end stations and the ATM network. This contrasts with the previous model, in which the PVCs are carried transparently across the network.

Figure 19-3   *In the VoATM Signaling Translate Model, the ATM Network Interprets the Signaling from Both Non-ATM and ATM Network Devices*

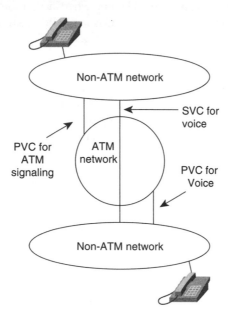

A signaling request from an end station causes the ATM network to create an SVC with the appropriate QoS to the desired end station. The creation of an SVC versus the prior establishment of PVCs is clearly more advantageous for three reasons:

- SVCs are more efficient users of bandwidth than PVCs.

- QoS for connections do not need to be constant, as with PVCs.

- The capability to switch calls within the network can lead to the elimination of the tandem PBX and potentially the edge PBX.

VoATM Addressing

ATM standards support both private and public addressing schemes. Both schemes involve addresses that are 20 bytes in length (shown in Figure 19-4). For further information on standard ATM addressing formats, refer to Figure 31-9 in Chapter 31.

Figure 19-4 *ATM Supports a 20-Byte Addressing Format*

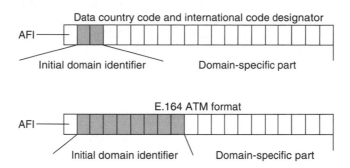

The *Authority and Format Identifier (AFI)* identifies the particular addressing format employed. Three identifiers are currently specified: data country code (DCC), international code designator (ICD), and E.164. Each is administered by a standards body. The second part of the address is the initial domain identifier (IDI). This address uniquely identifies the customer's network. The E.164 scheme has a longer IDI that corresponds to the 15-digit ISDN network number. The final portion, the domain-specific part (DSP), identifies logical groupings and ATM end stations.

In a transport model, you don't need to be aware of the underlying addresses used by the voice network. However, in the translate model, the capability to communicate from a non-ATM network device to an ATM network device implies a level of address mapping. Fortunately, ATM supports the E.164 addressing scheme, which is employed by telephone networks throughout the world.

VoATM Routing

ATM uses a *private network-to-network interface (PNNI)*, a hierarchical link-state routing protocol that is scalable for global usage. In addition to determining reachability and routing within an ATM network, it is also capable of call setup.

A virtual circuit (VC) call request causes a connection with certain QoS requirements to be requested through the ATM network. The route through the network is determined by the source ATM switch based on what it determines is the best path through the network, based on the PNNI protocol and the QoS request. Each switch along the path is checked to determine whether it has the appropriate resources for the connection.

When the connection is established, voice traffic flows between end stations as if a leased line existed between the two. This specification spells out routing in private networks. Within carrier networks, the switch-to-switch protocol is B-ICI. Current research and development of integrated non-ATM and ATM routing will yield new capabilities to build translate-level voice and ATM networks.

The B-ICI is an interface between two different public network providers or carriers. It is the demarcation point that designates the boundary between the public carriers' networks. The physical layer of the interface between the two carriers is based on the CCITT-defined Network Node Interface (NNI), with the addition of DS3 and E3 physical layers. The B-ICI specification also includes service-specific functions above the ATM layer that are required to transport, operate, and manage a variety of intercarrier services across the B-ICI.

VoATM and Delay

ATM has several mechanisms for controlling delay and delay variation. The QoS capabilities of ATM allow the specific request of constant-bit-rate traffic with bandwidth and delay variation guarantees. The use of VC queues allows each traffic stream to be treated uniquely. Priority can be given for the transmission of voice traffic. The use of small, fixed-size cells reduces queuing delay and the delay variation associated with variable-sized packets.

Voice over Frame Relay

Voice over Frame Relay enables a network to carry live voice traffic (for example, telephone calls and faxes) over a Frame Relay network. Frame Relay is a common and inexpensive transport that is provided by most of the large telcos.

VoFR Signaling

Historically, Frame Relay call setup has been proprietary by vendor. This has meant that products from different vendors would not interoperate. Frame Relay Forum FRF.11 establishes a standard for call setup, coding types, and packet formats for VoFR, and it provides the basis for interoperability between vendors.

VoFR Addressing

Address mapping is handled through static tables, dialed digits mapped to specific PVCs. How voice is routed depends on which routing protocol is chosen to establish PVCs and the hardware used in the Frame Relay network. Routing can be based on bandwidth limits, hops, delays, or some combination, but most routing implementations are based on maximizing bandwidth utilization.

A full mesh of voice and data PVCs is used to minimize the number of network transit hops and to maximize the capability to establish different QoS. A network designed in this fashion minimizes delay and improves voice quality, but it represents the highest network cost.

Most Frame Relay providers charge based on the number of PVCs used. To reduce costs, both data and voice segments can be configured to use the same PVC, thereby reducing the number of PVCs required. In this design, the central site switch reroutes voice calls. This design has the potential of creating a transit hop when voice needs to go from one remote office to another remote office. However, it avoids the compression and decompression that occurs when using a tandem PBX.

A number of mechanisms can minimize delay and delay variation on a Frame Relay network. The presence of long data frames on a low-speed Frame Relay link can cause unacceptable delays for time-sensitive voice frames. To reduce this problem, some vendors implement smaller frame sizes to help reduce delay and delay variation. FRF.12 proposes an industry-standard approach to do this, so products from different vendors will be capable of interoperating and consumers will know what type of voice quality to expect.

Methods for prioritizing voice frames over data frames also help reduce delay and delay variation. This—and the use of smaller frame sizes—is vendor-specific implementations. To ensure voice quality, the committed information rate (CIR) on each PVC should be set to ensure that voice frames are not discarded. Future Frame Relay networks will provide SVC signaling for call setup and may also allow Frame Relay DTEs to request a QoS for a call. This will enhance VoFR quality in the future.

Voice over IP

As stated previously, VoIP is an OSI Layer 3 solution rather than a Layer 2 solution. This feature allows VoIP to operate over Frame Relay and ATM networks autonomously. More importantly, VoIP operates over typical LANs to go all the way to the desktop. In this sense, VoIP is more of an application than a service, and VoIP protocols have evolved with this in mind.

VoIP protocols fall into two general categories: centralized and distributed. In general terms, centralized models follow a client/server architecture, while distributed models are based on peer-to-peer interactions. All VoIP technologies use common media by transmitting voice information in RTP packets over IP. They also agree by supporting a wide variety of compression codecs. The difference lies in signaling and where call logic and call state are maintained, whether at the endpoints or at a central, intelligent server. Both architectures have advantages and disadvantages. Distributed models tend to scale well and are more resilient (robust) because they lack a central point that could fail. Conversely, centralized call control models offer easier management and can support traditional supplementary services (such as conferencing) more easily, but they can have scaling limits based on the capacity of the central server. Hybrid and internetworking models being developed also offer the best of both approaches.

Distributed VoIP call management schemes include the oldest architecture, H.323, and the newest, Session Initiation Protocol (SIP). Centralized call management methods include Media Gateway Control Protocol (MGCP) and proprietary protocols, such as Skinny Client Control Protocol (SCCP) and the control protocol used in AVVID. A brief overview of each of these protocols is provided next.

Voice Codec Overview

Voice coder/decoder (codec) technology has advanced rapidly over the past few years thanks to advancements in DSP architectures as well as research into human speech and recognition. New codecs do more than simply provide analog-to-digital conversion. They can apply sophisticated predictive patterns to analyze voice input and, subsequently, transmit voice using a minimum of bandwidth. Some examples of voice codecs and the bandwidth used are discussed in this section. In all cases, voice is carried in RTP packets over IP.

Simple pulse code modulated (PCM) voice is defined by ITU-T G.711. It allows two basic variations of 64-Kbps PCM: Mu-law and A-law. The methods are similar in that they both use logarithmic compression to achieve 12 to 13 bits of linear PCM quality in 8 bits. However, they are different in relatively minor compression details (Mu-law has a slight advantage in low-level signal-to-noise ratio performance). Usage has historically been along country and regional boundaries, with North America using Mu-law and Europe using A-law modulation. Conversion from Mu-law to A-law is the responsibility of the Mu-law country. When troubleshooting PCM systems, a mismatch will result in terrible-sounding voice but will still be intelligible.

Another compression method often used is adaptive differential pulse code modulation (ADPCM). A commonly used instance of ADPCM, ITU-T G.726 encodes using 4-bit samples, giving a transmission rate of 32 Kbps. Unlike PCM, the 4 bits do not directly encode the amplitude of speech, but encode the differences in amplitude as well as the rate of change of that amplitude, employing some very rudimentary linear prediction.

PCM and ADPCM are examples of *waveform codecs*, compression techniques that exploit redundant characteristics of the waveform itself. New compression techniques have been developed over the past 10 to 15 years that further exploit knowledge of the source characteristics of speech generation. These techniques employ signal-processing techniques that compress speech by sending only simplified parametric information about the original speech excitation and vocal tract shaping, requiring less bandwidth to transmit that information. These techniques can be grouped generally as "source" codecs and include variations, such as linear predictive coding (LPC); code excited linear prediction (CELP); and multipulse, multilevel quantization (MP-MLQ).

There are also subcategories within these codec definitions. For example, code excited linear prediction (CELP) has been augmented by a low-delay version, predictably called *LD-CELP* (for low-delay CELP). It has also been augmented by a more sophisticated vocal tract modeling technique using conjugate structure algebraic transformations. This results in a codec called CSA-CELP. The list goes on and on, but it is important for network designers to understand only the trade-offs of these approaches as they apply to network and application design.

Advanced predictive codecs rely on a mathematical model of the human vocal tract and, instead of sending compressed voice, send mathematical representations so that voice can be generated at the receiving end. However, this required a great deal of research to get the bugs out. For example, some early predictive codecs did a good job of reproducing the developers' voices and were actively promoted—until it was discovered that they did not reproduce female voices or Asian dialects very well. These codecs then had to be redesigned to include a broader range of human voice types and sounds.

The ITU has standardized the most popular voice coding standards for telephony and packet voice to include the following:

- G.711, which describes the 64-Kbps PCM voice-coding technique outlined earlier. G.711-encoded voice is already in the correct format for digital voice delivery in the public phone network or through PBXs.

- G.726, which describes ADPCM coding at 40, 32, 24, and 16 Kbps. ADPCM voice may also be interchanged between packet voice and public phone or PBX networks, provided that the latter has ADPCM capability.

- G.728, which describes a 16-Kbps, low-delay variation of CELP voice compression. CELP voice coding must be transcoded to a public telephony format for delivery to or through telephone networks.

- G.729, which describes CELP compression that enables voice to be coded into 8-Kbps streams. Two variations of this standard (G.729 and G.729 Annex A) differ largely in computational complexity, and both generally provide speech quality as good as that of 32-Kbps ADPCM.

- G.723.1, which describes a compression technique that can be used for compressing speech or other audio signal components of multimedia service at a very low bit rate. As part of the overall H.324 family of standards, this coder has two bit rates associated with it: 5.3 and 6.3 Kbps. The higher bit rate is based on MP-MLQ technology and has greater quality; the lower bit rate is based on CELP, gives good quality, and provides system designers with additional flexibility.

As codecs rely increasingly on subjectively tuned compression techniques, standard objective quality measures, such as total harmonic distortion and signal-to-noise ratios, have less correlation with perceived codec quality. A common benchmark for quantifying the performance of the speech codec is the mean opinion score (MOS). Because voice quality and sound, in general, are subjective to the listener, it is important to get a wide range of listeners and sample material. MOS tests are given to a group of listeners who give each sample of speech material a rating of 1 (bad) to 5 (excellent). The scores are then averaged to get the mean opinion score. MOS testing is also used to compare how well a particular codec works under varying circumstances, including differing background noise levels, multiple encodes and decodes, and so on. This data can then be used to compare against other codecs.

MOS scoring for several ITU-T codecs is illustrated in Table 19-1. This table shows the relationship between several low-bit rate codecs and standard PCM.

Table 19-1   *Relative Processing Complexity and Mean Opinion Scores of Popular Voice Codecs*

Compression Method	Bit Rate (Kbps)	Processing[1] (MIPS)	Framing Size	MOS Score
G.711 PCM	64	0.34	0.125	4.1
G.726 ADPCM	32	14	0.125	3.85
G.728 LD-CELP	16	33	0.625	3.61
G.729 CS-ACELP	8	20	10	3.92
G.729 x2 Encodings	8	20	10	3.27
G.729 x3 Encodings	8	20	10	2.68
G.729a CS-ACELP	8	10.5	10	3.7
G.723.1 MPMLQ	6.3	16	30	3.9
G.723.1 ACELP	5.3	16	30	3.65

[1]   MIP processing power given for Texas Instruments 54x DSPs

This table provides information useful in comparing various popular voice codec implementations. The relative bandwidth as well as processing complexity (in millions of instructions per second [MIPS]) is useful in understanding the trade-offs associated with various codecs. In general, higher MOS are associated with more complex codecs or more bandwidth.

VoIP Network Design Constraints

After voice has been compressed and converted to data, the next step is to put it into a Real Time Protocol (RTP) stream for transmission across an IP network. Network designers must consider both bandwidth and delay when implementing VoIP. Bandwidth requirements are critical and are determined not only by the codec selected, but also by the overhead added by IP headers and other factors. Bandwidth is especially critical across expensive WAN links. Delay is affected by propagation delay (speed of light constraints), serialization delay (caused by buffering within devices in transit), quantization delay (A/D coding), and packetization delay.

Network Bandwidth Requirements

The bandwidth of a voice conversation over IP is affected by a variety of factors. First, as described previously, the codec employed for the conversation can vary widely from as little as 3 to 4 Kbps to as much as 64 Kbps. Layer 3 (IP) and Layer 2 (Ethernet) headers add additional overhead. Voice packets are typically very small and often contain no more than 20 bytes of information, so it is obvious that overhead can quickly overwhelm the bandwidth requirements.

Systems designers have several tools to help reduce the problem. First, voice activity detection (VAD) is used at the source to regulate the flow of packets by stopping transmission if the analog voice level falls below a threshold. This has the net result of reducing the bandwidth requirements by about half because most human conversations are silent at least half the time as the other person talks (unless there is a serious argument going on …).

There are a couple of problems with this solution. First, switch on/switch off times must be carefully tuned to avoid clipping. Cisco solves this problem by continuously sampling and coding, and then dropping the packet at the last moment if voice energy fails to exceed a certain minimum within the allotted time. In effect, a mostly empty voice packet is queued and prepared for transport, and will precede the speaker's first utterance, if necessary. The other problem created with VAD is the lack of noise at the receiver end. Human users of these early systems frequently complained that it sounded like they had been disconnected during the call because they no longer heard noise from the other end while they were talking. This proves that VAD is working, but is evidently not user-friendly.

Cisco and other manufacturers have solved this problem by adding *comfort noise* to the receive end of the conversation. When a receiver is in buffer underflow condition—that is, it is not receiving packets—the system generates a low-level pink or white noise signal to convince listeners that they are still connected. More advanced systems actually sample the ambient background noise at the far end and reproduce it during periods of silence.

Another tool often used by network designers is to compress the RTP headers. A great deal of information in RTP headers is duplicated or redundant in a stream. Cisco routers can compress the RTP headers on a hop-by-hop basis, reducing required bandwidth by a significant amount.

The end result of these steps is illustrated in Table 19-2. This table shows the relative bandwidth requirements of various codec implementations, along with additional overhead associated with typical network transport layers.

Delay

Network designers planning to implement VoIP must work within a delay budget imposed by the quality of the system to the users. As a typical rule, total end-to-end delay must be kept to less than about 150 ms.

Propagation delay is determined by the medium used for transmission. The speed of light in a vacuum is 186,000 miles per second, and electrons travel about 100,000 miles per second in copper. A fiber network halfway around the world (13,000 miles) would theoretically induce a one-way delay of about 70 milliseconds. Although this delay is almost imperceptible to the human ear, propagation delays in conjunction with handling delays can cause noticeable speech degradation. Users who have talked over satellite telephony links experience a delay approaching 1 second in some cases, with typical delays of about 250 ms being tolerable. Delays greater than 250 ms begin to interfere with natural conversation flow, as speakers interrupt each other.

Table 19-2 *VoIP/Channel Bandwidth Consumption*

Algorithm	Voice BW (Kbps)	MOS	Code Delay (msec)	Frame Size (Bytes)	Cisco Payload (Bytes)	Packets per Second	IP/UDP/RTP Header (Bytes)	CRTP Header (Bytes)	L2	Layer2 header (Bytes)	Total Bandwidth (Kbps no VAD)	Total Bandwidth (Kbps VAD)
G.729	8	3.9	15	10	20	50	40		Ether	14	29.6	14.8
G.729	8	3.9	15	10	20	50		2	Ether	14	14.4	7.2
G.729	8	3.9	15	10	20	50	40		PPP	6	26.4	13.2
G.729	8	3.9	15	10	20	50		2	PPP	6	11.2	5.6
G.729	8	3.9	15	10	20	50	40		FR	4	25.6	12.8
G.729	8	3.9	15	10	20	50		2	FR	4	10.4	5.2
G.729	8	3.9	15	10	20	50	40		ATM	2 cells	42.4	21.2
G.729	8	3.9	15	10	20	50		2	ATM	1 cell	21.2	10.6
G.711	64	4.1	1.5	160	160	50	40		Ether	14	85.6	42.8
G.711	64	4.1	1.5	160	160	50		2	Ether	14	70.4	35.2
G.711	64	4.1	1.5	160	160	50	40		PPP	6	82.4	41.2
G.711	64	4.1	1.5	160	160	50		2	PPP	6	67.2	33.6
G.711	64	4.1	1.5	160	160	50	40		FR	4	81.6	40.8
G.711	64	4.1	1.5	160	160	50		2	FR	4	66.4	33.2
G.711	64	4.1	1.5	160	160	50	40		ATM	5 cells	106.0	53.0
G.711	64	4.1	1.5	160	160	50		2	ATM	4 cells	84.8	42.4
G.729	8	3.9	15	10	30	33	40		PPP	6	20.3	10.1
G.729	8	3.9	15	10	30	33		2	PPP	6	10.1	5.1
G.729	8	3.9	15	10	30	33	40		FR	4	19.7	9.9
G.729	8	3.9	15	10	30	33		2	FR	4	9.6	4.8
G.729	8	3.9	15	10	30	33	40		ATM	2 cells	28.3	14.1

Table 19-2   *VoIP/Channel Bandwidth Consumption (Continued)*

Algorithm	Voice BW (Kbps)	MOS	Code Delay (msec)	Frame Size (Bytes)	Cisco Payload (Bytes)	Packets per Second	IP/UDP/RTP Header (Bytes)	CRTP Header (Bytes)	L2	Layer2 header (Bytes)	Total Bandwidth (Kbps no VAD)	Total Bandwidth (Kbps VAD)
G.729	8	3.9	15	10	30	33		2	ATM	1 cell	14.1	7.1
G.723.1	6.3	3.9	37.5	30	30	26	40		PPP	6	16.0	8.0
G.723.1	6.3	3.9	37.5	30	30	26		2	PPP	6	8.0	4.0
G.723.1	6.3	3.9	37.5	30	30	26	40		FR	4	15.5	7.8
G.723.1	6.3	3.9	37.5	30	30	26		2	FR	4	7.6	3.8
G.723.1	6.3	3.9	37.5	30	30	26	40		ATM	2 cells	22.3	11.1
G.723.1	6.3	3.9	37.5	30	30	26		2	ATM	1 cell	11.1	5.6
G.723.1	5.3	3.65	37.5	30	30	22	40		PPP	6	13.4	6.7
G.723.1	5.3	3.65	37.5	30	30	22		2	PPP	6	6.7	3.4
G.723.1	5.3	3.65	37.5	30	30	22	40		FR	4	13.1	6.5
G.723.1	5.3	3.65	37.5	30	30	22		2	FR	4	6.4	3.2
G.723.1	5.3	3.65	37.5	30	30	22	40		ATM	2 cells	18.7	9.4
G.723.1	5.3	3.65	37.5	30	30	22		2	ATM	1 cell	9.4	4.7

Handling delays can impact traditional circuit-switched phone networks, but they are a larger issue in packetized environments because of buffering of packets. Therefore, delay should be calculated to determine whether it stays below the threshold of 150 to 200 ms.

G.729 has an algorithmic delay of about 20 milliseconds because of look ahead. In typical VoIP products, the DSP generates a frame every 10 milliseconds. Two of these speech frames are then placed within one packet; the packet delay, therefore, is 20 milliseconds.

There are other causes of delay in a packet-based network: the time necessary to move the actual packet to the output queue, and queue delay. Cisco IOS software is quite good at moving and determining the destination of a packet. (This fact is mentioned because other packet-based solutions [PC-based and others] are not as good at determining packet destination and moving the actual packet to the output queue.) The actual queue delay of the output queue is another cause of delay. This factor should be kept to less than 10 milliseconds whenever possible by using whatever queuing methods are optimal for that network.

Table 19-3 shows that different codecs introduce different amounts of delay.

Table 19-3   *Codec-Introduced Delay*

Compression Method	Bit Rate (Kbps)	Compression Delay (ms)
G.711 PCM	64	0.75
G.726 ADPCM	32	1
G.728 LD-CELP	16	3 to 5
G.729 CS-ACELP	8	10
G.729a CS-ACELP	8	10
G.723.1 MPMLQ	6.3	30
G.723.1 ACELP	5.3	30

In addition to steady state delay, discussed previously, VoIP applications are sensitive to variations in that delay. Unlike circuit-based networks, the end-to-end delay over a packet network can vary widely depending on network congestion. Short-term variations in delay are called *jitter*, defined as the variation from when a packet was expected and when it actually is received. Voice devices have to compensate for jitter by setting up a playout buffer to play back voice in a smooth fashion and to avoid discontinuity in the voice stream. This adds to the overall system delay (and complexity). This receive buffer can be fixed at some value or, in the case of some advanced Cisco Systems devices, is adaptive.

Note that jitter is the primary impediment to transmitting VoIP over the Internet. A typical VoIP call over the Internet would traverse many different carrier systems, with widely varying latency and QoS management. As a result, VoIP over the public Internet results in poor quality and is typically discouraged by VoIP vendors. Nevertheless, many software applications exist to provide free voice services over the Internet. The common characteristic of these Voice over Internet systems is very large receive buffers, which can add more than 1 second of delay to voice calls. Free voice is attractive, but to business users, the poor quality means that these systems are worthless. However, some residential users are finding them adequate— especially for bypassing international toll charges.

In the future, as Internet service providers enhance the QoS features of their networks, Voice over Internet solutions will become more popular. In fact, many analysts predict that voice will eventually become free, as a bundled service with Internet access.

Quality of Service for VoIP

As seen previously, the quality of voice is greatly affected by latency and jitter in a packet network. Therefore, it is important for network designers to consider implementation of QoS policies on the network. In addition to protecting voice from data, this has the added benefit of protecting critical data applications from bandwidth starvation because of oversubscription of voice calls.

The elements of good QoS design include provisions for managing packet loss, delay, jitter, and bandwidth efficiency. Tools used to accomplish these goals are defined here:

- **Policing**—Provides simple limiting of packet rate, often by simply dropping packets that exceed thresholds to match capacities between different network elements. Policing can be performed on either input or output of a device. Examples include random early detection (RED) and WRED (weighted RED). These techniques help identify which packets are good candidates to drop, if necessary.

- **Traffic shaping**—Provides the capability to buffer and smooth traffic flows into and out of devices based on packet rate. Unlike policing, however, traffic shaping tries to avoid dropping packets, but it tends to add latency and jitter as they are buffered for later transmission.

- **Call admission control**—Provides the capability to reject requests for network bandwidth from applications. In the case of VoIP, an example might be the use of Resource Reservation Protocol (RSVP) to reserve bandwidth prior to completion of a call. Similarly, an H.323 gatekeeper might be used in signaling to manage a portion of available bandwidth on a per-call basis.

- **Queuing/scheduling**—These are used with buffering to determine the priority of packets to be transmitted. Separate queues for voice and data, for example, allow delay-sensitive voice packets to slip ahead of data packets. Examples useful for VoIP include weighted fair queuing and IP RTP priority queuing, among others.

- **Tagging/marking**—Includes various techniques to identify packets for special handling. In the case of VoIP packets, for example, the packets can be identified by RTP format, IP precedence bits (ToS bits), and so on. Tagging is also critical to preserve QoS across network boundaries. For example, tag switching preserves IP tagging across an ATM network, allowing VoIP to traverse an ATM network.

- **Fragmentation**—Refers to the capability of some network devices to subdivide large packets into smaller ones before traversing a narrow bandwidth link. This is critical to prevent voice packets from getting "frozen out" while waiting for a large data packet to go through. Fragmentation allows the smaller voice packets to be inserted within gaps in the larger packet. The large packet is subsequently reassembled by a router on the other end of the link so that the data application is unaffected.

H.323 Overview

H.323 is a derivative of the H.320 videoconferencing standard, but it assumes LAN connectivity rather than ISDN between conferencing components. As such, QoS is not assumed and is not implicitly supported. When used to support a VoIP application, the calls are treated as audio-only videoconferences.

Standards-based videoconferencing is generally governed by the ITU "H-series" recommendations, which include H.320 (ISDN protocol), H.323 (LAN protocol), and H.324 (POTS protocol). These standards specify the manner in which real-time audio, video, and data communications takes place over various communications topologies. Standards compliance promotes common capabilities and interoperability between networked multimedia building blocks that may be provided by multiple vendors.

The H.323 standard was ratified in 1996 and consists of the following component standards:

- **H.225**—Specifies messages for call control, including signaling, registration and admissions, and packetization/synchronization of media streams.

- **H.245**—Specifies messages for opening and closing channels for media streams and other commands, requests, and indications.

- **H.261**—Video codec for audiovisual services at P • 64 Kbps.

- **H.263**—Specifies a new video codec for video POTS.

- **G.711**—Audio codec, 3.1 kHz at 48, 56, and 64 Kbps (normal telephony).

- **G.722**—Audio codec, 7 kHz at 48, 56, and 64 Kbps; ratified.

- **G.728**—Audio codec, 3.1 kHz at 16 Kbps.

- **G.723**—Audio codec, for 5.3 and 6.3 Kbps modes.

- **G.729**—Audio codec (G.729a is a reduced complexity variant).

Following are H.323 device descriptions:

- **Terminal**—An H.323 terminal is an endpoint on the LAN that provides for real-time, two-way communications with another H.323 terminal, gateway, or multipoint control unit. This communication consists of control, indications, audio, moving color video pictures, and data between the two terminals. A terminal may provide speech only, speech and data, speech and video, or speech, data, and video.

- **Gateway**—An H.323 gateway (GW) is an endpoint on the LAN that provides for real-time, two-way communications between H.323 terminals on the LAN and other ITU terminals on a WAN, or to another H.323 gateway. Other ITU terminals include those complying with recommendations H.310 (H.320 on B-ISDN), H.320 (ISDN), H.321 (ATM), H.322 (GQOS-LAN), H.324 (GSTN), H.324M (mobile), and V.70 (DSVD).

- **Proxy**—The proxy is a special type of gateway that, in effect, relays H.323 to another H.323 session. The Cisco proxy is a key piece of the conferencing infrastructure that can provide QoS, traffic shaping, and policy management for H.323 traffic.

- **Gatekeeper**—The gatekeeper, which is optional in an H.323 system, provides call control services to the H.323 endpoints. More than one gatekeeper may be present and they can communicate with each other in an unspecified fashion. The gatekeeper is logically separate from the endpoints, but its physical implementation may coexist with a terminal, MCU, gateway, MC, or other non-H.323 LAN device.

- **Multipoint control unit**—The multipoint control unit (MCU) is an endpoint on the LAN that provides the capability for three or more terminals and gateways to participate in a multipoint conference. It may also connect two terminals in a point-to-point conference, which may later develop into a multipoint conference. The MCU generally operates in the fashion of an H.231 MCU, but an audio processor is not mandatory. The MCU consists of two parts: a mandatory multipoint controller and optional multipoint processors. In the simplest case, an MCU may consist of only an MC with no MPs.

- **Multipoint controller**—The multipoint controller (MC) is an H.323 entity on the LAN that provides for the control of three or more terminals participating in a multipoint conference. It may also connect two terminals in a point-to-point conference, which may later develop into a multipoint conference. The MC provides for capability negotiation with all terminals to achieve common levels of communications. It also may control conference resources, such as who is multicasting video. The MC does not perform mixing or switching of audio, video, and data.

- **Multipoint processor**—The multipoint processor (MP) is an H.323 entity on the LAN that provides for the centralized processing of audio, video, and data streams in a multipoint conference. The MP provides for the mixing, switching, or other processing of media streams under the control of the MC. The MP may process a single media stream or multiple media streams, depending on the type of conference supported.

- **Point-to-point conference**—A point-to-point conference is a conference between two terminals. It may be either directly between two H.323 terminals or between an H.323 terminal and an SCN terminal via a gateway. It is a call between two terminals.

- **Switched-circuit network (SCN)**—A public or private switched telecommunications network such as the GSTN, N-ISDN, or B-ISDN.

H.323 provides for fairly intelligent endpoints, which are responsible for maintaining their own call state. In its simplest form, H.323 is a peer-to-peer signaling system. Endpoints can call each other directly using the procedures provided by the standards if they know each other's IP address. Initial call setup signaling messages follow the traditional ISDN Q.931 model, using ASN.1-formatted information packets over TCP. As such, the signaling protocol relies on TCP retransmissions for QoS. After the call setup phase, the two endpoints do a capabilities exchange to negotiate which of several standard audio codecs to use, and, finally, they elect RTP port numbers to use for the voice media itself. Note that because RTP port numbers are assigned dynamically by the endpoints within a wide range, there are some difficulties operating through firewalls unless they maintain the call setup process itself.

H.323 Call Flow and Protocol Interworking

The provision of the communication is made in the steps shown in Figure 19-5.

Figure 19-5 *Call Flow Between H.323 Devices*

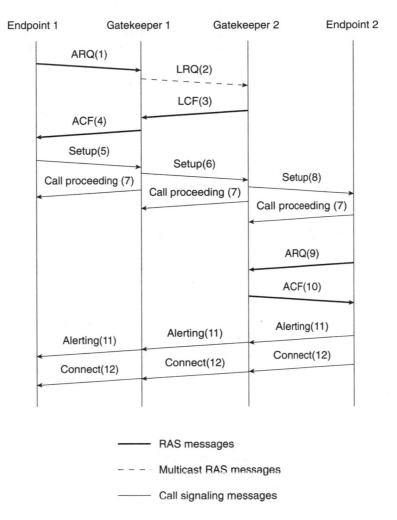

As can be seen from Figure 19-5, H.323 is designed to be robust and flexible, but at the cost of less efficiency.

General MGCP Overview

Media Gateway Control Protocol (MGCP) represents a relatively new set of client/server VoIP signaling protocols. These protocols have evolved in answer to the need for stateful, centralized management of relatively dumb endpoint devices. This capability greatly extends the utility of the system by making the VoIP system easier to design, configure, and manage because all major system changes occur at the server.

At the time of this writing, MGCP is an IETF draft. It may never be ratified as is by the IETF. Instead, a more advanced derivative protocol called MEGACO will probably be the ultimate solution. However, market demand has encouraged several vendors (including Cisco Systems) to announce support for MGCP in prestandard form. This has created the situation of a de facto standard with interoperability demonstrations among various vendors. This is generally good for the market because it has resulted in products with real customer value from various vendors.

As with most standards, MGCP has a colorful history. Initially, a client/server protocol called Simple Gateway Control Protocol was proposed jointly by Bellcore (now Telcordia) and Cisco Systems. This was the first step toward a truly stateless client. During the same period, another client/server protocol, called Internet Protocol Device Control (IPDC), was being developed by Level 3 in conjunction with Cisco Systems and other vendors. IPDC was conceived as a more generic control system for various IP multimedia devices. As the two protocols matured in the standards committees, they eventually merged to form MGCP.

MGCP Concepts

As stated before, MGCP uses simple endpoints called media gateways (MGs). An intelligent media gateway controller (MGC) or call agent (CA) provides services. The endpoint provides user interactions and interfaces, while the MGC provides centralized call intelligence. A master/slave relationship is preserved at all times between the MGC and the MGs. In fact, all changes of state are forwarded to the MGC via a series of relatively simple messages. The MG can then execute simple actions based on commands from the MGC.

It is important to understand the stateless nature of the MG endpoints. They have no local call intelligence. For example, in the case of an FXS type interface supporting an analog telephone, when the user goes off-hook, the gateway notifies the MGC, which then instructs the MG to play the dial tone. When the user enters digits (DTMF) to dial a number, each digit is relayed to the MGC individually because the MG has no concept of a dial plan. It doesn't know when the user has dialed enough digits to complete a call. In a sense, the MG becomes a logical extension of the MGC. If any new services are introduced (such as call waiting), they need be introduced only into the MGC.

Typically, MGCP messages are sent over IP/UDP between the MG and the MGC. Any special telephony signaling interfaces (such as the D channel of a Primary Rate Interface) are simply forwarded directly to the MGC for processing rather than terminating them in the MG. This means that for typical applications, the data connection between the MG and the MGC is critical to keep calls up.

The media connection (voice path) itself is usually over IP/RTP, but direct VoATM and VoFrame Relay can also be used. (In fact, MGCP does not specify the media.) For security, MGCP uses IPSec to protect the signaling information.

MGCP Advantages

MGCP offers several advantages over typical H.323 implementations. Although MGCP has not been ratified as an official standard, enough vendors have demonstrated interoperability that it can be safely deployed by customers without fear of being locked in. It leverages existing IETF protocols (SDP, SAP, RTSP). Probably most importantly, the centralized call control model in MGCP allows for much more efficient service creation environments, including billing, call agents, messaging services, and so on. Depending on vendor implementation, the MGC can support standard computer telephony integration (CTI) interfaces, such as Telephony Application Programming Interface (TAPI) used on PBXs.

MGCP Protocol Definitions

The MGCP model specifies the following:

- **Endpoints**—Specific trunk/port or service, such as an announcement server.
- **Connections**—The equivalent of a session. Connections offer several modes: send, receive, send/receive, inactive, loopback, and a continuity test.
- **Calls**—Groupings of connections.
- **Call agents**—The media gateway controller (MGC).

MGCP messages are composed from a short list of primitives:

- **NotificationRequest (RQNT)**—Instructs the gateway to watch for specific events.
- **Notify (NTFY)**—Informs the MGC when requested events occur.
- **CreateConnection (CRCX)**—Creates a connection to an endpoint inside the gateway.
- **ModifyConnection (MDCX)**—Changes the parameters associated with an established connection.
- **DeleteConnection**—Deletes an existing connection. Ack returns call statistics.
- **AuditEnpoint (AUEP)**—Audits an existing endpoint.
- **AuditConnection (AUCX)**—Audits an existing connection.
- **RestartInProgress (RSIP)**—Is a gateway notification to the MGC that an MG or an endpoint is restarting or stopping.

Of specific interest are the notification messages. The media gateway uses these messages to tell the MGC of a change of state. They typically involve signaling or events. Some examples of each are listed here:

- **Signals**—Ringing, distinctive ringing (0 to 7), ringback tone, dial tone, intercept tone, network congestion tone, busy tone, confirm tone, answer tone, call waiting tone, off-hook warning tone, pre-emption tone, continuity tone, continuity test, DTMF tones

- **Events**—Fax tones, modem tones, continuity tone, continuity detection (as a result of a continuity test), on-hook transition, off-hook transition, flash hook, receipt of DTMF digits

MGCP has a number of features that make it attractive for deployment of VoIP systems. First, messaging is UDP-based rather than TCP-based, which makes it more efficient. The centralized control model is subject to a single point of failure, so media gateways can be designed to revert to a standby MGC upon failure of the primary controller. This can result in the model being as reliable as any other call control model. MGCP scales well, typically depending only on the processing power of the MGC. When that becomes the limiting factor, the network can be subdivided into separate MGC domains. Therefore, an MGCP call control model can scale to millions of endpoints.

The protocol is also reliable, with an acknowledgment for each request consisting of one of three options: success, transient error, and permanent error. Requests that are not acknowledged can be retried. MGCP also relies on DNS to resolve names to IP addresses. This means that the IP address can be abstracted to multiple nodes, or a single node can have multiple IP addresses. Again, all this adds to the flexibility of the protocol.

Typical MGCP call flow is shown in Figure 19-6.

Figure 19-6 *Typical MGCP Flow*

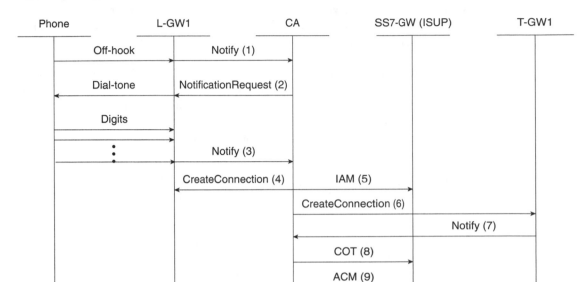

General SIP Tutorial

Session Initiation Protocol (SIP) is a new entry into the signaling arena, with a peer-to-peer architecture much like H.323. However, unlike H.323, SIP is an Internet-type protocol in philosophy and intent. It is described in RFC 2543, which was developed with the IETF MMUSIC Working Group in September 1999. Many technologists regard SIP as a competitor to H.323 and complementary to client/server protocols such as MGCP. As such, it will probably see deployment in mixed environments composed of combinations of SIP endpoints along with MGCP devices.

SIP depends on relatively intelligent endpoints, which require little or no interaction with servers. Each endpoint manages its own signaling, both to the user and to other endpoints. Fundamentally, the SIP protocol provides session control, while MGCP provides device control. This provides SIP with a number of advantages. First, the simple message structure provides for call setup in fewer steps than H.323 so that performance is better than H.323 using similar processing hardware. SIP is also more scalable than H.323 because it is inherently a distributed and stateless call model. Perhaps the key difference (and advantage) of SIP is the fact that it is truly an Internet-model protocol from inception. It uses simple ASCII messaging (instead of ASN.1) based on HTTP/1.1. This means that SIP messaging is easy to decode and troubleshoot—but more importantly, it means that Web-type applications can support SIP services with minimal changes. In fact, SIP fully supports URL (with DNS) naming in addition to standard E.164 North American Numbering Plan addressing. That means that in a SIP model, a user's e-mail address and phone address can be the same. It also means that the session is abstracted so that very different endpoints can communicate with each other.

SIP is modeled to support some or all of five facets of establishing and terminating multimedia communications. Each of these facets can be discovered or negotiated in a SIP session between two endpoints.

- User location
- User capabilities
- User availability
- Call setup
- Call handling

Although SIP is philosophically a peer-to-peer protocol, it is made up of logical clients and servers, often collocated within an endpoint. For example, a typical SIP client may be an IP phone, PC, or PDA; it contains both a user agent client (UAC) to originate SIP requests and a user agent server (UAS) to terminate SIP requests. Also supported are SIP proxy servers, SIP redirect servers (RS), registrars, and location servers. These servers are all optional, but also very valuable in actual SIP implementations.

SIP servers are defined here:

- **Proxy server**—Acts as a server and client; initiates SIP requests on behalf of a UAC.

- **Redirect server (RS)**—Receives a SIP request, maps the destination to one or more addresses, and responds with those addresses.

- **Registrar**—Accepts requests for the registration of a current location from UACs. Typically is collocated with a redirect server.

- **Location server**—Provides information about a callee's possible locations, typically contacted by a redirect server. A location server/service may co-exist with a SIP redirect server.

SIP Messages

SIP messages consist of a simple vocabulary of requests and responses. Requests are called *methods* and include these:

- **REGISTER**—Registers current location with the server.

- **INVITE**—Is sent by the caller to initiate a call.

- **ACK**—Is sent by the caller to acknowledge acceptance of a call by the callee. This message is not responded to.

- **BYE**—Is sent by either side to end a call.

- **CANCEL**—Is sent to end a call not yet connected.

- **OPTIONS**—Is sent to query capabilities.

SIP Addressing

As mentioned previously, SIP addressing is modeled after mailto URLs. For example, a typical SIP address might look like:

```
sip: "einstein" aeinstein@smartguy.com; transport=udp
```

However, standard E.164 addressing can also be supported by embedding it in the same URL format, like this:

```
+14085553426@smartguy.com; user=phone
```

The address structure also indicates parameters, such as transport type and multicast address.

SIP Call Flow

As seen in Figure 19-7, call setup with SIP is much simpler than H.323, even with a proxy server involved. Without the proxy server, the endpoints must know each other. However, call setup proceeds from a simple INVITE message directly from one endpoint to the other.

Figure 19-7 *Call Flow for Session Initiation Protocol (SIP)*

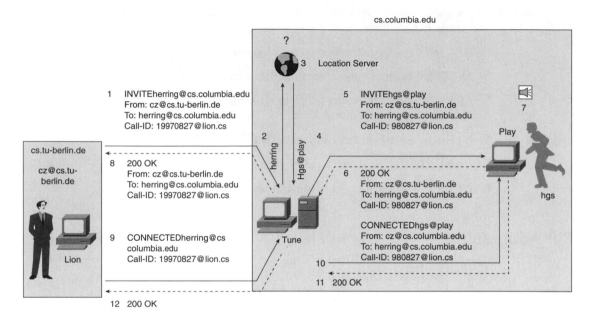

Skinny Client Control Protocol (SCCP)

SCCP, also referred to as "Skinny," is a Cisco Systems proprietary signaling and control protocol used for call establishment, teardown, and control in VoIP environments. It is the heart of the Cisco AVVID solution. It is widely deployed in VoIP enterprise solutions and is increasingly supported by third-party solutions in service provider environments.

It is a simple, lightweight stimulus protocol that is very feature-rich deployed in conjunction with Cisco IP Phones. The signaling path uses TCP port 2000, and the media path uses UDP. The message set for the control of the client has three basic areas: registration and management, call control (setup, teardown, and statistics), and media (audio) stream control. It was initially designed and deployed with Cisco Call Manager but has since gained much attention from third-party vendors. The Call Manager or SoftSwitch controls the endpoints, establishment, teardown, and accounting of calls, but the endpoints stream media directly between one another.

Comparison and Contrast of the Various VoIP Signaling Alternatives

The various signaling alternatives each offer advantages and disadvantages for system designers. A few highlights are presented here.

First, regarding MGCP and H.323, the scope of the protocols is different. MGCP is a simple device-control protocol, while H.323 is a full-featured multimedia conferencing protocol. H.323 is currently approved up to version 3, while MGCP has not been and may never be fully ratified; it is merely a de facto standard adopted by some manufacturers. As such, MGCP interoperability has been demonstrated, but not industry-wide. Likewise, the complexity of H.323 has inhibited interoperability as well.

MGCP can set up a call in as few as two round-trips, while H.323 typically requires seven or eight round-trips. (Note: H.323v2 provides for a fast start process to set up some calls in only two round-trips, but this is not widely implemented.) Call control is little more than device control for MGCP, while H.323 derives call flow from Q.931 ISDN signaling as a media control protocol. This control information is transmitted over UDP for MGCP, and over TCP for H.323.

SIP and H.323 are more direct competitors. They are both peer-to-peer, full-featured multimedia protocols. SIP is an IETF RFC, while H.323v3 has been approved by the ITU. Interoperability of both protocols has been demonstrated. SIP is more efficient than H.323, allowing some call setups in as little as a single round-trip. In addition, SIP uses existing Internet-type protocols, while H.323 continues to evolve new elements to fit into the Q.931 ISDN model.

Comparison of SIP to MGCP is similar to the comparison of H.323 to MGCP, in that SIP (like H.323) is a media-control protocol and MGCP is a device-control protocol. The same differences emerge as before between client/server and peer to peer. The fundamental difference is that peer-to-peer protocols, such as H.323 and SIP, tend to scale more gracefully, but client/server protocols, such as MGCP, are easier to design and maintain.

Evolution of Solutions for Voice over Data

The first products to integrate voice and data were targeted at eliminating long-distance telephone toll charges by providing tie lines between PBXs over a WAN infrastructure. These products were typically integrated into a router or another data device and provided simple point-to-point tie line service using simple analog trunk ports. As the products matured, more interface types were supported, including digital interfaces, E&M, and other types.

Later, as capabilities improved, support for analog telephone sets was introduced. This application was initially targeted at off-premises extensions from the PBXs using Private Line Automatic Ringdown (PLAR) circuits, but later DTMF detection was added within these gateway devices along with support for basic dial plans. Ultimately, this resulted in the capability of the WAN network devices to provide not only transport, but also tandem switching for the attached PBXs.

Over time, enterprise-wide call logic began to migrate toward the WAN data network elements. Each individual PBX at the edge of the WAN cloud needed only to forward intersite calls into the WAN gateways, without regard for further detailed trunk route calculations. Dial plans provisioned in data gateways, such as Cisco Systems-integrated voice/routers, which were sufficient to manage trunking between many sites.

This model worked very well, especially for smaller networks of 10 or fewer sites. However, as installations grew increasingly larger with greater numbers of sites, it became difficult to administer. Every time a new site was added or the dial plan was otherwise changed, network engineers would need to manually log in to every router in the network to make corresponding dial plan changes. This process with unwieldy and error-prone. Ultimately, vendors began introducing tools that made this job easier. For example, the Cisco Voice Manager (CVM) product provides a GUI interface for dial plan configuration and management, and allows network engineers to manage hundreds of voice gateways.

Again, these solutions were sufficient for many applications, but scaling again became an issue for even larger system sizes with many hundreds to thousands of nodes. As large enterprises and service providers began to evaluate the technology, they discovered scaling issues in two general areas: connection admission control (CAC) and dial plan centralization.

Connection admission control became more important as voice traffic grew. It became obvious that although a gateway could see another gateway across a logical flat mesh network, it was not always possible to complete a call. A method was needed for some central intelligence to act as traffic cop and to regulate the number of calls between critical nodes. Calls exceeding the defined number would be dropped or rerouted as necessary.

Dial plans also became too large to administer on small network elements. The flat mesh topology essentially made it necessary to store dial plan information about all sites in each node. Memory and processor limitations soon became the limiting factor to further growth.

The solution to both of these problems was the introduction of centralized call control. In the case of Voice over Frame Relay and Voice over ATM, virtual switch controller-type systems were introduced to centralize the call logic and intelligence. Likewise, for VoIP, the H.323 gatekeeper function was used to provide this centralized control function. In the case of Cisco Systems, for example, the Multimedia Conferencing Manager (MCM) H.323 gatekeeper application was deployed to support voice networks as well as the videoconferencing networks for which it was developed.

Note that centralized call control logic does not mean centralization of voice paths. Only the dial plan administration and call control are centralized. The actual switching of voice packets still occurs in the data network elements as it always has, so the inherent economies and efficiencies of packet voice solutions remain intact.

The Future: Telephony Applications

As integrated voice/data solutions continue to mature, a new wave of applications has emerged from various vendors. Instead of providing simple transport and switching functions for PBXs, packet voice solutions can now begin to replace those PBXs with an end-to-end solution. This means that packet voice technologies are no longer a service provided by the network, but they become an application running on the network. The distinction is critical in terms of how these products are marketed and administered. These products can be categorized by architecture and consist of the following general types:

- **Un-PBX**—In this architecture, a PC-based server contains both trunk gateway ports and analog telephone ports. Typically, special software and drivers running on an NT operating system provide all standard key system functions to the analog telephones. Supplementary functions, such as "hold" and "transfer", are activated via **hookflash** and * commands. The systems typically scale up to as many as 48 telephones. Note that there is no redundancy, but the overall cost of the system can be much less than that of older key systems. Many products include integrated voicemail by saving digitized voice messages on the hard disk.

- **LAN-PBX**—This is a general category of products that are based on LAN telephony all the way to the desktop. Some products offer LAN telephony services through the use of a software client on the user's PC, while others actually offer telephone instruments that plug into the LAN. Of the latter, products can be based on the MAC layer (Ethernet), ATM, or IP. Products at Layer 3 (those that are IP-based) offer greater flexibility and scaling because IP is a routable protocol. That means that these products can be used on different LAN segments. Products based on lower-layer protocols offer an attractive price point because client complexity is lower.

Over the long run, the greatest challenges facing LAN telephony are reliability and scalability. These issues must be addressed if voice/data integration is ever to replace the traditional PBX architecture. Products address these issues in a number of ways. For example, the Cisco Systems IP telephony solution provides for redundant call processing servers so that if one fails, the IP telephones switch to a backup unit. In addition, call control models that reduce server complexity provide for better scalability. In this case, the Cisco Systems products use a client/server call control model similar to MGCP, called Skinny Station Protocol. This allows a single server to manage thousands of telephone endpoints (telephones and gateway ports).

Incentives Toward Packet Telephony Applications

LAN-based telephony solutions offer attractive business models to consumers today. Typical "un-PBX" systems cost less than the key systems that they replace. Likewise, LAN-based PBX systems provide superior return on investment to traditional PBX systems. Although initial equipment costs are comparable, LAN PBXs typically cost much less to install than PBXs because they use the existing data infrastructure (Category 5 cabling) rather than separate voice wiring. Administration is also less burdensome because LAN and server administrators can manage the system without the need for dedicated telephony technicians. Finally, toll-bypass savings are also a byproduct of the system because calls between offices stay on the data network from end to end. Over time, these savings add up to the point that a LAN-based telephony system can offer considerable savings over traditional PBXs.

This is not to say that PBX systems will disappear overnight. Instead, traditional PBX vendors are actively migrating the existing products to become packet-enabled. Starting with simple data trunk cards to provide toll-bypass capability, PBX vendors are adding H.323 VoIP cards to allow the PBXs to manage H.323 clients as well. They see the PBX evolving into a voice server, much as the LAN PBX vendors are building from the ground up. Only time will tell which solution will be superior, but one thing is clear: Customers will have more choices than ever.

Perhaps the most compelling reason to consider IP telephony-type applications is the future integration of applications with voice. Over the years, a significant amount of work has gone into computer telephony integration (CTI) in traditional PBXs. These systems began to offer application programming interfaces, such as Telephony API (TAPI), Telephony Services API (TSAPI), and Java Telephony API (JTAPI). This work has resulted in advanced call center functions, including screen pops for agents and active call routing between call centers.

However, technologists believe that this is only the beginning. Integrated voice/data applications will revolutionize the way people use these systems. For example, Unified Messaging enables users to access voicemail, e-mail, and fax from one common server, using whatever media they choose. A user can retrieve voicemails on a PC (as .wav files) or, conversely, can retrieve written messages from a telephone utilizing text-to-speech capability in the system.

Fundamental to all these examples is a rethinking about the way people access and use information. It will become possible for the receiver of a message to determine the media rather than the sender. In addition, integration with intelligent assistant-type software from various vendors will enable users to set up rules for management of all incoming calls. In the call center, complex business rules (for example, checking credit before accepting new orders) can be applied to all forms of incoming communications (voice, e-mail, and so on) uniformly. The final result will be not only cost savings, but also increased efficiency for organizations that can learn to leverage this technology.

Summary

This chapter has provided an overview of technologies and applications of integrated voice/ data networking. Specific protocol and architectural definitions for Voice over Frame Relay, Voice over ATM, and VoIP were provided. However, more importantly, emphasis was placed on the reasons why these technologies have become prevalent. These technologies support a range of applications with very real business benefits for users. These benefits include cost savings from applications, such as toll bypass through total replacement of PBXs with VoIP technology. More importantly, new integrated applications can benefit from packet voice technologies.

Along with these technologies comes the pressure of deciding which one is appropriate for specific situations. The value of various solutions was reviewed, with Voice over ATM and Voice over Frame Relay shown as most appropriate for simple toll bypass and tandem switching; VoIP provides support for end-to-end voice applications to the desktop at the expense of greater complexity.

Review Questions

1   What are the three main packet voice technologies?

2   How are packet voice technologies used to provide toll bypass cost savings?

3   What are the primary voice-signaling protocols?

4   Describe how peer-to-peer voice signaling protocols are different from client/server protocols.

For More Information

Books

- Davidson, Jonathan. *Voice over IP Fundamentals*. Indianapolis: Cisco Press, March 2000.

- Newton, Harry. *Newton's Telecom Dictionary,* New York, March 2003.

- Dodd, Annabel Z. *The Essential Guide to Telecommunications,* New York, September 2001.

Objectives

- Introduce wireless concepts and terminology.
- Discuss Non-Line-of-Sight (NLOS) wireless.
- Introduce the elements of a total wireless solution.
- Introduce wireless local-area networks (WLANs).
- Discuss the benefits of using wireless technologies for communication.

CHAPTER 20

Wireless Technologies

Wireless technologies have existed in one form or another since the end of the 1800s. The methods used in transmissions, starting with arc transmitters and going up to the most sophisticated wireless communications systems, all have one main purpose. They are designed and built to transmit information through free space using electromagnetic waves. Many diverse methods are used to accomplish this, but they all share and are limited by the same laws of physics.

This chapter covers the basics of radio communications, starting with generic theories and concepts and moving on to the common, contemporary wireless systems we see today. Then it examines in greater detail the most popular wireless network type—wireless local-area networks (WLANs).

Wireless Concepts

The following sections introduce the physics behind radio communications, the building blocks of a radio system, and the main types of wireless systems commonly used today.

The basic goal of any communication system is to deliver information, commonly called *intelligence* in wireless circles, from source to destination. This data can be represented by either analog waveforms or digital pulses. In wireless communication, many basic physical properties govern the transmission, reception, and behavior of the electromagnetic waves as they are created, propagated, and ultimately received, complete with the intelligence they hold.

Radio Fundamentals

During discussions with peers about the networking issues we see today, it is amazing how many times discussions come all the way back to the basic physics we all learned in school.

Transmission theory, modulation theory, the concept of transmitted power, and receive sensitivity apply to every technology we work with today to one degree or another. With all technologies, including digital subscriber line, optical, cable, dial, and even simple RS-232, it's critical to understand the concepts and limitations inherent in communication between a transmitter and a receiver.

From a learning and development perspective, perhaps wireless is the best place to really learn and understand the fundamentals of communications.

The Components of a Wireless Communication System

The simplest form of wireless system consists of a transmitter, connected to an antenna with a transmission line, which is "connected" across the air interface to an antenna, which feeds a receiver via a transmission line. Although this description seems simple enough, in reality, the technology involved in this system is very sophisticated and constantly evolving. But after all is said and done, regardless of how advanced systems become, they all find their roots in the basic radio system shown in Figure 20-1.

Figure 20-1 *Wireless Communication System*

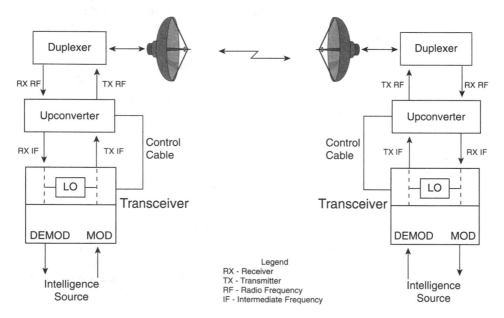

The main components of a radio communication system are as follows:

- **Intelligence source**—This is the information that is to be modulated and transmitted across the wireless link for delivery to the receiving site. It can be voice, data, or video and can be analog or digital originally.

- **Transceiver**—This is the "radio." It contains the functionality of a transmitter (TX) and a receiver (RX).

- **Modulator/demodulator**—The intelligence in its original state is combined with the frequency generated by a local oscillator.

- **Local oscillator (LO)**—The intelligence and the local oscillator frequency are combined in a filter, which produces the sum, difference, and two originals. Through the use of a band pass filter, the sum frequency is selected and coupled to a transmission line, where it is sent to an upconverter. This results in a signal called an intermediate frequency (IF). It is the local oscillator frequency with the intelligence modulated onto it. The LO frequency is typically the result of a crystal or synthesized frequency that is doubled, tripled, or quadrupled in stages until the LO frequency is achieved.

- **Upconverter**—The transceiver is connected to the upconverter or outdoor unit (ODU) via a transmission line, most often a coaxial cable. A variety of coaxial cables are available. The cable selected is based on the operating frequencies, power levels, and length. Transmission lines are explained later.

- **Control cable**—Depending on the type of ODU and transceiver, there also might be a control cable that provides communication between the two units. You might not always see radio systems where the IF and RF portions are in separate "boxes." Some radio systems have physical connections that connect directly to an antenna. The primary time to use a separate IF unit and RF unit is when there is a long distance between the intelligence point and the antenna. The transmission line properties, such as attenuation, of an IF signal at 70 MHz compared to an RF signal of 5.7 GHz are radically different. In a wireless design you try to keep the RF transmission lines to an absolute minimum length, especially as you use higher frequencies.

- **Duplexer**—The duplexer enables full-duplex wireless paths using a single antenna system for each location. Two unique frequencies, one for transmit and one for receive, are combined, yet they maintain their uniqueness. This is called frequency-division multiplexing (FDM). A common duplexing method is to use tuned cavities milled out of a metal, such as aluminum. The cavity attenuates frequencies, acting as a band pass filter for the frequencies of interest, yet attenuating all others greatly. In old voice radio systems that had simplex transmission paths, the antenna was coupled to the receiver until the transmitter was keyed, causing an RF relay to couple the transmitter output to the antenna system.

There are wireless systems whose architecture is not full-duplex. A simplex, or half-duplex, system is one in which communication between both endpoints is via the same radio frequency. Because both stations transmit on the same frequency when a conversation is ongoing, each party must make sure that the other party has stopped, or neither of them will hear the conversation.

This has been a simple introduction to a wireless communication system. Of course, there are many permutations in the way these technologies are implemented, but they all rely on the basic building blocks. Keep in mind that the goal is to accept data or intelligence from a source and modulate it onto an IF signal, where it can ultimately be unconverted to an RF signal and delivered across the open air.

The methods and physics that apply during this process are explained in subsequent sections, but first, let's take a look at the electromagnetic spectrum.

The Electromagnetic Spectrum

Electromagnetic (EM) spectrum is a term used to describe the sum of all forms of radiation. The EM spectrum refers collectively to all the components. Radiation is energy; it travels, theoretically, at the speed of light; and it is dispersed as it travels. There are many forms of EM energy:

- Visible light, which comes from a lamp in your house

- Radio waves from your favorite radio station

- Microwaves, used in point-to-point radio links and ovens

- Infrared and ultraviolet light, x-rays, and gamma rays

The EM spectrum is further divided into more finite pieces depending on the use. The important thing to remember is that most of the spectrum is used by *licensed users*, be they service providers, government agencies for such things as air traffic control, or the military.

The allocation of spectrum for use is normally the responsibility of government agencies, such as the Federal Communications Commission (FCC) in the U.S. or the Canadian Radio-Television and Telecommunications Commission (CRTC) in Canada. Both these agencies are excellent sources of reference material.

Radio frequencies are measured in hertz, which is equivalent to cycles per second. When we deal with the higher frequencies in the EM spectrum, we tend to use wavelength as a measure. This is common in optical technologies in which 850, 1310, and 1550 nanometers (nm) are common optical wavelengths. The reason for using this measurement system is the manageability of the numbers being dealt with.

The formula to determine frequency in hertz is

$$\lambda = c \, / \, F$$

where

- λ is the wavelength in meters

- c is the speed of light in a vacuum (3.0×10^8 meters per second)

- F is the frequency in hertz

The area of particular interest in our discussion of wireless technologies is the area of the EM spectrum called the radio waves portion. The major allocations in this portion of the EM spectrum are listed in Table 20-1.

Table 20-1   *Major Wireless Allocations*

Service	Frequency Spectrum	Comments
AM radio	535 to 1705 kHz	Commercial radio band
Analog television channels 2 to 6 (VHF)	54 to 88 MHz	Over-the-air broadcast television
FM radio	88 to 108 MHz	Commercial radio band
Analog television channels 7 to 13 (VHF)	174 to 216 MHz	These frequency ranges have been identified by the FCC as supporting digital television by 2007
Analog television channels 14 to 69 (UHF)	470 to 806 MHz	These frequency ranges have been identified by the FCC as supporting digital television by 2007
Cellular	825 to 894 MHz	Analog POTS
Industrial, scientific, and medical (ISM)	902 to 928 MHz	Unlicensed; proprietary systems
PCS	1850 to 1990 MHz	2G wireless
ISM	2.4 to 2.4835 GHz	Unlicensed; 802.11 and proprietary systems
Multichannel Multipoint Distribution Service (MMDS)	2.1 to 2.7 GHz	33 channels 6 MHz wide; earmarked for 3G wireless
Unlicensed National Information Infrastructure (U-NII)	5.15 to 5.35 GHz 5.725 to 5.825 GHz	Unlicensed; 802.11 and proprietary systems
Local Multipoint Distribution System (LMDS)	27.4 to 31.3 GHz	Two blocks of frequencies totaling 1.3 GHz
Free space optics	W-band 60 GHz	High bandwidth; optical replacement
Free space optics	IR 765 nm	High bandwidth; optical replacement

Table 20-1 describes only a small fraction of the EM spectrum, but it shows you the areas in which most data networking seen today occurs. For more information about the remaining spectrum allocations, consult the FCC Web site.

RF Transmission Theory

You have read about the wireless system, the electromagnetic spectrum, and the common frequency bands you will likely see in a networking environment. It is now time to look at the theory behind radio communications.

Electromagnetic Energy

To understand how wireless communications work, you must understand how electromagnetic energy is generated and propagated through free space. When current passes through a piece of wire, an electric field is created, which in turn creates a magnetic field. When the current is alternating, as opposed to direct, the electromagnetic field is created and collapses at the same rate as the frequency of the alternating current. The magnetic field also builds and collapses at the same rate as the electrical field. This action generates an electromagnetic wave, which is radiated from the wire, which at this point can be called an antenna.

The resulting electromagnetic wave or pulse is sinusoidal, so it has the three characteristics of this waveform—amplitude, phase, and frequency. These characteristics result from the original signal, which is coupled to the antenna after being generated in the transmitter.

The most important contributing factors to the success or failure of a wireless communication system are those that exist between the output of the final RF power amplifier and the front end of the receiver. This is where wireless systems either work or don't. The pieces involved in this RF transmission are the transmission lines, the antennas, and the air interface.

Power Measurement

The first pieces involved in the RF transmission are the transmission lines. Before we discuss transmission lines, you need to understand the importance and measurement of power, because it is one of the most important success factors in a communication system. The goal of the transmission line is to faithfully deliver the signal to the antenna while minimizing power loss in the transmission medium. The transmission line must also have certain electrical specifications, such as impedance, power-handling capabilities, and loss. These characteristics are all interrelated and interesting. However, they are outside the scope of this introductory discussion.

In wireless communications, power normally is expressed in watts or dBm. The reference for 0 dBm is 1 MW. With larger radio transmitters, power typically is measured in watts, but with lower power output devices, dBm is more manageable.

Table 20-2 compares dBm and watts.

Table 20-2 *Watts and dBm*

Power in dBm (Relative to 1 MW)	Power in Watts
50 dBm	100 W
40 dBm	10 W
30 dBm	1 W
20 dBm	100 MW
10 dBm	10 MW
0 dBm	1 MW
−10 dBm	100 uW
−20 dBm	10 uW
−30 dBm	1 uW

To quickly determine relative values when working in dBm, use the following calculations:

- If you have a power increase of 1 dBm, multiply the power by 1.25.

- If you have a power increase of 2 dBm, multiply the power by 1.5.

- If you have a power increase of 3 dBm, multiply the power by 2.

This also works in reverse. For instance, a drop of 3 dBm is a one half drop in power.

For example, given a power level of 20 dBm or 100 MW, if the power is increased by 5 dBm, the resulting power in watts would be 100 MW, doubled and then multiplied by a factor 1.5, which results in a power level of 300 MW.

Attenuation is the loss of signal power as it passes through a medium, whether it is the air, a physical transmission line, or even an electronic circuit, such as a filter. Just as you measure the *gain,* or the increase in a signal, you also need to be aware of a loss of power, or *attenuation.* In fact, you need to be able to calculate this in a loss budget to ensure that when a signal is transmitted, it arrives at the receiving station with enough strength. A receiver must be sensitive enough to be able to select the correct frequency. If the receiver is incapable of this, you will never be able to downconvert, producing an IF and, ultimately, demodulating your intelligence.

Transmission Lines

The purpose of a transmission line is to provide the physical connection between the transmitting device and the receiving device. Transmission lines come in various forms and materials. In wireless networks, the common types are

- Coaxial cables

- Waveguides

There are many versions of each, but regardless of the type chosen, here are the main characteristics you need to be aware of:

- RF attenuation
- Impedance
- DC loss (if you are also using it to provide DC power to an upconverter)
- Physical characteristics, such as weight and bend radius
- Cost

The first three characteristics are all related to a degree and are also related to the frequencies that are transmitted on the wire. The higher the frequency, the greater the attenuation, and, therefore, the greater the loss.

Impedance is critical, because it must match the devices at either end. An impedance mismatch means that there is a less-than-perfect transfer of energy at the mechanical connection points. Another problem that impedance mismatches compound is reflections. When 100% of the transmitted energy is not coupled into the sink, or destination circuit, the energy needs to go somewhere. This energy is either radiated into free space, which is called a leak, or it is reflected to the transmitting device.

This energy can cause many problems if it is reflected out of phase with the original. An original signal that is subjected to a reflection of itself that is equal in amplitude and 180 degrees out of phase effectively is reduced to 0. It is inconceivable that a reflection of 100% of the power, 180 degrees out of phase, would ever occur, but some percentage of reflection and, to some degree, being out of phase with the original always occurs. The result can be additive perfectly in phase, but it is subtractive if not.

In wireless these effects are measured and are called Voltage Standing Wave Ratio (VSWR). VSWR is a measure of impedance mismatch between the transmission line and its load, which is the antenna. The higher the VSWR, the greater the mismatch.

Antennas

The second piece of the RF transmission is the group of antennas. We have discussed the basic transceiver and connected a transmission line to it. Now we need to look at the other end of the transmission line. This is where the antenna fits. The antenna has two main functions. One is to accept RF power from the transmitter and radiate it in the right direction, to the receiving antenna. The second function is to receive the energy from the transmitter and couple it to the receiver. Antenna theory has several key concepts, as discussed next.

Full-Duplex Simultaneous Transmission

One thing that should be mentioned is the idea of full-duplex simultaneous transmission. Some radio systems offer full-duplex, full-time transmission. To do this from the perspective of an antenna, you need two unique antennas, or a device that can provide a signal path for the transmit and receive frequencies simultaneously using one antenna. This device is called a duplexer.

A duplexer essentially acts as a splitter/combiner that allows two unique frequencies to share one antenna. The transmit and receive frequencies need to be relatively close together, because they rely on the RF characteristics of one live antenna element. This use of a duplexer is called *frequency division multiplexing (FDM)*.

Many years ago, I was responsible for a microwave radio-relay system that used quadruplexers. This let us use one antenna with two transmit and two receive frequencies. The quadruplexer was fixed, meaning that we couldn't tune it, and it was manufactured of milled aluminum. The electrical behavior was that of a tuned cavity, acting similar to a waveguide, allowing the desired signals to pass while attenuating all others.

An isotropic antenna is a theoretical antenna that can radiate in all directions equally. It is used as a benchmark or reference when we express the properties of directional antennas. When we evaluate antennas, we refer to an antenna's gain, which is often measured in dBi—the power radiated or received with respect to an isotropic antenna. This provides a standard reference measurement that lets us compare antennas. Figure 20-2 illustrates antenna theory.

Figure 20-2 *Antenna Theory*

Antenna Theory

- A theoretical antenna (isotropic) has a perfect 360 degree vertical and horizontal beam width

**Side View
(Vertical Pattern)**

- This is a reference for ALL antennas

**Top View
(Horizontal Pattern)**

Effective Isotropic Radiated Power (EIRP)

Effective Isotropic Radiated Power (EIRP) is the result of the RF power delivered to the antenna multiplied by the gain as referenced to an isotropic radiator.

EIRP can be calculated as follows:

EIRP (dBW) = Ptx (dBW) + Gant (dBi) – Ltlc (dB)

where

- Ptx is the transmitter's power output in dBW

- Gant is the antenna gain, typically along the antenna's main lobe

- Ltlc is the loss of the transmission line, including connectors

EIRP is normally calculated and reported in dBW, but can also be calculated in dBm and simple watts.

Here's an example of EIRP in dBm:

EIRP (dBm) = Ptx (dBm) + Gant (dB) – Ltlc (dB)

For example, suppose a transmitter outputs 8.5 watts with an 11 dB gain antenna, the cable loss is 1.2 dB, and connector losses are 0.25 dB. The transmitter output must first be converted from watts to dBm. The EIRP is

EIRP = 39.29 dBm + 11.0 dB – 1.45 dB = 48.84 dBm EIRP

Antenna Types

There are many types of antennas. Which type you choose is directly related to the type of radiation pattern, frequency, and RF characteristics of the wireless network coverage. It is in selecting an antenna where the concept of EIRP needs to be evaluated, because it is a critical factor in antenna selection.

Many types of antennas are available for wireless systems. The most basic criterion for differentiation is the concept of directionality. In this respect, there are two basic antenna types:

- Omnidirectional

- Unidirectional

An omnidirectional antenna is one in which the transmitted power is radiated in all directions. A unidirectional antenna radiates its energy in a specific direction.

Before we proceed, we should qualify the phrase "in all directions." When we describe an antenna, we also need to consider another antenna trait—polarization. An antenna's polarization is the active element's physical placement relative to the Earth. The active element is the antenna element to which the power is applied and, therefore, radiated from. Antennas can be horizontally or vertically polarized. The difference between an isotropic and an omnidirectional antenna is that the omnidirectional antenna radiates in 360 degrees, but the radiation pattern is limited by the polarization of the active element.

An antenna's physical components include an active element or elements, reflectors, and directors. The active element is the element to which energy is applied and received. This element is coupled to the transceiver through a transmission line.

A unidirectional antenna directs its radiated energy in a specific direction, hence, concentrating it. This is done through the use of reflectors. Common types of unidirectional antennas are parabolic, semiparabolic, dish, panel, and yagi. They have a high gain and can be very directional. They are used for point-to-point and point-to-multipoint links. With careful engineering they can be directional to a degree, meaning that they can be used in a sector layout. For instance, in a mobile wireless or point-to-multipoint broadband deployment, a hub transmitter/receiver site may use three 120-degree antennas, thus concentrating the radiated energy in the desired sector (see Figure 20-3). In these three sectors, you also need to ensure that you effectively reuse the available frequencies efficiently. Consider that this particular area of coverage is bordered by identical areas of coverage. Because of the possibility of interference between cells if they use similar frequency plans, you need to ensure that the frequency plan prevents intercell frequency overlapping.

Figure 20-3 *Antenna Sectors—Three by 120 Degrees*

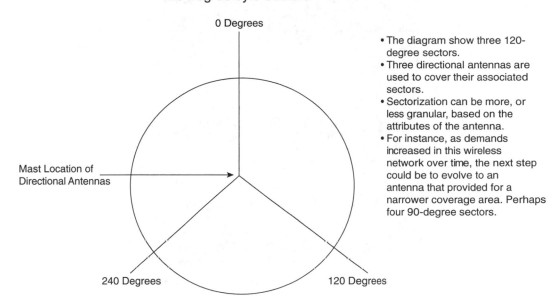

120 Degree by 3 Sectors

0 Degrees

Mast Location of Directional Antennas

240 Degrees

120 Degrees

- The diagram show three 120-degree sectors.
- Three directional antennas are used to cover their associated sectors.
- Sectorization can be more, or less granular, based on the attributes of the antenna.
- For instance, as demands increased in this wireless network over time, the next step could be to evolve to an antenna that provided for a narrower coverage area. Perhaps four 90-degree sectors.

An important concept in the selection and performance of a unidirectional cone (or dish) antenna is beam width. The energy that is transmitted is concentrated by virtue of the construction of the cone that provides the reflector function. A great analogy for this is the Maglite style of flashlight. When you rotate the lens collar on this kind of flashlight, you actually move the light bulb in and out. When you do so, the width of the beam of light narrows or widens. The same happens with energy propagated from a dish antenna. The actual level of transmitted energy (in this case, light) remains constant, but is dispersed over a greater area. Therefore, less energy is available across a great area at the receiving end. If you concentrate the beam, you can use lower power or perhaps reach farther.

Figure 20-4 shows one type of directional antenna.

Figure 20-4 *Common Directional Antenna*

Figure 20-5 shows a common form of omnidirectional antenna. You use an omnidirectional antenna when you want to radiate the transmitted signal from the base station or transmitter site to all possible locations in a 360-degree pattern. Common systems in which this is desirable are broadcast radio and navigation. Even with an omnidirectional antenna, you must keep in mind that as soon as you leave the antenna, you will not achieve a perfect circular coverage pattern. This is because of the antenna's radiation pattern, as well as the environment that the signal traverses in free space.

You have read about several key antenna concepts. You might have noticed that we keep mentioning antennas' transmit characteristics. Of course, an antenna must also be able to receive signals radiated from other sources. The signals received by an antenna and that are subsequently delivered to the receiver's front end are in the magnitude of microvolts and, in some systems, even lower. In order to effectively provide a survivable communication path in wireless communications, the antenna must possess particular qualities. These qualities let the antenna receive extremely weak signals and transmit them to the receiver at a level strong enough to recover the modulated information.

Figure 20-5 *Common Omnidirectional Antenna*

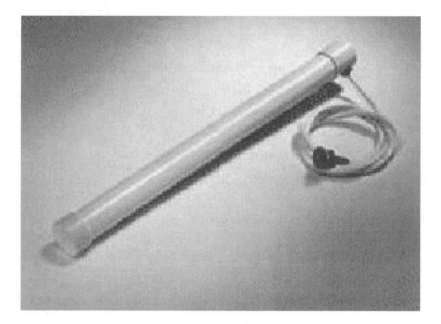

Free Space RF Propagation

The third piece of RF transmission is the air interface, or the free space between the transmitting and receiving antenna system. After the energy leaves the transmit antenna, it is radiated with sufficient power to reach the receiving antenna, and with sufficient strength for the receiver. However, the environment that the energy passes through is extremely hostile. You need to be aware of many factors and take them into account when designing a wireless system. Here are some of these factors:

- Free space loss
- Line of sight

- Fresnel zone

- Earth bulge

When radio waves depart the transmitting antenna, they are affected by the atmosphere, physical structures, and geography as they propagate to the receiving antenna. The first estimation you make when trying to understand a path is free space loss (FSL). This is a best-case calculation of the loss incurred in a transmission path. It is theoretical and assumes that there is no diffraction, refraction, obstructions, or scattering. It is just the loss in a path as a signal propagates farther from the source and spreads because of beam divergence. It can be calculated using this formula:

$$Lp = 36.6 + 20 \, LogF + 20 LogD$$

where

- Lp is the free space loss or attenuation between antennas in dB

- The constant 36.6 is the use of statute miles. If you use nautical miles, the constant is 37.8.

- F is the transmit frequency in MHz

- D is the path length in statute miles

Many FSL calculators are available on the WWW. You can just plug in your values to arrive at the answer. Use any search engine to look for "free space loss calculator."

A very important attribute in the behavior of radio waves is line of sight (LOS). Line of site with radio frequencies is more than the ability to see the receiving antenna from the transmitting antenna. To have true LOS, no objects, including trees, houses, and the Earth, can be in the Fresnel zone. The Fresnel zone is the area around the visual line of sight that radio waves propagate into after they leave the transmitting antenna. This area must be clear, or the signal's quality diminishes, because extra attenuation is present.

Fresnel zones are zones of radiated energy. In theory, there are an infinite number of them. In practice, however, we concern ourselves with only the first Fresnel zone. These zones are ellipsoid in shape and exist around the direct LOS path. The energy as it radiates from the antenna looks like a football.

In the first Fresnel zone, you need most of the energy that is present to reach the receiving antenna, notwithstanding the free space loss you expect based on the frequency and distance. For the maximum energy to be conveyed, you strive to ensure that no more than 40% of the LOS through the zone is obstructed. You also need to take into account the Earth's bulge, which is a result of the Earth's curvature. The compound effect of these two path attributes dictates the antenna's minimum height above ground. Figure 20-6 illustrates the effect of the Earth's bulge, and the concept of the Fresnel zone.

Figure 20-6 *Fresnel Zone and Earth Bulge*

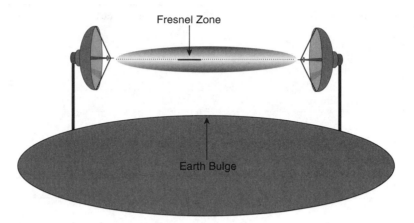

To calculate the radius of the first Fresnel zone, use this formula:

Rft= 72.1 * the square of D1 * D2 / FD

where

- Rft is the radius of the first Fresnel zone in feet
- D1 is the distance from the transmitter to the path obstacle
- D2 is the distance from the path obstacle to the receiver
- F is the frequency in GHz
- D is D1 + D2, the distance in miles

To calculate the effect of Earth bulge, use this formula:

Earth bulge in feet = D^2 / 8

where

- D^2 is the distance between antennas squared

Table 20-3 shows standard values for common distances.

Table 20-3 *Earth Bulge Values*

Distance in Miles	Bulge in Feet
2	0.5
4	2.0
6	4.5
8	8.0
10	12.5
12	18.0
14	24.5
16	32.0

To ensure that a particular radio path can perform satisfactorily, you must ensure that the Fresnel zone is adequately clear of obstructions and that the Earth bulge is allowed for. This might mean having to raise your antennas to higher elevations on antenna masts. You also need to understand the area's geography. A good path profile and survey are necessary to ensure that wireless systems perform as anticipated.

NLOS Wireless: Overcoming Multipath Signals in NLOS High Speed

This section introduces one of the biggest challenges in wireless communications. Modulation methods, encoding methods, and mitigation techniques also are discussed.

Multipath Signals

A multipath signal is the composition of a primary signal plus duplicate or echoed images caused by reflections of signals off objects between the transmitter and receiver. In Figure 20-7, the receiver hears the primary signal sent directly from the transmission facility, but it also sees secondary signals that are bounced off nearby objects.

Figure 20-7 *Multipath Signal Reception*

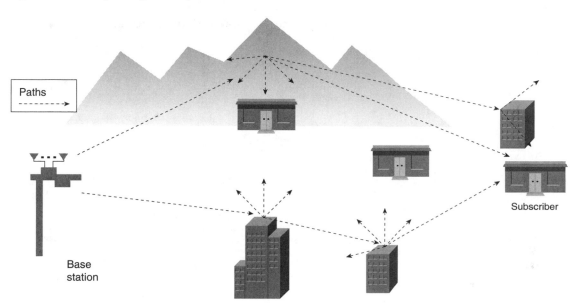

These bounced signals arrive at the receiver later than the incident signal. Because of this misalignment, the out-of-phase signals will cause intersymbol interference or distortion of the received signal. Although most of the multipath signals are caused by bounces off tall objects, multipath signals can also occur from bounces off low objects, such as lakes and pavement.

The actual received signal is a combination of a primary signal and several echoed signals. Because the distance traveled by the original signal is shorter than the bounced signal, the time differential causes two signals to be received. These signals overlap and combine into a single one. In real life, the time between the first received signal and the last echoed signal is called the delay spread. It can be as high as 4 μsec.

In Figure 20-8, the echoed signal is delayed in time and reduced in power. Both are caused by the additional distance that the bounced signal travels over the primary signal. The greater the distance, the longer the delay and the lower the power of the echoed signal. You might think that the longer the delay, the better off the reception would be. However, if the delay is too long, the reception of the echoed symbol (S1) and the primary symbol (S2) can also interact. Because there might not be a direct path for the incident signal in non-line-of-sight (NLOS) environments, the primary signal might be small in comparison to other secondary signals.

Figure 20-8 *Multipath Reception*

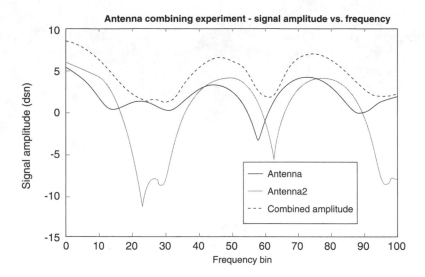

In analog systems, such as television, the human eye can actually see this multipath signals situation. Sometimes you see a ghost image on your television, and no matter how much you adjust the set, the image does not go away. In analog systems, this is an annoyance. In digital systems, it usually corrupts the data stream and causes loss of data or lower performance. Correction algorithms must be put into place to compensate for the multipath signals, resulting in a lower available data rate.

In digital systems, the input signal is sampled at the symbol rate. The echoed signal actually interferes with the reception of the second symbol, causing intersymbol interference (ISI). This ISI is the main result of multipath signals. Digital systems must be designed to deal with it.

Microwave Communication Links

Since the beginning of development of microwave wireless transmission equipment, manufacturers and operators have tried to mitigate the effects of reflected signals associated with signal propagation. These reflections are called multipath signals. In real-world situations, microwave systems involve careful design to overcome the effects of multipath signals. Most multipath signal mitigation approaches fall well short of the full reliable information rate potential of many wireless communications systems. This section discusses how to create a digital microwave transmission system that not only can tolerate multipath signals but that also can actually take advantage of them.

Digital microwave systems fall into two categories: wavelengths less than 10 GHz and wavelengths greater than 10 GHz (called millimeterwaves). Several bands exist below 10 GHz for high-speed transmissions. These may be licensed bands, such as MMDS (2.5 GHz), or unlicensed bands, such as U-NII (5.7 GHz). Bands that are below 10 GHz have long propagation distances (up to 30 miles). They are only mildly affected by climatic changes, such as rain. These frequencies are generally not absorbed by objects in the environment. They tend to bound and, thus, result in a high number of multipath signals.

Bands over 10 GHz, such as 24 GHz, LMDS (28 GHz), and 38 GHz, are very limited to distance (less than 5 miles). They are also quite susceptible to signal fades attributed to rain. Multipath signals tend not to be an issue because the transmission distances are less and because most of the multipath signal energy is absorbed by the physical environment. However, when these frequencies are used in highly dense urban areas, the signals tend to bounce off objects, such as metal buildings or metal window frames. The use of repeaters can add to the multipath signal propagation by delaying the received signal.

Multipath Signals in NLOS Environments

In LOS environments, multipath signals are usually minor and can be overcome easily. The amplitudes of the echoed signals are much smaller than the primary one and can be effectively filtered out using standard equalization techniques. However, in NLOS environments, the echoed signals might have higher power levels because the primary signal might be partially or totally obstructed and, generally, because more multipath signals are present. This makes the equalization design more difficult.

In all the previous discussions, multipath signals have been a semifixed event. However, other factors, such as moving objects, come into play. The particular multipath signals condition changes from one sample period to the next. This is called *time variation*. Digital systems must be capable of withstanding fast changes in multipath signal conditions, referred to as *fast fading*. To deal with this condition, digital systems need fast Automatic Gain Control (AGC) circuits. Adaptive equalizers, discussed next, need fast training times.

Modulation and Encoding Methods for QAM

Many modern fixed microwave communication systems are based on quadrature amplitude modulation (QAM). These systems have various levels of complexity.

Simpler systems, such as phase shift keying (PSK), are very robust and easy to implement because they have low data rates. In PSK modulation, the wave's shape is modified in neither amplitude nor frequency, but rather in phase. The phase can be thought of as a shift in time.

In binary phase shift keying (BPSK), the phases for the sine wave start at either 0 or 1/4. In BPSK modulation, only 1 bit is transmitted per cycle (called a symbol). In more-complex modulation schemes, more than 1 bit is transmitted per symbol. The modulation scheme quadrature phase shift keying (QPSK) is similar to BPSK. However, instead of only two separate phase states, QPSK uses four (0, 1/2, 1/4, and 3/2), carrying 2 bits per symbol. Like BPSK, QPSK is used because of its robustness. However, because it modulates only 2 bits per symbol, it still is not very efficient for high-speed communications. Hence, higher bit rates require the use of significant bandwidth.

Even though QPSK uses no state changes in amplitude, it is sometimes called 4-QAM. Four levels of amplitude combined with the four levels of phase result in 16-QAM. In 16-QAM, 2 bits are encoded on phase changes, and 2 bits are encoded on amplitude changes, yielding a total of 4 bits per symbol.

Figure 20-9 illustrates the modulation constellations for three common schemes—QPSK, 16-QAM, and 64-QAM.

In Figure 20-10, each unique phase is spaced equally in both the I and Q coordinates in the resulting modulation constellation. The angle of rotation indicates the phase, and the distance from the center point indicates the amplitude. This approach to modulation can be expanded to 64-QAM and 256-QAM or higher. Although 64-QAM is very popular in both cable and wireless broadband products, 256-QAM is also being tested. The higher the density in QAM, the higher signal-to-noise ratio (SNR) that must be maintained to meet the required bit error rates (BERs).

Figure 20-9   *QPSK, 16-QAM, and 64-QAM Modulation Constellations*

QPSK,16 QAM and 64 QAM Modulation Constellation

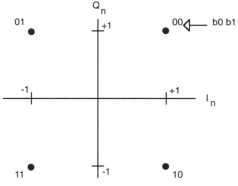

QPSK Signal Constellation.

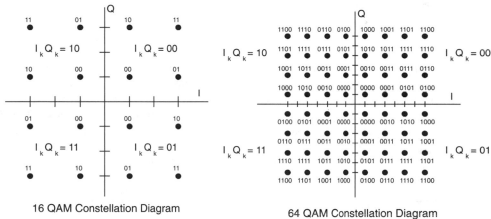

16 QAM Constellation Diagram

64 QAM Constellation Diagram

Figure 20-10 *Error Rates for PSK and QAM Systems*

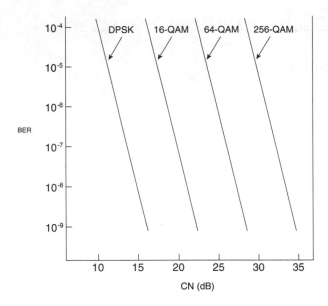

How the data is encoded also plays an important part in the equation. The data is usually scrambled, and a significant amount of forward error correction (FEC) data is also transmitted. Therefore, the system can recover bits that are lost because of noise, multipath signals, and interference. A significant improvement in BER is achieved using FEC for a given SNR at the receiver (see Figure 20-11).

Figure 20-11 *BER Against Signal-to-Noise for Coded and Uncoded Data Streams*

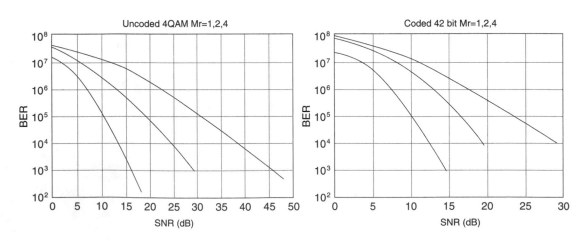

Advanced Signaling Techniques Used to Mitigate Multipath Signals

Several techniques make digital modulation schemes more robust: QAM with decision feedback equalization (DFE), direct sequence spread spectrum (DSSS), FDM, and orthogonal frequency-division multiplexing (OFDM).

QAM with DFE

In wireless QAM systems, DFE is used to mitigate the effects of ISI caused by multipath signals. When delay spread is present, the echoes of previous symbols corrupt the sampling instant for the current symbol. The DFE filter oversamples the incoming signal and filters out the echoed carriers. The complexity of DFE schemes causes them not to scale with increases in bandwidth. The complexity of the DFE filter (the number of taps) is proportional to the size of the delay spread. The number of required taps is proportional to the delay spread (in seconds) multiplied by the symbol rate.

For a QAM-based wireless system transmitting in the MMDS band (a 6-MHz-wide channel) to survive a 4-μsec delay spread, 24 taps are required. To equalize a system with 24 taps, a DFE system needs 72 feedforward and 24 feedback taps. In addition to the number of taps needed, the complexity of the math needed for each tap increases with the number of taps. Therefore, the increase in complexity becomes an exponential function of the carrier signal's bandwidth. Figure 20-12 compares the complexity rate of QAM/DFE and OFDM.

Figure 20-12 *Computational Complexity of QAM Versus OFDM*

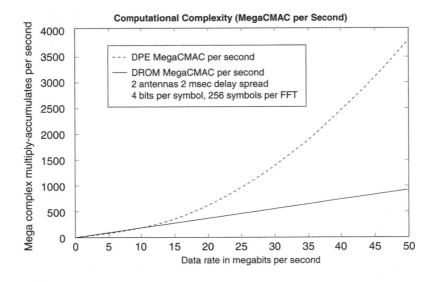

Spread Spectrum

Spread spectrum is a method commonly used to modulate information into manageable bits that are sent over the air wirelessly. Spread spectrum was invented by film actress Heddy Lamar, who received an award from the government for this accomplishment. She retains the patent to this day.

Essentially, spread spectrum refers to the concept of splitting information over a series of radio channels or frequencies. Generally, the number of frequencies is in the range of about 70, and the information is sent over all or most of the frequencies before being demodulated, or combined at the receiving end of the radio system.

Two kinds of spread spectrum are available:

- Direct sequence spread spectrum (DSSS)

- Frequency hopping spread spectrum (FHSS)

DSSS can provide higher data rates, with access rates up to 11 Mbps. FHSS systems can achieve 3 Mbps data rates. Because FHSS employs frequency-hopping schemes, more individual systems can exist in a given area without interfering with one another. However, direct sequence systems are more tolerant of local interference. When both systems use the same transmit power level, a DSSS system has a lower-power spectral density. This means that the same amount of power is radiated across a wider frequency range, which tends to lessen the effects on other local systems using the same frequency spectrum.

A commonly used analogy to understand spread spectrum is that of a series of trains departing a station at the same time. The payload is distributed relatively equally among the trains. When a train arrives at its destination, its payload is removed and collated. Duplications of payload are common in spread spectrum so that when data arrives excessively corrupted, or fails to arrive at all, the redundancies inherent in this architecture provide a more robust data link.

DSSS is a signaling method that avoids complexity and the need for equalization. Generally, a narrowband QPSK signal is used. This narrowband signal is then multiplied (or spread) across a much wider bandwidth. The amount of spectrum needed is expressed as 10 (SNR/10).

Therefore, if an SNR of 20 dB is required to achieve the appropriate BER, the total spread bandwidth needed to transmit a digital signal of 6 Mbps is 600 MHz.

This is not very bandwidth-efficient. In addition, the receiver's sampling rate needs to be about 100 times the data rate. Therefore, for this hypothetical system, the sampling rate also needs to be 600 megasamples per second.

With DSSS, all trains leave in an order beginning with Train 1 and ending with Train *N*, depending on how many channels the spread spectrum system allocates. In the DSSS architecture, the trains always leave in the same order, although the number of railroad tracks can be in the hundreds or even thousands.

Code division multiple access (CDMA) allows several simultaneous transmissions to occur. Each data stream is multiplied with a pseudorandom noise code (PN code). All users in a CDMA system use the same frequency band. Each signal is spread out and layered on top of each other and is overlaid using code spreading in the same time slot. The transmitted signal is recovered using the PN code.

Data transmitted by other users looks like white noise and drops out during the reception phase. Any narrowband noise is dispersed during the despreading of the data signal. The advantage of CMDA is that the amount of bandwidth required is shared over several users. However, in systems that have multiple transmitters and receivers, proper power management is needed to ensure that one user does not overpower other users in the same spectrum. These power-management issues are mainly confined to CMDA architectures.

FHHS

With the FHSS architecture, the trains leave in a different order—that is, not sequentially from Train 1 to Train N. In the best of FHSS systems, trains that run into interference are not sent out again until the interference abates. In FHSS systems, certain frequencies (channels) are avoided until the interference abates.

Interference tends to cover more than one channel at a time. Therefore, DSSS systems tend to lose more data from interference, because the data is sent over sequential channels. FHSS systems hop between channels in nonsequential order. The best FHSS systems adjust channel selection so that highly interfered channels are avoided, as measured by excessively low bit-error rates. Either approach is appropriate and depends on customer requirements, with the selection criteria primarily being that of severe multipath signals or an interfering RF environment.

FDM

In an FDM system, the available bandwidth is divided into multiple data carriers. The data to be transmitted is then divided among these subcarriers. Because each carrier is treated independently of the others, a frequency guard band must be placed around it. This guard band lowers the bandwidth efficiency. In some FDM systems, up to 50 percent of the available bandwidth is wasted. In most FDM systems, individual users are segmented to a particular subcarrier; therefore, their burst rate cannot exceed that subcarrier's capacity. If some subcarriers are idle, their bandwidth cannot be shared with other subcarriers.

OFDM

In OFDM (see Figure 20-13), multiple carriers (or tones) are used to divide the data across the available spectrum, similar to FDM. However, in an OFDM system, each tone is considered orthogonal (independent or unrelated) to the adjacent tones and, therefore, does not require a guard band. Because OFDM requires guard bands only around a set of tones, it is more efficient spectrally than FDM. Because OFDM is made up of many narrowband tones, narrowband interference degrades only a small portion of the signal and has little or no effect on the remainder of the frequency components.

Figure 20-13 *OFDM Tones*

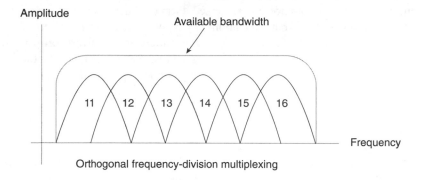

OFDM systems use bursts of data to minimize ISI caused by delay spread. Data is transmitted in bursts, and each burst consists of a cyclic prefix followed by data symbols. A typical OFDM signal occupying 6 MHz is made up of 512 individual carriers (or tones), each carrying a single QAM symbol per burst. The cyclic prefix absorbs transients from previous bursts caused by multipath signals. An additional 64 symbols are transmitted for the cyclic prefix.

For each symbol period, a total of 576 symbols are transmitted by only 512 unique QAM symbols per burst. In general, by the time the cyclic prefix is over, the resulting waveform created by the combining multipath signals is not a function of any samples from the previous burst. Hence, there is no ISI. The cyclic prefix must be greater than the delay spread of the multipath signals. In a 6-MHz system, the individual sample rate is $0.16\,\mu$secs. Therefore, the total time for the cyclic prefix is $10.24\,\mu$secs, greater than the anticipated $4\,\mu$secs delay spread.

VOFDM

In addition to the standard OFDM principles, the use of spatial diversity can increase the system's tolerance to noise, interference, and multipath signals. This is called vectored OFDM (VOFDM). Spatial diversity is a widely accepted technique for improving performance in multipath signal environments. Because multipath signals are a function of the collection of bounced signals, that collection is dependent on the location of the receiver antenna. If two or more antennas are placed in the system, each has a different set of multipath signals. The effects of each channel vary from one antenna to the next, so carriers that might be unusable on one antenna might be usable on another. Antenna spacing is at least 10 times the wavelength.

Significant gains in SNR are obtained by using multiple antennas. Typically, a second antenna adds about 3 dB in LOS environments and up to 10 dB in NLOS environments.

Elements of a Total Network Solution

The common elements of a total network solution are

- Premises networks
- Access networks
- Core networks
- Network management
- Deployment

Premises Networks

Premises networks are voice, data, or video distribution networks that exist or will exist within the subscriber premises. Typical points of demarcation between access and premises networks for the purposes of this discussion include channel banks, PBXs, routers, and multiservice access devices.

Customer premises equipment receives signals from the hub, translates them into customer-usable data, and transmits returning data back to the hub. The transmitter, the receiver, and the antenna are generally housed in a compact rooftop unit (RTU) that is smaller than a satellite TV minidish. It is mounted on the subscriber's roof in a location where it will have a clear LOS to the nearest LMDS hub site. Installation includes semiprecision pointing to ensure maximum performance of the RF link.

The indoor unit, the network interface unit (NIU), performs the modulation, demodulation, and in-building wire-line interface functions. It also provides an intermediate frequency to the RTU. Many interfaces required by end customer equipment require the NIU to have a breadth of physical and logical interfaces.

NIUs are designed to address a range of targeted subscribers whose connectivity requirements might include T1/E1, POTS, Ethernet, or any other standard network interface. The NIU provides these interfaces with interworking function (IWF) cards. Different types of IWF cards are required in the NIU to convert the inputs into ATM cells and provide the appropriate signaling. Common IWFs include 10BASE-T and T1/E1 circuit emulation. The NIU also has an IF that is translated by the CPE RTU.

Access Networks

Access networks are the transport and distribution networks that bridge the premises network and the core network demarcation points. For the purposes of this discussion, the primary means of providing the transport from an access network point of presence (POP) to the premises is radio, and the distribution between access network POPs is either fiber or radio.

Core Networks

Core networks are the public or private backbone networks that, in a general sense, the access network operators use to connect their multitude of regionally dispersed POPs and to interconnect to public service provider network elements. For the purposes of this discussion, the point of demarcation between the access network and the core network is a core switch that serves as an upstream destination point for a multitude of access network branches or elements.

Network Management

The glue that ties all the network elements together and supports the key information processing tasks that make a business run effectively is the Network Management System (NMS), which includes Operational Support System (OSS) functionality. In its full implementation, the NMS is an exceptionally complex set of moderately to highly integrated software platforms. For the purposes of this chapter, the element managers necessary within each system-level piece of the access network are assumed, but the overarching NMS is beyond the scope of this chapter.

Ideally, the NMS should provide end-to-end functionality throughout both the wireless and wireline elements of the network, including the backbone and the customer premises.

A network management system performs service, network, and element management across multivendor and multitechnology networks, including

- Topology management

- Connectivity management

- Event management

The functions of the network management system can be further outlined as follows:

- An integrated topology map that displays an entire set of nodes and links in the network, shown with mapped alarms

- A store of network-wide physical (nodes/links) and logical (circuits/PVCs) topology for inventory

- A customer care interface to provide network and end-user status
- Performance statistics on PCR, SCR, MBS, CDVT, and network/link status
- SLA reporting with customer partitioning and alerting of customer violations
- Alarm correlation and root-cause analysis
- A network simulation to test whether a problem was completely corrected
- Trouble ticketing/workforce management
- Performance reports based on statistics collected, with customer and network views
- Usage-based billing for ATM connections
- Read-only CNM for viewing network and connection

Deployment

Tier 1 customers use Cisco's ecosystem of deployment partners. Deployment for systems covering BTA, MTA, or nationwide footprints requires the following areas of expertise and resources:

- Construction (towers, masts)
- Licensing (FCC and local compliance for RF, construction, and access)
- Site survey (RF environment evaluation)
- Integration (selection and acquisition of various RF components)
- Prime (customer engagement through contract)
- Finance (securing or provisioning of project financing)
- Installation (assembly of components)
- Provisioning (spare components)
- Billing systems

Wireless Local-Area Networks (WLANs)

This section introduces what is most likely the fastest growing wireless technology today. The deployment of Wireless Local-Area Networks (WLANs) is quite common in many enterprises.

WLAN Overview

A WLAN is a data transmission system designed to offer traditional LAN service using a wireless physical layer. In September 1999, the IEEE ratified the 802.11b standard, which is the dominant WLAN standard. The IEEE 802.11 working groups continue working on the evolution of these standards.

The goal of 802.11b WLANs is to offer mobile users wired Ethernet-like performance, availability, and throughput, as well as freedom from the wired infrastructure.

Table 20-4 provides a brief comparison of WLAN standards.

Table 20-4   *A Brief Comparison of the Bluetooth and 802.11 WLAN Standards*

	Bluetooth	**802.11**
Physical layer	FHSS	FHSS, DSSS, infrared (IR)
Hop frequency	1600 hops per second	2.5 hops per second
Power output	100 MW	1 W
Data rates	1 Mbps	11 Mbps
Maximum number of devices supported	Up to 26	Up to 250
Security	0-bit, 40-bit, and 64-bit	40-bit to 128-bit RC4
Range	30 to 300 feet	400 feet indoors, 1000 feet LOS
Current version	V1.0	V1.0

Note the following in Table 20-4:

- 40-bit to 128-bit RC4 refers to data security algorithms.

- An 802.11 range of 1000 feet refers to outdoor conditions. Indoor conditions are more difficult for these types of RF systems.

- 802.11 power output of 1 W permitted by the FCC is substantial, although most 802.11 devices have a power output of 100 MW or less.

- The maximum number of devices supported depends on the data rate per device.

- The Cisco Aironet Products use 802.11.

Although three standards are in use in the U.S., and an additional two are in use in Europe (HyperLAN and HyperLAN2), the FCC thinks highly of the 802.11b standard, and a close relationship exists between the FCC and the IEEE, which backs the standard.

Table 20-5 lists the various 802.11 Working Groups.

Table 20-5   *802.11 Standard Working Groups*

Working Group	Technology Standard
802.11a	54 Mbps, 5 GHz, ratified in 1999
802.11b	11 Mbps, 2.4 GHz, ratified in 1999
802.11d	World mode and regulatory domains
802.11e	Quality of service
802.11f	Interaccess Point Protocol (IAPP)
802.11g	2.4 GHz, higher data rate (greater than 20 Mbps)
802.11h	Dynamic frequency allocation and transmit power control mechanisms
802.11i	Authentication and security

The 802.11 standard is composed of several components and services that interact to provide station mobility transparent to higher layers of the network stack.

The 802.11 WLAN defines two pieces of equipment:

- **Wireless LAN station or client**—The wireless station is the most basic component of a wireless network. A wireless LAN station is any piece of equipment that contains the 802.11 protocol functionality at both the MAC and physical layers and that has a connection to wireless media. Typically, the 802.11 protocol functionality is implemented in both the software and hardware of a Network Interface Card (NIC). A wireless station could be a PC, laptop, or handheld device.

- **Access point (AP)**—An access point acts as a bridge between the wireless and wired networks. An access point consists of a radio, a wired network interface (such as Ethernet or ATM), and bridging software. The access point acts as the base station for the wireless network, providing access to the wired network for multiple wireless stations. When an access point is present, all communication between wireless stations or between a wireless station and a wired network client go through the access point.

WLAN Architecture

The 802.11 architecture has five main components:

- Basic Service Set (BSS)
- Independent BSS
- Infrastructure BSS
- Distribution system
- Extended service set

The basic building block of an 802.11 wireless network is the BSS. It consists of wireless stations that communicate directly or indirectly with one another.

The independent BSS is the basic WLAN topology. It is a set of stations that recognize each other and establish communications in a peer-to-peer arrangement. Nodes communicate directly with one another and, therefore, must be within range of one another.

An infrastructure BSS has the added function of an access point. An access point allows clients that have connected to the WLAN to gain connectivity outside the WLAN when the access point is connected to the wired network. It also effectively doubles the radius of the wireless network, because two device that are connected at a maximum distance can communicate via the access point.

The distribution system is the wired network. It allows for backbone connectivity for access points.

An extended service set is the product of overlapping infrastructure BSSs, in which the access points can pass traffic via the distribution BSS. Clients that have associated with their respective APs thus can establish end-to-end communication.

The uniqueness of the WLAN technology exists at Layers 1 and 2 of the OSI model, the physical and data link layers, respectively. The 802.11 physical layer is the layer between the MAC layer and the wireless medium where frames are transmitted and received. The physical layer provides three functions.

The physical layer provides an interface to exchange frames with the MAC layer for transmission and reception of data. The physical layer uses signal carrier and spread spectrum modulation to transmit data frames over the wireless medium. The physical layer provides a carrier sense indication to the MAC layer to verify activity.

The 802.11 standard provides for the following physical layers:

- **Infrared**—Uses infrared light to transmit binary data at either 1 Mbps (the basic access rate) or 2 Mbps (the enhanced access rate).

- **FHSS**—Uses RF signals at 2.4 GHz to transmit data at 1 and 2 Mbps.

- **DSSS**—Uses RF signals at 2.4 GHz to transmit data at 1, 2, 5.5, and 11 Mbps.

The 802.11 MAC layer provides reliable data delivery for the upper layers over a wireless physical layer medium. Data delivery is based on asynchronous, best-effort, connectionless delivery. Here are the major attributes:

- There is no guarantee of successful delivery.

- The 802.11 MAC layer also provides a controlled access method to the shared wireless medium via Carrier Sense Multiple Access with Collision Avoidance (CSMA/CA). CSMA/CA is similar to the collision detection used by 802.3 Ethernet LANs.

- The 802.11 MAC layer also provides protection for the data being delivered by providing security and privacy services. Security is provided by both authentication and encryption.

Wired Equivalent Privacy (WEP) is defined as the 802.11 security protocol. Its goal is to achieve the level of security and privacy found in wired networks. RF communications are open, so transmissions can be intercepted. WEP is the feature used for data encryption between the client and access point. The minimum implementation is the use of a static 40-bit or 128-bit RC4 key. In the recent past, this encryption method had been compromised. This attack has been documented in white papers available on the Internet. This vulnerability is mitigated in the Cisco implementations by more-robust security measures. It is imperative that any network design consider the evaluation of network security in a WLAN environment.

Distribution Services

The distribution system must be able to offer certain services to clients of the WLAN. These distribution services are typically provided by access points. The five distribution services are

- Association
- Disassociation
- Reassociation
- Distribution
- Integration

The association service is responsible for the logical connections between an access point and a client. Each client must associate with an access point before it is allowed to send data through the access point into the distribution system. The connection is necessary for the distribution system to know where to send data to a particular client. The client typically forms an association service once, when the station enters the BSS. Each client can associate with one access point, but an access point can associate with multiple stations.

The disassociation service tears down an association between an access point and a client when that client no longer requires the services of the distribution system. When a station becomes disassociated, it must begin a new association to communicate with an access point again. The access point may force a client to disassociate because of resource restraints, because the access point is shutting down, or because the access point is no longer available. Clients disassociate when they leave a network. Disassociation is a notification and can be invoked by either associated party. Neither party can refuse termination of the association.

Reassociation lets a client change its current association with an access point, such as if it wants to again associate with an access point with which it was previously associated. The reassociation service is similar to the association service, but it includes information about the access point with which a mobile station has been previously associated.

Note that a client requires the reassociation service when it moves through the ESS, loses contact with the access point with which it is associated, and wants to become associated with a new access point. When reassociating, the client provides information to the access point it is about to associate with about the access point from which it is about to disassociate. The new associated access point contacts the previously associated access point to obtain data that might need to be forwarded to the client as well as other information relevant to the new association. The client always initiates reassociation.

The primary service used by an 802.11 client is the distribution service. A client uses the distribution service every time it sends data link layer MAC frames across the distribution system. The distribution service gives the client the necessary information to reach the proper destination BSS for its MAC frames. The three association services—association, reassociation, and disassociation—provide the necessary information for the distribution service to operate. Distribution within the distribution system does not necessarily involve any additional features outside the association services, but a client must be associated with an access point before the distribution service can successfully forward frames.

The integration service connects the 802.11 WLAN to other LANs, either wireless or wired. A network portal performs the integration service. The integration service allows for connectivity between these functionally unique local area networks.

Cisco Systems provides an array of hardware that enables feature-rich, scalable, wireless LAN solutions. Currently, 802.11a and 802.11b solutions are available. Access points, bridges, antennas, client adapters, and OSS and BSS solutions are offered.

The following list describes the Cisco Aironet family of WLAN devices:

- **Cisco Aironet 1200**—The Cisco Aironet 1200 series is the flagship of the Aironet line. It is the standard for next-generation high-performance, secure, manageable, reliable WLANs. It integrates seamlessly with an existing network as a wireless overlay or creates freestanding all-wireless networks, enabling mobility quickly and cost-effectively. The modular and upgradable platform protects current and future network infrastructure investments. Compliant with IEEE 802.11a and 802.11b standards, the Cisco Aironet 1200 series allows for both single- and dual-band configuration plus field upgradability to modify these configurations as your requirements and technology evolve. The Cisco Aironet 1200 series creates a wireless infrastructure that provides customers with maximum mobility and flexibility, enabling constant connection to all network resources from virtually anywhere wireless access is deployed.

- **Cisco Aironet 1100**—The Cisco Aironet 1100 series access point provides a secure, affordable, easy-to-use WLAN solution that combines mobility and flexibility with the enterprise-class features required by networking professionals. Taking advantage of the Cisco wireless security suite for the strongest enterprise security available and the Cisco IOS software for ease of use and familiarity, the Cisco Aironet 1100 series access point delivers manageability, performance, investment protection, and scalability in a cost-effective package with a low total cost of ownership. The Cisco Aironet 1100 series features a single, upgradable 802.11b radio, integrated diversity dipole antennas, and an innovative mounting system for easy installation in a variety of locations and orientations.

NOTE The preceding Aironet product descriptions are from the Cisco Systems Web site. For more information, see www.cisco.com/en/US/products/hw/wireless/index.html.

Summary

A basic understanding of wireless concepts is necessary to ensure that you make the correct choices when designing wireless networks. A good understanding of the basics is helpful when you're trying to understand an existing network that you might need to troubleshoot. When trying to determine higher-layer network behavior, the effect of the lower-layer network and its idiosyncrasies are very important.

In a new network design, it's important to determine the appropriate spectrum, as well as determine the ability of your network to coexist with other wireless communications. When you're trying to locate less-than-optimum performance in a wireless network, a solid understanding of the spectrum used is important.

Another critical design decision is selecting the hardware. Antenna, cable, and hardware selection are part of the design, and you must be careful to select the correct components based on the goals of your network design.

The limitations of NLOS communications and the methods available to overcome them are critical when you select a wireless technology. Modulation methods, schemes to more effectively enable the use of limited spectrum, and the prevention of interference are all considerations that must be factored into a design.

You must identify many components when developing a total network solution. Regardless of the equipment or technology choices, these are the end benefits of wireless deployment:

- **It completes the access technology portfolio**—Customers commonly use more than one access technology to service various parts of their network and during the migration phase of their networks, when upgrading occurs on a scheduled basis. Wireless lets a fully comprehensive access technology portfolio work with existing dial, cable, and DSL technologies.

- **It goes where cable and fiber cannot**—The inherent nature of wireless is that it doesn't require wires or lines to accommodate the data/voice/video pipeline. As such, the system carries information across geographic areas that are prohibitive in terms of distance, cost, access, or time. It also sidesteps the numerous issues of ILEC collocation.

  Although paying fees for access to elevated areas such, as masts, towers, and tops of buildings, is not unusual, these fees, the associated logistics, and contractual agreements are often minimal compared to the costs of trenching cable.

- **It involves reduced time to revenue**—Companies can generate revenue in less time through the deployment of wireless solutions than with comparable access technologies because a wireless system can be assembled and brought online in as little as two to three hours.

  This technology lets service providers sell access without having to wait for cable-trenching operations to complete or for incumbent providers to provide access or backhaul.

- **It provides broadband access extension**—Wireless commonly both competes with and complements existing broadband access. Wireless technologies play a key role in extending the reach of cable, fiber, and DSL markets, and they do so quickly and reliably. It also commonly provides a competitive alternative to broadband wireline or provides access in geographies that don't qualify for loop access.

Regardless of the provider of a wireless system, the fundamental elements remain relatively constant:

- Data or network
- Edge or access router
- DSP medium
- RF medium (coaxial, modulator/demodulator, antenna)
- RF management software

Like every access medium or technology, wireless has its pros and cons. Here are some of the pros:

- It's much less expensive to deploy than trenching for cabling.
- It's much quicker to deploy. A link can be up in a couple of hours.
- Wireless can go where cables can't, such as mountainous or inaccessible terrain.
- Less red tape is involved for deployment if roof rights or elevation access are available.

- It involves an inherent high degree of security, and additional security layers can be added.

- Wireless provides broadband mobility, portability that tethered access doesn't provide.

Review Questions

1 What are the main components of a wireless system?

2 What is the wavelength of an 850 MHz carrier?

3 What are some considerations when choosing a transmission line?

4 What are the two basic antenna types?

5 What does the acronym EIRP stand for?

6 What is a Fresnel zone?

7 What are multipath signals?

8 What are the five basic building blocks of an 802.11 reference architecture?

9 What five services does the distribution service offer?

10 What are four main benefits of using wireless technologies?

For More Information

- http://home.earthlink.net/~aareiter/introto.htm (guide to wireless Internet)

- http://http.cs.berkeley.edu/~gribble/cs294-7_wireless/summaries/index.html (UC Berkeley course in wireless)

- http://winwww.rutgers.edu/pub/Links.html (wireless links)

- www.airlinx.com/products.htm (RF product menu)

- www.allnetdevices.com/news/index.html (allNetDevices news)

- www.americasnetwork.com/issues/97issues/971001/100197_futurebb.html (broadband's evolution)

- www.broadbandforum.com (cable broadband forum)

- www.businesswire.com/cnn/wcii.htm (WinStar press releases)

- www.comet.columbia.edu/~angin/e6950/coolsites.html (wireless topics home page)

- www.ctimag.com/ (CTI newsletter)

- www.data.com/tutorials/web_connection.html (wireless web tutorial)
- www.dectweb.com/sitemap.htm (DECTweb)
- www.dnspublishing.com/rc/rcindex.cfm (reciprocal compensation site)
- www.ericsson.com/BN/dect2.html (Ericsson DECT)
- www.fcc.gov/Bureaus/Common_Carrier/Reports/FCC-State_Link/recent.html (FCC carrier data)
- www.fiberopticsonline.com (Fiberoptics Online)
- www.gbmarks.com/wireless.htm (Goodman's Wireless Telecomm links)
- www.globalwirelessnews.com/ (RCR Global Wireless News)
- www.herring.com/mag/issue48/comm.html (Ericsson's broadband plans)
- www.hometoys.com/htinews/oct99/articles/allied/allied.htm
- www.internettelephony.com (Internet telephony)
- www.internettelephony.com/archive/featurearchive/7.06.98.html (FSAN overview)
- www.it.kth.se/edu/gru/Fingerinfo/telesys.finger/Mobile.VT96/DECT.html (DECT)
- www.itu.int/imt/2-radio-dev/proposals/index.html (ITU world radio standards)
- www.mobilecomputing.com/ (mobile computing and communications)
- www.phonezone.com/tutorial/nextgen.htm (next-generation phone systems)
- http://www-star.stanford.edu/~osama/links.html (single-chip 2.4 GHz radio)
- www.tek.com/Measurement/App_Notes/ap-Wireless/welcome.html (wireless digital modulation)
- www.telecomweb.com/ct/ (Communications Today)
- www.ti.com/sc/data/wireless/panos1.pdf (wireless systems and technology overview)
- www.ti.com/sc/docs/wireless/cellterm.htm (glossary of wireless terms)
- www.tiap.org (guide to evolving wireless services)
- www.tr.com/ (Telecommunications Reports)
- www.trio.ca/annual/thrusts/mobsat.htm (Ontario, Canada wireless and mobile research)
- www.wapforum.org/what/technical.htm (WAP forum specs)
- www.webproforum.com/wpf_wireless.html (wireless tutorials)
- www.wirelessdata.org (wireless data forum)

- www.wirelessdata.org/news/currenttxt.asp (current newsletter)

- www.wirelessdesignonline.com (Wireless Design Online)

- www.wirelessweek.com/industry/indtoc.htm (Wireless Week industry information and statistics)

- www.wow-com.com/index.cfm (CTIA wireless web page: World of Wireless)

- www.wow-com.com/wirelesssurvey/1298datasurvey.pdf (1998 U.S. wireless survey)

- www.zdnet.com/anchordesk/story/story_1384.html (survey of access technologies by ZD Anchordesk)

- www.zdnet.com/intweek/print/971013/158897.html (October 1997 survey of access technologies)

Regulations and Government

- www.broadband-guide.com/lw/reg/index.html (Pennwell publications)

- www.commnow.com/3rd_Generation.html (article about TR-45 workshop on IMT-2000)

- www.fcc.gov/bandwidth/ (FCC bandwidth home page)

- www.itu.ch/imt/ (International Mobile Telecommunications-2000 [ITU R/T Initiative])

- www.ntia.doc.gov/osmhome/allochrt.html (U.S. spectrum chart)

WLL

- www.analysys.co.uk/publish/registered/locloop/default.htm#contents (LL competition)

- www.globaltelephony.com/archives/GT598/GT598cover.html (WLL cover feature)

- www.internettelephony.com/content/html/focus/feature1.html (February 1998 next-generation WLL)

- www.isir.com/wireless/ (WLL world)

- www.ntia.doc.gov/forums/wireless/index.html (WLL forum)

- www.verticom.com/cieee_1/index.htm (Steve Goldberg's IEEE talk on wireless LL)

- www.wavespan.com/solutions/ultraman.shtml (Wavespan Stratum 100)

LMDS/MMDS (Wireless Cable)

- http://businesstech.com/telecom/btfreetelecom9902.html (history of MMDS)
- http://grouper.ieee.org/groups/802/16/ (IEEE 802.16 BroadBand Fixed Wireless home page)
- http://nwest.nist.gov/ (Click News for current standards activity)
- http://nwest.nist.gov/tutorial_ets.pdf (a good LMDS context briefing)
- www.americasnetwork.com/issues/98issues/980801/980801_lmds.html
- www.americasnetwork.com/issues/99supplements/990601lmds/990601_toc.htm
- www.cabledatacomnews.com/wireless/cmic12.html (North American MMDS trials)
- www.fcc.gov/Bureaus/Wireless/Factsheets/lmds.html (FCC fact sheet on LMDS auction results)
- www.nmcfast.com (IBM and NewMedia partner in MMDS)
- www.teledotcom.com/1097/features/tdc1097telcos.html (BellSouth MMDS writeup)
- www.WCAI.com/index.htm (the WCA's home page for the Wireless Cable Association)
- www.webproforum.com/nortel4/ (Nortel tutorial on LMDS)
- www.zdnet.com/intweek/print/970630/inwk0009.html (broadband wireless alternatives)

Cordless

- www.broadband-guide.com/wi/techupdate/techupjf98.html (wireless in-building telephone systems)

Satellite

- http://sat-nd.com/news/ (satellite news)
- http://tcpsat.grc.nasa.gov/tcpsat/ (TCP over satellite WG)
- www.data.com/issue/990707/satellite.html (Internet satellite links)
- www.ee.surrey.ac.uk/Personal/L.Wood/constellations/ (the orbits)
- www.herring.com/mag/issue48/space.html (Loral portrait)
- www.iridium.com/index.html (Iridium home page)
- www.msua.org/mobile.htm (Mobile Satellite Users Association)

- www.project77.com Project77 (Iridium pricing)
- www.satphone.com/ (overview of programs)
- www.satphone.net (Iridium service provider satellite warehouse)
- www.skybridgesatellite.com/ (SkyBridge)
- www.skyreport.com/ (research and reporting for the satellite industry)
- www.spotbeam.com/links.htm (Internet and satellite links)
- www.spotbeam.com/mansum.htm (GEO summary)
- www.spotbeam.com/mansum99.htm (Internet and ISP summary)
- www.techweb.com/se/directlink.cgi?NWC19980315S0011 (satellite insecurity)
- www.techweb.com/se/directlink.cgi?NWC19980315S0017 (broadband Ka satellites)
- www.wizard.net/~vvaughn/sat.htm (satellite voice system comparisons)

Modulations

- http://diva.eecs.berkeley.edu/~linnartz/MCCDMA.html (OFDM definitions)
- http://propagation.jpl.nasa.gov/propdb/HELP/CLOUD.HTM (effects of clouds and rain)
- http://sss-mag.com/favlinks/index.html (many modulation links)
- http://wireless.stanford.edu/research.html (Stanford University wireless research)
- www.catv.org/modem/technical/ofdm.html (OFDM, the next upstream modulation)
- www.ee.mtu.edu/courses/ee465/groupe/index.html (CDMA class)
- www.gr.ssr.upm.es/~ana/ofdm_links.htm (OFDM sites)
- www.sm.luth.se/csee/sp/projects/ofdm/ofdm.html (OFDM description)

Interfaces

- http://cx667314-a.chnd1.az.home.com/1394Informer/990800.htm 1394 (news home page)
- http://skipstone.com/compcon.html (IEEE 1394 overview)
- http://www-europe.cisco.com/warp/public/459/8.html (HSSI)
- www.mfsdatanet.com/mfs-international/hssi.html (HSSI)
- www.sdlcomm.com/ (HSSI PCI module)

Glossary Terms

adjacent channel. A channel or frequency that is directly above or below a specific channel or frequency.

amplitude. The magnitude or strength of a varying waveform. Typically, this is represented as a curve along a graph's x-axis.

analog signal. The representation of information with a continuously variable physical quantity, such as voltage. Because of this constant change of the wave shape as it passes a given point in time or space, an analog signal may have a virtually indefinite number of states or values. This contrasts with a digital signal, which is expressed as a square wave and, therefore, has a very limited number of discrete states.

antenna. A device for transmitting or receiving a radio frequency (RF). Antennas are designed for specific and relatively tightly defined frequencies and are quite varied in design. An antenna for a 2.5 GHz (MMDS) system will not work for a 28 GHz (LMDS) design.

antenna gain. The measure of an antenna assembly performance relative to a theoretical antenna called an isotropic radiator (radiator is another term for antenna) when expressed in dBi. Certain antenna designs feature higher performance relative to vectors or frequencies.

bandwidth. The frequency range necessary to convey a signal measured in hertz (Hz). For example, voice signals typically require approximately 7 kHz of bandwidth, and data traffic typically requires approximately 50 kHz of bandwidth. A second meaning for the term bandwidth is the actual width or amount of spectrum used by a wireless system.

broadband. In general, an RF system is deemed broadband if it has a constant data rate at or in excess of 1.5 Mbps. Its corresponding opposite is narrowband.

broadcast. In general, this is the opposite of narrowcast and implies that a signal is sent to many points at the same time or is transmitted in an omnidirectional pattern.

BTA. Basic Trading Area. An area or footprint in which an entity is licensed to transmit its frequencies. BTAs were established by Rand McNally and are defined as county lines. Rand McNally licensed its mapping data to the FCC for ease of designation for site licenses.

CDMA. Code division multiple access. A transmission scheme that allows multiple users to share the same RF range of frequencies. In effect, the system divides a large set of frequencies into a smaller range and divides the data transmission among them. The transmitting device divides the data among a preselected set of nonsequential frequencies. The receiver then collates the various data pieces from the disparate frequencies into a coherent data stream. As part of the RF system setup, the receiver components are advised of the scrambled order of the incoming frequencies. An important aspect of this scheme is that the receiver system filters out any signal other than the ones specified for a given transmission.

channel. A communications path wide enough to permit a single RF transmission.

coaxial cable. A type of cable with a center conductor that is surrounded by a shield.

converter. RF systems have two fundamental frequencies: one that is sent over the air (carrier frequency), and one that is sent back and forth between Cisco equipment and the antennas (intermediate frequency). This is performed by a converter, also called an upconverter, downconverter, or transverter. The intermediate frequencies are split into a higher and lower frequency that are used for either transmission or reception of data between the antenna assembly and Cisco devices.

dB. Decibel. A unit for measuring relative power ratios in terms of gain or loss. Units are expressed in terms of the logarithm to base 10 of a ratio and typically are expressed in watts. dB is not an absolute value. Rather, it is the measure of power loss or gain between two devices. For example, a −3 dB loss indicates a 50 percent loss of power, and a +3 dB reading is a doubling of power. The rule of thumb is that 10 dB indicates an increase (or loss) by a factor of 10. Likewise, 20 dB indicates an increase (or loss) of a factor of 100, and 30 dB indicates an increase (or loss) of a factor of 1000. Because antennas and other RF devices/systems commonly have power gains or losses on the order of magnitude of 4, dB is a more easily used expression.

dBi. dB referencing an isotropic antenna (hence the "i") that is theoretically perfect in terms of symmetric patterns of radiation. Real-world antennas do not perform with even nominal amounts of symmetry, but this effect is generally used to the system designer's advantage.

dBm. dB referencing 1 milliwatt. 0 dBm is defined as 1 MW at 1 kHz of frequency at 600 ohms of impedance.

dBW. dB referencing 1 watt.

demodulator. A device for assembling signals after they have been received by an antenna. A demodulator is typically the first major device downstream from an antenna receiving system, and it exists on the block diagram before various Cisco devices. The corresponding device on the transmission side of a system is a modulator.

EIRP. Effective Isotropic Radiated Power. An expression of the performance of an antenna in a given direction relative to the performance of a theoretical (isotropic) antenna. This is expressed in watts or dBW. EIRP is the sum of the power sent to the antenna plus antenna gain.

electromagnetic spectrum. The full range of electromagnetic (same as magnetic) frequencies, the subset of which is used in commercial RF systems. Commercial RF systems are typically classified in ranges that include MF, HF, VHF, SHF, and EHF. Military systems typically include frequencies outside these types.

fixed wireless. The type of Cisco wireless in which neither the transmitter nor the receiver is mobile. Cisco wireless is always broadband wireless, with data rates in excess of 1.5 Mbps.

footprint. The geographic area in which an entity is licensed to broadcast its signal.

frequency reuse. One of the fundamental concepts on which commercial wireless systems are based. It involves partitioning an RF radiating area (cell) into segments. For Cisco purposes, this means that the cell is broken into three equal segments. One segment uses a frequency that is far enough away from the frequency in the bordering segment to prevent interference problems. The same frequency is used at least two cells apart from each other. This practice lets cellular providers have many times more customers for a given site license.

gain. The ratio of a signal's output amplitude to its input amplitude. This ratio is typically expressed in decibels. The higher the gain, the better the antenna receives or transmits, but also the more noise it includes.

license. The purchased right to transmit RF waves over a BTA is typically given for a ten-year period. The license tightly governs the design parameters of an RF system and its use. RF licenses are (typically) purchased from the FCC on an auction basis. The FCC provides licenses to ensure maximum competition in a free market (although this is not always obvious in how the FCC manages the auctions) and spectral efficiency, which is another way of saying efficient use of the RF spectrum.

LMDS. Local Multipoint Distribution Service. A relatively low-power license for broadcasting voice, video, and data. Typically, two licenses are granted in three frequencies, each to separate entities within a BTA. These licenses are known as Block A and Block B licenses. Block A licenses operate from 27.5 to 28.35 GHz, 29.10 to 29.25 GHz, and 31.075 to 31.225 GHz, for a total of 1.159 MHz of bandwidth. Block B licenses operate from 31.00 to 31.075 GHz and 31.225 to 31.300 GHz, for a total of 150 MHz of bandwidth. LMDS systems have a typical maximum transmission range of approximately 3 miles, as opposed to the transmission range of an MMDS system, which is typically 25 miles. This difference in range is primarily a function of physics and FCC-allocated output power rates.

LOS. Line of sight. Refers to the fact that there must be a clear, unobstructed path between transmitters and receivers. This is essential for LMDS products and enhances general performance in every RF deployment, compared to partial or completely obstructed data paths. The opposite of LOS is non-line-of-sight (NLOS).

MMDS. Multichannel Multipoint Distribution Service. As many as 33 discrete channels are transmitted in a pseudorandom order between the transmitters and receivers. The FCC has allocated two bands of frequencies for each BTA—2.15 to 2.161 GHz and 2.5 to 2.686 GHz.

mobile wireless. Cisco does not provide mobile wireless components. Instead, it provides backbone devices such as a GGSN that support mobile wireless infrastructures.

NLOS. Non-line-of-sight. Also known as obstructed path or pathway.

parabolic antenna. A dishlike antenna that sends RF waves in a highly focused manner. Such antennas provide very large power gains and are highly efficient. This antenna is typical of Cisco's LMDS, U-NII, and MMDS systems, but this is not the only design available or appropriate for those frequencies.

path loss. The power loss that occurs when RF waves are transmitted through the air. This loss occurs because the atmosphere filters the signal. Certain electromagnetic frequencies (very high and noncommercial) are completely blocked or filtered by the atmosphere.

point-to-multipoint. P2MP. Generally refers to the communication between a series of receivers and transmitters to a central location. Cisco P2MP is typically set up in three segments to enable frequency reuse. Cisco offers MMDS, U-NII, and LMDS systems in P2MP.

point-to-point. P2P. Has a higher bandwidth than P2MP because, among other things, it has less overhead to manage the data paths, and only one receiver exists per transmitter. Cisco offers MMDS, U-NII, and LMDS systems in P2P.

RF. Radio frequency. Generally refers to wireless communications with frequencies below 300 GHz.

TDMA. Time division multiplex access. A technique for splitting transmissions into time slots, which enables a greater number of users for a given frequency. A commonly used technique, as opposed to CDMA.

U-NII. Unlicensed National Information Infrastructure. Cisco offers a wireless product for this in the 5.7 GHz frequency. This frequency does not require the use or purchase of a site license, but, as with all electronic devices sold commercially, it does require registration with the FCC. NII is a term coined by federal regulators to describe citizens' and businesses' access to information. Equivalent to the term "information superhighway," it does not describe system architecture or topology.

Wireless Access Protocol. A language used for writing web pages that uses far less overhead, which makes it preferable for wireless access to the Internet. WAP's corresponding OS was created by 3COM for its Palm Pilot. Nokia recently adopted the Palm OS for its web-capable cellular phone.

Objectives

- Identify and discuss different types of digital subscriber line (DSL) technologies.

- Discuss the benefits of using xDSL technologies.

- Explain how ASDL works.

- Explain the basic concepts of signaling and modulation.

- Discuss additional DSL technologies (SDSL, HDSL, HDSL-2, G.SHDSL, IDSL, and VDSL).

CHAPTER 21

Digital Subscriber Line

Introduction

Digital Subscriber Line (DSL) technology is a modem technology that uses existing twisted-pair telephone lines to transport high-bandwidth data, such as multimedia and video, to service subscribers. The term *xDSL* covers a number of similar yet competing forms of DSL technologies, including ADSL, SDSL, HDSL, HDSL-2, G.SHDL, IDSL, and VDSL. xDSL is drawing significant attention from implementers and service providers because it promises to deliver high-bandwidth data rates to dispersed locations with relatively small changes to the existing telco infrastructure.

xDSL services are dedicated, point-to-point, public network access over twisted-pair copper wire on the local loop (last mile) between a network service provider's (NSP) central office and the customer site, or on local loops created either intrabuilding or intracampus. Currently, most DSL deployments are ADSL, mainly delivered to residential customers. This chapter focus mainly on defining ADSL.

Asymmetric Digital Subscriber Line

Asymmetric Digital Subscriber Line (ADSL) technology is asymmetric. It allows more bandwidth downstream—from an NSP's central office to the customer site—than upstream from the subscriber to the central office. This asymmetry, combined with always-on access (which eliminates call setup), makes ADSL ideal for Internet/intranet surfing, video-on-demand, and remote LAN access. Users of these applications typically download much more information than they send.

ADSL transmits more than 6 Mbps to a subscriber and as much as 640 Kbps more in both directions (shown in Figure 21-1). Such rates expand existing access capacity by a factor of 50 or more without new cabling. ADSL can literally transform the existing public information network from one limited to voice, text, and low-resolution graphics to a powerful, ubiquitous system capable of bringing multimedia, including full-motion video, to every home in the coming years.

Figure 21-1 *The Components of an ADSL Network Include a Telco and a CPE*

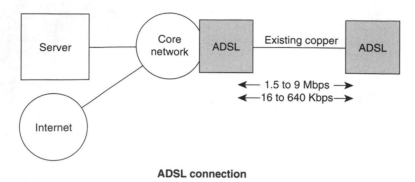

ADSL will play a crucial role over the next decade or more as telephone companies enter new markets for delivering information in video and multimedia formats. New broadband cabling will take decades to reach all prospective subscribers. Success of these new services depends on reaching as many subscribers as possible during the first few years. By bringing movies, television, video catalogs, remote CD-ROMs, corporate LANs, and the Internet into homes and small businesses, ADSL will make these markets viable and profitable for telephone companies and application suppliers alike.

ADSL Capabilities

An ADSL circuit connects an ADSL modem on each end of a twisted-pair telephone line, creating three information channels: a high-speed downstream channel, a medium-speed duplex channel, and a basic telephone service channel. The basic telephone service channel is split off from the digital modem by filters, thus guaranteeing uninterrupted basic telephone service, even if ADSL fails. The high-speed channel ranges from 1.5 to 9 Mbps, and duplex rates range from 16 to 640 Kbps. Each channel can be submultiplexed to form multiple lower-rate channels.

In ADSL networks, the filters are referred to as *Plain Old Telephone System Splitters*, or *POTS Splitters*. They function as band-pass filters for two distinct frequency ranges, above 15 KHz, and below 15 KHz. Their purpose is to effectively allow for the coexistence of both the lower-frequency voice and the higher-frequency modulated data signal on the same transmission line. This requires POTS splitters, or filters, at both the ADSL customer site and at the service provider's central office.

ADSL modems provide data rates consistent with North American T1 1.544 Mbps and European E1 2.048 Mbps digital hierarchies (see Figure 21-2), and can be purchased with various speed ranges and capabilities. The minimum configuration provides 1.5 or

2.0 Mbps downstream and a 16-Kbps duplex channel; others provide rates of 6.1 Mbps and 64 Kbps for duplex. Products with downstream rates up to 8 Mbps and duplex rates up to 640 Kbps are available today. ADSL modems accommodate Asynchronous Transfer Mode (ATM) transport with variable rates and compensation for ATM overhead, as well as IP protocols.

Figure 21-2 *This Chart Shows the Speeds for Downstream Bearer and Duplex Bearer Channels*

Downstream bearer channels	
n x 1.536 Mbps	1.536 Mbps
	3.072 Mbps
	4.608 Mbps
	6.144 Mbps
n x 2.048 Mbps	2.048 Mbps
	4.096 Mbps
Duplex bearer channels	
C channel	16 Kbps
	64 Kbps
Optional channels	160 Kbps
	384 Kbps
	544 Kbps
	576 Kbps

Downstream data rates depend on a number of factors, including the length of the copper line, its wire gauge, the presence of bridged taps, and cross-coupled interference. Line attenuation increases with line length and frequency, and decreases as wire diameter increases. Ignoring bridged taps, ADSL performs as shown in Table 21-1.

Table 21-1 *Claimed ADSL Physical-Media Performance*

Data Rate (Mbps)	Wire Gauge (AWG)	Distance (feet)	Wire Size (mm)	Distance (km)
1.5 or 2	24	18,000	0.5	5.5
1.5 or 2	26	15,000	0.4	4.6
6.1	24	12,000	0.5	3.7
6.1	26	9000	0.4	2.7

Two of the most destructive impairments in a DSL local loop environment are bridged taps and load coils.

A *bridged tap* is any portion of a loop that is not in the direct talking path between the CO and the service user's terminating equipment and that is unterminated. A bridged tap may be an unused cable pair connected at an intermediate point or an extension of the circuit beyond the service user's location. Line impairments, such as half-taps, shorts, or opens, will cause reflections, which degrades the reach, signal quality, and achievable data rate.

Load coils are used to modify the electrical characteristics of the local loop, allowing better quality voice-frequency transmission over extended distances (typically greater than 18,000 feet). In this extended-distance scenario, loading coils are placed every 6,000 feet on the line. Load coils are usually 88 millihenry (mH) inductors installed in cable splice cases or junction boxes. The load coils significantly improve the 3 kHz quality (frequency response) of long telephone cables, but effectively eliminate the ability of the cable to pass DSL frequencies. Load coils affect DSL frequencies by altering the inductive reactance of the transmission line.

Although the measure varies from telco to telco, these capabilities can cover up to 95 percent of a loop plant, depending on the desired data rate. Customers beyond these distances can be reached with fiber-based digital loop carrier (DLC) systems. As these DLC systems become commercially available, telephone companies can offer virtually ubiquitous access in a relatively short time.

Many applications envisioned for ADSL involve digital compressed video. As a real-time signal, digital video cannot use link- or network-level error control procedures commonly found in data communications systems. Therefore, ADSL modems incorporate forward-error correction that dramatically reduces errors caused by impulse noise. Error correction on a symbol-by-symbol basis also reduces errors caused by continuous noise coupled into a line. Two components of forward error correction are Reed-Solomon Coding and Byte Interleaving. Reed Solomon Coiding embeds overhead data bits in the forward direction, providing the receiving end with enough information to detect and correct errors, without the need for retransmission. Byte Interleaving takes the transmitted data stream and re-orders it in the time domain in order to mitigate the effect of short-duration impulse noise effects.

ADSL Technology

ADSL depends on advanced digital signal processing and creative algorithms to squeeze so much information through twisted-pair telephone lines. In addition, many advances have been required in transformers, analog filters, and analog/digital (A/D) converters. Long telephone lines may attcnuate signals at 1 MHz (the outer edge of the band used by ADSL) by as much as 90 dB, forcing analog sections of ADSL modems to work very hard to realize large dynamic ranges, separate channels, and maintain low noise figures. On the outside, ADSL looks simple—transparent synchronous data pipes at various data rates over ordinary telephone lines. The inside, where all the transistors work, is a miracle of modern technology. Figure 21-3 displays the ADSL transceiver–network end.

Figure 21-3 *This Diagram Provides an Overview of the Devices that Make Up the ADSL Transceiver-Network End of the Topology*

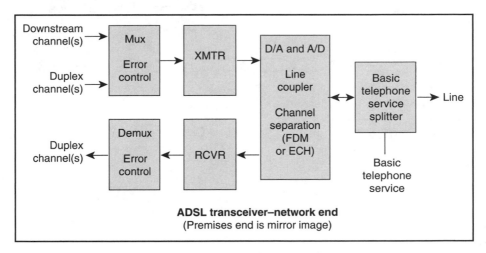

To create multiple channels, ADSL modems divide the available bandwidth of a telephone line in one of two ways: frequency-division multiplexing (FDM) or echo cancellation, as shown in Figure 21-4. FDM assigns one band for upstream data and another band for downstream data. The downstream path is then divided by time-division multiplexing into one or more high-speed channels and one or more low-speed channels. The upstream path is also multiplexed into corresponding low-speed channels. Echo cancellation assigns the upstream band to overlap the downstream, and separates the two by means of local echo cancellation, a technique well known in V.32 and V.34 modems. With either technique, ADSL splits off a 4-kHz region for basic telephone service at the DC end of the band.

Figure 21-4 depicts echo cancellation. Transmitting and receiving information using the same frequency spectrum creates interference within the single loop system itself. This interference differs from crosstalk because the offending transmit waveform is known to the receiver and can effectively be subtracted from the attenuated receive signals. Eliminating the effects of the transmitter is referred to as echo cancellation.

Figure 21-4 *Echo Cancellation*

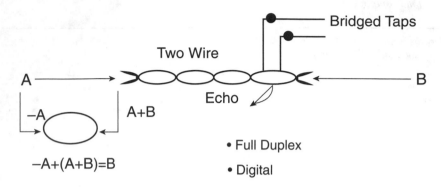

• Full-duplex Operation on a Two-wire Circuit

An ADSL modem organizes the aggregate data stream created by multiplexing downstream channels, duplex channels, and maintenance channels together into blocks, and it attaches an error correction code to each block. The receiver then corrects errors that occur during transmission, up to the limits implied by the code and the block length. At the user's option, the unit also can create superblocks by interleaving data within subblocks; this allows the receiver to correct any combination of errors within a specific span of bits. This, in turn, allows for effective transmission of both data and video signals.

Signaling and Modulation

This section includes the following:

• CAP and DMT Modulated ADSL

• ADSL Standards and Associations

CAP and DMT Modulated ADSL

DMT and *CAP* are line-coding methods for modulating the electrical signals sent over the copper wire in the local loop. Carrierless Amplitude and Phase (CAP) is a common line-coding method. CAP is a well-understood technology because of its similarity with QAM. Although CAP is well-understood and relatively inexpensive, some argue that it is difficult to scale because it is a single-carrier modulation technique and is susceptible to narrowband interference. Discrete Multi-Tone (DMT) uses multiple carriers. At this point, DMT is capable of more speed than CAP. This is one reason that the ANSI committee T1E1.4 accorded it standards status in document T1.413.

This standard calls for 256 subbands of 4 kHz each, thereby occupying 1.024MHz. Each subband can be modulated with QAM 64 for clean subbands, down to QPSK. If each of the subbands can support QAM-64 modulation, then the forward channel supports 6.1 Mbps. On the return path are 32 subbands, with a potential for 1.5 Mbps.

CAP and DMT Compared

CAP is a single-carrier technique that uses a wide passband. DMT is a multiple-carrier technique that uses many narrowband channels. The two have a number of engineering differences, even though, ultimately, they can offer similar service to the network layers discussed previously.

Adaptive Equalization

Adaptive equalizers are amplifiers that shape frequency response to compensate for attenuation and phase error. Adaptive equalization requires that the modems learn line characteristics and do so by sending probes and looking at the return signals. The equalizer then knows how it must amplify signals to get a nice, flat frequency response. The greater the dynamic range, the more complex the equalization. ADSL requires 50 dB of dynamic range, complicating adaptive equalization. Only with recent advances in digital signal processing (number crunching) has it become possible to have such equalization in relatively small packaging.

Adaptive equalization is required for CAP because noise characteristics vary significantly across the frequency passband. Adaptive equalization is not needed for DMT because noise characteristics do not vary across any given 4-kHz subband. A major issue in comparing DMT with CAP is determining the point at which the complexity of adaptive equalization surpasses the complexity of DMT's multiple Fourier transform calculations. This is determined by further implementation experience.

Power Consumption

Although DMT clearly scales and does not need adaptive equalization, other factors must be considered. First, with 256 channels, DMT has a disadvantage regarding power consumption (and, therefore, cost) when compared with CAP. DMT has a high peak-to-average power ratio because the multiple carriers can constructively interfere to yield a strong signal. DMT has higher computational requirements, resulting in more transistors than the transceiver chips. Numbers are mostly proprietary at this point, but it is estimated that a single transceiver will consume 5 W of power, even with further advances. Power consumption is important because hundreds or thousands (as carriers dearly hope) of transceivers might be at the central office, or CEV. This would require much more heat dissipation than CAP requires.

Latency

Another issue for DMT is that latencies are somewhat higher than with CAP (15). Because each subband uses only 4 kHz, no bit can travel faster than permitted by a QAM-64. The trade-off between throughput and latency is a historical one in data communications and has normally been settled in the marketplace.

Speed

DMT appears to have the speed advantage over CAP. Because narrow carriers have relatively few equalization problems, more aggressive modulation techniques can be used on each channel. For CAP to achieve comparable bit rates, it might be necessary to use more bandwidth, far beyond 1 MHz. This creates new problems associated with high frequencies on wires and would reduce CAP's current advantage in power consumption.

ADSL Standards and Associations

The American National Standards Institute (ANSI) Working Group T1E1.4 recently approved an ADSL standard at rates up to 6.1 Mbps (DMT/ANSI Standard T1.413). The European Technical Standards Institute (ETSI) contributed an annex to T1.413 to reflect European requirements. T1.413 currently embodies a single terminal interface at the premises end. Issue II expands the standard to include a multiplexed interface at the premises end, protocols for configuration and network management, and other improvements.

The ATM Forum and the Digital Audio-Visual Council (DAVIC) have both recognized ADSL as a physical layer transmission protocol for UTP media.

Additional DSL Technologies

This section discusses the following DSL technologies:

- SDSL
- HDSL
- HDSL-2
- G.SHDSL
- ISDN Digital Subscriber Line (DSL)
- VDSL

SDSL

Symmetric Digital Subscriber Line (SDSL) is a rate-adaptive version of HDSL and, like HDSL, is symmetric. It allows equal bandwidth downstream from an NSP's central office to the customer site as upstream from the subscriber to the central office. SDSL supports data only on a single line and does not support analog calls. SDSL uses 2B1Q line coding and can transmit up to 1.54 Mbps to and from a subscriber, or can be configured to offer a variable range of bandwidth up to 1.45 Mbps.

NOTE   *Two Binary, One Quaternary* is a line-coding technique that compresses two binary bits of data into one time state as a four-level code.

The symmetry that SDSL offers, combined with always-on access (which eliminates call setup), makes it a favorable WAN technology for small to medium businesses and branch offices, and can be an affordable alternative to dedicated leased lines and Frame Relay services. Because traffic is symmetrical, file transfer, web hosting, and distance-learning applications can effectively be implemented with SDSL.

HDSL

Originally developed by Bellcore, high bit-rate DSL (HDSL)/T1/E1 technologies have been standardized by ANSI in the United States and by ETSI in Europe. The ANSI standard covers two-pair T1 transmission, with a data rate of 784 Kbps on each twisted pair. ETSI standards exist both for a two-pair E1 system, with each pair carrying 1168 Kbps, and a three-pair E1 system, with 784 Kbps on each twisted pair.

HDSL became popular because it is a better way of provisioning T1 or E1 over twisted-pair copper lines than the long-used technique known as Alternative Mark Inversion (AMI). HDSL uses less bandwidth and requires no repeaters up to the CSA range. By using adaptive line equalization and 2B1Q modulation, HDSL transmits at 1.544 Mbps or 2.048 Mbps.

AMI is a *synchronous* clock-encoding technique that uses bipolar pulses to represent logical 1 values. It is, therefore, a three-level system. A logical 0 is represented by no symbol, and a logical 1 is represented by pulses of alternating polarity. AMI coding was used extensively in first-generation PCM networks, but suffers the drawback that a long run of 0s produces no transitions in the data stream and, therefore, does not contain sufficient transitions to guarantee lock of a DPLL.

T1 service can be installed in a day for less than $1,000 by installing HDSL modems at each end of the line. Installation via AMI costs much more and takes more time because of the requirement to add repeaters between the subscriber and the central office (CO). Depending on the length of the line, the cost to add repeaters for AMI could be up to $5,000 and could take more than a week. HDSL is heavily used in cellular telephone buildouts. Traffic from the base station is backhauled to the CO using HDSL in more than 50 percent of installations. Currently, the vast majority of new T1 lines are provisioned with HDSL. However, because of the embedded base of AMI, less than 30 percent of existing T1 lines are provisioned with HDSL.

HDSL does have drawbacks. First, no provision exists for analog voice because it uses the voice band. Second, ADSL achieves better speeds than HDSL because ADSL's asymmetry deliberately keeps the crosstalk at one end of the line. Symmetric systems, such as HDSL, have crosstalk at both ends.

HDSL-2

HDSL-2 is an emerging standard and a promising alternative to HDSL. The intention is to offer a symmetric service at T1 speeds using a single-wire pair rather than two pairs. This will enable it to operate for a larger potential audience. It will require more aggressive modulation, shorter distances (about 10,000 feet), and better phone lines.

Much of the SDSL equipment in the market today uses the 2B1Q line code developed for Integrated Services Digital Network. The Bell companies have insisted that using this SDSL at speeds higher than 768 Kbps can cause interference with voice and other services that are offered on copper wire within the same wire bundle.

The biggest advantage of HDSL-2, which was developed to serve as a standard by which different vendors' equipment could interoperate, is that it is designed not to interfere with other services. However, HDSL-2 is full rate only, offering services only at 1.5 Mbps.

G.SHDSL

G.SHDSL is a standards-based, multirate version of HDSL-2 and offers symmetrical service. The advantage of HDSL-2, which was developed to serve as a standard by which different vendors' equipment could interoperate, is that it is designed not to interfere with other services. However, the HDSL-2 standard addresses only services at 1.5 Mbps. Multirate HDSL-2 is part of Issue 2 of the standard known as G.SHDSL, and is ratified by the ITU. G.SHDSL builds upon the benefits of HDSL-2 by offering symmetrical rates of 2.3 Mbps.

ISDN Digital Subscriber Line

ISDN digital subscriber line (IDSL) is a cross between ISDN and xDSL. It is like ISDN in that it uses a single-wire pair to transmit full-duplex data at 128 Kbps and at distances of up to RRD range. Like ISDN, IDSL uses a 2B1Q line code to enable transparent operation through the ISDN "U" interface. Finally, the user continues to use existing CPE (ISDN BRI terminal adapters, bridges, and routers) to make the CO connections.

The big difference is from the carrier's point-of-view. Unlike ISDN, IDSL does not connect through the voice switch. A new piece of data communications equipment terminates the IDSL connection and shuts it off to a router or data switch. This is a key feature because the overloading of central office voice switches by data users is a growing problem for telcos.

The limitation of IDSL is that the customer no longer has access to ISDN signaling or voice services. But for Internet service providers, who do not provide a public voice service, IDSL is an interesting way of using POTS dial service to offer higher-speed Internet access, targeting the embedded base of more than five million ISDN users as an initial market.

VDSL

Very-High-Data-Rate Digital Subscriber Line (VDSL) transmits high-speed data over short reaches of twisted-pair copper telephone lines, with a range of speeds depending on actual line length. The maximum downstream rate under consideration is between 51 and 55 Mbps over lines up to 1000 feet (300 m) in length. Downstream speeds as low as 13 Mbps over lengths beyond 4000 feet (1500 m) are also common. Upstream rates in early models will be asymmetric, just like ADSL, at speeds from 1.6 to 2.3 Mbps. Both data channels will be separated in frequency from bands used for basic telephone service and ISDN, enabling service providers to overlay VDSL on existing services. Currently, the two high-speed channels are also separated in frequency. As needs arise for higher-speed upstream channels or symmetric rates, VDSL systems may need to use echo cancellation.

Summary

ADSL technology is asymmetric, allowing more bandwidth for downstream than upstream data flow. This asymmetric technology combined with always-on access makes ADSL ideal for users who typically download much more data than they send.

An ADSL modem is connected to both ends of a twisted-pair telephone line to create three information channels: a high-speed downstream channel, a medium-speed duplex channel, and a basic telephone service channel. ADSL modems create multiple channels by dividing the available bandwidth of a telephone line using either frequency-division multiplexing (FDM) or echo cancellation. Both techniques split off a 4-kHz region for basic telephone service at the DC-end of the band.

Synchronous Digital Subscriber Line (SDSL) provides variable, symmetric, high-speed data communication up to 1.54 Mbps. But SDSL doesn't allow analog on the same line, as ADSL does. SDSL uses 2B1Q line coding, a technology employed in ISDN and T1 services. SDSL is a viable business option because of its capability of transmitting high-speed data over longer distances from the CO and because of its ease of deployment made possible by its spectral compatibility.

High Bit-Rate DSL (HDSL) is a symmetric version of DSL that uses 2B1Q like SDSL, but over two-wire pairs. HDSL is targeted at business deployment because it offers full-rate symmetrical 1.5 Mbps service. HDSL-2 is a standards-based version of HDSL offering symmetrical 1.5 Mbps service like HDSL, but with a single twisted pair of wires. HDSL is full-rate and does not offer variable rates.

G.SHDSL does offer multirate service with symmetrical speeds of up to 2.3 Mbps. ISDN digital subscriber line (IDSL) is similar in many ways to ISDN. The primary difference is that IDSL is always on and can reach speeds up to 512 Kbps with compression. IDSL uses 2B1Q line coding and does not support analog. On the other hand, IDSL does allow data communications over longer distances than other DSL options (up to 26,000 feet) and is considerably less expensive than ISDN service, in most cases. Because IDSL supports existing ISDN CPE, it makes it easy to convert from ISDN to IDSL. Very-High-Data-Rate Digital Subscriber Line (VDSL) transmits high-speed data over short distances through twisted-pair copper telephone lines. VDSL technology is still in the definition stage, but additional research is required before it can be standardized. VSDL and ADSL are similar technologies. However, although VSDL transmits data at nearly 10 times the rate of ADSL, ADSL is the more complex transmission technology.

Review Questions

1   Name the current versions of DSL technology.

2   What are the two-line coding methods used for ADSL?

3   Which versions of DSL offer symmetrical service?

4   What symmetrical version of DSL offers multirate service over a single pair of wire?

5   How far of a reach can IDSL achieve from the CO?

6   What downstream and upstream rates are proposed for VDSL?

For More Information

- ADSL Forum (www.adsl.com/)

- Cisco DSL Depot (www.cisco.com/warp/public/779/servpro/promotions/dsldepot/)

Objectives

- Understand hybrid fiber coax (HFC) networking concepts as a viable data medium.

- Identify and characterize dominant HFC limitations associated with Data Over Cable Service Interface Specifications (DOCSIS) data transmission.

- Understand the (DOCSIS) standard for data transport over Cable Television System (CATV).

- Become familiar with DOCSIS hardware deployment and resulting capabilities.

- Become aware of future applications of the DOCSIS standard to support advanced services.

CHAPTER 22

Cable Access Technologies

Introduction

Historically, CATV has been a unidirectional medium designed to carry broadcast analog video channels to the maximum number of customers at the lowest possible cost. Since the introduction of CATV more than 50 years ago, little has changed beyond increasing the number of channels supported. The technology to provide high-margin, two-way services remained elusive to the operator.

During the 1990s, with the introduction of direct broadcast satellite (DBS) and digital subscriber line (DSL), the cable operators experienced a serious challenge to their existence by competing technologies threatening to erode market share of their single product.

DBS operators marketed more choice and better quality entertainment product through digital technology, whereas the incumbent local exchange carriers (ILEC) proposed to offer a combination of voice, video, and data by means of DSL.

Fearing loss of market share and the need to offer advanced services to remain economically viable, key multiple system operators (MSOs) formed the Multimedia Cable Network System Partners, Ltd. (MCNS), with the purpose of defining a product and system standard capable of providing data and future services over CATV plants. MCNS proposed a packet-based (IP) solution in contention with a cell-based (ATM) solution promoted by IEEE 802.14. MCNS partners included Comcast Cable Communications, Cox Communications, Tele-Communications Inc., Time Warner Cable, MediaOne, Rogers CableSystems, and Cable Television Laboratories (CableLabs).

The Data Over Cable Service Interface Specification (DOCSIS) 1.0 standard that resulted from the MCNS effort was unanimously accepted as the North American standard, and vendors aggressively introduced products in compliance with this standard. MSOs defined upgrade and construction programs to increase the supporting bandwidth of their plants and to provide two-way functionality.

The DOCSIS 1.0 standard prescribes multivendor interoperability and promotes a retail model for the consumer's direct purchase of a cable modem (CM) of choice. To ensure multivendor interoperability, CableLabs subjects all products offered to rigorous testing. Equipment successfully passing all tests will be CableLabs Qualified for head-end Cable Modem Terminating System (CMTS), and CableLabs Certified for CM devices.

To date, the DOCSIS 1.0 standard is proving to be a universal success, with deployments now in operation worldwide.

CableLabs, in conjunction with the vendor and user communities, has recently defined DOCSIS 1.1. With the enhancements to the protocol, it is now more capable of supporting Voice Over Internet Protocol (VoIP) and advanced security, and is also paving the way for advanced future multimedia services.

Evolution from One-Way Broadcast to Two-Way Hybrid Fiber Coax

A CATV network consists of a *head-end* location where all incoming signals are received and, regardless of their source, frequency-division multiplexing (FDM) is applied, amplified, and transmitted *downstream* for distribution to the complete cable plant.

Original CATV networks, as shown in Figure 22-1, were exclusively one-way, comprised of diverse amplifiers in cascade to compensate for the intrinsic signal loss of the coaxial cable in series with taps to couple video signal from the main trunks to subscriber homes via drop cables.

Figure 22-1 *A Simple, One-Way Video Broadcast Topology Using Coaxial Cabling Exclusively*

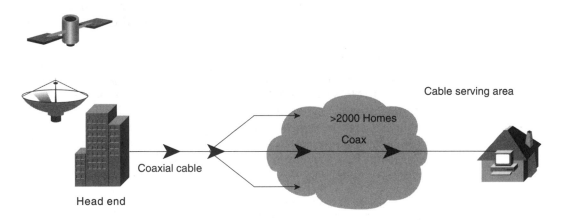

Besides being unidirectional, the long amplifier cascades resulted in a system with high noise that was inherently unreliable and failure-prone, in addition to being susceptible to lightning strikes and ingress noise from foreign radio frequency (RF) signals.

Ingress noise is unwanted electmagnetic energy that enters the Hybrid-Fiber Coax (HFC) plant. The result of this is to raise the noise floor of this transmission system, which is meant to be a closed system. This causes devices to transmit at higher power levels to achieve the same performance. Some sources of ingress noise are unterminated taps, loose connectors and fittings, and faulty equipment.

The first significant improvement to the CATV plant was the introduction of fiber-optic technology and the advent of the HFC plant (see Figure 22-2).

Figure 22-2 *Simple HFC Distribution Network*

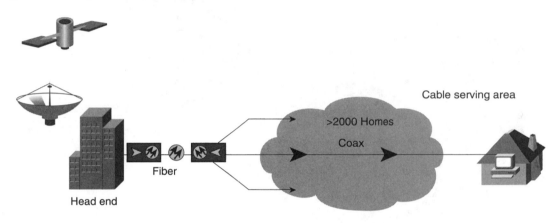

Portions of the coaxial cable and supporting amplification elements are replaced with multifiber optic cable from a head end or hub location. The aggregated video signal is used to modulate a downstream laser, which transmits the optical signal to an optical node, which, in turn, converts the signal from an optical to an electrical signal that can then be propagated downstream to the entire customer serving area.

It can be readily seen that the introduction of the fiber can significantly reduce the number of cascaded amplifiers consequently improving system reliability, the signal-to-noise ratio (SNR) of the downstream video signal, and potential system bandwidth. In addition, this makes the system ready for the next step to two-way operation. As an added benefit, HFC reduces operational and maintenance costs, and improves the immunity of the system to ingress noises.

Two-way operation is achieved by the addition of requisite upstream amplifiers in the amplifier housings, the addition of a narrow-band upstream laser in the optical node, a dedicated upstream fiber to the head end, and a compatible optical receiver to convert any upstream information to an electrical signal. When all components are in place, proper return path alignment is required.

By means of adding an optical RING topography, the cable network affords greater reliability, supports greater bandwidth with the capability to transport more information, and is ready to support two-way operation by the simple addition of requisite components, as illustrated in Figure 22-3.

Figure 22-3 *Advanced HFC Network with Ring Topography*

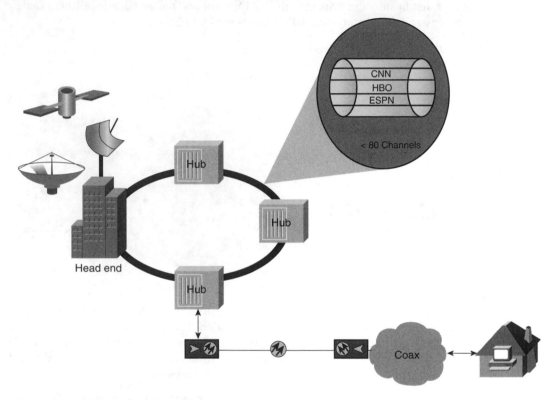

Network robustness, scalability, and flexibility is further improved by the introduction of the intermediate hub from which advanced services can ultimately be launched.

The HFC network and topography as outlined become the basic building blocks for developing access transport capabilities needed by the MSOs to compete in the dynamic communication environment.

Limitations and Specifications of the HFC Plant

The HFC network has the potential to offer tremendous bandwidth in the downstream or forward direction from the head end or hub to the customer. Depending upon the extent of the plant upgrade, the available bandwidth could be as much as from 54 to 860 MHz. Downstream channel bandwidths are determined by the individual country's video broadcast standards.

The historical broadcast video channel assignments limit the upstream or reverse direction from the customer to the spectrum between 5 to 42 MHz. This upstream spectrum is frequently hostile to return-path connectivity due to the ingress of foreign interfering signals, such as ham radio citizen band (CB), among other legitimate RF emissions.

Table 22-1 summarizes the specifications for the downstream direction, and Table 22-2 summarizes the specifications for the upstream direction.

A DOCSIS system must provide greater than 99 percent availability when forwarding 1500-byte packets at the rate of at least 100 packets per second. To achieve these criteria, certain CATV performance specifications are mandated on both the upstream and downstream spectrum.

Table 22-1 *Downstream Cable Specifications*

Downstream Parameter	Assumes nominal analog video carrier level (peak envelope power) in a 6-MHz channel with all conditions present concurrently and referenced to frequencies greater than 88 MHz
RF channel spacing (BW)	6 MHz
Transit delay, CMTS to most distant customer	Less than or equal to 0.800 ms
CNR in a 6-MHz band	Not less than 35 dB (analog video level)
C/I ratio for total power (discrete and broadband ingress signals)	Not less than 35 dB within the design BW
Composite triple-beat distortion for analog-modulated carriers	Not greater than 50 dBc within the design BW
Composite second-order distortion for analog-modulated carriers	Not greater than 50 dBc within the design BW
Cross-modulation level	Not greater than 40 dBc within the design BW
Amplitude ripple	0.5 dB within the design BW
Group delay ripple in the spectrum occupied by the CMTS	75 ns within the design BW

continues

Table 22-1   *Downstream Cable Specifications (Continued)*

Downstream Parameter	Assumes nominal analog video carrier level (peak envelope power) in a 6-MHz channel with all conditions present concurrently and referenced to frequencies greater than 88 MHz
Microreflections bound for dominant echo	10 dBc at less than or equal to 0.5 ms
	15 dBc at less than or equal to 1.0 ms
	20 dBc at less than or equal to 1.5 ms
	30 dBc at less than or equal to 1.5 ms
Carrier hum modulation	Not greater than 26 dBc (5 percent)
Burst noise	Less than 25 ms at a 10 Hz average rate
Seasonal and diurnal signal level variation	8 dB
Signal level slope (50 to 750 MHz)	16 dB
Maximum analog video carrier level at the CM input, inclusive of above signal level variations	17 dBmV
Lowest analog video carrier level at the CM input, inclusive of above signal level variation	5 dBmV

Good engineering, design, and maintenance practices for CATV plants ensure that these traditional video parameters can easily be met and maintained for operational systems. Parameters of primary concern, however, relate to signal level and noise.

Table 22-2   *Upstream Cable Specifications*

Upstream	Assumes all conditions present concurrently
Frequency range	5 to 42 MHz, edge to edge
Transit delay, most distant CM to nearest CM or CMTS	Less than or equal to 0.800 ms
Carrier-to-noise ratio	Not less than 25 dB
Carrier-to-ingress power (the sum of discrete and broadband ingress signals) ratio	Not less than 25 dB
Carrier-to-interference (the sum of noise, distortion, common path distortion, and cross-modulation) ratio	Not less than 25 dB
Carrier hum modulation	Not greater than 23 dBc (7 percent)
Burst noise	Not longer than 10 ms at a 1 kHz average rate for most cases

Table 22-2   *Upstream Cable Specifications (Continued)*

Upstream	Assumes all conditions present concurrently
Amplitude ripple	0.5 dB/MHz (5 42 MHz)
Group delay ripple	200 ns/MHz (5 42 MHz)
Microreflections: single echo	10 dBc at less than or equal to 0.5 ms
	20 dBc at less than or equal to 1.0 ms
	20 dBc at less than or equal to 1.0 ms
Seasonal and diurnal signal level variation	Not greater than 8 dB min to max

The greater challenge for the operator is to realize sufficient usable upstream bandwidth to achieve the systems throughput requirements for data or other services. The limited upstream bandwidth must often be shared with other services, ranging from impulse pay-per-view (IPPV), telemetry, and alarm gathering information from the active elements in the cable plant, as well as having to compete with interfering signals that radiate into the lower frequency range.

Because of the limited and often-hostile upstream bandwidth, the hardware design must implement diverse countermeasures to mitigate the effects of both fixed and transient harmful noise. In addition, the network designer must choose from the available remaining spectrum and often must implement bandwidth compromises for a DOCSIS deployment.

A combination of upstream signal quality measured by carrier-to-noise ratio (CNR), anticipated market penetration, services offered, and available upstream spectrum will ultimately dictate the physical configuration of the return-path physical layer.

DOCSIS Standards, Signaling Protocols, and Applications

The DOCSIS interface specifications enabled the development and deployment of data-over-cable systems on a nonproprietary, multivendor, interoperable basis for transparent bidirectional transfer of Internet Protocol (IP) traffic between the cable system head end and customer locations over an all-coaxial or HFC cable network.

The system consists of a CMTS located at the head end, a coaxial or HFC medium, and a CM located at the premises of the customer, in conjunction with DOCSIS-defined layers that support interoperability and evolutionary feature capabilities to permit future value-added services.

DOCSIS layer definitions are as follows:

- IP network layer
- Data link layer comprised of:
  - Logical Link Control (LLC) sublayer conforming to Ethernet standards
  - Link security sublayer for basic privacy, authorization, and authentication
  - Media Access Control (MAC) sublayer for operation supporting variable-length protocol data units (PDU) and featuring:
    - CMTS control of contention and reservation transmission opportunities
    - A stream of minislots in the upstream
    - Bandwidth efficiency through variable-length packets
    - Extensions for the future support of Asynchronous Transfer Mode (ATM) or other types of PDU
    - Support for multiple grade of service and wide range of data rates
- Physical (PHY) layer comprised of:
  - Downstream convergence layer conforming to MPEG-2 (Rec. H.222.0)
  - Physical Media Dependent (PMD) sublayer for:
    - Downstream based on ITU-T Rec J.83 Annex B with either 64 or 256 quadrature amplitude modulation (QAM), concatenation of Reed-Solomon and Trellis forward-error correction (FEC), in addition to variable-depth interleaving
    - Upstream, employing:
      - Quadrature phase shift keying (QPSK) or 16 QAM
      - Support for multiple symbol rates
      - CM controlled and programmable from the CMTS
      - Frequency agility
      - Support for fixed-frame and variable-length PDU formats
      - Time-division multiple access (TDMA), which works by dividing a radio frequency into time slots and then allocating slots to multiple calls. In this way, a single frequency can support multiple, simultaneous data channels.
      - Programmable Reed-Solomon FEC and preambles
      - Capability to support future physical layer technologies

In addition, the specification defines means by which a CM can self-discover the appropriate upstream and downstream frequencies, bit rates, modulation format, error correction, and power levels. To maintain equitable service levels, individual CMs are not allowed to transmit except under defined and controlled conditions.

The DOCSIS layers are represented by Figure 22-4 and are compared with the classic OSI layer.

Figure 22-4 *DOCSIS and OSI Protocol Layers*

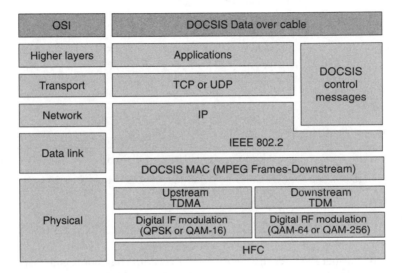

The DOCSIS physical layer permits considerable flexibility to ensure quality transmission can be achieved over cable plants of varying quality. Of significance are the optional upstream channel bandwidths and modulation choices available for both the upstream and downstream signal flows.

Based upon bandwidth and modulation options, in addition to DOCSIS-specified symbol rates, the total and effective data rates of DOCSIS facilities are summarized in Tables 22-3 through 22-5. The overhead generated by FEC inefficiency represents the difference between the respective rates.

Table 22-3   *Nominal DOCSIS Downstream Data Rates in 6-MHz Channel*

Modulation type	64 QAM	256 QAM
Symbol rate	5.057 MSs	5.360 MSs
Total data rate	30.34 Mbps	42.9 Mbps
Effective data rate	27 Mbps	38 Mbps

Table 22-4   *Nominal DOCSIS Upstream Data Rates for QPSK*

Bandwidth	200 kHz	400 kHz	800 kHz	1600 kHz	3200 kHz
Symbol rate	0.16 MSs	0.32 MSs	0.64 MSs	1.28 MSs	2.56 MSs
Total data rate	0.32 Mbps	0.64 Mbps	1.28 Mbps	2.56 Mbps	5.12 Mbps
Effective data rate	0.3 Mbps	0.6 Mbps	1.2 Mbps	2.3 Mbps	4.6 Mbps

Table 22-5   *Nominal DOCSIS Upstream Data Rates for 16 QAM*

Bandwidth	200 kHz	400 kHz	800 kHz	1600 kHz	3200 kHz
Symbol rate	0.16 MSs	0.32 MSs	0.64 MSs	1.28 MSs	2.56 MSs
Total data rate	0.64 Mbps	1.28 Mbps	2.56 Mbps	5.12 Mbps	10.24 Mbps
Effective data rate	0.6 Mbps	1.2 Mbps	2.3 Mbps	4.5 Mbps	9 Mbps

DOCSIS further specifies that for a system to become functional and operational, mandatory servers must interface the CMTS and CM deployments. These servers include the following:

- Dynamic Host Configuration Protocol (DHCP) server, as defined by RFC 2181. This server provides needed IP addresses for both the CM and subsequent PC devices that follow.

- Time of Day (TOD) server, as defined by RFC 868 for the purpose of time-stamping operational system events.

- Trivial File Transfer Protocol (TFTP) server, as defined by RFC 1350 for the purpose of registering and downloading CM configuration files for individual customer service. These configurations could include quality of service (QoS) parameters, baseline privacy (BPI) implementation, operating frequency assignments, the number of host devices, and so on.

For large-scale deployments, it is recommended that these servers be supported by dedicated hardware platforms to ensure rapid system response and scalability.

The DOCSIS specifications dictate a CM registration process as represented by Figure 22-5. In an environment equipped with a CMTS and supported with the required servers, a CM scans the downstream spectrum when it is initially powered on for a compatible RF channel carrying data adhering to DOCSIS physical layer characteristics. The CMTS periodically broadcasts upstream channel descriptors (UCD) over the DS channel, from which a CM will learn its assigned upstream operational frequency. The CM has now established both a US and a DS frequency.

Figure 22-5 *Cable Modem Registration Sequence*

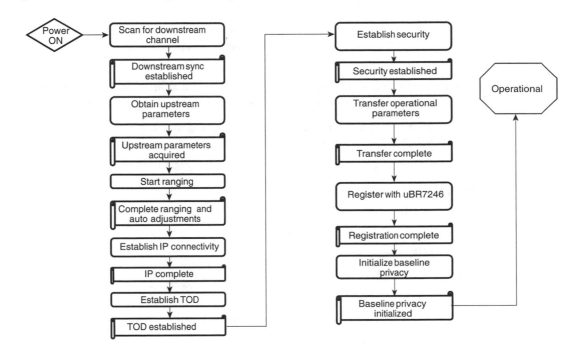

The CMTS periodically transmits upstream bandwidth allocation maps (henceforth referred to as MAP) in shared time slots in the DS direction.

The CMTS assigns a temporary service identifier (SID) (typically SID = 0) to the CM, which begins a coarse power ranging (R1 using 3 dB increments) and time synchronization process between itself and the CMTS on a contention basis using shared time slots.

The CMTS periodically sends keepalive messages to verify link continuity between itself and all CM units in the same domain. When a CM receives its first keepalive message, it reverts to a fine power ranging (R2 using 0.25 dB increments).

Following the R2 process, a CM is considered to have established a *link* between itself and the CMTS, but the link will be broken if 16 consecutive keepalive messages are lost.

On a contention basis in shared time slots, using a temporary SID, a CM forwards a bandwidth request to the CMTS, which, in turn, forwards a grant to the CM, permitting it to forward upstream information in allocated time slots. The CM subsequently makes a DHCP discovery followed by a DHCP request. The CMTS forwards a DHCP acknowledgment from the DHCP server containing an IP address, a default gateway, the addresses of a TFTP and TOD server, and a TFTP configuration file name.

The CM subsequently initiates the TOD and TFTP process. From the TFTP server, the CM receives a configuration file containing QoS, security, applicable frequency assignments, and any new software images.

The CM forwards this configuration file to the CMTS and initiates a registration request. If the configuration file is valid, the CMTS assigns the CM a permanent SID and registers the CM to online status.

Following registration, the CM optionally initiates the activation of the 56-bit DES encryption algorithm to provide security between the CMTS and itself over the cable plant.

As CMs register, their individual status can be monitored remotely via access commands to the CMTS. Table 22-6 defines status messages from a Cisco universal broadband router.

Table 22-6 *List and Definition of Show Cable Modem State Commands from a Cisco CMTS*

Message	Message Definition
Offline	Modem is considered offline
init(r1)	Modem is sent initial ranging
init(r2)	Modem is ranging
init(rc)	Ranging is complete
init(d)	DHCP request was received
init(i)	DHCP reply was received; IP address was assigned
init(t)	TOD request was received
init(o)	TFTP request was received
online	Modem is registered and enabled for data
online(d)	Modem is registered, but network access for the CM is disabled
online(pk)	Modem is registered, BPI is enabled, and KEK was assigned
online(pt)	Modem is registered, BPI is enabled, and TEK was assigned
reject(m)	Modem did attempt to register; registration was refused due to bad MIC
reject(c)	Modem did attempt to register; registration was refused due to bad COS
reject(pk)	KEK modem key assignment was rejected
reject(pt)	TEK modem key assignment was rejected

DOCSIS prescribes that data forwarding through the CMTS may be transparent bridging or, as an alternate, may employ network layer routing or IP switching. It also specifies that data forwarding through the CM is link layer transparent bridging with modifications allowing the support of multiple network layers.

In addition, DOCSIS defines generic CMTS and CM hardware specifications to ensure multivendor interoperability in field deployments. These are summarized in Table 22-7.

Table 22-7   *A Generic CMTS Hardware Specification*

Parameter	Characteristic	
Frequency range	Upstream	5 to 42 MHz (5 to 65 MHz offshore)
	Downstream	88 to 860 MHz
Bandwidth	Upstream	200, 400, 800, 1600, 3200 kHz
	Downstream	6 MHz (8 MHz offshore)
Modulation modes	Upstream	QPSK or 16 QAM
	Downstream	64 or 256 QAM
Symbol rates	Upstream	160, 320, 640, 1280, 2560 Ksymbols/sec
	Downstream	5.056941 or 5.360537 Msymbols/sec
CMTS power level range	Downstream	8 to 58 dBmV (QPSK), 8 to 55 dBmV (16 QAM)
	Upstream	−15 to +15 dBmV

For the DOCSIS availability criteria to be realized or exceeded, the hardware must support noise-mitigating countermeasures or properties to operate in the hostile upstream. For the upstream, the operator has a choice of either QPSK or 16 QAM enabling operation within a degraded CNR, but with reduced spectral efficiency.

Additionally, forward error correction (FEC) can be optionally configured to reduce the amount of data corrupted by noise. Furthermore, an optimal upstream BW can be selected by the operator to fit data channels between either noisy spectrum or spectrum assigned to other services.

The last countermeasure available is a concept of spectrum management, in which the selected upstream frequency, modulation, and channel bandwidth can be altered to ensure reliable access transmission between the CMTS and CM in case of transitory noise periods.

The physical characteristics of the generic DOCSIS 1.0 hardware, noise-mitigating countermeasures, and the associated cable plant parameters have been defined and specified in Table 22-8. Based on this information, and knowing the actual cable plants characteristics, the operator can now consider deploying hardware to develop a network.

Table 22-8 *Generic CM Hardware Specification*

Parameter	Characteristic
CM power level range:	
Output	QPSK: 8 to 58 dBmV
	16 QAM: 8 to 55 dBmV
Input	15 to 15 dBmV
Transmission level	6 to 10 dBc

DOCSIS Hardware Deployment and Resulting Service Capabilities

Assuming HFC CATV topography as shown in Figure 22-6, CMTS equipment could be deployed at both the hub and the head end locations. For the purpose of this application, the Cisco universal broadband router is considered. The uBR7246 is an integrated router with a capacity of up to four cable modem cards, with modem cards available with one or two downstream ports and from one to six upstream ports. In addition, the universal broadband router can be equipped for backbone connectivity from a large selection of port adapters, ranging from T1/E1 serial to Packet Over SONET (POS), to Dynamic Packet Transport (DPT) and from 10BaseT Ethernet, Gigabit Ethernet to High-Speed Serial Interface (HSSI).

The Cisco uBR10012 is Cisco's most recent CMTS. It has much greater capacity and integrates more redundancy, giving MSO's an opportunity to service more customers with a smaller footprint. Also available is a new modem card, the MC520, which supports five downstream and twenty upstream RF domains.

When selecting the backbone connection option, an assessment of the total backbone traffic and the available medium must be considered. In all likelihood, for our example, the backbone from the hub location would be transported optically to the head end, where all traffic would be aggregated by either a router or an IP switch before being forwarded to the Internet or to the public switched telephone network (PSTN). Often, the MSO will provision a cache engine at the head end to reduce the bandwidth to the Internet and, consequently, reduce the facility lease cost.

Connectivity to the PSTN is often required to support either dialup Internet service, voice, or Telco return data service.

Figure 22-6 *CMTS Deployment Possibilities in a Typical HFC CATV Plant*

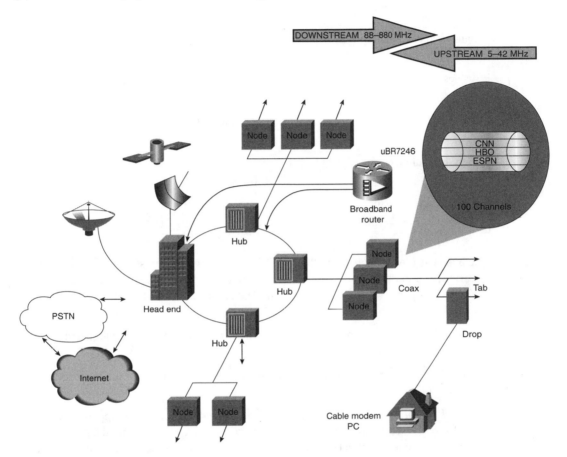

Telco return, if available from the MSO, is as an interim service offering because its plant topography has not been fully upgraded to two-way operation. In such applications, a high-speed downstream connection is established over the HFC plant, whereas the upstream connection is established via a Point-to-Point Protocol (PPP) connection over the telephone network, with a dialup modem at the customer premise and an access server collocated at the Service Providers Facility.

To emphasize the engineering considerations necessary for establishing a DOCSIS network, a simple business case model will be evaluated. The relevant business parameters are summarized in Table 22-9. The analysis considers only residential and limited business customers supported by the head end location.

Table 22-9   *Five-Year Business Plan Summary*

Plant Growth	0.75 Percent per Annum	
High-speed data service offered:		
Residential	256 Kbps DS	128 Kbps US
Business	1.5 Mbps DS	512 Kbps US
Penetration rates:		
Residential	3 percent in first year with 30 percent CAGR	
Business	Two in year two; add one per year thereafter	
Analysis assumptions:		
Residential activity factor	25 percent	
Business activity factor	25 percent	
Data peak factor	8 percent	

The business plan indicates that the DOCSIS service is for an existing serving area that will experience moderate growth, probably limited to new home construction, over the plan period. The operator intends to offer a single data product to each of the residential and business users within the serving area.

Penetration rate is the percentage of total homes passed in the serving area and represents the number of customers who buy the service.

The *activity factor* represents the percentage of subscribers who are actively online either uploading or downloading information.

The *peak factor* represents the relationship between the perceived or apparent bandwidth load of a system compared to the actual finite bandwidth available from the physical CMTS deployment. Peaking reflects the fact that data transfer to an individual user is typically during intervals of instantaneous duration.

The cable plant infrastructure (head end serving area) that is considered for this deployment has characteristics, assigned spectrum, and selected modulation as summarized in Table 22-10.

The head end supports a local serving area of 25,000 homes passed, distributed among 25 optical nodes with upstream CNR ranging from 30 to 36 dB. The CNR is a significant parameter because it dictates the number of nodes that can be combined into a single receive port. DOCSIS requires a CNR of 25 dB, irrespective of the upstream modulation chosen for certified operation.

Table 22-10 *Head End Serving Area Characteristics and Available Spectrum*

HFC characteristics	Downstream: 88 to 750 MHz
	Upstream: 5 to 42 MHz
Head end serving area	25,000 homes passed
	25 nodes (average of 1,000 homes each)
	CNR varying between 30 and 36 dB; average of 32 dB
Available spectrum	Downstream: EIA channel 60 at 439.25 MHz
	Upstream: 32 MHz, 800 kHz bandwidth
Modulation	Downstream: 64 QAM
	Upstream: QPSK

The selection of QPSK and bandwidth of 800 kHz will impact the return path data throughput rate.

From the business case variables, a five-year customer and traffic profile summary is prepared and summarized as in Table 22-11.

The table indicates that the number of homes passed and the penetration rates have increased considerably over the evaluation, with the resultant perceived bandwidth to be processed by the CMTS equipment at the head end.

The number of CMTS units to support the perceived load must be determined considering the use of the Cisco uBR-MC16C consisting of one downstream and six upstream ports. First, however, a valid upstream aggregation scenario must be established.

Consider combining three nodes, each having a CNR of 36 dB, resulting in an aggregated CNR of approximately 27 dB that comfortably exceeds the DOCSIS criteria.

We must now determine the quantity of CMTS units to satisfy this application:

> 25 nodes/3 nodes per receiver = 9 receivers, indicating a need for two uBR-MC16C units

Considering the 800 kHz QPSK upstream limitations, the hardware selection must be validated against the traffic analysis for the business plan, as summarized in Table 22-11.

Table 22-11 *Head End Customer and Traffic Profile*

	Year 1	Year 2	Year 3	Year 4	Year 5
Homes passed	25,000	25,188	25,376	25,666	25,758
Residential customer	750	982	1286	1685	2207
Business customer	—	2	3	4	5
Total traffic	DS 48M US 24M	DS 64M US 32M	DS 84M US 42M	DS 100M US 55M	DS 144M US 72M

- **Downstream Validation**

  Two uBR-MC16C resulting in $2 \times 27 = 54$ Mbps, compared to Year 5 requirement of $144/8 = 18.1$ Mbps (where 144 Mbps is the Year 5 apparent BW and 8 is the data peaking factor)

- **Upstream Validation**

  Two uBR-MC16C with 9 active receivers configured for QPSK and 800 kHz BW, resulting in $9 \times 1.2 = 10.8$ Mbps, compared to Year 5 requirement of $72/8 = 9$ Mbps (where 72 Mbps is the Year 5 apparent BW and 8 is the data peaking factor)

- **Subscriber Limit Validation**

  The total number of Year 5 subscribers is $2207 + 5 = 2212$, which is well within the suggested limit of 1200 subscribers per CMTS.

Based on the analysis of this simple business case, the initial deployment of CMTS hardware will meet the needs of the entire five-year plan and beyond, without compelling the operator to upgrade the configuration.

Future DOCSIS Applications

This chapter describes the DOCSIS 1.0 product definition intended to support high-speed data over a cable network. The most recent evolution of the DOCSIS standard is DOCSIS 1.1. It supports additional services today and will ease the deployment of future applications, which coincide with product enhancements to support the needs of the market to ensure network reliability, and high system availability.

Planned future services and applications include telephony based upon Voice over Internet Protocol (VoIP), video over IP using Motion Picture Expert Group (MPEG) frame format, QoS, and enhanced security definitions. At the same time, CM and set-top box (STB) devices capable of supporting these and other services are being introduced.

When considering the simultaneous support of these new services and applications, a more extensive planning concept must be considered.

The DOCSIS 1.1 specification provides the following functional enhancements over DOCSIS 1.0 coaxial cable networks:

- Enhanced QoS to give priority for real-time traffic, such as voice and video:
  - The DOCSIS 1.0 QoS model (a service ID (SID) associated with a QoS profile) has been replaced with a service-flow model that allows greater flexibility in assigning QoS parameters to different types of traffic and in responding to changing bandwidth conditions.
  - Support for multiple service flows per cable modem allows a single cable modem to support a combination of data, voice, and video traffic.
  - Greater granularity in QoS per cable modem in either direction, using unidirectional service flows.
  - Dynamic MAC messages create, modify, and delete traffic service flows to support on-demand traffic requests.

- Supported QoS models for the upstream are:
  - Best-effort—Data traffic sent on a non-guaranteed best-effort basis.
  - Committed information rate (CIR)—Guaranteed minimum bandwidth for data traffic.
  - Unsolicited grants (UGS)—Constant bit rate (CBR) traffic, such as voice, that is characterized by fixed-size packets at fixed intervals.
  - Real-time polling (RTPS)—Real-time service flows, such as video, that produce unicast, variable size packets at fixed intervals.
  - Unsolicited grants with activity detection (USG-AD)—Combination of UGS and RTPS to accommodate real-time traffic that might have periods of inactivity (such as voice using silence suppression). The service flow uses UGS fixed grants while active, but switches to RTPS polling during periods of inactivity to avoid wasting bandwidth.

- Enhanced time-slot scheduling mechanisms to support guaranteed delay and jitter-sensitive traffic on the shared multiple-access upstream link.

- Payload Header Suppression (PHS) conserves link-layer bandwidth by suppressing unnecessary packet headers on both upstream and downstream traffic flows.

- Layer 2 fragmentation on the upstream prevents large data packets from affecting real-time traffic, such as voice and video. Large data packets are fragmented and then transmitted in the time slots that are available between the time slots used for the real-time traffic.

- Concatenation allows a cable modem to send multiple MAC frames in the same time slot, as opposed to making an individual grant a request for each frame. This avoids wasting upstream bandwidth when sending a number of very small packets, such as TCP acknowledgment packets.

- Advanced authentication and security through X.509 digital certificates and Triple Data Encryption Standard (3DES) key encryption.

- Secure software download allows a service provider to remotely upgrade a cable modem's software, without risk of interception or alteration.

Summary

Historical coaxial broadcast networking was described in this chapter, and its inherent limitations to value-added services were identified. HFC networking was included, with a brief description of its advantages and benefits capable of supporting high-speed data connectivity.

The limitations of prevailing HFC designs, DOCSIS availability criteria, and requisite cable plant specifications and terminology were addressed as well.

In addition, this chapter summarized the DOCSIS standard, signaling protocol, requisite supporting servers, generic product specifications, and applications. Representative CM status messages as viewed at the CMTS were provided to reflect parameters and tools critical for the operational aspects of a DOCSIS system.

Finally, future services and applications were identified to coincide with the evolution to DOCSIS 1.1.

Review Questions

1 Describe the advantages or benefits offered by an HFC network.

2 Identify the process of providing two-way operation of an HFC cable plant.

3 Describe the upstream and downstream bandwidths associated with the DOCSIS standard.

4 Summarize the DOCSIS availability criteria.

5 Identify the DOCSIS-defined networking layers.

6 Identify the DOCSIS 1.0 servers, and describe their respective purposes in the network.

7 What are the facilities in which an MSO might deploy the universal broadband router?

8 Define Telco return and tell when this application might be considered.

9 List a few of the properties and future applications associated with DOCSIS 1.1.

For More Information

Books

- Azzam, Albert, and Niel Ransom. *Broadband Access Technology*. New York: McGraw-Hill, 1999.

- Ciciora, Walter, James Farmer, and David Large. *Modern Cable Television Technology*. Boston: Morgan Kaufmann Publishers, Inc., 1998.

- Grant, William. *Cable Television*, Third Edition. New York: GWG Associates, 1997.

- Raskin, Donald, and Dean Stoneback. *Broadband Return Systems for Hybrid Fiber/Coax Cable TV Networks*. New York: Prentice Hall PTR, 1997.

- Thomas, Jeff. *Cable Television: Proof of Performance*. New York: Prentice Hall PTR, 1995.

URLs

- www.cablelabs.com
- www.cablemodem.com
- www.cabletelephony.com
- www.catv.org

Magazines

- *Cablevision*. 8773 South Ridgeline Blvd., Highland Ranch, Co 80126. www.cablevisionmag.com.

- *Cableworld*. Intertec Publishing, a Primedia Company, 9800 Metcalf Ave., Overland Park, KS 66212-2215. www.cableworld.com.

- *CED* (*Communications Engineering & Design*). P.O. Box 266007, Highland Ranch, CO 80163-6007. www.cedmagazine.com.

Objectives

- Learn about different approaches to optical networking.
- Understand the different methods of building optical networks.
- Learn about different optical network topologies.

CHAPTER 23

Introduction to Optical Technologies

Optical networks provide the means to transport audio, video, and data across optical transmission and switching systems. This chapter investigates traditional architectures, such as SONET/SDH, and emerging paradigms, such as IP over DWDM, Gigabit Ethernet, and ATM. Recently, equipment and standards bodies have started developing the means to signal and switch optical networks. This chapter discusses recent developments in managing and controlling optical networks from the IETF, OIF, and ITU. Additionally, these organizations must decide how they will converge with the others' proposals.

What Is Optical Networking?

Optical networks are networks providing optical paths between service providers and customers. Optical networks are provided between corporations and homes through Fiber To The Home (FTTH). Optical networks provide the necessary infrastructure to meet bandwidth needs today and in the future. Optical media allows narrowband, wideband, and broadband applications to be networked. As the desire for bandwidth increases, optical networks are truly the only medium to meet the ever-expanding demands for data capacity increases.

Furthering the discussion of optical networking is what comprises the optical network. There are many opinions on what architecture is best for the devices, cross-connects, and switches used. This section focuses on real deployment only, emphasizing larger deployments. Optical networks also make use of electrical characteristics; therefore, this chapter covers legacy equipment in existing enterprise and service provider networks as well.

The following sections briefly describe the various types of optical networks.

Wave Division Multiplexing and Dense Wave Division Multiplexing

Wave Division Multiplexing (WDM) and Dense Wave Division Multiplexing (DWDM) provide optical paths to and from service providers while using tightly spaced optics. ITU spaced optical transmitters, which are filtered using a variety of filtering techniques (such as array wave guides), and optical amplifiers (such as EDFA) allow both circuit-switched and data circuits to be delivered.

Fiber to the Home

Optical networks are networks providing optical paths directly between service providers and customers' homes. Using leading-edge optical infrastructures allows service providers to cost-effectively provide bandwidth directly to customers. FTTH is truly broadband connectivity for telecommuters. FTTH allows for converged multimedia and its growth as the need for bandwidth grows.

All-Optical Networks

All-Optical Networks (AONs) are networks providing optical paths between service providers and customers. All optical networks are the means to transport and switch circuits and packets photonically. By transporting and switching photonically, enterprise and service providers can reduce the amount of equipment required to regenerate electrical signals. The advantage of using AONs is in reducing the cost of building and managing the optical network.

AONs are networks that allow services to run directly over fiber without intervening layers—in other words, staying in the physical or photonic layer. Because of various issues with transporting photons in optical fiber, network providers use electrical amplifiers and regenerators. AON uses techniques in the transportation of solitons with optical amplifiers (Raman) in optical fiber to allow signals to not require electrical regeneration, retiming, and reshaping. Much like photons, solitons have distance limitations; however, solitons can be tuned and reshaped in the physical layer. Switching AONs can also be accomplished photonically. Several optical techniques (such as MEMS) allow photonic signals to be switched.

All optical networks are broken into metro optical networks and core optical networks.

Metro Optical Networks

Explosive growth in Internet and enterprise applications is pushing global enterprise and service provider networks. For example, applications such as e-business, storage consolidation, and multiservice integration are changing the landscape for enterprise and service providers. Metro optical networks encompass metro access and metro core. Metro optical networks are between the central office and/or service points of presence (POPs) to major subscriber points (access network). Services are typically groomed into larger data/circuit pipes for transportation.

Core Optical Networks

Core optical networks lie between central offices and/or service POPs and connect each other with fiber suited for long-haul, extended long-haul, and ultra-long-haul transmission. Bulk services, which are groomed from metro optical networks, are transported over long distances to other central offices and/or service POPs. See the sections "Long-Haul Networks," "Extended Long-Haul Networks," and "Ultra-Long-Haul Networks" for more details.

Passive Optical Networks

Passive Optical Networks (PONs) can be broken into two markets—residential and business. Although PONs can be considered a mature and deployed technology, they fall very short of large-scale deployment. PONs consist of Optical Network Units (ONUs) and Optical Network Terminals (ONTs).

Typically, PONs are built for networks looking for cost advantages with asymmetrical bandwidth requirements. By using economical optical splitters, optical power (signals) can be transported to multiple locations. Generally downstream traffic (traffic from the service provider) to the customer is higher bandwidth than upstream traffic (from the customer). Also employed are lower-cost distributed feedback (DFB) optical transceivers. In most cases, PONs are used by companies, such as cable companies and utilities. PONs can also be part of a hybrid network. Hybrid networks make use of PONs' low cost to provide converged multimedia broadband services as well as existing legacy narrowband services.

Residential and Business PONs

There are two kinds of customers for PONs—business and residential. Business customers require higher bandwidth than residential customers; in fact, business customers might even sell services to residential customers on the same infrastructure. PONs are an optical access solution that requires no power and that serves multiple Small Office/Home Offices (SOHOs), businesses, and residential customers from a single fiber. Information is transported between the customer and business application services. Depending on the provider, customers get either their own separate wavelength or a data stream. Typically, residential customers' bandwidth requirements are within data stream limits. SOHOs and other business customers generally have higher bandwidth and are more symmetrical than the asymmetrical data stream used by residential customers. When building PONs, business and residential customer requirements are considered and are differentiated with different SLAs (Service Level Agreements).

Optical Network Units and Optical Network Terminals

ONUs are used to aggregate ONTs. ONTs are used at a business or residential customer to terminate services for delivery from the network and/or transmission into the network. Typically, up to 32 ONTs can be served from a single ONU. ONUs are typically found in the central office and/or a remote building; in some cases, they can be pole- and/or pedestal-mounted when the equipment is temperature-hardened.

Ethernet Passive Optical Networks

Ethernet Passive Optical Networks (EPONs) provide Ethernet or IP directly over fiber without the intervening layers of ATM and SONET. By using Gigabit Ethernet (GE) and/or 10

Gigabit Ethernet (10GE) directly mapped onto DWDM, service providers can economically provide customers broadband and narrowband Ethernet/IP services. See the section "Passive Optical Networks" to learn about PONs.

Metro Access Networks

Today's environments or enterprise and service providers have changed the landscape for traditional networks. Traditional access networks generally have included everything within 40 km of the service switching center (POP, TDM switch, and so on). Metro access networks now can comprise metro access and core networks by using integrated DWDM solutions. This lets enterprise and service providers have metro access networks of 40 to 80 km and metro core networks upwards of 200 km.

Both metro access networks and metro core networks let enterprise and service providers collect customer traffic and, in some cases, provide switching and routing within the network if required. If grooming and transportation are required, they are done in the POP and/or interoffice facility (IOF) switching center.

Transparent Optical Networks

Customers who need to transparently transport their services unintrusively use transparent optical networks. Typical customers have sensitive data as well as traffic that they or their customers don't want to reformat into existing legacy or newer next-generation systems. Transparent optical networks essentially allow customers to plug their optical signals into transponders that neither care about nor affect the optical line rate or framing technique. Transparent optical transponders can be found in access, metro, and transport networks.

Transport Networks

Transport networks provide optical interconnection between metro access networks and metro core networks. Transport networks use long-haul, extended long-haul, and ultra-long-haul equipment to give enterprise and service providers transport pipes for all services over distances of 80 to 200 km. OTNs employ engineered ITU and/or Telcordia (BellCore) systems to transport groomed or switched TDM and/or data traffic to and from other switching centers and IOF, SONET, SDH, and PDH systems are used in transport networks.

Long-Haul Networks

Being able to transport circuit and data services between large metro access networks is highly desirable. Long-haul (LH) networks provide transportation circuit and packet-aggregated and groomed services between central offices and between central offices and service POPs. This is accomplished with the use of WDM and DWDM lasers, filters, and optical amplifiers.

Packet and circuit traffic are groomed in switching and IOF centers and then are tightly packed into optical payloads to be optically transported upwards of 600 km to other switching and IOF centers or customers.

Optical line rates for long-haul networks are generally OC-48/STM-16 and OC-192/STM-64. Distances and capacity are governed by the type of laser, fiber, and optical spacing. Using back-to-back electrical transponders, optical signals can be electrically regenerated, retimed, and reframed to allow shaping of the optical signal, aiding in allowing the optical signal to be extended. Figure 23-1 shows an example of LHN.

Figure 23-1 *Metro Edge, Metro Core, Long-Haul, and Extended Long-Haul Optical Networks*

QPSK,16 QAM and 64 QAM Modulation Constellation

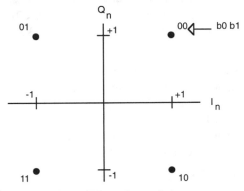

QPSK Signal Constellation.

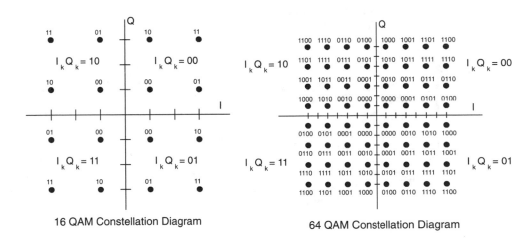

16 QAM Constellation Diagram

64 QAM Constellation Diagram

Extended Long-Haul Networks

This is a relatively new network topology that provides a solution for service providers between long-haul and ultra-long-haul networks. Using a hybrid technique of EDFA and Raman amplification, distances of 600 to 2500 km can be achieved. Extended long-haul (ELH) networks cost-effectively allow optical signals to transport packet and circuit traffic without having to employ optical regeneration for up to 2500 km (see Figure 23-1).

Ultra-Long-Haul Networks

Ultra-long-haul (ULH) networks are used for traffic requiring transport over distances greater than 600 km. ULH networks can also be used for the same area as LH and ELH networks. Even with overlap, ULH is predominantly used for distances in the thousands of kilometers, including subterranean or oceanic optical networks. Terrestrial optical networks use ULH networks where the use of electrical regenerators makes deployment economically challenging.

Usually AON technology is used, allowing optical signals to not require electrical regeneration, re-timing, and reshaping. Photonic transport systems require no optoelectronic (OEO) regeneration. For example, many electrical regenerators and add/drop multiplexers (ADMs) are required to provide ULH transportation. Operational and capital savings can be achieved without the use of electrical regenerators and add/drop multiplexers. ULH provides the same level of restoration, provisioning, and performance as traditional SONET/SDH.

Figure 23-2 shows the complexity required for ULH optical networks. By using Raman optical amplification, providers can reduce the amount of electrical regeneration and equipment. This point is important for operational and maintenance concerns, particularly with subterranean or oceanic optical networks.

Figure 23-2 *Ultra-Long-Haul Network*

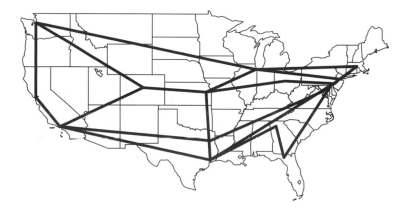

Gigabit and 10 Gigabit Ethernet Optical Networks

Directly mapping GE and 10GE to the optical network can cost-effectively meet customer broadband bandwidth requirements today and in the future. Direct IP over photonics does not require nonblocking cross-connects that require optical port scalability. GE and 10GE devices can use Layer 1, 2, and 3 functionalities, increasing service functionality, performance, and scalability. GE and 10GE optical networks can be connected by high-performance routers to provide scalability, restoration, and bit-rate transparency. Packet networks have no boundaries for both the service and physical layer.

Generalized Multiprotocol Label Switching

Generalized Multiprotocol Label Switching (GMPLS), as proposed by the Internet Engineering Task Force (IETF), will allow routers, switches (packet and circuit), DWDM networks, ADMs, photonic cross-connects (PXCs), and optical cross-connects (OXCs) to dynamically provision resources. GMPLS will also provide protection and restoration to the provisioned services.

GMPLS can support an overlay, peer, and augmented model used to provide the control plane for TDM networks (such as PDH, SDH/SONET, and G.709), DWDM networks, and photonic switching. Timing, signaling, and routing are all part of these models.

The following sections cover only high-level aspects of GMPLS. For further information, review RFCs 3031 and 2026 and visit the IETF forum.

Label Switch Routers

RFC 3031 does not recognize packet and cell boundaries, which precludes it from forwarding data derived from the information in the packet or cell headers. Label Switch Routers (LSRs), which carry these packets and cells, can. The following LSRs, as defined by the IETF, support forwarding decisions based on time slots, wavelengths, and optical ports:

- **Packet Switch-Capable (PSC) interfaces**—Interfaces that recognize packet boundaries and can forward data based on the content of the packet header. Examples include interfaces on routers that forward data based on the header's content and interfaces on routers that forward data based on the content of the multiprotocol label switching (MPLS) "shim" header.

- **Layer 2 Switch-Capable (L2SC) interfaces**—Interfaces that recognize frame/cell boundaries and can forward data based on the content of the frame/cell header. Examples include interfaces on Ethernet bridges that forward data based on the content of the MAC header and interfaces on ATM-LSRs that forward data based on the ATM VPI/VCI.

- **Time-Division Multiplexing (TDM) Capable interfaces**—Interfaces that forward data based on the data's time slot in a repeating cycle. Examples include SDH/SONET cross-connects (XCs), terminal multiplexers (TMs), and ADMs. Other examples include interfaces providing G.709 TDM capabilities (the "digital wrapper") and PDH interfaces.

- **Lambda Switch-Capable (LSC) interfaces**—Interfaces that forward data based on the wavelength on which the data is received. An example of such an interface is a Photonic Cross-Connect (PXC) or Optical Cross-Connect (OXC) that can operate at the level of an individual wavelength. Additional examples include PXC interfaces that can operate at the level of a group of wavelengths—a waveband and G.709 interfaces providing optical capabilities.

- **Fiber Switch-Capable (FSC) interfaces**—Forward data based on the data's position in physical (real-world) space. An example of such an interface is a PXC or OXC that can operate at the level of a single fiber or multiple fibers.

A circuit can be established only between or through interfaces of the same type. Depending on the particular technology being used for each interface, different circuit names can be used, such as SDH circuit, optical trail, and light path. In the context of GMPLS, all these circuits are referenced by a common name: *Label-Switched Path (LSP)*.

The concept of nested LSPs (LSPs within LSPs), already available in traditional MPLS, facilitates building a forwarding hierarchy—a hierarchy of LSPs. This hierarchy of LSPs can occur on the same interface or between different interfaces. For example, a hierarchy can be built if an interface can multiplex several LSPs from the same technology (layer)—that is, a lower-order SDH/SONET LSP (VC-12) nested in a higher-order SDH/SONET LSP (VC-4). Several levels of signal (LSP) nesting are defined in the SDH/SONET multiplexing hierarchy.

The nesting can also occur between interfaces. At the top of the hierarchy are FSC interfaces, followed by LSC interfaces, TDM interfaces, L2SC interfaces, and PSC interfaces. This way, an LSP that starts and ends on a PSC interface can be nested (with other LSPs) in an LSP that starts and ends on an L2SC interface. This LSP, in turn, can be nested (with other LSPs) in an LSP that starts and ends on a TDM interface. In turn, this LSP can be nested (with other LSPs) in an LSP that starts and ends on an LSC interface, which, in turn, can be nested (with other LSPs) in an LSP that starts and ends on an FSC interface.

Link Management Protocol

GMPLS is based primarily on extended routing and signaling protocols using IPv4 (and IPv6 in the future) for addressing. But LSPs need to consider framing, protection switching, and so on. Thus, Link Management Protocol (LMP) is needed for signaling. LMP is generally considered where shortest path first (SPF) routing is insufficient. Discovery of resource state and domain topology are dependent on these routing protocols. GMPLS control and data planes are separated, so LMP is required to provide knowledge between TE links and neighboring nodes.

LMP provides mechanisms to maintain control channel connectivity (IP control channel maintenance), verify the physical connectivity of the data-bearing links (link verification), correlate the link property information (link property correlation), and manage link failures (fault localization and fault notification).

The majority of control channels for GMPLS require IP to transport the signaling and routing protocols (such as LMP). GMPLS does not specify how this is done. That is up to the manufacturer. Control channels for GMPLS can be either in-band or out-of-band.

LMP provides control channel management (multiple wavelengths between optical switches) and link property correlation. Link connectivity verification and fault management can also be considered for LMP but are optional as per IETF.

LMP Control Channel and Control Channel Management

LMP Control Channel (CC) and Control Channel Management (CCM) are used to establish and maintain nodal control channels. CC is used to exchange MPLS control plane information. Routing, signaling, and link management can be shared between nodes. These CCs can be dynamic or statically configured. Each CC is allowed to negotiate and maintain connectivity using the hello protocol. The hello protocol can be considered lightweight keep-alive for channel failures allowing link-state adjacencies. LMP requires that one control channel always be available.

CCM manages and/or negotiates the exchange of control-plane information. Fault management, link provisioning, path management, and label distribution are shared between the link within one or more bidirectional control channels. Provisioning a control channel is done either statically or automatically, with CCM provisioning the IP address on the far end of the control channel. CCM uses signaling protocols, such as RSVP-TE (RFC 3209), and traffic engineering extensions of protocols, such as OSPF-TE and IS-IS-TE, for link distribution and path management, respectively.

Link Property

LMP also defines link property correlation, which is used to aggregate multiple (data) links. Component links are bundled and correlated, exchanged, or modified. Link property (LP) correlation can be set up when the link is available, but not during the verification stage.

PSC and non-PSC interfaces, along with IP hosts and routers, can readily be identified by IP addresses. With IP routing protocols, routes for IP datagrams can be routed via SPF algorithm. Conversely, non-PSC circuits can find routes using a CSPF algorithm.

User-to-Network Interface

What is significant for GMPLS is that existing IP routing protocols can be used for non-PSC layers. Rich development in these protocols' functionality, such as intradomain (link-state) routing and interdomain (policy) routing, can be used. This is of particular interest for providers in an overlay model. The non-PSC layer can be autonomous. Interdomain routing (such as BGP) can be used to route information over autonomous networks. This obviously has a huge benefit to existing interdomain providers. Segmentation of intradomain areas can provide routing domains by using IS-IS or OSPF (link-state) routing for TE.

User-to-Network Interface (UNI) is the link between the GMPLS node and a GMPLS LSR (network side). Network-to-Network Interface (NNI) is the interface between two network LSRs. The history of GMPLS is one that considered UNI and NNI at the same time and created a distinction for GMPLS. This section does not review this distinction; it only points out that there is one. The OIF UNI specification is the client specification for SDH/SONET, which is designed for an overlay model. Currently, the OIF UNI does not support G.709 Digital Wrapper or other photonic network models. GMPLS assumes that OIF UNI is a subset of GMPLS.

G.ASON

ITU's G.ASON (Automatic Switched Optical Networks) uses transport network architecture recommendations (G.803, G.805, G.872, and I.326), among others.

G.ASON uses a control plane to configure switched and soft permanent connections at the transport layer. Reconfiguration for connections or the ability to modify connections while providing restoration is required. For specific technical details on G.ASON, refer to ITU's T-REC-G.8080 recommendation.

G.ASON is essentially the architecture and requirements for the control plane components in SDH and PDH to allow transport network resources to set up, maintain, and release connections for G.ASON to perform signaling and connection services for the control plane between the three distinct planes—control, management, and transport. Call control and connection control are provided via signaling, where the control plane sets up and tears down the connection(s). Restoration is also included.

Interaction (fault, QoS, and so on) between the transport plane and control plane allows the transport plane to update the connection's status to the control plane as required.

Control Plane

The control plane performs link status (capacity, failure) to support connection setup/teardown and restoration.

Domains are used to allow subdivision of control planes. If desired, transport planes can also be subdivided into the same planes. Subdividing domains lets them be administered— something highly desirable for service providers who want geographic or equipment diversity. UNI is the reference point between the administrative point and an end user. E-NNI is the reference point between domains. I-NNI is the reference point between routing areas and sets of control components where applicable.

Policies are used across the various reference points (UNI, I-NNI, and E-NNI) and are unique to them. Table 23-1 shows various policies applied to call control, connection control, and routing. Addressing for various entities in a G.ASON control plane is needed for multiple entities, including connection control, SNNP, routing area, calling/called party call control, network call control, and UNI transport. Addressing entities can be uniquely assigned by the G.ASON and can then be used globally and/or within an area. Resource discovery is done statically or automatically across UNI, E-NNI, and I-NNI functions.

Table 23-1   *Policy Functions*

	UNI	I-NNI	E-NNI
Call control	Yes	—	Yes
Resource discovery	Yes	Yes	Yes
Connection control	Yes	Yes	Yes
Connection selection	Yes	Yes	Yes
Connection routing	—	Yes	Yes

As operating experience is gained with employing current transport network technologies and new technologies evolve (such as variable-size packets, high-speed transport networks, and ASON), these recommendations need to be enhanced, or new recommendations need to be developed, in close cooperation with the standardization activities on transport network systems and equipment. Enhancements are also needed to the requirements for the management capabilities of transport networks. Moreover, requirements for new transport network interfaces need to be studied.

Unified Control Plane

There are several approaches to controlling the optical control plane. One common trait is that direct signaling is required. Unified Control Plane (UCP) is one technique that lets OTNs signal individual nodes. The benefit of UCP is that bandwidth (typically high bandwidth) can be enabled more cost-effectively. Service providers can use UCP. Most, if not all, developed UCP can be defined as proprietary. This does not mean that it cannot or will not interoperate with other UCP implementations.

UCP is software that comprises addressing, routing, and signaling protocols. It runs on IP routers (such as GSR and 7600) and optical network elements (such as 15454, 15600, 15801, and 15200) where control functions are unified across the disparate technology layers, making control independent of transport.

Different models are defined by the industry. The overlay model and peer model are the most popular. The peer model has just one common control plane for Layer 3 and optical networks.

Overlay Model

The overlay model defines two administrative domains—one for the IP layer and one for the optical layer. Each layer uses its own control plane and Optical User Network Interface (O-UNI) to communicate with the other (see Figure 23-3).

Figure 23-3 *Common Control Plane*

Edge-LSR   LSR   OXC-LSR   OXC-LSR   LSR   Edge-LSR

Peer Model

Several Optical Control Plane (OCP) initiatives are under way within the telecom industry. The end goal of all these standards bodies' activities is to provide automated end-to-end optical network provisioning with the addition of mesh restoration. The following are brief descriptions of the standards bodies and their OCP initiatives' focus:

- The Optical Internetworking Forum (OIF) is working on an implementation agreement for a UNI between optical network clouds and clients.

- The IETF is working on a standard that extends the capabilities of MPLS to control wavelength and circuits in addition to packets.

- The ITU is working on a standard for optical control.

Overlay Network Configuration

For an overlay network that not everyone needs to route, they do need to be able to signal the connection requests. Typically, an overlay model is used when the optical network service provider and the user of the facility require no trust. O-UNI defines optical interface requirements for this interaction.

GMPLS routes client requests within the optical network, statically or dynamically providing the service. Routing information stays in the optical backbone and is not shared with subnetworks, because it is unnecessary to do so. Packet clients use the optical network as point-to-point IP links. For TDM clients, optical LSPs are fixed-bandwidth paths.

With the overlay model, scalability can be an issue as the optical network capacity grows. Due to the lack of routing information, clients cannot select the correct router or light path. In today's networks, this issue does not appear to be significant. This warrants further study as the optical network grows.

Peer Model

The overlay model fails to provide end-to-end optimal routes. This is the price we pay for having administrative constraints. The peer model addresses this problem and is more suitable for cases in which such administrative measures need not be observed. Use a single control plane for all devices (such as routers and optical switches) and no UNI, as implied in MPLS.

Full Peering Model

A full peering model has a single IGP instance for the entire network, including IP routers and optical switches. There are two possible implementations:

- **Single-area implementation**—Common IGP. Use a flat network organization with a common IGP running in IP and optical networks.

- **Multiarea solution**—IGP with summarization. Use hierarchical routing within IGP with multiple areas and summarization of reachability and resource information.

Filtered-Pair Model and Augmented Model

Filtered-pair and augmented models do not share topology information. The optical control plane and IP/router control planes are separated and have no knowledge of each other. Using this model allows IP/routers to learn about peers and associated optical endpoints by sharing or exchanging information with each other.

Optical Control Plane User Network Interface

The *Optical Control Plane User Network Interface (OCP-UNI)* is a set of software functions based on an emerging standards protocol that lets systems initiate and complete circuit and light-path connections across optical networks. These elements may include ADMs, cross-connects, optical switches, routers, and ATM switches.

For example, Cisco's 15454 implementation of the OCP-UNI allows customers to extend "A-to-Z" provisioning beyond the domain of a single ONS 15454 SDCC-connected network without requiring the use of a higher-layer management system to "bind" the path between subnetworks. This feature is similar to the ONS 15454's A-to-Z provisioning feature but includes a number of enhancements.

Signaling over the UNI is used to invoke services that optical networks offer to clients. Use of the UNI interface requires

- Defining the services offered over the UNI

- Defining how these services are invoked

- Defining the signaling mechanism for invoking the services

In the UNI 1.0 implementation, these services are used to invoke connection creation, deletion, and status inquiry. To provide these services, the UNI must offer the following procedures:

- **Neighbor discovery**—Allows a client system to inform the network element of its connectivity.

- **Service discovery**—Allows the network elements to convey information about available services to the client systems. Service discovery uses the information from neighbor discovery to convey service information to the client systems.

- **Signaling control channel maintenance**—A control channel that connects the client side and the network side.

- **Address resolution**—Allows clients to obtain optical network points of attachment, because there is a separation between the two entities. Registration (a request to associate client layer addresses with an optical network point of attachment) and query (obtaining the network point-of-attachment address for a remote client by its address) are covered by this service.

OCP-UNI also includes features that automate optical networks across various equipment-based network elements. These features are the auto-discovery of adjacent network elements and automated address registration with these auto-discovered network elements or networks.

Client networks request services of the optical network using UNI signaling. UNI signaling messages are transported over IP control channels—in-band (IB) or out-of-band (OB). Various protocols, such as LDP and RSVP-TE, allow UNI signaling, but are not the only solutions.

Optical Control Plane Optical Network-to-Network Interface

OCP is a modular software feature set that provides functions related to networking control capabilities, such as routing, signaling, provisioning, and resource and service discovery. OCP is being developed by equipment manufacturers to automate end-to-end optical network provisioning. Mesh restoration capability is also being considered for implementation as a restoration technique for OCP.

Manual processes are used in today's optical networks that require the use of multiple management systems to set up multiple segments for end-to-end circuit provisioning. OCP alleviates this by allowing optical networks to be constructed in new ways. For OCP optical networks, more intelligence in network elements (such as bandwidth awareness and service-level support) reduces capital and operational costs.

NNI is an optical subnetwork interface for signaling and routing in a network domain. At this time, GMPLS technology is likely to evolve as the preferred implementation in an OCP O-NNI. This does not mean that G.ASON will not be part of NNI. In fact, G.8080 makes a provision for NNI and other optical interface signaling and routing protocols.

At this time, network elements are considering NNI for signaling and routing exchange between the optical network elements (such as switches and routers) to set up light-path requests through the optical core network.

NNI is another emerging industry-standard protocol. While NNI is in development, UNI extensions and propriety extensions will be used by equipment vendors. For example, standard IP routing using OSPF protocols can be used to support circuit provisioning, and signaling can be accomplished with RSVP-TE with optical, UNI, and proprietary extensions.

Next-Generation Protection and Restoration

Protection and restoration will evolve to offer more than just "premium" and "protected" options for private-line circuits. Most new service offerings now include class-of-service capability. SDH/SONET APS rings typically have the highest level of protection available in optical networks. With 50 ms for APS optical networks, they are viewed as the kings of the telecom world and are viewed as typical by most customers.

Other types of restoration can and will evolve to allow customers with protected service restoration within several seconds. Mesh or other networking principles can reserve or engineer bandwidth by priority, diversity, and latency. In consideration of bandwidth, a backup route would not be required to be dedicated or planned for, thus saving money and allowing for optimization of bandwidth while serving customer needs.

Unprotecting service protection using manual restoration is another service that can be offered to customers who already invoke Layer 3 protection schemes. Service would be provided when repair is complete or when manual restoration is done.

Protection routes can also be virtual (1:n). When a light path is created, a precalculated protection path is recalculated, but not reserved. This technique allows constant reoptimization of the optical network.

Preempted service using protection bandwidth provides service to other customers. Preempted service is not new to the RBOC and ILEC community. If the protected traffic requires protections, the preempted service on the protected route is affected (unavailable).

Mixed services, such as IP and TDM, can also use OCP to convert light-path requests across optical networks. OCP promises the ability to converge service layers and applications. Security and privacy of the light path can be guaranteed, allowing service and enterprise providers to manage resources within their domains and allow extension into other domains.

Service providers need multiple solutions for offering UCP and/or any other type of signaling protocols. Optical networks are predominantly legacy network builds or next-generation builds. Legacy optical network builds were built for circuit-switched traffic. Typically, next-generation networks are built for both circuit-switched and packet-switched traffic. Several other types of optical architectures employ other physical layer routing and switching, but they are not covered here.

Summary

Optical networks provide the means to transport audio, video, and data across optical transmission and switching systems. Managing and controlling optical network development is well under way by the IETF, OIF, and ITU. Signaling and switching optical networks provide cost-effectively integrated voice, video, data, and storage applications. Secure and scalable networks using optical control planes will offer new SLAs for service providers and additional bandwidth for enterprise providers.

Several methods of implementation will be used by providers and customers alike. With manufacturers and service and enterprise providers belonging to one or more of the standards and working groups, implementation is deliberately reserved. However, there are ongoing efforts from all these organizations in how they will converge with each others' proposals.

Even in today's optical networks, fiber capacity is underused. As a medium, fiber-optic cable has no challenger for bandwidth capacity. Optical networking with the use of signaling and managing next-generation equipment and existing legacy equipment allows service and enterprise providers and customers to garner the benefit of optical networking. Obviously, not every aspect of optical networking was discussed in this chapter. You are encouraged to review the reference materials and to visit the standards bodies' Web sites.

Review Questions

1 What are the LSR's interfaces?

2 What three planes are used in G.8080 to perform signaling and connection services?

3 What is the purpose of domains used in G.ASON?

4 When you use PONs, which traffic, upstream or downstream, requires more bandwidth? Why?

5 What two domains are used for administration in the OTN for the overlay model?

6 What type of optical network allows customers to directly plug optical signals regardless of optical line rate or framing?

7 In G.ASON, what is used as the reference point between domains?

8 Which protocol is used to provide link and neighboring node knowledge? Why?

For More Information

- ITU-T Recommendation G.8080/Y.1304, www.itu.int/rec/ recommendation.asp?type=items&lang=E&parent=T-REC-G.8080-200111-I
- draft-ietf-ccamp-gmpls-architecture-04, http://www1.ietf.org/mail-archive/ ietf-announce/Current/msg22930.html
- RFC 2026, www.ietf.org/rfc/rfc2026.txt
- RFC 2748, www.ietf.org/rfc/rfc2748.txt
- RFC 3031, www.ietf.org/rfc/rfc3031.txt
- RFC 3035, www.ietf.org/rfc/rfc3035.txt
- RFC 3036, www.ietf.org/rfc/rfc3036.txt
- UNI 1.0, OIF2001.125, www.oiforum.com/
- NNI 1.0, www.oiforum.com/
- NNI DDRP, OIF2002.023, www.oiforum.com/
- draft-ietf-mpls-generalized-signaling, http://www1.ietf.org/mail-archive/ ietf-announce/Current/msg20113.html
- draft-ietf-mpls-lsp-hierarchy, http://www1.ietf.org/mail-archive/ietf-announce/ Current/msg20272.html
- draft-ietf-mpls-bundle, www.ietf.org/proceedings/02nov/I-D/draft-ietf-mpls- bundle-04.txt

- draft-ietf-ccamp-gmpls-sonet-sdh, http://www1.ietf.org/mail-archive/ietf-announce/Current/msg23580.html

- draft-ietf-ccamp-gmpls-sonet-sdh-extensions, http://www1.ietf.org/mail-archive/ietf-announce/Current/msg18647.html

- draft-ietf-ccamp-gmpls-routing, http://www1.ietf.org/mail-archive/ietf-announce/Current/msg20086.html

- draft-ietf-mpls-ldp-state, http://www1.ietf.org/mail-archive/ietf-announce/Current/msg12101.html

- draft-ietf-mpls-crldp, http://www1.ietf.org/mail-archive/ietf-announce/Current/msg21677.html

- draft-ietf-mpls-crlsp-modify, www.ietf.org/proceedings/01mar/I-D/mpls-crlsp-modify-03.txt

- draft-ietf-mpls-generalized-cr-ldp, http://www1.ietf.org/mail-archive/ietf-announce/Current/msg20114.html

- draft-ietf-mpls-crldp-unnum, http://www1.ietf.org/mail-archive/ietf-announce/Current/msg21677.html

- draft-ietf-mpls-ldp, http://www1.ietf.org/mail-archive/ietf-announce/Current/msg08973.html

- draft-ietf-mpls-lmp, www.ietf.org/proceedings/01mar/I-D/mpls-lmp-02.txt

- draft-nadeau-ccamp-gmpls-tc-mib, http://www1.ietf.org/mail-archive/ietf-announce/Current/msg16480.html

- draft-nadeau-ccamp-gmpls-label-mib, http://www1.ietf.org/mail-archive/ietf-announce/Current/msg16481.html

- draft-nadeau-ccamp-gmpls-te-mib, http://www1.ietf.org/mail-archive/ietf-announce/Current/msg16483.html

- draft-nadeau-ccamp-gmpls-lsr-mib, http://www1.ietf.org/mail-archive/ietf-announce/Current/msg15246.html

Objectives

- Understand H.323 network devices.

- Work with the H.323 protocol suite.

- Know the Session Initiation Protocol (SIP).

- Describe connecting VoIP networks with the SS7 network.

CHAPTER 24

VoIP

Chances are that even if you are new to the networking industry, you have heard of voice over Internet Protocol (VoIP). VoIP is the transport of voice traffic over an IP infrastructure rather than over the traditional time-division multiplexing (TDM)-based telephone network, also called the public switched telephone network (PSTN). VoIP refers to the transport of voice at the network layer of the International Organization for Standardization's (ISO's) open systems interconnection (OSI) model.

VoIP has been gaining momentum in the industry over the past few years with the support of industry heavyweights, such as Cisco. Many enterprise companies, competitive local exchange carriers (CLECs), and incumbent local exchange carriers (ILECs) deploy VoIP solutions of varying degrees. Like anything in business, the main driving force behind VoIP deployments is money. The deployment of private IP infrastructures to transport voice saves companies on leased circuit costs, management overhead, and equipment required.

For example, as shown in Figure 24-1, a typical service provider network contains switches, intermachine trunks (IMTs) that are high-speed links between switches, Signaling System 7 (SS7) equipment, such as signaling transfer points (STPs), and a staff to run the infrastructure (not shown in the figure). These are very high costs, particularly for CLECs, which might not have this capital up front.

Figure 24-1 *Service Provider and Basic VoIP Infrastructures*

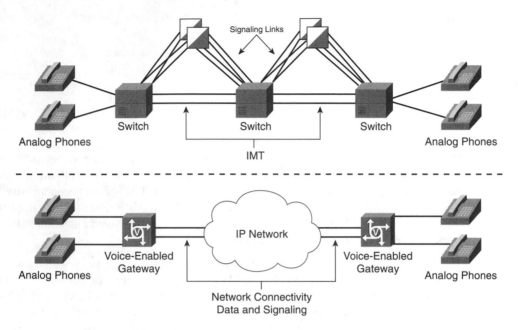

Figure 24-1 is not meant to show everything in a network, because that would take quite a large figure. Instead, it is meant to show how each network can be deployed in its most basic way.

VoIP equipment, such as IP phones, voice-enabled gateways, and call managers, can be purchased and installed in existing IP networks for a small fraction of the TDM network. For individuals or companies that need to offer voice transport and services, but that do not have the capital for large expenditures, VoIP might be a good alternative for increasing voice services. The primary reason for VoIP is the savings on per-call toll access.

VoIP is used for internal voice transport, as a Private Branch Exchange (PBX) replacement in the office, and as a long-haul voice transport in enterprise or service provider networks. Some speculate that VoIP will soon replace the legacy TDM network, and it might someday. However, with the amount of legacy TDM equipment deployed throughout the world, VoIP will likely complement the TDM network for many years to come rather than replace it.

Another noted area of cost savings has to do with the IP infrastructure. Particularly for companies that already have an IP infrastructure in place, long-haul voice services can be added much less expensively than creating a separate TDM-based network for voice services. The feasibility depends on the current network traffic load and how much voice traffic needs to be supported. For example, if a corporation has offices in New York and New Jersey, VoIP can be used to transport the intersite voice traffic rather than making the company pay for toll access on a per-call basis. The ability to provide this type of service also depends on the available bandwidth and the ability to provide the proper quality of service (QoS).

Another cost savings can be seen not with the equipment itself, but with the staff that is needed to run it. Although staffing typically includes individuals who understand wide-area network (WAN) connections, there is a natural overlap with the same individuals who maintain the routers, because VoIP is based on IP transport. The learning curve is often a lot less for someone to come up to speed on VoIP and associated configuration steps than for someone who must learn the entire service provider network and technologies such as SS7.

NOTE   SS7 is a protocol suite that service providers use for call signaling, circuit maintenance, and billing of services for worldwide voice services.

This overlap is not observed in all corporations. Many companies separate pure IP and voice job roles. This is mentioned to identify other ways in which smaller companies can save money.

H.323 Network Devices

To most people, VoIP means almost exclusive use of a suite of protocols from the International Telecommunication Union (ITU) under the umbrella of H.323, but protocols such as Session Initiation Protocol (SIP) when used with Session Description Protocol (SDP), can provide the same type of VoIP call management functionality. SIP is discussed later in this chapter.

Before we discuss the primary protocols that make up the H.323 protocol suite, it is important that you understand the devices in the H.323 network and what functions each performs. Figure 24-2 shows some of the more common H.323 devices. Their approximate location in the H.323 network is indicated.

Figure 24-2 *H.323 Network Devices and Approximate Network Location*

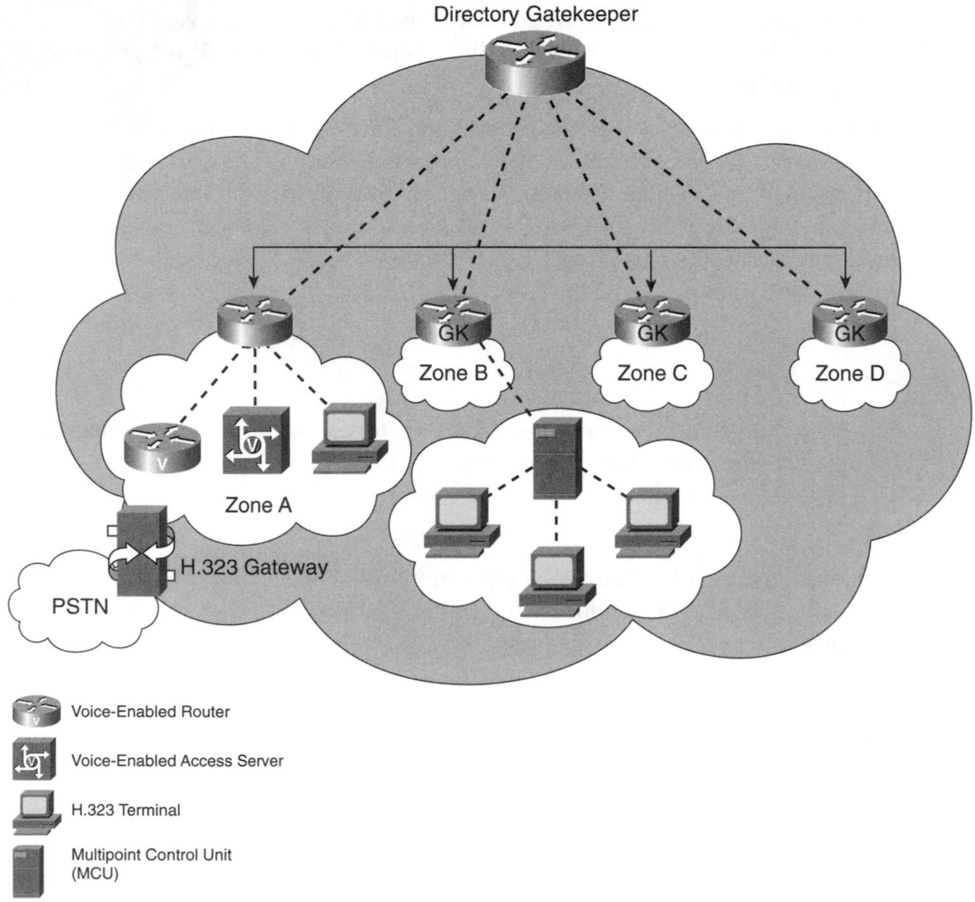

H.323 Terminals

An H.323 terminal is identified in the H.323 specification as a device that provides real-time, two-way communication with another H.323 terminal, gateway, or multipoint control unit (MCU). For H.323 terminals, support for voice is required, and video and data are optional. An H.323 terminal is more easily described as a device that directly supports and understands H.323 and does not need a gateway for translation. This is similar to terminal equipment type 1 (TE1) devices in an ISDN network. Examples of H.323 devices are IP Phones, voice-enabled routers, and voice-enabled access servers. The router and access server are included in Figure 24-2 because they are discussed in more detail later when dial peers are discussed.

H.323 Gatekeepers

H.323 gatekeepers are devices that allow the H.323 network to be scaled. During normal H.323 configuration on a voice-enabled router or access server, dial peers are used to identify the destinations for numbers or groups of numbers that are to be analyzed and passed through said devices. A dial peer is required for each destination in the H.323 network that calls must be routed to. In a small implementation, configuring dial peers is not an issue, but as the network grows, configuring dial peers becomes more of an administrative burden. For instance, if you have 45 voice-enabled routers and you need a minimum of 1980 dial peers for a fully meshed network (44 per device), this does not include any additional dial peers required for multiple groups for the same destination.

Instead of having to configure that many dial peers, gatekeepers can be used to manage this function. Gatekeepers are responsible for managing H.323 zones. H.323 zones are groups of H.323 devices within a logical control domain. This concept is similar to an IP network subnet. An H.323 zone can have only one gatekeeper, but gatekeepers may serve as the control device for multiple zones. Some of the other management functions include security, call admission, bandwidth control, resource reporting, and alias and number translation or resolution.

As H.323 devices, such as voice-enabled routers, are added to the network, they register with the gatekeeper using the H.225 Registration, Admission, and Status (RAS) protocol. H.225 RAS operation is discussed in detail in the section "H.225 RAS."

The H.225 RAS protocol allows the H.323 devices to identify to the gatekeeper which group of phone numbers they are responsible for. The gatekeeper builds this table dynamically, and when calls are placed through H.323 devices, they query the gatekeeper for the call's destination H.323 device. The gatekeeper either finds the number locally or queries a neighbor gatekeeper for the destination H.323 device and then returns that information to the origination H.323 device.

H.323 Directory Gatekeepers

Directory gatekeepers (DGKs) are devices that allow you to further scale the H.323 network infrastructure. The DGK is responsible for keeping track of the location of all the H.323 gatekeepers. To communicate with each other, gatekeepers need to know where all the other gatekeepers are. As with dial peers on H.323 devices, it is possible for the network to become large enough that identifying the location of all the gatekeepers can become an administrative burden.

The DGK is configured with a list of gatekeepers. As calls come through the gatekeepers, they in turn query the DGK for the location of the remote gatekeeper that is responsible for a call that is not locally served.

H.323 Gateways

By pure definition, a gateway is a device that connects two dissimilar networks. For instance, it might translate between an IP network and an IPX network. In the context of H.323, a gateway is a device that connects an H.323 network to a non-H.323 network, such as the PSTN. A growing interest over the past few years in the VoIP world has been the ability to interconnect the service provider SS7 network with private H.323 networks.

Multipoint Control Unit (MCU)

The purpose of the MCU is to provide the ability to conference three or more H.323 devices. Multipoint conferencing has two basic modes of operation—centralized and decentralized. In centralized multipoint conferencing, all H.323 devices communicate directly with the MCU in a point-to-point fashion, and the MCU directly manages the conference.

In decentralized multipoint conferencing, each H.323 device uses multicast to send all information to the other conference participants and bypasses a MCU. Typically, MCUs are used only in centralized multipoint conferences, but they can be used in a hybrid fashion between the two methods. MCUs can act as a bridge between centralized and decentralized devices, thereby allowing a hybrid conference to take place.

H.323 Protocol Suite

Although the most common use of H.323 is for VoIP transport, the specification does include the capability to transport video and data. The initial design for H.323 was to be a multimedia transport, not just voice. Table 24-1 describes some of the different protocol standards that are included under the H.323 umbrella and their intended use.

Table 24-1   *Specifications Under the H.323 Umbrella*

Specification Subheading	Specification Name	Intended Use
Main systems operation	H.323	H.323 is the overall operations specification set forth by the ITU. H.323 specifies the interactions between the various protocols used in the H.323 protocol suite. There are several versions of the standard. Version 4 from 11/2000 is the most current specification being used.
System control	H.225	H.225 is used for call management functions, such as call setup and teardown. H.225 is based on the Q.931 specification for ISDN.

Table 24-1 *Specifications Under the H.323 Umbrella (Continued)*

Specification Subheading	Specification Name	Intended Use
System control (continued)	H.225 RAS	H.225 RAS messages are used for communication between H.323 gateways and H.323 gatekeepers. These messages include the ability to implement scalability, security, billing, and bandwidth control.
	H.245	H.245 specifies the use of a control channel to provide reliable in-band transport for capability exchange. H.245 allows the originating and terminating parties to agree on functions, such as compression/decompression (CODEC) methods.
Video specifications	H.261	H.261 specifies the methodology for the coding and decoding of video signals. This includes bit rate, source coding algorithm, sampling frequency, and error handling.
	H.263	H.263 identifies the compression of video streams at lower bit rates. It is based on the H.261 specification.
Audio specifications	G.711, G.723.1, G.729	These are not all of the available CODECS, but they are some of the more common ones in use. They allow the compression of voice to varying degrees over an IP network.

NOTE The H.261 and H.263 video specifications are out of the scope of this chapter and are not discussed further.

H.323

H.323 describes the overall H.323 network and how the different protocols under the H.323 umbrella interact with each other. This specification is important because without it, there would be just individual protocol specifications without any cohesive relationship between them.

H.323 also identifies which specifications are to be used for video and data communications, which parameters are required, and which are optional.

H.323 calls are set up in sections known as call legs. A call leg is a logical connection between two H.323 terminals. Each endpoint along the call setup path has two identifiable call legs—in and out. Figure 24-3 illustrates the call legs between two gateways in a call.

Figure 24-3 *H.323 Call Legs*

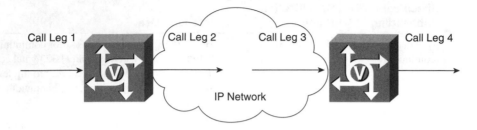

The rule of thumb is that there are two call legs for each endpoint that performs call processing in the call path. The important point to remember is that only endpoints that process call messages have call legs. In other words, the routers that are used to transport IP packets between the two gateways do not have call legs. So a call that travels from one H.323 gateway through five IP routers to another H.323 gateway has four call legs.

H.225

H.225 is the protocol responsible for call setup and teardown between H.323 endpoints (see Figure 24-4). H.225 is based on Q.931. It works in tandem with H.245, RTP, and RTCP to complete the call setup and cut through the voice stream. It is important to note that the H.225 channel is open before any other channels used for call setup and is completely separate from H.225 RAS and H.245. H.225 uses port 1720 for initial call setup and can use dynamic ports thereafter.

Figure 24-4 *H.225 Call Setup Messages*

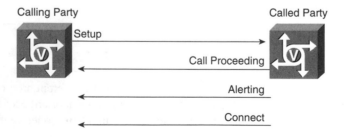

The blank lined sections in Figure 24-4 represent the H.245 capability exchange process and the RTP/RTCP stream creation process for voice transport. Both of these procedures take place after the initial H.225 call setup messages. They are discussed in the sections "H.245" and "RTP and RTCP."

As shown in Figure 24-4, H.225 uses several messages for basic call setup between H.323 endpoints:

- Setup
- Call Proceeding
- Alerting
- Connect

Setup

The first message sent during the H.225 call setup process is the Setup message. This message is a forward message, or a message that travels from the call's originator (the calling party) to the terminating party (the called party). The Setup message contains information similar to that of a Q.931 Setup message, but several key areas are worth pointing out.

Several mandatory information elements (IEs) from Q.931 are required in the H.225 Setup message—protocol discriminator, call reference, message type, bearer capability, and user-user IE. All other IEs are optional or forbidden for use. Table 24-2 describes some of the most important contents within the user-user IE.

Table 24-2 *Partial Contents of the User-User IE from an H.225 Setup Message*

Subheading	Description
protocolIdentifier	Identifies the version of H.225 that is supported with this call.
sourceAddress	The listed alias of the call's origination endpoint.
sourceInfo	Identifies the type of endpoint that originates the call.
destinationAddress	The destination address of this call setup request.
conferenceID	A unique identifier for this conference. All conferences are assigned a unique ID.
conferenceGoal	Identifies whether the purpose of this conference is to create, join, invite, exchange capability, or apply supplementary services.
cryptoTokens	Can be used for a simple authentication method between gateways or between a gateway and a gatekeeper. This token is recalculated at each leg of the call setup.
fastStart	Used only if the fast connect procedure is to be used between endpoints.
neededFeatures	A list of features that need to be included for the call to complete.
desiredFeatures	A list of optional features that can be included for the call. These features are not required for call completion.

continues

Table 24-2   *Partial Contents of the User-User IE from an H.225 Setup Message (Continued)*

Subheading	Description
supportedFeatures	A list of features that are supported by the call's originator.
h245SecurityCapability	A set of features that can be used to secure the H.245 channel between the endpoints.
callIdentifier	A unique identifier for this call that is assigned by the call's originator.

NOTE   The sourceAddress and destinationAddress portions of the user-user IE in essence are the call's originating and destination nodes. However, the source address number (E.164 number) also is included in the calling party number IE, as in Q.931 Setup messages. Furthermore, the destination address is included in the called party number IE. The destinationAddress is a required field for H.323 devices compliant with version 2 or later.

You should be aware that there are four different versions of H.323, and they differ in how the relationship between protocols is handled. Of notable importance is the fastStart field. As mentioned in Table 24-2, the fastStart field works in conjunction with the fast connect procedure, first available in version 2. Fast connect provides the ability to open a logical channel for capability exchange, thereby cutting down on the number of round trips required for call setup.

In other words, version 1 specifies a total of seven or eight round trips between H.323 devices required for call setup. Version 2's fast connect procedure allows call setup to take place over two round trips between H.323 devices. The fast connect procedure was created to decrease the amount of time that call setup takes.

Call Proceeding

The Call Proceeding message is sent in the backward direction—from called party to calling party. The Call Proceeding message specifies that the call setup process has begun. This can be seen as the acknowledgment that the Setup message was received by the called party and is being acted on. Like the Setup message, several fields are required—protocol discriminator, call reference, message type, and user-user IE.

Notice the absence of the bearer capability field. This field is not present because the calling party typically is responsible for stating the bearer capability in the initial Setup message. For Call Proceeding, Alerting, and Connect messages, the bearer capability IE is optional. Table 24-3 describes some of the notable fields that are included in the user-user IE of the Call Proceeding message.

Table 24-3 *Partial Contents of the User-User IE from an H.225 Call Proceeding Message*

Subheading	Description
protocolIdentifier	Identifies the version of H.225 that is in use.
destinationInfo	Allows the called party to identify whether a gateway is included within the call path.
callIdentifier	A unique identifier for this call that is assigned by the call's originator.
h245Address	A specific transport address on which the called endpoint or gatekeeper handling the call wants to establish H.245 signaling.
h245SecurityMode	h245SecurityMode is listed in the Call Proceeding, Alerting, and Connect messages if security is requested in the initial Setup message for the H.245 channel.
fastConnectRefused	A called party returns this field to the calling party if fast connect procedures are not supported.
featureSet	A listing of the supported features for this call.

When the Call Proceeding message is returned to the calling party, several fields serve as answers to the calling party requests in the call Setup. First, notice that the callIdentifier is listed. This field is important so that both parties can keep track of which messages are for which call IDs. When a called party receives a setup message with the h245SecurityCapability set, it responds by setting the appropriate h245SecurityMode in the Call Proceeding, Alerting, and Connect messages. Also notice the fastConnectRefused field. The called party uses this field to notify the calling party that the fast connect procedure is not supported from either vendor implementation or version support.

The h245Address field is used in the Call Proceeding and Alerting messages. This field identifies the address that is requested for use for the H.245 signaling channel. The Setup message can use this field, but only if the calling party supports H.245 signaling before the connect statement. It's more common for the Call Proceeding and Alerting messages to use this field than it is for Setup to use it.

Alerting

The Alerting message is also sent in the backward direction to notify the calling party that the proper endpoint has been identified and is ringing. As with the Call Proceeding message, some fields are required—protocol discriminator, call reference, message type, and user-user IE. Within the user-user IE, there are fields to note for the Alerting message. Table 24-4 describes several of the common fields that are used in the Alerting messages.

Table 24-4   *Partial Contents of the User-User IE from an H.225 Alerting Message*

Subheading	Description
protocolIdentifier	Identifies the version of H.225 that is in use.
destinationInfo	Allows the called party to identify whether a gateway is included in the call path.
callIdentifier	A unique identifier for this call that is assigned by the call's originator.
h245Address	A specific transport address on which the called endpoint or gatekeeper handling the call wants to establish H.245 signaling.
h245SecurityMode	h245SecurityMode is listed in the call Proceeding, Alerting, and Connect messages if security is requested in the initial Setup message for the H.245 channel.
alertingAddress	Identifies the address of the party being alerted for this call.
screeningIndicator	Identifies whether the alerted device's address is visible in this message.
capacity	Lists the called party's current call capacity.

The Alerting message has certain fields that should be noted. The alertingAddress and the screeningIndicator work together in the event that the called party is to be screened from the calling party. By screening addresses, a level of security can be instituted during the call setup process.

The capacity field is the current call capacity of the called party. It's important for obvious reasons. If the called party endpoint has no more resources, the call cannot complete. This resource reporting and management functionality can be performed by a gatekeeper. Offloading resource reporting and management to the gatekeeper allows the gatekeeper to make smart decisions on call routing if resources are unavailable.

Connect

The Connect message tells the calling party that the called party has answered the call, and that voice path cut-through can now commence. The Connect message uses a lot of the same fields that the Alerting and Call Proceeding messages do, with the addition of several more. The connectedAddress field identifies to the calling party the alias address of the called party that answers the call. The presentationIndicator field identifies whether the connectedAddress is shown to the calling party.

Release and Release Complete

The Release (REL) and Release Complete (RLC) messages are where H.225 differs more significantly from ISDN Q.931—particularly in the fact that H.323 endpoints do not use the REL message:

> The disconnect/release/release complete sequence is not used since the only added value is that a network-to-user information element can be appended to the release message. As this does not apply to the packet-based network environment, the single step method of sending only Release Complete is used.
>
> —ITU H.225 Specification 11/2000, page 40

Figure 24-5 illustrates the single RLC sent from the calling party to the called party when the calling party wants to disconnect the call. H.323 endpoints use the RLC message only when call termination is required.

Figure 24-5 *H.225 Call Teardown with an RLC Message*

Table 24-5 describes some of the fields shown in the Release Complete message's user-user IE.

Table 24-5 *Release Complete Message Fields and Release Codes*

Subheading	Description
reason	Specifies why the call was terminated.
busyAddress	The alias address of the busy called party.
capacity	Specifies the sending device's capacity. The difference is that with the RLC message, the capacity is the call capacity of the sending device after the current call has been released.

The following list describes some of the more common call release cause codes:

- **noBandwidth**—No channel is available for the call to complete.

- **gatekeeperResources**—No available resources.

- **unreachableDestination**—No route to the destination. This typically means that there is no IP path to the destination, whether through routing or the lack of a dial peer.

- **destinationRejection**—Normal call clearing.

- **invalidRevision**—The endpoint that rejected this call is incompatible.

- **unreachableGatekeeper**—The gatekeeper is unavailable, usually because of a network infrastructure problem.

- **gatewayResources**—There is congestion in the switching equipment, typically in the destination gateway or endpoint.

- **badFormatAddress**—Invalid or unrecognized number format.

- **inConf**—The endpoint that was requested in the Setup message is already "in conference." The called party is busy.

- **facilityCallDeflection**—A normal call-clearing message.

- **securityDenied**—The security check did not match, and the call was rejected.

- **calledPartyNotRegistered/callerNotRegistered**—These messages are sent when an endpoint is not registered with a gatekeeper and a call request is sent or the endpoint is not registered with the proper gatekeeper.

- **neededFeatureNotSupported**—One of the call's required features is not supported by the called party.

- **tunneledSignalingRejected**—H.225 tunneled signaling has been requested by the calling party but is not supported by the called party.

H.225 tunneled signaling can be used for different applications. Specific to H.323 networks that connect with the service provider SS7 network, as soon as the SS7 call signaling hits the H.323 network, many SS7 call features are lost. H.225 tunneled signaling can be used to tunnel those features across the H.323 network to be provided at the called party location or between calling and called parties.

Within the fast connect procedure, an H.245 control channel can be opened in an H.225 tunnel to reduce the number of required round trips between endpoints.

H.245

H.245 is used between H.323 devices for several different functions for call control management. When you think about H.245, capability exchange probably comes to mind. Although that is a very important aspect of H.245, it is not the only function that is served with H.245. Other responsibilities of H.245 are master/slave determination, control channel management, round-trip delay determination, maintenance loop signaling, and mode requests.

Capability Exchange

The capability exchange between endpoints happens before a logical H.245 control channel is opened between them. The capability exchange identifies what capabilities each endpoint in the call prefers and can handle. Capabilities that are exchanged include CODEC lists (in order of preference) and video or data specifications if needed.

The capabilities are ordered into a capabilityTable and then into an alternativeCapabilitySet. The purpose of the alternativeCapabilitySet is to identify to the destination endpoint (in either direction) all the available operational capabilities and to specify that one must be selected. For instance, it would list all the supported audio CODECs, but only one could be selected for use from that set. More than one operational CODEC at a time is not supported.

After the alternativeCapabilitySets have been created, they are grouped into simultaneousCapabilitySets. These sets identify which of the alternativeCapabilitySets may be used in conjunction with each other. For instance, they might identify a video and audio CODEC that may be used together.

Capabilities are also grouped into transmit, receive, and transmit-receive groupings, although this is a logical grouping. These groups identify transmit, receive, and capabilities that must be the same in both directions (transmit-receive).

Master/Slave Determination

Master/slave determination, as set forth by the H.323 specification, is used to settle conflicts between H.323 endpoints. The H.323 endpoints set a terminal type that identifies what type of terminal they are, and they generate a random number to be disclosed in the statusDeterminationNumber field. Four different types of terminals can be assigned, as shown in Table 24-6.

Table 24-6   *Terminal Types to Be Used in Master/Slave Determination*

Terminal Type Value Table	H.323 Terminal Types			
Feature Set	**Terminal**	**Gateway**	**Gatekeeper**	**MCU**
Entity with no MC	50	60	—	—
Entity contains an MC but no MP	70	80	120	160
Entity contains MC with data MP	—	90	130	170
Entity contains MC with data and audio MP	—	100	140	180
Entity contains MC with data, audio, and video MP	—	110	150	190

Table taken from ITU H.323 version 4, 12/00, page 27

The purpose of this table is to identify which terminal types take priority (become the master). Entries that have a—identify that terminal type's inability to use the listed feature set. The endpoint with the higher value from the table as terminal type becomes the master for the connection. It is possible for an endpoint to be the master in one connection and a slave in another. If the two terminal types are the same, the endpoint with the higher feature set becomes the master.

One of the main uses of the master/slave determination is deciding the preferred order of items, such as audio CODECs. For example, if the master lists the order of preference as G.723 and then G.729, but the slave has an ordered list of G.729 and then G.723, the slave should reorder its CODEC preference to match that of the master endpoint.

Control Channel Management

After the exchange of capability and the identification of the master and slave endpoints, H.245 opens a control channel. The logical control channel is used for control message transport and is always assigned as logical channel 0. That channel remains open until the call's termination. H.245 is also responsible for closing the control channel when necessary.

Figure 24-6 shows the steps that typically take place during a call setup negotiation.

Figure 24-6 *H.245 Call Setup Messages*

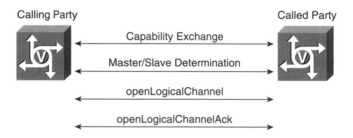

The control channel is opened using the openLogicalChannel message. Because voice is the most common application of H.323, we will focus on the procedure for voice transport. When audio is to be used with an RTP stream, the mediaControlChannel parameter is included with the openLogicalChannel message. The forward mediaControlChannel message includes the address of the reverse RTCP channel. The receiving endpoint replies with an openLogicalChannelAck that contains the mediaTransportChannel and the mediaControlChannel. The mediaTransportChannel contains the RTP transport channel for the media channel, and the mediaControlChannel contains the transport address for the forward RTCP channel.

Round-Trip Delay Determination

The round-trip delay determination serves two different functions in the H.323 network. It identifies the round-trip delay between the endpoints, and it verifies that the remote endpoint is still functional and communicating with the H.323 network. This function can be used as a type of "heartbeat" to verify network operation within the H.323 network.

Maintenance Loop Signaling

The maintenance loop signaling method in H.245 lets the control channel perform loops to provide testing to the network. Three different types of loops are specified:

- **System**—Refers to all present logical channels.
- **Media**—The media stream that is used by the call.
- **Logical channel**—A loop of a specific logical channel.

NOTE   H.323 specifies only the use of a media loop. The system and logical channel loops are marked as forbidden.

Mode Request

The mode request is the receivers' ability to request the mode that the transmitters will use. The two methods available to endpoints are unicast and multicast. Unicast is used in point-to-point H.323 terminal connections, and multicast is used in H.323 terminal-to-MCU connections for centralized or decentralized conference requests.

RTP and RTCP

Real-time protocol (RTP), also called real-time transport protocol, is responsible for creating the avenues that the medium (audio, video, or data) takes. RTP is identified by the Internet Engineering Task Force (IETF) in RFC 1889. RTP is used extensively in H.323 networks along with RTP Control Protocol (RTCP) for both unicast and multicast operation.

RTP streams between endpoints are unidirectional. Bidirectional communication requires an RTP stream in both directions, as shown in Figure 24-7.

Figure 24-7 *RTP Streams and the RTCP Connection*

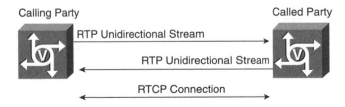

Figure 24-7 also shows the RTCP connection. RTCP is used to report to endpoints on the quality of data distribution that is provided on the link. RTP streams are opened on even UDP port numbers that are in a range of unused port numbers. RTCP uses the next-higher odd UDP port in that same range.

Endpoints that are engaged in a connection using RTP form an RTP session. This RTP session includes destination transport addresses for each participant in unicast conferences or a common destination transport address in multicast conferences. A destination transport address consists of a network address and a pair of ports for RTP and RTCP. So, for a unicast conference between endpoints, each endpoint has its own network address but shares the same port pair for RTP and RTCP.

RTP does not provide a mechanism for QoS. Instead, it relies on other protocols, such as resource reservation protocol (RSVP).

H.450

H.450 is a set of specifications that were designed to offer services to the end users in an H.323 network. These services are intended to emulate the services that are offered in the service provider's SS7 network so that providers of H.323 can compete with existing services in the PSTN. Table 24-7 describes the H.450 specifications and their uses.

Table 24-7   *H.450 Services Issued for Customer Use*

Specification	Name	Description
H.450.2	Call transfer	Transfers calls from one endpoint to another.
H.450.3	Call redirection	Redirects a call from one endpoint to another. This entails redirecting the call before answering.
H.450.4	Call hold	Places the call in a hold state to be answered later from the same endpoint.
H.450.5	Call park	Places the call in a hold state to be answered from the same endpoint or a different endpoint.
H.450.6	Call waiting	The ability to receive incoming call notification as soon as a call has been established on an endpoint.
II.450.7	Message Waiting Indicator (MWI)	Specifies that a message is waiting for the user.
H.450.8	Name identification (caller ID)	Identifies the user who is placing the call (calling party identification).

Table 24-7   *H.450 Services Issued for Customer Use (Continued)*

Specification	Name	Description
H.450.9	Call completion	Completes a call that was rejected because of a busy endpoint after that endpoint becomes available.
H.450.10	Call offer	Decides whether to answer the call or reject the call after another call has been established.
H.450.11	Call intrusion	Interrupts a call between parties in an H.323 call to place a new call with either of the two involved parties.

Audio CODECs

Audio CODECs are used to transport audio (typically voice) at varying compressed bit rates. A CODEC is a very important addition to the transport of VoIP networks because it allows more-efficient use of resources.

NOTE   There are several ways to interpret the acronym CODEC. Some say it stands for coder/decoder, and others say it stands for compression/decompression. Although they are both correct in their own right, CODEC in the context of H.323 is more appropriately thought of as compression/decompression.

CODECs are processed by digital signal processors (DSPs) within the fabric of the H.323 hardware. DSPs are devices that are used to process digital signal forms at very high speeds.

In a legacy TDM-based network, a voice call uses a single 64-Kbps channel called a digital signal level 0 (DS0). A voice call does not require the use of all 64-Kbps, but because no method is in place to reallocate unused bandwidth, excess bandwidth is wasted.

A standard call in H.323 also uses what is equivalent to a 64-Kbps channel by default. The most basic of CODECs is the G.711a or G.711u CODEC. They specify that voice calls use a full 64 Kbps in either A-law (E1) or mu-Law (T1) companding. So if 24 DS0s worth of traffic are supported on a gateway, there can be a maximum of only 24 voice calls.

CODECs are broken into two groups—medium-complexity and high-complexity. These groups identify how complex the algorithm is that is used for the CODEC. Higher-complexity CODECs take more processing power than medium-complexity CODECs and, therefore, typically allow fewer calls on the same H.323 device. Medium-complexity CODECs allow four calls per DSP, whereas high-complexity CODECs allow only two calls per DSP. Table 24-8 lists the medium- and high-complexity CODECs and their individual compression ratios.

Table 24-8   *Complexity Groups for CODECs and Associated Bit Rates*

CODEC	Complexity	Bit Rate in Kbps	Handling Delay in ms
G.711 A-law and mu-law	Medium	64	5
G.726	Medium	32, 24, or 16	1
G.729a	Medium	8	15
G.729ab	Medium	8	15
G.723.1 MP-MLQ	High	6.3	30
G.723.1 ACELP	High	5.3	30
G.723.1 Annex A MP-MLQ (VAD)	High	6.3	30
G.723.1 Annex A ACELP (VAD)	High	5.3	30
G.728 LD-CELP	High	16	Less than 2
G.729	High	8	15
G.729B	High	8	15
G.729 Annex B (VAD)	High	8	15

ACELP—Algebraic Code-Excited Linear Prediction

LD-CELP—Low-Delay Code-Excited Linear Prediction

CS-ACELP—Conjugate Structure Algebraic Code-Excited Linear Prediction

MP-MLQ—Multipulse Multilevel Quantization

NOTE   G.729 (g729r8) is the default CODEC in the Cisco IOS.

Notice that G.729 Annex B and G.723.1 Annex A have "VAD" listed next to them. This means that voice activity detection is integrated into the CODEC and cannot be disabled.

VAD is a feature that helps the H.323 network devices use bandwidth more efficiently. For example, if two people are talking to each other over an H.323 network, there will be times in this conversation during which neither party is speaking. Keep in mind that the transport network is an IP infrastructure, and even silence is sent over the network as IP packets. For network infrastructures that pay on a per-packet basis, this is cause for concern, because it wastes money.

VAD alleviates this problem by detecting the silence and suppressing any packets from being sent during those periods. During these periods of inactivity, comfort noise is generated on the call so that it does not sound as if the call has been disconnected. Figure 24-8 illustrates the basic difference between devices when VAD is used and when VAD is turned off.

Figure 24-8 *H.323 Calls with and Without VAD*

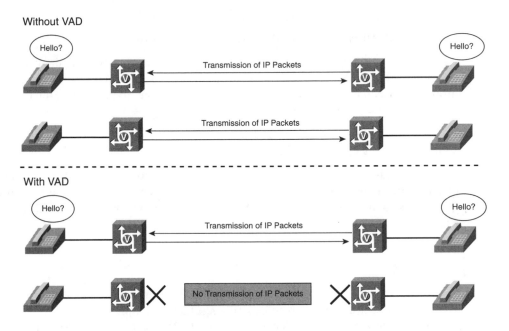

Not all CODECs interoperate. Great care must be taken to ensure that the proper CODECs are selected on both ends of the connection. If the CODECs that are selected do not match or are incompatible, the call setup fails. If the remote CODEC is unknown, CODEC classes can be created in Cisco IOS to allow CODEC negotiation to occur between endpoints. Configuration of CODEC classes is covered later in this chapter. Here are the CODECs that can interoperate:

- G.729 and G.729A
- G.729 and G.729
- G.729A and G.729A
- G.729 Annex B and G.729A Annex B
- G.729 Annex B and G.729 Annex B
- G.729A Annex B and G.729A Annex B
- G.723.1 (5.3 Kbps) and G.723.1 (6.3 Kbps)
- G.723.1 (5.3 Kbps) and G.723.1 (5.3 Kbps)
- G.723.1 (6.3 Kbps) and G.723.1 (6.3 Kbps)

- G.723.1 Annex A (5.3 Kbps) and G.723.1 Annex A (6.3 Kbps)

- G.723.1 Annex A (5.3 Kbps) and G.723.1 Annex A (5.3 Kbps)

- G.723.1 Annex A (6.3 Kbps) and G.723.1 Annex A (6.3 Kbps)

As is the case with any voice network (IP or otherwise), delay is a very important issue. Too much delay in the network causes poor, choppy voice quality and possibly even call drops and disconnects. There are two general types of delay (typically measured in ms)—propagation delay and handling delay.

Propagation delay is experienced as data is transmitted from one location to another. It is simply the amount of time it takes the information to traverse the network.

Handling delay is the amount of time that endpoints take to process the information. For example, the amount of time that is required to compress or decompress the call with a CODEC is a handling delay. Table 24-8 lists the compression or handling delay for each CODEC.

H.225 RAS

Gatekeepers and directory gatekeepers are optional components that allow the H.323 network to be scaled more easily by centralizing H.323 endpoint management. Gatekeepers use the suite of RAS messages identified in the H.225 specification to communicate with each other as well as with H.323 endpoints. Earlier in this chapter, H.225 was mentioned as a protocol under the H.323 umbrella. It is separated from H.225 in this chapter because of its application in H.323 networks. However, H.225 RAS is actually part of the H.225 specification; it is not a specific subsection.

Two main types of gatekeeper signaling are widely used—directed call signaling and gate-keeper routed signaling (GRS). Directed signaling uses the gatekeeper for destination location but relies on the gateways to set up the calls between endpoints. GRS uses the gate-keepers for endpoint location as well as for the call signaling path. The easiest way to tell the difference between them is that directed signaling shows only RAS message communication between the gateway and gatekeeper (no H.225 call setup).

NOTE   Because Cisco gatekeepers support only the directed call signaling method, this method is used for all subsequent RAS call flows.

Table 24-9 lists the RAS message types and whether they are used for gateway-to-gatekeeper communication (1), gatekeeper-to-gateway communication (2), or gatekeeper-to-gatekeeper communication (3).

Table 24-9 *RAS Message Types and Message Direction*

RAS Message	Message Name	Communication Direction
GRQ	Gatekeeper Request	1
GCF	Gatekeeper Confirm	2
GRJ	Gatekeeper Reject	2
RRQ	Registration Request	1
RCF	Registration Confirm	2
RRJ	Registration Reject	2
URQ	Unregistration Request	1
UCF	Unregistration Confirm	2
URJ	Unregistration Reject	2
ARQ	Admission Request	1
ACF	Admission Confirm	2
ARJ	Admission Reject	2
LRQ	Location Request	3
LCF	Location Confirm	3
LRJ	Location Reject	3
RIP	Request In Progress	2
DRQ	Disengage Request	1 or 2
DCF	Disengage Confirm	1 or 2
DRJ	Disengage Reject	1 or 2
BRQ	Bandwidth Change Request	1
BCF	Bandwidth Change Confirm	2
BRJ	Bandwidth Change Reject	2

continues

Table 24-9 *RAS Message Types and Message Direction (Continued)*

RAS Message	Message Name	Communication Direction
IRQ	Information Request	2
IRR	Information Response	1
IACK	Information Acknowledgment	2
INACK	Information Negative Acknowledgment	2
RAI	Resource Availability Indicator	1
RAC	Resource Availability Confirm	2

As you can see, there is a pattern with RAS messages. Request, Confirm, and Reject are the three primary message types that are used, with the exception of information-gathering messages.

Gatekeeper Discovery

Gatekeeper discovery is the process in which the gateway locates the gatekeeper. Before the gateway registers with the gatekeeper, discovery must be performed. Typically, this can be accomplished in two ways. The gateway can locate the gatekeeper by a unicast request or by a multicast request, as shown in Figure 24-9.

- If a unicast GRQ is sent, the receiving gatekeeper responds directly with either a GCF or GRJ to the requesting gateway.

- If a multicast GRQ is sent, only a gatekeeper that wants to grant the gateway discovery responds with a GCF. If no suitable gatekeeper is present, no response is made. If more than one gatekeeper responds, the first response received is used.

Gateway Registration

Gateway registration is the process in which the H.323 gateway registers with the gatekeeper and tells the gatekeeper about all the numbers or addresses it is responsible for. If an RRQ has been sent to a gatekeeper from a gateway, the discovery procedure has completed. The RRQ is answered with an RCF to confirm the addition of the gateway or an RRJ to decline it.

Figure 24-9 *Unicast and Multicast Gatekeeper Discovery*

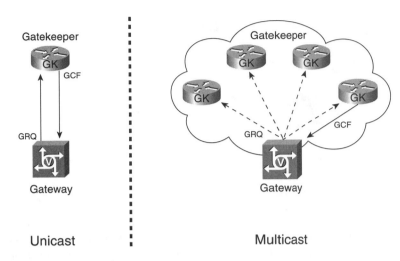

The gatekeeper can decline registration for several reasons, not the least of which is security. Gatekeepers can be configured to accept or decline registrations based on the requester's subnet or specific IP address, among other things.

Gateway registration has been improved since H.323 version 1. In version 1, the gateway required a registration every 30 seconds, which could consume considerable bandwidth in large networks. H.323 version 2 instituted a new registration method called lightweight registration. It requires that a gateway send a partial registration after the initial registration is complete. The caveat is that no changes may be made to the gateway configuration. Otherwise, a full registration is again required.

Gateway Unregistration

If a gateway wants to unregister from its gatekeeper, it must send a URQ to the gatekeeper. For the gateway to unregister, it must receive a UCF in response. In the case of a gatekeeper failure, recovery measures should be instituted to allow the gateway to register with a different gatekeeper after a timeout or failover.

Call Admission

After the registration process has successfully completed, the gateway is ready to place calls. For calls placed between gateways using the same gatekeeper, this is known as an intrazone call. Figure 24-10 illustrates the procedure that is used for gateways to place calls using a gatekeeper.

Figure 24-10   *Call Admission Request (ARQ) Procedure for Intrazone Calls*

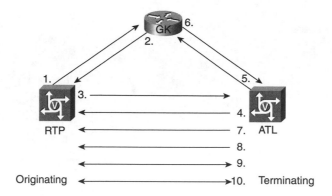

Step 1   When a call is placed, the gateway sends an ARQ to its local gatekeeper. The ARQ is used to ask permission to place the call. The gatekeeper can block the call and send an ARJ or allow the call to complete by sending back an ACF. Embedded in the ARQ is the requested H.323 alias or number.

NOTE   A common way to use a gatekeeper is to use it for bandwidth control. On many gatekeepers, you can set limits for items such as bandwidth or number of calls per gateway. For example, if Gateway A is allowed to place only seven concurrent calls, the gatekeeper sends back an ARJ on the eighth request.

Step 2   In this case, the call is allowed to proceed. The gatekeeper looks at the incoming call request and looks for the called number-to-IP address mapping that is stored in its dynamic database. The database is built as gateways register with the gatekeeper and identify which number they are responsible for. After the proper gateway IP address has been located, the gatekeeper returns that information, embedded in the ACF, to the originating gateway.

Step 3   The originating gateway takes the ACF and attempts to set up a call directly to the remote gateway.

Step 4   Upon receipt of the call setup request, the terminating gateway sends a Call Proceeding response back to the originating gateway.

Step 5   Before sending the Alerting or Connect messages to the originating gateway, the terminating gateway also has to query the gatekeeper with an ARQ to ask for permission to answer the call. The bandwidth constraints can work on both inbound and outbound calls, so the gateway must make sure that it is allowed to accept the call.

Step 6   The gatekeeper responds with an ACF, allowing the terminating gateway to accept the incoming call.

Step 7   The terminating gateway sends the Alerting message back to the originating gateway.

Step 8   The terminating gateway sends the Connect message back to the originating gateway.

Step 9   The H.245 exchange occurs.

Step 10 The RTP streams and RTCP control channel are opened for voice path cut-through.

NOTE   This list mentions every step. However, remember that if the fast connect procedure is used, the H.225 and H.245 sequences are combined, and the number of round trips between endpoints is reduced.

Location Request

If the called number is not served by the local gatekeeper, it might be necessary for the local gatekeeper to query a remote gatekeeper to find the terminating endpoint. Because the call is passed to another gatekeeper, it is said to be an interzone call. The message the gatekeeper sends to the remote gatekeeper is in the form of an LRQ. An LRQ is a gatekeeper's way of saying, "This is not one of my numbers. Do you know where it is?" Figure 24-11 illustrates the procedure for interzone calling.

Figure 24-11 *Interzone Calling Using Gatekeepers*

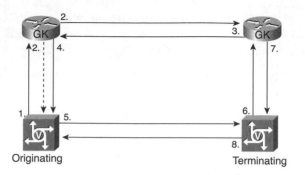

NOTE	The final stages of the call setup (H.245, RTP, RTCP) will not be mentioned again and are assumed to complete successfully.

Step 1   The originating gateway sends an ARQ to its gatekeeper.

Step 2   The gatekeeper identifies that the dialed number belongs to a remote gatekeeper and sends an LRQ to the proper gatekeeper. At the same time, the gatekeeper sends a RIP message to the originating gateway to notify the gateway that it is in the process of locating the proper endpoint. The purpose of the RIP message is to keep the call from terminating or timing out before a response is received from the remote gatekeeper.

Step 3   The terminating gatekeeper looks at the incoming LRQ and looks for the called number-to-IP address mapping that is stored in its dynamic database. After the proper gateway IP address has been located, the gatekeeper returns that information, embedded in an LCF, to the originating gatekeeper.

Step 4   The originating gatekeeper translates the LCF into an ACF and sends it to the originating gateway.

Step 5   The originating gateway takes the ACF and uses it to set up a call directly to the terminating gateway.

Step 6   The terminating gateway requests permission to answer the call using an ARQ of its own.

Step 7   The terminating gatekeeper allows the terminating gateway to answer the call by sending it an ACF.

Step 8   The terminating gateway completes the call signaling process and sets up the call.

Call Disengage

When a party involved with a call that was set up with the aid of a gatekeeper wants to end the call, it sends a DRQ to the gatekeeper. The gatekeeper may also send the DRQ to the gateway if it wants to end the call itself. After the gatekeeper receives the DRQ from the gateway, it responds with a DCF to complete the call disconnect or a DRJ to reject the gateway's request.

The DRQ can also be used to send billing information about the call being ended to the gatekeeper.

Bandwidth Modification

Bandwidth modification (BRQ, BCF, BRJ) allows a gateway to update or modify its bandwidth usage to a gatekeeper. When a call is initially connected through a gatekeeper, the call is assumed to be a full 64 Kbps, regardless of the CODEC used. If bandwidth is limited for the gateway, it can send a BRQ to the gatekeeper to update it after the call has been connected to tell the gatekeeper, "Hey, I'm using G.729, so I'm using only 8 Kbps for this call, not 64 Kbps." The gatekeeper responds with a BCF or BRJ.

Information Request

Gatekeepers can request call and status information from gateways using the IRQ message. The receiving gateway should respond with an IRR that includes the proper status information. A gateway may send the IRR messages to the gatekeeper unsolicited as a way of identifying itself as a "live" gateway to the gatekeeper.

If the IRR's needResponse field is populated in an unsolicited IRR to the gatekeeper, the gatekeeper may use the IACK or INACK acknowledgment messages to acknowledge the IRR in a positive or negative manner.

Resource Availability

A gateway generates an RAI message to notify a gatekeeper of its current call capacity. This message can be used for informational purposes or to tell the gatekeeper that the sending gateway cannot take any more calls. The gatekeeper responds with a RAC to confirm the state and to stop sending calls to that gateway. As soon as the congestive state has cleared, the gateway sends another RAI, saying that it can again handle incoming call requests.

Session Initiation Protocol (SIP)

SIP (RFC 2543) is a part of the IETF Multiparty Multimedia Session Control (IETF-MMSC) protocol suite. It is used for end-to-end call signaling and management in a packet network to provide voice, video, and other real-time services to two or more endpoints. SIP is an ASCII-based protocol that operates at the application layer of the OSI model. These key properties are seen as advantages over H.323:

- **Ease of use, implementation, and troubleshooting**—Because SIP is ASCII-based, the messages are presented in clear text. The clear-text messages are written in an easy-to-understand method that allows for quick troubleshooting and a smaller message size.

- **Supports existing protocols**—SIP is an IETF specification that works seamlessly with existing protocols, such as Domain Name System (DNS), Session Description Protocol (SDP), and RTP.

- **Designed to integrate with existing applications**—SIP was designed to integrate with data applications, such as chat and e-mail.

- **Designed for enhanced mobility**—Services can follow customers regardless of where they are on the SIP network.

SIP Messages

SIP messages are ASCII-based. The actual formatting uses the syntax of HTTP version 1.1, which is an IETF standard for message encoding. Using this format, you will notice that the SIP address URLs look a lot like the addresses you find on the WWW. This is not by mistake. It goes back to ease of decoding, use, and troubleshooting. If host names are used instead of IP addresses, DNS servers can be queried for name resolution.

SIP messages are placed in two main groups—request and response. Requests are messages sent from a UAC to a UAS. Responses are messages sent from a UAS to a UAC.

On SIP networks, requests are also called methods. Six main types of methods are identified in RFC 2543:

- **INVITE**—A request to set up a new SIP session. This session setup method is used on SIP networks.

- **REGISTER**—Registers a SIP endpoint. A REGISTER method is sent when a SIP terminal registers with a SIP proxy server to identify itself and its numbers for use.

- **ACK**—Final acknowledgment of an INVITE. Until the ACK is received, all methods after the INVITE are considered provisional and part of the session setup process.

- **OPTIONS**—A request for capabilities. The OPTION method is used to query a server or another UA for its session capabilities.

- **CANCEL**—Cancels a request that has not yet been completed. This is sent if a voice call is placed over SIP, but the session is terminated (the user hangs up) before the session is answered.

- **BYE**—A request for session teardown or disconnect. This is similar to a Disconnect message in ISDN.

Example 24-1 shows a sample INVITE method. Table 24-10 explains the major headers.

Example 24-1 *SIP INVITE Method Output*

```
INVITE sip:2029033000@10.15.2.6:5060;user=phone SIP/2.0
Via: SIP/2.0/UDP 10.15.1.6:5060
From: <sip:2019033000@10.15.1.6>;tag=1E11E574-8FC
To: <sip:2029033000@10.15.2.6;user=phone>
Date: Thu, 12 Dec 2002 20:08:06 GMT
Call-ID: D2A1FE73-C3AB11D3-8039C64F-9EF784A8@10.15.1.6
Supported: timer,100rel
Min-SE: 1800
Cisco-Guid: 3533831795-3282768339-2151073359-2667021480
User-Agent: Cisco-SIPGateway/IOS-12.x
CSeq: 101 INVITE
Max-Forwards: 6
Timestamp: 947189286
Contact: <sip:2019033000@10.15.1.6:5060;user=phone>
Expires: 180
Allow-Events: telephone-event
Content-Type: application/sdp
Content-Length: 233
```

Table 24-10 *Major SIP INVITE Headers*

Header	Description
INVITE sip:2029033000@10.15.2.6:5060;user=phone SIP/2.0	The SIP method being sent is an INVITE for a voice call at 10.15.2.6:5060. The well-known port is 5060, and the called number is 2029033000. The user type is a phone, and the version of SIP being used is 2.0.
Via: SIP/2.0/UDP 10.15.1.6:5060	VIA contains the SIP version, the transport protocol, and the call's originator with its well-known port (5060). If this session were to pass through proxy servers, each server would add a VIA header with its own address.
From: <sip:2019033000@10.15.1.6>;tag=1E11E574-8FC	Identifies who the call is from. Here the SIP URL is identified as *number@IPaddress*, but host names can be used in the same format, such as johndoe@cisco.com.

continues

Table 24-10 *Major SIP INVITE Headers (Continued)*

Header	Description
To: <sip:2029033000@10.15.2.6;user=phone>	Identifies who the call is intended for. The SIP URL and originator user type are also included.
Date: Thu, 12 Dec 2002 20:08:06 GMT	Method timestamp.
Call-ID: D2A1FE73-C3AB11D3-8039C64F-9EF784A8@10.15.1.6	A unique call identifier that is used to keep track of the call state. The random number is followed by the *@host* format.
Min-SE: 1800	Session timer.
User-Agent: Cisco-SIPGateway/IOS-12.x	Identifies exactly the type of agent that is placing the call. In this case, it is a Cisco gateway running Cisco IOS 12.2.
CSeq: 101 INVITE	CSeq stands for command sequence number. It contains the SIP method type and a numerical value used to identify this method in a unique manner. Each subsequent request increments this number.
Max-Forwards: 6	The maximum number of times this message may be forwarded through the network.
Contact: <sip:2019033000@10.15.1.6:5060;user=phone>	The location where the terminating UA can find the originating UA.
Expires: 180	Method timeout value.
Content-Type: application/sdp	Identifies the intended content and media type. The "SDP" stands for Session Description Protocol. It is used for media negotiation (capability exchange). It is discussed in the next section.
Content-Length: 233	The length of the current message.

RFC 2543 also identifies six classes of messages. Each class of messages deals with either in-progress or completed actions. They identify different types of call progress messages or session errors. Table 24-11 lists the main numerical groups of SIP response messages and describes their use on the network.

Table 24-11 *SIP Response Code Classes*

Message Class	Description
100 PROVISIONAL	The 100 series of messages specifies that a request is in progress, but has not successfully completed or failed yet. Here are some common messages: 100—Trying 180—Ringing 181—Call is being forwarded 182—Call is queued 183—Session progress
200 SUCCESS	The 200 series of messages specifies a successful completion of a particular request. There is really only the 200 OK message in this class.
300 REDIRECTION	The SIP session request needs to be directed to a new location.
400 CLIENT ERROR	An error with the client must be corrected.
500 SERVER ERROR	An error with the server must be corrected.
600 GLOBAL FAILURE	The user has been declined within the network, and all other attempts by this user will also fail.

Session Description Protocol

SIP works in conjunction with several established protocols. Probably the most important is the Session Description Protocol (SDP). SDP is used to exchange capabilities. You find this protocol syntax directly following SIP INVITE, 183 Session Progress, and the 200 OK response for an INVITE. The purpose of SDP in the SIP network is the same purpose that H.245 serves in H.323 networks. SDP lets media negotiation take place between UAs, including such information as audio CODECs and RTP information. Example 24-2 shows the output of the SDP parameters from a SIP INVITE method. Table 24-12 discusses each of these fields in detail.

Example 24-2 *SIP INVITE SDP Parameters*

```
v=0
o=CiscoSystemsSIP-GW-UserAgent 762 3453 IN IP4 10.15.1.6
s=SIP Call
c=IN IP4 10.15.1.6
t=0 0
m=audio 16952 RTP/AVP 18 100
a=rtpmap:18 G729/8000
a=fmtp:18 annexb=no
a=rtpmap:100 X-NSE/8000
a=fmtp:100 192-194
a=ptime:10
```

Table 24-12 *SIP INVITE SDP Parameters*

Header	Description
v=0	The version of SDP that is in use.
o=CiscoSystemsSIP-GW-UserAgent 762 3453 IN IP4 10.15.1.6	Originator information, including UA type, network type, and contact name.
s=SIP Call	Session name.
c=IN IP4 10.15.1.6	Information about the media type, as in IPv4 or IPv6, and the connection address. The connection address is the address of the sending UA.
t=0 0	Start and stop times.
m=audio 16952 RTP/AVP 18 100	Media type and transport port to be used.
a=rtpmap:18 G729/8000 a=fmtp:18 annexb=no a=rtpmap:100 X-NSE/8000 a=fmtp:100 192-194 a=ptime:10	Attributes as they apply to the media field. In this case, includes items such as the CODEC in use (G.729).

SIP Network Devices

SIP uses a client/server model when transporting messages between endpoints. The two entities identified are the user agent client (UAC) and the user agent server (UAS). The UAC is the client device that initiates the SIP request. The UAS is the server that responds to that SIP request.

All SIP devices must be able to act as both a UAC and a UAS. As shown in Figure 24-12, when Bill sends a request to Nancy, Bill is the UAC, and Nancy is the UAS. However, if Nancy sends a request to Bill, the roles are reversed.

User agents are endpoint devices in the SIP network, such as SIP phones or gateways. More recently, other UAs have been added, such as chat clients with SIP support or even wireless phones and personal digital assistants (PDAs).

Figure 24-12 *SIP UAC and UAS Relationship*

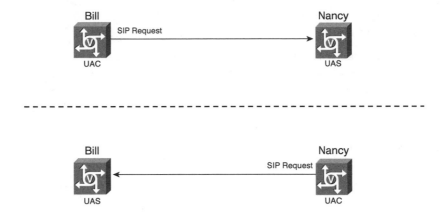

Also defined in RFC 2543 are SIP servers. They typically handle one or all of the following tasks:

- Registration

- Redirection

- Proxy

SIP sessions may be set up directly between UAs or through intermediaries, such as a SIP registrar, redirect, or proxy server.

A SIP registrar server manages the registration of endpoints and associated numbers in much the same way gatekeepers handle the registration of H.323 gateways. SIP UAs do not have to use a SIP registrar server, but a registrar server makes managing the UAs easier.

A SIP redirect server diverts SIP sessions to other locations. Applications include call forwarding for busy, no answer, or manually redirected numbers. Much like the directed call signaling used with H.323 gatekeepers, the SIP redirect server finds out the SIP session's new destination and reports it to the SIP UA. The SIP UA is then responsible for sending the SIP INVITE message to the new destination.

A SIP proxy server is an active intermediary between UAs. It receives inbound session requests and responses, performs name and/or number resolution, provides security services, and acts on behalf of all connected SIP UAs.

The SIP proxy server can be either stateful or stateless. A stateful SIP proxy keeps detailed information about the messages' transaction status and, in some cases, call state as well. The stateless SIP proxy simply forwards the messages as received and doesn't worry about keeping track of what messages went where.

SIP proxy servers can also perform session *forking,* in which they send a SIP session request to several locations simultaneously. A SIP proxy might need to use this feature to locate the proper destination party if a "follow-me" service is used. Think of this as yelling into a room for someone and then waiting for the proper person to respond.

Because forking sends messages to multiple locations, the proxy server must be able to keep track of each of their states. For this reason, to use forking, the SIP proxy must be stateful in nature. Upon receiving responses from multiple parties, it is up to the SIP proxy to filter the unnecessary replies and forward the proper response to the originating SIP UA. Figure 24-13 illustrates call forking and the return filtering performed.

Figure 24-13   *SIP Session Forking and Return Filtering*

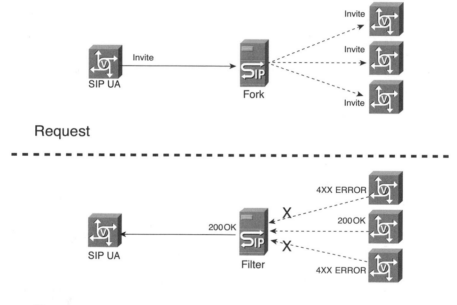

<table>
<tr><td>NOTE</td><td>Although the definitions of these SIP server functions are different, it is common to find SIP servers that have all three functions.</td></tr>
</table>

SIP Call Flows

Three basic call flows are discussed in this chapter. The first call flow is between two SIP UAs. In this case, it is between two SIP gateways. The top of Figure 24-14 shows the SIP method transfer between SIP UAs.

Figure 24-14 *SIP UA-to-SIP UA Call Flow*

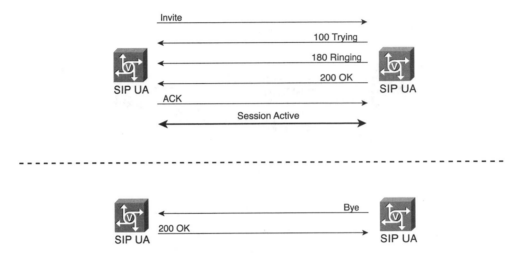

The following list describes the five steps shown at the top of Figure 24-14. These steps represent a basic session setup in SIP:

- When the originating SIP UA initiates the SIP session, it sends an INVITE request similar to the one discussed earlier.

- The terminating SIP UA responds with a 100 Trying message to notify the requester that the message has been received.

- After the terminating SIP UA locates the resource and finds it to be available, the terminating SIP UA sends a 180 Ringing message to alert the originating SIP UA.

- When the called party answers the phone, the terminating SIP UA sends a 200 OK message to the originating SIP UA.

- This message must be answered with an ACK message. At this time, the SIP session is active.

The bottom of Figure 24-14 shows the call teardown or disconnect procedure. Disconnecting the call is simple, because the party that decides to hang up sends a BYE message. This message is responded to with a 200 OK message.

The second call flow is between two SIP UAs, but a SIP proxy server acts as an intermediary between them, as shown in Figure 24-15. In pure proxy mode, the only thing that is different is that the SIP proxy server intercepts and "proxies" the messages between SIP UAs.

Figure 24-15 *SIP UA-to-SIP UA Call Flow with SIP Proxy Server*

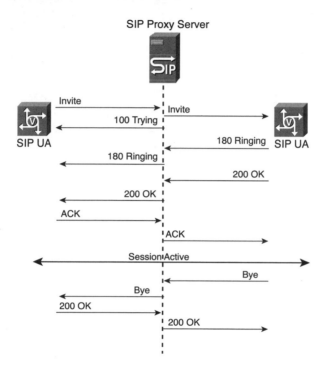

When a SIP proxy is involved with a SIP session, it has the option of turning on a feature called *record route*. The record route header allows the proxy server to stay in the signaling path for the session as long as that session is active. If the call goes through more than one proxy, each subsequent proxy can also be added to the record route header. That way, a backward-traceable path to the session's origin exists.

The last call flow involves the use of a SIP redirect server. With this call flow, the message exchanges are slightly different. Figure 24-16 shows the call flow between two SIP UAs that are using a SIP redirect server.

Figure 24-16 *SIP UA-to-SIP UA Call Flow with SIP Redirect Server*

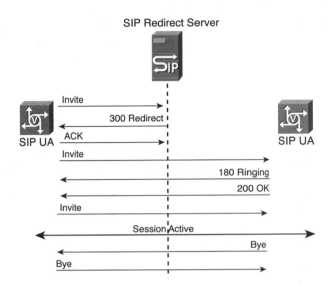

The redirect server is used in much the same way a gatekeeper is with directed call signaling. The redirect server is used only to identify the location of the terminating UA. After that has been established through a 300-series multiple-choice message, the originating UA is responsible for communicating directly with the terminating UA. All other communication, including session disconnect, is handled between the two UAs.

Connecting VoIP Networks with the SS7 Network

VoIP is used for many applications. In a lot of instances, connectivity into the legacy service provider network is required to communicate with non-VoIP networks. The service provider SS7 network is an international network that reaches even the most remote spots on the planet. The SS7 network's coverage is in almost every part of every country.

Millions of miles of land-line phone cable are deployed throughout the world, and connecting into that infrastructure gives users of VoIP networks many possibilities. For voice providers, the private IP network can serve as a cost-saving long-haul transport mechanism. For ISPs, the dial traffic can be offloaded from the service provider network before it ties up valuable resources for extended periods of time. Merging the data and voice networks creates an intricate combination of service possibilities, such as two-stage dial (phone cards), resource pool management (RPM), and even SIP-based message clients.

Although H.323 and SIP are both emerging as popular methods for deploying voice services, the fact remains that the service provider networks throughout the world have been deployed for several decades. With that in mind, H.323 and SIP might help provide increasingly advanced services to end users, but they will likely complement instead of replace it for the near future.

Summary

Voice over IP (VoIP) has emerged in recent years as a hot topic among entrepreneurs, enterprise networkers, and multimillion-dollar service providers. As with anything in the industry, it has to do with money. The ability to transport voice over a private IP infrastructure allows companies to save on costly legacy TDM-based connections and per-minute charges for long-distance calls. In effect, these companies become their own long-distance providers.

Within the realm of VoIP are two competing yet very similar technologies—H.323 and SIP. To many, VoIP automatically means H.323. The ITU developed the H.323 protocol suite as a multimedia suite of protocols for packet-based networks. Although the video and data portions of this protocol suite have not been used to the same depth as the voice aspects, they do exist. Voice transport has been widely deployed throughout the world. Every day, service providers put more voice ports into their H.323 networks.

H.323 specifies a number of different devices for use under the protocol umbrella. H.323 terminals are endpoint devices that interact directly with the H.323 network, such as IP phones or H.323-enabled software packages on PCs. H.323 gatekeepers and directory gatekeepers are optional devices that allow you to scale the H.323 network. Gatekeepers keep track of which gateways can service which numbers, and directory gatekeepers keep track of where the different gatekeepers are located (as well as which gateways they contain).

H.323 gateways are devices that connect the H.323 network to a non-H.323 network, such as a gateway that connects a private H.323 network to a service provider's TDM-based network. Multipoint control units are devices that control H.323 conferences within an H.323 network. Many devices incorporate some sort of MCU functionality within their code, and MCUs are becoming less and less common in active deployments.

H.323 is a suite of protocols that work together to provide reliable voice call setup, teardown, and management. The H.323 specification is used as an umbrella specification that acts as the "glue" for all the other specifications included. H.225 is used for call setup and teardown. It is loosely based on ISDN Q.931 signaling, and it has many of the same characteristics.

H.245 is used for capability exchange. The capabilities exchanged are items such as audio CODECs. Another advantage of the VoIP network is the ability to use the same amount of bandwidth to transport more calls using CODECs. CODECs compress the voice stream to varying degrees and to varying quality. G.729 can transport eight times more calls in a single DS0 than a traditional service provider network. Also functioning with H.245 are RTP and RTCP.

RTP is used specifically to manage the voice paths between endpoints. RTP provides the real-time services that are required to transport voice calls over an IP network. RTCP provides feedback on the RTP streams.

SIP is a newer technology that was created by the IETF. It is included under IETF-MMSC. RFC 2543 was the initial version of the SIP protocol. SIP was designed to help alleviate some of the shortcomings experienced with H.323. SIP was developed as a true multimedia protocol that works seamlessly with established, protocols, such as DNS and SDP.

SIP is an ASCII-based clear-text structure that uses the HTTP 1.1 encoding scheme. This allows for easy decoding and troubleshooting of SIP networks. SIP messages were designed in a client/server model using UACs and UASs. Every device in the SIP network must be capable of functioning in either mode.

SIP UAs are devices that are typically associated with being an end-user device, such as a SIP phone. However, this can also include SIP gateways. SIP UAs can set up SIP sessions directly with each other or through a SIP proxy server.

SIP proxy servers can perform three distinct functions. They can be used as a registrar server, proxy server, or redirect server, or a combination of all three. SIP proxy servers provide centralized management of UAs, call route determination, security, translation, and SIP network services.

For several years now, IP networks and service provider networks have been merging. This integration is inevitable due to the rising demand for coverage and services and the quest to lower costs. SS7 interconnect solutions connect next-generation IP networks to legacy service provider networks. Although VoIP doesn't appear to be going anywhere, it's not likely to overtake the service provider infrastructure anytime soon.

Review Questions

1 What is an H.323 gatekeeper?

2 What is the purpose of SDP?

3 What is the main reason that companies deploy H.323 and/or SIP networks?

4 What protocol are the messages in H.225 based on—Q.921, Q.931, Q.932, or Q.703?

5 Which device is responsible for processing voice streams and performing complex CODEC algorithms?

6 What message must follow a 200 OK message when it is received?

For More Information

H.323

- www.cisco.com/pcgi-bin/Support/browse/
  psp_view.pl?p=Internetworking:H323&s=Implementation_and_Configuration
- www.cisco.com/en/US/tech/tk652/tk90/
  technologies_tech_note09186a008010fed1.shtml#intro
- www.cisco.com/en/US/products/sw/iosswrel/ps1833/
  products_feature_guide_chapter09186a00800ca70f.html#1019911
- www.cisco.com/en/US/tech/tk652/tk698/
  technologies_tech_note09186a0080094ae2.shtml#topic2
- www.cisco.com/en/US/products/hw/routers/ps221/
  products_configuration_guide_chapter09186a0080089519.html#35804
- www.cisco.com/en/US/tech/tk652/tk698/
  technologies_white_paper09186a00800a8993.shtml#sourceofdelay

SIP

- www.ietf.org/rfc/rfc2543.txt
- www.cisco.com/en/US/products/sw/voicesw/ps2157/
  products_administration_guide_chapter09186a00800c7943.html

SS7 Interconnect for Voice Gateways

- www.cisco.com/en/US/tech/tk652/tk653/
  technologies_white_paper09186a0080113758.shtml

Glossary Terms

call leg. A logical connection between two H.323 terminals. Each endpoint along the call setup path has two identifiable call legs—in and out.

CLEC. Competitive Local Exchange Carrier. A startup service provider that competes with the established RBOCs for voice, data, and service customers. Most were created after the Telecommunications Act of 1996 instilled competition in a classically monopoly-dominated industry.

CODEC. Compression/decompression (or coder/decoder). Compresses voice streams to varying degrees to provide more-efficient use of bandwidth in an H.323 network.

H.225. An ITU specification based on ISDN's Q.931. Provides call setup and teardown messaging for H.323 calls between endpoints. Works with H.245, RTP, and RTCP for complete call setup. Uses a single RLC for call teardown.

H.245. An ITU specification used for capability exchange between endpoints during H.323 call setup.

H.323. A protocol suite created by the ITU for multimedia transport in a packet-based network. Used widely for VoIP transport. The H.323 specification describes the interaction between all included protocols.

H.323 directory gatekeeper. Lets you scale an H.323 network to a level above gatekeeper. The directory gatekeeper keeps track of the different gatekeepers and which numbers should be routed to them.

H.323 gatekeeper. A device that allows you to scale the H.323 network by maintaining lists of H.323 gateways and which numbers those gateways can serve.

H.323 gateway. A device that connects an H.323 network to a non-H.323 network, such as the PSTN.

H.323 terminal. A device that interacts directly with the H.323 network, such as an IP phone.

ILEC. Incumbent Local Exchange Carrier. An established national service provider in the U.S. Also called an RBOC.

MCU. Multipoint Control Unit. Lets you conference three or more H.323 devices.

OSI model. Open Systems Interconnection model. The ISO created the OSI model in 1984 to help facilitate equipment interoperation between vendors by providing a seven-layer common framework for all vendors to develop against.

RBOC. Regional Bell Operating Company. The regional phone companies that were created after the breakup of AT&T at the end of 1983. Bell South, Southwest Bell, and Bell Atlantic are all RBOCs.

RTCP. Real-Time Control Protocol. Reports to endpoints on the quality of data distribution provided on the link.

RTP. Real-Time Protocol. Transports real-time streams of voice in an IP environment for both unicast and multicast traffic. RTP streams are unidirectional, so a call between two endpoints has two RTP streams.

SIP. Session Initiation Protocol. Part of the IETF-MMSC protocol suite. Used for end-to-end call signaling and management in a packet network to provide voice, video, and other real-time services to two or more endpoints.

SIP Method. SIP request messages.

SS7. Signaling System 7. The signaling system used internationally to provide signaling setup, teardown, link management, and service capacity to subscribers. (Known as C7 internationally.)

TDM. Time-Division Multiplexing. The process of dividing time into portions called timeslots. Each timeslot is a moment in time and is allotted a specific channel to transmit data on the network. For example, a T1 circuit has 24 timeslots. Timeslot #1 transmits, and then 2, and then 3, and so on.

UAC. User Agent Client. Originates requests in the SIP network.

UAS. User Agent Server. The device that responds to the request from the UAC.

VAD. Voice Activity Detection. Used in H.323 networks to provide more efficient use of network resources. During a typical VoIP call, even silence is transported across the IP network. When VAD is used, silence is detected and is not transmitted.

VoIP. Voice over Internet Protocol. A term coined to describe the transport of voice over an IP infrastructure. Although most people associate the H.323 protocol suite exclusively with VoIP, other standards may be used, such as SIP.

Objectives

- Describe the background of DPT/SRP.

- Explain the DPT/SRP architecture.

- Understand bandwidth reuse.

- Describe the DPT/SRP packet format.

CHAPTER 25

Dynamic Packet Transport/Spatial Reuse Protocol

This chapter introduces Dynamic Packet Transport (DPT) and Spatial Reuse Protocol (SRP). It examines the DPT architecture and SRP's features, including bandwidth optimization, packet priority, the fairness algorithm, and topology discovery. The packet formats of both control and data planes are explained. Finally, this chapter looks at how DPT supports multicast traffic.

Cisco developed DPT technology, based on the MAC-layer SRP, to provide a bandwidth-efficient ring technology optimized for packet transport. It provides scalability of nodes, plug-and-play operation, support for priority traffic, fair bandwidth usage to all nodes on the ring, and fast recovery from ring faults.

The SRP protocol is being considered as part of the standardization for IEEE 802.17 Resilient Packet Ring. SRP is media-independent. DPT implements SRP over fiber in SONET/SDH framing; hence, DPT can be deployed transparently over SONET/SDH, WDM, or dark fiber infrastructure. Support of both multimode and single-mode fiber allows DPT to deployed within the POP and also as MAN and WAN links, typically at OC-12c/STM-4c (622 Mbps) speeds and above.

DPT Architecture

DPT connects nodes (also called stations) to two counterrotating fiber rings. These are called the inner and outer rings. Both rings are part of the same IP subnet. Unlike other dual-ring technologies, such as FDDI, there is no idle or standby ring. Both rings transmit packets concurrently.

Figure 25-1 illustrates the connection of DPT nodes via the two rings.

Figure 25-1 *DPT Connectivity*

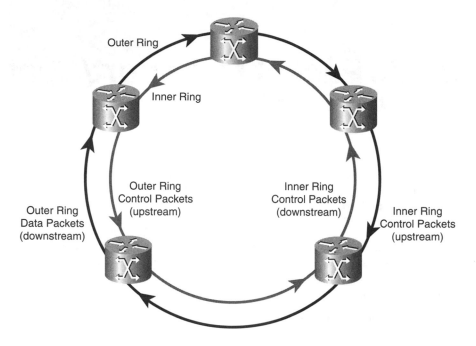

As shown in Figure 25-1, each node sends the data packets in one direction (downstream) on one ring and the control packets in the opposite direction (upstream) on the other ring. The control packets provide features, such as topology discovery and failure recovery. The decision of which direction to send packets to reach another node is made by the Address Resolution Protocol (ARP) process. An ARP packet is sent on one ring, and the target responds via the shortest-hop path as determined by the topology discovery process. The ARP originator uses the ring that the ARP response was received on to send future packets to that target node.

As part of the goal of plug-and-play deployment, additional nodes can be added to the ring at any stage without reconfiguring any of the existing nodes or management system intervention. The ring heals (wraps) around the disconnection while the new node is added. This resiliency is discussed later in this chapter.

SRP Bandwidth Optimization

Unlike other packet ring technologies, such as Token Ring, SRP has no token circulating the ring, so multiple stations can transmit on the rings at the same time. SRP uses destination stripping, which occurs when the receiving station removes the packet from the ring. There is no need to wait for the transmitting station to receive the packet after it has circulated the entire ring and removed it from the ring. Hence, greater bandwidth utilization can be achieved.

Figure 25-2 shows multiple packets circulating the rings simultaneously.

Figure 25-2 *SRP Bandwidth Reuse*

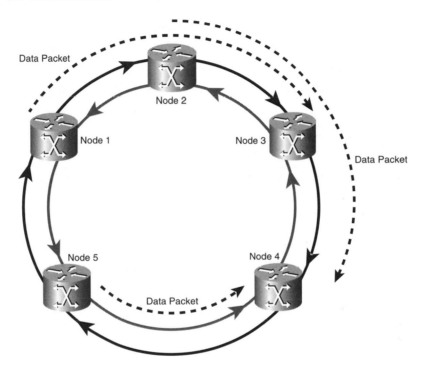

In Figure 25-2, SRP provides the mechanism for Node 1 to send to Node 3. At the same time, Node 2 sends to Node 4 because the packets are on different segments of the outer ring. Meanwhile, Node 5 also sends a packet to Node 4 via the inner ring. It is possible for each node to have full access to the medium's transmission speed.

Note that multicast packets are source-stripped rather than destination-stripped to ensure that all nodes receive the multicast packet. If multicast packets were destination-stripped, the first multicast-enabled node receiving the packet would strip it from the ring. Instead, each node makes a copy of the multicast packet for its own use and forwards the original packet to the next node. When the multicast packet arrives back at the originating node, it is stripped from the ring.

When a node receives an incoming data packet, it may do one of the following:

- **Strip the packet from the ring**—The packet circulated the ring and was removed by the sending node (for example, a multicast packet returned to the originator).

- **Receive and strip the packet**—The packet is destined for this node's Layer 3 address.

- **Receive and forward the packet**—It is a multicast packet and must be passed on.

- **Forward the packet on the ring**—The packet is not addressed for this node.

- **Wrap the packet back onto the other ring**—A ring fault or other disconnection has occurred, and ring wrap is in effect.

- **Pass-through the packet on the ring**—This node's control plane is not in operation.

SRP Packet Priority

SRP provides four transmission queues—two queues for traffic sourced (or transmitted) by a node and two queues for traffic transiting the ring through that node. The two transmit queues are designated as high- or low-priority transmission queues. Similarly, for transit traffic, the node also has a high- and low-priority queue for each ring. The IP Precedence and SRP Priority fields support eight priority levels, which are mapped to either the high- or low-priority queues. This mapping can be customized.

Packets are transmitted from the four queues in the following order:

1 High-priority transit packets

2 High-priority transmit packets

3 Low-priority transmit packets

4 Low-priority transit packets

Thresholds and feedback mechanisms are used to ensure that transit traffic is not dropped by the transmitting of new traffic by a node. This is defined in the SRP Fairness Algorithm.

SRP Fairness Algorithm

The *SRP Fairness Algorithm (SRP-fa)* ensures that no one node can monopolize the ring and prevent other nodes from accessing their fair share of the bandwidth while at the same time allowing a node to use any free bandwidth.

This flexibility is achieved via an algorithm executing on each node. When a node experiences congestion, it reports its transmit bandwidth usage via control packets to its upstream neighbor. The upstream node uses this value in a feedback loop to adjust (throttle) its transmission rate on the ring. This node may, in turn, advise its upstream neighbor. The details of the algorithm's operation are complex. Refer to the "For More Information" section at the end of this chapter to learn more.

NOTE   SRP-fa operates only on low-priority traffic.

DPT Resiliency

DPT rings use Intelligent Protection Switching (IPS) to provide fast ring recovery from node or fiber faults. IPS can detect Layer 1 faults and self-heal within 50 ms without causing Layer 3 reconvergence. Ring recovery is achieved by ring wraps.

A ring wrap may occur automatically as a result of signal failure or degradation in signal quality or manually as commanded by an operator. If both rings are cut together, the nodes on either side of the break immediately wrap. If only one ring is cut, the node in the downstream side of the cut detects the signal failure and sends the upstream node an IPS control message via the other ring. Then that upstream node also wraps. In both cases, the nodes detecting the failure also notify other stations by sending control messages.

Figure 25-3 illustrates a dual-fiber failure and a node that has experienced a Layer 3 control plane failure whose DPT interface is operating in pass-through mode.

In normal fault-free operation, data packets from node 1 destined for node 4 are sent on the inner ring via node 5. After the fiber break occurs and the ring wraps, node 1 sends data packets to node 4 via the same inner ring as before because the topology discovery process is as of yet unaware of any shorter paths. Node 5 then wraps this packet back onto the outer ring, where each node passes the packet via its transit buffer until it reaches node 4. Note that node 4 does not receive and strip the packet directly off the outer ring. Rather, it wraps the packet back onto the inner ring before the normal packet-receiving process handles the packet.

In the header of each SRP packet, the ring identifier field indicates whether the packet originated on the inner or outer ring. In a wrap condition, the intermediate nodes note that the ring-ID is that of the other ring and do not attempt to process it, only forward it. Not until the packet is wrapped back onto the original ring can any node, including the intended receiver, process the packet.

At some point, the topology discovery process determines the new ring order, and traffic from node 1 travels directly via the outer ring to node 4 rather than following the suboptimal wrapped path via node 5.

Figure 25-3 *DPT Resiliency*

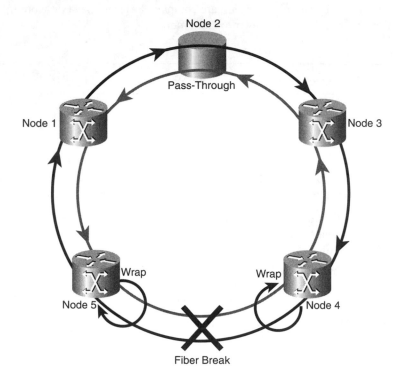

Also in Figure 25-3, note that node 2 has lost its software control plane through either failure or operator intervention. Because the DPT interface still has power, it operates in pass-through mode—merely repeating all packets it receives back onto the ring, thus both minimizing disruption and preserving bandwidth, because both rings are still operational. If node 2 experiences a power outage, nodes 1 and 3 see this as a dual fiber break and perform the necessary ring wraps to recover.

When the fault is cleared, the ring automatically unwraps.

Topology Discovery

Each node on the ring periodically sends topology discovery packets to the outer ring. Each node appends its MAC address and specifies whether its interface is wrapped. The topology discovery packet eventually returns to the source node. When two consecutive discovery packets are sent and received with the same ring information, the node builds a topology map of the ring. This map is used to respond to ARP requests via the shortest path to the source MAC. If the paths are equal distance, a hash is done to select the ring.

DPT/SRP Packet Formats

There are two types of packet formats—control packets and data packets. SRP's Maximum Transfer Unit (MTU) is 9216 bytes, and the minimum is 55 bytes. The current Cisco default is 4470 bytes. Both packets types use the same generic header.

SRP Version 2 Generic Header

All SRP packets have a common 16-bit header format, as shown in Figure 25-4.

Figure 25-4 *SRP Version 2 Generic Header*

This header contains the following fields:

- **Time to live (TTL)**—8 bits. Decremented by 1 each time the packet transits a node. To safeguard against endlessly looping packets, when the TTL reaches 0, the packet is stripped from the ring. The initial TTL must be twice the number of nodes on a ring to handle wrap conditions. Hence, the theoretical maximum number of nodes on a ring is 256 / 2 = 128.

- **Ring identifier (R)**—1 bit. Indicates whether the packet originated on the inner or outer ring. A value of 0 indicates the outer ring, and a value of 1 indicates the inner ring.

- **Mode**—3 bits. Identifies the type of SRP packet as a control packet or data packet. Table 25-1 lists the values.

- **Priority (Pri)**—3 bits. A packet priority of 0 to 7, copied from the IP Precedence bits. The SRP implements only two levels of priority queue to which the eight Priority values are mapped.

- **Parity (P)**—1 bit. An odd parity calculated on the SRP generic header.

Table 25-1 *Mode Values*

Value	Description
000	Reserved
001	Reserved
010	Reserved
011	ATM data cell

continues

Table 25-1   *Mode Values (Continued)*

Value	Description
100	Control message (pass to host)
101	Control message (locally buffered for host)
110	Usage packet
111	Data packet

SRP Data Packet

Figure 25-5 shows the format of an SRP data packet. Note that the Mode field within the header is set to 0x7 (binary 111), indicating a data packet.

Figure 25-5   *SRP Version 2 Data Packet Format*

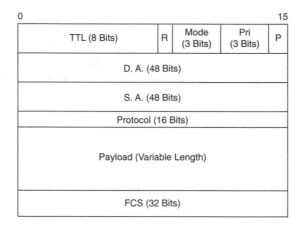

In addition to the SRP generic header, the following fields are included:

- **Destination MAC Address (DA)**—48 bits. The globally unique IEEE MAC address.
- **Source MAC Address (SA)**—48 bits. The globally unique IEEE MAC address.
- **Protocol Type**—16 bits. Note that the value cannot be 0x2007, because this indicates a control packet. Refer to Table 25-2 for the values.
- **Payload**—Variable length.
- **Frame Check Sum (FCS)**—32 bits. The 32-bit CRC.

Table 25-2   *Protocol Types*

Value	Description
0x2007	SRP control (discussed in the next section)
0x0800	IP V4
0x0806	ARP

SRP Control Packet

Figure 25-6 shows the format of an SRP control packet. Note that in the generic header, the TTL is normally set to 1, because the control message will be processed by the next node anyway. The priority should be set to 7 to ensure that control packets are treated with priority on the ring.

Figure 25-6   *SRP Version 2 Control Packet*

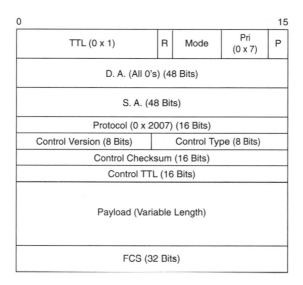

In addition to the SRP generic header, the following fields are included:

- **Destination MAC Address (DA)**—48 bits. This is set to all 0's for control packets because they will be received by the next node anyway.

- **Source MAC Address (SA)**—48 bits. The globally unique IEEE MAC address.

- **Protocol Type**—16 bits. SRP control packets are 0x2007.

- **Control Version**—8 bits. The version number for the Control Type field. Currently all control message types are version 0.

- **Control Type**—8 bits. Identifies the type of control message. Table 25-3 lists the values.

- **Control Checksum**—16 bits.

- **Control TTL**—16 bits. This value should be set to the same generic SRP header TTL that the originator uses for data packets (that is, at least twice the number of nodes on the ring). The generic SRP header TTL for control packets is still set to 1.

- **Payload**—Variable length.

- **Frame Check Sum (FCS)**—32 bits. The 32-bit CRC.

Table 25-3   *Control Type Values*

Value	Description
0x00	Reserved
0x01	Topology discovery
0x02	IPS message
0x03 to 0xFF	Reserved

Multicast Support

SRP directly supports IP multicast (Class D) packets. The MAC addresses 00:00:5E:xx:xx:xx are reserved for multicast. Also, the least-significant bit of the most-significant byte is set as the multicast bit. Finally, the lower 23 bits of the Class D IP address are mapped to the remainder of the MAC address.

All multicast-enabled nodes match a DA address of 01:00:5E:xx:xx:xx, and both receive and forward the packet. As mentioned earlier, the multicast packet eventually is source-stripped after circulating the entire ring.

Summary

Cisco developed Dynamic Packet Transport/Spatial Reuse Protocol to provide a bandwidth-efficient ring technology optimized for packet transport. Nodes are connected to two counterrotating fiber rings—the inner and outer rings. Both rings transmit packets. Because packets are destination-stripped and no token is required for ring access, multiple nodes can transmit simultaneously on different segments of the ring giving greater bandwidth.

The SRP packet format supports eight priority levels copied from the IP precedence bits, which can be used for internal queuing of packets transmitted by a node. The actual SRP interfaces have only two levels of queues—a low- and high-priority queue for transmit and transit traffic to which the eight levels are mapped. The SRP Fairness Algorithm ensures that each node has fair access to the ring during congestion, but can use more than its fair share when there is no congestion.

DPT/SRP is resilient and supports plug-and-play deployment because of its ability to heal ring breaks by implementing ring wraps and transparent pass-through mode features.

Review Questions

1   How does DPT/SRP differ from other ring technologies such as Token Ring and FDDI?

2   How does DPT/SRP implement packet priority?

3   What mechanism determines which ring a node should send a data packet to reach another node?

4   How does DPT/SRP recover from a fiber break?

For More Information

- White paper: "Dynamic Packet Transport Technology and Performance," Cisco Systems, 2000, www.cisco.com.

- White paper: "Spatial Reuse Protocol Technology," Cisco Systems, 2000, www.cisco.com.

- Informational RFC 2892: *The Cisco SRP MAC Layer Protocol*, Tsiang, D. (Cisco Systems) and G. Suwala (Cisco Systems), August 2000, www.ietf.org.

Glossary Terms

transiting traffic.   Packets that the DPT node receives on its DPT interface and that are forwarded unchanged to the next DPT node in the ring. An example is a DPT packet with a destination MAC address for a station other than this node.

transmitted traffic.   Packets for which this DPT node is the source MAC station. This includes packets generated by the node itself and also traffic that the node receives on another of its interfaces and forwards out its DPT interface.

Objectives

- Describe EAP.

- Understand PKI support with EAP.

- Describe EAP Transport Layer Security (TLS).

- Understand Protected EAP (PEAP).

- Introduce various EAP implementations.

CHAPTER 26

Extensible Authentication Protocol (EAP)

Extensible Authentication Protocol (EAP) is an authentication protocol that was defined to support multiple authentication mechanisms. Point-to-Point Protocol (PPP) connections typically negotiate the authentication protocol during the connection's Link Control Protocol (LCP) phase. This requires PPP to support the authentication method being used.

Although authentication is not required for PPP connections during the connection's LCP phase, the endpoints negotiate which authentication protocol to use to establish the connection. They may choose no-auth, PAP, or CHAP authentication. EAP defers the negotiation of this authentication mechanism until more information about the connection can be gathered. There has been growing concern as to the integrity of authentication mechanisms, and EAP is an attempt to provide a foundation to secure this part of network access control. Many vendors are building support for EAP into both client and server applications.

This chapter explores the protocol itself. EAP is defined in RFC 2284, and this chapter covers some of the specifics defined in that RFC to help you understand the basis of the protocol. You will see some of the advantages of using EAP, along with the security concerns that make this protocol so attractive in a variety of implementations. Remote Authentication Dial-In User Service (RADIUS) is helpful in addressing these concerns. This chapter describes how RADIUS can be used as a back-end service to provide authentication support for the user. With this more-complete picture of the EAP authentication process, you will look at different implementations of EAP in the network.

The EAP Protocol

The protocol specification for EAP is not complicated. The authentication process has only a few steps. You will take a closer look at each of the steps and see some of the different options available for the client and the authenticator.

EAP starts when the link establishment phase is complete. The EAP negotiation takes place in the Information field of the PPP data link layer packet. Figure 26-1 shows the different fields for EAP packets and the length of each field in octets.

Figure 26-1 *EAP Packet Format*

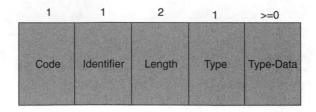

Figure 26-1 shows the five different elements of an EAP packet. The first three fields are required. Depending on the type of EAP packet being sent, the other fields may also be present. Each field is discussed in the following list:

- **Code**—The Code field of an EAP packet identifies the type of EAP packet being sent. This field is one octet in length and has one of four codes:

  — Request

  — Response

  — Success

  — Failure

- **Identifier**—The Identifier field is also one octet in length. It contains an identifier number for the packet. It is used to match request packets with the proper reply packet. There might be a need for the client to retransmit a request. This retransmission is required to use the same identifier as the previous attempt so that the authenticator can properly distinguish between retransmissions and new request packets.

- **Length**—The Length field is a two-octet field that defines the length of the EAP packet. The value of the Length field includes the length of the EAP packet's Code, Identifier, Length, and Data fields. Any data after the range identified by the Length field should be considered padding of the PPP data link layer and should be ignored by EAP.

- **Type**—The Type field of the EAP packet indicates the type of data contained in the packet. This field depends on the packet's Code field. A code of request or response indicates that the Type field is set. This field is one octet in length. The Negative Acknowledgment (NAK) type may be used in a response packet only to indicate that the authentication type is not supported. All EAP implementations are required to support the first four types listed next. Note that if the packet is a success or failure code packet, this field has no requirement. The different types are as follows:

  - **Identity**—The authenticator generally uses the identity type in the first packet of the authentication process to query the client. This is the initial request for the client to send its identity for authentication.

- **Notification**—Displays a message to the client from the authenticator. This can be a warning message or a password expiration time. This message is not required to be sent, although the EAP implementation must support its use.

- **NAK**—This type is valid only in response packets. It is used when an unacceptable authentication type is requested. For example, the authenticator might request PAP authentication, and the client might support only CHAP. The client sends a NAK so that the authenticator requests an alternative authentication type.

- **MD5-Challenge**—The challenge message to the peer, much like a CHAP request in a standard PPP negotiation. The peer must respond with either another MD5-Challenge or a NAK.

- **One-Time Password (OTP)**—The challenge message for performing the authentication via an OTP system. The response to an OTP type packet must be either NAK or a type of OTP.

- **Generic Token Card**—Defined for use with various token card implementations. The authenticator sends the message type containing a message requiring user input.

- **Type-data**—The Type-data field is 0 bytes or greater, depending on the Type field of the EAP packet. Mostly this field contains display messages to the client in a request packet. If the packet is a NAK packet, this field contains information on what authentication method is acceptable. If the Type field is MD5-Challenge, the contents of the Type-data field correlate to the PPP CHAP fields of Value-size, Value, and Name. (See the PPP CHAP RFC [1994].) If the Type field is representative of an OTP or generic token card, the Type-data field contains information required by the server for the authentication.

Using RADIUS for EAP Authentication

One of EAP's best properties is the ability to add RADIUS as a back-end authentication service. With the use of a RADIUS server, the EAP authentication varies a little from a traditional RADIUS authentication. In a traditional RADIUS authentication, the Network Access Server (NAS) prompts the user for the authentication method to be used. When the client responds to the request by the NAS, the NAS creates an access-request packet to send to the RADIUS server by translating that authentication method into the appropriate RADIUS attributes for the server. The server responds with either an access-accept or access-reject response packet. When the NAS receives the response, it interprets the results from the authentication method and sends them to the client, either accepting or rejecting the user authentication. This is slightly different with the use of EAP as the authentication mechanism.

When the NAS uses RADIUS as a back-end server for the EAP authentication, the NAS is not required to support the authentication method being used. In this case, the NAS operates as a proxy for the authentication between the client and the RADIUS server and transparently passes the authentication messages between the client and the back-end server. The NAS is no longer involved in the authentication process. It operates in proxy mode, sending the EAP messages between the two remote peers. This generic platform for authentication now allows vendors to develop and use different authentication methods that are understood by the client and the server, without concern for support on the NAS. The NAS is required only to bundle the EAP messages and send them to the RADIUS server.

Two new RADIUS attributes have been added to support EAP. They work together to provide RADIUS EAP support.

The first is the EAP-Message attribute. It sends the EAP information from the client to the server, and vice versa. The NAS can send the information in one or more EAP-Messages. The server can also use this attribute to respond with a challenge, accept, or reject packet. It is assumed that this authentication method will be used for strong cryptography or other sensitive authentication methods.

The second RADIUS attribute that was added is Message-Authenticator. The Message-Authenticator attribute maintains the integrity of the RADIUS packets and thwarts attacks to the RADIUS EAP server by protecting the data inside the packet. This attribute must be used anytime there is an EAP-Message attribute in the RADIUS request, accept, or challenge packets. If the Message-Authenticator attribute is not present with the EAP-Message attribute, the packet should be discarded, because the packet's integrity cannot be verified. Table 26-1 shows the two new RADIUS attributes and their IETF attribute numbers.

Table 26-1 *IETF Attribute Numbers for RADIUS EAP Authentication*

IETF Number	Attribute	Description
79	EAP-Message	Encapsulates EAP information to be transferred between the client and the RADIUS server
80	Message-Authenticator	Ensures message integrity by encrypting the EAP messages with the RADIUS secret key

A Typical Authentication Conversation

Now that you have a better idea of how EAP works, and you have seen the role of a back-end RADIUS server in the authentication process, let's look at a typical authentication conversation with an EAP client, a NAS, and the RADIUS server. There are different implementations of EAP in several different network architectures. Each implementation follows the same basic premise for the authentication flow. Figure 26-2 illustrates a basic authentication packet flow for RADIUS EAP involving a client, a NAS, and a RADIUS server.

Figure 26-2 *RADIUS EAP Authentication Packet Flow*

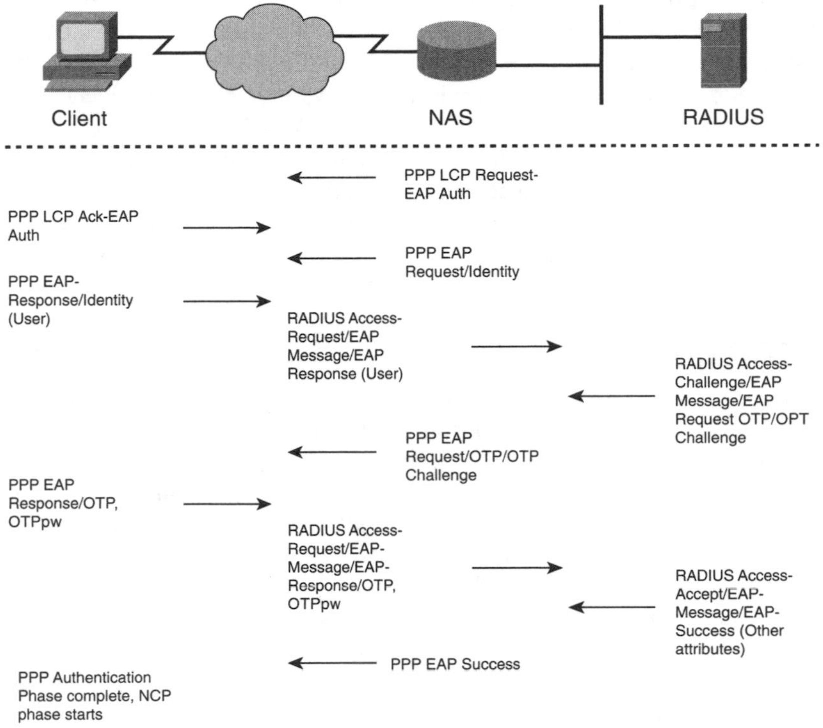

PKI Support with EAP

What about the ability to use digital certificates when performing user authentication with EAP? Public Key Infrastructure (PKI) is the use of digital certificates. PKI is a system designed to manage asymmetric cryptographic keys to ensure the validity of the data being passed. This data is likely authentication data for a specific user and for a specific use, which is valid for only a period of time.

Two new emerging standards for EAP use these certificates—EAP-TLS and PEAP. Each offers a different perspective. Neither is better or worse than the other. However, each method has distinct properties and is suited to different implementation requirements. The use of digital certificates for user authentication is a little more complicated simply because of its nature. The next two sections discuss these extensions to EAP because they are a growing requirement for new EAP implementations.

EAP Transport Layer Security (EAP-TLS)

Transport Layer Security (TLS) is the newest IETF version for the Secure Socket Layer (SSL) protocol. TLS is SSL version 3.0. TLS authenticates the user's identity for both the authentication server and the client. Each uses its private key and certificate to verify the other endpoint. First the server sends its identity information. The client verifies the certificate with a trusted Certificate Authority (CA) server. After the client identifies the server, it sends its certificate to the server to identify the user attempting to authenticate. The server checks the certificate for its validity on the CA server to confirm the user's identity. This is known as mutual authentication. Each party verifies the identity of the other to have EAP success without transmitting any passwords across the link.

Protected EAP (PEAP)

Protected EAP (PEAP) uses the same principles as EAP-TLS. However, with PEAP the authentication is a little different. It uses PKI only to authenticate the server to the client. This is called server-side certificates. The purpose of this type of authentication is three-fold. First, it allows the client to ask the server to prove its identity with its certificate. This is much like any public Web site that uses SSL. When a user visits a Web site using SSL (HTTPS in the browser), the server is required to provide its certificate to prove that it is the host you are trying to establish a connection with. The second purpose of using PEAP is to allow for flexibility in the user authentication. It is not always practical for every client to be issued a certificate to be used for client authentication. PEAP allows for alternative client-side authentication methods, including OTP. The third, and final, purpose of using the server side certificate is that the session is encrypted with the server certificate before the user sends their username to the server. This prevents attackers from extracting usernames from the authentication packet.

EAP Implementations

Now that you have a better understanding of what EAP is and some of the protocol's different extensions, we can look at a few of the different implementations of such a powerful authentication mechanism.

The use of this protocol is growing. EAP was introduced in the wireless access authentication model. The advantages of requiring authentication for Layer 2 access to the network are clear. It prohibits hosts from obtaining a Layer 3 address until after authentication. This concept was expanded to LAN-switched environments. By using EAP for Layer 2 access on a switch port, network administrators have complete control over which users are allowed to access the LAN. Additionally, this method of authentication provides a means of controlling that user's VLAN, regardless of the physical switch port. It uses RADIUS to provide the attributes for such administrative control.

In addition to these implementations, EAP has been extended to remote-access methods. EAP can be applied to traditional dialup connections, as well as to VPDN connections where the endpoint is a router. The NAS needs only to support EAP as a PPP authentication type for this implementation. The authentication method used inside EAP need not be supported by the NAS itself, as discussed earlier. The NAS simply proxies the authentication to the RADIUS server. Figure 26-3 shows each of these EAP implementations—wireless, remote access via dialup, and switched LAN.

Figure 26-3 *Physical Topologies for Different Implementations of EAP Authentication*

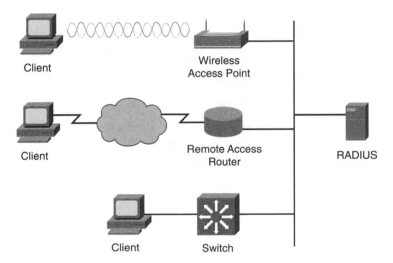

With the growing use of EAP in network authentication, we are seeing an increase in native support for such authentication mechanisms. Microsoft Windows operating systems now ship with native support for EAP authentication of network connections. Linux distributions also support EAP as a valid authentication method. Cisco Systems has already built in support for all these network authentication implementations. Other vendors are working toward this end.

Summary

As you have seen, EAP is a powerful means of providing user authentication for network access. Its popularity is growing as network administrators and vendors recognize its flexibility. From a traditional MD5-Challenge to digital certificates, administrators can use a strong authentication mechanism that meets the requirements of their security policies. EAP currently covers implementations from wireless to switched LAN authentication. It is clear that EAP is an emerging standard that will continue to expand its role in the networks of tomorrow.

Review Questions

1 What field of an EAP packet identifies whether the message is a request, response, success, or failure?

2 What is the primary benefit of using EAP as an authentication mechanism?

3 What two RADIUS attributes are used in EAP authentication?

4 Does EAP support server-side certificates, client-side certificates, or both?

For More Information

- RFC 2284, *PPP Extensible Authentication Protocol,* ftp://ftp.isi.edu/in-notes/rfc2284.txt

- RFC 2716, *PPP EAP-TLS Authentication Protocol,* ftp://ftp.isi.edu/in-notes/rfc2716.txt

- RFC 2869, *RADIUS Extensions,* www.ietf.org/rfc/rfc2869.txt

- Internet Draft: *Protected EAP Protocol,* www.ietf.org/internet-drafts/ draft-josefsson-pppext-eap-tls-eap-05.txt

Bridging and Switching

Objectives

- Understand transparent bridge processes of learning, filtering, forwarding, and flooding.
- Explain the purpose of the spanning-tree algorithm.
- Describe the bridge and port modes in a spanning-tree network.

CHAPTER 27

Transparent Bridging

Transparent bridges were first developed at Digital Equipment Corporation (Digital) in the early 1980s. Digital submitted its work to the Institute of Electrical and Electronic Engineers (IEEE), which incorporated the work into the IEEE 802.1 standard. Transparent bridges are very popular in Ethernet/IEEE 802.3 networks. This chapter provides an overview of transparent bridging's handling of traffic and protocol components.

Transparent Bridging Operation

Transparent bridges are so named because their presence and operation are transparent to network hosts. When transparent bridges are powered on, they learn the workstation locations by analyzing the source address of incoming frames from all attached networks. For example, if a bridge sees a frame arrive on port 1 from Host A, the bridge concludes that Host A can be reached through the segment connected to port 1. Through this process, transparent bridges build a table (the learning process), such as the one in Figure 27-1.

Figure 27-1 *Transparent Bridges Build a Table That Determines a Host's Accessibility*

Host address	Network number
15	1
17	1
12	2
13	2
18	1
9	1
14	3
.	.
.	.
.	.

The bridge uses its table as the basis for traffic forwarding. When a frame is received on one of the bridge's interfaces, the bridge looks up the frame's destination address in its internal table. If the table contains an association between the destination address and any of the bridge's ports aside from the one on which the frame was received, the frame is forwarded out the indicated port. If no association is found, the frame is flooded to all ports except the inbound port. Broadcasts and multicasts also are flooded in this way.

Transparent bridges successfully isolate intrasegment traffic, thereby reducing the traffic seen on each individual segment. This is called *filtering* and occurs when the source and destination MAC addresses reside on the same bridge interface. Filtering usually improves network response times, as seen by the user. The extent to which traffic is reduced and response times are improved depends on the volume of intersegment traffic relative to the total traffic, as well as the volume of broadcast and multicast traffic.

Bridging Loops

Without a bridge-to-bridge protocol, the transparent-bridge algorithm fails when multiple paths of bridges and local-area networks (LANs) exist between any two LANs in the internetwork. Figure 27-2 illustrates such a bridging loop.

Suppose that Host A sends a frame to Host B. Both bridges receive the frame and correctly learn that Host A is on segment 2. Each bridge then forwards the frame onto segment 2. Unfortunately, not only will Host B receive two copies of the frame (once from bridge 1 and once from bridge 2), but each bridge now believes that Host A resides on the same segment as Host B. When Host B replies to Host A's frame, both bridges will receive and subsequently filter the replies because the bridge table will indicate that the destination (Host A) is on the same network segment as the frame's source.

Figure 27-2 *Bridging Loops Can Result in Inaccurate Forwarding and Learning in Transparent Bridging Environments*

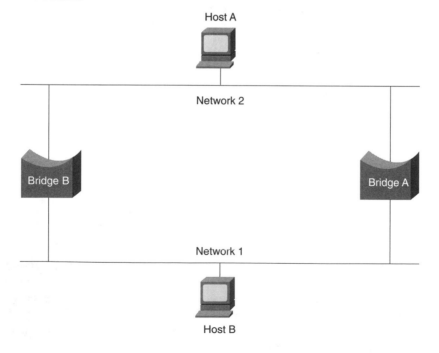

In addition to basic connectivity problems, the proliferation of broadcast messages in networks with loops represents a potentially serious network problem. Referring again to Figure 27-2, assume that Host A's initial frame is a broadcast. Both bridges forward the frames endlessly, using all available network bandwidth and blocking the transmission of other packets on both segments.

A topology with loops, such as that shown in Figure 27-2, can be useful as well as potentially harmful. A loop implies the existence of multiple paths through the internetwork, and a network with multiple paths from source to destination can increase overall network fault tolerance through improved topological flexibility.

Spanning-Tree Algorithm

The *spanning-tree algorithm (STA)* was developed by Digital Equipment Corporation, a key Ethernet vendor, to preserve the benefits of loops while eliminating their problems. Digital's algorithm subsequently was revised by the IEEE 802 committee and was published in the IEEE 802.1d specification. The Digital algorithm and the IEEE 802.1d algorithm are not compatible.

The STA designates a loop-free subset of the network's topology by placing those bridge ports that, if active, would create loops into a standby (blocking) condition. Blocking bridge ports can be activated in the event of a primary link failure, providing a new path through the internetwork.

The STA uses a conclusion from graph theory as a basis for constructing a loop-free subset of the network's topology. Graph theory states the following:

> For any connected graph consisting of nodes and edges connecting pairs of nodes, a spanning tree of edges maintains the connectivity of the graph but contains no loops.

Figure 27-3 illustrates how the STA eliminates loops. The STA calls for each bridge to be assigned a unique identifier. Typically, this identifier is one of the bridge's *Media Access Control (MAC)* addresses, plus an administratively assigned priority. Each port in every bridge also is assigned a unique identifier (within that bridge), which is typically its own MAC address. Finally, each bridge port is associated with a path cost, which represents the cost of transmitting a frame onto a LAN through that port. In Figure 27-3, path costs are noted on the lines emanating from each bridge. Path costs are usually defaulted but can be assigned manually by network administrators.

Figure 27-3 *STA-Based Bridges Use Designated and Root Ports to Eliminate Loops*

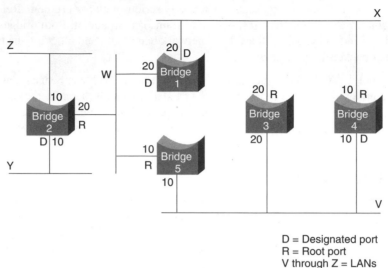

D = Designated port
R = Root port
V through Z = LANs

The first activity in spanning-tree computation is the selection of the *root bridge*, which is the bridge with the lowest-value bridge identifier. In Figure 27-3, the root bridge is Bridge 1. Next, the *root port* on all other bridges is determined. A bridge's root port is the port through which the root bridge can be reached with the least aggregate path cost, a value that is called the *root path cost*.

Finally, designated bridges and their designated ports are determined. A designated bridge is the bridge on each LAN that provides the minimum root path cost. A LAN's *designated bridge* is the only bridge allowed to forward frames to and from the LAN for which it is the designated bridge. A LAN's *designated port* is the port that connects it to the designated bridge.

In some cases, two or more bridges can have the same root path cost. In Figure 27-3, for example, Bridges 4 and 5 can both reach Bridge 1 (the root bridge) with a path cost of 10. In this case, the bridge identifiers are used again, this time to determine the designated bridges. Bridge 4's LAN V port is selected over Bridge 5's LAN V port.

Using this process, all but one of the bridges directly connected to each LAN are eliminated, thereby removing all two-LAN loops. The STA also eliminates loops involving more than two LANs, while still preserving connectivity. Figure 27-4 shows the results of applying the STA to the network shown in Figure 27-3. Figure 27-4 shows the tree topology more clearly. It also shows that the STA has placed both Bridge 3 and Bridge 5's ports to LAN V in standby mode.

Figure 27-4 *A Loop-Free Tree Topology and an STA-Based Transparent-Bridge Network*

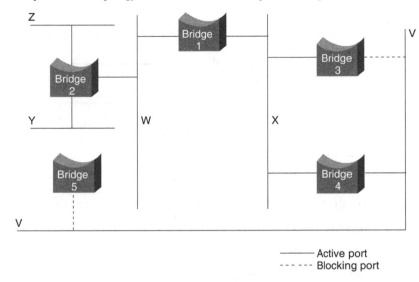

——— Active port
- - - - - Blocking port

The spanning-tree calculation occurs when the bridge is powered up and whenever a topology change is detected. The calculation requires communication between the spanning-tree bridges, which is accomplished through *configuration messages* (sometimes called *bridge protocol data units*, or *BPDUs*). Configuration messages contain information identifying the bridge that is presumed to be the root (root identifier) and the distance from the sending bridge to the root bridge (root path cost). Configuration messages also contain the bridge and port identifier of the sending bridge, as well as the age of information contained in the configuration message.

Bridges exchange configuration messages at regular intervals (typically 1 to 4 seconds). If a bridge fails (causing a topology change), neighboring bridges will detect the lack of configuration messages and will initiate a spanning-tree recalculation.

All transparent-bridge topology decisions are made locally by each bridge. Bridges exchange configuration messages with neighboring bridges, and no central authority exists to determine network topology or administration.

Frame Format

Transparent bridges exchange *configuration messages* and *topology-change messages*. Configuration messages are sent between bridges to establish a network topology. Topology-change messages are sent after a topology change has been detected to indicate that the STA should be rerun. This forces bridges to relearn the location of hosts because a host may originally have been accessed from port 1, although after the topology change it may be reached through port 2.

Figure 27-5 illustrates the IEEE 802.1d configuration-message format.

Figure 27-5 *Twelve Fields Comprise the Transparent-Bridge Configuration Message*

Field length, in bytes

2	1	1	1	8	4	8	2	2	2	2	2
Protocol identifier	Version	Message type	Flags	Root ID	Root path cost	Bridge ID	Port ID	Message age	Maximum age	Hello time	Forward delay

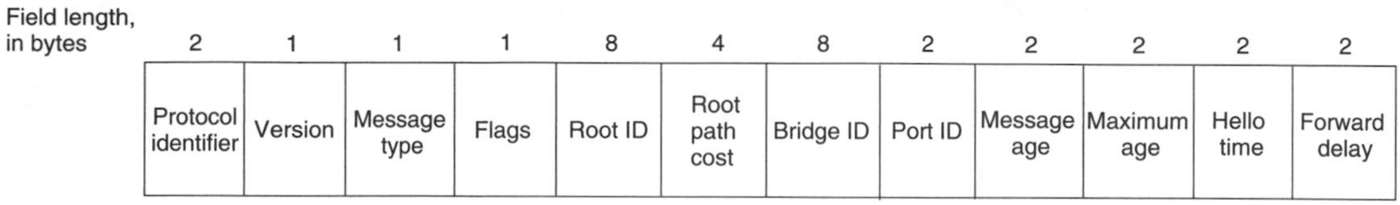

The fields of the transparent bridge configuration message are as follows:

- **Protocol Identifier**—Contains the value zero.

- **Version**—Contains the value zero.

- **Message Type**—Contains the value zero.

- **Flag**—Contains 1 byte, of which only 2 bits are used. The topology-change (TC) least significant bit signals a topology change. The topology-change acknowledgment (TCA) most significant bit is set to acknowledge receipt of a configuration message with the TC bit set.

- **Root ID**—Identifies the root bridge by listing its 2-byte priority followed by its 6-byte ID.

- **Root Path Cost**—Contains the cost of the path from the bridge sending the configuration message to the root bridge.

- **Bridge ID**—Identifies the priority and ID of the bridge sending the message.

- **Port ID**—Identifies the port from which the configuration message was sent. This field allows loops created by multiple attached bridges to be detected and handled.

- **Message Age**—Specifies the amount of time since the root sent the configuration message on which the current configuration message is based.

- **Maximum Age**—Indicates when the current configuration message should be deleted.

- **Hello Time**—Provides the time period between root bridge configuration messages.

- **Forward Delay**—Provides the length of time that bridges should wait before transitioning to a new state after a topology change. If a bridge transitions too soon, not all network links might be ready to change their state, and loops can result.

Topology-change messages consist of only 4 bytes. These include a Protocol-Identifier field, which contains the value zero; a *Version* field, which contains the value zero; and a Message-Type field, which contains the value 128.

Review Questions

1 What three frame types does a transparent bridge flood?

2 How does a bridge learn the relative location of a workstation?

3 What two bridge PDUs does a transparent bridge generate, and what are they used for?

4 What is the difference between forwarding and flooding?

5 After bridges determine the spanning-tree topology, they will take on various roles and configure ports into various modes. Specifically, the roles are root and designated bridges, and the modes are designated ports and root ports. If there are 10 bridges and 11 segments, how many of each are there in the broadcast domain?

For More Information

- Clark, Kennedy, and Kevin Hamilton. *CCIE Professional Development: Cisco LAN Switching*. Indianapolis: Cisco Press, 1999.

- Perlman, Radia. *Interconnections*, Second Edition: *Bridges, Routers, Switches, and Internetworking Protocols*. Boston: Addison Wesley, 1999.

Objectives

- Understand bridging in a mixed Ethernet and Token Ring environment.
- Describe the differences between source-route transparent and translational bridging.
- List some of the challenges of translational bridging.

CHAPTER 28

Mixed-Media Bridging

Background

Transparent bridges are found predominantly in Ethernet networks, and source-route bridges (SRBs) are found almost exclusively in Token Ring networks. Both transparent bridges and SRBs are popular, so it is reasonable to ask whether a method exists to directly bridge between them. Several solutions have evolved.

Translational bridging provides a relatively inexpensive solution to some of the many problems involved with bridging between transparent bridging and SRB domains. Translational bridging first appeared in the mid- to late-1980s but has not been championed by any standards organization. As a result, many aspects of translational bridging are left to the implementor.

In 1990, IBM addressed some of the weaknesses of translational bridging by introducing source-route transparent (SRT) bridging. SRT bridges can forward traffic from both transparent and source-route end nodes and can form a common spanning tree with transparent bridges, thereby allowing end stations of each type to communicate with end stations of the same type in a network of arbitrary topology. SRT is specified in the IEEE 802.1d Appendix C.

Ultimately, the goal of connecting transparent bridging and SRB domains is to allow communication between transparent bridges and SRB end stations. This chapter describes the technical problems that must be addressed by algorithms attempting to do this and presents two possible solutions: translational bridging and SRT bridging.

Translation Challenges

Many challenges are associated with allowing end stations from the Ethernet/transparent bridging domain to communicate with end stations from the SRB/Token Ring domain:

- **Incompatible bit ordering**—Although both Ethernet and Token Ring support 48-bit Media Access Control (MAC) addresses, the internal hardware representation of these addresses differs. In a serial bit stream representing an address, Token Ring considers the first bit encountered to be the high-order bit of a byte. Ethernet, on the other hand, considers the first bit encountered to be the low-order bit. The Ethernet format is referred to as canonical format, and the Token Ring method is noncanonical. To translate between canonical and noncanonical formats, the translational bridge reverses the bit order for each byte of the address. For example, an Ethernet address of 0C-00-01-38-73-0B (canonical) translates to an address of 30-00-80-1C-CE-D0 (noncanonical) for Token Ring.

- **Embedded MAC addresses**—In some cases, MAC addresses actually are carried in the data portion of a frame. The Address Resolution Protocol (ARP), a popular protocol in Transmission Control Protocol/Internet Protocol (TCP/IP) networks, for example, places hardware addresses in the data portion of a link layer frame. Conversion of addresses that might or might not appear in the data portion of a frame is difficult because these must be handled on a case-by-case basis. IPX also embeds Layer 2 addresses in the data portion of some frames. Translational bridges should resequence the bit order of these embedded addresses, too. Many protocols respond to the MAC addresses embedded in the protocol rather than in the Layer 2 headers. Therefore, the translational bridge must resequence these bytes as well, or the device will not be capable of responding to the correct MAC address.

- **Incompatible maximum transfer unit (MTU) sizes**—Token Ring and Ethernet support different maximum frame sizes. Ethernet's MTU is approximately 1500 bytes, whereas Token Ring frames can be much larger. Because bridges are not capable of frame fragmentation and reassembly, packets that exceed the MTU of a given network must be dropped.

- **Handling of frame-status bit actions**—Token Ring frames include three frame-status bits: A, C, and E. The purpose of these bits is to tell the frame's source whether the destination saw the frame (A bit set), copied the frame (C bit set), or found errors in the frame (E bit set). Because Ethernet does not support these bits, the question of how to deal with them is left to the Ethernet-Token Ring bridge manufacturer.

- **Handling of exclusive Token Ring functions**—Certain Token Ring bits have no corollary in Ethernet. For example, Ethernet has no priority mechanism, whereas Token Ring does. Other Token Ring bits that must be thrown out when a Token Ring frame is converted to an Ethernet frame include the token bit, the monitor bit, and the reservation bits.

- **Handling of explorer frames**—Transparent bridges do not inherently understand what to do with SRB explorer frames. Transparent bridges learn about the network's topology through analysis of the source address of incoming frames. They have no knowledge of the SRB route-discovery process.

- **Handling of routing information field (RIF) information within Token Ring frames**—The SRB algorithm places routing information in the RIF field. The transparent-bridging algorithm has no RIF equivalent, and the idea of placing routing information in a frame is foreign to transparent bridging.

- **Incompatible spanning-tree algorithms**—Transparent bridging and SRB both use the spanning-tree algorithm to try to avoid loops, but the particular algorithms employed by the two bridging methods are incompatible.

- **Handling of frames without route information**—SRBs expect all inter-LAN frames to contain route information. When a frame without a RIF field (including transparent bridging configuration and topology-change messages, as well as MAC frames sent from the transparent-bridging domain) arrives at an SRB bridge, it is ignored.

Translational Bridging

Because there has been no real standardization in how communication between two media types should occur, no single translational bridging implementation can be called correct. This section describes several popular methods for implementing translational bridging.

Translational bridges reorder source and destination address bits when translating between Ethernet and Token Ring frame formats. The problem of embedded MAC addresses can be solved by programming the bridge to check for various types of MAC addresses, but this solution must be adapted with each new type of embedded MAC address. Some translational-bridging solutions simply check for the most popular embedded addresses. If translational-bridging software runs in a multiprotocol router, the router can successfully route these protocols and avoid the problem entirely.

The RIF field has a subfield that indicates the largest frame size that can be accepted by a particular SRB implementation. Translational bridges that send frames from the transparent-bridging domain to the SRB domain usually set the MTU size field to 1500 bytes to limit the size of Token Ring frames entering the transparent-bridging domain. Some hosts cannot correctly process this field, in which case translational bridges are forced to drop those frames that exceed Ethernet's MTU size.

Bits representing Token Ring functions that have no Ethernet corollary typically are thrown out by translational bridges. For example, Token Ring's priority, reservation, and monitor bits (contained in the access-control byte) are discarded. Token Ring's frame status bits (contained in the byte following the ending delimiter, which follows the data field) are treated differently depending on the bridge manufacturer. Some bridge manufacturers simply ignore the bits. Others have the bridge set the C bit (to indicate that the frame has been copied) but not the A bit (which indicates that the destination station recognizes the address). In the former case, a Token Ring source node determines whether the frame it sent has become lost. Proponents of this approach suggest that reliability mechanisms, such as the tracking of lost frames, are better left for implementation in Layer 4 of the OSI model. Proponents of setting the C bit contend that this bit must be set to track lost frames but that the A bit cannot be set because the bridge is not the final destination.

Translational bridges can create a software gateway between the two domains. To the SRB end stations, the translational bridge has a ring number and a bridge number associated with it, so it looks like a standard SRB. The ring number, in this case, actually reflects the entire transparent-bridging domain. To the transparent-bridging domain, the translational bridge is another transparent bridge.

When bridging from the SRB domain to the transparent-bridging domain, SRB information is removed. RIFs usually are cached for use by subsequent return traffic. When bridging from the transparent bridging to the SRB domain, the translational bridge can check the frame to see if it has a unicast destination. If the frame has a multicast or broadcast destination, it is sent into the SRB domain as a spanning-tree explorer. If the frame has a unicast address, the translational bridge looks up the destination in the RIF cache. If a path is found, it is used, and the RIF information is added to the frame; otherwise, the frame is sent as a spanning-tree explorer.

Figure 28-1 shows a mix of Token Ring and Ethernet, with a translational bridge interconnecting the Token Ring to the Ethernet. A unicast transfer sourced by station 1 on the Token Ring to station 2 on the Ethernet segment passes through two bridges. Station 1 generates a frame with a RIF that lists Ring1-Bridge1-Ring2-Bridge2-Ring3 as the path. Note that Ring3 is really the Ethernet segment. Station 1 does not know that Station 2 is on Ethernet. When station 2 responds to station 1, it generates a frame without a RIF. Bridge 2, the translational bridge, notices the destination MAC address (station 1), inserts a RIF in the frame, and forwards it toward station 1.

Figure 28-1 *A Network to Demonstrate a Unicast Transfer Between a Token Ring and an Ethernet-Attached Station*

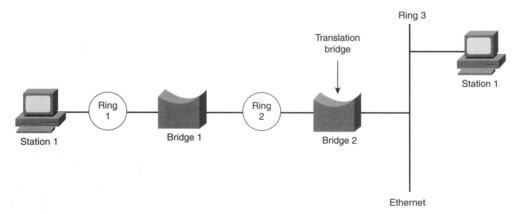

Because the two spanning-tree implementations are not compatible, multiple paths between the SRB and the transparent-bridging domains typically are not permitted. Figures 28-2 through 28-4 illustrate frame conversions that can take place in translational bridging.

Figure 28-2 illustrates the frame conversion between IEEE 802.3 and Token Ring. The destination and source addresses (DASA), service-access point (SAP), Logical Link Control (LLC) information, and data are passed to the corresponding fields of the destination frame. The destination and source address bits are reordered. When bridging from IEEE 802.3 to Token Ring, the length field of the IEEE 802.3 frame is removed. When bridging from Token Ring to IEEE 802.3, the access-control byte and the RIF are removed. The RIF can be cached in the translational bridge for use by return traffic.

Figure 28-2   *Four Fields Remain the Same in Frame Conversion Between IEEE 802.3 and Token Ring*

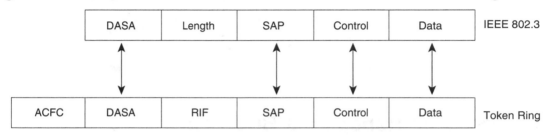

Figure 28-3 illustrates the frame conversion between Ethernet Type II and Token Ring Subnetwork Access Protocol (SNAP). (SNAP adds vendor and type codes to the Data field of the Token Ring frame.) The destination and source addresses, type information, and data are passed to the corresponding fields of the destination frame, and the DASA bits are reordered. When bridging from Token Ring SNAP to Ethernet Type II, the RIF information, SAP, LLC information, and vendor code are removed. The RIF can be cached in the translational bridge for use by return traffic. When bridging from Ethernet Type II to Token Ring SNAP, no information is removed.

Figure 28-3   *Three Fields Remain the Same in Frame Conversion Between Ethernet Type II and Token Ring SNAP*

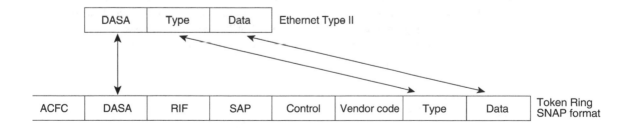

Figure 28-4 illustrates the frame conversion between Ethernet Type II 0x80D5 format and Token Ring. (Ethernet Type II 0x80D5 carries IBM SNA data in Ethernet frames.) The DASA, SAP, LLC information, and data are passed to the corresponding fields of the destination frame, and the destination and source address bits are reordered. When bridging from Ethernet Type II 0x80D5 to Token Ring, the Type and 80D5 Header fields are removed. When bridging from Token Ring to Ethernet Type II 0x80D5, the RIF is removed. The RIF can be cached in the translational bridge for use by return traffic.

Figure 28-4 *Four Fields Remain the Same in Frame Conversion Between Ethernet Type II 0x80D5 Format and Token Ring*

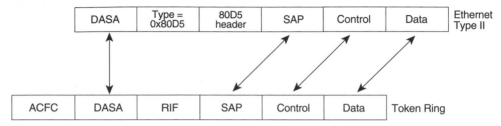

Source-Route Transparent Bridging

SRT bridges combine implementations of the transparent-bridging and SRB algorithms. SRT bridges use the routing information indicator (RII) bit to distinguish between frames employing SRB and frames employing transparent bridging. If the RII bit is 1, a RIF is present in the frame, and the bridge uses the SRB algorithm. If the RII bit is 0, a RIF is not present, and the bridge uses transparent bridging.

As with translational bridges, SRT bridges are not perfect solutions to the problems of mixed-media bridging. SRT bridges still must deal with the Ethernet/Token Ring incompatibilities described earlier. SRT bridging is likely to require hardware upgrades to SRBs to allow them to handle the increased burden of analyzing every packet. Software upgrades to SRBs also might be required. Furthermore, in environments of mixed SRT bridges, transparent bridges, and SRBs, source routes chosen must traverse whatever SRT bridges and SRBs are available. The resulting paths potentially can be substantially inferior to spanning-tree paths created by transparent bridges. Finally, mixed SRB/SRT bridging networks lose the benefits of SRT bridging, so users feel compelled to execute a complete cutover to SRT bridging at considerable expense. Still, SRT bridging permits the coexistence of two incompatible environments and allows communication between SRB and transparent-bridging end nodes.

Review Questions

1 Translational bridging addresses several issues when interconnecting different media types such as Ethernet and Token Ring. List and describe four of the methods described in the chapter.

2 One of the challenges of translational bridging is the reordering of bits whenever a frame moves from an Ethernet to a Token Ring segment. If an Ethernet station targets a Token Ring station with a destination MAC address of 00-00-0C-11-22-33 (canonical format), what would the MAC address look like on Token Ring (noncanonical format)?

3 Can a translational bridge work for all Ethernet and Token Ring networks and protocols?

4 What is the difference between a source-route bridge and a source-route transparent bridge?

For More Information

- Clark, Kennedy, and Kevin Hamilton. *CCIE Professional Development: Cisco LAN Switching.* Indianapolis: Cisco Press, 1999.

- Perlman, Radia. *Interconnections, Second Edition: Bridges, Routers, Switches, and Internetworking Protocols*. Boston: Addison Wesley, 1999.

Objectives

- Describe when to use source-route bridging.
- Understand the difference between SRB and transparent bridging.
- Know the mechanism that end stations use to specify a source-route.
- Understand the basics of source-route frame formats.

CHAPTER 29

Source-Route Bridging

Background

The source-route bridging (SRB) algorithm was developed by IBM and was proposed to the IEEE 802.5 committee as the means to bridge between all LANs. Since its initial proposal, IBM has offered a new bridging standard to the IEEE 802 committee: the source-route transparent (SRT) bridging solution. SRT bridging eliminates pure SRBs, proposing that the two types of LAN bridges be transparent bridges and SRT bridges. Although SRT bridging has achieved support, SRBs are still widely deployed. SRT is covered in Chapter 28, "Mixed-Media Bridging." This chapter summarizes the basic SRB frame-forwarding algorithm and describes SRB frame fields.

SRB Algorithm

SRBs are so named because they assume that the complete source-to-destination route is placed in all inter-LAN frames sent by the source. SRBs store and forward the frames as indicated by the route appearing in the appropriate frame field. Figure 29-1 illustrates a sample SRB network.

In Figure 29-1, assume that Host X wants to send a frame to Host Y. Initially, Host X does not know whether Host Y resides on the same LAN or a different LAN. To determine this, Host X sends out a test frame. If that frame returns to Host X without a positive indication that Host Y has seen it, Host X assumes that Host Y is on a remote segment.

Figure 29-1 *An SRB Network Contains LANs and Bridges*

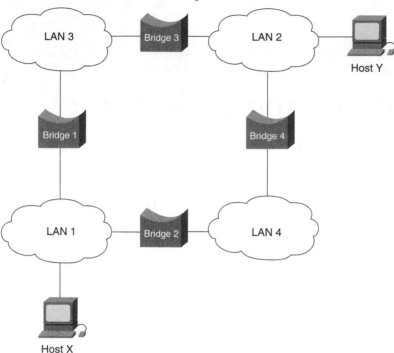

To determine the exact remote location of Host Y, Host X sends an explorer frame. Each bridge receiving the explorer frame (Bridges 1 and 2, in this example) copies the frame onto all outbound ports. Route information is added to the explorer frames as they travel through the internetwork. When Host X's explorer frames reach Host Y, Host Y replies to each individually, using the accumulated route information. Upon receipt of all response frames, Host X chooses a path based on some predetermined criteria.

In the example in Figure 29-1, this process will yield two routes:

- LAN 1 to Bridge 1 to LAN 3 to Bridge 3 to LAN 2
- LAN 1 to Bridge 2 to LAN 4 to Bridge 4 to LAN 2

Host X must select one of these two routes. The IEEE 802.5 specification does not mandate the criteria that Host X should use in choosing a route, but it does make several suggestions, including the following:

- First frame received
- Response with the minimum number of hops
- Response with the largest allowed frame size
- Various combinations of the preceding criteria

In most cases, the path contained in the first frame received is used.

After a route is selected, it is inserted into frames destined for Host Y in the form of a *routing information field (RIF)*. A RIF is included only in those frames destined for other LANs. The presence of routing information within the frame is indicated by setting the most significant bit within the Source Address field, called the *routing information indicator (RII)* bit.

Frame Format

The IEEE 802.5 RIF is structured as shown in Figure 29-2.

The RIF illustrated in Figure 29-2 consists of two main fields: Routing Control and Routing Designator. These fields are described in the summaries that follow.

Figure 29-2 *An IEEE 802.5 RIF Is Present in Frames Destined for Other LANs*

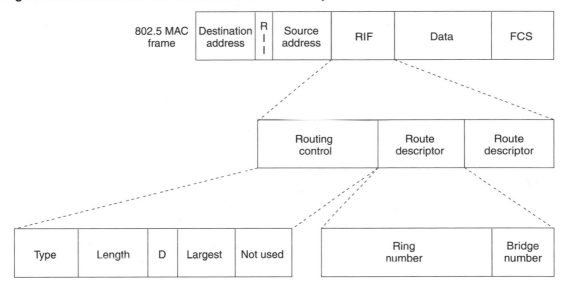

Routing Control Field

The Routing Control field consists of four subfields: Type, Length, D Bit, and Largest Frame. The fields are summarized in the following list:

- **Type**—Consists of three possible types of routing controls:
    - **Specifically routed**—Used when the source node supplies the route in the RIF header. The bridges route the frame by using the route designator field(s).

- **All paths explorer**—Used to find a remote node. The route is collected as the frame traverses the network. Bridges add to the frame their bridge number and the ring number onto which the frame is forwarded. (The first bridge also adds the ring number of the first ring.) The target destination will receive as many frames as routes to that destination.

- **Spanning-tree explorer**—Used to find a remote node. Only bridges in the spanning tree forward the frame, adding their bridge number and attached ring number as it is forwarded. The spanning-tree explorer reduces the number of frames sent during the discovery process.

- **Length**—Indicates the total length (in bytes) of the RIF. The value can range from 2 to 30 bytes.

- **D Bit**—Indicates and controls the direction (forward or reverse) that the frame traverses. The D bit affects whether bridges read the ring number/bridge number combinations in the route designators from right to left (forward) or from left to right (reverse).

- **Largest Frame**—Indicates the largest frame size that can be handled along a designated route. The source initially sets the largest frame size, but bridges can lower it if they cannot accommodate the requested size.

Routing Designator Fields

Each routing designator field consists of two subfields:

- **Ring Number (12 bits)**—Assigns a value that must be unique within the bridged network.

- **Bridge Number (4 bits)**—Assigns a value that follows the ring number. This number does not have to be unique unless it is parallel with another bridge connecting two rings.

Bridges add to the frame their bridge number and the ring number onto which the frame is forwarded. (The first bridge also adds the ring number of the first ring.)

Routes are alternating sequences of ring and bridge numbers that start and end with ring numbers. A single RIF can contain more than one routing designator field. The IEEE specifies a maximum of 14 routing designator fields (a maximum of 13 bridges or hops because the last bridge number always equals zero).

Until recently, IBM specified a maximum of eight routing designator fields (a maximum of seven bridges or hops), and most bridge manufacturers followed IBM's implementation. Newer IBM bridge software programs combined with new LAN adapters support 13 hops.

Review Questions

1 Describe a basic difference between transparent bridges and source-route bridges relative to the forwarding processes.

2 Recall that the SRB standards do not specify how a source selects a path to the destination whenever multiple choices exist. The chapter listed four methods that a source could use to make the decision and said that the first received frame (path) was the most commonly used method. What assumptions might the source make about the network when using this method?

3 How do stations and bridges know if there is a source route defined in the frame?

4 What problems might you anticipate in a large SRB network with many alternate paths?

5 Because only 4 bits are used to define bridge numbers, does this mean that there can be only 16 bridges ($2^4=16$)? Why or why not?

6 Can you have a large number of bridges attached to a central ring, all with the same bridge value?

7 A 12-bit value defines ring numbers. Can you have more than 4096 rings in the network ($2^{12}=4096$)? Why or why not?

For More Information

- Computer Technology Research Corporation. *The IBM Token Ring Network*. New York: Prentice Hall, 1990.

- IEEE. "IEEE Standard for Local Area Networks: Token Ring Physical Layer Specifications." June 1989.

- Although not directly related to source-route bridging, an effort to define a high-speed Token Ring standard for IEEE 802.5 is underway. Details may be monitored at the Web site http://www.hstra.com/.

Objectives

- Understand the relationship of LAN switching to legacy internetworking devices such as bridges and routers.
- Understand the advantages of VLANs.
- Know the difference between access and trunk links.
- Know the purpose of a trunk protocol.
- Understand Layer 3 switching concepts.

CHAPTER **30**

LAN Switching and VLANs

A *LAN switch* is a device that provides much higher port density at a lower cost than traditional bridges. For this reason, LAN switches can accommodate network designs featuring fewer users per segment, thereby increasing the average available bandwidth per user. This chapter provides a summary of general LAN switch operation and maps LAN switching to the OSI reference model.

The trend toward fewer users per segment is known as *microsegmentation*. Microsegmentation allows the creation of private or dedicated segments—that is, one user per segment. Each user receives instant access to the full bandwidth and does not have to contend for available bandwidth with other users. As a result, collisions (a normal phenomenon in shared-medium networks employing hubs) do not occur, as long as the equipment operates in full-duplex mode. A LAN switch forwards frames based on either the frame's Layer 2 address (Layer 2 LAN switch) or, in some cases, the frame's Layer 3 address (multilayer LAN switch). A LAN switch is also called a frame switch because it forwards Layer 2 frames, whereas an ATM switch forwards cells.

Figure 30-1 illustrates a LAN switch providing dedicated bandwidth to devices and illustrates the relationship of Layer 2 LAN switching to the OSI data link layer.

Figure 30-1 *A LAN Switch Is a Data Link Layer Device*

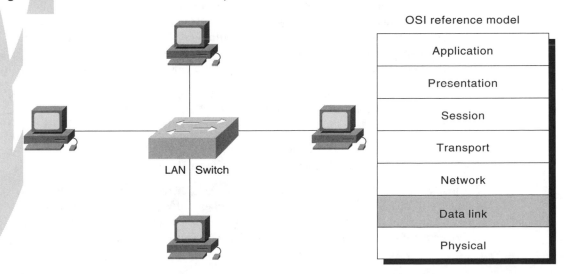

History

The earliest LAN switches were developed in 1990. They were Layer 2 devices (bridges) dedicated to solving desktop bandwidth issues. Recent LAN switches evolved to multilayer devices capable of handling protocol issues involved in high-bandwidth applications that historically have been solved by routers. Today, LAN switches are used to replace hubs in the wiring closet because user applications demand greater bandwidth.

LAN Switch Operation

LAN switches are similar to transparent bridges in functions such as learning the topology, forwarding, and filtering. These switches also support several new and unique features, such as dedicated communication between devices through full-duplex operations, multiple simultaneous conversations, and media-rate adaption.

Full-duplex communication between network devices increases file-transfer throughput. Multiple simultaneous conversations can occur by forwarding, or switching, several packets at the same time, thereby increasing network capacity by the number of conversations supported. Full-duplex communication effectively doubles the throughput, while with media-rate adaption, the LAN switch can translate between 10 and 100 Mbps, allowing bandwidth to be allocated as needed.

Deploying LAN switches requires no change to existing hubs, network interface cards (NICs), or cabling.

VLANs Defined

A VLAN is defined as a *broadcast domain* within a switched network. Broadcast domains describe the extent that a network propagates a broadcast frame generated by a station. Some switches may be configured to support a single or multiple VLANs. Whenever a switch supports multiple VLANs, broadcasts within one VLAN never appear in another VLAN. Switch ports configured as a member of one VLAN belong to a different broadcast domain, as compared to switch ports configured as members of a different VLAN.

Creating VLANs enables administrators to build broadcast domains with fewer users in each broadcast domain. This increases the bandwidth available to users because fewer users will contend for the bandwidth.

Routers also maintain broadcast domain isolation by blocking broadcast frames. Therefore, traffic can pass from one VLAN to another only through a router.

Normally, each subnet belongs to a different VLAN. Therefore, a network with many subnets will probably have many VLANs. Switches and VLANs enable a network administrator to assign users to broadcast domains based upon the user's job need. This provides a high level of deployment flexibility for a network administrator.

Advantages of VLANs include the following:

- Segmentation of broadcast domains to create more bandwidth
- Additional security by isolating users with bridge technologies
- Deployment flexibility based upon job function rather than physical placement

Switch Port Modes

Switch ports run in either access or trunk mode. In access mode, the interface belongs to one and only one VLAN. Normally a switch port in access mode attaches to an end user device or a server. The frames transmitted on an access link look like any other Ethernet frame.

Trunks, on the other hand, multiplex traffic for multiple VLANs over the same physical link. Trunk links usually interconnect switches, as shown in Figure 30-2. However, they may also attach end devices such as servers that have special adapter cards that participate in the multiplexing protocol.

Figure 30-2 *Switches Interconnected with Trunk Links*

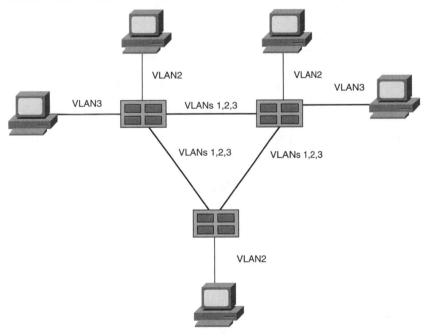

Note that some of the devices attach to their switch using access links, while the connections between the switches utilize trunk links.

To multiplex VLAN traffic, special protocols exist that encapsulate or tag (mark) the frames so that the receiving device knows to which VLAN the frame belongs. Trunk protocols are either proprietary or based upon IEEE 802.1Q. For example, a proprietary trunk protocol may be like Cisco's proprietary Inter-Switch Link (ISL), which enables Cisco devices to multiplex VLANs in a manner optimized for Cisco components. Or, an intervendor solution may be implemented, such as 802.1Q, which enables products from more than one vendor to multiplex VLANs on a trunk link.

Without trunk links, multiple access links must be installed to support multiple VLANs between switches. This is not cost-effective and does not scale well, so trunks are preferable for interconnecting switches in most cases.

LAN Switching Forwarding

LAN switches can be characterized by the forwarding method that they support. In the store-and-forward switching method, error checking is performed and erroneous frames are discarded. With the cut-through switching method, latency is reduced by eliminating error checking.

With the store-and-forward switching method, the LAN switch copies the entire frame into its onboard buffers and computes the cyclic redundancy check (CRC). The frame is discarded if it contains a CRC error or if it is a *runt* (less than 64 bytes, including the CRC) or a *giant* (more than 1518 bytes, including the CRC). If the frame does not contain any errors, the LAN switch looks up the destination address in its forwarding, or switching, table and determines the outgoing interface. It then forwards the frame toward its destination.

With the cut-through switching method, the LAN switch copies only the destination address (the first 6 bytes following the preamble) into its onboard buffers. It then looks up the destination address in its switching table, determines the outgoing interface, and forwards the frame toward its destination. A cut-through switch provides reduced latency because it begins to forward the frame as soon as it reads the destination address and determines the outgoing interface.

Some switches can be configured to perform cut-through switching on a per-port basis until a user-defined error threshold is reached, when they automatically change to store-and-forward mode. When the error rate falls below the threshold, the port automatically changes back to store-and-forward mode.

LAN switches must use store-and-forward techniques to support multilaycr switching. The switch must receive the entire frame before it performs any protocol-layer operations. For this reason, advanced switches that perform Layer 3 switching are store-and-forward devices.

LAN Switching Bandwidth

LAN switches also can be characterized according to the proportion of bandwidth allocated to each port. Symmetric switching provides evenly distributed bandwidth to each port, while asymmetric switching provides unlike, or unequal, bandwidth between some ports.

An *asymmetric LAN switch* provides switched connections between ports of unlike bandwidths, such as a combination of 10BaseT and 100BaseT. This type of switching is also called *10/100 switching*. Asymmetric switching is optimized for client/server traffic flows in which multiple clients simultaneously communicate with a server, requiring more bandwidth dedicated to the server port to prevent a bottleneck at that port.

A *symmetric switch* provides switched connections between ports with the same bandwidth, such as all 10BaseT or all 100BaseT. Symmetric switching is optimized for a reasonably distributed traffic load, such as in a peer-to-peer desktop environment.

A network manager must evaluate the needed amount of bandwidth for connections between devices to accommodate the data flow of network-based applications when deciding to select an asymmetric or symmetric switch.

LAN Switch and the OSI Model

LAN switches can be categorized according to the OSI layer at which they filter and forward, or switch, frames. These categories are: Layer 2, Layer 2 with Layer 3 features, or multilayer.

A Layer 2 LAN switch is operationally similar to a multiport bridge but has a much higher capacity and supports many new features, such as full-duplex operation. A Layer 2 LAN switch performs switching and filtering based on the OSI data link layer (Layer 2) MAC address. As with bridges, it is completely transparent to network protocols and user applications.

A Layer 2 LAN switch with Layer 3 features can make switching decisions based on more information than just the Layer 2 MAC address. Such a switch might incorporate some Layer 3 traffic-control features, such as broadcast and multicast traffic management, security through access lists, and IP fragmentation.

A multilayer switch makes switching and filtering decisions based on OSI data link layer (Layer 2) and OSI network layer (Layer 3) addresses. This type of switch dynamically decides whether to switch (Layer 2) or route (Layer 3) incoming traffic. A multilayer LAN switch switches within a workgroup and routes between different workgroups.

Layer 3 switching allows data flows to bypass routers. The first frame passes through the router as normal to ensure that all security policies are observed. The switches watch the way that the router treats the frame and then replicate the process for subsequent frames. For example, if a series of FTP frames flows from a 10.0.0.1 to 192.168.1.1, the frames normally pass through a router. Multilayer switching observes how the router changes the Layer 2 and Layer 3 headers and imitates the router for the rest of the frames. This reduces the load on the router and the latency through the network.

Review Questions

1 A multilayer switch mimics the actions of a router when an initial frame passes through a router. What things does the multilayer switch do to the Layer 2 and Layer 3 headers to thoroughly imitate the router?

2 A LAN switch most closely resembles what type of internetworking device?

3 Two trunk protocols were described. For what situation would you use the IEEE 802.1Q mode?

4 Which switching method protects network segment bandwidth from errored frames?

5 How does a store-and-forward switch know if a frame is errored?

6 Do VLAN borders cross routers?

7 How does a trunk link differ from an access link?

8 Before switches and VLANs, administrators assigned users to a network based not on the user's needs, but on something else. What determined the user network assignment?

For More Information

- Breyer, Robert, and Sean Riley. *Switched and Fast Ethernet*. New York: Ziff-Davis Press, 1997.

- Clark, Kennedy, and Kevin Hamilton. *CCIE Professional Development: Cisco LAN Switching*. Indianapolis: Cisco Press, 1999.

- Hein, Mathias, and David Griffiths. *Switching Technology in the Local Network*. New York: International Thomson Publishing, 1997.

- Perlman, Radia. *Interconnections*, Second Edition: *Bridges, Routers, Switches, and Internetworking Protocols*. Boston: Addison Wesley, 1999.

Objectives

- Understand the ATM cell structure.
- Identify the ATM model layers.
- Know the ATM connection types.
- Describe the call establishment process.
- Understand the purpose of each LANE component.
- Describe LANE operations.
- Know the purpose of MPOA.

CHAPTER 31

Asynchronous Transfer Mode Switching

Asynchronous Transfer Mode (ATM) is an International Telecommunication Union–Telecommunications Standards Section (ITU-T) standard for cell relay wherein information for multiple service types, such as voice, video, or data, is conveyed in small, fixed-size cells. ATM networks are connection-oriented. This chapter provides summaries of ATM protocols, services, and operation. Figure 31-1 illustrates a private ATM network and a public ATM network carrying voice, video, and data traffic.

Figure 31-1 *A Private ATM Network and a Public ATM Network Both Can Carry Voice, Video, and Data Traffic*

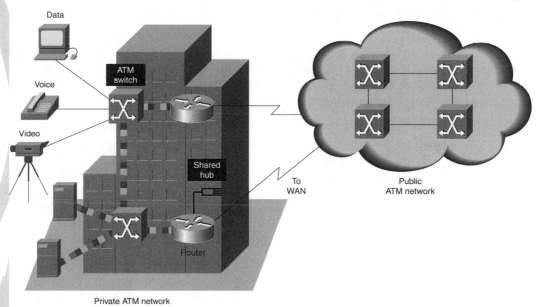

Standards

ATM is based on the efforts of the ITU-T Broadband Integrated Services Digital Network (B-ISDN) standard. It was originally conceived as a high-speed transfer technology for voice, video, and data over public networks. The ATM Forum extended the ITU-T's vision of ATM for use over public and private networks. The ATM Forum has released work on the following specifications:

- User-to-Network Interface (UNI) 2.0
- UNI 3.0
- UNI 3.1
- UNI 4.0
- Public-Network Node Interface (P-NNI)
- LAN Emulation (LANE)
- Multiprotocol over ATM

ATM Devices and the Network Environment

ATM is a cell-switching and multiplexing technology that combines the benefits of circuit switching (guaranteed capacity and constant transmission delay) with those of packet switching (flexibility and efficiency for intermittent traffic). It provides scalable bandwidth from a few megabits per second (Mbps) to many gigabits per second (Gbps). Because of its asynchronous nature, ATM is more efficient than synchronous technologies, such as *time-division multiplexing (TDM)*.

With TDM, each user is assigned to a time slot, and no other station can send in that time slot. If a station has much data to send, it can send only when its time slot comes up, even if all other time slots are empty. However, if a station has nothing to transmit when its time slot comes up, the time slot is sent empty and is wasted. Because ATM is asynchronous, time slots are available on demand with information identifying the source of the transmission contained in the header of each ATM cell.

ATM Cell Basic Format

ATM transfers information in fixed-size units called *cells*. Each cell consists of 53 octets, or bytes. The first 5 bytes contain cell-header information, and the remaining 48 contain the payload (user information). Small, fixed-length cells are well suited to transferring voice and video traffic because such traffic is intolerant of delays that result from having to wait for a large data packet to download, among other things. Figure 31-2 illustrates the basic format of an ATM cell.

Figure 31-2 *An ATM Cell Consists of a Header and Payload Data*

ATM Devices

An *ATM network* is made up of an *ATM switch* and *ATM endpoints*. An ATM switch is responsible for cell transit through an ATM network. The job of an ATM switch is well defined: It accepts the incoming cell from an ATM endpoint or another ATM switch. It then reads and updates the cell header information and quickly switches the cell to an output interface toward its destination. An ATM endpoint (or end system) contains an ATM network interface adapter. Examples of ATM endpoints are workstations, routers, digital service units (DSUs), LAN switches, and video coder-decoders (CODECs). Figure 31-3 illustrates an ATM network made up of ATM switches and ATM endpoints.

Figure 31-3 *An ATM Network Comprises ATM Switches and Endpoints*

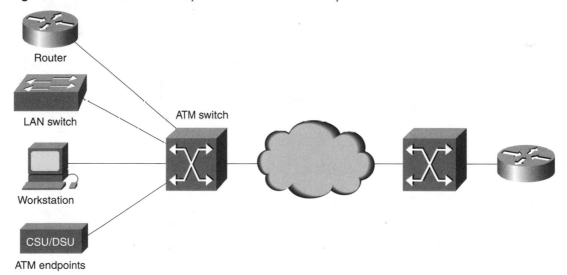

ATM Network Interfaces

An ATM network consists of a set of ATM switches interconnected by point-to-point ATM links or interfaces. ATM switches support two primary types of interfaces: UNI and NNI. The UNI connects ATM end systems (such as hosts and routers) to an ATM switch. The NNI connects two ATM switches.

Depending on whether the switch is owned and located at the customer's premises or is publicly owned and operated by the telephone company, UNI and NNI can be further subdivided into public and private UNIs and NNIs. A private UNI connects an ATM endpoint and a private ATM switch. Its public counterpart connects an ATM endpoint or private switch to a public switch. A private NNI connects two ATM switches within the same private organization. A public one connects two ATM switches within the same public organization.

An additional specification, the *broadband intercarrier interface (B-ICI)*, connects two public switches from different service providers. Figure 31-4 illustrates the ATM interface specifications for private and public networks.

Figure 31-4 *ATM Interface Specifications Differ for Private and Public Networks*

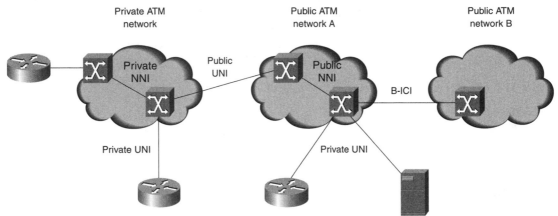

ATM Cell Header Format

An ATM cell header can be one of two formats: UNI or NNI. The UNI header is used for communication between ATM endpoints and ATM switches in private ATM networks. The NNI header is used for communication between ATM switches. Figure 31-5 depicts the basic ATM cell format, the ATM UNI cell header format, and the ATM NNI cell header format.

Figure 31-5 *An ATM Cell, ATM UNI Cell, and ATM NNI Cell Header Each Contain 48 Bytes of Payload*

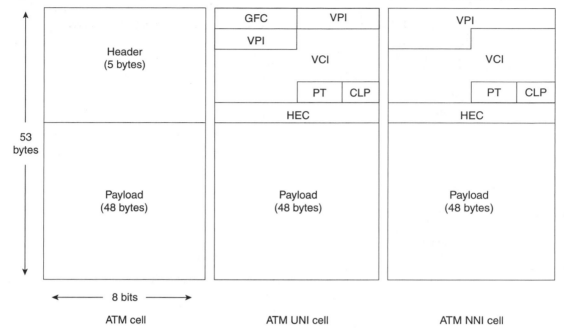

Unlike the UNI, the NNI header does not include the Generic Flow Control (GFC) field. Additionally, the NNI header has a Virtual Path Identifier (VPI) field that occupies the first 12 bits, allowing for larger trunks between public ATM switches.

ATM Cell Header Fields

In addition to GFC and VPI header fields, several others are used in ATM cell header fields. The following descriptions summarize the ATM cell header fields illustrated in Figure 31-5:

- **Generic Flow Control (GFC)**— Provides local functions, such as identifying multiple stations that share a single ATM interface. This field is typically not used and is set to its default value of 0 (binary 0000).

- **Virtual Path Identifier (VPI)**—In conjunction with the VCI, identifies the next destination of a cell as it passes through a series of ATM switches on the way to its destination.

- **Virtual Channel Identifier (VCI)**—In conjunction with the VPI, identifies the next destination of a cell as it passes through a series of ATM switches on the way to its destination.

- **Payload Type (PT)**—Indicates in the first bit whether the cell contains user data or control data. If the cell contains user data, the bit is set to 0. If it contains control data, it is set to 1. The second bit indicates congestion (0 = no congestion, 1 = congestion), and the third bit indicates whether the cell is the last in a series of cells that represent a single AAL5 frame (1 = last cell for the frame).

- **Cell Loss Priority (CLP)**—Indicates whether the cell should be discarded if it encounters extreme congestion as it moves through the network. If the CLP bit equals 1, the cell should be discarded in preference to cells with the CLP bit equal to 0.

- **Header Error Control (HEC)**—Calculates checksum only on the first 4 bytes of the header. HEC can correct a single bit error in these bytes, thereby preserving the cell rather than discarding it.

ATM Services

Three types of ATM services exist: permanent virtual circuits (PVC), switched virtual circuits (SVC), and connectionless service (which is similar to SMDS).

PVC allows direct connectivity between sites. In this way, a PVC is similar to a leased line. Among its advantages, PVC guarantees availability of a connection and does not require call setup procedures between switches. Disadvantages of PVCs include static connectivity and manual setup. Each piece of equipment between the source and the destination must be manually provisioned for the PVC. Furthermore, no network resiliency is available with PVC.

An SVC is created and released dynamically and remains in use only as long as data is being transferred. In this sense, it is similar to a telephone call. Dynamic call control requires a signaling protocol between the ATM endpoint and the ATM switch. The advantages of SVCs include connection flexibility and call setup that can be handled automatically by a networking device. Disadvantages include the extra time and overhead required to set up the connection.

ATM Virtual Connections

ATM networks are fundamentally connection-oriented, which means that a virtual channel (VC) must be set up across the ATM network prior to any data transfer. (A virtual channel is roughly equivalent to a virtual circuit.)

Two types of ATM connections exist: *virtual paths*, which are identified by virtual path identifiers, and *virtual channels*, which are identified by the combination of a VPI and a *virtual channel identifier (VCI)*.

A virtual path is a bundle of virtual channels, all of which are switched transparently across the ATM network based on the common VPI. All VPIs and VCIs, however, have only local significance across a particular link and are remapped, as appropriate, at each switch.

A transmission path is the physical media that transports virtual channels and virtual paths. Figure 31-6 illustrates how VCs concatenate to create VPs, which, in turn, traverse the media or transmission path.

Figure 31-6 *VCs Concatenate to Create VPs*

ATM Switching Operations

The basic operation of an ATM switch is straightforward: The cell is received across a link on a known VCI or VPI value. The switch looks up the connection value in a local translation table to determine the outgoing port (or ports) of the connection and the new VPI/VCI value of the connection on that link. The switch then retransmits the cell on that outgoing link with the appropriate connection identifiers. Because all VCIs and VPIs have only local significance across a particular link, these values are remapped, as necessary, at each switch.

ATM Reference Model

The ATM architecture uses a logical model to describe the functionality that it supports. ATM functionality corresponds to the physical layer and part of the data link layer of the OSI reference model.

The ATM reference model is composed of the following planes, which span all layers:

- **Control**—This plane is responsible for generating and managing signaling requests.
- **User**—This plane is responsible for managing the transfer of data.
- **Management**—This plane contains two components:
    - Layer management manages layer-specific functions, such as the detection of failures and protocol problems.
    - Plane management manages and coordinates functions related to the complete system.

The ATM reference model is composed of the following ATM layers:

- **Physical layer**—Analogous to the physical layer of the OSI reference model, the ATM physical layer manages the medium-dependent transmission.

- **ATM layer**—Combined with the ATM adaptation layer, the ATM layer is roughly analogous to the data link layer of the OSI reference model. The ATM layer is responsible for the simultaneous sharing of virtual circuits over a physical link (cell multiplexing) and passing cells through the ATM network (cell relay). To do this, it uses the VPI and VCI information in the header of each ATM cell.

- **ATM adaptation layer (AAL)**—Combined with the ATM layer, the AAL is roughly analogous to the data link layer of the OSI model. The AAL is responsible for isolating higher-layer protocols from the details of the ATM processes. The adaptation layer prepares user data for conversion into cells and segments the data into 48-byte cell payloads.

Finally, the higher layers residing above the AAL accept user data, arrange it into packets, and hand it to the AAL. Figure 31-7 illustrates the ATM reference model.

Figure 31-7 *The ATM Reference Model Relates to the Lowest Two Layers of the OSI Reference Model*

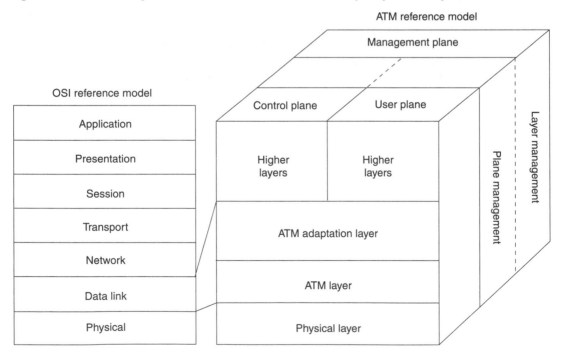

The ATM Physical Layer

The ATM physical layer has four functions: Cells are converted into a bitstream, the transmission and receipt of bits on the physical medium are controlled, ATM cell boundaries are tracked, and cells are packaged into the appropriate types of frames for the physical medium. For example, cells are packaged differently for SONET than for DS-3/E-3 media types.

The ATM physical layer is divided into two parts: the physical medium-dependent (PMD) sublayer and the transmission convergence (TC) sublayer.

The PMD sublayer provides two key functions. First, it synchronizes transmission and reception by sending and receiving a continuous flow of bits with associated timing information. Second, it specifies the physical media for the physical medium used, including connector types and cable. Examples of physical medium standards for ATM include Synchronous Digital Hierarchy/Synchronous Optical Network (SDH/SONET), DS-3/E3, 155 Mbps over multimode fiber (MMF) using the 8B/10B encoding scheme, and 155 Mbps 8B/10B over shielded twisted-pair (STP) cabling.

The TC sublayer has four functions: cell delineation, header error control (HEC) sequence generation and verification, cell-rate decoupling, and transmission frame adaptation. The cell delineation function maintains ATM cell boundaries, allowing devices to locate cells within a stream of bits. HEC sequence generation and verification generates and checks the header error control code to ensure valid data. Cell-rate decoupling maintains synchronization and inserts or suppresses idle (unassigned) ATM cells to adapt the rate of valid ATM cells to the payload capacity of the transmission system. Transmission frame adaptation packages ATM cells into frames acceptable to the particular physical layer implementation.

ATM Adaptation Layers: AAL1

AAL1, a connection-oriented service, is suitable for handling constant bit rate sources (CBR), such as voice and videoconferencing. ATM transports CBR traffic using circuit-emulation services. Circuit-emulation service also accommodates the attachment of equipment currently using leased lines to an ATM backbone network. AAL1 requires timing synchronization between the source and the destination. For this reason, AAL1 depends on a medium, such as SONET, that supports clocking.

The AAL1 process prepares a cell for transmission in three steps. First, synchronous samples (for example, 1 byte of data at a sampling rate of 125 microseconds) are inserted into the Payload field. Second, Sequence Number (SN) and Sequence Number Protection (SNP) fields are added to provide information that the receiving AAL1 uses to verify that it has received cells in the correct order. Third, the remainder of the Payload field is filled with enough single bytes to equal 48 bytes. Figure 31-8 illustrates how AAL1 prepares a cell for transmission.

Figure 31-8 *AAL1 Prepares a Cell for Transmission So That the Cells Retain Their Order*

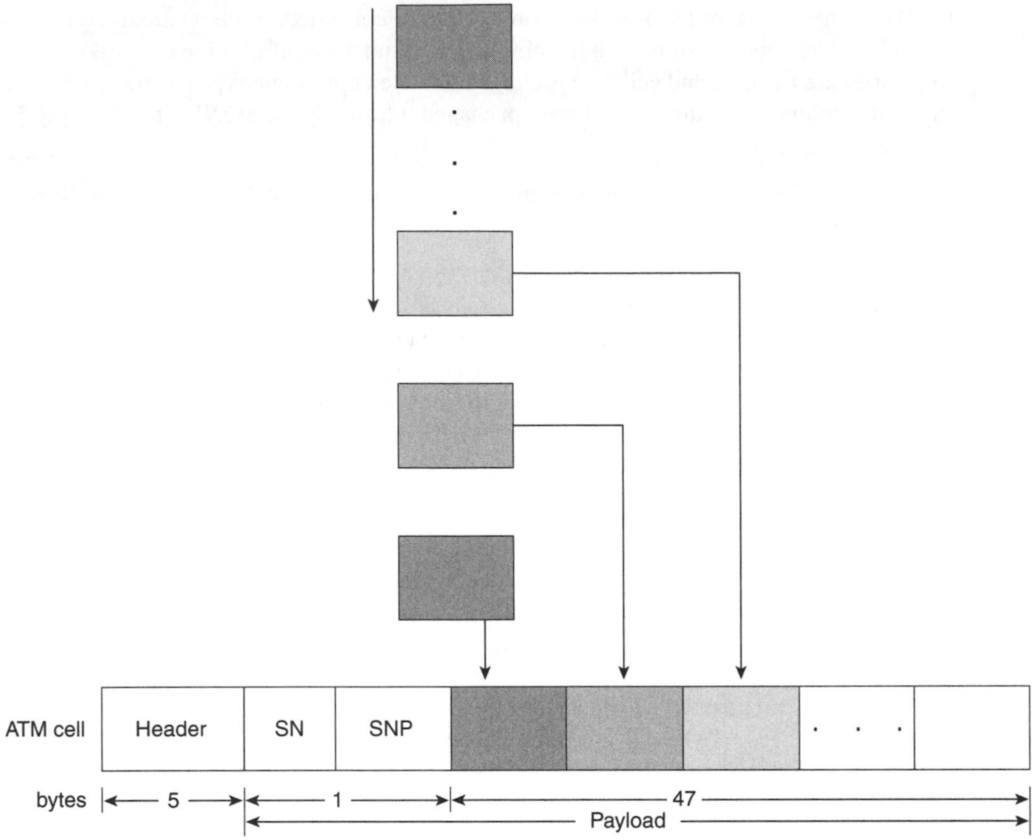

ATM cell	Header	SN	SNP				. . .	
bytes	← 5 →	← 1 →	← 47 →
		← Payload →

ATM Adaptation Layers: AAL2

Another traffic type has timing requirements like CBR but tends to be bursty in nature. This is called variable bit rate (VBR) traffic. This typically includes services characterized as packetized voice or video that do not have a constant data transmission speed but that do have requirements similar to constant bit rate services. AAL2 is suitable for VBR traffic. The AAL2 process uses 44 bytes of the cell payload for user data and reserves 4 bytes of the payload to support the AAL2 processes.

VBR traffic is characterized as either real-time (VBR-RT) or as non-real-time (VBR-NRT). AAL2 supports both types of VBR traffic.

ATM Adaptation Layers: AAL3/4

AAL3/4 supports both connection-oriented and connectionless data. It was designed for network service providers and is closely aligned with Switched Multimegabit Data Service (SMDS). AAL3/4 is used to transmit SMDS packets over an ATM network.

AAL3/4 prepares a cell for transmission in four steps. First, the convergence sublayer (CS) creates a protocol data unit (PDU) by prepending a beginning/end tag header to the frame and appending a length field as a trailer. Second, the segmentation and reassembly (SAR) sublayer fragments the PDU and prepends a header to it. Then the SAR sublayer appends a CRC-10 trailer to each PDU fragment for error control. Finally, the completed SAR PDU becomes the Payload field of an ATM cell to which the ATM layer prepends the standard ATM header.

An AAL 3/4 SAR PDU header consists of Type, Sequence Number, and Multiplexing Identifier fields. Type fields identify whether a cell is the beginning, continuation, or end of a message. Sequence number fields identify the order in which cells should be reassembled. The Multiplexing Identifier field determines which cells from different traffic sources are interleaved on the same virtual circuit connection (VCC) so that the correct cells are reassembled at the destination.

ATM Adaptation Layers: AAL5

AAL5 is the primary AAL for data and supports both connection-oriented and connectionless data. It is used to transfer most non-SMDS data, such as classical IP over ATM and LAN Emulation (LANE). AAL5 also is known as the simple and efficient adaptation layer (SEAL) because the SAR sublayer simply accepts the CS-PDU and segments it into 48-octet SAR-PDUs without reserving any bytes in each cell.

AAL5 prepares a cell for transmission in three steps. First, the CS sublayer appends a variable-length pad and an 8-byte trailer to a frame. The pad ensures that the resulting PDU falls on the 48-byte boundary of an ATM cell. The trailer includes the length of the frame and a 32-bit cyclic redundancy check (CRC) computed across the entire PDU. This allows the AAL5 receiving process to detect bit errors, lost cells, or cells that are out of sequence. Second, the SAR sublayer segments the CS-PDU into 48-byte blocks. A header and trailer are not added (as is in AAL3/4), so messages cannot be interleaved. Finally, the ATM layer places each block into the Payload field of an ATM cell. For all cells except the last, a bit in the Payload Type (PT) field is set to 0 to indicate that the cell is not the last cell in a series that represents a single frame. For the last cell, the bit in the PT field is set to 1.

ATM Addressing

The ITU-T standard is based on the use of E.164 addresses (similar to telephone numbers) for public ATM (B-ISDN) networks. The ATM Forum extended ATM addressing to include private networks. It decided on the subnetwork or overlay model of addressing, in which the ATM layer is responsible for mapping network layer addresses to ATM addresses. This subnetwork model is an alternative to using network layer protocol addresses (such as IP and IPX) and existing routing protocols (such as IGRP and RIP). The ATM Forum defined an address format based on the structure of the OSI network service access point (NSAP) addresses.

Subnetwork Model of Addressing

The subnetwork model of addressing decouples the ATM layer from any existing higher-layer protocols, such as IP or IPX. Therefore, it requires an entirely new addressing scheme and routing protocol. Each ATM system must be assigned an ATM address, in addition to any higher-layer protocol addresses. This requires an ATM address resolution protocol (ATM ARP) to map higher-layer addresses to their corresponding ATM addresses.

NSAP Format ATM Addresses

The 20-byte NSAP-format ATM addresses are designed for use within private ATM networks, whereas public networks typically use E.164 addresses, which are formatted as defined by ITU-T. The ATM Forum has specified an NSAP encoding for E.164 addresses, which is used for encoding E.164 addresses within private networks, but this address can also be used by some private networks.

Such private networks can base their own (NSAP format) addressing on the E.164 address of the public UNI to which they are connected and can take the address prefix from the E.164 number, identifying local nodes by the lower-order bits.

All NSAP-format ATM addresses consist of three components: the authority and format identifier (AFI), the initial domain identifier (IDI), and the domain-specific part (DSP). The AFI identifies the type and format of the IDI, which, in turn, identifies the address allocation and administrative authority. The DSP contains actual routing information.

NOTE   Summarized another way, the first 13 bytes form the NSAP *prefix* that answers the question, "Which switch?" Each switch must have a prefix value to uniquely identify it. Devices attached to the switch inherit the prefix value from the switch as part of their NSAP address. The prefix is used by switches to support ATM routing.

The next 6 bytes, called the *end station identifier (ESI)*, identify the ATM element attached to the switch. Each device attached to the switch must have a unique ESI value.

The last byte, called the *selector* (SEL) byte, identifies the intended process within the device that the connection targets.

Three formats of private ATM addressing differ by the nature of the AFI and IDI. In the NSAP-encoded E.164 format, the IDI is an E.164 number. In the DCC format, the IDI is a data country code (DCC), which identifies particular countries, as specified in ISO 3166. Such addresses are administered by the ISO National Member Body in each country. In the ICD format, the IDI is an international code designator (ICD), which is allocated by the ISO 6523 registration authority (the British Standards Institute). ICD codes identify particular international organizations.

The ATM Forum recommends that organizations or private network service providers use either the DCC or the ICD formats to form their own numbering plan.

Figure 31-9 illustrates the three formats of ATM addresses used for private networks.

Figure 31-9 *Three Formats of ATM Addresses Are Used for Private Networks*

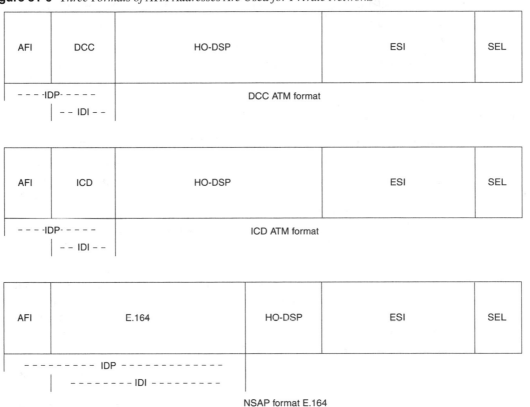

ATM Address Fields

The following descriptions summarize the fields illustrated in Figure 31-9:

- **AFI**—Identifies the type and format of the address (E.164, ICD, or DCC).

- **DCC**—Identifies particular countries.

- **High-Order Domain-Specific Part (HO-DSP)**—Combines the routing domain (RD) and the area identifier (AREA) of the NSAP addresses. The ATM Forum combined these fields to support a flexible, multilevel addressing hierarchy for prefix-based routing protocols.

- **End System Identifier (ESI)**—Specifies the 48-bit MAC address, as administered by the Institute of Electrical and Electronic Engineers (IEEE).

- **Selector (SEL)**—Is used for local multiplexing within end stations and has no network significance.

- **ICD**—Identifies particular international organizations.

- **E.164**—Indicates the BISDN E.164 address.

ATM Connections

ATM supports two types of connections: point-to-point and point-to-multipoint.

Point-to-point connects two ATM end systems and can be unidirectional (one-way communication) or bidirectional (two-way communication). Point-to-multipoint connects a single-source end system (known as the root node) to multiple destination end systems (known as leaves). Such connections are unidirectional only. Root nodes can transmit to leaves, but leaves cannot transmit to the root or to each other on the same connection. Cell replication is done within the ATM network by the ATM switches where the connection splits into two or more branches.

It would be desirable in ATM networks to have bidirectional multipoint-to-multipoint connections. Such connections are analogous to the broadcasting or multicasting capabilities of shared-media LANs, such as Ethernet and Token Ring. A broadcasting capability is easy to implement in shared-media LANs, where all nodes on a single LAN segment must process all packets sent on that segment.

Unfortunately, a multipoint-to-multipoint capability cannot be implemented by using AAL5, which is the most common AAL to transmit data across an ATM network. Unlike AAL3/4, with its Message Identifier (MID) field, AAL5 does not provide a way within its cell format to interleave cells from different AAL5 packets on a single connection. This means that all AAL5 packets sent to a particular destination across a particular connection must be received in sequence; otherwise, the destination reassembly process will be incapable of reconstructing the packets.

This is why AAL5 point-to-multipoint connections can be only unidirectional. If a leaf node were to transmit an AAL5 packet onto the connection, for example, it would be received by both the root node and all other leaf nodes. At these nodes, the packet sent by the leaf could be interleaved with packets sent by the root and possibly other leaf nodes, precluding the reassembly of any of the interleaved packets.

ATM and Multicasting

ATM requires some form of multicast capability. AAL5 (which is the most common AAL for data) currently does not support interleaving packets, so it does not support multicasting.

If a leaf node transmitted a packet onto an AAL5 connection, the packet could be intermixed with other packets and be improperly reassembled. Three methods have been proposed for solving this problem: VP multicasting, multicast server, and overlaid point-to-multipoint connection.

Under the first solution, a multipoint-to-multipoint VP links all nodes in the multicast group, and each node is given a unique VCI value within the VP. Interleaved packets hence can be identified by the unique VCI value of the source. Unfortunately, this mechanism would require a protocol to uniquely allocate VCI values to nodes, and such a protocol mechanism currently does not exist. It is also unclear whether current SAR devices could easily support such a mode of operation.

A multicast server is another potential solution to the problem of multicasting over an ATM network. In this scenario, all nodes wanting to transmit onto a multicast group set up a point-to-point connection with an external device known as a multicast server (perhaps better described as a resequencer or serializer). The multicast server, in turn, is connected to all nodes wanting to receive the multicast packets through a point-to-multipoint connection. The multicast server receives packets across the point-to-point connections and then retransmits them across the point-to-multipoint connection—but only after ensuring that the packets are serialized (that is, one packet is fully transmitted before the next is sent). In this way, cell interleaving is precluded.

An overlaid point-to-multipoint connection is the third potential solution to the problem of multicasting over an ATM network. In this scenario, all nodes in the multicast group establish a point-to-multipoint connection with each other node in the group and, in turn, become leaves in the equivalent connections of all other nodes. Hence, all nodes can both transmit to and receive from all other nodes. This solution requires each node to maintain a connection for each transmitting member of the group, whereas the multicast-server mechanism requires only two connections. This type of connection also requires a registration process for informing the nodes that join a group of the other nodes in the group so that the new nodes can form the point-to-multipoint connection. The other nodes must know about the new node so that they can add the new node to their own point-to-multipoint connections. The multicast-server mechanism is more scalable in terms of connection resources but has the problem of requiring a centralized resequencer, which is both a potential bottleneck and a single point of failure.

ATM Quality of Service

ATM supports QoS guarantees comprising traffic contract, traffic shaping, and traffic policing.

A *traffic contract* specifies an envelope that describes the intended data flow. This envelope specifies values for peak bandwidth, average sustained bandwidth, and burst size, among others. When an ATM end system connects to an ATM network, it enters a contract with the network, based on QoS parameters.

Traffic shaping is the use of queues to constrain data bursts, limit peak data rate, and smooth jitters so that traffic will fit within the promised envelope. ATM devices are responsible for adhering to the contract by means of traffic shaping. ATM switches can use *traffic policing* to enforce the contract. The switch can measure the actual traffic flow and compare it against the agreed-upon traffic envelope. If the switch finds that traffic is outside of the agreed-upon parameters, it can set the cell-loss priority (CLP) bit of the offending cells. Setting the CLP bit makes the cell *discard eligible*, which means that any switch handling the cell is allowed to drop the cell during periods of congestion.

ATM Signaling and Connection Establishment

When an ATM device wants to establish a connection with another ATM device, it sends a signaling-request packet to its directly connected ATM switch. This request contains the ATM address of the desired ATM endpoint, as well as any QoS parameters required for the connection.

ATM signaling protocols vary by the type of ATM link, which can be either UNI signals or NNI signals. UNI is used between an ATM end system and ATM switch across ATM UNI, and NNI is used across NNI links.

The ATM Forum UNI 3.1 specification is the current standard for ATM UNI signaling. The UNI 3.1 specification is based on the Q.2931 public network signaling protocol developed by the ITU-T. UNI signaling requests are carried in a well-known default connection: VPI = 0, VPI = 5.

The ATM Connection-Establishment Process

ATM signaling uses the one-pass method of connection setup that is used in all modern telecommunication networks, such as the telephone network. An ATM connection setup proceeds in the following manner. First, the source end system sends a connection-signaling request. The connection request is propagated through the network. As a result, connections are set up through the network. The connection request reaches the final destination, which either accepts or rejects the connection request.

Connection-Request Routing and Negotiation

Routing of the connection request is governed by an ATM routing protocol (Private Network-Network Interface [PNNI], which routes connections based on destination and source addresses), traffic, and the QoS parameters requested by the source end system. Negotiating a connection request that is rejected by the destination is limited because call routing is based on parameters of initial connection; changing parameters might affect the connection routing. Figure 31-10 highlights the one-pass method of ATM connection establishment.

Figure 31-10 *ATM Devices Establish Connections Through the One-Pass Method*

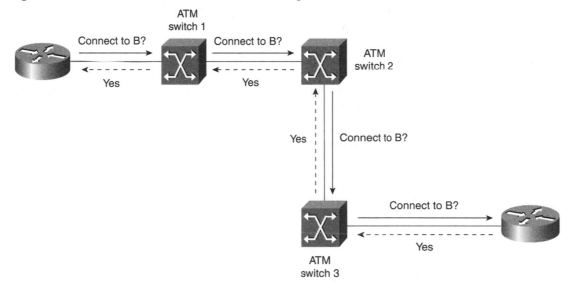

ATM Connection-Management Messages

A number of connection-management message types, including setup, call proceeding, connect, and release, are used to establish and tear down an ATM connection. The source end system sends a setup message (including the address of the destination end system and any traffic QoS parameters) when it wants to set up a connection. The ingress switch sends a call proceeding message back to the source in response to the setup message. The destination end system next sends a connect message if the connection is accepted.

The destination end system sends a release message back to the source end system if the connection is rejected, thereby clearing the connection.

Connection-management messages are used to establish an ATM connection in the following manner. First, a source end system sends a setup message, which is forwarded to the first ATM switch (ingress switch) in the network. This switch sends a call proceeding message and invokes an ATM routing protocol. The signaling request is propagated across the network. The exit switch (called the egress switch) that is attached to the destination end system receives the setup message. The egress switch forwards the setup message to the end system across its UNI, and the ATM end system sends a connect message if the connection is accepted. The connect message traverses back through the network along the same path to the source end system, which sends a connect acknowledge message back to the destination to acknowledge the connection. Data transfer can then begin.

PNNI

PNNI provides two significant services: ATM topology discovery and call establishment. For switches to build connections between end points, the switch must know the ATM network topology. PNNI is the ATM routing protocol that enables switches to automatically discover the topology and the characteristics of the links interconnecting the switches. A link-state protocol much like OSPF, PNNI tracks things such as bandwidth on links. When a significant event occurs that changes the characteristics of a link, PNNI announces the change to the other switches.

When a station sends a call setup request to its local switch, the ingress switch references the PNNI routing table to determine a path between the source and the intended destination that meets the QoS requirements specified by the source. The switch attached to the source then builds a list defining each switch hop to support the circuit to the destination. This is called the *designated transit list (DTL)*.

VCI = 18 is reserved for PNNI.

Integrated Local Management Interface

Integrated Local Management Interface (ILMI) enables devices to determine status of components at the other end of a physical link and to negotiate a common set of operational parameters to ensure interoperability. ILMI operates over a reserved VCC of VPI = X, VCI = 16.

Administrators may enable or disable ILMI at will, but it is highly recommended to enable it. Doing so allows the devices to determine the highest UNI interface level to operate (3.0, 3.1, 4.0), UNI vs. NNI, as well as numerous other items. Furthermore, ILMI allows devices to share information such as NSAP addresses, peer interface names, and IP addresses. Without ILMI, many of these parameters must be manually configured for the ATM attached devices to operate correctly.

NOTE   The VCI values of 0 through 31 are reserved and should not be used for user traffic. Three
frequently encountered VCI values are shown in Table 31-1.

Table 31-1   *Commonly Used VCI Values*

VCI	Function
5	Signaling from an edge device to its switch (ingress switch)
16	ILMI for link parameter exchanges
18	PNNI for ATM routing

LAN Emulation

LAN Emulation (LANE) is a standard defined by the ATM Forum that gives to stations
attached via ATM the same capabilities that they normally obtain from legacy LANs, such
as Ethernet and Token Ring. As the name suggests, the function of the LANE protocol is to
emulate a LAN on top of an ATM network. Specifically, the LANE protocol defines
mechanisms for emulating either an IEEE 802.3 Ethernet or an 802.5 Token Ring LAN.
The current LANE protocol does not define a separate encapsulation for FDDI. (FDDI
packets must be mapped into either Ethernet or Token Ring-emulated LANs [ELANs] by
using existing translational bridging techniques.) Fast Ethernet (100BaseT) and IEEE
802.12 (100VG-AnyLAN) both can be mapped unchanged because they use the same
packet formats. Figure 31-11 compares a physical LAN and an ELAN.

Figure 31-11 *ATM Networks Can Emulate a Physical LAN*

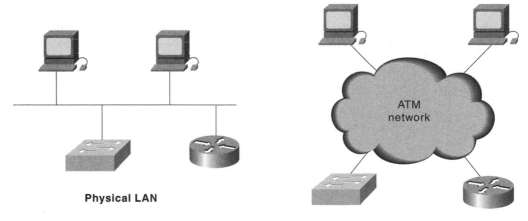

Physical LAN

**ATM
network**

Emulated LAN

The LANE protocol defines a service interface for higher-layer (that is, network layer) protocols that is identical to that of existing LANs. Data sent across the ATM network is encapsulated in the appropriate LAN MAC packet format. Simply put, the LANE protocols make an ATM network look and behave like an Ethernet or Token Ring LAN—albeit one operating much faster than an actual Ethernet or Token Ring LAN network.

It is important to note that LANE does not attempt to emulate the actual MAC protocol of the specific LAN concerned (that is, CSMA/CD for Ethernet or token passing for IEEE 802.5). LANE requires no modifications to higher-layer protocols to enable their operation over an ATM network. Because the LANE service presents the same service interface of existing MAC protocols to network layer drivers (such as an NDIS- or ODI-like driver interface), no changes are required in those drivers.

The LANE Protocol Architecture

The basic function of the LANE protocol is to resolve MAC addresses to ATM addresses. The goal is to resolve such address mappings so that LANE end systems can set up direct connections between themselves and then forward data. The LANE protocol is deployed in two types of ATM-attached equipment: ATM network interface cards (NICs) and internetworking and LAN switching equipment.

ATM NICs implement the LANE protocol and interface to the ATM network but present the current LAN service interface to the higher-level protocol drivers within the attached end system. The network layer protocols on the end system continue to communicate as if they were on a known LAN by using known procedures. However, they are capable of using the vastly greater bandwidth of ATM networks.

The second class of network gear to implement LANE consists of ATM-attached LAN switches and routers. These devices, together with directly attached ATM hosts equipped with ATM NICs, are used to provide a virtual LAN (VLAN) service in which ports on the LAN switches are assigned to particular VLANs independently of physical location. Figure 31-12 shows the LANE protocol architecture implemented in ATM network devices.

Figure 31-12 *LANE Protocol Architecture Can Be Implemented in ATM Network Devices*

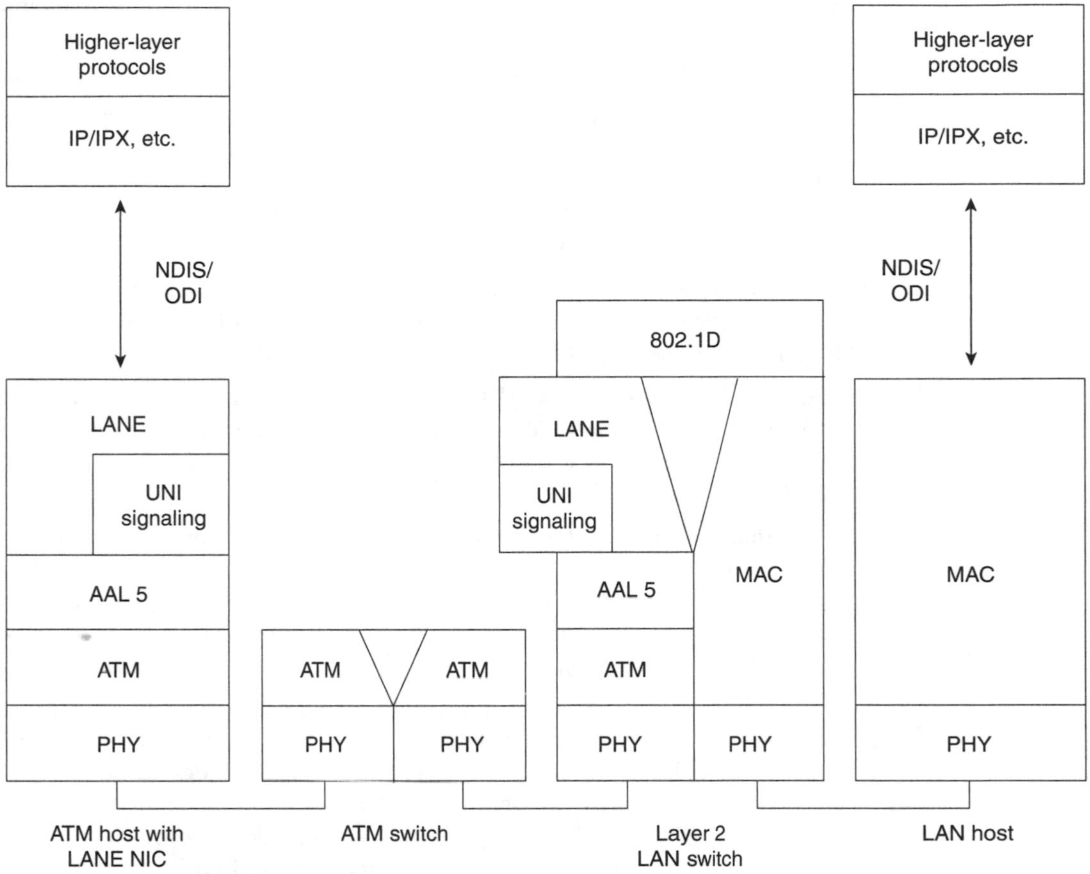

| ATM host with LANE NIC | ATM switch | Layer 2 LAN switch | LAN host |

NOTE   The LANE protocol does not directly affect ATM switches. As with most of the other ATM internetworking protocols, LANE builds on the overlay model. As such, the LANE protocols operate transparently over and through ATM switches, using only standard ATM signaling procedures.

LANE Components

The LANE protocol defines the operation of a single ELAN or VLAN. Although multiple ELANs can simultaneously exist on a single ATM network, an ELAN emulates either an Ethernet or a Token Ring and consists of the following components:

- **LAN Emulation client (LEC)**—The LEC is an entity in an end system that performs data forwarding, address resolution, and registration of MAC addresses with the LAN Emulation Server (LES). The LEC also provides a standard LAN interface to higher-level protocols on legacy LANs. An ATM end system that connects to multiple ELANs has one LEC per ELAN.

- **LES**—The LES provides a central control point for LECs to forward registration and control information. (Only one LES exists per ELAN.) The LES maintains a list of MAC addresses in the ELAN and the corresponding NSAP addresses.

- **Broadcast and Unknown Server (BUS)**—The BUS is a multicast server that is used to flood unknown destination address traffic and to forward multicast and broadcast traffic to clients within a particular ELAN. Each LEC is associated with only one BUS per ELAN.

- **LAN Emulation Configuration Server (LECS)**—The LECS maintains a database of LECs and the ELANs to which they belong. This server accepts queries from LECs and responds with the appropriate ELAN identifier—namely, the ATM address of the LES that serves the appropriate ELAN. One LECS per administrative domain serves all ELANs within that domain.

Because single server components lack redundancy, Cisco has overcome this shortcoming by implementing a proprietary solution called Simple Server Redundancy Protocol. SSRP works with any vendors LECs; however, it requires the use of Cisco devices as server components. It allows up to 16 LECSs per ATM LANE network and an infinite number of LES/BUS pairs per ELAN. The ATM Forum also released a vendor-independent method of providing server redundancy: Lane Emulation Network-Network Interface (LNNI). Therefore, servers from different vendors can provide interoperable redundancy.

Figure 31-13 illustrates the components of an ELAN.

Figure 31-13 *An ELAN Consists of Clients, Servers, and Various Intermediate Nodes*

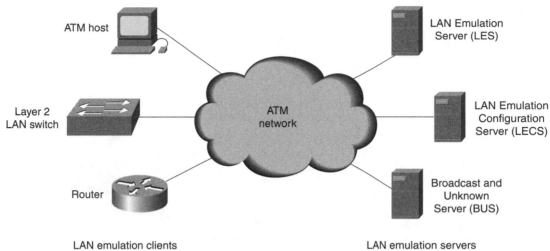

LAN Emulation Connection Types

The Phase 1 LANE entities communicate with each other by using a series of ATM VCCs. LECs maintain separate connections for data transmission and control traffic. The LANE data connections are data-direct VCC, multicast send VCC, and multicast forward VCC.

Data-direct VCC is a bidirectional point-to-point VCC set up between two LECs that want to exchange data. Two LECs typically use the same data-direct VCC to carry all packets between them rather than opening a new VCC for each MAC address pair. This technique conserves connection resources and connection setup latency.

Multicast send VCC is a bidirectional point-to-point VCC set up by the LEC to the BUS.

Multicast forward VCC is a unidirectional VCC set up to the LEC from the BUS. It typically is a point-to-multipoint connection, with each LEC as a leaf.

Figure 31-14 shows the LANE data connections.

Control connections include configuration-direct VCC, control-direct VCC, and control-distribute VCC. Configuration-direct VCC is a bidirectional point-to-point VCC set up by the LEC to the LECS. Control-direct VCC is a bidirectional VCC set up by the LEC to the LES. Control-distribute VCC is a unidirectional VCC set up from the LES back to the LEC (this is typically a point-to-multipoint connection). Figure 31-15 illustrates LANE control connections.

Figure 31-14 *LANE Data Connections Use a Series of VCLs to Link a LAN Switch and ATM Hosts*

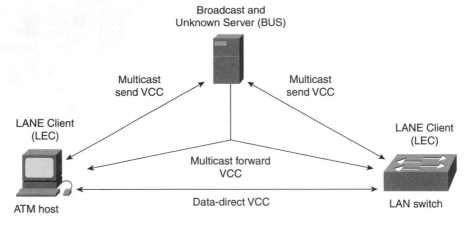

LAN emulation data connections

Figure 31-15 *LANE Control Connections Link the LES, LECS, LAN Switch, and ATM Host*

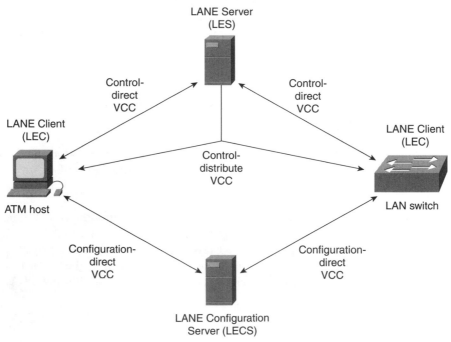

LAN emulation control connections

LANE Operation

The operation of a LANE system and components is best understood by examining these stages of LEC operation: performing initialization and configuration, joining and registering with the LES, finding and joining the BUS, and performing data transfer.

Initialization and Configuration

Upon initialization, an LEC finds the LECS to obtain required configuration information. It begins this process when the LEC obtains its own ATM address, which typically occurs through address registration.

The LEC must then determine the location of the LECS. To do this, the LEC first must locate the LECS by one of the following methods: by using a defined ILMI procedure to determine the LECS address, by using a well-known LECS address, or by using a well-known permanent connection to the LECS (VPI = 0, VCI = 17). (The well-known permanent connection is not commonly used.)

After the LEC discovers the LECS's NSAP, the LEC sets up a configuration-direct VCC to the LECS and sends an LE_CONFIGURE_REQUEST message. If a matching entry is found, the LECS returns a LE_CONFIGURE_RESPONSE message to the LEC with the configuration information that it requires to connect to its target ELAN, including the following: ATM address of the LES, type of LAN being emulated, maximum packet size on the ELAN, and ELAN name (a text string for display purposes).

Joining and Registering with the LES

When an LEC joins the LES and registers its own ATM and MAC addresses, it does so by following three steps:

1 After the LEC obtains the LES address, the LEC optionally clears the connection to the LECS, sets up the control-direct VCC to the LES, and sends an LE_JOIN_REQUEST message on that VCC. This allows the LEC to register its own MAC and ATM addresses with the LES and (optionally) any other MAC addresses for which it is proxying. This information is maintained so that no two LECs will register the same MAC or ATM address.

2 After receipt of the LE_JOIN_REQUEST message, the LES checks with the LECS via its open connection, verifies the request, and confirms the client's membership.

3 Upon successful verification, the LES adds the LEC as a leaf of its point-to-multipoint control-distribute VCC and issues the LEC a successful LE_JOIN_RESPONSE message that contains a unique LAN Emulation client ID (LECID). The LECID is used by the LEC to filter its own broadcasts from the BUS.

Finding and Joining the BUS

After the LEC has successfully joined the LECS, its first task is to find the BUS's ATM address to join the broadcast group and become a member of the emulated LAN.

First, the LEC creates an LE_ARP_REQUEST packet with the MAC address 0xFFFFFFFF. Then the LEC sends this special LE_ARP packet on the control-direct VCC to the LES. The LES recognizes that the LEC is looking for the BUS and responds with the BUS's ATM address on the control-distribute VCC.

When the LEC has the BUS's ATM address, it joins the BUS by first creating a signaling packet with the BUS's ATM address and setting up a multicast-send VCC with the BUS. Upon receipt of the signaling request, the BUS adds the LEC as a leaf on its point-to-multipoint multicast forward VCC. The LEC is now a member of the ELAN and is ready for data transfer.

Data Transfer

The final state, data transfer, involves resolving the ATM address of the destination LEC and actual data transfer, which might include the flush procedure.

When a LEC has a data packet to send to an unknown destination MAC address, it must discover the ATM address of the destination LEC through which the particular address can be reached. To accomplish this, the LEC first sends the data frame to the BUS (via the multicast send VCC) for distribution to all LECs on the ELAN via the multicast forward VCC. This is done because resolving the ATM address might take some time, and many network protocols are intolerant of delays.

The LEC then sends a LAN Emulation Address Resolution Protocol Request (LE_ARP_Request) control frame to the LES via a control-direct VCC.

If the LES knows the answer, it responds with the ATM address of the LEC that owns the MAC address in question. If the LES does not know the answer, it floods the LE_ARP_REQUEST to some or all LECs (under rules that parallel the BUS's flooding of the actual data frame, but over control-direct and control-distribute VCCs instead of the multicast send or multicast forward VCCs used by the BUS). If bridge/switching devices with LEC software participating in the ELAN exist, they respond to the LE_ARP_REQUEST if they service the LAN device with the requested MAC address. This is called a *proxy service*.

In the case of actual data transfer, if an LE_ARP message is received, the LEC sets up a data-direct VCC to the destination LEC and uses this for data transfer rather than the BUS path. Before it can do this, however, the LEC might need to use the LANE flush procedure, which ensures that all packets previously sent to the BUS were delivered to the destination prior to the use of the data-direct VCC. In the flush procedure, a control frame is sent down the first transmission path following the last packet. The LEC then waits until the destination acknowledges receipt of the flush packet before using the second path to send packets.

Multiprotocol over ATM

Multiprotocol over ATM (MPOA) provides a method of transmitting data between ELANs without needing to continuously pass through a router. Normally, data passes through at least one router to get from one ELAN to another. This is normal per-hop routing as experienced in LAN environments. MPOA, however, enables devices in different ELANs to communicate without needing to travel hop by hop.

Figure 31-16 illustrates the process without MPOA in part A and with MPOA in part B. With MPOA-enabled devices, only the first few frames between devices pass through routers. This is called the *default path*. The frames pass from ELAN to ELAN through appropriate routers. After a few frames follow the default path, the MPOA devices discover the NSAP address of the other device and then build a direct connection called the *shortcut* for the subsequent frames in the flow.

The edge devices that generate the ATM traffic are called multiprotocol clients (MPC) and may be an ATM-attached workstation, or a router. The inter-ELAN routers are called multiprotocol servers (MPS) and assist the MPCs in discovering how to build a shortcut. MPSs are always routers.

This reduces the load on routers because the routers do not need to sustain the continuous flow between devices. Furthermore, MPOA can reduce the number of ATM switches supporting a connection, freeing up virtual circuits and switch resources in the ATM network. Figure 31-16 illustrates the connection before and after the shortcut is established.

Note that MPOA does not replace LANE. In fact, MPOA requires LANE version 2.

Figure 31-16 *A Comparison of Inter-ELAN Communications Without (Part A) and with (Part B) MPOA*

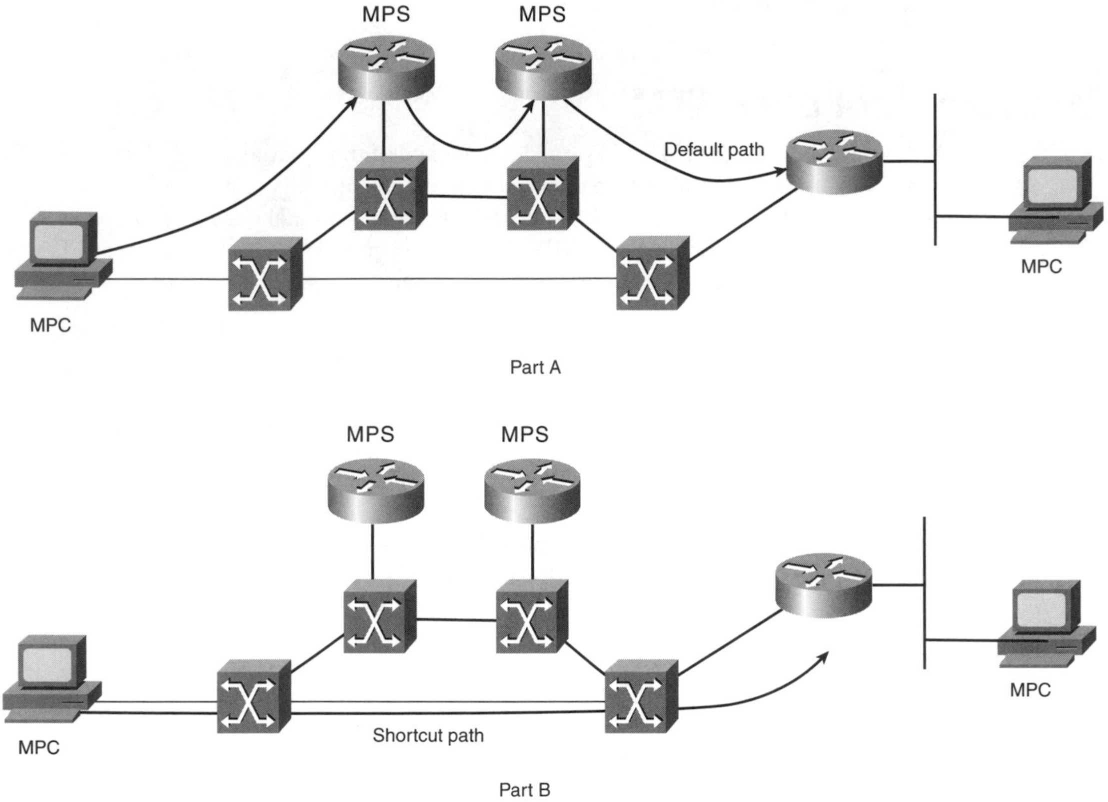

Part A

Part B

Review Questions

1 Name the four components of LANE.

2 Which LANE component maintains an ATM ARP table?

3 Which LANE component maintains policy for ELAN membership?

4 List two functions of PNNI.

5 Which field in the ATM header checks the header integrity?

6 What is the primary difference between the UNI header and the NNI header?

7 Which adaptation mode is most appropriate to interconnect T1 signals from PBXs over ATM?

8 Which adaptation mode is most frequently implemented for data transport over ATM?

9 What VCI value is reserved for call setup requests from an ATM edge device?

10 What ATM protocol simplifies the ATM administrator's life by automatically ensuring that certain ATM parameters are compatible between two devices connected to the same link?

11 What ATM protocol communicates exclusively between ATM switches?

12 Describe the difference between PVC and SVC.

13 What is the purpose of the adaptation layer?

14 What advantage is there to implementing MPOA?

For More Information

- Clark, Kennedy, and Kevin Hamilton. *CCIE Professional Development: Cisco LAN Switching*. Indianapolis: Cisco Press, 1999.

- Ginsburg, David. *ATM: Solutions for Enterprise Internetworking.* Boston: Addison-Wesley Publishing Co, 1996.

- McDysan, David E., and Darren L. Spohn. *ATM Theory and Application*. New York: McGraw-Hill, 1998

- http://www.atmforum.com for ATM standards document

Objectives

- Understand the advantages of MPLS.

- Learn the components of an MPLS system.

- Compare and contrast MPLS and hop-by-hop routing.

- Describe the two methods of label distribution.

- Explain the purpose of MPLS traffic engineering.

CHAPTER 32

MPLS

In a typical router-based network, Layer 3 datagrams pass from a source to a destination on a hop-by-hop basis. Transit routers evaluate each datagram's Layer 3 header and perform a routing table lookup to determine the next hop toward the destination. Although some routers implement hardware and software switching techniques (for example, Cisco Express Forwarding [CEF]) to accelerate the evaluation process by creating high-speed cache entries, these methods rely on the Layer 3 routing protocol to determine the path to the destination.

Unfortunately, routing protocols have little, if any, visibility into the network's Layer 2 characteristics, particularly in regard to quality of service (QoS) and link load. Rapid changes in the type (and quantity) of traffic handled by the Internet and the explosion in the number of Internet users is putting an unprecedented strain on the Internet's infrastructure. This pressure mandates new traffic-management solutions. Multiprotocol label switching (MPLS) and its predecessor, tag switching, are intended to resolve many of the challenges facing the evolving Internet and high-speed data communications in general.

To meet these new demands, MPLS changes the hop-by-hop paradigm by letting edge routers specify paths in the network based on a variety of user-defined criteria, including QoS requirements and the applications' bandwidth needs. In other words, path selection in a router-only network can now take into account Layer 2 attributes. This solution lets Internet service providers (ISPs) and large enterprise networks deploy a unified Layer 3 infrastructure that can support requirements that in the past were supported only with the Layer 2 backbone (such as a Frame Relay or ATM backbone).

In essence, the MPLS technology combines the richness of IP routing and the simplicity of hop-by-hop label switching of Frame Relay or ATM to provide seamless integration of connection-oriented Layer 2 forwarding with the connectionless IP world. Because of their dual nature (they operate on the IP layer and on the label-switching layer), MPLS devices are called Label Switch Routers (LSRs).

Based on Cisco's proprietary tag-switching protocol, the IETF has defined MPLS as a vendor-independent protocol. The two protocols have much in common. The only major difference is in the details of the protocol used between adjacent MPLS devices, giving network administrators an opportunity for gradual migration from tag-switching networks to standards-based MPLS networks.

MPLS Terminology

MPLS uses a number of new terms. Here are the most significant:

- **Label header**—A header created by an edge LSR and used by LSRs to forward packets. The header format varies based on the network media type. In an ATM network, the label is placed in the VPI/VCI fields of each ATM cell header. In all other environments (for example, LANs or point-to-point links), the header is a "shim" located between the Layer 2 and Layer 3 headers, as shown in Figure 32-1. The label header can contain one label or a stack of labels.

- **Label Forwarding Information Base (LFIB)**—A table created by an LSR-capable device that indicates where and how to forward frames with specific label values.

- **LSR**—A device, such as a switch or router, that forwards labeled entities based on the label value.

- **Edge LSR**—A device that initially adds the label to or ultimately removes the label from the packet. An edge LSR has some interfaces connected to other LSRs and some interfaces connected to non-MPLS-enabled devices (for example, IP hosts).

- **Core LSR**—A device that primarily switches labeled packets based on the label value present in the label header. All interfaces of a core LSR are connected to other LSRs.

- **Label-switched**—When an LSR makes a forwarding decision based on the value of a label in the MPLS header of a frame/cell.

- **Label-Switched Path (LSP)**—The path defined by the labels through LSRs between a pair of edge LSRs.

Figure 32-1   *Position of the MPLS Label Header in a Layer 2 Frame*

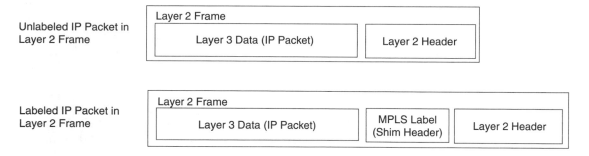

A few additional terms are defined for MPLS operation in the ATM environment:

- **Label Virtual Circuit (LVC)**—An LSP through an IP+ATM (MPLS-enabled ATM) system.

- **Label Switch Controller (LSC)** — An LSR attached to an ATM switch that communicates with the ATM switch to provide and provision LVC cross-connects in the ATM switch.

- **Label Distribution Protocol (LDP)** — A set of messages defined to distribute label information among LSRs.

- **XmplsATM** — The virtual interface between an ATM switch and an LSC.

MPLS Operations

This section illustrates the passage of a frame through an MPLS system to highlight the function of several key MPLS components. Specifically, it illustrates MPLS through a frame-based infrastructure as opposed to a cell-based (ATM) system.

In Figure 32-2, a series of LSRs (edge and core) interconnect, forming a physical path between two elements, Station A and Station B.

Figure 32-2 *Series of Interconnected LSRs*

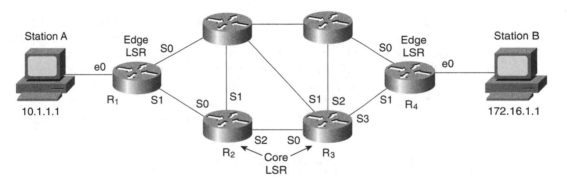

Router	Incoming Label	Incoming Interface	Destination Network	Outgoing Interface	Outgoing Label
R₁	—	e0	172.16.1	S1	6
R₂	6	S0	172.16.1	S2	11
R₃	11	S0	172.16.1	S3	7
R₄	7	S1	172.16.1	e0	—

The Ethernet frame carrying an IP datagram generated by Station A follows the standard Ethernet format with a normal Layer 2 header followed by a Layer 3 header. Because the destination address resides in a different network, Station A targets the Layer 2 header to its default gateway (R1). In this case, the default gateway also serves as the edge LSR (ingress side). The ingress LSR references its internal IP switching table (Forwarding Information Base [FIB]) and determines that it needs to forward the IP datagram through interface S1 toward the next LSR.

Furthermore, the FIB entry for network 172.16.1.0/24 in the ingress LSR indicates that the ingress LSR must insert a label between the Layer 2 and Layer 3 headers to indicate what path the frame should take on its way to Station B. The ingress LSR, therefore, inserts an MPLS header between the Point-to-Point Protocol (PPP) Layer 2 header and the IP header (this process is called label imposition) and forwards the labeled packet toward R2. Router 2 looks at the frame entering port 1 and determines that a label is embedded between Layers 2 and 3 based on the information in the frame's Layer 2 header (for example, PPP packet type or EtherType field in LAN packets). Therefore, the router treats the frame according to the configuration in its LFIB, which says to forward the frame out port 2 and replace the incoming label 6 with outgoing label 11. Each of the subsequent routers handles the frame in a similar manner until the frame reaches the egress LSR.

The egress edge LSR performs the label lookup in the same way as all the previous LSRs, finding no outgoing label to use. It, therefore, strips off all label information (this is called *label removal*) and passes a standard IP datagram encapsulated in an Ethernet frame to Station B. Because each of the routers between Stations A and B can switch the frame based on content in the LFIB and does not need to perform the usual routing operation, the IP datagram forwarding across the network is handled more efficiently. Furthermore, the LSP between R1 and R4 can take different links than the ones indicated in the IP routing table.

MPLS/Tag-Switching Architecture

MPLS relies on two principal components: forwarding and control. The control component is responsible for maintaining correct label-forwarding information among a group of interconnected LSRs. The forwarding component uses labels carried by packets and the label-forwarding information maintained by an LSR to perform packet forwarding. Details about MPLS forwarding and control mechanisms follow.

Control Component

All devices in an MPLS network run IP routing protocols on their *control plane* to build IP routing tables. In MPLS devices that support IP forwarding (for example, edge LSR), the IP routing tables are used to build IP forwarding tables (FIBs). In MPLS devices that support only label forwarding (such as ATM switches with MPLS functionality), the IP routing FIB does not exist. Figure 32-3 shows the IP routing operation of the MPLS control plane.

Figure 32-3 *LSRs Build the IP Routing Table*

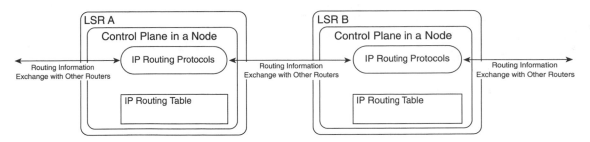

After the IP routing tables have been built, MPLS labels are assigned to individual entries in the IP routing table (individual IP prefixes) and are propagated to adjacent MPLS devices through an LDP.

NOTE   In usual MPLS operation, labels are not assigned to Border Gateway Protocol (BGP) destinations, because the router always reaches BGP destinations through recursive lookup on the BGP next hop. BGP destinations, therefore, can be reached through the label associated with the BGP next hop for those destinations, as explained in the section "Hierarchical Routing."

Each MPLS device uses its own local label space. There is no need for globally unique labels or centralized label assignment, making MPLS extremely robust and scalable. Every label assigned by an MPLS device is entered as an input label in its LFIB—the forwarding table that is used for label switching. Figure 32-4 shows label assignment and distribution for an MPLS device.

Most label assignments, both local and those made by adjacent devices, are entered into a table called the Label Information Base (LIB). The label assigned by the IP next hop for a particular IP prefix is entered as an output label in the local LFIB to enable pure label forwarding. In devices that support IP forwarding, such a label is also entered in the FIB to support IP-to-label forwarding.

NOTE   The LIB contains all the labels assigned to an IP prefix by the local LSR and its neighbors. The LFIB contains only the inbound-to-outbound label mapping used to forward labeled packets. Information in the LFIB is, therefore, always a subset of information in the LIB.

Figure 32-4 *Control Plane Operations in an LSR*

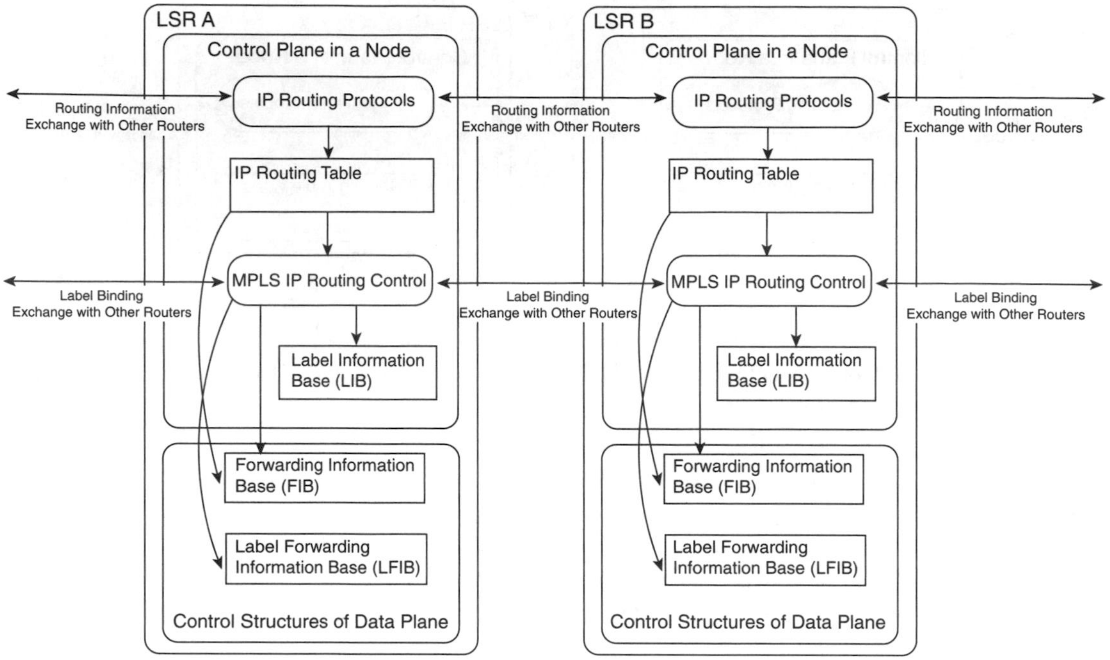

Label Distribution Protocol

With destination-based routing, a router makes a forwarding decision based on the Layer 3 destination address carried in a packet and the information stored in FIB maintained by the router. A router constructs its FIB using information the router receives from routing protocols, such as OSPF and BGP.

To support destination-based routing with MPLS, an LSR participates in routing protocols and constructs its LFIB using information it receives from these protocols. In this way, it operates much like a router.

An LSR, however, must distribute and use allocated labels for LSR peers to correctly forward the frame. LSRs distribute labels using an LDP. A label binding associates a destination subnet with a locally significant label. (Labels can be locally significant because they are replaced at each hop.) Whenever an LSR discovers a neighbor LSR, the two establish a TCP connection to transfer label bindings. LDP exchanges subnet/label bindings using one of two methods: downstream unsolicited distribution or downstream-on-demand distribution. Both LSRs must agree on which mode to use.

Downstream unsolicited distribution disperses labels if a downstream LSR needs to establish a new binding with its neighboring upstream LSR. For example, an edge LSR may enable a new interface with another subnet. The edge LSR then announces to the upstream LSR a binding to reach this network.

In downstream-on-demand distribution, on the other hand, a downstream LSR sends a binding upstream only if the upstream LSR requests it. For each route in its route table, the LSR identifies the next hop for that route. It then issues a request (via LDP) to the next hop for a label binding for that route. When the next hop receives the request, it allocates a label, creates an entry in its LFIB with the incoming label set to the allocated label, and then returns the binding between the (incoming) label and the route to the LSR that sent the original request. When the LSR receives the binding information, it creates an entry in its LFIB and sets the outgoing label in the entry to the value received from the next hop. In a network using downstream-on-demand distribution, this process is repeated recursively until the destination is reached.

Forwarding Component

The forwarding paradigm employed by MPLS is based on the notion of label swapping. When an LSR receives a packet with a label, the switch uses the label as an index in its LFIB. Each entry in the LFIB consists of an incoming label and one or more subentries (of the form outgoing label, outgoing interface, outgoing link-level information). If the switch finds an entry with the incoming label equal to the label carried in the packet, for each component in the entry, the switch replaces the label in the packet with the outgoing label, replaces the link-level information (such as the MAC address) in the packet with the outgoing link-level information, and forwards the packet over the outgoing interface. Some MPLS devices (edge LSR) can receive IP datagrams, perform a lookup in the FIB, insert an MPLS label in front of the IP datagram based on information stored in the FIB, and forward the labeled packet to the next-hop LSR. The switching paths supported in an edge LSR are shown in Figure 32-5.

Figure 32-5 *Switching Paths in an Edge LSR*

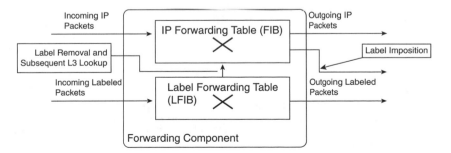

From the previous description of the forwarding component, you can make several observations. First, the forwarding decision is based on the exact-match algorithm using a fixed-length, fairly short label as an index. This enables a simplified forwarding procedure, relative to longest-match forwarding, traditionally used at the network layer.

This, in turn, enables higher forwarding performance (higher packets per second). The forwarding procedure is simple enough to allow a straightforward hardware implementation. A second observation is that the forwarding decision is independent of the label's forwarding granularity. The same forwarding algorithm, for example, applies to both unicast and multicast: A unicast entry would have a single subentry (outgoing label, outgoing interface, outgoing link-level information), and a multicast entry might have one or more subentries. This illustrates how the same forwarding paradigm can be used in label switching to support different routing functions.

The simple forwarding procedure, thus, is essentially decoupled from the control component of label switching. New routing (control) functions can readily be deployed without disturbing the forwarding paradigm. This means that it is not necessary to reoptimize forwarding performance (by modifying either hardware or software) as new routing (control plane) functionality is added. For example, a large number of MPLS applications sharing common LFIB are already supported in Cisco routers, as shown in Figure 32-6.

Figure 32-6 *Multiple MPLS Applications Sharing a Common LFIB*

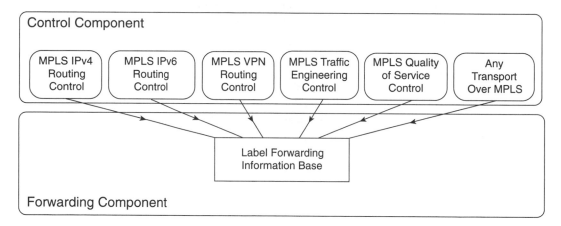

Label Encapsulation

Label information can be carried in a packet in a variety of ways:

- As a small shim label header inserted between the Layer 2 and network layer headers (see Figure 32-7)

- As part of the Layer 2 header if the Layer 2 header provides adequate semantics (such as ATM)

Figure 32-7 *MPLS Label Header Format*

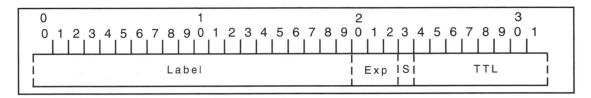

As a result, MPLS can be implemented over any media type, including point-to-point links, multiaccess links, and ATM. The label-forwarding component is independent of the network layer protocol. Use of control component(s) specific to a particular network layer protocol enables the use of label switching with different network layer protocols.

Label Switching with ATM

Because the MPLS forwarding paradigm is based on label swapping, as is ATM forwarding, MPLS technology can be applied to ATM switches by implementing the control component. The label information needed for MPLS switching is carried in the VPI and VCI field of every ATM cell.

NOTE   The combination of ATM, MPLS, and IP technology in the ATM switches is usually called IP+ATM.

In most IP+ATM networks, the ATM switches support additional label setup mechanisms (for example, ATM Forum signaling), and the VPI field is used to allocate parts of available label space to the various label setup mechanisms. For most networks, a single VPI value allocated to the MPLS LDP is adequate.

Implementing MPLS on an ATM switch simplifies integration of ATM switches and routers. An ATM switch capable of MPLS appears as a router to an adjacent packet-based router. This provides a scalable alternative to the overlay model and removes the need for ATM addressing, routing, and signaling schemes. Because destination-based forwarding is topology-driven rather than traffic-driven, applying this approach to ATM switches does not involve high call-setup rates, nor does it depend on the longevity of flows.

Implementing MPLS on an ATM switch does not preclude the capability to support a traditional ATM control plane (such as PNNI) on the same switch. The two components, MPLS and the ATM control plane, operate independently with VPI/VCI space and other resources partitioned so that the components do not interact.

Hierarchical Routing

Essential to MPLS is the notion of binding between a label and network layer routes. MPLS supports a wide range of forwarding granularities to provide good scaling characteristics while also accommodating diverse routing functionality. At one extreme, a label can be associated (bound) to all routes announced into an IP network from an edge router through BGP. This MPLS functionality can be used very successfully to build highly scalable IP networks, as explained in this section.

The IP routing architecture models a network as a collection of routing domains. Within a domain, routing is provided via interior routing (such as OSPF), and routing across domains is provided via exterior routing (such as BGP). However, all routers within domains that carry transit traffic (such as domains formed by ISPs) must maintain information provided by exterior routing, not just interior routing.

MPLS decouples interior and exterior routing so that only LSRs at the border of a domain are required to maintain routing information provided by exterior routing. All other switches within the domain maintain routing information provided by the domain's interior routing, which usually is smaller than the exterior routing information. This, in turn, reduces the routing load on nonborder switches and shortens routing convergence time.

To support this functionality, edge LSRs do not assign labels to individual BGP routes, but reuse the labels assigned to BGP next hops for all BGP destinations that can be reached through them, as shown in Figure 32-8.

Figure 32-8 *MPLS Forwarding Across a BGP-Based IP Backbone*

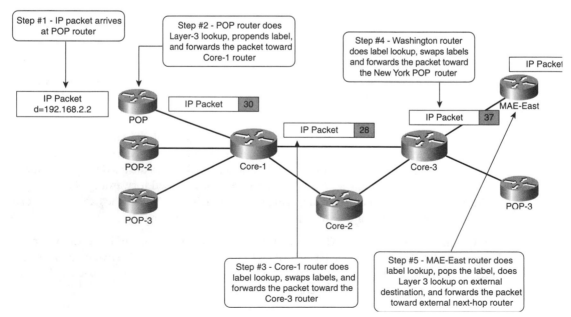

This figure shows a small ISP network that has a few Point-of-Presence (POP) routers connected to a network core composed of three LSRs. The network is also connected to a peering point (MAE-East in the example) through which it receives the BGP route for network 192.168.3.0/24. The IP packet forwarding from a POP router toward the external destination within 192.168.3.0/24 (or any other destination advertised via BGP from MAE-East) is performed as follows:

Step 1   A POP router receives an IP datagram for a destination within IP network 192.168.3.0/24.

Step 2   The POP router performs Layer 3 lookup, inserts an MPLS label header in front of the IP datagram, and forwards the labeled packet toward the next-hop router. The label in the MPLS label header is the label assigned to the BGP next hop, not to the external IP network.

Step 3   The Core-1 LSR forwards the labeled packet toward the destination indicated in the MPLS label stack—the BGP next hop.

Step 4   The same process is repeated at the Core-3 LSR.

Step 5   The egress edge LSR (MAE-East) removes the MPLS label header, performs Layer 3 lookup, and forwards the IP datagram toward the external destination.

Throughout this process, the core LSRs never perform a Layer 3 lookup for an external IP address. Thus, it's not necessary to run BGP on the core LSRs, reducing their memory utilization and CPU load while increasing the core network's stability.

MPLS-Based Virtual Private Networks

One of the most popular MPLS applications today is the implementation of virtual private networks (VPNs) with the help of MPLS technology. To support MPLS-based VPNs, Cisco IOS was modified to support a large number of independent IP routing tables within a single router—a global IP routing table and a number of Virtual Routing and Forwarding (VRF) tables. As shown in Figure 32-9, each VRF has its own set of routing protocols, operating as an independent router from an IP routing perspective (but not from a network management perspective, where the whole router is still managed as one device). The total independence of the VRF tables allows different VPN networks to use overlapping IP address space. For example, VPN-A and VPN-B could both use network 10.0.0.0/8.

Figure 32-9 *VRF Architecture*

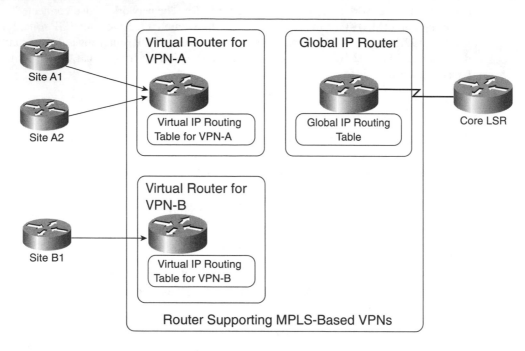

The potential for overlapping address space between the VPN customers prevents the simple MPLS forwarding paradigm used in hierarchical IP routing to be used in the MPLS VPN architecture. A more complex forwarding process using a label stack is needed (see Figure 32-10). The label stack is composed of two labels:

- The top label (marked IL or IGP label in the figure), pointing toward the egress LSR, is assigned through LDP.

- The bottom label (marked VL or VPN label in the figure), pointing toward a VPN destination, is assigned by the egress LSR and is propagated directly to other edge LSRs through multiprotocol BGP.

Figure 32-10 *MPLS VPN Forwarding*

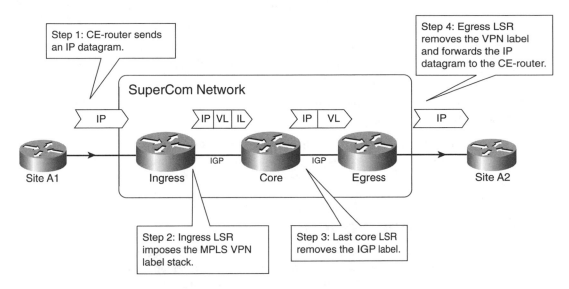

A packet sent from Site A1 to Site A2 is forwarded through the MPLS VPN backbone in the following steps:

Step 1   The IP datagram is sent from Site A1 to the ingress router.

Step 2   Ingress performs an IP lookup and prepends an MPLS header consisting of two labels—a label assigned via LDP (the IGP label [IL]), identifying the path toward the egress router, and a VPN label (VL) assigned by the egress router.

Step 3   The penultimate core router (the Core router in Figure 32-10) in the service provider network removes the IGP label, leaving only the VPN label in the MPLS header.

Step 4   The egress router performs label lookup on the VPN label, removes the MPLS header, and forwards the IP datagram toward Site A2.

MPLS Quality of Service

An important MPLS capability is QoS support. Two mechanisms provide a range of QoS to packets passing through a router or tag switch:

- Classification of packets into different classes

- Handling of packets via appropriate QoS characteristics (such as bandwidth and loss)

MPLS provides an easy way to mark packets as belonging to a particular class after they have been classified the first time. Initial classification uses information carried in the network layer or higher-layer headers. The packet marking can be done in two ways:

- In ATM environments, a label corresponding to the resultant class is applied to the packet. Labeled packets can be handled efficiently by LSRs in their path without needing to be reclassified.

- In all other environments, the packet's precedence is stored in 3 bits in the MPLS label header.

The actual packet scheduling and queuing are largely orthogonal. The key point here is that MPLS lets you use simple logic to find the state that identifies how the packet should be scheduled.

MPLS Traffic Engineering

One of the fundamental properties of destination-based routing is that the only information from a packet that is used to forward the packet is the destination address. Although this property enables highly scalable routing, it also limits the capability to influence the actual paths taken by packets. This limits the capability to evenly distribute traffic among multiple links, taking the load off highly utilized links and shifting it toward less-utilized links.

For ISPs that support different classes of service, destination-based routing also limits their capability to segregate different classes with respect to the links used by these classes. Some ISPs today use Frame Relay or ATM to overcome the limitations imposed by destination-based routing. Because of the flexible granularity of labels, MPLS can overcome these limitations without using either Frame Relay or ATM. To provide forwarding along the paths that are different from the paths determined by destination-based routing, the control component of MPLS allows installation of label bindings in LSRs that do not correspond to the destination-based routing paths.

Traffic engineering allows a network administrator to make the path deterministic and bypass the normal routed hop-by-hop paths. An administrator may elect to explicitly define the path between network endpoints to ensure QoS or may have the traffic follow a specified path to reduce traffic loading across certain links. In other words, the network administrator can reduce congestion by forcing the frame to travel around the overloaded segments. Traffic engineering, then, lets an administrator define a policy for forwarding frames rather than depending on dynamic routing protocols.

Traffic engineering is similar to source routing in that an explicit path is defined for the frame to travel. However, unlike source routing, the hop-by-hop definition is not carried with every frame. Rather, the hops are configured in the LSRs ahead of time along with the appropriate label values.

A number of existing protocols were modified to support the needs of MPLS traffic engineering:

- Extensions to OSPF and IS-IS have been defined to allow these link-state protocols to propagate the link utilization information across the network.

- Constraint-based routing has been implemented in Cisco IOS to allow the headend routers to find optimal paths across the network based on operator-established criteria.

- Resource Reservation Protocol (RSVP) has been extended to support the establishment and maintenance of explicitly routed LSPs.

Summary

Multiprotocol Label Switching (MPLS) is a technology that combines the benefits of connection-oriented Layer 2 forwarding with the benefits of connectionless Layer 3 Internet Protocol (IP). In MPLS-enabled networks, all network devices become IP-aware. They run IP routing protocols on the control plane while performing the actual packet forwarding based on labels allocated to IP prefixes with a variety of label distribution protocols.

The ability to perform packet forwarding in the core of an IP network without performing an IP lookup at every hop enables a variety of new solutions:

- Internet routing with greatly reduced IP routing tables on the core routers

- MPLS-based traffic engineering (MPLS TE)

- MPLS-based Virtual Private Networks (MPLS VPNs)

Review Questions

1 In downstream-on-demand distribution, how does the upstream LSR know it needs a label?

2 How does FIB differ from LFIB?

3 What are the two LDP modes?

4 It is highly recommended that neighbor LSRs operate in the same LDP mode. What might happen if an upstream LSR operates in downstream unsolicited distribution mode and the downstream LSR runs in downstream-on-demand mode?

5 If a vendor's router already uses high-speed switching and caching techniques to forward frames, performance might not be a valid motivation for using MPLS. Is there any other reason that might merit deployment of MPLS in such a network?

For More Information

- McDysan, David Ph.D., *QoS and Traffic Management in IP and ATM Networks*, McGraw-Hill Professional Publishing: New York, 2000.

- Pepelnjak, Ivan, Jim Guichard, and Jeff Apcar, *Advanced MPLS and VPN Architectures, Volume II,* Cisco Press, 2003.

- Pepelnjak Ivan, and Jim Guichard, *MPLS and VPN Architectures, CCIP Edition,* Cisco Press, 2002.

- www.cisco.com/warp/public/732/Tech/mpls/

- www.ietf.org/html.charters/mpls-charter.html

- www.ietf.org/rfc/rfc2702.txt

- www.mplsrc.com/

Objectives

- Describe the need for DLSw.
- Know the advantages of DLSw over source-route bridging.
- Specify the transport protocol between DLSw switches.
- Understand the basic structure of DLSw.
- Recognize DLSw processes by name and function.
- Understand the circuit establishment process.

Data-Link Switching

Background

Data-link switching (DLSw) provides a means of transporting IBM Systems Network Architecture (SNA) and network basic input/output system (NetBIOS) traffic over an IP network. It serves as an alternative to *source-route bridging (SRB)*, a protocol for transporting SNA and NetBIOS traffic in Token Ring environments that was widely deployed before the introduction of DLSw. In general, DLSw addresses some of the shortcomings of SRB for certain communication requirements—particularly in WAN implementations. This chapter contrasts DLSw with SRB, summarizes underlying protocols, and provides a synopsis of normal protocol operations.

DLSw initially emerged as a proprietary IBM solution in 1992. It was first submitted to the IETF as RFC 1434 in 1993. DLSw is now documented in detail by IETF RFC 1795, which was submitted in April 1995. DLSw was jointly developed by the Advanced Peer-to-Peer Networking (APPN) Implementors Workshop (AIW) and the Data-Link Switching Related Interest Group (DLSw RIG).

RFC 1795 describes three primary functions of DLSw:

- The Switch-to-Switch Protocol (SSP) is the protocol maintained between two DLSw nodes or routers.
- The termination of SNA data-link control (DLC) connections helps to reduce the likelihood of link layer timeouts across WANs.
- The local mapping of DLC connections to a DLSw circuit.

Each of these functions is discussed in detail in this chapter.

In 1997, the IETF released DLSw version 2 (RFC 2166) which provides enhancements to RFC 1795 document. The additional features include these:

- IP multicast
- UDP unicast responses to DLSw broadcasts
- Enhanced peer-on-demand routing
- Expedited TCP connections

Each of these features enables DLSw as a scalable technology over WANs. In DLSw Version 1, transactions occur with TCP. As a result, many operations in a DLSw environment consumed circuits between peers. For example, a multicast required multiple TCP connections from the source to each peer. With DLSw Version 2, multicast is distributed using unreliable transport following traditional multicast methods.

Note that RFC 2166 does not supercede 1795, but it adds functionality and maintains backward compatibility.

Cisco supports a third version of DLSw called DLSw+. DLSw+ predates DLSw Version 2 and provides even further enhancements to basic DLSw. DLSw+ is fully compliant with RFC 1795. The enhancements may be used when both peers are Cisco devices running DLSw+.

This chapter focuses on the basic function of DLSw as defined in RFC 1795.

Figure 33-1 illustrates a generalized DLSw environment.

Figure 33-1 *A DLSw Circuit Facilitates SNA Connectivity over an IP WAN*

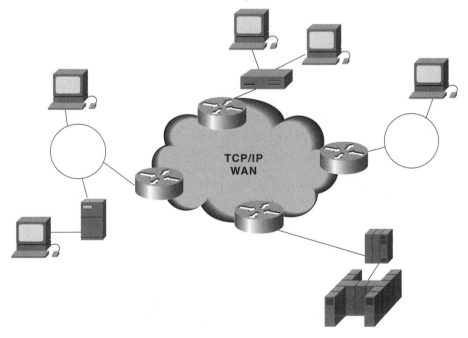

DLSw Contrasted with Source-Route Bridging

The principal difference between SRB and DLSw involves support of local termination. SNA and NetBIOS traffic rely on link layer acknowledgments and keepalive messages to ensure the integrity of connections and the delivery of data. For connection-oriented data, the local DLSw node or router terminates data-link control. Therefore, link layer acknowledgments and keepalive messages do not have to traverse a WAN. By contrast, DLC for SRB is handled on an end-to-end basis, which results in increased potential for DLC timeouts over WAN connections.

Although SRB has been a viable solution for many environments, several issues limit its usefulness for transport of SNA and NetBIOS in WAN implementations. Chief among them are the following constraints:

- SRB hop-count limitation of seven hops
- Broadcast traffic handling (from SRB explorer frames or NetBIOS name queries)
- Unnecessary traffic forwarding (acknowledgments and keepalives)
- Lack of flow control and prioritization

Figure 33-2 illustrates the basic end-to-end nature of an SRB connection over a WAN link.

Figure 33-2 *SRB Provides an End-to-End Connection over an IP WAN*

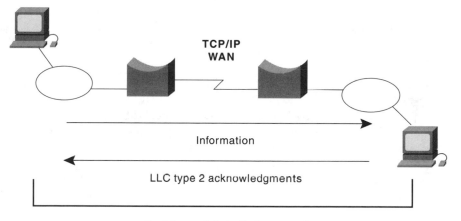

End-to-end data link control

Local termination of DLC connections by DLSw provides a number of advantages over SRB-based environments. DLSw local termination eliminates the requirement for link layer acknowledgments and keepalive messages to flow across a WAN. In addition, local termination reduces the likelihood of link layer timeouts across WANs. Similarly, DLSw ensures that the broadcast of search frames is controlled by the DLSw when the location of a target system is discovered. Figure 33-3 illustrates the flow of information and the use of local acknowledgment in a DLSw environment.

Figure 33-3 *DLSw Uses Local Acknowledgment to Control Data Flow*

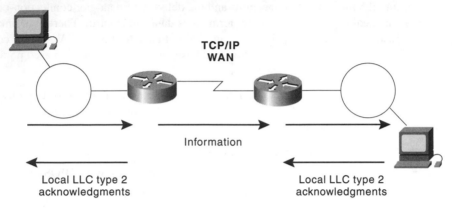

DLSw SNA Support

One of the advantages inherent in DLSw is that it supplies broader device and media support than previously available with SRB. DLSw accommodates a number of typical SNA environments and provides for IEEE 802.2-compliant LAN support, which includes support for SNA physical unit (PU) 2, PU 2.1, and PU 4 systems and NetBIOS-based systems.

DLSw provides for Synchronous Data Link Control (SDLC) support, covering PU 2 (primary or secondary) and PU 2.1 systems. With SDLC-attached systems, each SDLC PU is presented to the DLSw Switch-to-Switch Protocol (SSP) as a unique Media Access Control (MAC)/service access point (SAP) address pair. With Token Ring–attached systems, a DLSw node appears as a source-route bridge. Remote Token Ring systems accessed via a DLSw node are seen as attached to an adjacent ring. This apparent adjacent ring is known as a virtual ring created within each DLSw node. Figure 33-4 illustrates various IBM nodes connected to a TCP/IP WAN through DLSw devices, which, in this case, are routers.

Figure 33-4 *SNA Nodes Connect Through TCP/IP WAN via DLSw*

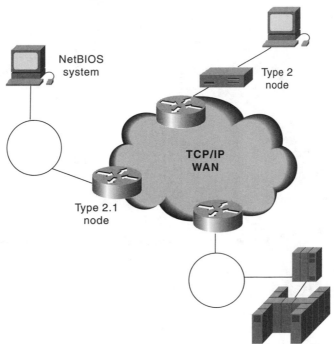

DLSw Switch-to-Switch Protocol

Switch-to-Switch Protocol (SSP) is a protocol used between DLSw nodes (routers) to establish connections, locate resources, forward data, and handle flow control and error recovery. This is truly the essence of DLSw. In general, SSP does not provide for full routing between nodes because this is generally handled by common routing protocols such as RIP, OSPF, or IGRP/EIGRP. Instead, SSP switches packets at the SNA data link layer. It also encapsulates packets in TCP/IP for transport over IP-based networks and uses TCP as a means of reliable transport between DLSw nodes. Figure 33-5 illustrates where SSP falls in the overall SNA architecture, and shows its relationship to the OSI reference model.

Figure 33-5 *SSP Maps to the Data Link Components of SNA and the OSI Reference Model*

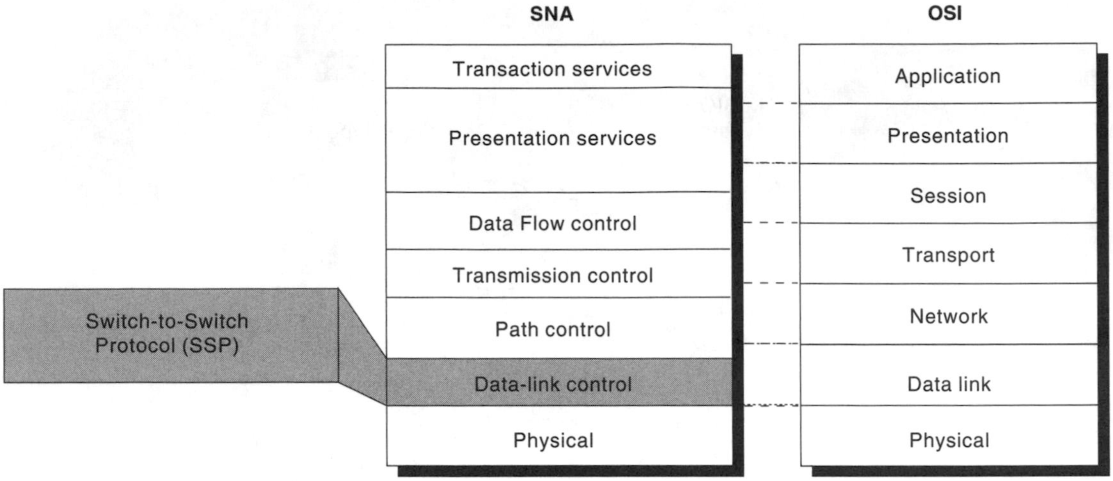

DLSw Operation

DLSw involves several operational stages. Two DLSw partners establish two TCP connections with each other. TCP connections provide the foundation for the DLSw communication. Because TCP provides for reliable and guaranteed delivery of IP traffic, it ensures the delivery and integrity of the traffic that is being encapsulated in the IP protocol, which, in this case, is SNA and NetBIOS traffic. After a connection is established, the DLSw partners exchange a list of supported capabilities. This is particularly vital when the DLSw partners are manufactured by different vendors. Next, the DLSw partners establish circuits between SNA or NetBIOS end systems, and information frames can flow over the circuit.

DLSw Processes

The overall DLSw operational process can be broken into three basic components: capabilities exchange, circuit establishment, and flow control. In the context of DLSw, *capabilities exchange* involves the trading of information about capabilities associated with a DLSw session. This exchange of information is negotiated when the session is initiated and during the course of session operations. *Circuit establishment* in DLSw occurs between end systems. It includes locating the target end system and setting up data-link control connections between each end system and its local router. DLSw *flow control* enables the establishment of independent, unidirectional flow control between partners. Each process in discussed in the sections that follow.

DLSw Capabilities Exchange

DLSw capabilities exchange is based on a switch-to-switch control message that describes the capabilities of the sending data-link switch. A capabilities exchange control message is sent after the switch-to-switch connection is established or during run time, if certain operational parameters that must be communicated to the partner switch have changed. During the capabilities exchange, a number of capabilities are identified and negotiated. Capabilities exchanged between DLSw partners include the following:

- DLSw version number
- Initial pacing window size (receive window size)
- NetBIOS support
- List of supported link SAPs (LSAPs)
- Number of TCP sessions supported
- MAC address lists
- NetBIOS name lists
- Search frames support

DLSw Circuit Establishment

The process of circuit establishment between a pair of end systems in DLSw involves locating the target end system and setting up data-link control (DLC) connections between each end system and its local router. The specifics of circuit establishment differ based on traffic type.

One of the primary functions of DLSw is to provide a transport mechanism for SNA traffic. SNA circuit establishment involves several distinct stages and is illustrated in Figure 33-6.

First, SNA devices on a LAN find other SNA devices by sending an explorer frame with the MAC address of the target SNA device. When a DLSw internetworking node receives an explorer frame, that node sends a *canureach frame* to each of its DLSw partners. The function of this frame is to query each of the DLSw partners to see whether it can locate the device in question. If one of the DLSw partners can reach the specified MAC address, the partner replies with an *icanreach frame*, which indicates that a specific DLSw partner can provide a communications path to the device in question.

After the canureach and icanreach frames have been exchanged, the two DLSw partners establish a circuit that consists of a DLC connection between each router and the locally attached SNA end system (for a total of two connections) and a TCP connection between the DLSw partners. The resulting circuit is uniquely identified by the source and destination circuit IDs. Each SNA DLSw circuit ID includes a MAC address, a link-service access point (LSAP), and the DLC port ID. Circuit priority is negotiated at circuit setup time.

Figure 33-6 *DLSw Circuit Establishment Flow*

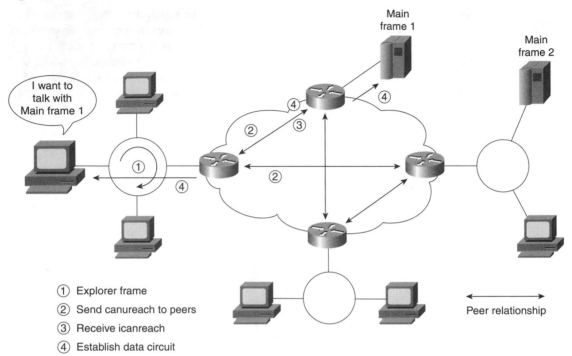

① Explorer frame
② Send canureach to peers
③ Receive icanreach
④ Establish data circuit

NetBIOS circuit establishment parallels SNA circuit establishment, with a few differences. First, with NetBIOS circuit establishment, DLSw nodes send a name query with a NetBIOS name (not a canureach frame specifying a MAC address). Similarly, the DLSw nodes establishing a NetBIOS circuit send a name recognized frame (not an icanreach frame).

DLSw Flow Control

DLSw flow control involves *adaptive pacing* between DLSw routers. During the flow-control negotiation, two independent, unidirectional flow-control mechanisms are established between DLSw partners. Adaptive pacing employs a windowing mechanism that dynamically adapts to buffer availability. Windows can be incremented, decremented, halved, or reset to zero. This allows the DLSw nodes to control the pace of traffic forwarded through the network to ensure integrity and delivery of all data.

DLSw Flow-Control Indicators

Granted units (the number of units that the sender has permission to send) are incremented with a flow-control indication (one of several possible indicators) from the receiver. DLSw flow control provides for the following indicator functions:

- **Repeat**—Increments granted units by the current window size.

- **Increment**—Increases the window size by 1 and increases granted units by the new window size.

- **Decrement**—Decrements window size by 1 and increments granted units by the new window size.

- **Reset**—Decreases window size to 0 and sets granted units to 0, which stops all transmission in one direction until an increment flow-control indicator is sent.

- **Half**—Cuts the current window size in half and increments granted units by the new window size.

- **Flow**—Control indicators and flow-control acknowledgments can be piggybacked on information frames or sent as independent flow-control messages. Reset indicators are always sent as independent messages.

Adaptive-Pacing Examples

Examples of adaptive-pacing criteria include buffer availability, transport utilization, outbound queue length, and traffic priority. Examples of how each can be used to influence pacing follow:

- **Buffer availability**—If memory buffers in a DLSw node are critically low, the node can decrement the window size to reduce the flow of traffic. As buffer availability increases, the node then can increase the window size to increase traffic flow between the DLSw partners.

- **Transport utilization**—If the link between two DLSw partners reaches a high level of utilization, the window size can be reduced to lower the level of link utilization and to prevent packet loss between the nodes.

- **Outbound queue length**—Traffic forwarded by a DLSw node typically is placed into an outbound queue, which is a portion of memory dedicated to traffic being forwarded by one device to another. If this queue reaches a specified threshold or perhaps becomes full, the number of granted units can be reduced until the queue utilization is reduced to a satisfactory level.

- **Traffic priority**—One of the unique capabilities of the SSP is its capability to prioritize specific traffic. These priorities are identified by the Circuit Priority field in the DLSw message frame. By providing a varying number of granted units to specific DLSw circuits, the nodes can maintain different levels of priority to each circuit.

DLSw Message Formats

Two message header formats are exchanged between DLSw nodes:

- Control
- Information

The control message header is used for all messages except information frames (Iframes) and independent flow control messages (IFCMs), which are sent in information header format.

Figure 33-7 illustrates the format of the DLSw Control and Information fields. These fields are discussed in detail in the subsequent descriptions.

Figure 33-7 *DLSw Control and Information Frames Have Their First 16 Bytes in Common*

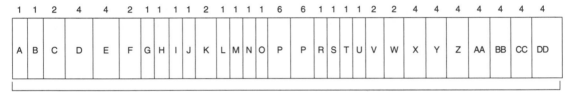

Field length, in bytes

1	1	2	4	4	2	1	1	1	1	2	1	1	1	1	6	6	1	1	1	1	2	2	4	4	4	4	4	4	4
A	B	C	D	E	F	G	H	I	J	K	L	M	N	O	P	P	R	S	T	U	V	W	X	Y	Z	AA	BB	CC	DD

DLSw information message (16 bytes)

DLSw control message (72 bytes)

DLSw information message (16 bytes)

- A = Version number
- B = Header length
- C = Message length
- D = Remote data-link correlator
- E = Remote data-link control (DLC) port ID
- F = Reserved
- G = Message type
- H = Flow-control byte

DLSw control message format

- A = Version number
- B = Header length
- C = Message length
- D = Remote data-link correlator
- E = Remote data-link-control (DLC) port ID
- F = Reserved
- G = Message type
- H = Flow-control byte
- I = Protocol ID
- J = Header number
- K = Reserved
- L = Largest frame size
- M = SSP flags
- N = Circuit priority
- O = Message type

- P = Target MAC address
- Q = Origin MAC address
- R = Origin link service access point (LSAP)
- S = Target LSAP
- T = Frame direction
- U = Reserved
- V = Reserved
- W = Data-link control (DLC) port ID
- Y = Origin data-link control (DLC) port ID
- Z = Origin transport ID
- AA = Target data-link correlator
- CC = Target transport ID
- DD = 2 reserved fields

The following fields are illustrated in Figure 33-7 (fields in the first 16 bytes of all DLSw message headers are the same):

- **Version number**—When set to 0x31 (ASCII 1), indicates a decimal value of 49, which identifies this device as utilizing DLSw version 1. This will allow future interoperability between DLSw nodes using different versions of the DLSw standard. Currently, all devices utilize DLSw version 1, so this field will always have the decimal value of 49.

- **Header length**—When set to 0x48 for control messages, indicates a decimal value of 72 bytes. This value is set to 0x10 for information and independent flow control messages, indicating a decimal value of 16 bytes.

- **Message length**—Defines the number of bytes within the data field following the header.

- **Remote data-link correlator**—Works in tandem with the remote DLC port ID to form a 64-bit circuit ID that identifies the DLC circuit within a single DLSw node. The circuit ID is unique in a single DLSw node and is assigned locally. An end-to-end circuit is identified by a pair of circuit IDs that, along with the data-link IDs, uniquely identifies a single end-to-end circuit. Each DLSw node must keep a table of these circuit ID pairs: one for the local end of the circuit and the other for the remote end of the circuit. The remote data-link correlator is set equal to the target data-link correlator if the Frame Direction field is set to 0x01. It is equal to the origin data-link correlator if the Frame Direction field is set to 0x02.

- **Remote DLC port ID**—Works in tandem with the remote data-link correlator to form a 64-bit circuit ID that identifies the DLC circuit within a single DLSw node. The circuit ID is unique in a single DLSw node and is assigned locally. The end-to-end circuit is identified by a pair of circuit IDs that, along with the data-link IDs, uniquely identifies a single end-to-end circuit. Each DLSw device must keep a table of these circuit ID pairs: one for the local end of the circuit and the other for the remote end of the circuit. The remote DLC port ID is set equal to the target DLC port ID if the Frame Direction field is set to 0x01. It is equal to the origin DLC port ID if the Frame Direction field is set to 0x02.

- **Message type**—Indicates a specific DLSw message type. The value is specified in two different fields (offset 14 and 23 decimal) of the control message header. Only the first field is used when parsing a received SSP message. The second field is ignored by new implementations on reception, but it is retained for backward compatibility with RFC 1434 implementations and can be used in future versions, if needed.

- **Flow-control byte**—Carries the flow-control indicator, flow-control acknowledgment, and flow-control operator bits.

- **Protocol ID**—When set to 0x42, indicates a decimal value of 66.

- **Header number**—When set to 0x01, indicates a value of 1.

- **Largest frame size**—Carries the largest frame size bits across the DLSw connection. This field is implemented to ensure that the two end stations always negotiate a frame size to be used on a circuit that does not require DLSw partners to resegment frames.

- **SSP flags**—Contains additional information about the SSP message. Flag definitions (bit 7 is the most significant bit, and bit 0 is the least significant bit of the octet) are shown in Table 33-1.

Table 33-1 *SSP Flag Definitions*

Bit Position	Name	Meaning
7	SSPex	1 = Explorer message (canureach or icanreach).
6 through 0	Reserved	None. Reserved fields are set to 0 upon transmission and are ignored upon receipt.

- **Circuit priority**—Provides for unsupported, low, medium, high, and highest circuit priorities in the 3 low-order bits of this byte. At circuit start time, each circuit endpoint provides priority information to its circuit partner. The initiator of the circuit chooses which circuit priority is effective for the life of the circuit. If the priority is not implemented by the nodes, the unsupported priority is used.

- **Target MAC address**—Combines with the target link SAP, origin MAC address, and origin SAP to define a logical end-to-end association called a data-link ID.

- **Origin MAC address**—Serves as the MAC address of the origin end station.

- **Origin LSAP**—Serves as the SAP of the source device. The SAP is used to logically identify the traffic being transmitted.

- **Target LSAP**—Serves as the SAP of the destination device.

- **Frame direction**—Contains the value 0x01 for frames sent from the origin DLSw to the target DLSw node, or 0x02 for frames sent from the target DLSw to the origin DLSw node.

- **DLC header length**—When set to 0 for SNA and 0x23 for NetBIOS datagrams, indicates a length of 35 bytes. The NetBIOS header includes the following information:

  — Access Control (AC) field

  — Frame Control (FC) field

  — Destination MAC address (DA)

  — Source MAC address (SA)

  — Routing Information (RI) field (padded to 18 bytes)

  — Destination service access point (DSAP)

  — Source SAP (SSAP)

  — LLC control field (UI)

- **Origin DLC port ID**—Works in tandem with the origin data-link correlator to form a 64-bit circuit ID that identifies the DLC circuit within a single DLSw node. The circuit ID is unique in a single DLSw node and is assigned locally. The end-to-end circuit is identified by a pair of circuit IDs that, along with the data-link IDs, uniquely identify a single end-to-end circuit. Each DLSw node must keep a table of these circuit ID pairs: one for the local end of the circuit and one for the remote end of the circuit.

- **Origin data-link correlator**—Works in tandem with the origin DLC port ID to form a 64-bit circuit ID that identifies the DLC circuit within a single DLSw node. The circuit ID is unique in a single DLSw and is assigned locally. The end-to-end circuit is identified by a pair of circuit IDs that, along with the data-link IDs, uniquely identify a single end-to-end circuit. Each DLSw node must keep a table of these circuit ID pairs: one for the local end of the circuit and one for the remote end of the circuit.

- **Origin transport ID**—Identifies the individual TCP/IP port on a DLSw node. Values have only local significance. Each DLSw node must reflect the values, along with the associated values for the DLC port ID and the data-link correlator, when returning a message to a DLSw partner.

- **Target data-link correlator**—Works in tandem with the target DLC port ID to form a 64-bit circuit ID that identifies the DLC circuit within a single DLSw node. The circuit ID is unique in a single DLSw node and is assigned locally. The end-to-end circuit is identified by a pair of circuit IDs that, along with the data-link IDs, uniquely identifies a single end-to-end circuit. Each DLSw node must keep a table of these circuit ID pairs: one for the local end of the circuit and one for the remote end of the circuit.

- **Transport ID**—Identifies the individual TCP/IP port on a DLSw node. Values have only local significance. Each DLSw node must reflect the values, along with the associated values for the DLC port ID and the data-link correlator, when returning a message to a DLSw partner.

Review Questions

1 DLSw provides link layer acknowledgments. What is meant by link layer acknowledgments? Why is this advantageous?

2 DLSw SSP uses what transport protocol? What are the advantages and disadvantages of this selection?

3 List and describe the three operational phases of DLSw.

4 What protocols does DLSw support?

5 What is the normal Layer 2 process employed without DLSw?

6 DLSw defines two message types. What are they, which has the larger header, and is there anything in common between them?

Network Protocols

Objectives

- Introduce the OSI protocol, used primarily to facilitate multivendor equipment interoperability.
- Discuss the structures and functioning of this protocol, from its introduction in the early 1980s.

CHAPTER 34

Open System Interconnection Protocols

Background

The *Open System Interconnection (OSI)* protocol suite is comprised of numerous standard protocols that are based on the OSI reference model. These protocols are part of an international program to develop data-networking protocols and other standards that facilitate multivendor equipment interoperability. The OSI program grew out of a need for international networking standards and is designed to facilitate communication between hardware and software systems despite differences in underlying architectures.

The OSI specifications were conceived and implemented by two international standards organizations: the International Organization for Standardization (ISO) and the International Telecommunication Union–Telecommunications Standards Sector (ITU-T). This chapter provides a summary of the OSI protocol suite and illustrates its mapping to the general OSI reference model.

OSI Networking Protocols

Figure 34-1 illustrates the entire OSI protocol suite and its relation to the layers of the OSI reference model. Each component of this protocol suite is discussed briefly in this chapter. The OSI routing protocols are addressed in more detail in Chapter 48, "Open System Interconnection (OSI) Routing Protocols."

Figure 34-1   *The OSI Protocol Suite Maps to All Layers of the OSI Reference Model*

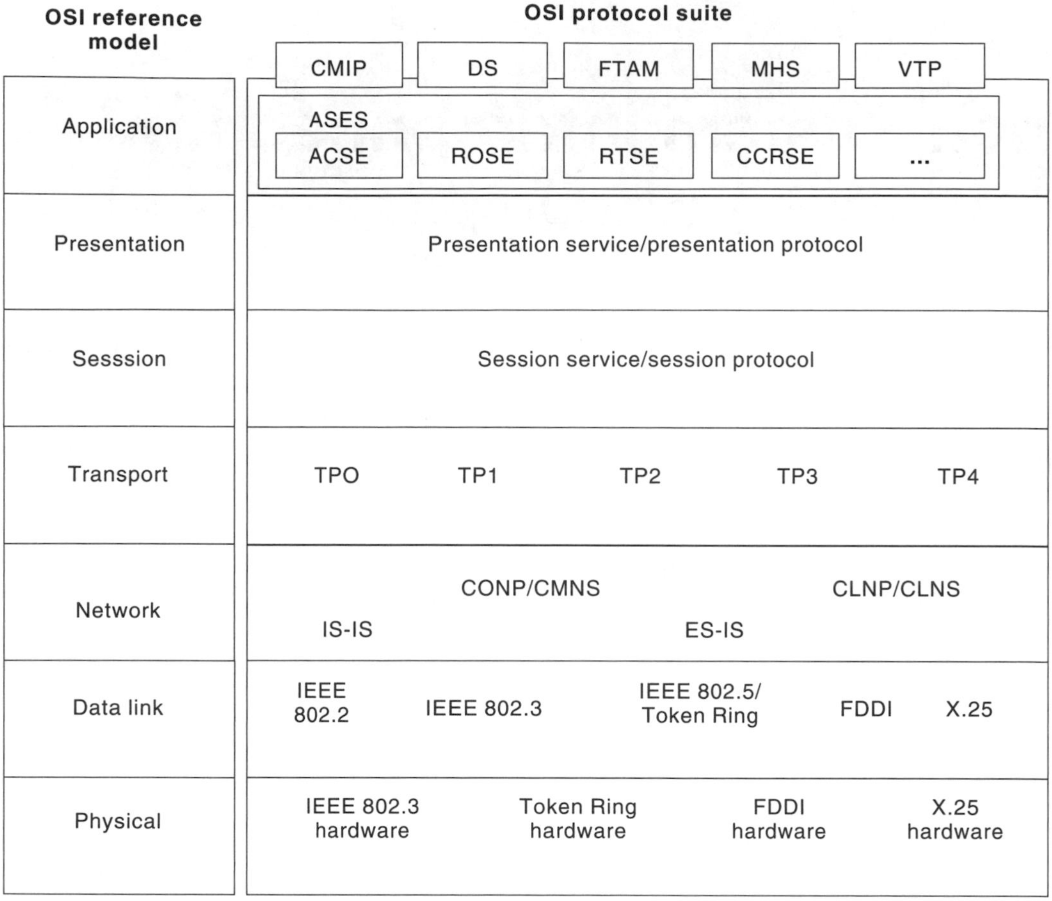

OSI reference model	OSI protocol suite				
Application	CMIP / DS / FTAM / MHS / VTP ASES ACSE / ROSE / RTSE / CCRSE / ...				
Presentation	Presentation service/presentation protocol				
Sesssion	Session service/session protocol				
Transport	TPO	TP1	TP2	TP3	TP4
Network	CONP/CMNS CLNP/CLNS IS-IS ES-IS				
Data link	IEEE 802.2	IEEE 802.3	IEEE 802.5/ Token Ring	FDDI	X.25
Physical	IEEE 802.3 hardware	Token Ring hardware	FDDI hardware	X.25 hardware	

OSI Physical and Data Link layers

The OSI protocol suite supports numerous standard media-access protocols at the physical and data link layers. The wide variety of media-access protocols supported in the OSI protocol suite allows other protocol suites to exist easily alongside OSI on the same network media. Supported media-access protocols include IEEE 802.2 LLC, IEEE 802.3, Token Ring/IEEE 802.5, Fiber Distributed Data Interface (FDDI), and X.25.

OSI Network Layer

The OSI protocol suite specifies two routing protocols at the network layer: End System-to-Intermediate System (ES-IS) and Intermediate System-to-Intermediate System (IS-IS).

In addition, the OSI suite implements two types of network services: connectionless service and connection-oriented service.

OSI Layer Standards

In addition to the standards specifying the OSI network layer protocols and services, the following documents describe other OSI network layer specifications:

- **ISO 8648**—This standard defines the internal organization of the network layer (IONL), which divides the network layer into three distinct sublayers to support different subnetwork types.

- **ISO 8348**—This standard defines network layer addressing and describes the connection-oriented and connectionless services provided by the OSI network layer.

- **ISO TR 9575**—This standard describes the framework, concepts, and terminology used in relation to OSI routing protocols.

OSI Connectionless Network Service

OSI connectionless network service is implemented by using the Connectionless Network Protocol (CLNP) and Connectionless Network Service (CLNS). CLNP and CLNS are described in the ISO 8473 standard.

CLNP is an OSI network layer protocol that carries upper-layer data and error indications over connectionless links. CLNP provides the interface between the Connectionless Network Service (CLNS) and upper layers.

CLNS provides network layer services to the transport layer via CLNP.

CLNS does not perform connection setup or termination because paths are determined independently for each packet that is transmitted through a network. This contrasts with Connection-Mode Network Service (CMNS).

In addition, CLNS provides best-effort delivery, which means that no guarantee exists that data will not be lost, corrupted, misordered, or duplicated. CLNS relies on transport layer protocols to perform error detection and correction.

OSI Connection-Oriented Network Service

OSI connection-oriented network service is implemented by using the Connection-Oriented Network Protocol (CONP) and Connection-Mode Network Service (CMNS).

CONP is an OSI network layer protocol that carries upper-layer data and error indications over connection-oriented links. CONP is based on the X.25 Packet-Layer Protocol (PLP) and is described in the ISO 8208 standard, "X.25 Packet-Layer Protocol for DTE."

CONP provides the interface between CMNS and upper layers. It is a network layer service that acts as the interface between the transport layer and CONP, and it is described in the ISO 8878 standard.

CMNS performs functions related to the explicit establishment of paths between communicating transport layer entities. These functions include connection setup, maintenance, and termination. CMNS also provides a mechanism for requesting a specific quality of service (QoS). This contrasts with CLNS.

Network Layer Addressing

OSI network layer addressing is implemented by using two types of hierarchical addresses: network service access point addresses and network entity titles.

A *network service access point (NSAP)* is a conceptual point on the boundary between the network and the transport layers. The NSAP is the location at which OSI network services are provided to the transport layer. Each transport layer entity is assigned a single NSAP, which is individually addressed in an OSI internetwork using NSAP addresses.

Figure 34-2 illustrates the format of the OSI NSAP address, which identifies individual NSAPs.

Figure 34-2   *The OSI NSAP Address Is Assigned to Each Transport Layer Entity*

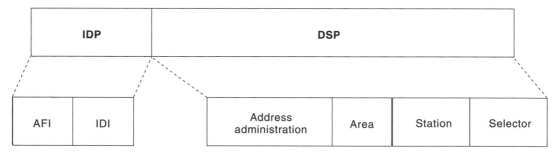

NSAP Address Fields

Two NSAP Address fields exist: the initial domain part (IDP) and the domain-specific part (DSP).

The IDP field is divided into two parts: the authority format identifier (AFI) and the initial domain identifier (IDI). The AFI provides information about the structure and content of the IDI and DSP fields, such as whether the IDI is of variable length and whether the DSP uses decimal or binary notation. The IDI specifies the entity that can assign values to the DSP portion of the NSAP address.

The DSP is subdivided into four parts by the authority responsible for its administration. The Address Administration fields allow for the further administration of addressing by adding a second authority identifier and by delegating address administration to subauthorities. The Area field identifies the specific area within a domain and is used for routing purposes. The Station field identifies a specific station within an area and also is used for routing purposes. The Selector field provides the specific n-selector within a station and, much like the other fields, is used for routing purposes. The reserved n-selector 00 identifies the address as a network entity title (NET).

End-System NSAPs

An OSI end system (ES) often has multiple NSAP addresses, one for each transport entity that it contains. If this is the case, the NSAP address for each transport entity usually differs only in the last byte (called the n-selector). Figure 34-3 illustrates the relationship between a transport entity, the NSAP, and the network service.

Figure 34-3 *The NSAP Provides a Link Between a Transport Entity and a Network Service*

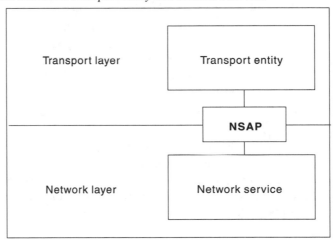

A network entity title (NET) is used to identify the network layer of a system without associating that system with a specific transport layer entity (as an NSAP address does). NETs are useful for addressing intermediate systems (ISs), such as routers, that do not interface with the transport layer. An IS can have a single NET or multiple NETs, if it participates in multiple areas or domains.

OSI Protocols Transport Layer

The OSI protocol suite implements two types of services at the transport layer: connection-oriented transport service and connectionless transport service.

Five connection-oriented transport layer protocols exist in the OSI suite, ranging from Transport Protocol Class 0 through Transport Protocol Class 4. Connectionless transport service is supported only by Transport Protocol Class 4.

Transport Protocol Class 0 (TP0), the simplest OSI transport protocol, performs segmentation and reassembly functions. TP0 requires connection-oriented network service.

Transport Protocol Class 1 (TP1) performs segmentation and reassembly, and offers basic error recovery. TP1 sequences protocol data units (PDUs) and will retransmit PDUs or reinitiate the connection if an excessive number of PDUs are unacknowledged. TP1 requires connection-oriented network service.

Transport Protocol Class 2 (TP2) performs segmentation and reassembly, as well as multiplexing and demultiplexing of data streams over a single virtual circuit. TP2 requires connection-oriented network service.

Transport Protocol Class 3 (TP3) offers basic error recovery and performs segmentation and reassembly, in addition to multiplexing and demultiplexing of data streams over a single virtual circuit. TP3 also sequences PDUs and retransmits them or reinitiates the connection if an excessive number are unacknowledged. TP3 requires connection-oriented network service.

Transport Protocol Class 4 (TP4) offers basic error recovery, performs segmentation and reassembly, and supplies multiplexing and demultiplexing of data streams over a single virtual circuit. TP4 sequences PDUs and retransmits them or reinitiates the connection if an excessive number are unacknowledged. TP4 provides reliable transport service and functions with either connection-oriented or connectionless network service. It is based on the Transmission Control Protocol (TCP) in the Internet Protocols suite and is the only OSI protocol class that supports connectionless network service.

OSI Protocols Session Layer

The session layer implementation of the OSI protocol suite consists of a session protocol and a session service. The session protocol allows session-service users (SS-users) to communicate with the session service. An SS-user is an entity that requests the services of the session layer. Such requests are made at session-service access points (SSAPs), and SS-users are uniquely identified by using an SSAP address. Figure 34-4 shows the relationship between the SS-user, the SSAP, the session protocol, and the session service.

Session service provides four basic services to SS-users. First, it establishes and terminates connections between SS-users and synchronizes the data exchange between them. Second, it performs various negotiations for the use of session layer tokens, which the SS-user must possess to begin communicating. Third, it inserts synchronization points in transmitted data that allow the session to be recovered in the event of errors or interruptions. Finally, it enables SS-users to interrupt a session and resume it later at a specific point.

Figure 34-4 *Session Layer Functions Provide Service to Presentation Layer Functions via an SSAP*

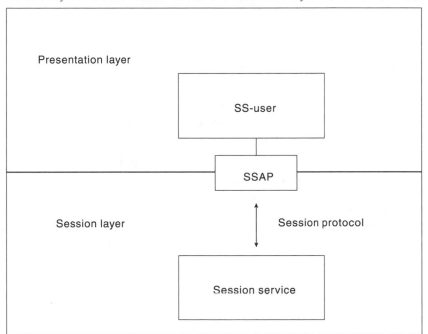

Session service is defined in the ISO 8306 standard and in the ITU-T X.215 recommendation. The session protocol is defined in the ISO 8307 standard and in the ITU-T X.225 recommendation. A connectionless version of the session protocol is specified in the ISO 9548 standard.

OSI Protocols Presentation Layer

The presentation layer implementation of the OSI protocol suite consists of a presentation protocol and a presentation service. The presentation protocol enables presentation-service users (PS-users) to communicate with the presentation service.

A PS-user is an entity that requests the services of the presentation layer. Such requests are made at presentation-service access points (PSAPs). PS-users are uniquely identified by using PSAP addresses.

Presentation service negotiates transfer syntax and translates data to and from the transfer syntax for PS-users, which represent data using different syntaxes. The presentation service is used by two PS-users to agree upon the transfer syntax that will be used. When a transfer syntax is agreed upon, presentation-service entities must translate the data from the PS-user to the correct transfer syntax.

The OSI presentation layer service is defined in the ISO 8822 standard and in the ITU-T X.216 recommendation. The OSI presentation protocol is defined in the ISO 8823 standard and in the ITU-T X.226 recommendation. A connectionless version of the presentation protocol is specified in the ISO 9576 standard.

OSI Protocols Application Layer

The application layer implementation of the OSI protocol suite consists of various application entities. An application entity is the part of an application process that is relevant to the operation of the OSI protocol suite. An application entity is composed of the user element and the application service element (ASE).

The user element is the part of an application entity that uses ASEs to satisfy the communication needs of the application process. The ASE is the part of an application entity that provides services to user elements and, therefore, to application processes. ASEs also provide interfaces to the lower OSI layers. Figure 34-5 portrays the composition of a single application process (composed of the application entity, the user element, and the ASEs) and its relation to the PSAP and presentation service.

Figure 34-5 *An Application Process Relies on the PSAP and Presentation Service*

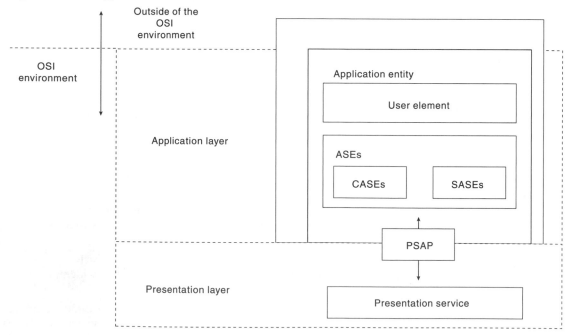

ASEs fall into one of the two following classifications: common-application service elements (CASEs) and specific-application service elements (SASEs). Both of these might be present in a single application entity.

Common-Application Service Elements

Common-application service elements (CASEs) are ASEs that provide services used by a wide variety of application processes. In many cases, multiple CASEs are used by a single application entity. The following four CASEs are defined in the OSI specification:

- **Association control service element (ACSE)**—Creates associations between two application entities in preparation for application-to-application communication
- **Remote operations service element (ROSE)**—Implements a request-reply mechanism that permits various remote operations across an application association established by the ACSE
- **Reliable transfer service element (RTSE)**—Allows ASEs to reliably transfer messages while preserving the transparency of complex lower-layer facilities
- **Commitment, concurrence, and recovery service elements (CCRSE)**— Coordinates dialogues among multiple application entities

Specific-Application Service Elements

Specific-application service elements (SASEs) are ASEs that provide services used only by a specific application process, such as file transfer, database access, and order entry, among others.

OSI Protocols Application Processes

An application process is the element of an application that provides the interface between the application itself and the OSI application layer. Some of the standard OSI application processes include the following:

- **Common management-information protocol (CMIP)**—Performs network-management functions, allowing the exchange of management information between ESs and management stations. CMIP is specified in the ITU-T X.700 recommendation and is functionally similar to the Simple Network Management Protocol (SNMP) and NetView.
- **Directory services (DS)**—Serves as a distributed directory that is used for node identification and addressing in OSI internetworks. DS is specified in the ITU-T X.500 recommendation.
- **File transfer, access, and management (FTAM)**—Provides file-transfer service and distributed file-access facilities.

- **Message handling system (MHS)**—Provides a transport mechanism for electronic messaging applications and other applications by using store-and-forward services.
- **Virtual terminal protocol (VTP)**—Provides terminal emulation that allows a computer system to appear to a remote ES as if it were a directly attached terminal.

Review Questions

1 What are the two routing protocols specified in the OSI suite?

2 Describe the OSI connectionless network protocol.

3 Describe the OSI connection-oriented network protocol.

4 How are requests to services at the session layer made within OSI protocols?

5 Describe common-application service elements (CASEs).

6 Name some of the media types that the OSI protocol suite supports.

7 Why was the OSI protocol suite created?

8 Describe the session layer protocols within the OSI protocol suite.

9 Describe the presentation layer protocols of the OSI protocol suite.

10 What are the two types of ASEs?

Objectives

- Introduce the IP protocol, one of the most prolific and popular protocols used today.
- Discuss the structures and addressing of this protocol.

CHAPTER 35

Internet Protocols

Background

The Internet protocols are the world's most popular open-system (nonproprietary) protocol suite because they can be used to communicate across any set of interconnected networks and are equally well suited for LAN and WAN communications. The Internet protocols consist of a suite of communication protocols, of which the two best known are the Transmission Control Protocol (TCP) and the Internet Protocol (IP).

The Internet protocol suite not only includes lower-layer protocols (such as TCP and IP), but it also specifies common applications such as electronic mail, terminal emulation, and file transfer. This chapter provides a broad introduction to specifications that comprise the Internet protocols. Discussions include IP addressing and key upper-layer protocols used in the Internet. Specific routing protocols are addressed individually in Part VII, "Routing Protocols."

Internet protocols were first developed in the mid-1970s, when the Defense Advanced Research Projects Agency (DARPA) became interested in establishing a packet-switched network that would facilitate communication between dissimilar computer systems at research institutions. With the goal of heterogeneous connectivity in mind, DARPA funded research by Stanford University and Bolt, Beranek, and Newman (BBN). The result of this development effort was the Internet protocol suite, completed in the late 1970s.

TCP/IP later was included with Berkeley Software Distribution (BSD) UNIX and has since become the foundation on which the Internet and the World Wide Web (WWW) are based.

Documentation of the Internet protocols (including new or revised protocols) and policies are specified in technical reports called Request For Comments (RFCs), which are published and then reviewed and analyzed by the Internet community. Protocol refinements are published in the new RFCs. To illustrate the scope of the Internet protocols, Figure 35-1 maps many of the protocols of the Internet protocol suite and their corresponding OSI layers. This chapter addresses the basic elements and operations of these and other key Internet protocols.

Figure 35-1 *Internet Protocols Span the Complete Range of OSI Model Layers*

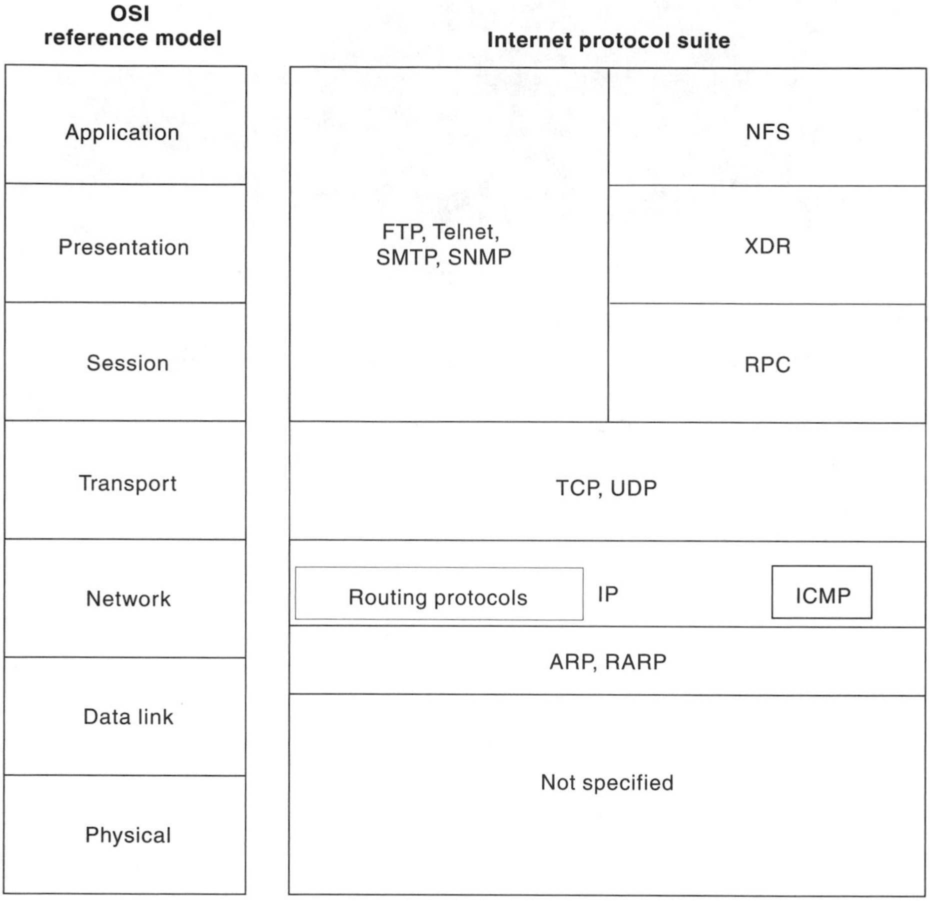

OSI reference model	Internet protocol suite		
Application	FTP, Telnet, SMTP, SNMP		NFS
Presentation			XDR
Session			RPC
Transport	TCP, UDP		
Network	Routing protocols	IP	ICMP
Data link	ARP, RARP		
Physical	Not specified		

Internet Protocol

The Internet Protocol (IP) is a network layer (Layer 3) protocol that contains addressing information and some control information that enables packets to be routed. IP is documented in RFC 791 and is the primary network layer protocol in the Internet protocol suite. Along with the Transmission Control Protocol (TCP), IP represents the heart of the Internet protocols. IP has two primary responsibilities: providing connectionless, best-effort delivery of datagrams through an internetwork; and providing fragmentation and reassembly of datagrams to support data links with different maximum transmission unit (MTU) sizes.

IP Packet Format

An IP packet contains several types of information, as illustrated in Figure 35-2.

Figure 35-2 *Fourteen Fields Comprise an IP Packet*

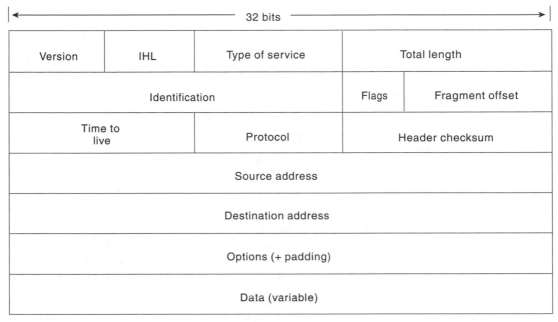

The following discussion describes the IP packet fields illustrated in Figure 35-2:

- **Version**—Indicates the version of IP currently used.
- **IP header length (IHL)**—Indicates the datagram header length in 32-bit words.
- **Type-of-service**—Specifies how an upper-layer protocol would like a current datagram to be handled, and assigns datagrams various levels of importance.
- **Total length**—Specifies the length, in bytes, of the entire IP packet, including the data and the header.
- **Identification**—Contains an integer that identifies the current datagram. This field is used to help piece together datagram fragments.
- **Flags**—Consists of a 3-bit field of which the two low-order (least-significant) bits control fragmentation. The low-order bit specifies whether the packet can be fragmented. The middle bit specifies whether the packet is the last fragment in a series of fragmented packets. The third or high-order bit is not used.

- **Fragment offset**—Indicates the position of the fragment's data relative to the beginning of the data in the original datagram, which allows the destination IP process to properly reconstruct the original datagram.

- **Time-to-live**—Maintains a counter that gradually decrements down to zero, at which point the datagram is discarded. This keeps packets from looping endlessly.

- **Protocol**—Indicates which upper-layer protocol receives incoming packets after IP processing is complete.

- **Header checksum**—Helps ensure IP header integrity.

- **Source address**—Specifies the sending node.

- **Destination address**—Specifies the receiving node.

- **Options**—Allows IP to support various options, such as security.

- **Data**—Contains upper-layer information.

IP Addressing

As with any other network layer protocol, the IP addressing scheme is integral to the process of routing IP datagrams through an internetwork. Each IP address has specific components and follows a basic format. These IP addresses can be subdivided and used to create addresses for subnetworks, as discussed in more detail later in this chapter.

Each host on a TCP/IP network is assigned a unique 32-bit logical address that is divided into two main parts: the network number and the host number. The network number identifies a network and must be assigned by the Internet Network Information Center (InterNIC) if the network is to be part of the Internet. An Internet service provider (ISP) can obtain blocks of network addresses from the InterNIC and can itself assign address space as necessary. The host number identifies a host on a network and is assigned by the local network administrator.

IP Address Format

The 32-bit IP address is grouped 8 bits at a time, separated by dots and represented in decimal format (known as dotted decimal notation). Each bit in the octet has a binary weight (128, 64, 32, 16, 8, 4, 2, 1). The minimum value for an octet is 0, and the maximum value for an octet is 255. Figure 35-3 illustrates the basic format of an IP address.

Figure 35-3 *An IP Address Consists of 32 Bits, Grouped into 4 Octets*

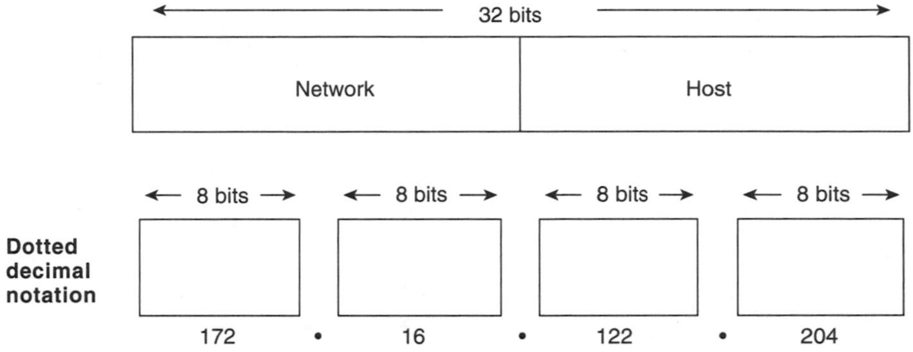

IP Address Classes

IP addressing supports five different address classes: A, B, C, D, and E. Only classes A, B, and C are available for commercial use. The left-most (high-order) bits indicate the network class. Table 35-1 provides reference information about the five IP address classes.

Table 35-1 *Reference Information About the Five IP Address Classes*

IP Address Class	Format	Purpose	High-Order Bit(s)	Address Range	Number of Bits Network/ Host	Max. Hosts
A	N.H.H.H[1]	Few large organizations	0	1.0.0.0 to 126.0.0.0	7/24	$16,777,214^2 (2^{24}\text{-}2)$
B	N.N.H.H	Medium-size organizations	1,0	128.1 to 191.254.0.0	14/16	$65,543(2^{16}\text{-}2)$
C	N.N.N.H	Relatively small organizations	1,1,0	192.0.1.0 to 223.255.254.0	22/8	$245(2^8\text{-}2)$
D	—	Multicast groups (RFC 1112)	1,1,1,0	224.0.0.0 to 239.255.255.255	Not for commercial use	—
E	—	Experimental	1,1,1,1	240.0.0 to 254.255.255.255	—	—

[1] N = Network number, H = Host number

[2] One address is reserved for the broadcast address, and one address is reserved for the network.

Figure 35-4 illustrates the format of the commercial IP address classes. (Note the high-order bits in each class.)

Figure 35-4 *IP Address Formats A, B, and C Are Available for Commercial Use*

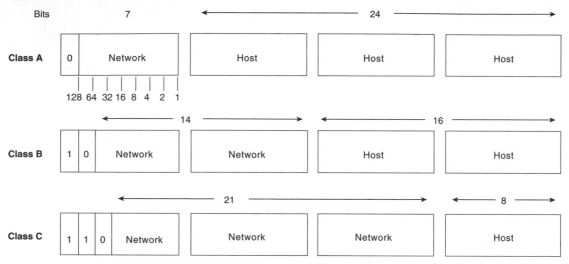

The class of address can be determined easily by examining the first octet of the address and mapping that value to a class range in the following table. In an IP address of 172.31.1.2, for example, the first octet is 172. Because 172 falls between 128 and 191, 172.31.1.2 is a Class B address. Figure 35-5 summarizes the range of possible values for the first octet of each address class.

Figure 35-5 *A Range of Possible Values Exists for the First Octet of Each Address Class*

Address class	First octet in decimal	High-order bits
Class A	1 – 126	0
Class B	128 – 191	10
Class C	192 – 223	110
Class D	224 – 239	1110
Class E	240 – 254	1111

IP Subnet Addressing

IP networks can be divided into smaller networks called subnetworks (or subnets). Subnetting provides the network administrator with several benefits, including extra flexibility, more efficient use of network addresses, and the capability to contain broadcast traffic (a broadcast will not cross a router).

Subnets are under local administration. As such, the outside world sees an organization as a single network and has no detailed knowledge of the organization's internal structure.

A given network address can be broken up into many subnetworks. For example, 172.16.1.0, 172.16.2.0, 172.16.3.0, and 172.16.4.0 are all subnets within network 172.16.0.0. (All 0s in the host portion of an address specifies the entire network.)

IP Subnet Mask

A subnet address is created by borrowing bits from the host field and designating them as the Subnet field. The number of borrowed bits varies and is specified by the subnet mask. Figure 35-6 shows how bits are borrowed from the Host address field to create the Subnet address field.

Figure 35-6 *Bits Are Borrowed from the Host Address Field to Create the Subnet Address Field*

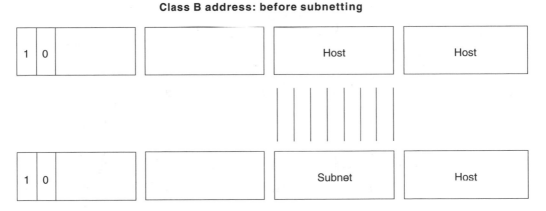

Class B address: before subnetting

Class B address: after subnetting

Subnet masks use the same format and representation technique as IP addresses. The subnet mask, however, has binary 1s in all bits specifying the Network and Subnetwork fields, and binary 0s in all bits specifying the Host field. Figure 35-7 illustrates a sample subnet mask.

Figure 35-7 *A Sample Subnet Mask Consists of All Binary 1s and 0s*

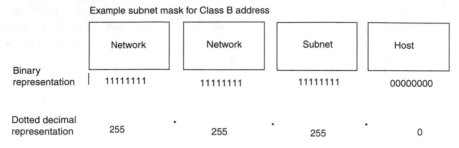

Example subnet mask for Class B address

Network	Network	Subnet	Host

Binary
representation   11111111   11111111   11111111   00000000

Dotted decimal
representation   255   .   255   .   255   .   0

Subnet mask bits should come from the high-order (left-most) bits of the host field, as Figure 35-8 illustrates. Details of Class B and C subnet mask types follow. Class A addresses are not discussed in this chapter because they generally are subnetted on an 8-bit boundary.

Figure 35-8 *Subnet Mask Bits Come from the High-Order Bits of the Host Field*

128	64	32	16	8	4	2	1		
1	0	0	0	0	0	0	0	=	128
1	1	0	0	0	0	0	0	=	192
1	1	1	0	0	0	0	0	=	224
1	1	1	1	0	0	0	0	=	240
1	1	1	1	1	0	0	0	=	248
1	1	1	1	1	1	0	0	=	252
1	1	1	1	1	1	1	0	=	254
1	1	1	1	1	1	1	1	=	255

Various types of subnet masks exist for Class B and C subnets.

The default subnet mask for a Class B address that has no subnetting is 255.255.0.0, while the subnet mask for a Class B address 171.16.0.0 that specifies 8 bits of subnetting is

255.255.255.0. The reason for this is that 8 bits of subnetting, or $2^8 - 2$ (1 for the network address and 1 for the broadcast address) = 254 subnets possible, with $2^8 - 2 = 254$ hosts per subnet.

The subnet mask for a Class C address 192.168.2.0 that specifies 5 bits of subnetting is 255.255.255.248. With 5 bits available for subnetting, $2^5 - 2 = 31$ subnets possible, with $2^3 - 2 = 6$ hosts per subnet.

The reference charts shown in Table 35-2 and Table 35-3 can be used when planning Class B and C networks to determine the required number of subnets and hosts, and the appropriate subnet mask.

Table 35-2   *Class B Subnetting Reference Chart*

Number of Bits	Subnet Mask	Number of Subnets	Number of Hosts
2	255.255.192.0	2	16,382
3	255.255.224.0	6	8190
4	255.255.240.0	14	4094
5	255.255.248.0	30	2046
6	255.255.252.0	62	1022
7	255.255.254.0	126	510
8	255.255.255.0	254	254
9	255.255.255.128	510	126
10	255.255.255.192	1022	62
11	255.255.255.224	2046	30
12	255.255.255.240	4094	14
13	255.255.255.248	8190	6
14	255.255.255.252	16,382	2

Table 35-3   *Class C Subnetting Reference Chart*

Number of Bits	Subnet Mask	Number of Subnets	Number of Hosts
2	255.255.255.192	2	62
3	255.255.255.224	6	30
4	255.255.255.240	14	14
5	255.255.255.248	30	6
6	255.255.255.252	62	2

How Subnet Masks Are Used to Determine the Network Number

The router performs a set process to determine the network (or, more specifically, the subnetwork) address. First, the router extracts the IP destination address from the incoming packet and retrieves the internal subnet mask. It then performs a logical AND operation to obtain the network number. This causes the host portion of the IP destination address to be removed, while the destination network number remains. The router then looks up the destination network number and matches it with an outgoing interface. Finally, it forwards the frame to the destination IP address. Specifics regarding the logical AND operation are discussed in the following section.

Logical AND Operation

Three basic rules govern using a logical AND on two binary numbers. First, 1 "ANDed" with 1 yields 1. Second, 1 "ANDed" with 0 yields 0. Finally, 0 "ANDed" with 0 yields 0. The truth table provided in Table 35-4 illustrates the rules for logical AND operations.

Table 35-4   *Rules for Logical AND Operations*

Input	Input	Output
1	1	1
1	0	0
0	1	0
0	0	0

Two simple guidelines exist for remembering logical AND operations: Using a logical AND on a 1 with a 1 yields the original value, and using a logical AND on a 0 with any number yields 0.

Figure 35-9 illustrates that when a logical AND of the destination IP address and the subnet mask is performed, the subnetwork number remains, which the router uses to forward the packet.

Figure 35-9 *Applying a Logical AND to the Destination IP Address—the Subnet Mask Produces the Subnetwork Number*

		Network	Subnet	Host
Destination IP address	171.16.1.2		00000001	00000010
Subnet mask	255.255.255.0		11111111	00000000
			00000001	00000000
			1	0

Address Resolution Protocol Overview

For two machines on a given network to communicate, they must know the other machine's physical (or MAC) addresses. By broadcasting Address Resolution Protocols (ARPs), a host can dynamically discover the MAC-layer address corresponding to a particular IP network layer address.

After receiving a MAC-layer address, IP devices create an ARP cache to store the recently acquired IP-to-MAC address mapping, thus avoiding having to broadcast ARPs when they want to recontact a device. If the device does not respond within a specified time frame, the cache entry is flushed.

In addition, the Reverse Address Resolution Protocol (RARP) is used to map MAC-layer addresses to IP addresses. RARP, which is the logical inverse of ARP, might be used by diskless workstations that do not know their IP addresses when they boot. RARP relies on the presence of a RARP server with table entries of mappings from MAC layer to IP address mappings.

Internet Routing

Internet routing devices traditionally have been called gateways. In today's terminology, however, the term *gateway* refers specifically to a device that performs application layer protocol translation between devices. Interior gateways refer to devices that perform these protocol functions between machines or networks under the same administrative control or authority, such as a corporation's internal network. These are known as autonomous systems. Exterior gateways perform protocol functions between independent networks.

Routers within the Internet are organized hierarchically. Routers used for information exchange within autonomous systems are called interior routers, which use a variety of Interior Gateway Protocols (IGPs) to accomplish this purpose. The Routing Information Protocol (RIP) is an example of an IGP.

Routers that move information between autonomous systems are called exterior routers. These routers use an Exterior Gateway Protocol to exchange information between autonomous systems. The Border Gateway Protocol (BGP) is an example of an Exterior Gateway Protocol.

NOTE   Specific routing protocols, including BGP and RIP, are addressed in individual chapters presented in Part VII, later in this book.

IP Routing

IP routing protocols are dynamic. Dynamic routing calls for routes to be calculated automatically at regular intervals by software in routing devices. This contrasts with static routing, in which routers are established by the network administrator and do not change until the network administrator changes them.

An IP routing table, which consists of destination address/next-hop pairs, is used to enable dynamic routing. An entry in this table, for example, would be interpreted as follows: To get to network 172.31.0.0, send the packet out Ethernet interface 0 (E0).

IP routing specifies that IP datagrams travel through internetworks one hop at a time. The entire route is not known at the onset of the journey, however. Instead, at each stop, the next destination is calculated by matching the destination address within the datagram with an entry in the current node's routing table.

Each node's involvement in the routing process is limited to forwarding packets based on internal information. The nodes do not monitor whether the packets get to their final destination, nor does IP provide for error reporting back to the source when routing anomalies occur. This task is left to another Internet protocol, the Internet Control Message Protocol (ICMP), which is discussed in the following section.

Internet Control Message Protocol

The Internet Control Message Protocol (ICMP) is a network layer Internet protocol that provides message packets to report errors and other information regarding IP packet processing back to the source. ICMP is documented in RFC 792.

ICMP Messages

ICMPs generate several kinds of useful messages, including destination unreachable, echo request and reply, redirect, time exceeded, and router advertisement and router solicitation messages. If an ICMP message cannot be delivered, no second one is generated. This is to avoid an endless flood of ICMP messages.

When an ICMP destination unreachable message is sent by a router, it means that the router is incapable of sending the package to its final destination. The router then discards the original packet. Two reasons exist for why a destination might be unreachable. Most commonly, the source host has specified a nonexistent address. Less frequently, the router does not have a route to the destination.

Destination unreachable messages include four basic types: network unreachable, host unreachable, protocol unreachable, and port unreachable. Network unreachable messages usually mean that a failure has occurred in routing or addressing a packet. Host unreachable messages usually indicate delivery failure, such as a wrong subnet mask. Protocol unreachable messages generally mean that the destination does not support the upper-layer protocol specified in the packet. Port unreachable messages imply that the TCP socket or port is not available.

An ICMP echo request message, which is generated by the **ping** command, is sent by any host to test node reachability across an internetwork. The ICMP echo reply message indicates that the node can be successfully reached.

An ICMP redirect message is sent by the router to the source host to stimulate more efficient routing. The router still forwards the original packet to the destination. ICMP redirects allow host routing tables to remain small because it is necessary to know the address of only one router, even if that router does not provide the best path. Even after receiving an ICMP redirect message, some devices might continue using the less-efficient route.

An ICMP time-exceeded message is sent by the router if an IP packet's Time-to-Live field (expressed in hops or seconds) reaches zero. The Time-to-Live field prevents packets from continuously circulating the internetwork if the internetwork contains a routing loop. The router then discards the original packet.

ICMP Router-Discovery Protocol

ICMP Router-Discovery Protocol (IDRP) uses router advertisement and router solicitation messages to discover the addresses of routers on directly attached subnets. Each router periodically multicasts router advertisement messages from each of its interfaces. Hosts then discover addresses of routers on directly attached subnets by listening for these messages. Hosts can use router solicitation messages to request immediate advertisements rather than waiting for unsolicited messages.

IRDP offers several advantages over other methods of discovering addresses of neighboring routers. Primarily, it does not require hosts to recognize routing protocols, nor does it require manual configuration by an administrator.

Router advertisement messages enable hosts to discover the existence of neighboring routers, but not which router is best to reach a particular destination. If a host uses a poor first-hop router to reach a particular destination, it receives a redirect message identifying a better choice.

Transmission Control Protocol

The Transmission Control Protocol (TCP) provides reliable transmission of data in an IP environment. TCP corresponds to the transport layer (Layer 4) of the OSI reference model. Among the services that TCP provides are stream data transfer, reliability, efficient flow control, full-duplex operation, and multiplexing.

With stream data transfer, TCP delivers an unstructured stream of bytes identified by sequence numbers. This service benefits applications because they do not have to chop data into blocks before handing it off to TCP. Instead, TCP groups bytes into segments and passes them to IP for delivery.

TCP offers reliability by providing connection-oriented, end-to-end reliable packet delivery through an internetwork. It does this by sequencing bytes with a forwarding acknowledgment number that indicates to the destination the next byte that the source expects to receive. Bytes not acknowledged within a specified time period are retransmitted. The reliability mechanism of TCP allows devices to deal with lost, delayed, duplicate, or misread packets. A timeout mechanism allows devices to detect lost packets and request retransmission.

TCP offers efficient flow control, which means that, when sending acknowledgments back to the source, the receiving TCP process indicates the highest sequence number that it can receive without overflowing its internal buffers.

Full-duplex operation means that TCP processes can both send and receive at the same time.

Finally, TCP's multiplexing means that numerous simultaneous upper-layer conversations can be multiplexed over a single connection.

TCP Connection Establishment

To use reliable transport services, TCP hosts must establish a connection-oriented session with one another. Connection establishment is performed by using a three-way handshake mechanism.

A *three-way handshake* synchronizes both ends of a connection by allowing both sides to agree upon initial sequence numbers. This mechanism also guarantees that both sides are ready to transmit data and know that the other side is ready to transmit as well. This is necessary so that packets are not transmitted or retransmitted during session establishment or after session termination.

Each host randomly chooses a sequence number used to track bytes within the stream that it is sending and receiving. Then, the three-way handshake proceeds in the following manner:

The first host (Host A) initiates a connection by sending a packet with the initial sequence number (X) and SYN bit set to indicate a connection request. The second host (Host B) receives the SYN, records the sequence number X, and replies by acknowledging the SYN (with an ACK = X + 1). Host B includes its own initial sequence number (SEQ = Y). An ACK of 20 means that the host has received bytes 0 through 19, and expects byte 20 next. This technique is called forward acknowledgment. Host A then acknowledges all bytes that Host B sent with a forward acknowledgment indicating the next byte Host A expects to receive (ACK = Y + 1). Data transfer then can begin.

Positive Acknowledgment and Retransmission

A simple transport protocol might implement a reliability and flow control technique in which the source sends one packet, starts a timer, and waits for an acknowledgment before sending a new packet. If the acknowledgment is not received before the timer expires, the source retransmits the packet. Such a technique is called *positive acknowledgment and retransmission (PAR)*.

By assigning each packet a sequence number, PAR enables hosts to track lost or duplicate packets caused by network delays that result in premature retransmission. The sequence numbers are sent back in the acknowledgments so that the acknowledgments can be tracked.

PAR is an inefficient use of bandwidth, however, because a host must wait for an acknowledgment before sending a new packet, and only one packet can be sent at a time.

TCP Sliding Window

A TCP sliding window provides more efficient use of network bandwidth than PAR because it enables hosts to send multiple bytes or packets before waiting for an acknowledgment.

In TCP, the receiver specifies the current window size in every packet. Because TCP provides a byte-stream connection, window sizes are expressed in bytes. This means that a window is the number of data bytes that the sender is allowed to send before waiting for an acknowledgment. Initial window sizes are indicated at connection setup but might vary throughout the data transfer to provide flow control. A window size of zero, for instance, means "Send no data."

In a TCP sliding-window operation, for example, the sender might have a sequence of bytes to send (numbered 1 to 10) to a receiver who has a window size of 5. The sender then would place a window around the first 5 bytes and transmit them together. It would then wait for an acknowledgment.

The receiver would respond with an ACK of 6, indicating that it has received bytes 1 to 5 and is expecting byte 6 next. In the same packet, the receiver would indicate that its window size is 5. The sender then would move the sliding window 5 bytes to the right and transmit bytes 6 to 10. The receiver would respond with an ACK of 11, indicating that it is expecting sequenced byte 11 next. In this packet, the receiver might indicate that its window size is 0 (because, for example, its internal buffers are full). At this point, the sender cannot send any more bytes until the receiver sends another packet with a window size greater than 0.

TCP Packet Format

Figure 35-10 illustrates the fields and overall format of a TCP packet.

Figure 35-10 *Twelve Fields Comprise a TCP Packet*

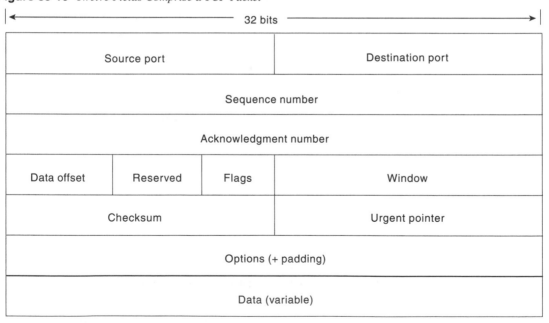

TCP Packet Field Descriptions

The following descriptions summarize the TCP packet fields illustrated in Figure 35-10:

- **Source port and destination port**—Identifies points at which upper-layer source and destination processes receive TCP services.
- **Sequence number**—Usually specifies the number assigned to the first byte of data in the current message. In the connection-establishment phase, this field also can be used to identify an initial sequence number to be used in an upcoming transmission.
- **Acknowledgment number**—Contains the sequence number of the next byte of data that the sender of the packet expects to receive.
- **Data offset**—Indicates the number of 32-bit words in the TCP header.
- **Reserved**—Remains reserved for future use.
- **Flags**—Carries a variety of control information, including the SYN and ACK bits used for connection establishment, and the FIN bit used for connection termination.
- **Window**—Specifies the size of the sender's receive window (that is, the buffer space available for incoming data).
- **Checksum**—Indicates whether the header was damaged in transit.
- **Urgent pointer**—Points to the first urgent data byte in the packet.
- **Options**—Specifies various TCP options.
- **Data**—Contains upper-layer information.

User Datagram Protocol

The *User Datagram Protocol (UDP)* is a connectionless transport layer protocol (Layer 4) that belongs to the Internet protocol family. UDP is basically an interface between IP and upper-layer processes. UDP protocol ports distinguish multiple applications running on a single device from one another.

Unlike the TCP, UDP adds no reliability, flow control, or error-recovery functions to IP. Because of UDP's simplicity, UDP headers contain fewer bytes and consume less network overhead than TCP.

UDP is useful in situations in which the reliability mechanisms of TCP are not necessary, such as in cases where a higher-layer protocol might provide error and flow control.

UDP is the transport protocol for several well-known application layer protocols, including Network File System (NFS), Simple Network Management Protocol (SNMP), Domain Name System (DNS), and Trivial File Transfer Protocol (TFTP).

The UDP packet format contains four fields, as shown in Figure 35-11. These include Source Port, Destination Port, Length, and Checksum fields.

Figure 35-11 *A UDP Packet Consists of Four Fields*

The Source and Destination port fields contain the 16-bit UDP protocol port numbers used to demultiplex datagrams for receiving application layer processes. A Length field specifies the length of the UDP header and data. The Checksum field provides an (optional) integrity check on the UDP header and data.

Internet Protocols Application Layer Protocols

The Internet protocol suite includes many application layer protocols that represent a wide variety of applications, including the following:

- **File transfer protocol (FTP)**—Moves files between devices

- **Simple network management protocol (SNMP)**—Primarily reports anomalous network conditions and sets network threshold values

- **Telnet**—Serves as a terminal emulation protocol

- **X windows**—Serves as a distributed windowing and graphics system used for communication between X terminals and UNIX workstations

- **Network file system (NFS), External data representation (XDR), and Remote procedure call (RPC)**—Work together to enable transparent access to remote network resources

- **Simple mail transfer protocol (SMTP)**—Provides electronic mail services

- **Domain name system (DNS)**—Translates the names of network nodes into network addresses

Table 35-5 lists these higher-layer protocols and the applications that they support.

Table 35-5   *Higher-Layer Protocols and Their Applications*

Application	Protocols
File transfer	FTP
Network management	SNMP
Terminal emulation	Telnet
Distributed file services	NFS, XDR, RPC, X Windows
Electronic mail	SMTP
Distributed naming services	DNS

Summary

TCP/IP defines the large suite of protocols that are most widely used today. IP addresses are used on the Internet to deliver data to computers worldwide. The protocol suite includes transport protocols such as TCP that provide connection-oriented guaranteed delivery of data. There are also non-connection-oriented transport protocols such as UDP that provide best-effort delivery of data. The TCP/IP protocol suite also includes application layer protocols that are open standards. This open standard and ease of interoperability between computing systems is what has made TCP/IP the most popular protocol used today.

Review Questions

1 How are Internet protocols documented?

2 What are the two primary responsibilities of IP?

3 Which field in the IP packet keeps packets from looping endlessly in a malconfigured network?

4 How is an IP address generally represented?

5 How is the class of an IP address determined?

6 What is the purpose of the subnet mask in an IP address?

7 What is the purpose of Address Resolution Protocol (ARP)?

8 What is the function of Internet Control Message Protocol (ICMP)?

9 What type of data delivery does TCP provide?

10 How does User Datagram Protocol (UDP) differ from Transmission Control Protocol (TCP)?

Objective

- Provide an overview of IPv6, the newest version of the most popular protocol used today.

CHAPTER 36

IPv6

One of the newest major standards on the horizon is IPv6. Although IPv6 has not officially become a standard, it is worth some overview. It is very possible that this information will change as we move closer to IPv6 as a standard, so you should use this as a guide into IPv6, not the definitive information.

A number of books are now being published that cover in detail this emerging standard; if you are looking for more details you should refer to these books. All the RFCs available on the Internet have the raw details on how this standard is developing. However, these documents are difficult to interpret at first glance and require some commitment to going through any number of RFCs pertaining to many subjects all related to IPv6 development.

Internet Protocol Version 4 is the most popular protocol in use today (see Chapter 35, "Internet Protocols"), although there are some questions about its capability to serve the Internet community much longer. IPv4 was finished in the 1970s and has started to show its age. The main issue surrounding IPv6 is addressing—or, the lack of addressing—because many experts believe that we are nearly out of the four billion addresses available in IPv4. Although this seems like a very large number of addresses, multiple large blocks are given to government agencies and large organizations. IPv6 could be the solution to many problems, but it is still not fully developed and is not a standard—yet!

Many of the finest developers and engineering minds have been working on IPv6 since the early 1990s. Hundreds of RFCs have been written and have detailed some major areas, including expanded addressing, simplified header format, flow labeling, authentication, and privacy.

Expanded addressing moves us from 32-bit address to a 128-bit addressing method. It also provides newer unicast and broadcasting methods, injects hexadecimal into the IP address, and moves from using "." to using ":" as delimiters. Figure 36-1 shows the IPv6 packet header format.

Figure 36-1 *IPv6 Packet Header Format*

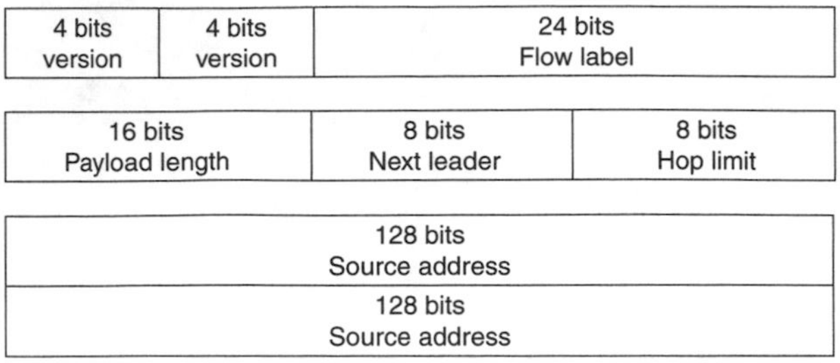

4 bits version	4 bits version	24 bits Flow label	

16 bits Payload length	8 bits Next leader	8 bits Hop limit

128 bits Source address
128 bits Source address

Description of IPv6 Packet Header

The simplified header is 40 bits long and the format consists of Version, Class, Flow Label, Payload Length, Next Header, Hop Limit, Source Address, Destination Address, Data, and Payload fields.

Hexadecimal "Hex"

At its simplest, hex numbers are base 16. Decimal is base 10, counting from 0 to 9, as we do in decimal, and then adding a column to make 10. Counting in hex goes from 0 to F before adding a column. The characters A through F represent the decimal values of 10 through 15, as illustrated in Figure 36-2.

Figure 36-2 *Hex Characters A Through F Represent the Numbers 10 Through 15*

Decimal	0 1 2 3 4 5 6 7 8 9 10 11 12 13 14 15
Hex	0 1 2 3 4 5 6 7 8 9 A B C D E F

Counting in hex goes as follows: 0 1 2 3 4 5 6 7 8 9 A B C D E F 10 11 12 13 14 15 16 17 18 19 1A 1B 1C 1D 1E 1F 20 21 and up, as far as you want to go.

Addressing Description

Let's look at an example of IPv6 address. The address is an eight-part hex address separated by colons (":"). Each part *n* can equal a 16-bit number and is eight parts long, providing a 128-bit address length ($16 \times 8 = 128$),

Addresses are n:n:n:n:n:n:n:n n = 4 digit hexadecimal integer, $16 \times 8 = 128$ address.

```
1080:0:0:0:8:800:200C:417A Unicast address
FF01:0:0:0:0:0:0:101Multicast address
```

Broadcasting Methods

Included in IPv6 are a number of new broadcasting methods:

- Unicast
- Multicast
- Anycast

Unicast

Unicast is a communication between a single host and a single receiver. Packets sent to a unicast address are delivered to the interface identified by that address, as seen in Figure 36-3.

Figure 36-3 *Unicast Sends Packets to a Specified Interface*

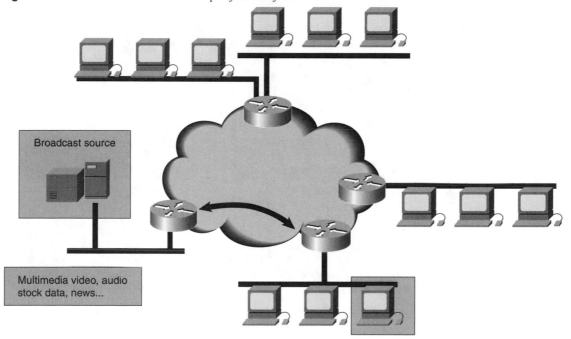

Multicast

Multicast is communication between a single host and multiple receivers. Packets are sent to all interfaces identified by that address, as seen in Figure 36-4.

Figure 36-4 *Multicast Sends Packets to a Subnet, and Defined Devices Listen for Multicast Packets*

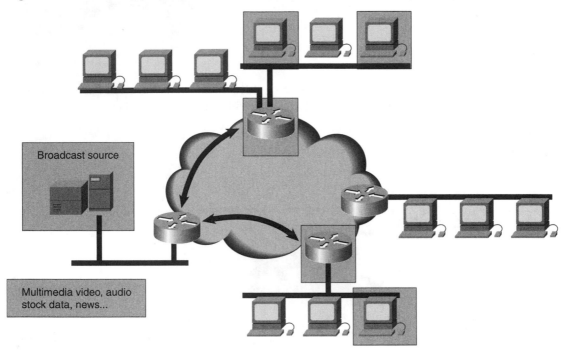

Anycast

Packets sent to an anycast address or list of addresses are delivered to the nearest interface identified by that address. Anycast is a communication between a single sender and a list of addresses, as shown in Figure 36-5.

Figure 36-5 *Anycast Sends Packets to Specified Interface List and Can Contain End Nodes and Routers*

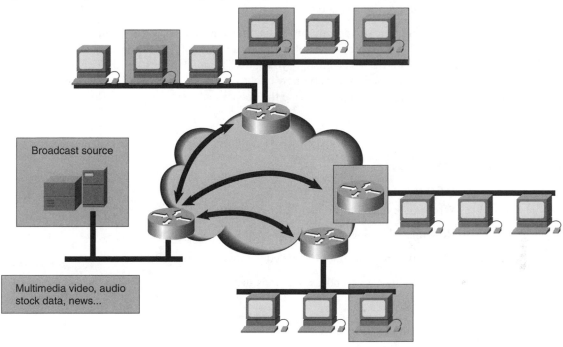

Summary

Some of the benefits of IPv6 seem obvious: greater addressing space, built-in QoS, and better routing performance and services. However, a number of barriers must be overcome before the implementation of IPv6. The biggest question for most of us will be what the business need is for moving from current IPv4 to IPv6. The killer app has not appeared yet, but it may be closer than we think. The second consideration is the cost—it may not have much to do with hardware replacement cost. All the larger routers have upgradable OSs IOS; the only necessity is the commitment to upgrading IOS. More likely to do with training and support of minor IP devices such as printers and network faxes, they will support the new address space. IPv6 has schemes to support old and new, however, so this may not even be a barrier. The last issue to consider is training: This will need to happen sooner or later because we all need to start thinking about 128-bit addressing based on MAC addresses in HEX. This involves all new ways of addressing and will be an uncomfortable change for many people.

This conclusion may seem negative, but the greater good will overpower all the up-front issues. The issue is not whether you will have to move to IPv6, but when! We all need IPv6; the increased address space, which is quadrupled, is needed for the growth of IP appliances that we are starting to hear about weekly. IP-ready cars are already shipping today. This requires mobility, which is addressed in IPv6.

Of course, a number of very important features have not been discussed in this section, including QoS, mobile IP, autoconfiguration, and security. All these areas are extremely important, and until IPv6 is finished, you should keep referring to the IETF Web site for the most current information. Several new books on IPv6 also are starting to show up on bookstore shelves and should provide the deeper technical detail on address headers and full packet details.

Review Questions

1   What is the current standard?

2   What is the main reason for IPv6 being developed?

3   How many bits does the new expanded addressing provide?

4   What other benefits does expanded addressing provide?

5   What are the new broadcast methods included in IPv6?

6   What is unicast?

7   What is multicast?

8   What is anycast?

For More Information

- http://www-6bone.lbl.gov/6bone
- http://www.cisco.com/warp/customer/732/ipv6/index.html
- http://www.ietf.org/html.charters/ipngwg-charter.html
- http://playground.Sun.COM:80/pub/ipng/html

Objectives

- Introduce the NetWare protocol IPX/SPX, used primarily in Novell-based networks.
- Discuss the structures and functioning of this protocol, from its introduction in the early 1980s to its current form.

CHAPTER 37

NetWare Protocols

Background

NetWare is a network operating system (NOS) that provides transparent remote file access and numerous other distributed network services, including printer sharing and support for various applications such as electronic mail transfer and database access. NetWare specifies the upper five layers of the OSI reference model and, as such, runs on any media-access protocol (Layer 2). Additionally, NetWare runs on virtually any kind of computer system, from PCs to mainframes. This chapter summarizes the principal communications protocols that support NetWare.

NetWare was developed by Novell, Inc., and was introduced in the early 1980s. It was derived from Xerox Network Systems (XNS), which was created by Xerox Corporation in the late 1970s, and is based on a client-server architecture. Clients (sometimes called workstations) request services, such as file and printer access, from servers.

NetWare's client/server architecture supports remote access that is transparent to users through remote procedure calls. A remote procedure call begins when the local computer program running on the client sends a procedure call to the remote server. The server then executes the remote procedure call and returns the requested information to the local client.

Figure 37-1 illustrates the NetWare protocol suite, the media-access protocols on which NetWare runs, and the relationship between the NetWare protocols and the OSI reference model. This chapter addresses the elements and operations of these protocol components.

Figure 37-1 *The NetWare Protocol Suite Maps to All OSI Layers*

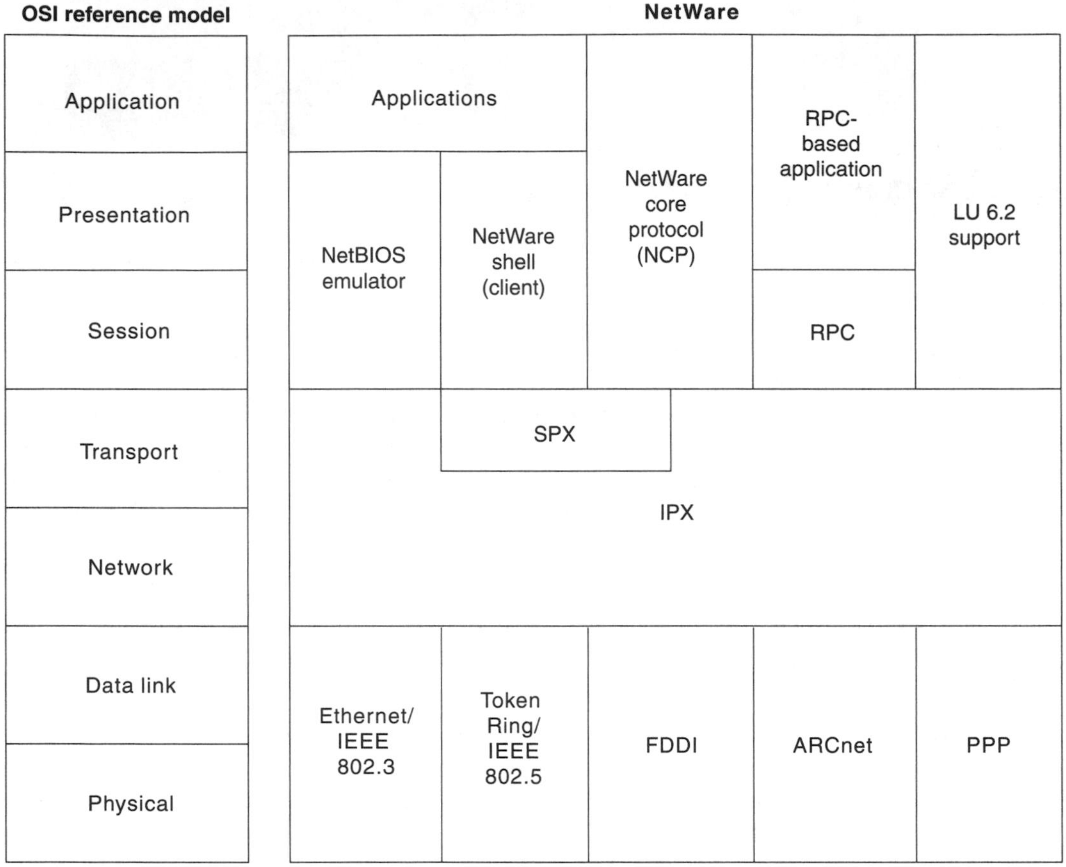

NetWare Media Access

The NetWare suite of protocols supports several media-access (Layer 2) protocols, including Ethernet/IEEE 802.3, Token Ring/IEEE 802.5, Fiber Distributed Data Interface (FDDI), and Point-to-Point Protocol (PPP). Figure 37-2 highlights NetWare's breadth of media-access support.

Figure 37-2 *NetWare Supports Most Common Media-Access Protocols*

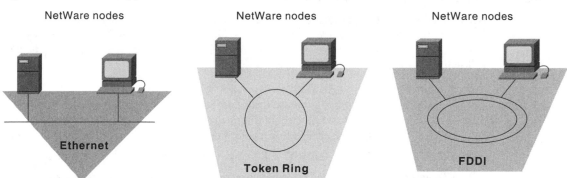

Internetwork Packet Exchange Overview

Internetwork Packet Exchange (IPX) is the original NetWare network layer (Layer 3) protocol used to route packets through an internetwork. IPX is a connectionless datagram-based network protocol and, as such, is similar to the Internet Protocol found in TCP/IP networks.

IPX uses the services of a dynamic distance vector routing protocol (Routing Information Protocol [RIP]) or a link-state routing protocol (NetWare Link-State Protocol [NLSP]). IPX RIP sends routing updates every 60 seconds. To make best-path routing decisions, IPX RIP uses a *tick* as the metric, which in principle is the delay expected when using a particular length. One tick is 1/18th of a second. In the case of two paths with an equal tick count, IPX RIP uses the hop count as a tie-breaker. (A hop is the passage of a packet through a router.) IPX's RIP is not compatible with RIP implementations used in other networking environments.

As with other network addresses, Novell IPX network addresses must be unique. These addresses are represented in hexadecimal format and consist of two parts: a network number and a node number. The IPX network number, which is assigned by the network administrator, is 32 bits long. The node number, which usually is the Media Access Control (MAC) address for one of the system's network interface cards (NICs), is 48 bits long.

IPX's use of a MAC address for the node number enables the system to send nodes to predict what MAC address to use on a data link. (In contrast, because the host portion of an IP network address has no correlation to the MAC address, IP nodes must use the Address Resolution Protocol [ARP] to determine the destination MAC address.)

IPX Encapsulation Types

Novell NetWare IPX supports multiple encapsulation schemes on a single router interface, provided that multiple network numbers are assigned. Encapsulation is the process of packaging upper-layer protocol information and data into a frame. NetWare supports the following four encapsulation schemes:

- **Novell Proprietary**—Also called 802.3 raw or Novell Ethernet_802.3, Novell proprietary serves as the initial encapsulation scheme that Novell uses. It includes an Institute of Electrical and Electronic Engineers (IEEE) 802.3 Length field, but not an IEEE 802.2 (LLC) header. The IPX header immediately follows the 802.3 Length field.

- **802.3**—Also called Novell_802.2, 802.3 is the standard IEEE 802.3 frame format.

- **Ethernet version 2**—Also called Ethernet-II or ARPA, Ethernet version 2 includes the standard Ethernet Version 2 header, which consists of Destination and Source Address fields followed by an EtherType field.

- **SNAP**—Also called Ethernet_SNAP, SNAP extends the IEEE 802.2 header by providing a type code similar to that defined in the Ethernet version 2 specification.

Figure 37-3 illustrates these encapsulation types.

Figure 37-3 *Four IPX Encapsulation Types Exist*

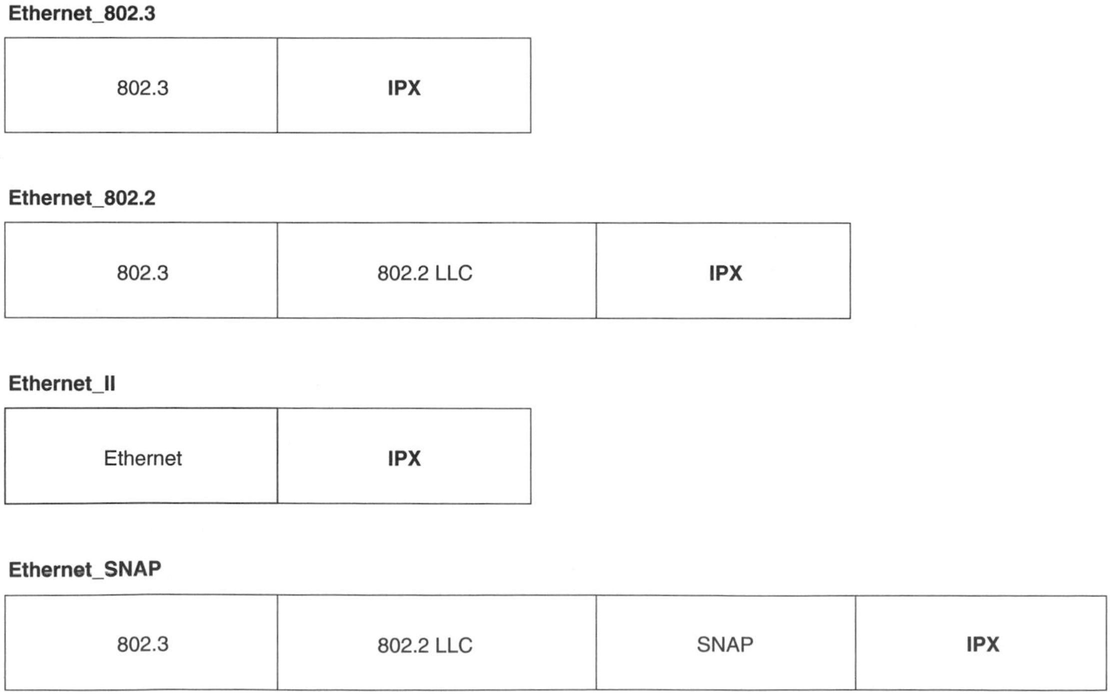

Ethernet_802.3

802.3	IPX

Ethernet_802.2

802.3	802.2 LLC	IPX

Ethernet_II

Ethernet	IPX

Ethernet_SNAP

802.3	802.2 LLC	SNAP	IPX

Service Advertisement Protocol

The *Service Advertisement Protocol (SAP)* is an IPX protocol through which network resources such as file servers and print servers advertise their addresses and the services that they provide. Advertisements are sent via SAP every 60 seconds. Services are identified by a hexadecimal number, which is called a SAP identifier (for example, 4 = file server, and 7 = print server).

A SAP operation begins when routers listen to SAPs and build a table of all known services along with their network address. Routers then send their SAP table every 60 seconds. Novell clients can send a query requesting a particular file, printer, or gateway service. The local router responds to the query with the network address of the requested service, and the client then can contact the service directly.

SAP is pervasive in current networks based on NetWare 3.11 and earlier, but it is utilized less frequently in NetWare 4.0 networks because workstations can locate services by consulting a NetWare Directory Services (NDS) Server. SAP, however, still is required in NetWare 4.0 networks for workstations when they boot up to locate an NDS server.

SAP Filters

Using the SAP identifier, SAP advertisements can be filtered on a router's input or output port, or from a specific router. SAP filters conserve network bandwidth and are especially useful in large Novell installations where hundreds of SAP services exist.

In general, the use of SAP filters is recommended for services that are not required for a particular network. Remote sites, for example, probably do not need to receive SAP advertising print services located at a central site. A SAP output filter at the central site (preferred), or a SAP input filter that uses the SAP identifier for a print server at the remote site prevents the router from including print services in SAP updates.

NetWare Transport Layer

The *Sequenced Packet Exchange (SPX)* protocol is the most common NetWare transport protocol at Layer 4 of the OSI model. SPX resides atop IPX in the NetWare Protocol Suite. SPX is a reliable, connection-oriented protocol that supplements the datagram service provided by the IPX, NetWare's network layer (Layer 3) protocol. SPX was derived from the Xerox Networking Systems (XNS) Sequenced Packet Protocol (SPP). Novell also offers Internet Protocol support in the form of the User Datagram Protocol (UDP). IPX datagrams are encapsulated inside UDP/IP headers for transport across an IP-based internetwork.

NetWare Upper-Layer Protocols and Services

NetWare supports a wide variety of upper-layer protocols, including NetWare Shell, NetWare Remote Procedure Call, NetWare Core Protocol, and Network Basic Input/Output System.

The NetWare shell runs clients (often called workstations in the NetWare community) and intercepts application input/output (I/O) calls to determine whether they require network access for completion. If the application request requires network access, the NetWare shell packages the request and sends it to lower-layer software for processing and network transmission. If the application request does not require network access, the request is passed to the local I/O resources. Client applications are unaware of any network access required for completion of application calls.

NetWare Remote Procedure Call (NetWare RPC) is another more general redirection mechanism similar in concept to the NetWare shell supported by Novell.

NetWare Core Protocol (NCP) is a series of server routines designed to satisfy application requests coming from, for example, the NetWare shell. The services provided by NCP include file access, printer access, name management, accounting, security, and file synchronization.

NetWare also supports the Network Basic Input/Output System (NetBIOS) session layer interface specification from IBM and Microsoft. NetWare's NetBIOS emulation software allows programs written to the industry-standard NetBIOS interface to run within the NetWare system.

NetWare Application Layer Services

NetWare application layer services include NetWare message-handling service (NetWare MHS), Btrieve, NetWare loadable modules (NLMs), and IBM Logical Unit (LU) 6.2 network-addressable units (NAUs). NetWare MHS is a message-delivery system that provides electronic mail transport. Btrieve is Novell's implementation of the binary tree (btree) database-access mechanism. NLMs are add-on modules that attach into a NetWare system. NLMs currently available from Novell and third parties include alternate protocol stacks, communication services, and database services. In terms of IBM LU 6.2 NAU support, NetWare allows peer-to-peer connectivity and information exchange across IBM networks. NetWare packets are encapsulated within LU 6.2 packets for transit across an IBM network.

IPX Packet Format

The IPX packet is the basic unit of Novell NetWare internetworking. Figure 37-4 illustrates the format of a NetWare IPX packet.

Figure 37-4 *A NetWare IPX Packet Consists of 11 Fields*

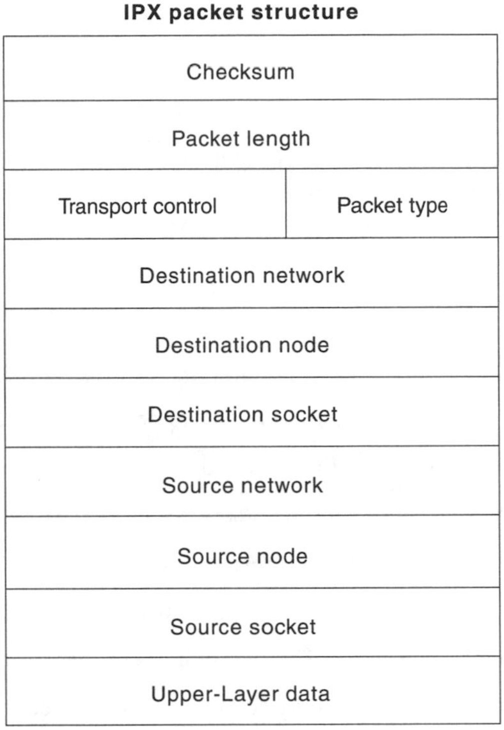

IPX packet structure

Checksum

Packet length

Transport control	Packet type

Destination network

Destination node

Destination socket

Source network

Source node

Source socket

Upper-Layer data

The following descriptions summarize the IPX packet fields illustrated in Figure 37-4:

- **Checksum**—Indicates that the checksum is not used when this 16-bit field is set to 1s (FFFF).

- **Packet length**—Specifies the length, in bytes, of a complete IPX datagram. IPX packets can be any length, up to the media maximum transmission unit (MTU) size (no packet fragmentation allowed).

- **Transport control**—Indicates the number of routers through which the packet has passed. When this value reaches 16, the packet is discarded under the assumption that a routing loop might be occurring.

- **Packet type**—Specifies which upper-layer protocol should receive the packet's information. It has two common values:

    - **5**—Specifies Sequenced Packet Exchange (SPX)

    - **17**—Specifies NetWare Core Protocol (NCP)

- **Destination network, Destination node, and Destination socket**—Specify destination information.

- **Source network, Source node, and Source socket**—Specify source information.
- **Upper-Layer data**—Contains information for upper-layer processes.

Summary

IPX is still installed in millions of computers in the NetWare networks. However, there has been a large change from IPX to IP within those environments, and this trend is likely to continue, with Novell supporting native IP within its networking environments.

Review Questions

1 What are the two types of routing protocols used by IPX?

2 What information is used by IPX RIP to determine a path for network traffic?

3 What are the two parts of an IPX address?

4 How do Novell stations discover services available on the network?

5 What protocol is used at the transport layer?

6 How do IPX stations map the MAC address to an IPX address?

7 What enhancement in NetWare 4.0 reduces the need for SAPs?

8 What services are provided by NetWare Core Protocol?

9 Describe NetWare's support of NetBIOS.

10 Would you want to filter SAPs?

Objectives

- Describe the development history of the AppleTalk protocol, used almost exclusively in Macintosh computers.

- Describe the components of AppleTalk networks and extended network.

- Discuss the primary characteristics of the AppleTalk protocol.

- Discuss the addressing methods of AppleTalk.

- Describe additional protocols implemented in AppleTalk networks, including protocols used in the upper layers of the OSI reference model.

CHAPTER 38

AppleTalk

Introduction

AppleTalk, a protocol suite developed by Apple Computer in the early 1980s, was developed in conjunction with the Macintosh computer. AppleTalk's purpose was to allow multiple users to share resources, such as files and printers. The devices that supply these resources are called servers, while the devices that make use of these resources (such as a user's Macintosh computer) are referred to as clients. Hence, AppleTalk is one of the early implementations of a distributed client/server networking system. This chapter provides a summary of AppleTalk's network architecture.

AppleTalk was designed with a transparent network interface—that is, the interaction between client computers and network servers requires little interaction from the user. In addition, the actual operations of the AppleTalk protocols are invisible to end users, who see only the result of these operations. Two versions of AppleTalk exist: AppleTalk Phase 1 and AppleTalk Phase 2.

AppleTalk Phase 1, which is the first AppleTalk specification, was developed in the early 1980s strictly for use in local workgroups. Phase 1 therefore has two key limitations: Its network segments can contain no more than 135 hosts and 135 servers, and it can support only nonextended networks. Extended and nonextended networks will be discussed in detail later in the sections "Extended Networks" and "Nonextended Networks."

AppleTalk Phase 2, which is the second enhanced AppleTalk implementation, was designed for use in larger internetworks. Phase 2 addresses the key limitations of AppleTalk Phase 1 and features a number of improvements over Phase 1. In particular, Phase 2 allows any combination of 253 hosts or servers on a single AppleTalk network segment and supports both nonextended and extended networks.

AppleTalk Network Components

AppleTalk networks are arranged hierarchically. Four basic components form the basis of an AppleTalk network: sockets, nodes, networks, and zones. Figure 38-1 illustrates the hierarchical organization of these components in an AppleTalk internetwork. Each of these concepts is summarized in the sections that follow.

Figure 38-1   *The AppleTalk Internetwork Consists of a Hierarchy of Components*

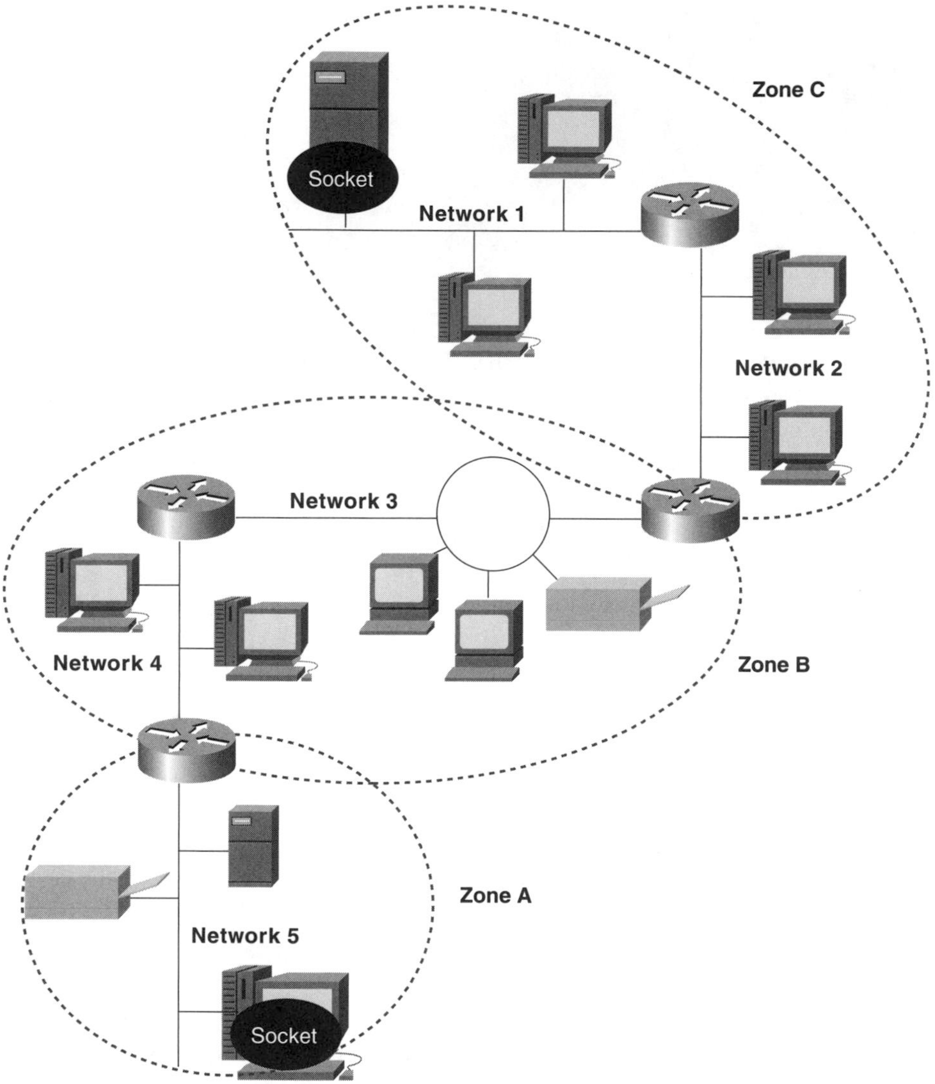

Sockets

An *AppleTalk socket* is a unique, addressable location in an AppleTalk node. It is the logical point at which upper-layer AppleTalk software processes and the network layer Datagram Delivery Protocol (DDP) interact. These upper-layer processes are known as socket clients. Socket clients own one or more sockets, which they use to send and receive datagrams. Sockets can be assigned statically or dynamically. Statically assigned sockets are reserved for use by certain protocols or other processes. Dynamically assigned sockets are assigned by DDP to socket clients upon request. An AppleTalk node can contain up to 254 different socket numbers. Figure 38-2 illustrates the relationship between the sockets in an AppleTalk node and DDP at the network layer.

Figure 38-2 *Socket Clients Use Sockets to Send and Receive Datagrams*

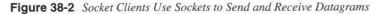
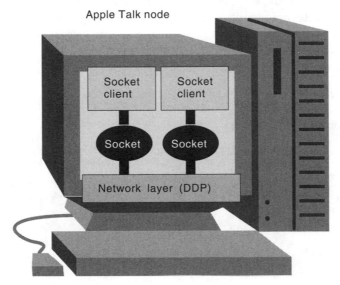

Nodes

An *AppleTalk node* is a device that is connected to an AppleTalk network. This device might be a Macintosh computer, a printer, an IBM PC, a router, or some other similar device. Within each AppleTalk node exist numerous software processes called sockets. As discussed earlier, the function of these sockets is to identify the software processes running in the device. Each node in an AppleTalk network belongs to a single network and a specific zone.

Networks

An *AppleTalk network* consists of a single logical cable and multiple attached nodes. The logical cable is comprised of either a single physical cable or multiple physical cables interconnected by using bridges or routers. AppleTalk networks can be nonextended or extended. Each is discussed briefly in the following sections.

Nonextended Networks

A *nonextended AppleTalk network* is a physical network segment that is assigned only a single network number, which can range between 1 and 1024. Network 100 and network 562, for example, are both valid network numbers in a nonextended network. Each node number in a nonextended network must be unique, and a single nonextended network segment cannot have more than one AppleTalk Zone configured on it. (A zone is a logical group of nodes or networks.) AppleTalk Phase 1 supports only nonextended networks, but as a rule, nonextended network configurations are no longer used in new networks because they have been superseded by extended networks. Figure 38-3 illustrates a nonextended AppleTalk network.

Figure 38-3 *A Nonextended Network Is Assigned Only One Network Number*

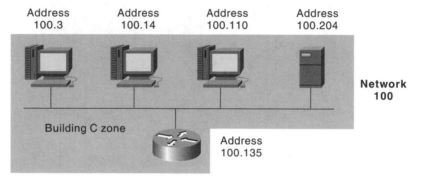

Extended Networks

An *extended AppleTalk network* is a physical network segment that can be assigned multiple network numbers. This configuration is known as a cable range. AppleTalk cable ranges can indicate a single network number or multiple consecutive network numbers. The cable ranges network 3-3 (unary) and network 3-6, for example, are both valid in an extended network. Just as in other protocol suites, such as TCP/IP and IPX, each combination of network number and node number in an extended network must be unique, and its address must be unique for identification purposes. Extended networks can have multiple AppleTalk zones configured on a single network segment, and nodes on extended networks can belong to any single zone associated with the extended network. As a rule, extended network configurations have replaced nonextended network configurations. Figure 38-4 illustrates an extended network.

Figure 38-4 *An Extended Network Can Be Assigned Multiple Network Numbers*

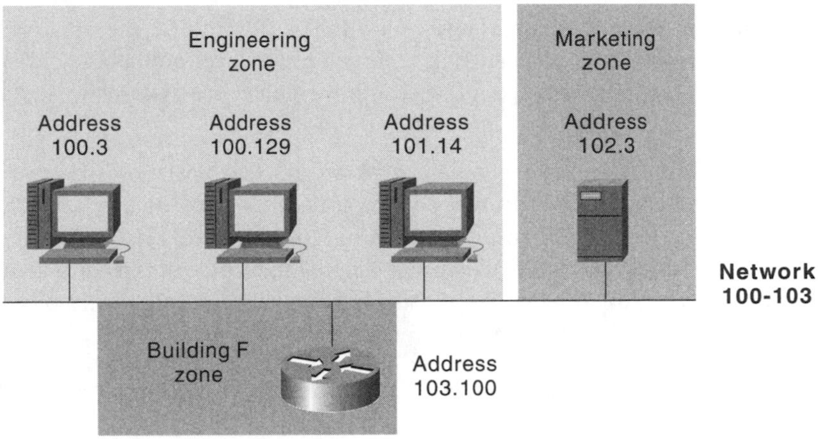

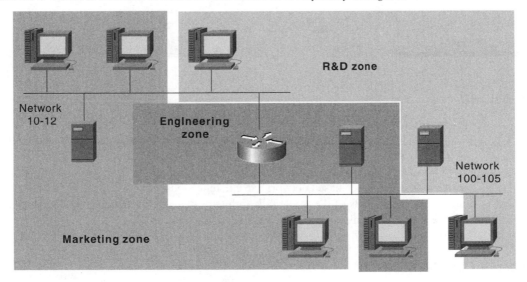

Zones

An *AppleTalk zone* is a logical group of nodes or networks that is defined when the network administrator configures the network. The nodes or networks need not be physically contiguous to belong to the same AppleTalk zone. Figure 38-5 illustrates an AppleTalk internetwork composed of three noncontiguous zones.

Figure 38-5 *Nodes or Networks in the Same Zone Need Not be Physically Contiguous*

AppleTalk Physical and Data Link Layers

As with other popular protocol suites, such as TCP/IP and IPX, the AppleTalk architecture maintains media-access dependencies on such lower-layer protocols as Ethernet, Token Ring, and FDDI. Four main media-access implementations exist in the AppleTalk protocol suite: EtherTalk, LocalTalk, TokenTalk, and FDDITalk.

These data link layer implementations perform address translation and other functions that allow proprietary AppleTalk protocols to communicate over industry-standard interfaces, which include IEEE 802.3 (using EtherTalk), Token Ring/IEEE 802.5 (using TokenTalk), and FDDI (using FDDITalk). In addition, AppleTalk implements its own network interface, known as LocalTalk. Figure 38-6 illustrates how the AppleTalk media-access implementations map to the OSI reference model.

Figure 38-6 *AppleTalk Media-Access Implementations Map to the Bottom Two Layers of the OSI Reference Model*

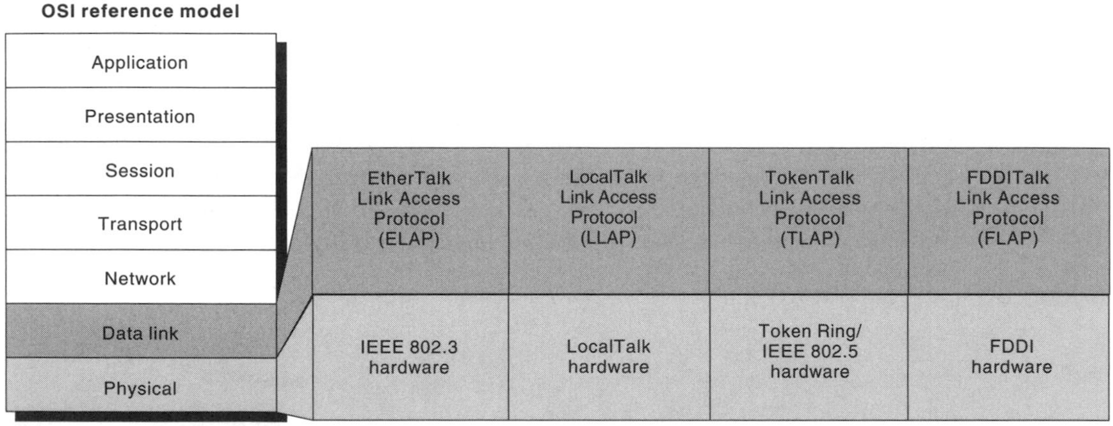

EtherTalk

EtherTalk extends the data link layer to enable the AppleTalk protocol suite to operate atop a standard IEEE 802.3 implementation. EtherTalk networks are organized exactly as IEEE 802.3 networks, supporting the same speeds and segment lengths, as well as the same number of active network nodes. This allows AppleTalk to be deployed over any of the thousands of Ethernet-based networks in existence today. Communication between the upper-layer protocols of the AppleTalk architecture and the Ethernet protocols is handled by the EtherTalk Link Access Protocol (ELAP).

EtherTalk Link Access Protocol

The *EtherTalk Link Access Protocol (ELAP)* handles the interaction between the proprietary AppleTalk protocols and the standard IEEE 802.3 data link layer. Upper-layer

AppleTalk protocols do not recognize standard IEEE 802.3 hardware addresses, so ELAP uses the Address Mapping Table (AMT) maintained by the AppleTalk Address Resolution Protocol (AARP) to properly address transmissions.

ELAP handles the interaction between upper-layer protocols of AppleTalk and the data link layer by encapsulating or enclosing the data inside the protocol units of the 802.3 data link layer. ELAP performs three levels of encapsulation when transmitting DDP packets:

- Subnetwork Access Protocol (SNAP) header
- IEEE 802.2 Logical Link Control (LLC) header
- IEEE 802.3 header

This process of encapsulation performed by the ELAP is detailed in the following section.

ELAP Data Transmission Process

ELAP uses a specific process to transmit data across the physical medium. First, ELAP receives a DDP packet that requires transmission. Next, it finds the protocol address specified in the DDP header and checks the AMT to find the corresponding IEEE 802.3 hardware address. ELAP then prepends three different headers to the DDP packet, beginning with the SNAP and 802.2 LLC headers. The third header is the IEEE 802.3 header. When prepending this header to the packet, the hardware address taken from the AMT is placed in the Destination Address field. The result, an IEEE 802.3 frame, is placed on the physical medium for transmission to the destination.

LocalTalk

LocalTalk, which is a proprietary data link layer implementation developed by Apple Computer for its AppleTalk protocol suite, was designed as a cost-effective network solution for connecting local workgroups. LocalTalk hardware typically is built into Apple products, which are easily connected by using inexpensive twisted-pair cabling. LocalTalk networks are organized in a bus topology, which means that devices are connected to each other in series. Network segments are limited to a 300-meter span with a maximum of 32 active nodes, and multiple LocalTalk networks can be interconnected by using routers or other similar intermediate devices. The communication between the data link layer protocol LocalTalk and upper-layer protocols is the LocalTalk Link Access Protocol (LLAP).

LocalTalk Link Access Protocol

The *LocalTalk Link Access Protocol (LLAP)* is the media-access protocol used in LocalTalk networks to provide best-effort, error-free delivery of frames between AppleTalk nodes. This means that delivery of datagrams is not guaranteed by the LLAP; such a function is performed only by higher-layer protocols in the AppleTalk architecture. LLAP is responsible for regulating node access to the physical media and dynamically acquiring data link layer node addresses.

Regulating Node Access to the Physical Media

LLAP implements a media-access scheme known as carrier sense multiple access collision avoidance (CSMA/CA), whereby nodes check the link to see whether it is in use. The link must be idle for a certain random period of time before a node can begin transmitting data. LLAP uses data exchanges known as handshakes to avoid collisions (that is, simultaneous transmissions by two or more nodes). A successful handshake between nodes effectively reserves the link for their use. If two nodes transmit a handshake simultaneously, the transmissions collide. In this case, both transmissions are damaged, causing the packets to be discarded. The handshake exchange is not completed, and the sending nodes infer that a collision occurred. When the collision occurs, the device remains idle for a random period of time and then retries its transmission. This process is similar to the access mechanism used with Ethernet technology.

Acquiring Node Addresses

LLAP acquires data link layer node addresses dynamically. The process allows a unique data link layer address to be assigned without permanently assigning the address to the node. When a node starts up, LLAP assigns the node a randomly chosen node identifier (node ID). The uniqueness of this node ID is determined by the transmission of a special packet that is addressed to the randomly chosen node ID. If the node receives a reply to this packet, the node ID is not unique. The node therefore is assigned another randomly chosen node ID and sends out another packet addressed to that node until no reply returns. If the acquiring node does not receive a reply to the first query, it makes a number of subsequent attempts. If there is still no reply after these attempts, the node ID is considered unique, and the node uses this node ID as its data link layer address.

TokenTalk

TokenTalk extends the data link layer to allow the AppleTalk protocol suite to operate atop a standard IEEE 802.5/Token Ring implementation. TokenTalk networks are organized exactly as IEEE 802.5/Token Ring networks, supporting the same speeds and the same number of active network nodes. Communication between the data link layer protocols used with Token Ring and upper-layer protocols is the TokenTalk Link Access Protocol (TLAP).

TokenTalk Link Access Protocol

The *TokenTalk Link Access Protocol (TLAP)* handles the interaction between the proprietary AppleTalk protocols and the standard IEEE 802.5 data link layer. Upper-layer AppleTalk protocols do not recognize standard IEEE 802.5 hardware addresses, so TLAP uses the AMT maintained by the AARP to properly address transmissions. TLAP performs three levels of encapsulation when transmitting DDP packets:

- Subnetwork Access Protocol (SNAP) header
- IEEE 802.2 Logical Link Control (LLC) header
- IEEE 802.5 header
- TLAP data transmission process

TLAP data transmission involves a number of steps to transmit data across the physical medium. When TLAP receives a DDP packet that requires transmission, it finds the protocol address specified in the DDP header and then checks the AMT to find the corresponding IEEE 802.5/Token Ring hardware address. Next, TLAP prepends three different headers to the DDP packet, beginning with the SNAP and 802.2 LLC headers. When the third header, IEEE 802.5/Token Ring, is prepended to the packet, the hardware address received from the AMT is placed in the Destination Address field. The result, an IEEE 802.5/Token Ring frame, is placed on the physical medium for transmission to the destination.

FDDITalk

FDDITalk extends the data link layer to allow the AppleTalk protocol suite to operate atop a standard ANSI FDDI implementation. FDDITalk networks are organized exactly as FDDI networks, supporting the same speeds and the same number of active network nodes.

FDDITalk Link Access Protocol

The *FDDITalk Link Access Protocol (FLAP)* handles the interaction between the proprietary AppleTalk protocols and the standard FDDI data link layer. Upper-layer AppleTalk protocols do not recognize standard FDDI hardware addresses, so FLAP uses the AMT maintained by the AARP to properly address transmissions. FLAP performs three levels of encapsulation when transmitting DDP packets:

- Subnetwork Access Protocol (SNAP) header
- IEEE 802.2 Logical Link Control (LLC) header
- FDDI header
- FLAP data transmission process

As with TLAP, FLAP involves a multistage process to transmit data across the physical medium. When FLAP receives a DDP packet requiring transmission, it finds the protocol address specified in the DDP header and then checks the AMT to find the corresponding FDDI hardware address. FLAP then prepends three different headers to the DDP packet, beginning with the SNAP and 802.2 LLC headers. When the third header, the FDDI header, is prepended to the packet, the hardware address received from the AMT is placed in the Destination Address field. The result, an FDDI frame, is placed on the physical medium for transmission to the destination.

Network Addresses

AppleTalk utilizes addresses to identify and locate devices on a network in a manner similar to the process utilized by such common protocols as TCP/IP and IPX. These addresses, which are assigned dynamically as discussed in the following section, are composed of three elements:

- **Network number**—A 16-bit value that identifies a specific AppleTalk network (either nonextended or extended)

- **Node number**—An 8-bit value that identifies a particular AppleTalk node attached to the specified network

- **Socket number**—An 8-bit number that identifies a specific socket running on a network node

AppleTalk addresses usually are written as decimal values separated by a period. For example, 10.1.50 means network 10, node 1, socket 50. This also might be represented as 10.1, socket 50. Figure 38-7 illustrates the AppleTalk network address format.

Figure 38-7 *The AppleTalk Network Address Consists of Three Distinct Numbers*

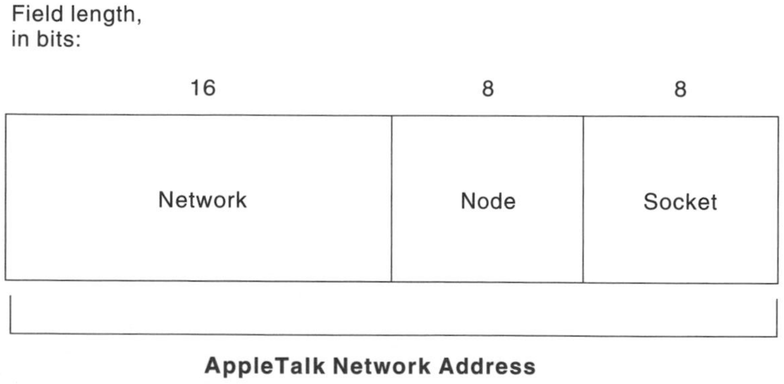

AppleTalk Network Address

Network Address Assignment

One of the unique characteristics of AppleTalk is the dynamic nature of device addresses. It is not necessary to statically define an address to an AppleTalk device. Instead, AppleTalk nodes are assigned addresses dynamically when they first attach to a network.

When an AppleTalk network node starts up, it receives a provisional network layer address. The network portion of the provisional address (the first 16 bits) is selected from the startup range, which is a reserved range of network addresses (values 65280 to 65534). The node portion (the next 8 bits) of the provisional address is chosen randomly.

Using the Zone Information Protocol (ZIP), the node communicates with a router attached to the network. The router replies with the valid cable range for the network to which the node is attached. Next, the node selects a valid network number from the cable range supplied by the router and then randomly chooses a node number. A broadcast message is used to determine whether the selected address is in use by another node.

If the address is not being used (that is, no other node responds to the broadcast within a specific period of time), the node has successfully been assigned an address. However, if another node is using the address, that node responds to the broadcast with a message indicating that the address is in use. The new node must choose another address and repeat the process until it selects an address that is not in use.

AppleTalk Address Resolution Protocol

AppleTalk Address Resolution Protocol (AARP) is a network layer protocol in the AppleTalk protocol suite that associates AppleTalk network addresses with hardware addresses. AARP services are used by other AppleTalk protocols. When an AppleTalk protocol has data to transmit, for example, it specifies the network address of the destination. It is the job of AARP to find the hardware address that is associated with the device using that network address.

AARP uses a request-response process to learn the hardware address of other network nodes. Because AARP is a media-dependent protocol, the method used to request a hardware address from a node varies depending on the data link layer implementation. Typically, a broadcast message is sent to all AppleTalk nodes on the network.

Address Mapping Table

Each AppleTalk node contains an *Address Mapping Table (AMT)*, where hardware addresses are associated with network addresses. Each time AARP resolves a network and hardware address combination, the mapping is recorded in the AMT.

Over time, the potential for an AMT entry to become invalid increases. For this reason, each AMT entry typically has a timer associated with it. When AARP receives a packet that verifies or changes the entry, the timer is reset.

If the timer expires, the entry is deleted from the AMT. The next time an AppleTalk protocol wants to communicate with that node, another AARP request must be transmitted to discover the hardware address.

Address Gleaning

In certain implementations, incoming DDP packets are examined to learn the hardware and network addresses of the source node. DDP then can place this information in the AMT. This is one way in which a device, such as a router, workstation, or server, can discover devices within an AppleTalk network.

This process of obtaining address mappings from incoming packets is known as *address gleaning*. Address gleaning is not widely used, but in some situations it can reduce the number of AARP requests that must be transmitted.

AARP Operation

The AppleTalk Address Resolution Protocol (AARP) maps hardware addresses to network addresses. When an AppleTalk protocol has data to send, it passes the network address of the destination node to AARP. It is the job of AARP to supply the hardware address associated with that network address.

AARP checks the AMT to see whether the network address is already mapped to a hardware address. If the addresses are already mapped, the hardware address is passed to the inquiring AppleTalk protocol, which uses it to communicate with the destination. If the addresses are not mapped, AARP transmits a broadcast requesting that the node using the network address in question supply its hardware address.

When the request reaches the node using the network address, that node replies with its hardware address. If no node exists with the specified network address, no response is sent. After a specified number of retries, AARP assumes that the protocol address is not in use and returns an error to the inquiring AppleTalk protocol. If a response is received, the hardware address is associated to the network address in the AMT. The hardware address then is passed to the inquiring AppleTalk protocol, which uses it to communicate with the destination node.

Datagram Delivery Protocol Overview

The *Datagram Delivery Protocol (DDP)* is the primary network layer routing protocol in the AppleTalk protocol suite that provides a best-effort connectionless datagram service between AppleTalk sockets. As with protocols such as TCP, no virtual circuit or connection is established between two devices. The function of guaranteeing delivery instead is handled by upper-layer protocols of the AppleTalk protocol suite. These upper-layer protocols will be discussed later in this chapter.

DDP performs two key functions: packet transmission and receipt.

- **Transmission of packets**—DDP receives data from socket clients, creates a DDP header by using the appropriate destination address, and passes the packet to the data link layer protocol.

- **Reception of packets**—DDP receives frames from the data link layer, examines the DDP header to find the destination address, and routes the packet to the destination socket.

DDP maintains the cable range of the local network and the network address of a router attached to the local network in every AppleTalk node. In addition to this information, AppleTalk routers must maintain a routing table by using the Routing Table Maintenance Protocol (RTMP).

DDP Transmission Process

DDP operates much like any routing protocol. Packets are addressed at the source, are passed to the data link layer, and are transmitted to the destination. When DDP receives data from an upper-layer protocol, it determines whether the source and destination nodes are on the same network by examining the network number of the destination address.

If the destination network number is within the cable range of the local network, the packet is encapsulated in a DDP header and is passed to the data link layer for transmission to the destination node. If the destination network number is not within the cable range of the local network, the packet is encapsulated in a DDP header and is passed to the data link layer for transmission to a router. Intermediate routers use their routing tables to forward the packet toward the destination network. When the packet reaches a router attached to the destination network, the packet is transmitted to the destination node.

AppleTalk Transport Layer

The transport layer in AppleTalk implements reliable internetwork data-transport services that are transparent to upper layers. Transport layer functions typically include flow control, multiplexing, virtual circuit management, and error checking and recovery.

Five key implementations exist at the transport layer of the AppleTalk protocol suite:

- Routing Table Maintenance Protocol (RTMP)
- Name Binding Protocol (NBP)

- AppleTalk Update-Based Routing Protocol (AURP)
- AppleTalk Transaction Protocol (ATP)
- AppleTalk Echo Protocol (AEP)

Each of these protocol implementations is addressed briefly in the discussions that follow.

Routing Table Maintenance Protocol Overview

The *Routing Table Maintenance Protocol (RTMP)* is a transport layer protocol in the AppleTalk protocol suite that establishes and maintains routing tables in AppleTalk routers.

RTMP is based on the Routing Information Protocol (RIP); as with RIP, RTMP uses hop count as a routing metric. Hop count is calculated as the number of routers or other intermediate nodes through which a packet must pass to travel from the source network to the destination network.

RTMP Routing Tables

RTMP is responsible for establishing and maintaining routing tables for AppleTalk routers. These routing tables contain an entry for each network that a packet can reach.

Routers periodically exchange routing information to ensure that the routing table in each router contains the most current information and that the information is consistent across the internetwork. An RTMP routing table contains the following information about each of the destination networks known to the router:

- Network cable range of the destination network
- Distance in hops to the destination network
- Router port that leads to the destination network
- Address of the next-hop router
- Current state of the routing-table entry (good, suspect, or bad)

Figure 38-8 illustrates a typical RTMP routing table.

Name Binding Protocol Overview

The *Name Binding Protocol (NBP)* is a transport layer protocol in the AppleTalk protocol suite that maps the addresses used at lower layers to AppleTalk names. Socket clients within AppleTalk nodes are known as Network-Visible Entities (NVEs). An NVE is a network-addressable resource, such as a print service, that is accessible over the internetwork. NVEs are referred to by character strings known as entity names. NVEs also have a zone and various attributes, known as entity types, associated with them.

Figure 38-8   *An RTMP Routing Table Contains Information About Each Destination Network Known to the Router*

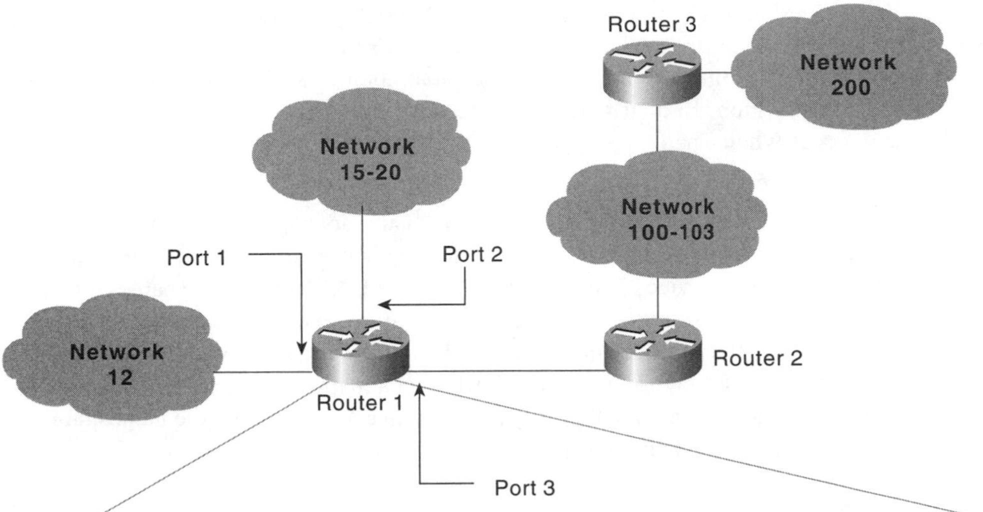

Network cable range	Distance	Port	Next hop	Entry State
RTMP routing table				
12	0	1	0	Good
15-20	0	2	0	Good
100-103	1	3	Router 2	Good
200	2	3	Router 2	Good

Two key reasons exist for using entity names rather than addresses at the upper layers. First, network addresses are assigned to nodes dynamically and, therefore, change regularly. Entity names provide a consistent way for users to refer to network resources and services, such as a file server. Second, using names instead of addresses to refer to resources and services preserves the transparency of lower-layer operations to end users.

Name Binding

Name binding is the process of mapping NVE entity names with network addresses. Each AppleTalk node maps the names of its own NVEs to its network addresses in a names table. The combination of all the names tables in all internetwork nodes is known as the names directory, which is a distributed database of all name-to-address mappings. Name binding can occur when a node is first started up or dynamically immediately before the named entity is accessed.

NBP performs the following four functions: name lookup, name recognition, name confirmation, and name deletion. Name lookup is used to learn the network address of an NVE before the services in that NVE are accessed. NBP checks the names directory for the name-to-address mapping. Name registration allows a node to create its names table. NBP confirms that the name is not in use and then adds the name-to-address mappings to the table. Name confirmation is used to verify that a mapping learned by using a name lookup is still accurate. Name deletion is used to remove an entry from the names table in such instances as when the node is powered off.

AppleTalk Update-Based Routing Protocol

The *AppleTalk Update-Based Routing Protocol (AURP)* is a transport layer protocol in the AppleTalk protocol suite that allows two or more AppleTalk internetworks to be interconnected through a Transmission Control Protocol/Internet Protocol (TCP/IP) network to form an AppleTalk WAN. AURP encapsulates packets in User Datagram Protocol (UDP) headers, allowing them to be transported transparently through a TCP/IP network. An AURP implementation has two components: exterior routers and AURP tunnels.

Exterior routers connect a local AppleTalk internetwork to an AURP tunnel. Exterior routers convert AppleTalk data and routing information to AURP and perform encapsulation and de-encapsulation of AppleTalk traffic. An exterior router functions as an AppleTalk router in the local network and as an end node in the TCP/IP network. When exterior routers first attach to an AURP tunnel, they exchange routing information with other exterior routers. Thereafter, exterior routers send routing information only under the following circumstances:

- When a network is added to or removed from the routing table
- When the distance to a network is changed
- When a change in the path to a network causes the exterior router to access that network through its local internetwork rather than through the tunnel, or through the tunnel rather than through the local internetwork

An AURP tunnel functions as a single, virtual data link between remote AppleTalk internetworks. Any number of physical nodes can exist in the path between exterior routers, but these nodes are transparent to the AppleTalk networks. Two kinds of AURP tunnels exist: point-to-point tunnels and multipoint tunnels. A point-to-point AURP tunnel connects only two exterior routers. A multipoint AURP tunnel connects three or more exterior routers. Two kinds of multipoint tunnels also exist. A fully connected multipoint tunnel enables all connected exterior routers to send packets to one another. With a partially connected multipoint tunnel, one or more exterior routers are aware only of some, not all, of the other exterior routers. Figure 38-9 illustrates two AppleTalk LANs connected via a point-to-point AURP tunnel.

Figure 38-9 *An AURP Tunnel Acts as a Virtual Link Between Remote Networks*

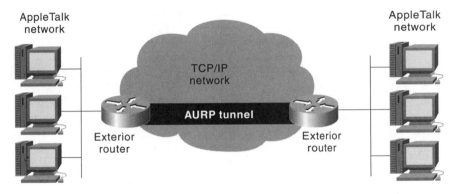

AURP Encapsulation

When exchanging routing information or data through an AURP tunnel, AppleTalk packets must be converted from RTMP, ZIP, and (in the Cisco implementation) Enhanced IGRP to AURP. The packets then are encapsulated in User Datagram Protocol (UDP) headers for transport across the TCP/IP network. The conversion and encapsulation are performed by exterior routers, which receive AppleTalk routing information or data packets that must be sent to a remote AppleTalk internetwork. The exterior router converts the packets to AURP packets, and these packets then are encapsulated in UDP headers and are sent into the tunnel (that is, the TCP/IP network).

The TCP/IP network treats the packets as normal UDP traffic. The remote exterior router receives the UDP packets and removes the UDP header information. The AURP packets then are converted back into their original format, whether as routing information or data packets. If the AppleTalk packets contain routing information, the receiving exterior router updates its routing tables accordingly. If the packets contain data destined for an AppleTalk node on the local network, the traffic is sent out the appropriate interface.

AppleTalk Transaction Protocol

The *AppleTalk Transaction Protocol (ATP)* is a transport layer protocol in the AppleTalk protocol suite that handles transactions between two AppleTalk sockets. A transaction consists of transaction requests and transaction responses, which are exchanged by the involved socket clients.

The requesting socket client sends a transaction request asking that the receiving client perform some action. Upon receiving the request, the client performs the requested action and returns the appropriate information in a transaction response. In transmitting transaction requests and responses, ATP performs most of the important transport layer functions, including acknowledgment and retransmission, packet sequencing, and segmentation and reassembly.

Several session layer protocols run over ATP, including the AppleTalk Session Protocol (ASP) and the Printer Access Protocol (PAP). These two upper-layer AppleTalk protocols are discussed later in this chapter.

Responding devices behave differently depending on which of two types of transaction services is being used: At-Least-Once (ALO) or Exactly-Once (XO) transactions. ALO transactions are used when repetition of the transaction request is the same as executing it once. If a transaction response is lost, the source retransmits its request. This does not adversely affect protocol operations because repetition of the request is the same as executing it once. XO transactions are used when repetition of the transaction request might adversely affect protocol operations. Receiving devices keep a list of every recently received transaction so that duplicate requests are not executed more than once.

AppleTalk Echo Protocol

The *AppleTalk Echo Protocol (AEP)* is a transport layer protocol in the AppleTalk protocol suite that generates packets that test the reachability of network nodes. AEP can be implemented in any AppleTalk node and has the statically assigned socket number 4 (the Echoer socket).

To test the reachability of a given node, an AEP request packet is passed to the DDP at the source. DDP addresses the packet appropriately, indicating in the Type field that the packet is an AEP request. When the packet is received by the destination, DDP examines the Type field and sees that it is an AEP request. In this process, the packet is copied, changed to an AEP reply (by changing a field in the AEP packet), and returned to the source node.

AppleTalk Upper-Layer Protocols

AppleTalk implements services at the session, presentation, and application layers of the OSI model. Four key implementations at the session layer are included in the AppleTalk protocol suite. (The session layer establishes, manages, and terminates communication sessions between presentation layer entities).

Communication sessions consist of service requests and service responses that occur between applications located in different network devices. These requests and responses are coordinated by protocols implemented at the session layer.

The session layer protocol implementations supported by AppleTalk include the AppleTalk Data Stream Protocol (ADSP), Zone Information Protocol (ZIP), AppleTalk Session Protocol (ASP), and Printer Access Protocol (PAP).

The AppleTalk Filing Protocol (AFP) is implemented at the presentation and application layers of the AppleTalk protocol suite. In general, the presentation layer provides a variety of coding and conversion functions that are applied to application layer data. The application layer interacts with software applications (which are outside the scope of the OSI model) that implement a communicating component. Application layer functions typically include identifying communication partners, determining resource availability, and synchronizing communication. Figure 38-10 illustrates how the upper layers of the AppleTalk protocol suite map to the OSI model.

Figure 38-10 *AppleTalk Upper-Layer Protocols Map to Three Layers of the OSI Model*

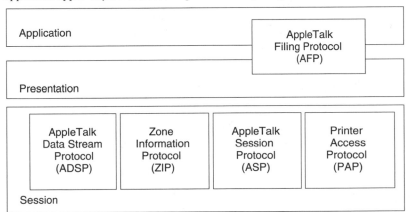

AppleTalk Data Stream Protocol

The *AppleTalk Data Stream Protocol (ADSP)* is a session layer protocol in the AppleTalk protocol suite that establishes and maintains full-duplex communication between two AppleTalk sockets. ADSP guarantees that data is correctly sequenced and that packets are not duplicated. ADSP also implements a flow-control mechanism that allows a destination to slow source transmissions by reducing the size of the advertised receive window. ADSP runs directly on top of the DDP.

Zone Information Protocol

The *Zone Information Protocol (ZIP)* is a session layer protocol in the AppleTalk protocol suite that maintains network number-to-zone name mappings in AppleTalk routers. ZIP is used primarily by AppleTalk routers. Other network nodes, however, use ZIP services at startup to choose their zone. ZIP maintains a zone information table (ZIT) in each router. ZITs are lists maintained by ZIP that map specific network numbers to one or more zone names. Each ZIT contains a network number-to-zone name mapping for every network in the internetwork. Figure 38-11 illustrates a basic ZIT.

Figure 38-11 *Zone Information Tables Assist in Zone Identification*

Network number	Zones
10	Marketing
20-25	Documentation, training
50	Finance
100-120	Engineering
100-120	Facilities, administration

AppleTalk Session Protocol

The *AppleTalk Session Protocol (ASP)* is a session layer protocol in the AppleTalk protocol suite that establishes and maintains sessions between AppleTalk clients and servers. ASP allows a client to establish a session with a server and to send commands to that server. Multiple client sessions to a single server can be maintained simultaneously. ASP uses many of the services provided by lower-layer protocols, such as ATP and NBP.

Printer Access Protocol Overview

The *Printer Access Protocol (PAP)* is a session layer protocol in the AppleTalk protocol suite that allows client workstations to establish connections with servers, particularly printers. A session between a client workstation and a server is initiated when the workstation requests a session with a particular server. PAP uses the NBP to learn the network address of the requested server and then opens a connection between the client and the server. Data is exchanged between client and server using the ATP. When the communication is complete, PAP terminates the connection. Servers implementing PAP can support multiple simultaneous connections with clients. This allows a print server, for example, to process jobs from several different workstations at the same time.

AppleTalk Filing Protocol

The *AppleTalk Filing Protocol (AFP)* permits AppleTalk workstations to share files across a network. AFP performs functions at the presentation and application layers of the AppleTalk protocol suite. This protocol preserves the transparency of the network by allowing users to manipulate remotely stored files in exactly the same manner as locally stored files. AFP uses the services provided by the ASP, the ATP, and the AEP.

AppleTalk Protocol Suite

Figure 38-12 illustrates the entire AppleTalk protocol suite and shows how it maps to the OSI reference model.

DDP Packet Format

The following descriptions summarize the fields associated with the DDP packets. This packet has two forms:

- **Short DDP packet**—The short format is used for transmissions between two nodes on the same network segment in a nonextended network only. This format is seldom used in new networks.
- **Extended DDP packet**—The extended format is used for transmissions between nodes with different network numbers (in a nonextended network) and for any transmissions in an extended network.

Figure 38-13 illustrates the format of the extended DDP packet.

Figure 38-12 *The AppleTalk Protocol Suite Maps to Every Layer of the OSI Model*

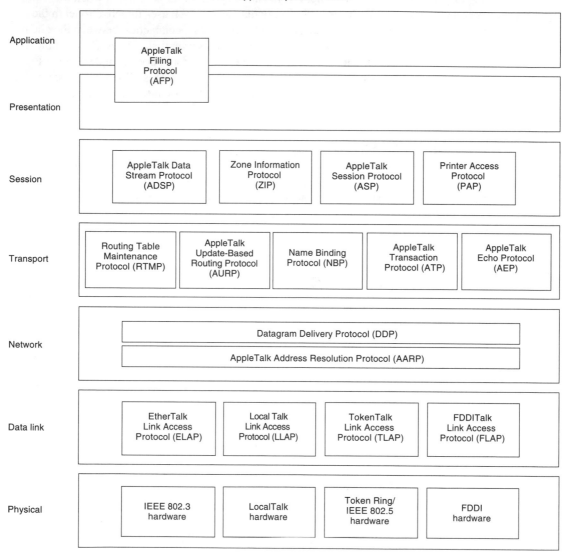

Figure 38-13 *An Extended DDP Packet Consists of 13 Fields*

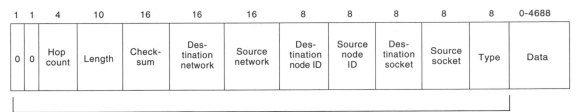

The extended DDP packet fields illustrated in Figure 25-13 are summarized in the discussion that follows:

- **Hop count**—Counts the number of intermediate devices through which the packet has passed. At the source, this field is set to 0. Each intermediate node through which the packet passes increases the value of this field by 1. The maximum number of hops is 15.

- **Length**—Indicates the total length, in bytes, of the DDP packet.

- **Checksum**—Contains a checksum value used to detect errors. If no checksum is performed, the bits in this optional field are set to 0.

- **Destination network**—Indicates the 16-bit destination network number.

- **Source network**—Indicates the 16-bit source network number.

- **Destination node ID**—Indicates the 8-bit destination node ID.

- **Source node ID**—Indicates the 8-bit source node ID.

- **Destination socket**—Indicates the 8-bit destination socket number.

- **Source socket**—Indicates the 8-bit source socket number.

- **Type**—Indicates the upper-layer protocol to which the information in the Data field belongs.

- **Data**—Contains data from an upper-layer protocol.

Summary

This chapter has introduced you to the AppleTalk protocol suite. The AppleTalk protocol uses zones to group nodes or networks into logical groups. In AppleTalk, data link layer addresses are assigned dynamically.

AppleTalk includes an address-resolution method much like TCP/IP's ARP. The AppleTalk version is called AARP. AARP uses broadcasts to discover the hardware address of a node.

The primary network layer routing protocol in AppleTalk is the Datagram Delivery Protocol (DDP). DDP provides a best-effort connectionless datagram service.

There are five key implementations of the transport layer in AppleTalk: RTMP, NBP, AURP, ATP, and AEP.

Review Questions

1   Describe an AppleTalk Zone.

2   What are the four main media-access implementations for the AppleTalk protocol?

3   How are node addresses assigned to workstations?

4   What is the primary network layer routing protocol used by AppleTalk?

5   Name the five key transport layer protocols in AppleTalk.

For More Information

- http://www.apple.com
- http://www.cisco.com/univercd/cc/td/doc/cisintwk/ito_doc/applet.htm

Objectives

- Introduce the SNA protocol, used primarily by mainframe systems and terminals.
- Describe the structures and functioning of this protocol, from its introduction in the early 1970s to its current form.
- Describe IBM peer-based networking.
- Describe the basic information unit (BIU) format.
- Describe the path information unit (PIU) format.

CHAPTER 39

IBM Systems Network Architecture Protocols

Background

IBM networking today consists of essentially two separate architectures that branch, more or less, from a common origin. Before contemporary networks existed, IBM's Systems Network Architecture (SNA) ruled the networking landscape, so it often is referred to as traditional or legacy SNA.

With the rise of personal computers, workstations, and client/server computing, the need for a peer-based networking strategy was addressed by IBM with the creation of Advanced Peer-to-Peer Networking (APPN) and Advanced Program-to-Program Computing (APPC).

Although many of the legacy technologies associated with mainframe-based SNA have been brought into APPN-based networks, real differences exist. This chapter discusses each branch of the IBM networking environment, beginning with legacy SNA environments and following with a discussion of APPN. The chapter closes with summaries of the IBM basic-information unit (BIU) and path-information unit (PIU).

IBM-based routing strategies are covered in a separate chapter. Refer to Chapter 43, "IBM Systems Network Architecture Routing," for details about IBM routing protocols.

Traditional SNA Environments

SNA was developed in the 1970s with an overall structure that parallels the OSI reference model. With SNA, a mainframe running Advanced Communication Facility/Virtual Telecommunication Access Method (ACF/VTAM) serves as the hub of an SNA network. ACF/VTAM is responsible for establishing all sessions and for activating and deactivating resources. In this environment, resources are explicitly predefined, thereby eliminating the requirement for broadcast traffic and minimizing header overhead. The underlying architecture and key components of traditional SNA networking are summarized in the sections that follow.

IBM SNA Architecture

IBM SNA model components map closely to the OSI reference model. The descriptions that follow outline the role of each SNA component in providing connectivity among SNA entities.

- **Data link control (DLC)**—Defines several protocols, including the Synchronous Data Link Control (SDLC) protocol for hierarchical communication, and the Token Ring Network communication protocol for LAN communication between peers

- **Path control**—Performs many OSI network layer functions, including routing and datagram segmentation and reassembly (SAR)

- **Transmission control**—Provides a reliable end-to-end connection service, as well as encrypting and decrypting services

- **Data flow control**—Manages request and response processing, determines whose turn it is to communicate, groups messages, and interrupts data flow on request

- **Presentation services**—Specifies data-transformation algorithms that translate data from one format to another, coordinate resource sharing, and synchronize transaction operations

- **Transaction services**—Provides application services in the form of programs that implement distributed processing or management services

SNA does not define specific protocols for its physical control layer. The physical control layer is assumed to be implemented via other standards.

Figure 39-1 illustrates how these elements of the IBM SNA model map to the general ISO OSI networking model.

Figure 39-1 *IBM SNA Maps to All Seven Levels of the OSI Model*

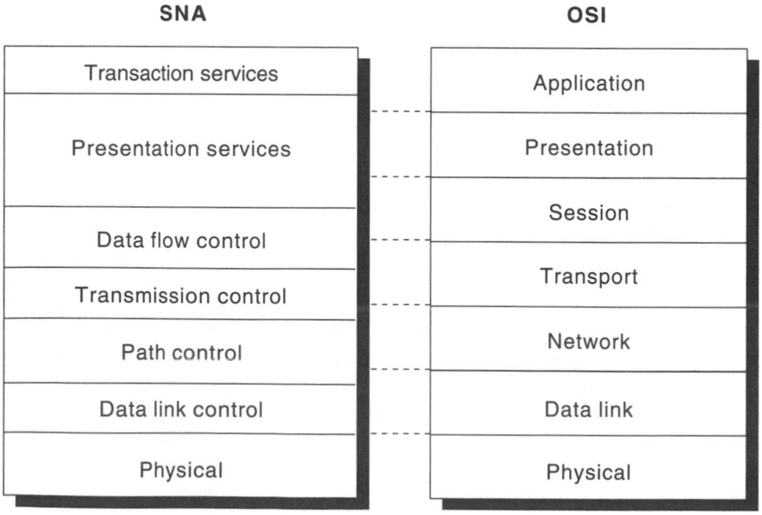

SNA	OSI
Transaction services	Application
Presentation services	Presentation
Data flow control	Session
Transmission control	Transport
Path control	Network
Data link control	Data link
Physical	Physical

A key construct defined within the overall SNA network model is the path control network, which is responsible for moving information between SNA nodes and facilitating internetwork communication between nodes on different networks. The path control network environment uses functions provided by the path control and data link control (DLC). The path control network is a subset of the IBM transport network.

IBM SNA Physical Entities

Traditional SNA physical entities assume one of the following four forms: hosts, communications controllers, establishment controllers, and terminals. Hosts in SNA control all or part of a network and typically provide computation, program execution, database access, directory services, and network management. (An example of a host device within a traditional SNA environment is an S/370 mainframe.) Communications controllers manage the physical network and control communication links. In particular, communications controllers—also called front-end processors (FEPs)—are relied upon to route data through a traditional SNA network. (An example of a communications controller is a 3745.)

Establishment controllers are commonly called cluster controllers. These devices control input and output operations of attached devices, such as terminals. (An example of an establishment controller is a 3174.) Terminals, also referred to as workstations, provide the user interface to the network. (A typical example would be a 3270. Figure 39-2 illustrates each of these physical entities in the context of a generalized SNA network diagram.)

Figure 39-2 *SNA Physical Entities Can Assume One of Four Forms*

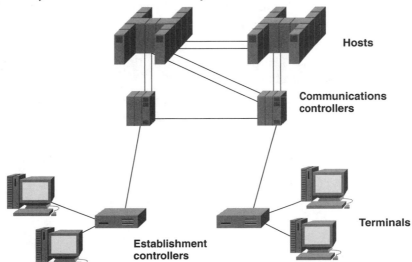

IBM SNA Data Link Control

The *SNA data link control (DLC)* layer supports a number of media, each of which is designed to provide access to devices and users with differing requirements. SNA-supported media types include mainframe channels, SDLC, X.25, and Token Ring, among other media.

A standard SNA mainframe channel attachment provides a parallel-data channel that uses direct memory access (DMA) data-movement techniques. A mainframe channel connects IBM hosts to each other and to communications controllers via multiwire cables. Each cable can be up to several hundred feet in length. A standard mainframe channel can transfer data at a rate of 3 to 4.5 Mbps.

IBM's Enterprise Systems Connection (ESCON) mainframe attachment environment permits higher throughput and can cover greater physical distances. In general, ESCON transfers data at 18 Mbps and supports a point-to-point connection, ranging up to several kilometers, and transfers. To allow higher data rates and longer distances, ESCON uses optical fiber for its network medium.

SDLC has been widely implemented in SNA networks to interconnect communications and establishment controllers, and to move data via telecommunications links.

X.25 networks have long been implemented for WAN interconnections. In general, an X.25 network is situated between two SNA nodes and is treated as a single link. SNA implements X.25 as the access protocol, and SNA nodes are considered adjacent to one another in the context of X.25 networks. To interconnect SNA nodes over an X.25-based WAN, SNA requires DLC protocol capabilities that X.25 does not provide. Several specialized DLC protocols are employed to fill the gap, such as the physical services header, Qualified Logical Link Control (QLLC), and Enhanced Logical Link Control (ELLC).

Token Ring networks are the primary SNA DLC method for providing media access to LAN-based devices. Token Ring, as supported by IBM, is virtually the same as the IEEE 802.5 link access protocol running under IEEE 802.2 Logical Link Control Type 2 (LLC2).

In addition to the basic suite of media types, IBM added support for several other widely implemented media, including IEEE 802.3/Ethernet, Fiber Distributed Data Interface (FDDI), and Frame Relay.

Figure 39-3 illustrates how the various media generally fit into an SNA network.

Figure 39-3 *SNA Has Evolved to Support a Variety of Media*

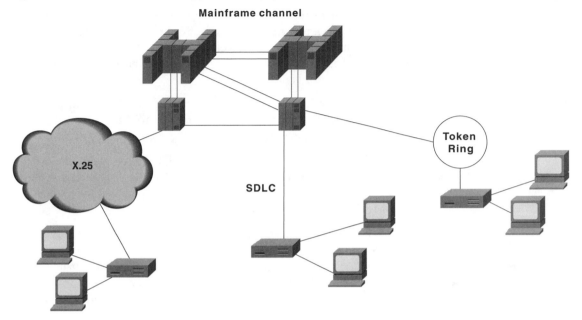

IBM Network Addressable Units

SNA defines three essential network addressable units (NAUs): logical units, physical units, and control points. Each plays an important role in establishing connections between systems in an SNA network.

Logical units (LUs) function as end-user access ports into an SNA network. LUs provide users with access to network resources, and they manage the transmission of information between end users.

Physical units (PUs) are used to monitor and control attached network links and other network resources associated with a particular node. PUs are implemented on hosts by SNA access methods, such as the virtual telecommunication access method (VTAM). PUs also are implemented within communications controllers by network control programs (NCPs).

Control points (CPs) manage SNA nodes and their resources. CPs generally are differentiated from PUs in that CPs determine which actions must be taken, while PUs cause actions to occur. An example of a CP is the SNA system services control point (SSCP). An SSCP can be the CP residing in a PU 5 node or an SSCP as implemented under an SNA access method, such as VTAM.

IBM SNA Nodes

Traditional SNA nodes belong to one of two categories: subarea nodes and peripheral nodes. SNA subarea nodes provide all network services, including intermediate node routing and address mapping between local and network-wide addresses. No relationship exists between SNA node types and actual physical devices. Two subarea nodes are of particular interest: node type 4 and node type 5.

Node type 4 (T4) usually is contained within a communications controller, such as a 3745. An example of a T4 node is an NCP, which routes data and controls flow between a front-end processor and other network resources.

Node type 5 (T5) usually is contained in a host, such as an S/370 mainframe. An example of a T5 node is the VTAM resident within an IBM mainframe. A VTAM controls the logical flow of data through a network, provides the interface between application subsystems and a network, and protects application subsystems from unauthorized access.

SNA peripheral nodes use only local addressing and communicate with other nodes through subarea nodes. Node type 2 (T2) is generally the peripheral node type of interest, although SNA does specify a node type 1 peripheral node. T2 typically resides in intelligent terminals (such as a 3270) or establishment controllers (such as a 3174). Node Type 1 (T1) is now obsolete, but when implemented, it resided in unintelligent terminals. Figure 39-4 illustrates the various SNA nodes and their relationships to each other.

Figure 39-4 *Peripheral Nodes Communicate with Other Nodes Through Subarea Nodes*

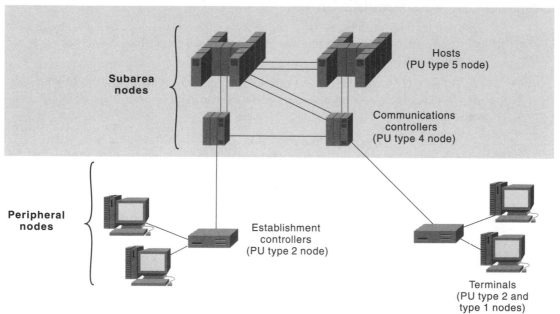

IBM Peer-Based Networking

Changes in networking and communications requirements caused IBM to evolve (and generally overhaul) many of the basic design characteristics of SNA. The emergence of peer-based networking entities (such as routers) resulted in a number of significant changes in SNA. Internetworking among SNA peers hinges on several IBM-developed networking components.

Advanced Peer-to-Peer Networking (APPN) represents IBM's second-generation SNA. In creating APPN, IBM moved SNA from a hierarchical, mainframe-centric environment to a peer-based networking environment. At the heart of APPN is an IBM architecture that supports peer-based communications, directory services, and routing between two or more APPC systems that are not directly attached.

APPN Components

In addition to the APPN environment, peer-based SNA networking specifies three additional key networking concepts: logical units (LUs), Advanced Program-to-Program Computing (APPC), and node type 2.1. Each plays an important role in the establishment of communication among SNA peers within the context of an SNA-based peer internetwork.

Logical Unit (LU) 6.2 governs peer-to-peer communications in an SNA environment. In addition, LU 6.2 supports general communication between programs in a distributed processing environment and between both similar and dissimilar node types. APPC enables SNA applications to communicate directly with peer SNA applications, and it provides a set of programming conventions and protocols that implement LU 6.2. Node type 2.1s (T2.1) are logical entities that permit direct communication among peripheral nodes capable of supporting T2.1. The T2.1 entity facilitates point-to-point communications by providing data transport support for peer-level communications supported by APPC. In addition, a T2.1 contains a peripheral node control point (PNCP) that combines the traditional functions of a physical unit (PU) and a control point (CP).

IBM APPN Node Types

Under APPN, peer-based communication occurs among several well-defined node types. These nodes can be broken down into three basic types: low-entry nodes (LENs), end nodes (ENs), and network nodes (NNs).

The *low-entry network (LEN)* node is a pre-APPN era peer-to-peer node. A LEN node participates in APPN networking by taking advantage of services provided by an adjacent network node (NN). The CP of the LEN node manages local resources but does not establish a CP-to-CP session with the adjacent NN. Before a session can start, session partners must be defined for a LEN node, and the LEN node must be defined for its service-providing adjacent NN.

An *end node (EN)* contains a subset of full APPN support. An end node accesses the network through an adjacent NN and uses the routing services of the same adjacent NN. To communicate on a network, an EN establishes a CP-to-CP session with an adjacent NN and uses the CP-to-CP session to register resources, request directory services, and request routing information.

A *network node (NN)* contains full APPN functionality. The CP in an NN manages the resources of the NN, as well as the attached ENs and LEN nodes. In addition, the CP in an NN establishes CP-to-CP sessions with adjacent ENs and NNs, and maintains the network topology and directory databases created and updated by gathering information dynamically from adjacent NNs and ENs.

Figure 39-5 illustrates where each of these peer types might be found in a generalized APPN environment.

Figure 39-5 *APPN Supports Several Well-Defined Node Types*

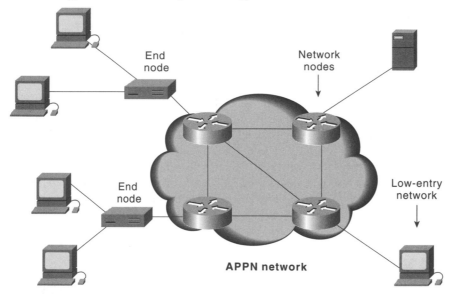

IBM APPN Services

Basic APPN services fall into four general categories: configuration, directors, topology, and routing and session services. Each is summarized in the sections that follow.

IBM APPN Configuration Services

APPN configuration services are responsible for activating connections to the APPN network. Connection activation involves establishing a connection, establishing a session, and selecting an adjacency option.

The connect phase of connection activation enables the initial establishment of communications between nodes. This initial communication involves exchanging characteristics and establishing roles, such as primary versus secondary. Connection establishment is accomplished by the transmission of exchange identification type 3 (XID3) frames between nodes.

During session establishment, CP-to-CP sessions are established with an adjacent EN or NN. Minimally, each node must establish at least one pair of CP-to-CP sessions with one adjacent node. An EN can establish a maximum of one pair of CP-to-CP sessions but can be attached to more than one NN. Between NNs, pairs of CP-to-CP sessions with all adjacent nodes or a subset of adjacent nodes can be established. The minimum requirement is a single pair of sessions to one adjacent NN, which ensures proper topology updating.

Adjacency among APPN nodes is determined by using CP-to-CP sessions. Two configurable options are available for determining node adjacency. A node can be specified as adjacent to a single node, or as logically adjacent to every possible adjacent node. Selecting an adjacency option for a specific situation depends on a given network's connectivity requirements. The reduction in CP-to-CP sessions associated with single-node adjacency can reduce network overhead associated with topology updates, as well as the number of buffers required to distribute topology updates. Reducing the number of adjacent nodes, however, also increases the time required to synchronize routers.

IBM APPN Directory Services

APPN directory services are intended to help network devices locate service providers. These services are essential to establishing a session between end users. Directory services in APPN call for each NN to maintain a directory of local resources and a network directory that associate end users with NNs providing service. A distributed directory service then is formed from the collection of individual NN network directories. This section summarizes the nature of APPN databases, node-directory service handling, and the role of a centralized directory service.

The local and network directory databases support three service-entry types: configured entries, registered entries, and cached entries. Configured database entries usually are local low-entry network nodes that must be configured because no CP-to-CP session can be established over which to exchange information. Other nodes might be configured to reduce broadcast traffic, which is generated as part of the discovery process. Registered entries are local resource entries about which an end node has informed its associated network node server when CP-to-CP sessions are established. A registered entry is added by an NN to its local directory. Cached database entries are directory entries created as session requests and received by an NN. The total number of cached entries permitted can be controlled through user configurations to manage memory requirements.

The end-node directory service negotiation process involves several steps. An EN first sends a LOCATE request to the NN providing network services. The local and network directory databases next are searched to determine whether the destination end user is already known. If the destination end user is known, a single directed LOCATE request is sent to ensure its current availability. If the destination end user is not found in the existing databases, the NN sends a LOCATE request to adjacent ENs to determine whether the destination end user is a local resource. If the destination is not local, the NN sends a broadcast LOCATE request to all adjacent NNs for propagation throughout the network. A message is sent back to the originating NN indicating that the destination is found when the NN providing network services for the destination end user locates the end-user resource. Finally, both origin and destination NNs cache the information.

Directory services for LEN nodes are handled by a proxy service process. First, a LEN node sends a bind session (BIND) request for attached resources. This contrasts with the LOCATE request sent by ENs. To receive any directory services, an NN must provide proxy services for a LEN node. When a proxy service NN is linked to the LEN node, the NN broadcasts LOCATE requests as needed for the LEN node.

A central directory service usually exists within an ACF/VTAM and usually is implemented to help minimize LOCATE broadcasts. This kind of database can be used to maintain a centrally located directory for an entire network because it contains configured, registered, and cached entries. Under a centralized directory service process, an NN sends a directed LOCATE broadcast to the central directory server, which then searches the central database and broadcasts when necessary.

IBM APPN Topology and Routing Services

In an APPN network topology, network nodes are connected by transmission groups (TGs). Each TG consists of a single link, and all NNs maintain a network topology database that contains a complete picture of all NNs and TGs in the network. Transmission groups are discussed in Chapter 43.

A network's topology database is updated by information received in a topology database update (TDU) message. These TDU messages flow over CP-to-CP sessions whenever a change occurs in the network, such as when a node or link becomes active or inactive, when congestion occurs, or when resources are limited.

The network topology database contains information used when calculating routes with a particular class of service (CoS). This information includes NN and TG connectivity and status, and NN and TG characteristics, such as TG capacity.

APPN's routing services function uses information from directory and topology databases to determine a route based on CoS. Route determination starts when an end node first receives a session request from a logical unit. A LOCATE request is sent from the EN to its NN to request destination information and to obtain a route through the network. The NN then identifies the properties associated with the requested level of service. The identified properties are compared to properties of each TG and NN in the network, and all routes that meet the specified criteria are cached as applicable. Each EN, NN, and TG in the network is assigned a weight based on CoS properties, such as capacity, cost, security, and delay. Properties also can be user-defined. Finally, a least-cost path is determined by totaling the weights on the paths that meet the routing criteria.

IBM APPN Session Services

Following route establishment, the APPN session-establishment process varies depending on the node type. If the originating end user is attached to an EN, a LOCATE reply containing the location of the destination and route is returned to the originating EN by the NN adjacent to the destination EN. The originating EN then sends a BIND on a session route. If originating, the end user is attached to a LEN node that sends a BIND to its adjacent NN. The adjacent NN converts the LEN BIND to APPN BIND, and sends a BIND on the session path.

A BIND is a specific type of request message sent from one LU to another LU. A BIND carries the route being used for a session. It specifies NNs and TGs, a unique session identifier for each TG, the transmission priority for the session, and window information to support adaptive pacing to limit traffic on the network.

Basic Information Unit Format

IBM SNA NAUs employ basic information units (BIUs) to exchange requests and responses. Figure 39-6 illustrates the BIU format.

BIU Fields

The following field descriptions summarize the content of the BIU, as illustrated in Figure 39-6.

Figure 39-6 *A Basic Information Unit (BIU) Can Be Either a Request or a Response*

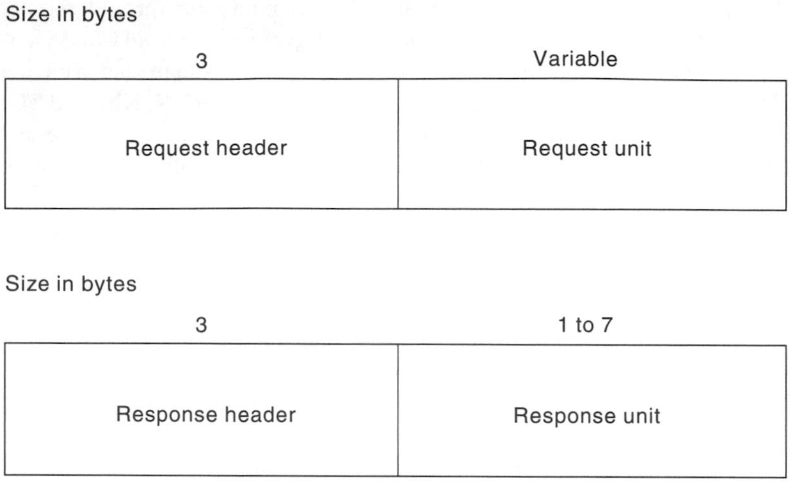

Size in bytes

3	Variable
Request header	Request unit

Size in bytes

3	1 to 7
Response header	Response unit

- **Request header**—Identifies the type of data in the associated request units. This header provides information about the format of the data and specifies protocols for the session. Only NAUs use request header information.

- **Request unit**—Contains either end-user data or SNA commands. End-user data is sent in data request units. SNA commands are sent in command request units that control the network and contain information exchanged between end users.

- **Response header**—Identifies the type of data associated with the response unit. The request/response indicator bit distinguishes a response header from a request header. A receiving NAU indicates whether the response being returned to the request sender is positive or negative by setting the response type indicator (RTI) bit in the response header.

- **Response unit**—Contains information about the request indicating either a positive or negative response. Positive responses to command requests usually contain a 1- to 3-byte response unit that identifies the command request. Positive responses to data requests contain response headers but no response unit.

Negative response units are 4 to 7 bytes long and always are returned with a negative response. A receiving NAU returns a negative response to the requesting NAU under one of three conditions:

- Sender violates SNA protocol

- Receiver does not understand the transmission

- Unusual condition, such as a path failure, occurs

When a negative response is transmitted, the first 4 bytes of a response unit contain data that explains why the request is unacceptable. The receiving NAU sends up to 3 additional bytes that identify the rejected request.

Path Information Unit Format

The path information unit (PIU) is an SNA message unit formed by path control elements by adding a transmission header to a BIU. Figure 39-7 illustrates the PIU format.

PIU Fields

The following field descriptions summarize the content of the PIU, as illustrated in Figure 39-7.

Figure 39-7 *The Path Information Unit (PIU) Requests and Responses Each Consist of Three Fields*

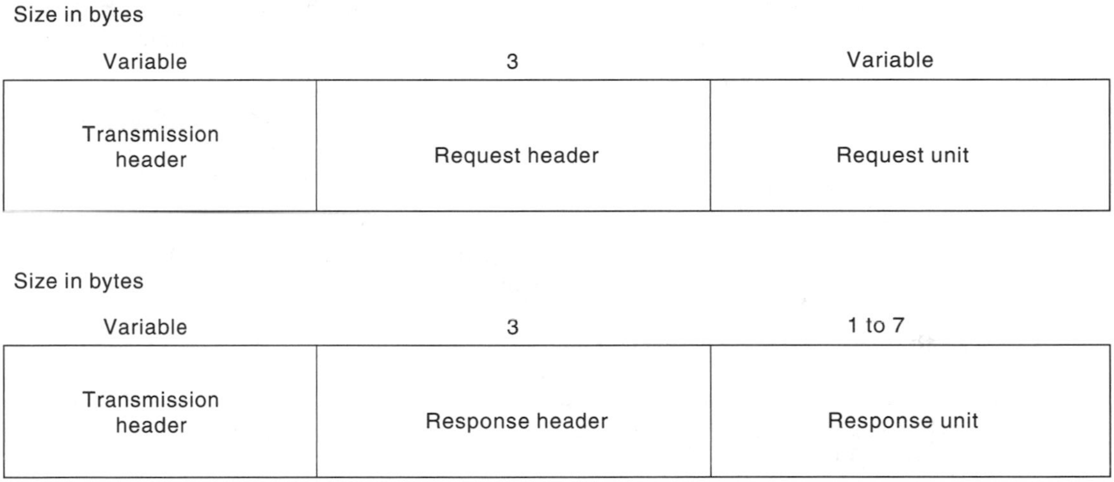

Size in bytes

Variable	3	Variable
Transmission header	Request header	Request unit

Size in bytes

Variable	3	1 to 7
Transmission header	Response header	Response unit

- **Transmission header**—Routes message units through the network. This header contains routing information for traditional SNA subarea networking. Transmission header formats are differentiated by the format identification (FID) type. Path control uses the FID types to route data among SNA nodes.

  Three FID types are implemented in PIUs:

  — FID0 is used to route data between adjacent subarea nodes for non-SNA devices. FID0 generally is rendered obsolete by the FID4 bit set to indicate whether a device is an SNA or non-SNA device.

—   FID1 is used to route data between adjacent subarea nodes when one or both of the nodes do not support explicit and virtual route protocols.

—   FID2 is used to route data between a subarea boundary node and an adjacent peripheral node, or between adjacent type 2.1 nodes.

In general, the transmission header is used to route data between adjacent subarea nodes when both the subarea nodes support explicit and virtual route protocols.

• **Request header**—Identifies the type of data in the associated request units. This header provides information about the format of the data and specifies protocols for the session. Only NAUs use request header information.

• **Request unit**—Contains either end-user data or SNA commands. End-user data is sent in data request units. SNA commands are sent in command request units that control the network and contain information exchanged between end users.

• **Response header**—Identifies the type of data associated with a response unit. The request/response indicator bit distinguishes a response header from a request header. A receiving NAU indicates whether the response being returned to the request sender is positive or negative by setting the RTI bit in the response header.

• **Response unit**—Contains information about the request indicating either a positive or a negative response. Positive responses to command requests usually contain a 1- to 3-byte response unit that identifies the command request. Positive responses to data requests contain response headers but no response unit.

Negative response units are 4 to 7 bytes long and always are returned with a negative response. A receiving NAU returns a negative response to the requesting NAU under one of three conditions: The sender violates SNA protocol, a receiver does not understand the transmission, or an unusual condition, such as a path failure, occurs.

When a negative response is transmitted, the first 4 bytes of a response unit contain data that explains why the request is unacceptable. The receiving NAU sends up to 3 additional bytes that identify the rejected request.

Summary

IBM's SNA was one of the first networking protocols. Although it is now considered a legacy networking protocol, it is still widely deployed. SNA was designed around the host-to-terminal communication model that IBM's mainframes use.

IBM expanded the SNA protocol to support peer-to-peer networking. This expansion was deemed Advanced Peer-to-Peer Networking (APPN) and Advanced Program-to-Program Communication (APPC).

Review Questions

1 What did IBM create to accommodate peer-based networking?

2 What are the types of physical entities that IBM SNA supports?

3 What are the three types of network addressable units in SNA?

4 What is the function of an LU?

5 What is the function of a PU?

6 What is the function of a CP?

7 Under APPN, what are the well-defined node types?

8 What are the four basic service categories for APPN?

9 For what is the network topology database used?

For More Information

- http://www.networking.ibm.com/app/aiwconf/cpic.htm

Objectives

- Describe the development history of the DECnet protocol, used primarily in Digital Equipment Corporation minicomputers.

- Describe the architecture of DECnet networks.

- Discuss the addressing methods of DECnet.

- Describe implementation and access methods of DECnet.

- Describe additional protocols implemented in DECnet networks, including protocols used in the upper layers of the OSI reference model.

CHAPTER 40

DECnet

Introduction

DECnet is a group of data communications products, including a protocol suite, developed and supported by Digital Equipment Corporation (Digital). The first version of DECnet, released in 1975, allowed two directly attached PDP-11 minicomputers to communicate. In recent years, Digital has included support for nonproprietary protocols, but DECnet remains the most important of Digital's network product offerings. This chapter provides a summary of the DECnet protocol suite, Digital's networking architectures, and the overall operation of DECnet traffic management.

Figure 40-1 illustrates a DECnet internetwork, with routers interconnecting two LANs that contain workstations and VAXs.

Several versions of DECnet have been released. The first allowed two directly attached minicomputers to communicate.

Subsequent releases expanded the DECnet functionality by adding support for additional proprietary and standard protocols, while remaining compatible with the immediately preceding release. This means that the protocols are backward compatible. Currently, two versions of DECnet are in wide use: DECnet Phase IV and DECnet/OSI.

Figure 40-1 *In a DECnet-Based Internetwork, Routers Interconnect Workstations and VAXs*

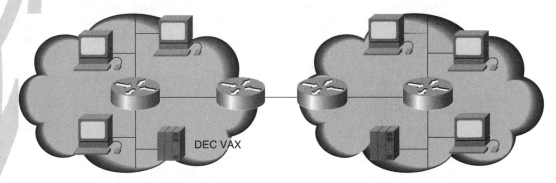

DEC VAX

DECnet Phase IV is the most widely implemented version of DECnet. However, DECnet/OSI is the most recent release. DECnet Phase IV is based on the Phase IV Digital Network Architecture (DNA), and it supports proprietary Digital protocols and other proprietary and standard protocols. DECnet Phase IV is backward compatible with DECnet Phase III, the version that preceded it.

DECnet/OSI (also called DECnet Phase V) is backward compatible with DECnet Phase IV and is the most recent version of DECnet. This version is based on the DECnet/OSI DNA. DECnet/OSI supports a subset of the OSI protocols, multiple proprietary DECnet protocols, and other proprietary and standard protocols.

DECnet Phase IV Digital Network Architecture

The *Digital Network Architecture (DNA)* is a comprehensive layered network architecture that supports a large set of proprietary and standard protocols. The Phase IV DNA is similar to the architecture outlined by the OSI reference model. As with the OSI reference model, the Phase IV DNA utilizes a layered approach, whereby specific layer functions provide services to protocol layers above it and depend on protocol layers below it. Unlike the OSI model, however, the Phase IV DNA is comprised of eight layers. Figure 40-2 illustrates how the eight layers of the Phase IV DNA relate to the OSI reference model.

The following section details the functionality and role of each of these layers and identifies the similarities between the Phase IV DNA architecture and the OSI reference model.

Phase IV DNA Layers

The DECnet Phase IV DNA defines an eight-layer model, as illustrated in Figure 40-2. The user layer represents the User-Network Interface, supporting user services and programs with a communicating component. The user layer corresponds roughly to the OSI application layer. The network management layer represents the user interface to network-management information. This layer interacts with all the lower layers of the DNA and corresponds roughly with the OSI application layer. The network application layer provides various network applications, such as remote file access and virtual terminal access. This layer corresponds roughly to the OSI presentation and application layers.

The session control layer manages logical link connections between end nodes and corresponds roughly to the OSI session layer. The end communications layer handles flow control, segmentation, and reassembly functions and corresponds roughly to the OSI transport layer. The routing layer performs routing and other functions, and corresponds roughly to the OSI network layer. The data link layer manages physical network channels and corresponds to the OSI data link layer. The physical layer manages hardware interfaces and determines the electrical and mechanical functions of the physical media; this layer corresponds to the OSI physical layer.

Figure 40-2 *Phase IV Consists of Eight Layers That Map to the OSI Layers*

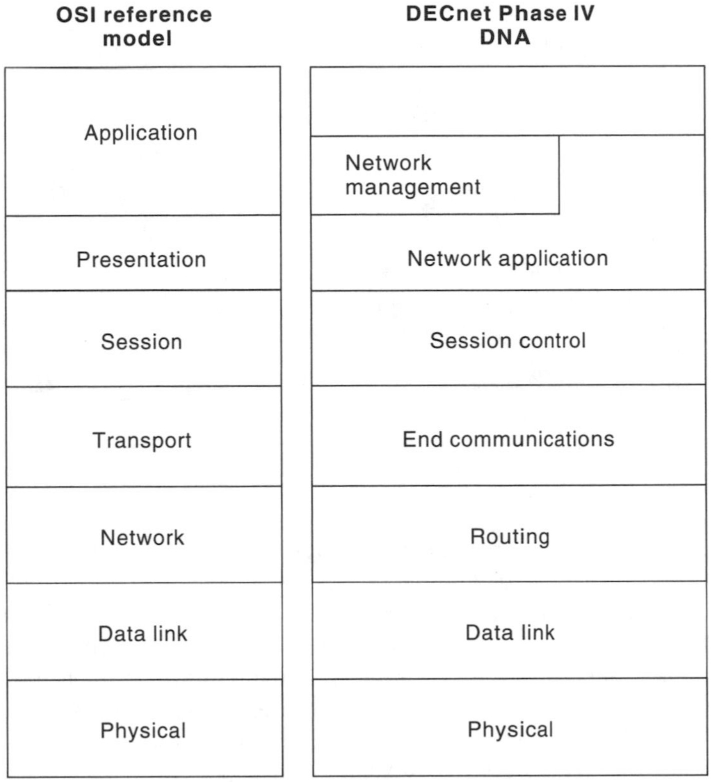

OSI reference model	DECnet Phase IV DNA
Application	Network management
	Network application
Presentation	
Session	Session control
Transport	End communications
Network	Routing
Data link	Data link
Physical	Physical

Phase IV DECnet Addressing

DECnet addresses are not associated with the physical networks to which the nodes are connected. Instead, DECnet locates hosts using area/node address pairs. An area's value ranges from 1 to 63, inclusive. Likewise, a node address can be between 1 and 1023, inclusive. Therefore, each area can have 1023 nodes, and approximately 65,000 nodes can be addressed in a DECnet network. Areas can span many routers, and a single cable can support many areas. Therefore, if a node has several network interfaces, it uses the same area/node address for each interface. Figure 40-3 illustrates a sample DECnet network with several addressable entities.

Figure 40-3 *DECnet Locates Hosts Using Area/Node Address Pairs*

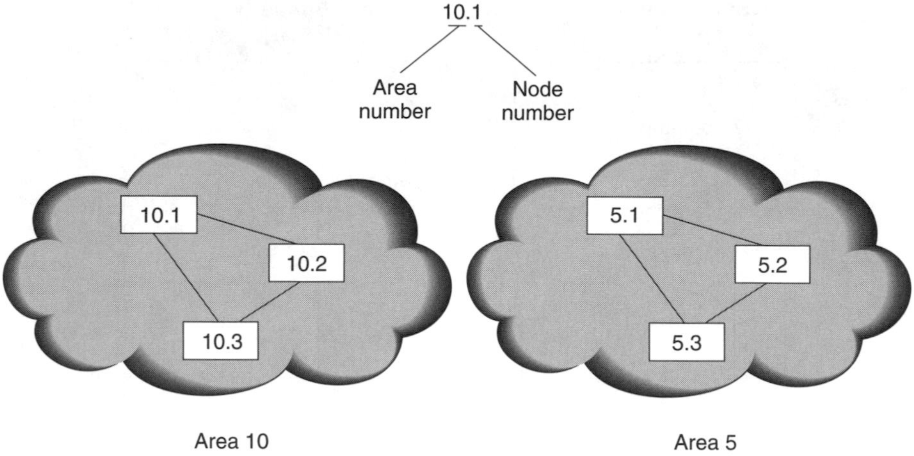

DECnet hosts do not use manufacturer-assigned Media Access Control (MAC)-layer addresses. Instead, network level addresses are embedded in the MAC-layer address according to an algorithm that multiplies the area number by 1024 and adds the node number to the product. The resulting 16-bit decimal address is converted to a hexadecimal number and is appended to the address AA00.0400 in byte-swapped order, with the least-significant byte first. For example, DECnet address 12.75 becomes 12363 (base 10), which equals 304B (base 16). After this byte-swapped address is appended to the standard DECnet MAC address prefix, the address is AA00.0400.4B30.

DECnet/OSI Digital Network Architecture

The DECnet/OSI (DECnet Phase V) DNA is very similar to the architecture outlined by the OSI reference model. DECnet Phase V utilizes a layered approach that achieves a high degree of flexibility in terms of support for upper-layer protocol suites. As the following section discusses, DECnet OSI actually allows for the support of multiple protocol suites.

DECnet/OSI DNA Implementations

The DECnet/OSI DNA defines a layered model that implements three protocol suites: OSI, DECnet, and Transmission Control Protocol/Internet Protocol (TCP/IP). The OSI implementation of DECnet/OSI conforms to the seven-layer OSI reference model and supports many of the standard OSI protocols. The Digital implementation of DECnet/OSI provides backward compatibility with DECnet Phase IV and supports multiple proprietary Digital protocols. The TCP/IP implementation of DECnet/OSI supports the lower-layer

TCP/IP protocols and enables the transmission of DECnet traffic over TCP transport protocols. Figure 40-4 illustrates the three DECnet/OSI implementations.

Figure 40-4 *The OSI, DECnet, and TCP Are All Supported by DECnet/OSI DNA*

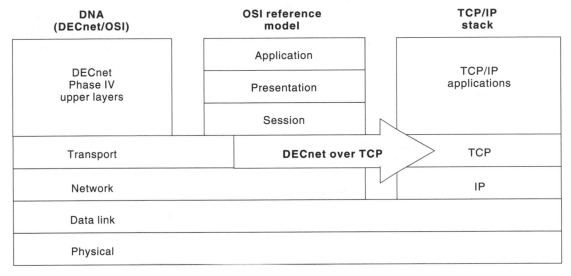

DECnet Media Access

DECnet Phase IV and DECnet/OSI support a variety of media-access implementations at the physical and data link layers. This has contributed to the relatively wide acceptance of DECnet in the computer networking industry. As explained in the following sections, both DECnet Phase IV and Phase V can support many of the common physical and data-link technologies in use today.

At the physical layer, DECnet Phase IV and DECnet/OSI support most of the popular physical implementations, including Ethernet/IEEE 802.3, Token Ring/IEEE 802.5, and Fiber Distributed Data Interface (FDDI). In addition, DECnet/OSI supports Frame Relay and X.21bis.

At the data link layer, DECnet Phase IV and DECnet/OSI support IEEE 802.2 Logical Link Control (LLC), Link Access Procedure, Balanced (LAPB), Frame Relay, and High-Level Data Link Control (HDLC). Both DECnet Phase IV and DECnet/OSI also support the proprietary Digital data-link protocol, Digital Data Communications Message Protocol (DDCMP), which provides point-to-point and multipoint connections; full-duplex or half-duplex communication over synchronous and asynchronous channels; and error correction, sequencing, and management.

DECnet Routing

DECnet routing occurs at the routing layer of the DNA in DECnet Phase IV and at the network layer of the OSI model in DECnet/OSI. The routing implementations in both DECnet Phase IV and DECnet/OSI, however, are similar.

DECnet Phase IV routing is implemented by the DECnet Routing Protocol (DRP), which is a relatively simple and efficient protocol whose primary function is to provide optimal path determination through a DECnet Phase IV network. Figure 40-5 provides a sample DECnet network to illustrate how the routing function is performed in a DECnet Phase IV network.

Figure 40-5 *The DRP Determines the Optimal Route Through a DECnet Phase IV Network*

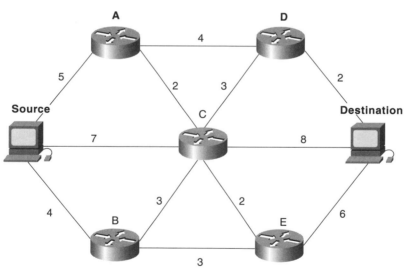

DECnet routing decisions are based on cost, an arbitrary measure assigned by network administrators to be used in comparing various paths through an internetwork environment. Costs typically are based on hop count or media bandwidth, among other measures. The lower the cost, the better the path. When network faults occur, the DRP uses cost values to recalculate the best paths to each destination.

DECnet/OSI routing is implemented by the standard OSI routing protocols (ISO 8473, ISO 9542, and ISO 10589) and by DRP. Detailed information on the OSI routing protocols can be found in Chapter 48, "Open System Interconnection Routing Protocol."

DECnet End Communications Layer

DECnet Phase IV supports a single transport protocol at the DNA end communications layer: the Network-Services Protocol (NSP).

Network-Services Protocol

The *Network-Services Protocol (NSP)* is a proprietary, connection-oriented, end communications protocol developed by Digital that is responsible for creating and terminating connections between nodes, performing message fragmentation and reassembly, and managing error control.

NSP also manages two types of flow control: a simple start/stop mechanism in which the receiver tells the sender when to terminate and resume data transmission, and a more complex scheme in which the receiver tells the sender how many messages it can accept.

DECnet/OSI Transport Layer

DECnet/OSI supports NSP, three standard OSI transport protocols, and the Transmission Control Protocol (TCP).

DECnet/OSI supports Transport Protocol classes (TP) 0, TP2, and TP4. TP0 is the simplest OSI connection-oriented transport protocol. Of the classic transport layer functions, it performs only segmentation and reassembly. This means that TP0 will note the smallest maximum-size protocol data unit (PDU) supported by the underlying subnetworks and will break the transport packet into smaller pieces that are not too big for network transmission. TP2 can multiplex and demultiplex data streams over a single virtual circuit. This capability makes TP2 particularly useful over public data networks (PDNs), in which each virtual circuit incurs a separate charge. As with TP0 and TP1, TP2 also segments and reassembles PDUs, while TP3 combines the features of TP1 and TP2. TP4, the most popular OSI transport protocol, is similar to the Internet protocol suite's TCP and, in fact, was based on that model. In addition to performing TP3's features, TP4 provides reliable transport service and assumes a network in which problems are not detected.

Request For Comments (RFC) 1006 and RFC 1006 Extensions define an implementation of OSI transport layer protocols atop the TCP. RFC 1006 defines the implementation of OSI Transport Protocol class 0 (TP0) on top of TCP. RFC 1006 extensions define the implementation of Transport Protocol class 2 (TP2) on top of TCP.

DECnet Phase IV Upper Layers

The DECnet Phase IV DNA specifies four upper layers to provide user interaction services, network-management capabilities, file transfer, and session management. Specifically, these are referred to as the user layer, network management layer, network application layer, and session control layer. The upper layers of the DECnet Phase IV architecture are discussed in more detail in the following sections.

User Layer

The DNA user layer supports user services and programs that interact with user applications. The end user interacts directly with these applications, and the applications use the services and programs provided by the user layer.

Network Management Layer

The network-management protocol widely used in DECnet networks is the proprietary Digital Network Information and Control Exchange (NICE) protocol. NICE is a command-response protocol. Commands, which request an action, are issued to a managed node or process; responses, in the form of actions, are returned by those nodes or processes. NICE performs a variety of network management-related functions and can be used to transfer an operating system from a local system into a remote system, as well as enable an unattended remote system to dump its memory to the local system. Protocols using NICE can examine or change certain characteristics of the network. NICE supports an event logger that automatically tracks important network events, such as an adjacency change or a circuit-state change. NICE supports functions that accommodate hardware and node-to-node loop tests.

Certain network management functions can use the *Maintenance Operations Protocol (MOP)*, a collection of functions that can operate without the presence of the DNA layers between the network management and data link layers. This allows access to nodes that exist in a state in which only data link layer services are available or operational.

Network Application Layer

Data-Access Protocol (DAP), a proprietary Digital protocol, is used by DECnet Phase IV at the network application layer. DAP supports remote file access and remote file transfer, services that are used by applications at the network management layer and the user layer. Other proprietary Digital protocols operating at the network application layer include MAIL, which allows the exchange of mail messages, and CTERM, which allows remote interactive terminal access.

Session Control Layer

The *Session Control Protocol (SCP)* is the DECnet Phase IV session control-layer protocol that performs a number of functions. In particular, SCP requests a logical link from an end device, receives logical-link requests from end devices, accepts or rejects logical-link requests, translates names to addresses, and terminates logical links.

DECnet/OSI Upper Layers

The DECnet/OSI DNA is based on the OSI reference model. DECnet/OSI supports two protocol suites at each of the upper layers: the OSI protocols and the DECnet Phase IV protocols (for backward compatibility). DECnet/OSI supports functionality in the application, presentation, and session layers.

Application Layer

DECnet/OSI implements the standard OSI application layer implementations, as well as standard application layer processes such as Common Management-Information Protocol (CMIP) and File Transfer, Access, and Management (FTAM), among others. DECnet/OSI also supports all the protocols implemented by DECnet Phase IV at the user and network-management layers of the DNA, such as the Network Information and Control Exchange (NICE) protocol.

The OSI application layer includes actual applications, as well as application service elements (ASEs). ASEs allow easy communication from applications to lower layers. The three most important ASEs are Association Control Service Element (ACSE), Remote Operations Service Element (ROSE), and Reliable Transfer Service Element (RTSE). ACSE associates application names with one another in preparation for application-to-application communications. ROSE implements a generic request-reply mechanism that permits remote operations in a manner similar to that of remote procedure calls (RPCs). RTSE aids reliable delivery by making session layer constructs easy to use.

Presentation Layer

DECnet/OSI implements all the standard OSI presentation layer implementations. DECnet/OSI also supports all the protocols implemented by DECnet Phase IV at the network application layer of the DNA. The most important of these is the Data-Access Protocol (DAP).

The OSI presentation layer typically is just a pass-through protocol for information from adjacent layers. Although many people believe that Abstract Syntax Notation 1 (ASN.1) is OSI's presentation layer protocol, ASN.1 is used for expressing data formats in a machine-independent format. This allows communication between applications on diverse computer systems (ESs) in a manner transparent to the applications.

Session Layer

DECnet/OSI implements all the standard OSI session layer implementations. DECnet/OSI also supports all the protocols implemented by DECnet Phase IV at the session control layer of the DNA. The primary session control layer protocol is the Session Control Protocol (SCP). The OSI session layer protocol turns the data streams provided by the lower four layers into sessions by implementing various control mechanisms. These mechanisms include accounting, conversation control, and session-parameter negotiation. Session conversation control is implemented by use of a token, the possession of which provides the right to communicate. The token can be requested, and ESs can be granted priorities that provide for unequal token use.

Figure 40-6 illustrates the complete DECnet Phase IV and DECnet/OSI protocol suites, including the implementation of DECnet/OSI over TCP.

Figure 40-6 *DECnet Phase IV and DECnet/OSI Support the Same Data Link and Physical Layer Specifications*

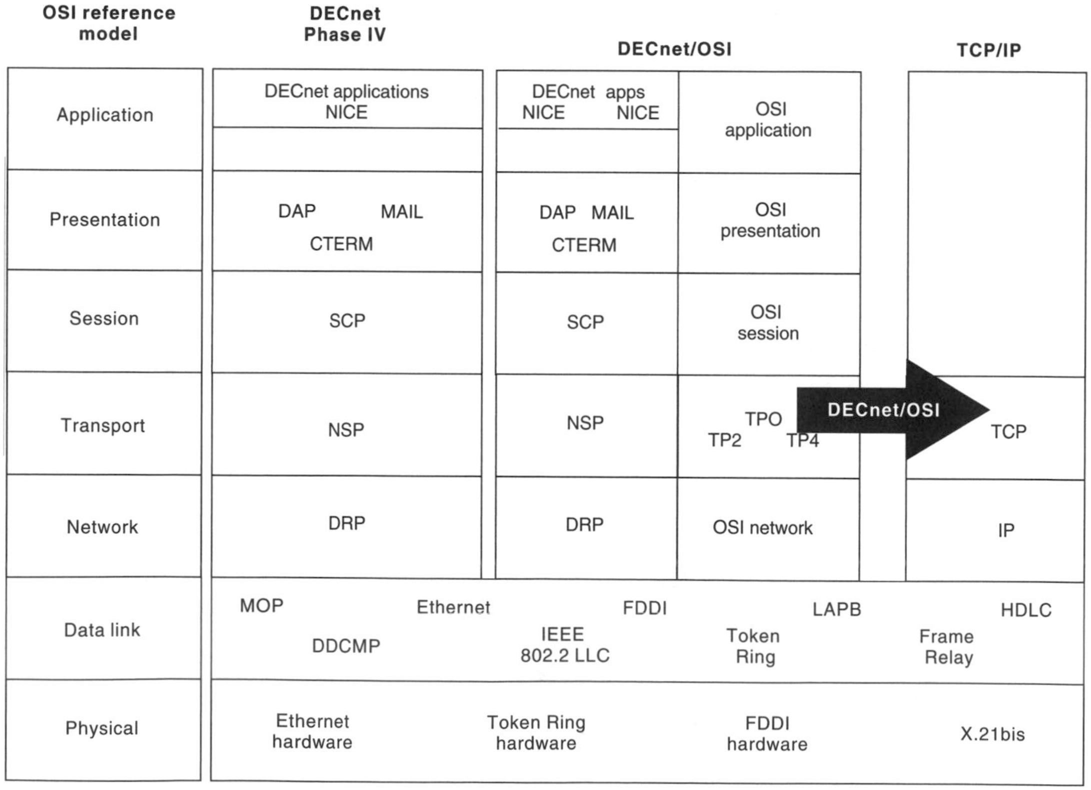

Summary

The benefits of the DECnet protocol are realized in specific networks using Digital equipment. Few networks still use DECnet, but you may encounter them in some legacy systems.

Review Questions

1   How do DECnet hosts use the manufacturer-assigned Media Access Control (MAC) address?

2   What protocol in DECnet Phase IV is responsible for routing?

3   What functions does Network-Services Protocol (NSP) provide?

4   What functions does the Session Control Protocol (SCP) provide?

5   The user layer provides what types of functions in DECnet?

Routing Protocols

Objectives

- Understand the purpose of the Border Gateway Protocol.
- Explain BGP attributes and their use in route selection.
- Examine the BGP route selection process.

CHAPTER 41

Border Gateway Protocol

Introduction

The *Border Gateway Protocol (BGP)* is an interautonomous system routing protocol. An autonomous system is a network or group of networks under a common administration and with common routing policies. BGP is used to exchange routing information for the Internet and is the protocol used between Internet service providers (ISP). Customer networks, such as universities and corporations, usually employ an Interior Gateway Protocol (IGP) such as RIP or OSPF for the exchange of routing information within their networks. Customers connect to ISPs, and ISPs use BGP to exchange customer and ISP routes. When BGP is used between autonomous systems (AS), the protocol is referred to as External BGP (EBGP). If a service provider is using BGP to exchange routes within an AS, then the protocol is referred to as Interior BGP (IBGP). Figure 41-1 illustrates this distinction.

Figure 41-1 *External and Interior BGP*

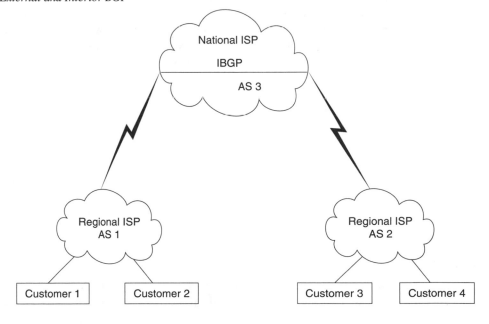

BGP is a very robust and scalable routing protocol, as evidenced by the fact that BGP is the routing protocol employed on the Internet. At the time of this writing, the Internet BGP routing tables number more than 90,000 routes. To achieve scalability at this level, BGP uses many route parameters, called attributes, to define routing policies and maintain a stable routing environment.

In addition to BGP attributes, classless interdomain routing (CIDR) is used by BGP to reduce the size of the Internet routing tables. For example, assume that an ISP owns the IP address block 195.10.x.x from the traditional Class C address space. This block consists of 256 Class C address blocks, 195.10.0.x through 195.10.255.x. Assume that the ISP assigns a Class C block to each of its customers. Without CIDR, the ISP would advertise 256 Class C address blocks to its BGP peers. With CIDR, BGP can supernet the address space and advertise one block, 195.10.x.x. This block is the same size as a traditional Class B address block. The class distinctions are rendered obsolete by CIDR, allowing a significant reduction in the BGP routing tables.

BGP neighbors exchange full routing information when the TCP connection between neighbors is first established. When changes to the routing table are detected, the BGP routers send to their neighbors only those routes that have changed. BGP routers do not send periodic routing updates, and BGP routing updates advertise only the optimal path to a destination network.

BGP Attributes

Routes learned via BGP have associated properties that are used to determine the best route to a destination when multiple paths exist to a particular destination. These properties are referred to as BGP attributes, and an understanding of how BGP attributes influence route selection is required for the design of robust networks. This section describes the attributes that BGP uses in the route selection process:

- Weight
- Local preference
- Multi-exit discriminator
- Origin
- AS_path
- Next hop
- Community

Weight Attribute

Weight is a Cisco-defined attribute that is local to a router. The weight attribute is not advertised to neighboring routers. If the router learns about more than one route to the same destination, the route with the highest weight will be preferred. In Figure 41-2, Router A is receiving an advertisement for network 172.16.1.0 from routers B and C. When Router A receives the advertisement from Router B, the associated weight is set to 50. When Router A receives the advertisement from Router C, the associated weight is set to 100. Both paths for network 172.16.1.0 will be in the BGP routing table, with their respective weights. The route with the highest weight will be installed in the IP routing table.

Figure 41-2 *BGP Weight Attribute*

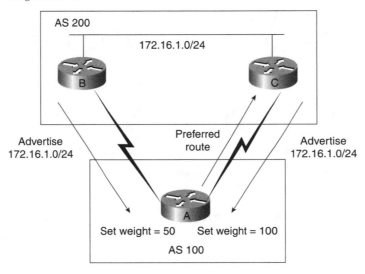

Local Preference Attribute

The *local preference* attribute is used to prefer an exit point from the local autonomous system (AS). Unlike the weight attribute, the local preference attribute is propagated throughout the local AS. If there are multiple exit points from the AS, the local preference attribute is used to select the exit point for a specific route. In Figure 41-3, AS 100 is receiving two advertisements for network 172.16.1.0 from AS 200. When Router A receives the advertisement for network 172.16.1.0, the corresponding local preference is set to 50. When Router B receives the advertisement for network 172.16.1.0, the corresponding local preference is set to 100. These local preference values will be exchanged between routers A and B. Because Router B has a higher local preference than Router A, Router B will be used as the exit point from AS 100 to reach network 172.16.1.0 in AS 200.

Figure 41-3 *BGP Local Preference Attribute*

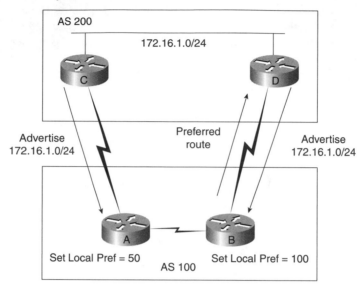

Multi-Exit Discriminator Attribute

The *multi-exit discriminator (MED)* or *metric attribute* is used as a suggestion to an external AS regarding the preferred route into the AS that is advertising the metric.

The term *suggestion* is used because the external AS that is receiving the MEDs may be using other BGP attributes for route selection. We will cover the rules regarding route selection in the next section. In Figure 41-4, Router C is advertising the route 172.16.1.0 with a metric of 10, while Route D is advertising 172.16.1.0 with a metric of 5. The lower value of the metric is preferred, so AS 100 will select the route to router D for network 172.16.1.0 in AS 200. MEDs are advertised throughout the local AS.

Origin Attribute

The *origin attribute* indicates how BGP learned about a particular route. The origin attribute can have one of three possible values:

- **IGP**—The route is interior to the originating AS. This value is set when the network router configuration command is used to inject the route into BGP.
- **EGP**—The route is learned via the Exterior Border Gateway Protocol (EBGP).
- **Incomplete**—The origin of the route is unknown or learned in some other way. An origin of incomplete occurs when a route is redistributed into BGP.

The origin attribute is used for route selection and will be covered in the next section.

Figure 41-4 *BGP Multi-Exit Discriminator Attribute*

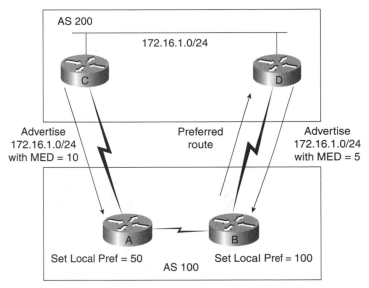

AS_path Attribute

When a route advertisement passes through an autonomous system, the AS number is added to an ordered list of AS numbers that the route advertisement has traversed. Figure 41-5 shows the situation in which a route is passing through three autonomous systems.

AS1 originates the route to 172.16.1.0 and advertises this route to AS 2 and AS 3, with the AS_path attribute equal to {1}. AS 3 will advertise back to AS 1 with AS-path attribute {3,1}, and AS 2 will advertise back to AS 1 with AS-path attribute {2,1}. AS 1 will reject these routes when its own AS number is detected in the route advertisement. This is the mechanism that BGP uses to detect routing loops. AS 2 and AS 3 propagate the route to each other with their AS numbers added to the AS_path attribute. These routes will not be installed in the IP routing table because AS 2 and AS 3 are learning a route to 172.16.1.0 from AS 1 with a shorter AS_path list.

Next-Hop Attribute

The EBGP *next-hop* attribute is the IP address that is used to reach the advertising router. For EBGP peers, the next-hop address is the IP address of the connection between the peers. For IBGP, the EBGP next-hop address is carried into the local AS, as illustrated in Figure 41-6.

Figure 41-5 *BGP AS-path Attribute*

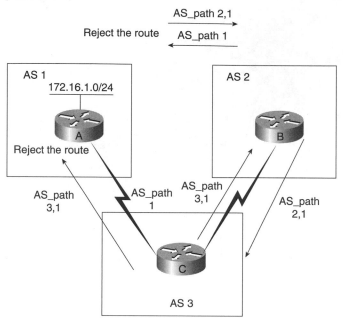

Figure 41-6 *BGP Next-Hop Attribute*

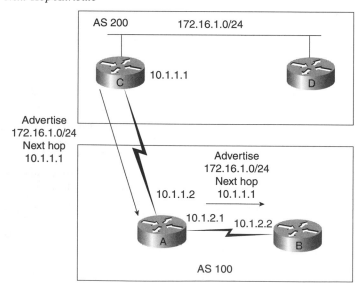

Router C advertises network 172.16.1.0 with a next hop of 10.1.1.1. When Router A propagates this route within its own AS, the EBGP next-hop information is preserved. If Router B does not have routing information regarding the next hop, the route will be discarded. Therefore, it is important to have an IGP running in the AS to propagate next-hop routing information.

Community Attribute

The community attribute provides a way of grouping destinations, called communities, to which routing decisions (such as acceptance, preference, and redistribution) can be applied. Route maps are used to set the community attribute. Predefined community attributes are listed here:

- **no-export**—Do not advertise this route to EBGP peers.
- **no-advertise**—Do not advertise this route to any peer.
- **internet**—Advertise this route to the Internet community; all routers in the network belong to it.

Figure 41-7 illustrates the no-export community. AS 1 advertises 172.16.1.0 to AS 2 with the community attribute no-export. AS 2 will propagate the route throughout AS 2 but will not send this route to AS 3 or any other external AS.

Figure 41-7 *BGP no-export Community Attribute*

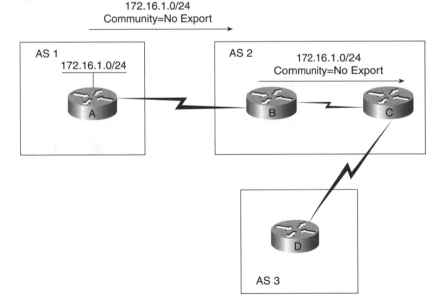

In Figure 41-8, AS 1 advertises 172.16.1.0 to AS 2 with the community attribute no-advertise. Router B in AS 2 will not advertise this route to any other router.

Figure 41-8 *BGP no-advertise Community Attribute*

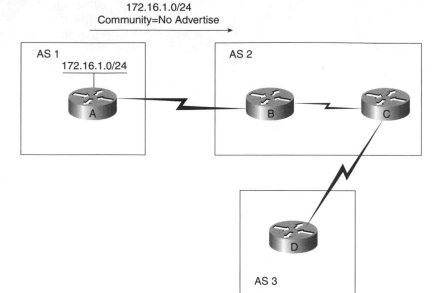

Figure 41-9 demonstrates the internet community attribute. There are no limitations to the scope of the route advertisement from AS 1.

Figure 41-9 *BGP internet Community Attribute*

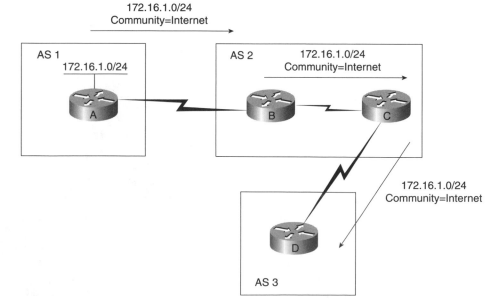

BGP Path Selection

BGP could possibly receive multiple advertisements for the same route from multiple sources. BGP selects only one path as the best path. When the path is selected, BGP puts the selected path in the IP routing table and propagates the path to its neighbors. BGP uses the following criteria, in the order presented, to select a path for a destination:

- If the path specifies a next hop that is inaccessible, drop the update.
- Prefer the path with the largest weight.
- If the weights are the same, prefer the path with the largest local preference.
- If the local preferences are the same, prefer the path that was originated by BGP running on this router.
- If no route was originated, prefer the route that has the shortest AS_path.
- If all paths have the same AS_path length, prefer the path with the lowest origin type (where IGP is lower than EGP, and EGP is lower than incomplete).
- If the origin codes are the same, prefer the path with the lowest MED attribute.
- If the paths have the same MED, prefer the external path over the internal path.
- If the paths are still the same, prefer the path through the closest IGP neighbor.
- Prefer the path with the lowest IP address, as specified by the BGP router ID.

Review Questions

1 Can IBGP be used in place of an IGP (RIP, IGRP, EIGRP, OSPF, or ISIS)?

2 Assume that a BGP router is learning the same route from two different EBGP peers. The AS_path information from peer 1 is {2345,86,51}, and the AS_path information from peer 2 is {2346,51}. What BGP attributes could be adjusted to force the router to prefer the route advertised by peer 1?

3 Can BGP be used only by Internet service providers?

4 If a directly connected interface is redistributed into BGP, what value will the origin attribute have for this route?

For More Information

- RFC 1771, "BGP4"
- Halabi, Bassam. *Internet Routing Architectures*. Cisco Press: Indianapolis, 1997.
- Parkhurst, William R., and David R. Jackson. *Practical BGP for Internet Routing*. Cisco Press: Indianapolis, in press.

- BGP4 Case Studies/Tutorial Section 1, http://www.cisco.com/warp/customer/459/13.html
- BGP4 Case Studies/Tutorial Section 2, http://www.cisco.com/warp/customer/459/14.html
- BGP4 Case Studies/Tutorial Section 3, http://www.cisco.com/warp/customer/459/15.html
- BGP4 Case Studies/Tutorial Section 4, http://www.cisco.com/warp/customer/459/16.html
- BGP4 Case Studies/Tutorial Section 5, http://www.cisco.com/warp/customer/459/17.html

Objectives

- Identify the four key technologies employed by Enhanced IGRP (EIGRP).
- Understand the Diffusing Update Algorithm (DUAL), and describe how it improves the operational efficiency of EIGRP.
- Learn how to use EIGRP to interconnect networks with different routing protocols as well as different routed protocols.
- Discover how it is possible to migrate gradually to EIGRP.

CHAPTER 42

Enhanced IGRP

The Enhanced Interior Gateway Routing Protocol (EIGRP) represents an evolution from its predecessor IGRP (refer to Chapter 44, "Interior Gateway Routing Protocol"). This evolution resulted from changes in networking and the demands of diverse, large-scale internetworks. Enhanced IGRP integrates the capabilities of link-state protocols into distance vector protocols. Additionally, EIGRP contains several important protocols that greatly increase its operational efficiency relative to other routing protocols. One of these protocols is the *Diffusing update algorithm (DUAL)* developed at SRI International by Dr. J.J. Garcia-Luna-Aceves. DUAL enables EIGRP routers to determine whether a path advertised by a neighbor is looped or loop-free, and allows a router running EIGRP to find alternate paths without waiting on updates from other routers.

Enhanced IGRP provides compatibility and seamless interoperation with IGRP routers. An automatic-redistribution mechanism allows IGRP routes to be imported into Enhanced IGRP, and vice versa, so it is possible to add Enhanced IGRP gradually into an existing IGRP network. Because the metrics for both protocols are directly translatable, they are as easily comparable as if they were routes that originated in their own autonomous systems (ASs). In addition, Enhanced IGRP treats IGRP routes as external routes and provides a way for the network administrator to customize them.

This chapter provides an overview of the basic operations and protocol characteristics of Enhanced IGRP.

Enhanced IGRP Capabilities and Attributes

Key capabilities that distinguish Enhanced IGRP from other routing protocols include fast convergence, support for variable-length subnet mask, support for partial updates, and support for multiple network layer protocols.

A router running Enhanced IGRP stores all its neighbors' routing tables so that it can quickly adapt to alternate routes. If no appropriate route exists, Enhanced IGRP queries its neighbors to discover an alternate route. These queries propagate until an alternate route is found.

Its support for variable-length subnet masks permits routes to be automatically summarized on a network number boundary. In addition, Enhanced IGRP can be configured to summarize on any bit boundary at any interface.

Enhanced IGRP does not make periodic updates. Instead, it sends partial updates only when the metric for a route changes. Propagation of partial updates is automatically bounded so that only those routers that need the information are updated. As a result of these two capabilities, Enhanced IGRP consumes significantly less bandwidth than IGRP.

Enhanced IGRP includes support for AppleTalk, IP, and Novell NetWare. The AppleTalk implementation redistributes routes learned from the Routing Table Maintenance Protocol (RTMP). The IP implementation redistributes routes learned from OSPF, Routing Information Protocol (RIP), Intermediate System-to-Intermediate System (IS-IS), Exterior Gateway Protocol (EGP), or Border Gateway Protocol (BGP). The Novell implementation redistributes routes learned from Novell RIP or Service Advertisement Protocol (SAP).

Underlying Processes and Technologies

To provide superior routing performance, Enhanced IGRP employs four key technologies that combine to differentiate it from other routing technologies: neighbor discovery/recovery, reliable transport protocol (RTP), DUAL finite-state machine, and protocol-dependent modules.

The *neighbor discovery/recovery* mechanism enables routers to dynamically learn about other routers on their directly attached networks. Routers also must discover when their neighbors become unreachable or inoperative. This process is achieved with low overhead by periodically sending small hello packets. As long as a router receives hello packets from a neighboring router, it assumes that the neighbor is functioning, and the two can exchange routing information.

Reliable Transport Protocol (RTP) is responsible for guaranteed, ordered delivery of Enhanced IGRP packets to all neighbors. It supports intermixed transmission of multicast or unicast packets. For efficiency, only certain Enhanced IGRP packets are transmitted reliably. On a multiaccess network that has multicast capabilities, such as Ethernet, it is not necessary to send hello packets reliably to all neighbors individually. For that reason, Enhanced IGRP sends a single multicast hello packet containing an indicator that informs the receivers that the packet need not be acknowledged. Other types of packets, such as updates, indicate in the packet that acknowledgment is required. RTP contains a provision for sending multicast packets quickly when unacknowledged packets are pending, which helps ensure that convergence time remains low in the presence of varying speed links.

The *DUAL finite-state machine* embodies the decision process for all route computations by tracking all routes advertised by all neighbors. DUAL uses distance information to select efficient, loop-free paths and selects routes for insertion in a routing table based on feasible successors. A *feasible successor* is a neighboring router used for packet forwarding that is a least-cost path to a destination that is guaranteed not to be part of a routing loop. When a neighbor changes a metric, or when a topology change occurs, DUAL tests for feasible successors. If one is found, DUAL uses it to avoid recomputing the route unnecessarily. When no feasible successors exist but neighbors still advertise the destination, a recomputation (also known as a diffusing computation) must occur to determine a new successor. Although recomputation is not processor-intensive, it does affect convergence time, so it is advantageous to avoid unnecessary recomputations.

Protocol-dependent modules are responsible for network layer protocol-specific requirements. The IP-Enhanced IGRP module, for example, is responsible for sending and receiving Enhanced IGRP packets that are encapsulated in IP. Likewise, IP-Enhanced IGRP is also responsible for parsing Enhanced IGRP packets and informing DUAL of the new information that has been received. IP-Enhanced IGRP asks DUAL to make routing decisions, the results of which are stored in the IP routing table. IP-Enhanced IGRP is responsible for redistributing routes learned by other IP routing protocols.

Routing Concepts

Enhanced IGRP relies on four fundamental concepts: neighbor tables, topology tables, route states, and route tagging. Each of these is summarized in the discussions that follow.

Neighbor Tables

When a router discovers a new neighbor, it records the neighbor's address and interface as an entry in the *neighbor table*. One neighbor table exists for each protocol-dependent module. When a neighbor sends a hello packet, it advertises a hold time, which is the amount of time that a router treats a neighbor as reachable and operational. If a hello packet is not received within the hold time, the hold time expires and DUAL is informed of the topology change.

The neighbor-table entry also includes information required by RTP. Sequence numbers are employed to match acknowledgments with data packets, and the last sequence number received from the neighbor is recorded so that out-of-order packets can be detected. A transmission list is used to queue packets for possible retransmission on a per-neighbor basis. Round-trip timers are kept in the neighbor-table entry to estimate an optimal retransmission interval.

Topology Tables

The *topology table* contains all destinations advertised by neighboring routers. The protocol-dependent modules populate the table, and the table is acted on by the DUAL finite-state machine. Each entry in the topology table includes the destination address and a list of neighbors that have advertised the destination. For each neighbor, the entry records the advertised metric, which the neighbor stores in its routing table. An important rule that distance vector protocols must follow is that if the neighbor advertises this destination, it must use the route to forward packets.

The metric that the router uses to reach the destination is also associated with the destination. The metric that the router uses in the routing table, and to advertise to other routers, is the sum of the best-advertised metric from all neighbors and the link cost to the best neighbor.

Route States

A topology-table entry for a destination can exist in one of two states: active or passive. A destination is in the *passive state* when the router is not performing a recomputation; it is in the *active state* when the router is performing a recomputation. If feasible successors are always available, a destination never has to go into the active state, thereby avoiding a recomputation.

A recomputation occurs when a destination has no feasible successors. The router initiates the recomputation by sending a query packet to each of its neighboring routers. The neighboring router can send a reply packet, indicating that it has a feasible successor for the destination, or it can send a query packet, indicating that it is participating in the recomputation. While a destination is in the active state, a router cannot change the destination's routing-table information. After the router has received a reply from each neighboring router, the topology-table entry for the destination returns to the passive state, and the router can select a successor.

Route Tagging

Enhanced IGRP supports internal and external routes. Internal routes originate within an Enhanced IGRP AS. Therefore, a directly attached network that is configured to run Enhanced IGRP is considered an internal route and is propagated with this information throughout the Enhanced IGRP AS. External routes are learned by another routing protocol or reside in the routing table as static routes. These routes are tagged individually with the identity of their origin.

External routes are tagged with the following information:

- Router ID of the Enhanced IGRP router that redistributed the route
- AS number of the destination
- Configurable administrator tag
- ID of the external protocol
- Metric from the external protocol
- Bit flags for default routing

Route tagging allows the network administrator to customize routing and maintain flexible policy controls. Route tagging is particularly useful in transit ASs, where Enhanced IGRP typically interacts with an interdomain routing protocol that implements more global policies, resulting in a very scalable, policy-based routing.

Enhanced IGRP Packet Types

Enhanced IGRP uses the following packet types: hello and acknowledgment, update, and query and reply.

Hello packets are multicast for neighbor discovery/recovery and do not require acknowledgment. An *acknowledgment* packet is a hello packet that has no data. Acknowledgment packets contain a nonzero acknowledgment number and always are sent by using a unicast address.

Update packets are used to convey reachability of destinations. When a new neighbor is discovered, unicast update packets are sent so that the neighbor can build up its topology table. In other cases, such as a link-cost change, updates are multicast. Updates always are transmitted reliably.

Query and reply packets are sent when a destination has no feasible successors. *Query* packets are always multicast. Reply packets are sent in response to query packets to instruct the originator not to recompute the route because feasible successors exist. *Reply* packets are unicast to the originator of the query. Both query and reply packets are transmitted reliably.

Summary

Cisco Systems's EIGRP is one of the most feature-rich and robust routing protocols to ever be developed. Its unique combination of features blends the best attributes of distance vector protocols with the best attributes of link-state protocols. The result is a hybrid routing protocol that defies easy categorization with conventional protocols.

EIGRP is also remarkably easy to configure and use, as well as remarkably efficient and secure in operation. It can be used in conjunction with IPv4, AppleTalk, and IPX. More importantly, its modular architecture will readily enable Cisco to add support for other routed protocols that may be developed in the future.

Review Questions

1 Name the four key technologies that are used by EIGRP.

2 Explain why EIGRP is more efficient in operation than IGRP.

3 How does RTP enable improved convergence times?

4 Why does EIGRP tag certain routes?

For More Information

- Pepelnjak, Ivan. *EIGRP Network Design Solutions.* Indianapolis: Cisco Press, 2000.
- Sportack, Mark A. *IP Routing Fundamentals.* Indianapolis: Cisco Press, 1999.
- http://www.cisco.com/cpress/cc/td/cpress/ccie/ndcs798/nd2017.htm

Objectives

- Describe Class of Service, what it is, and how to use it.
- Describe how to use subareas to break up the network.
- Describe how peer-to-peer routing works.
- Describe types of PtP routing.

CHAPTER 43

IBM Systems Network Architecture Routing

Background

IBM's networking architecture has evolved considerably as computing in general has evolved away from domination by centralized computing solutions to peer-based computing. Today, IBM Systems Network Architecture (SNA) routing involves two separate kinds of environments, although a number of key concepts are central to all SNA routing situations. This chapter addresses functions and services that make both SNA subarea routing and Advanced Peer-to-Peer Networking (APPN) routing possible. Topics covered include session connections, transmission groups, explicit and virtual routes, and Class of Service (COS). Refer to Chapter 43, "IBM Systems Network Architecture Protocols," for general information about traditional IBM SNA and APPN. Figure 43-1 illustrates the concepts addressed in this chapter in the context of a traditional SNA environment.

IBM SNA Session Connectors

IBM SNA session connectors are used to bridge address spaces when sessions traverse multiple address spaces. Three types of session connectors exist: boundary functions, SNA network interconnection (SNI) gateways, and APPN intermediate routing functions. Boundary functions reside in subarea nodes and map between subarea and peripheral address spaces. SNI gateways act as bridges between SNA networks, accepting data from one network and transmitting it to the appropriate destination in another network. SNI gateways are transparent to endpoint network attachment units (NAUs). APPN intermediate nodes perform intermediate routing within APPN networks. Refer to Figure 43-1 for the relative position of a session connector in a traditional SNA environment.

Figure 43-1 *SNA Routing Relies on Transmission Groups to Interconnect Subarea Entities*

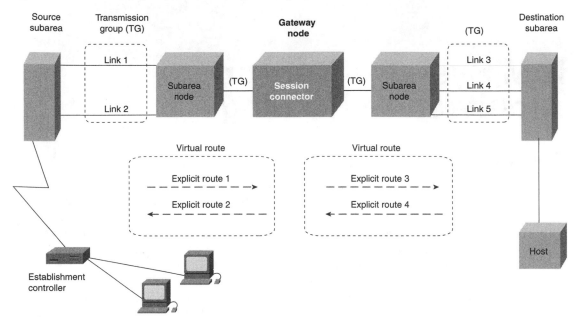

IBM SNA Transmission Groups

IBM SNA transmission groups (TGs) are logical connections formed between adjacent IBM SNA nodes that are used to pass SNA session traffic. TGs are comprised of one or more SNA links and their assigned transmission priorities. Multilink TGs, which provide added reliability and bandwidth, are used to bundle multiple physical links into a single logical SNA link. Multilink TGs are supported only between T4 nodes. TG sequence numbers are used to resequence out-of-order messages at each hop. Four transmission priorities are supported at each transmission group: low, medium, high, and network-service traffic (the highest priority). Refer to Figure 43-1 for an illustration of the relationship of TGs with respect to other common SNA routing components within the context of a subarea routing environment.

IBM SNA Explicit and Virtual Routes

Routes between subareas assume either an explicit or virtual route form. Explicit routes are the physical connections between two subarea nodes, and they serve as the ordered sequences of subareas and connecting transmission groups. Explicit routes are unidirectional, and two explicit routes are required to create a full-duplex path.

Virtual routes are two-way logical connections formed between two subarea nodes. A virtual route flows over both an explicit route and a reverse explicit route that follows the same physical path. Virtual routes do not cross network boundaries; instead, they use an SNA network interconnect session connector to bridge two virtual routes. Virtual routes include values defining transmission priority and global flow control, which is provided by pacing, in which a receiver with sufficient buffer space grants pacing windows to the sender. Each pacing window enables the sender to transmit a certain amount of information before the sender must request the next pacing window. Refer to Figure 43-1 for an illustration of the relationship between explicit routes and virtual routes, and their relative position in the context of an SNA subarea routing environment.

IBM SNA Class of Service

The *IBM SNA Class of Service (COS)* function designates the transport network characteristics of a given session. Depending on user requirements, different COSs can be specified in an SNA network. COS provides the mechanism to determine all SNA routes and describes acceptable service levels for a session. COS also specifies the collection of session characteristics, including response time, security, and availability. In addition, COS can be established automatically when logging in, or manually (by the user) when the session is initiated. Each COS name is associated with a list of virtual routes that meet the desired service-level requirement. Relevant information for a given session is captured in COS subarea and APPN tables. The differences between COS implementation in subarea and APPN routing are summarized in the following sections.

COS in Subarea Routing

In subarea routing, the user defines COS support required for a particular session. Specific virtual routes are mapped to identified services, while COS characteristics are associated with the underlying explicit routes. The System Services Control Point (SSCP) uses the COS table to provide information on virtual routes and transmission priority to the path control function. Path control, in turn, selects a virtual route and transmission priority for use in a session. Figure 43-2 illustrates the subarea routing COS table-entry format.

Figure 43-2 *A Subarea Routing COS Table Holds Data on Virtual Routes and Transmission Priorities*

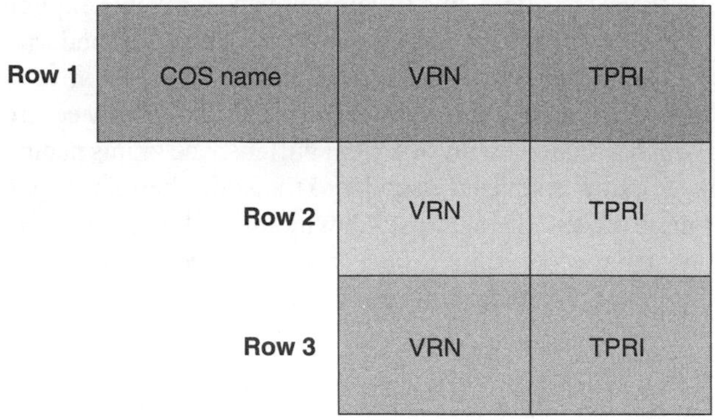

Subarea routing COS table entries include COS name, virtual route number (VRN), and subarea transmission priority (TRPI).

COS name is a standard name, such as SEC3, that is agreed upon by conventions.

The VRN identifies a specific route between subareas. Up to eight virtual route numbers can be assigned between two subarea nodes. Each virtual route can be assigned with up to three different transmission priorities, and up to 24 virtual routes are possible between two subareas.

TPRI identifies the priority of logical unit-to-logical unit (LU-to-LU) session data flowing over an explicit route. Users can select one of three priorities for each virtual route: 0 (lowest), 1, or 2 (highest).

COS in APPN Routing

COS in APPN is defined explicitly with COS table parameters. COS is more granular in APPN than subarea SNA. In particular, COS for APPN allows a route to be defined based on capacity, cost, security, propagation delay, and user-defined characteristics. It extends service to end nodes (ENs) and is not limited to communications controllers, as in subarea SNA. APPN COS permits the topology database to maintain a tree for every COS that tracks all routes and costs. APPN COS also provides a configuration option to control memory dedicated to COS trees. Figure 43-3 illustrates the APPN routing COS table-entry format.

Figure 43-3 *An APPN Routing COS Table Can Include Special Character Returns and Route-Weighting Information*

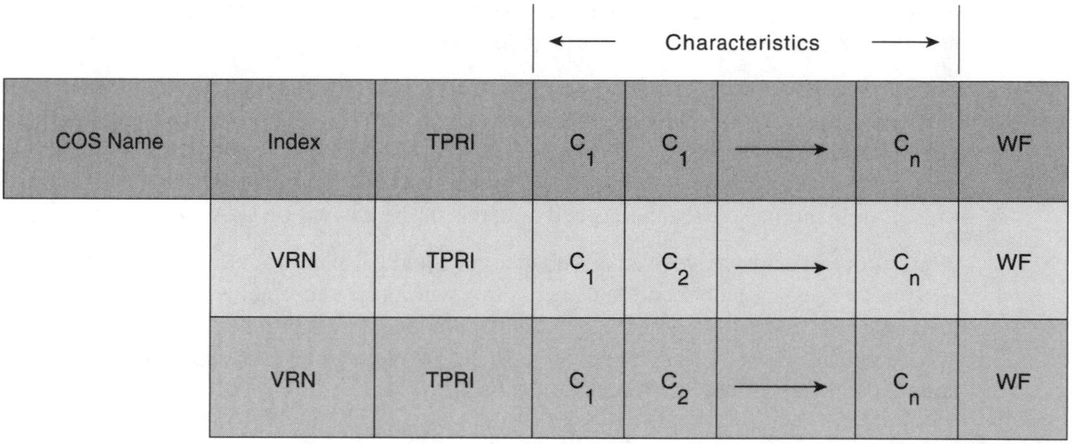

			← Characteristics →				
COS Name	Index	TPRI	C_1	C_1	→	C_n	WF
	VRN	TPRI	C_1	C_2	→	C_n	WF
	VRN	TPRI	C_1	C_2	→	C_n	WF

APPN routing COS table entries include COS name, index, APPN transmission priority (TPRI) characteristics, and APPN COS Weighted Field (WF).

The COS name is a standard name, such as SEC3, that is agreed upon by conventions.

The Index field entry enables computed weight values for route components to be stored and retrieved. This entry points to the entry in the COS weight array where the weights for the COS are stored.

APPN TPRI identifies the priority of LU-to-LU session data flowing over an explicit route. It specifies only one TPRI field for each COS table entry. APPN TPRI requires that traffic over a given session with the same COS in a particular APPN network flow with the same transmission priority.

Node and transmission group (TG) characteristics consist of a user-specified list of characteristics acceptable for an identified COS. Each row defines either a set of node characteristics or a set of TG characteristics. Entries can include security, cost per connect time, and available capacity. The field representing a characteristic contains a range of acceptable values.

The APPN COS WF enables routes-selection services (RSS) to assign a weight to a given possible route component (node or TG). WF is used by RSS to determine relative desirability of a particular route component. The WF can contain a constant or the name of a function that RSS uses in weight calculation.

IBM SNA Subarea Routing

SNA logical areas and node addressing are two central components of traditional routing in SNA environments. This section addresses these topics in the context of traditional SNA networking.

SNA networks are divided into logical areas: subareas and domains. Subareas consist of a subarea node and its attached peripherals. Domains consist of a system services control point (SSCP) and the network resources that it can control. SSCPs in different domains can cooperate with each other to compensate for host processor failures. Figure 43-4 illustrates the relationship between subareas and domains in the context of SNA subarea routing.

Node addresses are categorized as subarea-node and peripheral-node addresses. Subarea-node addresses are global and must be unique within the entire network. These addresses are assigned to NAUs when activated. Subarea-node addresses generally consist of a subarea portion and an element portion. All NAUs within a given subarea share the same subarea address but have different element addresses.

Figure 43-4 *Subareas Exist Within Domains in SNA Subarea Routing*

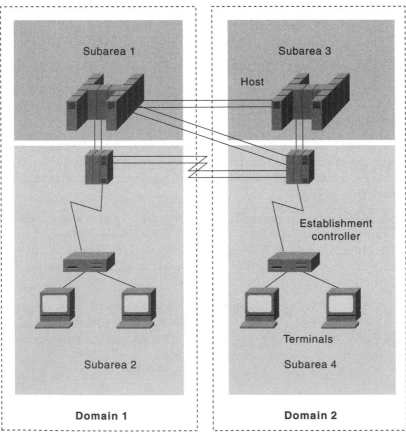

Peripheral-node addresses, which are considered local addresses, differ depending on whether the node is T2 or T2.1. T2 addresses refer to NAUs and are statically assigned, while T2.1 addresses are dynamically assigned for the duration of a session and identify the session rather than the NAU. Peripheral-node addresses are referred to as local form-session identifiers.

IBM Advanced Peer-to-Peer Networking Routing

IBM Advanced Peer-to-Peer Networking (APPN) routing is dynamic and is based on a least-weight path calculated from input received from all APPN network nodes. Each APPN network node is responsible for reporting changes in its local topology (that is, the node itself and the attached links). Topology information is passed until all APPN nodes receive it. When a node receives data that it already has, it stops forwarding the data to other nodes. Duplicate information is recognized via a check of update sequence numbers. Figure 43-5 illustrates where APPN network nodes fit into the general scheme of an APPN environment with ENs and low-entry network (LEN) nodes.

Figure 43-5 *APPN Network Nodes Link to ENs, LENs, and Other Network Nodes*

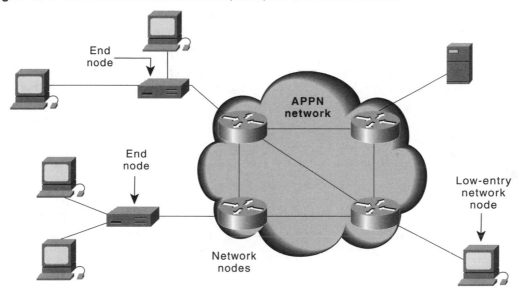

Several underlying functions and capabilities enable APPN routing. These include node type 2.1 routing, Dependent Logical-Unit Requester/Server (DLUR/S) routing, connections networks, and border nodes.

IBM APPN Node Type 2.1 Routing

Node type 2.1 routing involves routing traffic between one or more APPN network nodes. Two node type 2.1 routing processes are supported: intermediate session routing (ISR) and high-performance routing (HPR).

Intermediate Session Routing

The *ISR* process involves bind session BIND requests and responses flowing from network node to network node. In this environment, session connectors are built and used in place of routing tables in APPN. With ISR, a map is generated of the session identifier and port from one side of a node to the other. A unique session identifier in the session connector header is swapped for an outgoing identifier and then is sent out from the appropriate port.

ISR-supported subarea SNA features include node-to-node error and flow-control processing, as well as session switching around network failures. Node-to-node error and flow-control processing are considered redundant and unnecessary because these processes reduce end-to-end throughput.

High-Performance Routing

The HPR protocol, an alternative to ISR, is based on two key components: Rapid-Transport Protocol (RTP) and Automatic Network Routing (ANR). RTP is a reliable, connection-oriented protocol that ensures delivery and manages end-to-end network error and flow control. RTP creates new routes following a network failure. ANR is a connectionless service that is responsible for node-to-node source-routed service.

The RTP layer is invoked only at the edges of an APPN network. In intermediate nodes, only the ANR layer is invoked. RTP nodes establish RTP connections to carry session data. All traffic for a single session flows over the same RTP-to-RTP connection and is multiplexed with traffic from other sessions using the same connection. Figure 43-6 illustrates the overall architecture of an HPR-based routing environment.

Figure 43-6 *RTP Is Supported Only in APPN Edge Network Nodes*

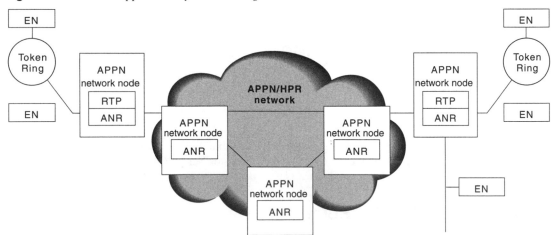

A typical HPR routing process involves several stages. First, a route is selected while it is using ISR. To establish a connection between the edge RTP nodes, either an existing RTP-to-RTP connection is used or a route-services request (RSR) is sent. The returned route-services reply (RSP) carries information showing forward and reverse paths through the network.

Paths represent the forward and reverse port lists and include the port identifier used in each ANR node. These lists are carried on every message, eliminating the need for routing tables or session connectors in the ANR nodes.

HPR provides for link-failure recovery. If a link fails and an alternate path exists between the RTP endpoints for a particular COS, a new RTP-to-RTP connection can be selected, and a session can be moved without disruption. If a connection does not exist along the new path, RSR and RSP messages are sent to obtain the new port lists. Sending a new BIND is not required because the session is not disrupted.

Flow control in an HRP environment uses a technique called adaptive rate-based (ARB) flow control. ARB flow control monitors and controls the amount of traffic introduced into the network. Under ARB flow control, the sending and receiving RTP nodes exchange messages at regular intervals. Traffic introduced into the network is modified to adapt to network conditions.

IBM APPN DLUR/S Routing

The *Dependent Logical-Unit Requester/Server (DLUR/S)* is an APPN feature that allows legacy SNA traffic to flow on an APPN network.

Under DLUR/S, a client/server relationship is established between a Dependent Logical-Unit Server (DLUS) and a Dependent Logical-Unit Requester (DLUR). A DLUS is typically an ACF/UTAM4.2 entity, and a DLUR is typically a router. A pair of LU 6.2 sessions is established between the DLUR and DLUS. These LU 6.2 sessions transport legacy SNA control messages. Those messages not recognized in an APPN environment are encapsulated on the LU 6.2 session. Messages then are de-encapsulated by DLUR and are passed to the legacy SNA LU. The DLU session initiation is then passed to the DLUS and is processed by the DLUS as legacy traffic. The DLUS sends a message to the application host, and the application host sends the BIND. Finally, legacy SNA data flows natively with APPN traffic.

IBM APPN Connection Network

An *IBM APPN connection network* is a logical construct used to provide direct connectivity between APPN ENs without the configuration overhead of defining direct connections between every pair of ENs. In general, the process of creating a connection network starts when a LOCATE request is received from an EN.

A network node (NN) then is used to locate the destination specified in the LOCATE request. If the NN sees that the two ENs (source and destination) are attached to the same transport medium (such as Token Ring), a virtual node (VN) is used to connect the two endpoints and form a connection network. The NN defines the session path as a direct connection from EN1 to VN to EN2, and then traffic is permitted to flow.

IBM APPN Border Node

A border node is an APPN entity that enables multiple APPN networks to interconnect. Presently, border nodes are implemented only in ACF/VTAM and OS/400. Border nodes are responsible for tying directories and topology databases together for connected networks, and rebuilding BIND requests to show separate routes in each network.

With border nodes, topology and directory databases in NNs are reduced to sizes required for individual subnetworks rather than the composite network. In addition, cross-network sessions are routed through the border node. Figure 43-7 illustrates the position of border nodes (ACF/VTAM and OS/400 devices) in a multinetwork APPN environment:

Figure 43-7 *Border Nodes (ACF/VTAM and OS/400 Devices) Can Connect APPN Networks*

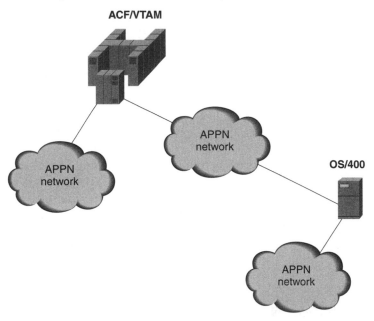

Review Questions

1 What are SNA session connectors used for?

2 What is created when a network node determines via the LOCATE request that the two end nodes are attached to the same medium?

3 True or false: All NAUs within a subarea have the same element address.

Objectives

- Identify the metrics that IGRP uses to compare routes.
- Explain how an administrator can influence route selection.
- Understand multipath routing.
- Identify IGRP's native stability features.
- Identify IGRP's timing mechanisms and explain their purpose.

CHAPTER 44

Interior Gateway Routing Protocol

Background

The *Interior Gateway Routing Protocol (IGRP)* is a routing protocol that was developed in the mid-1980s by Cisco Systems, Inc. Cisco's principal goal in creating IGRP was to provide a robust protocol for routing within an autonomous system (AS). Such protocols are known as Interior Gateway Routing Protocols.

In the mid-1980s, the most popular Interior Gateway Routing Protocol was the Routing Information Protocol (RIP). Although RIP was quite useful for routing within small- to moderate-sized, relatively homogeneous internetworks, its limits were being pushed by network growth. In particular, RIP's small hop-count limit (16) restricted the size of internetworks; single metric (hop count) support of only equal-cost load balancing (in all-Cisco networks only!) did not allow for much routing flexibility in complex environments. The popularity of Cisco routers and the robustness of IGRP encouraged many organizations with large internetworks to replace RIP with IGRP.

Cisco's initial IGRP implementation worked in Internet Protocol (IP) networks. IGRP was designed to run in any network environment, however, and Cisco soon ported it to run in OSI Connectionless-Network Protocol (CLNP) networks. Cisco developed Enhanced IGRP in the early 1990s to improve the operating efficiency of IGRP. This chapter discusses IGRP's basic design and implementation. Enhanced IGRP is discussed in Chapter 42, "Enhanced IGRP."

IGRP Protocol Characteristics

IGRP is a *distance vector* Interior Gateway Protocol (IGP). Distance vector routing protocols mathematically compare routes using some measurement of distance. This measurement is known as the distance vector. Routers using a distance vector protocol must send all or a portion of their routing table in a routing-update message at regular intervals to each of their neighboring routers. As routing information proliferates through the network, routers can identify new destinations as they are added to the network, learn of failures in the network, and, most importantly, calculate distances to all known destinations.

Distance vector routing protocols are often contrasted with link-state routing protocols, which send local connection information to all nodes in the internetwork. For a discussion of Open Shortest Path First (OSPF) and Intermediate System-to-Intermediate System (IS-IS), two popular link-state routing algorithms, see Chapter 47, "Open Shortest Path First," and Chapter 48, "Open System Interconnection Routing Protocol," respectively.

IGRP uses a composite metric that is calculated by factoring weighted mathematical values for internetwork delay, bandwidth, reliability, and load. Network administrators can set the weighting factors for each of these metrics, although great care should be taken before any default values are manipulated. IGRP provides a wide range for its metrics. Reliability and load, for example, can take on any value between 1 and 255; bandwidth can take on values reflecting speeds from 1200 bps to 10 Gbps, while delay can take on any value from 1 to 2^{24}. These wide metric ranges are further complemented by a series of user-definable constants that enable a network administrator to influence route selection. These constants are hashed against the metrics, and each other, in an algorithm that yields a single, composite metric. Thus, the network administrator can influence route selection by giving higher or lower weighting to specific metrics. This flexibility allows administrators to fine-tune IGRP's automatic route selection.

To provide additional flexibility, IGRP permits multipath routing. Dual equal-bandwidth lines can run a single stream of traffic in round-robin fashion, with automatic switchover to the second line if one line goes down. Multiple paths can have unequal metrics yet still be valid multipath routes. For example, if one path is three times better than another path (its metric is three times lower), the better path will be used three times as often. Only routes with metrics that are within a certain range or variance of the best route are used as multiple paths. Variance is another value that can be established by the network administrator.

Stability Features

IGRP provides a number of features that are designed to enhance its stability. These include holddowns, split horizons, and poison-reverse updates.

Holddowns are used to prevent regular update messages from inappropriately reinstating a route that might have gone bad. When a router goes down, neighboring routers detect this via the lack of regularly scheduled update messages. These routers then calculate new routes and send routing update messages to inform their neighbors of the route change. This activity begins a wave of triggered updates that filter through the network. These triggered updates do not instantly arrive at every network device. Thus, it is possible for a device that has yet to be informed of a network failure to send a regular update message, which advertises a failed route as being valid to a device that has just been notified of the network failure. In this case, the latter device would contain (and potentially advertise) incorrect routing information. Holddowns tell routers to hold down any changes that might affect routes for some period of time. The holddown period usually is calculated to be just greater than the period of time necessary to update the entire network with a routing change.

Split horizons derive from the premise that it is never useful to send information about a route back in the direction from which it came. Figure 44-1 illustrates the split-horizon rule. Router 1 (R1) advertises that it has a route to Network A. There is no reason for Router 2 (R2) to include this route in its update back to R1 because R1 is closer to Network A. The split-horizon rule says that R2 should strike this route from any updates that it sends to R1. The split-horizon rule helps prevent routing loops. Consider, for example, the case in which R1's interface to Network A goes down. Without split horizons, R2 continues to inform R1 that it can get to Network A (through R1). If R1 does not have sufficient intelligence, it actually might pick up R2's route as an alternative to its failed direct connection, causing a routing loop. Although holddowns should prevent this, split horizons are implemented in IGRP because they provide extra algorithm stability.

Figure 44-1 *The Split-Horizon Rule Helps Protect Against Routing Loops*

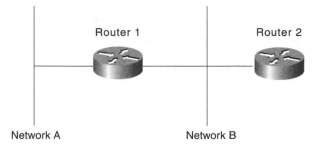

Router 1   Router 2

Network A   Network B

Split horizons should prevent routing loops between adjacent routers, but *poison-reverse updates* are necessary to defeat larger routing loops. Increases in routing metrics generally indicate routing loops. Poison-reverse updates then are sent to remove the route and place it in holddown. In Cisco's implementation of IGRP, poison-reverse updates are sent if a route metric has increased by a factor of 1.1 or greater.

Timers

IGRP maintains a number of timers and variables containing time intervals. These include an update timer, an invalid timer, a hold-time period, and a flush timer. The *update timer* specifies how frequently routing update messages should be sent. The IGRP default for this variable is 90 seconds. The *invalid timer* specifies how long a router should wait in the absence of routing-update messages about a specific route before declaring that route invalid. The IGRP default for this variable is three times the update period. The *hold-time variable* specifies the holddown period. The IGRP default for this variable is three times the update timer period plus 10 seconds. Finally, the *flush timer* indicates how much time should pass before a route should be flushed from the routing table. The IGRP default is seven times the routing update period.

Summary

IGRP has proven to be one of the most successful routing protocols of all time. No small part of its success has been due to its functional similarity to RIP, a simple yet highly successful and widely deployed routing protocol. Cisco took great pains to carefully preserve many of the effective features of RIP, while greatly expanding its capabilities. Today, IGRP is showing its age; it lacks support for variable-length subnet masks (VLSM). Rather than develop an IGRP version 2 to incorporate that capability, Cisco has built upon IGRP's legacy of success with Enhanced IGRP. Enhanced IGRP is examined in Chapter 42 of this book.

Review Questions

1 Name the benefits of using IGRP instead of RIP.

2 How can an administrator influence route selection?

3 What is variance, and how does it affect multipath routing?

4 Identify and explain IGRP's stability features.

5 What timers are used by IGRP, and what is their function?

For More Information

- Sportack, Mark A. *IP Routing Fundamentals.* Indianapolis: Cisco Press, 1999.
- http://www.cisco.com/univercd/cc/td/doc/product/software/ios113ed/ 113ed_cr/np1_c/1cigrp.htm

Objectives

- Explain IP multicast addressing.
- Learn the basics of Internet Group Management Protocol (IGMP).
- Explain how multicast in Layer 2 switching works.
- Define multicast distribution trees.
- Learn how multicast forwarding works.
- Explain the basics of protocol-independent multicast (PIM).
- Define multiprotocol BGP.
- Learn how Multicast Source Discovery Protocol (MSDP) works.
- Explain reliable multicast: PGM.

CHAPTER 45

Internet Protocol Multicast

Background

Internet Protocol (IP) multicast is a bandwidth-conserving technology that reduces traffic by simultaneously delivering a single stream of information to thousands of corporate recipients and homes. Applications that take advantage of multicast include videoconferencing, corporate communications, distance learning, and distribution of software, stock quotes, and news.

IP Multicast delivers source traffic to multiple receivers without adding any additional burden on the source or the receivers while using the least network bandwidth of any competing technology. Multicast packets are replicated in the network by Cisco routers enabled with Protocol Independent Multicast (PIM) and other supporting multicast protocols resulting in the most efficient delivery of data to multiple receivers possible. All alternatives require the source to send more than one copy of the data. Some even require the source to send an individual copy to each receiver. If there are thousands of receivers, even low-bandwidth applications benefit from using Cisco IP Multicast. High-bandwidth applications, such as MPEG video, may require a large portion of the available network bandwidth for a single stream. In these applications, the only way to send to more than one receiver simultaneously is by using IP Multicast. Figure 45-1 demonstrates how data from one source is delivered to several interested recipients using IP multicast.

Figure 45-1   *Multicast Transmission Sends a Single Multicast Packet Addressed to All Intended Recipients*

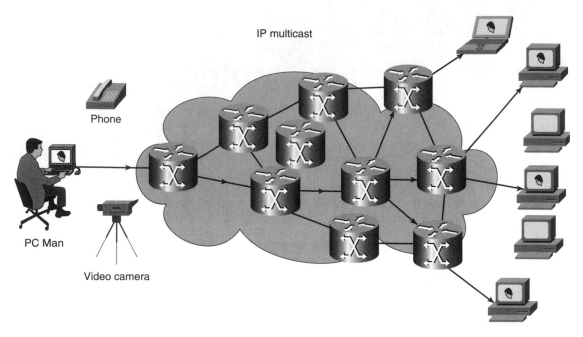

Multicast Group Concept

Multicast is based on the concept of a group. An arbitrary group of receivers expresses an interest in receiving a particular data stream. This group does not have any physical or geographical boundaries—the hosts can be located anywhere on the Internet. Hosts that are interested in receiving data flowing to a particular group must join the group using IGMP. Hosts must be a member of the group to receive the data stream.

IP Multicast Addresses

Multicast addresses specify an arbitrary group of IP hosts that have joined the group and want to receive traffic sent to this group.

IP Class D Addresses

The *Internet Assigned Numbers Authority (IANA)* controls the assignment of IP multicast addresses. It has assigned the old Class D address space to be used for IP multicast. This means that all IP multicast group addresses will fall in the range of 224.0.0.0 to 239.255.255.255.

NOTE   This address range is only for the group address or destination address of IP multicast traffic. The source address for multicast datagrams is always the unicast source address.

Reserved Link Local Addresses

The IANA has reserved addresses in the 224.0.0.0 through 224.0.0.255 to be used by network protocols on a local network segment. Packets with these addresses should never be forwarded by a router; they remain local on a particular LAN segment. They are always transmitted with a time-to-live (TTL) of 1.

Network protocols use these addresses for automatic router discovery and to communicate important routing information. For example, OSPF uses 224.0.0.5 and 224.0.0.6 to exchange link state information. Table 45-1 lists some of the well-known addresses.

Table 45-1   *Link Local Addresses*

Address	Usage
224.0.0.1	All systems on this subnet
224.0.0.2	All routers on this subnet
224.0.0.5	OSPF routers
224.0.0.6	OSPF designated routers
224.0.0.12	DHCP server/relay agent

Globally Scoped Address

The range of addresses from 224.0.1.0 through 238.255.255.255 are called globally scoped addresses. They can be used to multicast data between organizations and across the Internet.

Some of these addresses have been reserved for use by multicast applications through IANA. For example, 224.0.1.1 has been reserved for Network Time Protocol (NTP).

More information about reserved multicast addresses can be found at http://www.isi.edu/in-notes/iana/assignments/multicast-addresses.

Limited Scope Addresses

The range of addresses from 239.0.0.0 through 239.255.255.255 contains limited scope addresses or administratively scoped addresses. These are defined by RFC 2365 to be constrained to a local group or organization. Routers are typically configured with filters to prevent multicast traffic in this address range from flowing outside an autonomous system (AS) or any user-defined domain. Within an autonomous system or domain, the limited scope address range can be further subdivided so those local multicast boundaries can be defined. This also allows for address reuse among these smaller domains.

Glop Addressing

RFC 2770 proposes that the 233.0.0.0/8 address range be reserved for statically defined addresses by organizations that already have an AS number reserved. The AS number of the domain is embedded into the second and third octets of the 233.0.0.0/8 range.

For example, the AS 62010 is written in hex as F23A. Separating out the two octets F2 and 3A, we get 242 and 58 in decimal. This would give us a subnet of 233.242.58.0 that would be globally reserved for AS 62010 to use.

Layer 2 Multicast Addresses

Normally, network interface cards (NICs) on a LAN segment will receive only packets destined for their burned-in MAC address or the broadcast MAC address. Some means had to be devised so that multiple hosts could receive the same packet and still be capable of differentiating among multicast groups.

Fortunately, the IEEE LAN specifications made provisions for the transmission of broadcast and/or multicast packets. In the 802.3 standard, bit 0 of the first octet is used to indicate a broadcast and/or multicast frame. Figure 45-2 shows the location of the broadcast/multicast bit in an Ethernet frame.

Figure 45-2 *IEEE 802.3 MAC Address Format*

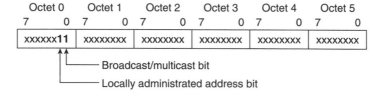

This bit indicates that the frame is destined for an arbitrary group of hosts or all hosts on the network (in the case of the broadcast address, 0xFFFF.FFFF.FFFF).

IP multicast makes use of this capability to transmit IP packets to a group of hosts on a LAN segment.

Ethernet MAC Address Mapping

The IANA owns a block of Ethernet MAC addresses that start with 01:00:5E in hexadecimal. Half of this block is allocated for multicast addresses. This creates the range of available Ethernet MAC addresses to be 0100.5e00.0000 through 0100.5e7f.ffff.

This allocation allows for 23 bits in the Ethernet address to correspond to the IP multicast group address. The mapping places the lower 23 bits of the IP multicast group address into these available 23 bits in the Ethernet address (shown in Figure 45-3).

Figure 45-3 *Mapping of IP Multicast to Ethernet/FDDI MAC Address*

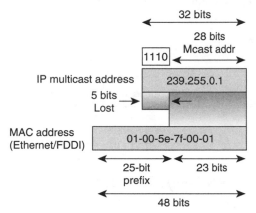

Because the upper 5 bits of the IP multicast address are dropped in this mapping, the resulting address is not unique. In fact, 32 different multicast group IDs all map to the same Ethernet address (see Figure 45-4).

Figure 45-4 *MAC Address Ambiguities*

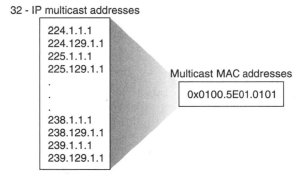

Internet Group Management Protocol

IGMP is used to dynamically register individual hosts in a multicast group on a particular LAN. Hosts identify group memberships by sending IGMP messages to their local multicast router. Under IGMP, routers listen to IGMP messages and periodically send out queries to discover which groups are active or inactive on a particular subnet.

IGMP Version 1

RFC 1112 defines the specification for IGMP Version 1. A diagram of the packet format is found in Figure 45-5.

Figure 45-5 *IGMP Version 1 Packet Format*

0
4
7
15
23
31
Version
Type
Unused
Checksum
Group address

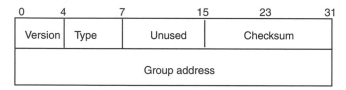

In Version 1, there are just two different types of IGMP messages:

- Membership query
- Membership report

Hosts send out IGMP membership reports corresponding to a particular multicast group to indicate that they are interested in joining that group. The router periodically sends out an IGMP membership query to verify that at least one host on the subnet is still interested in receiving traffic directed to that group. When there is no reply to three consecutive IGMP membership queries, the router times out the group and stops forwarding traffic directed toward that group.

IGMP Version 2

RFC 2236 defines the specification for IGMP Version 2.

A diagram of the packet format follows in Figure 45-6.

Figure 45-6 *IGMPv2 Message Format*

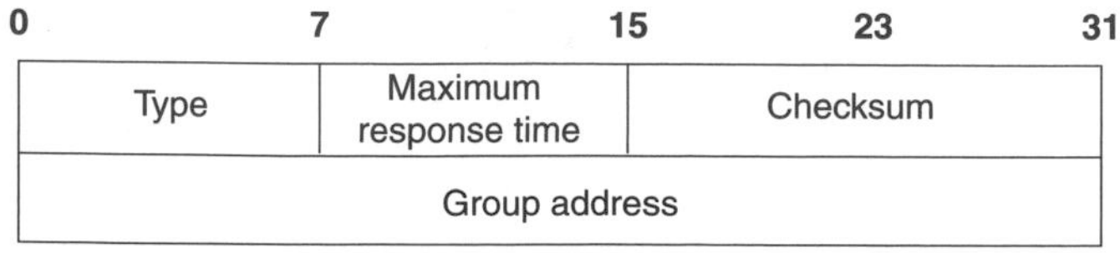

0
7
15
23
31
Type
Maximum response time
Checksum
Group address

In Version 2, there are four types of IGMP messages:

- Membership query
- Version 1 membership report
- Version 2 membership report
- Leave group

IGMP Version 2 works basically the same as Version 1. The main difference is that there is a leave group message. The hosts now can actively communicate to the local multicast router their intention to leave the group. The router then sends out a group-specific query and determines whether there are any remaining hosts interested in receiving the traffic. If there are no replies, the router times out the group and stops forwarding the traffic. This can greatly reduce the leave latency compared to IGMP Version 1. Unwanted and unnecessary traffic can be stopped much sooner.

Multicast in the Layer 2 Switching Environment

The default behavior for a Layer 2 switch is to forward all multicast traffic to every port that belongs to the destination LAN on the switch. This would defeat the purpose of the switch, which is to limit traffic to the ports that need to receive the data.

Two methods exist by which to deal with multicast in a Layer 2 switching environment efficiently—Cisco Group Management Protocol (CGMP) and IGMP snooping.

Cisco Group Management Protocol

CGMP is a Cisco-developed protocol that allows Catalyst switches to leverage IGMP information on Cisco routers to make Layer 2 forwarding decisions. CGMP must be configured both on the multicast routers and on the Layer 2 switches. The net result is that with CGMP, IP multicast traffic is delivered only to those Catalyst switch ports that are interested in the traffic. All other ports that have not explicitly requested the traffic will not receive it.

The basic concept of CGMP is shown in Figure 45-7. When a host joins a multicast group (part A), it multicasts an unsolicited IGMP membership report message to the target group (224.1.2.3, in this example). The IGMP report is passed through the switch to the router for the normal IGMP processing. The router (which must have CGMP enabled on this interface) receives this IGMP report and processes it as it normally would, but in addition it creates a CGMP join message and sends it to the switch.

The switch receives this CGMP join message and then adds the port to its content addressable memory (CAM) table for that multicast group. Subsequent traffic directed to this multicast group will be forwarded out the port for that host. The router port is also added to the entry for the multicast group. Multicast routers must listen to all multicast traffic for every group because the IGMP control messages are also sent as multicast traffic. With CGMP, the switch must listen only to CGMP join and CGMP leave messages from the router. The rest of the multicast traffic is forwarded using its CAM table exactly the way the switch was designed.

Figure 45-7 *Basic CGMP Operation*

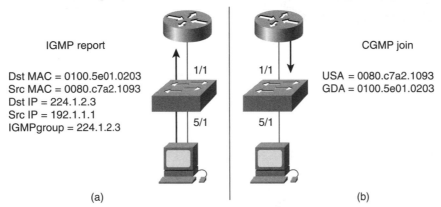

IGMP report

Dst MAC = 0100.5e01.0203
Src MAC = 0080.c7a2.1093
Dst IP = 224.1.2.3
Src IP = 192.1.1.1
IGMPgroup = 224.1.2.3

CGMP join

USA = 0080.c7a2.1093
GDA = 0100.5e01.0203

(a)

(b)

IGMP Snooping

IGMP snooping requires the LAN switch to examine, or snoop, some Layer 3 information in the IGMP packets sent between the hosts and the router. When the switch hears the IGMP host report from a host for a particular multicast group, the switch adds the host's port number to the associated multicast table entry. When the switch hears the IGMP leave group message from a host, it removes the host's port from the table entry.

Because IGMP control messages are transmitted as multicast packets, they are indistinguishable from multicast data at Layer 2. A switch running IGMP snooping examine every multicast data packet to check whether it contains any pertinent IGMP must control information. If IGMP snooping has been implemented on a low-end switch with a slow CPU, this could have a severe performance impact when data is transmitted at high rates. The solution is to implement IGMP snooping on high-end switches with special ASICs that can perform the IGMP checks in hardware. CGMP is ideal for low-end switches without special hardware.

Multicast Distribution Trees

Multicast-capable routers create distribution trees that control the path that IP multicast traffic takes through the network to deliver traffic to all receivers. The two basic types of multicast distribution trees are source trees and shared trees.

Source Trees

The simplest form of a multicast distribution tree is a *source tree* whose root is the source of the multicast tree and whose branches form a spanning tree through the network to the receivers. Because this tree uses the shortest path through the network, it is also referred to as a shortest path tree (SPT).

Figure 45-8 shows an example of an SPT for group 224.1.1.1 rooted at the source, Host A, and connecting two receivers, hosts B and C.

Figure 45-8 *Host A Shortest Path Tree*

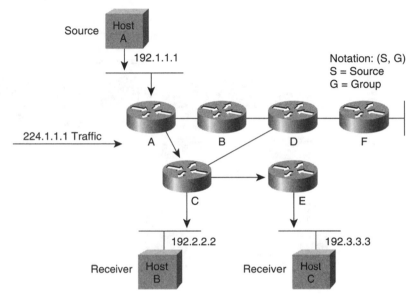

The special notation of (S,G), pronounced "S comma G," enumerates an SPT in which S is the IP address of the source and G is the multicast group address. Using this notation, the SPT for the example in Figure 45-7 would be (192.1.1.1, 224.1.1.1).

The (S,G) notation implies that a separate SPT exists for each individual source sending to each group, which is correct. For example, if Host B is also sending traffic to group 224.1.1.1 and hosts A and C are receivers, then a separate (S,G) SPT would exist with a notation of (192.2.2.2,224.1.1.1).

Shared Trees

Unlike source trees that have their root at the source, *shared trees* use a single common root placed at some chosen point in the network. This shared root is called the *rendezvous point (RP)*.

Figure 45-9 shows a shared tree for the group 224.2.2.2 with the root located at Router D. When using a shared tree, sources must send their traffic to the root, and then the traffic is forwarded down the shared tree to reach all receivers.

Figure 45-9 *Shared Distribution Tree*

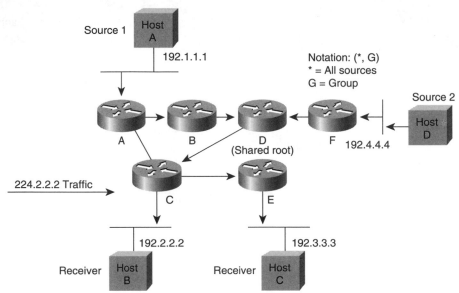

In this example, multicast traffic from the source hosts A and D travels to the root (Router D) and then down the shared tree to the two receivers, hosts B and C. Because all sources in the multicast group use a common shared tree, a wildcard notation written as (*, G), pronounced "star comma G," represents the tree. In this case, * means all sources, and the G represents the multicast group. Therefore, the shared tree shown in Figure 45-8 would be written as (*, 224.2.2.2).

Both SPT and shared trees are loop-free. Messages are replicated only where the tree branches.

Members of multicast groups can join or leave at any time, so the distribution trees must be dynamically updated. When all the active receivers on a particular branch stop requesting the traffic for a particular multicast group, the routers prune that branch from the distribution tree and stop forwarding traffic down that branch. If one receiver on that branch becomes active and requests the multicast traffic, the router dynamically modifies the distribution tree and starts forwarding traffic again.

Shortest path trees have the advantage of creating the optimal path between the source and the receivers. This guarantees the minimum amount of network latency for forwarding multicast traffic. This optimization does come with a price, though: The routers must maintain path information for each source. In a network that has thousands of sources and thousands of groups, this can quickly become a resource issue on the routers. Memory consumption from the size of the multicast routing table is a factor that network designers must take into consideration.

Shared trees have the advantage of requiring the minimum amount of state in each router. This lowers the overall memory requirements for a network that allows only shared trees. The disadvantage of shared trees is that, under certain circumstances, the paths between the source and receivers might not be the optimal paths—which might introduce some latency in packet delivery. Network designers must carefully consider the placement of the RP when implementing an environment with only shared trees.

Multicast Forwarding

In unicast routing, traffic is routed through the network along a single path from the source to the destination host. A unicast router does not really care about the source address—it only cares about the destination address and how to forward the traffic towards that destination. The router scans through its routing table and then forwards a single copy of the unicast packet out the correct interface in the direction of the destination.

In multicast routing, the source is sending traffic to an arbitrary group of hosts represented by a multicast group address. The multicast router must determine which direction is upstream (toward the source) and which direction (or directions) is downstream. If there are multiple downstream paths, the router replicates the packet and forwards the traffic down the appropriate downstream paths—which is not necessarily all paths. This concept of forwarding multicast traffic away from the source, rather than to the receiver, is called *reverse path forwarding*.

Reverse Path Forwarding

Reverse path forwarding (RPF) is a fundamental concept in multicast routing that enables routers to correctly forward multicast traffic down the distribution tree. RPF makes use of the existing unicast routing table to determine the upstream and downstream neighbors. A router forwards a multicast packet only if it is received on the upstream interface. This RPF check helps to guarantee that the distribution tree will be loop-free.

RPF Check

When a multicast packet arrives at a router, the router performs an RPF check on the packet. If the RPF check is successful, the packet is forwarded. Otherwise, it is dropped.

For traffic flowing down a source tree, the RPF check procedure works as follows:

Step 1   Router looks up the source address in the unicast routing table to determine whether it has arrived on the interface that is on the reverse path back to the source.

Step 2   If packet has arrived on the interface leading back to the source, the RPF check is successful and the packet is forwarded.

Step 3   If the RPF check in Step 2 fails, the packet is dropped.

Figure 45-10 shows an example of an unsuccessful RPF check.

Figure 45-10 *RPF Check Fails*

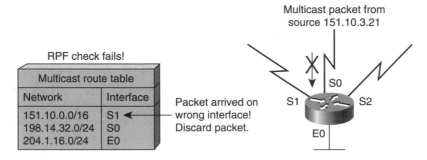

A multicast packet from source 151.10.3.21 is received on interface S0. A check of the unicast route table shows that the interface that this router would use to forward unicast data to 151.10.3.21 is S1. Because the packet has arrived on S0, the packet will be discarded.

Figure 45-11 shows an example of a successful RPF check.

Figure 45-11 *RPF Check Succeeds*

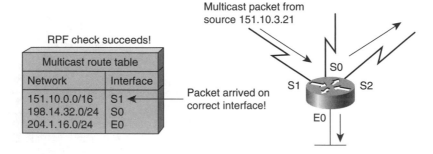

This time the multicast packet has arrived on S1. The router checks the unicast routing table and finds that S1 is the correct interface. The RPF check passes and the packet is forwarded.

Protocol-Independent Multicast

Protocol-independent multicast (PIM) gets its name from the fact that it is IP routing protocol-independent. PIM can leverage whichever unicast routing protocols are used to populate the unicast routing table, including EIGRP, OSPF, BGP, or static routes. PIM uses this unicast routing information to perform the multicast forwarding function, so it is IP protocol-independent. Although PIM is called a multicast routing protocol, it actually uses the unicast routing table to perform the reverse path forwarding (RPF) check function instead of building up a completely independent multicast routing table. PIM does not send and receive multicast routing updates between routers like other routing protocols do.

PIM Dense Mode

PIM Dense Mode (PIM-DM) uses a push model to flood multicast traffic to every corner of the network. This is a brute-force method for delivering data to the receivers, but in certain applications, this might be an efficient mechanism if there are active receivers on every subnet in the network.

PIM-DM initially floods multicast traffic throughout the network. Routers that do not have any downstream neighbors prune back the unwanted traffic. This process repeats every 3 minutes.

The flood and prune mechanism is how the routers accumulate their state information—by receiving the data stream. These data streams contain the source and group information so that downstream routers can build up their multicast forwarding tables. PIM-DM can support only source trees—(S,G) entries. It cannot be used to build a shared distribution tree.

PIM Sparse Mode

PIM Sparse Mode (PIM-SM) uses a pull model to deliver multicast traffic. Only networks that have active receivers that have explicitly requested the data will be forwarded the traffic. PIM-SM is defined in RFC 2362.

PIM-SM uses a shared tree to distribute the information about active sources. Depending on the configuration options, the traffic can remain on the shared tree or switch over to an optimized source distribution tree. The latter is the default behavior for PIM-SM on Cisco routers. The traffic starts to flow down the shared tree, and then routers along the path determine whether there is a better path to the source. If a better, more direct path exists, the designated router (the router closest to the receiver) will send a join message toward the source and then reroute the traffic along this path.

PIM-SM has the concept of an RP, since it uses shared trees—at least initially. The RP must be administratively configured in the network. Sources register with the RP, and then data is forwarded down the shared tree to the receivers. If the shared tree is not an optimal path between the source and the receiver, the routers dynamically create a source tree and stop traffic from flowing down the shared tree. This is the default behavior in IOS. Network administrators can force traffic to stay on the shared tree by using a configuration option (lp pim spt-threshold infinity).

PIM-SM scales well to a network of any size, including those with WAN links. The explicit join mechanism prevents unwanted traffic from flooding the WAN links.

Sparse-Dense Mode

Cisco has implemented an alternative to choosing just dense mode or just sparse mode on a router interface new IP. This was necessitated by a change in the paradigm for forwarding multicast traffic via PIM that became apparent during its development. It turned out that it was more efficient to choose sparse or dense on a per group basis rather than a per router interface basis. Sparse-dense mode facilitates this ability.

Network administrators can also configure sparse-dense mode. This configuration option allows individual groups to be run in either sparse or dense mode, depending on whether RP information is available for that group. If the router learns RP information for a particular group, it will be treated as sparse mode; otherwise, that group will be treated as dense mode.

Multiprotocol Border Gateway Protocol

Multiprotocol Border Gateway Protocol (MBGP) gives a method for providers to distinguish which route prefixes they will use for performing multicast RPF checks. The RPF check is the fundamental mechanism that routers use to determine the paths that multicast forwarding trees will follow and successfully deliver multicast content from sources to receivers.

MBGP is described in RFC 2283, Multiprotocol Extensions for BGP-4. Since MBGP is an extension of BGP, it brings along all the administrative machinery that providers and customers like in their interdomain routing environment. Including all the inter-AS tools to filter and control routing (e.g., route maps). Therefore, by using MBGP, any network utilizing internal or external BGP can apply the multiple policy control knobs familiar in BGP to specify routing (and thereby forwarding) policy for multicast.

Two path attributes, MP_REACH_NLRI and MP_UNREACH_NLRI have been introduced in BGP4+. These new attributes create a simple way to carry two sets of routing information—one for unicast routing and one for multicast routing. The routes associated with multicast routing are used to build the multicast distribution trees.

The main advantage of MBGP is that an internet can support noncongruent unicast and multicast topologies. When the unicast and multicast topologies are congruent, MBGP can support different policies for each. MBGP provides a scalable policy based interdomain routing protocol.

Multicast Source Discovery Protocol

In the PIM Sparse mode model, multicast sources and receivers must register with their local Rendezvous Point (RP). Actually, the closest router to the sources or receivers registers with the RP but the point is that the RP knows about all the sources and receivers for any particular group. RPs in other domains have no way of knowing about sources located in other domains. MSDP is an elegant way to solve this problem. MSDP is a mechanism that connects PIM-SM domains and allows RPs to share information about active sources. When RPs in remote domains know about active sources they can pass on that information to their local receivers and multicast data can be forwarded between the domains. A nice feature of MSDP is that it allows each domain to maintain an independent RP which does not rely on other domains, but it does enable RPs to forward traffic between domains.

The RP in each domain establishes an MSDP peering session using a TCP connection with the RPs in other domains or with border routers leading to the other domains. When the RP learns about a new multicast source within its own domain (through the normal PIM register mechanism), the RP encapsulates the first data packet in a Source Active (SA) message and sends the SA to all MSDP peers. The SA is forwarded by each receiving peer using a modified RPF check, until it reaches every MSDP router in the interconnected networks—theoretically the entire multicast internet. If the receiving MSDP peer is an RP, and the RP has a (*,G) entry for the group in the SA (there is an interested receiver), the RP will create (S,G) state for the source and join to the shortest path tree for the state of the source. The encapsulated data is decapsulated and forwarded down that RP's shared tree. When the packet is received by a receiver's last hop router, the last-hop may also join the shortest path tree to the source. The source's RP periodically sends SAs, which include all sources within that RP's own domain. Figure 45-12 shows how data would flow between a source in domain A to a receiver in domain E.

Figure 45-12 *MSDP Example*

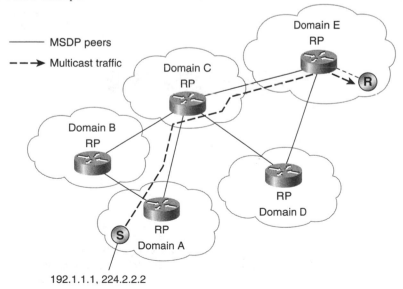

192.1.1.1, 224.2.2.2

MDSP was developed for peering between Internet Service Providers (ISPs). ISPs did not want to rely on an RP maintained by a competing ISP to service their customers. MSDP allows each ISP to have their own local RP and still forward and receive multicast traffic to the Internet.

Anycast RP—Logical RP

A very useful application of MSDP is called anycast RP. This is a technique for configuring a multicast sparse-mode network to provide for fault tolerance and load sharing within a single multicast domain.

Two or more RPs are configured with the same IP address on loopback interfaces—say, 10.0.0.1, for example (refer to Figure 45-13). The loopback address should be configured as a 32 bit address. All the downstream routers are configured so that they know that their local RP's address is 10.0.0.1. IP routing automatically selects the topologically closest RP for each source and receiver. Because some sources might end up using one RP and some receivers a different RP, there needs to be some way for the RPs to exchange information about active sources. This is done with MSDP. All the RPs are configured to be MSDP peers of each other. Each RP will know about the active sources in the other RP's area. If any of the RPs fail, IP routing will converge and one of the RPs will become the active RP in both areas.

NOTE   The Anycast RP example above uses IP addresses from RFC 1918. These IP addresses are normally blocked at interdomain borders and therefore are not accessible to other ISPs. You must use valid IP addresses if you want the RPs to be reachable from other domains.

Figure 45-13 *Anycast RP*

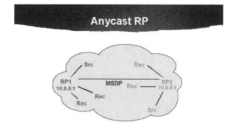

NOTE   The RPs are used only to set up the initial connection between sources and receivers. After the last-hop routers join the shortest path tree, the RP is no longer necessary.

Multicast Address Dynamic Client Allocation Protocol

The *Multicast Address Dynamic Client Allocation Protocol (MADCAP)* is defined in RFC 2730 as a protocol that allows hosts to request a multicast address allocation dynamically from a MADCAP server. The concept is very similar to the way DHCP works today and is built on a client/server model.

Multicast-Scope Zone Announcement Protocol

Multicast-Scope Zone Announcement Protocol (MZAP) is defined in RFC 2776 as a protocol that allows networks to automatically discover administratively scoped zones relative to a particular location.

Reliable Multicast—Pragmatic General Multicast

Pragmatic General Multicast (PGM) is a reliable multicast transport protocol for applications that require ordered, duplicate-free, multicast data delivery from multiple sources to multiple receivers. PGM guarantees that a receiver in a multicast group either receives all data packets from transmissions and retransmissions, or can detect unrecoverable data packet loss.

The PGM Reliable Transport Protocol itself is implemented on the sources and the receivers. The source maintains a transmit window of outgoing data packets and retransmits individual packets when it receives a negative acknowledgment (NAK). The network elements (routers) assist in suppressing an implosion of NAKs (when a failure does occur) and aids in efficient forwarding of the retransmitted data just to the networks that need it.

PGM is intended as a solution for multicast applications with basic reliability requirements. The specification for PGM is network layer-independent. The Cisco implementation of PGM Router Assist supports PGM over IP.

Today, the specification for PGM is an Internet draft that can be found on the IETF web site (http://www.ietf.org) under the name "PGM Reliable Transport Protocol."

Review Questions

1 What is the range of available IP multicast addresses?

2 What is the purpose of IGMP?

3 What is an advantage of IGMPv2 over IGMPv1?

4 What is a potential disadvantage of IGMP snooping over CGMP on a low-end Layer 2 switch?

5   What is an advantage of shortest path (or source) trees compared to shared trees?

6   What is an advantage of using shared trees?

7   What information does the router use to do an RPF check?

8   Why is protocol-independent multicast called "independent"?

9   What is the main advantage of MBGP?

10   How do RPs learn about sources from other RPs with MSDP?

11   What is the purpose of the anycast RP?

For More Information

- Williamson, Beau. *Developing IP Multicast Networks*. Indianapolis: Cisco Press, 2000.

- Multicast Quick Start Configuration Guide (http://www.cisco.com/warp/customer/105/48.html)

Objectives

- Describe the Network Link-Service Protocol.
- Describe routing with NLSP.
- Describe the data packet used by NLSP.

NetWare Link-Services Protocol

Background

The *NetWare Link-Services Protocol (NLSP)* is a link-state routing protocol from Novell designed to overcome some of the limitations associated with the IPX Routing Information Protocol (RIP) and its companion protocol, the Service Advertisement Protocol (SAP). NLSP is based on the OSI Intermediate System-to-Intermediate System (IS-IS) protocol and was designed to replace RIP and SAP, Novell's original routing protocols that were designed when internetworks were local and relatively small. As such, RIP and SAP are not well suited for today's large, global internetworks. This chapter summarizes the routing processes and protocol components of NLSP.

Compared to RIP and SAP, NLSP provides improved routing, better efficiency, and scalability. In addition, NLSP-based routers are backward compatible with RIP-based routers. NLSP-based routers use a reliable delivery protocol, so delivery is guaranteed. Furthermore, NLSP facilitates improved routing decisions because NLSP-based routers store a complete map of the network, not just next-hop information such as RIP-based routers use. Routing information is transmitted only when the topology has changed, not every 60 seconds as RIP-based routers do, regardless of whether the topology has changed. Additionally, NLSP-based routers send service-information updates only when services change, not every 60 seconds as SAP does.

NLSP is efficient in several ways. It is particularly useful over a WAN link because its support of IPX header compression makes it possible to reduce the size of packets. NLSP also supports multicast addressing so that routing information is sent only to other NLSP routers, not to all devices, as RIP does.

In addition, NLSP supports load balancing across parallel paths and improves link integrity. It periodically checks links for connectivity and for the data integrity of routing information. If a link fails, NLSP switches to an alternate link and updates the network topology databases stored in each node when connectivity changes occur anywhere in the routing area.

In terms of scalability, NLSP can support up to 127 hops (RIP supports only 15 hops) and permits hierarchical addressing of network nodes, which allows networks to contain thousands of LANs and servers.

NLSP Hierarchical Routing

NLSP supports hierarchical routing with area, domain, and global internetwork components. An *area* is a collection of connected networks that all have the same area address. A *domain* is a collection of areas that belong to the same organization. A *global internetwork* is a collection of domains that usually belong to different organizations, but with an arms-length relationship. Areas can be linked to create routing domains, and domains can be linked to create a global internetwork.

NLSP supports three levels of hierarchical routing: Level 1, Level 2, and Level 3 routing. A Level 1 router connects network segments within a given routing area. A Level 2 router connects areas and also acts as a Level 1 router within its own area. A Level 3 router connects domains and also acts as a Level 2 router within its own domain. Figure 46-1 illustrates the three routing levels NLSP defines.

Figure 46-1 *NLSP Defines Three Routing Levels*

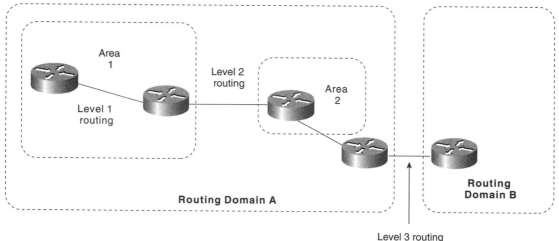

Hierarchical Routing Efficiencies

Hierarchical routing simplifies the process of enlarging a network by reducing the amount of information that every router must store and process to route packets within a domain. A Level 1 router is required to keep detailed information only about its own area instead of storing link-state information for every router and network segment in its domain. To exchange traffic with other areas, a Level 1 router must find only the nearest Level 2 router. Between areas, Level 2 routers advertise the area address(es) only for their respective areas, not their entire link-state databases. Level 3 routers perform similarly between domains.

NLSP Adjacencies

By exchanging hello packets, a router determines the reachability of its neighbors and uses this information to establish adjacency. Adjacency is a record that a router keeps about the state of its connectivity with a neighbor and the attributes of the neighboring router. The router stores these records in its adjacency database.

Adjacency-establishment procedures vary depending upon whether the router is establishing and maintaining adjacencies over a WAN or a LAN.

Establishing router adjacency over a WAN involves first establishing the underlying data-link connection (details depend upon the medium). The routers then exchange identities by using the IPX WAN Version 2 protocol and determine certain operational characteristics of the link. Hello packets are exchanged, and the routers update their adjacency databases. The routers then exchange both link-state packets (LSPs) describing the state of their links and IPX data packets over the link. To maintain a WAN link, the router maintains a state variable indicating whether the link is up, down, or initializing for each adjacency. If the router does not hear from a neighbor within the time specified in a holding timer, the router generates a message indicating that the link is down and deletes the adjacency.

WAN hello packets enable routers to discover each other's identity, to decide whether they are in the same routing area, and to determine whether other routers and links are operational. A router sends hello packets when the circuit is first established, when a timer expires, or when the contents of the next hello to be transmitted are different than the contents of the previous hello transmitted by this system (and one or more seconds have elapsed since the previous hello). Hello packets are sent as long as the circuit exists.

Establishing a New WAN Adjacency

A typical startup procedure between two routers (A and B) on a WAN link begins with the link in the down state. Router A sends a WAN hello indicating the down state to Router B, which changes its state for the link to initializing. Router B sends a WAN hello with a field indicating its initializing state to Router A. Router A then changes its state for the link to initializing and sends a WAN hello with a field indicating this to Router B. Router B changes its state for the link to the up state and sends a WAN hello with a field indicating its new state. Finally, Router A changes its state for the link to up.

Maintaining Adjacencies over LANs

When a broadcast circuit, such as an 802.3 Ethernet and 802.5 Token Ring, is enabled on a router, the router begins sending and accepting hello packets from other routers on the LAN and starts the designated router election process.

The designated router represents the LAN as a whole in the link-state database, makes routing decisions on behalf of the whole, and originates LSPs on behalf of the LAN. This ensures that the size of the link-state databases that each router must construct and manage stay within reasonable limits.

Periodically, every router sends a multicast hello packet on the LAN. The router with the highest priority (a configurable parameter) becomes the Level 1 designated router on the LAN. In case of a tie, the router with the higher MAC address wins.

Sending LAN Hello Packets

Hello packets enable routers on the broadcast circuit to discover the identity of the other Level 1 routers in the same routing area on that circuit. The packets are sent immediately when any circuit has been enabled to a special multicast destination address. Routers listen on this address for arriving hello packets.

NLSP Operation

An NLSP router extracts certain information from the adjacency database and adds locally derived information. Using this information, the router constructs a link-state packet (LSP) that describes its immediate neighbors. All LSPs constructed by all routers in the routing area make up the link-state database for the area.

The NLSP specification intends for each router to maintain a copy of the link-state database and to keep these copies synchronized with each other. The link-state database is synchronized by reliably propagating LSPs throughout the routing area when a router observes a topology change. Two methods ensure that accurate topology-change information is propagated: flooding and receipt confirmation.

Flooding is instigated when a router detects a topology change. When such a change is detected, the router constructs a new LSP and transmits it to each of its neighbors. Such LSPs are directed packets on a WAN and multicast packets on a LAN. Upon receiving an LSP, the router uses the sequence number in the packet to decide whether the packet is newer than the current copy stored in its database. If it is a newer LSP, the router retransmits it to all its neighbors (except on the circuit over which the LSP was received).

The receipt-confirmation process is different for LANs and WANs. On WANs, a router receiving an LSP replies with an acknowledgment. On LANs, no explicit acknowledgment occurs, but the designated router periodically multicasts a packet called a complete sequence number packet (CSNP) that contains all the LSP identifiers and sequence numbers that it has in its database for the entire area. This ensures that other routers can detect whether they are out of synchronization with the designated router.

NLSP Hierarchical Addressing

NLSP supports a hierarchical addressing scheme. Each routing area is identified by two 32-bit quantities: a network address and a mask. This pair of numbers is called an area address. Expressed in hexadecimal, an example of an area address follows:

- **01234500**—This number is the network address for this routing area. Every network number within that area starts with the identification code 012345.

- **FFFFFF00**—This number is the mask that identifies how much of the network address refers to the area itself and how much refers to individual networks within the area.

In this example area address, the first 24 bits (012345) identify the routing area. The remaining 8 bits are used to identify individual network numbers within the routing area (for example, 012345AB, 012345C1, 01234511). Figure 46-2 highlights these addressing concepts with three different networks in a single area.

Figure 46-2 *NLSP Addresses Consist of a Network Address and a Mask*

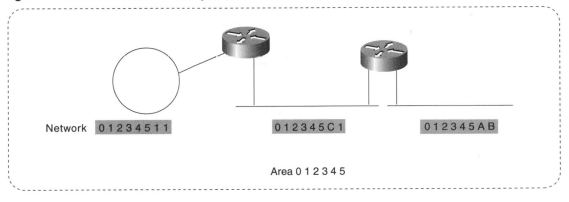

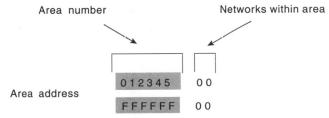

A routing area can have as many as three different area addresses, each with a different mask. Having more than one area address allows the routing area to be reorganized without interrupting operations. Any combination of area addresses can be used within a domain.

NLSP Hello Packets

Two types of NLSP hello packets exist: WAN hello and Level 1 LAN hello packets.

WAN Hello Packet

Figure 46-3 illustrates the fields of a WAN hello packet.

Figure 46-3 *Fourteen Fields Make Up a WAN Hello Packet*

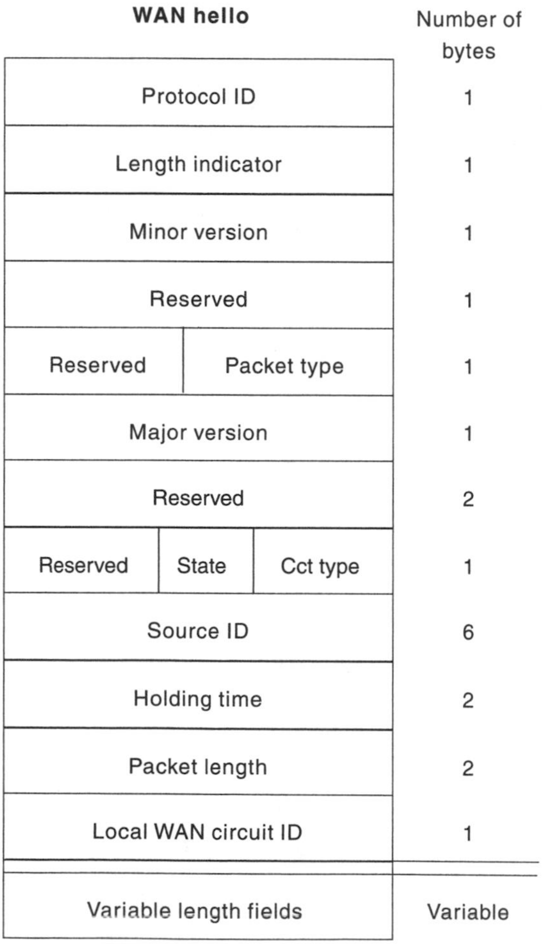

WAN hello — Number of bytes

Field	Number of bytes
Protocol ID	1
Length indicator	1
Minor version	1
Reserved	1
Reserved / Packet type	1
Major version	1
Reserved	2
Reserved / State / Cct type	1
Source ID	6
Holding time	2
Packet length	2
Local WAN circuit ID	1
Variable length fields	Variable

WAN Hello Packet Fields

The following WAN hello packet field descriptions summarize each field illustrated in Figure 46-3.

- **Protocol ID**—Identifies the NLSP routing layer with the 0x83 hex number.
- **Length indicator**—Determines the number of bytes in the fixed portion of the header.
- **Minor version**—Contains one possible decimal value and is ignored on receipt.
- **Reserved**—Contains no decimal values and is ignored on receipt.
- **Packet type (5 bits)**—Contains 17 possible decimal values.
- **Major version**—Contains one possible decimal value.
- **Reserved**—Contains no decimal values and is ignored on receipt.
- **State (2 bits)**—Sends the router's state associated with the link (0 = up, 1 = initializing, 2 = down).
- **Circuit type (Cct type)**—Consists of 2 bits. This field can have one of the following values:
    - **0**—Reserved value; ignore entire packet.
    - **1**—Level 1 routing only.
    - **2**—Level 2 routing only. (The sender uses this link for Level 2 routing.)
    - **3**—Both Level 1 and Level 2. (The sender is a Level 2 router and uses this link for Level 1 and Level 2 traffic.)
- **Source ID**—Serves as the system identifier of the sending router.
- **Holding time**—Contains the holding timer, in seconds, to be used for the sending router.
- **Packet length**—Determines the entire length of the packet, in bytes, including the NLSP header.
- **Local WAN circuit ID**—Acts as a unique identifier assigned to this circuit when it is created by the router.
- **Variable length field**—Consists of a series of optional fields.

NLSP LAN Hello Packets

Figure 46-4 illustrates the fields of a LAN Level 1 hello packet.

Figure 46-4 *A LAN Level 1 Hello Packet Consists of 16 Fields*

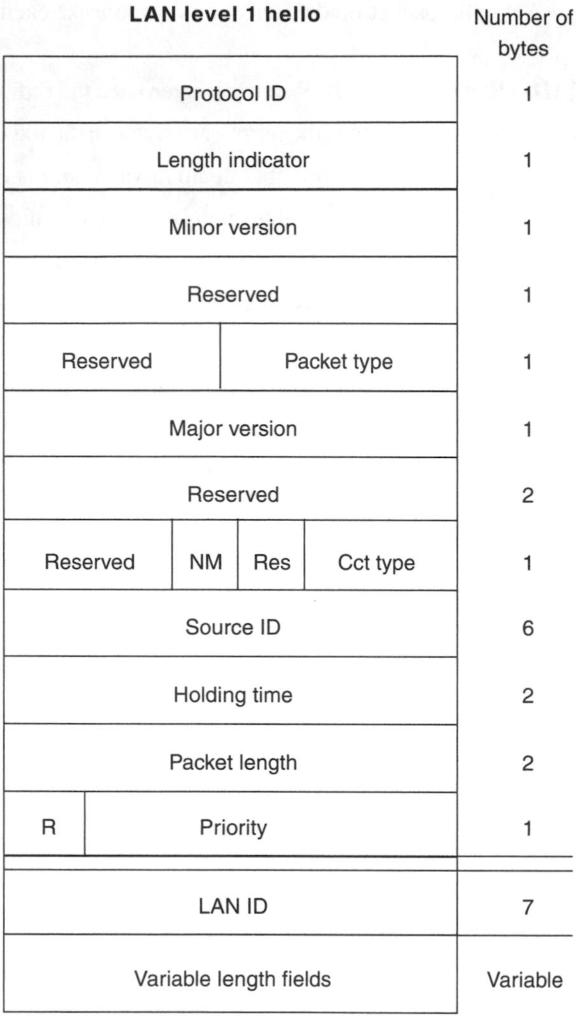

LAN level 1 hello	Number of bytes
Protocol ID	1
Length indicator	1
Minor version	1
Reserved	1
Reserved / Packet type	1
Major version	1
Reserved	2
Reserved / NM / Res / Cct type	1
Source ID	6
Holding time	2
Packet length	2
R / Priority	1
LAN ID	7
Variable length fields	Variable

Level 1 LAN Hello Packet Fields

The following Level 1 LAN Hello packet field descriptions summarize each field illustrated in Figure 46-4:

- **Protocol ID**—Identifies the NLSP routing layer with the 0x83 hex number.
- **Length indicator**—Determines the number of bytes in the fixed portion of the header (up to and including the LAN ID field).
- **Minor version**—Contains one possible decimal value and is ignored on receipt.

- **Reserved**—Contains no possible decimal values and is ignored on receipt.
- **Packet type (5 bits)**—Contains 15 possible decimal values.
- **Major version**—Contains one possible decimal value.
- **Reserved**—Contains no possible decimal values and is ignored on receipt.
- **No multicast (NM) (1 bit)**—Indicates, when set to 1, that the packet sender cannot receive traffic addressed to a multicast address. (Future packets on this LAN must be sent to the broadcast address.)
- **Circuit type (Cct Type) (2 bits)**—Can have one of the following values:
  - **0**—Reserved value; ignore entire packet.
  - **1**—Level 1 routing only.
  - **2**—Level 2 routing only. (The sender uses this link for Level 2 routing.)
  - **3**—Both Level 1 and Level 2. (The sender is a Level 2 router and uses this link for Level 1 and Level 2 traffic.)
- **Source ID**—Contains the system ID of the sending router.
- **Holding time**—Contains the holding timer, in seconds, to be used for the sending router.
- **Packet length**—Determines the entire length of the packet, in bytes, including the NLSP header.
- **R**—Contains no possible decimal values and is ignored on receipt.
- **Priority (7 bits)**—Serves as the priority associated with being the LAN Level 1 designated router. (Higher numbers have higher priority.)
- **LAN ID**—Contains the system ID (6 bytes) of the LAN Level 1 designated router, followed by a field assigned by that designated router.
- **Variable length fields**—Consists of a series of optional fields.

Review Questions

1 What is the purpose of a Layer 2 router within the NLSP hierarchical routing scheme?

2 How long are hello packets sent after a router is initialized and reaches a fully functional state?

3 What type of LSPs are sent over a WAN—directed or multicast?

Objectives

- Discuss the use of autonomous systems.
- Describe the use of the Sorts Path First algorithm.
- Discuss the additional features of OSPF.

CHAPTER 47

Open Shortest Path First

Background

Open Shortest Path First (OSPF) is a routing protocol developed for Internet Protocol (IP) networks by the Interior Gateway Protocol (IGP) working group of the Internet Engineering Task Force (IETF). The working group was formed in 1988 to design an IGP based on the Shortest Path First (SPF) algorithm for use in the Internet. Similar to the Interior Gateway Routing Protocol (IGRP), OSPF was created because in the mid-1980s, the Routing Information Protocol (RIP) was increasingly incapable of serving large, heterogeneous internetworks. This chapter examines the OSPF routing environment, underlying routing algorithm, and general protocol components.

OSPF was derived from several research efforts, including Bolt, Beranek, and Newman's (BBN's) SPF algorithm developed in 1978 for the ARPANET (a landmark packet-switching network developed in the early 1970s by BBN), Dr. Radia Perlman's research on fault-tolerant broadcasting of routing information (1988), BBN's work on area routing (1986), and an early version of OSI's Intermediate System-to-Intermediate System (IS-IS) routing protocol.

OSPF has two primary characteristics. The first is that the protocol is open, which means that its specification is in the public domain. The OSPF specification is published as Request For Comments (RFC) 1247. The second principal characteristic is that OSPF is based on the SPF algorithm, which sometimes is referred to as the Dijkstra algorithm, named for the person credited with its creation.

OSPF is a link-state routing protocol that calls for the sending of link-state advertisements (LSAs) to all other routers within the same hierarchical area. Information on attached interfaces, metrics used, and other variables is included in OSPF LSAs. As OSPF routers accumulate link-state information, they use the SPF algorithm to calculate the shortest path to each node.

As a link-state routing protocol, OSPF contrasts with RIP and IGRP, which are distance-vector routing protocols. Routers running the distance-vector algorithm send all or a portion of their routing tables in routing-update messages to their neighbors.

Routing Hierarchy

Unlike RIP, OSPF can operate within a hierarchy. The largest entity within the hierarchy is the autonomous system (AS), which is a collection of networks under a common administration that share a common routing strategy. OSPF is an intra-AS (interior gateway) routing protocol, although it is capable of receiving routes from and sending routes to other ASs.

An AS can be divided into a number of areas, which are groups of contiguous networks and attached hosts. Routers with multiple interfaces can participate in multiple areas. These routers, which are called Area Border Routers, maintain separate topological databases for each area.

A topological database is essentially an overall picture of networks in relationship to routers. The topological database contains the collection of LSAs received from all routers in the same area. Because routers within the same area share the same information, they have identical topological databases.

The term *domain* sometimes is used to describe a portion of the network in which all routers have identical topological databases. Domain is frequently used interchangeably with AS.

An area's topology is invisible to entities outside the area. By keeping area topologies separate, OSPF passes less routing traffic than it would if the AS were not partitioned.

Area partitioning creates two different types of OSPF routing, depending on whether the source and the destination are in the same or different areas. Intra-area routing occurs when the source and destination are in the same area; interarea routing occurs when they are in different areas.

An OSPF backbone is responsible for distributing routing information between areas. It consists of all Area Border Routers, networks not wholly contained in any area, and their attached routers. Figure 47-1 shows an example of an internetwork with several areas.

In the figure, routers 4, 5, 6, 10, 11, and 12 make up the backbone. If Host H1 in Area 3 wants to send a packet to Host H2 in Area 2, the packet is sent to Router 13, which forwards the packet to Router 12, which sends the packet to Router 11. Router 11 then forwards the packet along the backbone to Area Border Router 10, which sends the packet through two intra-area routers (Router 9 and Router 7) to be forwarded to Host H2.

The backbone itself is an OSPF area, so all backbone routers use the same procedures and algorithms to maintain routing information within the backbone that any area router would. The backbone topology is invisible to all intra-area routers, as are individual area topologies to the backbone.

Areas can be defined in such a way that the backbone is not contiguous. In this case, backbone connectivity must be restored through virtual links. Virtual links are configured between any backbone routers that share a link to a nonbackbone area and function as if they were direct links.

Figure 47-1 *An OSPF AS Consists of Multiple Areas Linked by Routers*

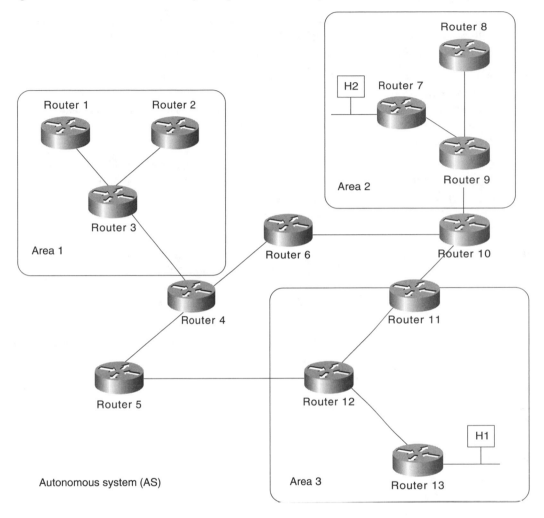

AS border routers running OSPF learn about exterior routes through exterior gateway protocols (EGPs), such as Exterior Gateway Protocol (EGP) or Border Gateway Protocol (BGP), or through configuration information. For more information about these protocols, see Chapter 41, "Border Gateway Protocol."

SPF Algorithm

The *Shortest Path First (SPF)* routing algorithm is the basis for OSPF operations. When an SPF router is powered up, it initializes its routing-protocol data structures and then waits for indications from lower-layer protocols that its interfaces are functional.

After a router is assured that its interfaces are functioning, it uses the OSPF Hello protocol to acquire neighbors, which are routers with interfaces to a common network. The router sends hello packets to its neighbors and receives their hello packets. In addition to helping acquire neighbors, hello packets also act as keepalives to let routers know that other routers are still functional.

On multiaccess networks (networks supporting more than two routers), the Hello protocol elects a designated router and a backup designated router. Among other things, the designated router is responsible for generating LSAs for the entire multiaccess network. Designated routers allow a reduction in network traffic and in the size of the topological database.

When the link-state databases of two neighboring routers are synchronized, the routers are said to be adjacent. On multiaccess networks, the designated router determines which routers should become adjacent. Topological databases are synchronized between pairs of adjacent routers. Adjacencies control the distribution of routing-protocol packets, which are sent and received only on adjacencies.

Each router periodically sends an LSA to provide information on a router's adjacencies or to inform others when a router's state changes. By comparing established adjacencies to link states, failed routers can be detected quickly, and the network's topology can be altered appropriately. From the topological database generated from LSAs, each router calculates a shortest-path tree, with itself as root. The shortest-path tree, in turn, yields a routing table.

Packet Format

All OSPF packets begin with a 24-byte header, as illustrated in Figure 47-2.

Figure 47-2 *OSPF Packets Consist of Nine Fields*

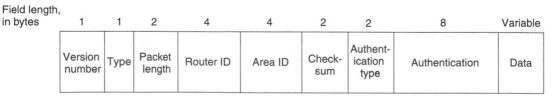

The following descriptions summarize the header fields illustrated in Figure 47-2.

- **Version number**—Identifies the OSPF version used.

- **Type**—Identifies the OSPF packet type as one of the following:
  - **Hello**—Establishes and maintains neighbor relationships.
  - **Database description**—Describes the contents of the topological database. These messages are exchanged when an adjacency is initialized.
  - **Link-state request**—Requests pieces of the topological database from neighbor routers. These messages are exchanged after a router discovers (by examining database-description packets) that parts of its topological database are outdated.
  - **Link-state update**—Responds to a link-state request packet. These messages also are used for the regular dispersal of LSAs. Several LSAs can be included within a single link-state update packet.
  - **Link-state acknowledgment**—Acknowledges link-state update packets.
- **Packet length**—Specifies the packet length, including the OSPF header, in bytes.
- **Router ID**—Identifies the source of the packet.
- **Area ID**—Identifies the area to which the packet belongs. All OSPF packets are associated with a single area.
- **Checksum**—Checks the entire packet contents for any damage suffered in transit.
- **Authentication type**—Contains the authentication type. All OSPF protocol exchanges are authenticated. The authentication type is configurable on per-area basis.
- **Authentication**—Contains authentication information.
- **Data**—Contains encapsulated upper-layer information.

Additional OSPF Features

Additional OSPF features include equal-cost, multipath routing, and routing based on upper-layer type-of-service (TOS) requests. TOS-based routing supports those upper-layer protocols that can specify particular types of service. An application, for example, might specify that certain data is urgent. If OSPF has high-priority links at its disposal, these can be used to transport the urgent datagram.

OSPF supports one or more metrics. If only one metric is used, it is considered to be arbitrary, and TOS is not supported. If more than one metric is used, TOS is optionally supported through the use of a separate metric (and, therefore, a separate routing table) for each of the eight combinations created by the three IP TOS bits (the delay, throughput, and reliability bits). For example, if the IP TOS bits specify low delay, low throughput, and high reliability, OSPF calculates routes to all destinations based on this TOS designation.

IP subnet masks are included with each advertised destination, enabling variable-length subnet masks. With variable-length subnet masks, an IP network can be broken into many subnets of various sizes. This provides network administrators with extra network-configuration flexibility.

Review Questions

1   When using OSPF, can you have two areas attached to each other where only one AS has an interface in Area 0?

2   Area 0 contains five routers (A, B, C, D, and E), and Area 1 contains three routers (R, S, and T). What routers does Router T know exists? Router S is the ABR.

Objectives

- Understand the background and role of ES-IS, IS-IS, and IDRP.

- Describe the general operation of ES-IS.

- Explain the IS-IS routing architecture.

- Examine the use of IS-IS for CLNS routing and IP routing.

- Describe the IS-IS packet types and formats.

- Look at some of the additional features supported by IS-IS.

- Describe the general operation of IDRP.

CHAPTER 48

Open System Interconnection Routing Protocols

Intermediate System–to–Intermediate System (IS-IS) is based on work originally done at Digital Equipment Corporation (Digital) for DECnet/OSI (DECnet Phase V). IS-IS originally was developed to route in ISO Connectionless Network Protocol (CLNP) networks. A version has since been created that supports both CLNP and IP networks; this version usually is called Integrated IS-IS (it also has been called Dual IS-IS).

Open System Interconnection (OSI) routing protocols are summarized in several International Organization for Standardization (ISO) documents, including ISO 10589, which defines IS-IS. The American National Standards Institute (ANSI) X3S3.3 (network and transport layers) committee was the motivating force behind ISO standardization of IS-IS. Other ISO documents include ISO 9542, which defines ES-IS, and ISO 10747, which defines IDRP.

The ISO developed a complete suite of routing protocols for use in the OSI protocol suite. These include End System–to–Intermediate System (ES-IS), IS-IS, and Interdomain Routing Protocol (IDRP). This chapter addresses the basic operations of each of these protocols. Also covered is terminology specific to OSI routing and an overview of routing operation. The extension of IS-IS to support not only Connectionless Network Service (CLNS) but also IP networks is described, introducing features such as black hole avoidance and MPLS traffic engineering.

OSI Networking Terminology

The world of OSI networking uses some specific terminology, such as *end system (ES)*, which refers to any nonrouting network node, and *intermediate system (IS)*, which refers to a router. These terms form the basis of the ES-IS and IS-IS OSI protocols. The ES-IS protocol lets ESs and ISs discover each other. The IS-IS protocol provides routing between ISs.

Other important OSI networking terms include area, domain, Level 1 routing, and Level 2 routing. An *area* is a group of contiguous networks and attached hosts that is designated as an area by a network administrator or manager. A *domain* is a collection of connected areas. Routing domains provide full connectivity to all end systems within them. *Level 1 routing* is routing within a Level 1 area, and *Level 2 routing* is routing between Level 1 areas. Figure 48-1 illustrates the relationship between areas and domains and shows the levels of routing between the two.

Figure 48-1 *Areas Exist Within a Larger Domain and Use Level 2 Routing to Communicate*

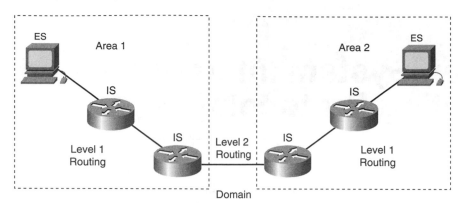

Overview of OSI Routing Operation

Each ES lives in a particular area. OSI routing begins when the ESs discover the nearest IS by listening to IS hello (ISH) message packets. When an ES wants to send a packet to another ES, it sends the packet to one of the ISs on its directly attached network. The router then looks up the destination address and forwards the packet along the best route. If the destination ES is on the same subnetwork, the local IS knows this from listening to ES hello (ESH) messages and forwards the packet appropriately. The IS also might provide a redirect message back to the source to tell it that a more-direct route is available.

If the destination address is an ES on another subnetwork in the same area, the IS knows the correct route and forwards the packet appropriately. If the destination address is an ES in another area, the Level 1 IS sends the packet to the nearest Level 2 IS. Forwarding through Level 2 ISs continues until the packet reaches a Level 2 IS in the destination area. Within the destination area, ISs forward the packet along the best path until the destination ES is reached.

ES-IS

ES-IS is an OSI protocol that defines how end systems (hosts) and intermediate systems (routers) learn about each other, a process known as configuration. Configuration must happen before routing between ESs can occur.

ES-IS is more of a discovery protocol than a routing protocol. It distinguishes among three different types of subnetworks: point-to-point, broadcast, and general topology (see Figure 48-2).

Figure 48-2 *ES-IS Can Be Deployed in Point-to-Point, Broadcast, and General Topology Subnetworks*

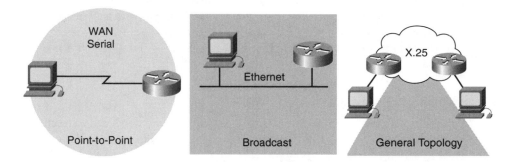

Point-to-point subnetworks, such as WAN serial links, provide a point-to-point link between two systems. Broadcast subnetworks, such as Ethernet and IEEE 802.3, direct a single physical message to all nodes on the subnetwork. General topology subnetworks, such as X.25, support an arbitrary number of systems. Unlike broadcast subnetworks, however, the cost of an *n*-way transmission scales directly with the subnetwork size on a general topology subnetwork.

ES-IS Configuration

ES-IS configuration is the process whereby ESs and ISs discover each other so that routing between ESs can occur. ES-IS configuration information is transmitted at regular intervals through ESHs and ISHs. ESHs are generated by ESs and are sent to every IS on the subnetwork. ISHs are generated by ISs and are sent to all ESs on the subnetwork. These hello messages primarily are intended to convey the subnetwork and network layer addresses of the systems that generate them.

Where possible, ES-IS attempts to send configuration information simultaneously to many systems. On broadcast subnetworks, ES-IS hello messages are sent to all ISs through a special multicast address that designates all end systems. When operating on a general topology subnetwork, ES-IS generally does not transmit configuration information because of the high cost of multicast transmissions.

ES-IS Addressing Information

The ES-IS configuration protocol conveys both OSI network layer addresses and OSI subnetwork addresses. OSI network layer addresses identify either the network service access point (NSAP), which is the interface between OSI Layer 3 and Layer 4, or the network entity title (NET), which is the network layer entity in an OSI IS.

OSI subnetwork addresses, or subnetwork point of attachment (SNPA) addresses, are the points at which an ES or IS is physically attached to a subnetwork. The SNPA address uniquely identifies each system attached to the subnetwork. In an Ethernet network, for example, the SNPA is the 48-bit Media Access Control (MAC) address. Part of the configuration information transmitted by ES-IS is the NSAP-to-SNPA or NET-to-SNPA mapping.

IS-IS

Originally supporting OSI CLNS networks, IS-IS has been extended to also support routing of classless IP networks. This extended version is called Integrated IS-IS or sometimes Dual IS-IS.

Regardless of the network type supported, IS-IS is a link-state protocol and, therefore, shares many of the advantages of OSPF over distance-vector-based protocols, such as IP RIP.

It provides fast convergence and rapid flooding of network changes. It supports a hierarchical routing design through the use of areas, which provides scalability. Additionally, this protocol has been enhanced to increase its flexibility, such as for use as the Interior Gateway Protocol (IGP) in networks using Multiprotocol Label Switching (MPLS) traffic engineering (TE).

Integrated IS-IS

As mentioned, IS-IS was extended to support IP routing in addition to CLNS. IP support is defined in RFC 1195. This protocol is popular with large service providers and often is used in pure IP-only networks. Integrated IS-IS can support both IP and CLNS networks either singularly or concurrently. There is no need for a network to run two completely independent routing protocols and associated control planes to support both OSI and IP traffic.

IS-IS Routing Architecture Support

IS-IS supports hierarchical routing design through the use of areas. A large network is divided into smaller areas. IS-IS routers that route wholly within an area are called Level 1 routers. IS-IS routers that route between areas are called Level 2 routers.

The IS-IS backbone is not a single area 0 as in OSPF. It is the grouping of all contiguously connected Level 2 routers. Each Level 2 router resides in only a single area, but may have links that connect to a Level 2 router in another area or areas. Note that the area border is not the Level 2 router, but the link between the Level 2 routers. Figure 48-3 illustrates the IS-IS hierarchy.

Figure 48-3 *IS-IS Routing Architecture*

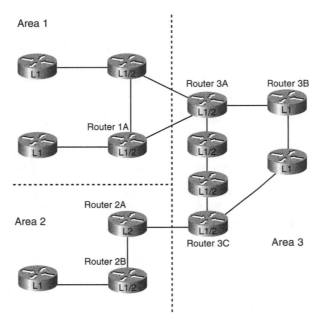

Generally, Level 1 routers know only the networking information within that area. If a Level 1 router cannot route a packet using the information within the area, it sends the packet to the closest Level 2 router, which then routes it to the appropriate area. At the destination area, the packet is then forwarded by the Level 1 routers for that area.

If a Level 1/2 router is connected to another area, it alerts the Level 1 routers in its own area by setting the attached bit in the routing advertisement. Level 1 routers see this and know that the Level 1/2 router can be used to reach networks outside the current area. In Integrated IS-IS, the Level 1/2 router originates an IP default route into its own area. In Figure 48-3, Routers 1A and 1B both set the attached bit and/or originate default routes to the other routers in Area 1.

Level 2 routers know only about the interarea routes, not the routes in their own area. Level 2 routers should not be configured in an OSI-only network, because all OSI routers need to know the topology of their own area. A router can be configured as a Level 1/2 router; in which case, it knows both the local area routes and the interarea routes. The Level 1/2 Integrated IS-IS router leaks the Level 1 IP information into Level 2 and can be summarized during this process.

Depending on the network design, the closest Level 2 router might not be the optimum traffic path, but the Level 1 router does not know this, because it can see only the Level 1 routes. For example, in Figure 48-3, the Level 1 Router 3B chooses Router 3A as its closest

Level 2 router. If the traffic were destined for Area 2, Router 3A would have to forward it via a longer path than if Router 3B initially chose to send the traffic toward the other Level 2 router, Router 3C.

To address this issue, an enhancement to Integrated IS-IS allows a Level 2 router to leak selected routes into the Level 1 area. The Level 1 routers can then make a more intelligent or optimal forwarding decision. However, the increase in routing information is a trade-off against the scalability of the original IS-IS routing architecture.

IS-IS routers discover their neighbors automatically by sending out hello packets. On point-to-point links, they form a direct peering and flood their routing information in link-state packets (LSPs). The information in the LSP is used to build the link-state database (LSDB) from which a shortest-path tree is constructed and also is used to populate the forwarding table.

On broadcast networks, the hello packets are sent on well-known multicast MAC addresses. A Designated Intermediate System (DIS) is elected and does the flooding of LSPs on behalf of the other routers on that segment.

Packet Types

As discussed, IS-IS routers send hello packets for automatic neighbor discovery of both Level 1- and Level 2-capable routers.

Figure 48-4 shows the fields in the IS-IS Level 1 and Level 2 hello packet.

Here are descriptions of the packet fields:

- **Intradomain Routing Protocol Discriminator**—8 bits. The network layer identifier for the IS-IS protocol (0x83).

- **Length Indicator**—8 bits. The header length in bytes.

- **Version/Protocol ID Extension**—8 bits. Set to 1.

- **ID Length**—8 bits. The length of the Source ID field. A value of 0 means a default ID Length field size of 6 bytes.

- **Reserved/Type**—3 bits/5 bits. The first 3 bits are reserved. The last 5 bits define the type of PDU. Hello packets have the PDU type values shown in Table 48-1.

Table 48-1   *PDU Type Values for Hello Packets*

Type	Value
15	Level 1 LAN IS-IS hello
16	Level 2 LAN IS-IS hello
17	Point-to-point IS-IS hello

Version—8 bits. The current version is 1.

Maximum Area Addresses—8 bits. The number of area addresses allowed within this area, from 1 to 254. A value of 0 implies three area addresses.

Reserved/Circuit Type—6 bits/2 bits. The circuit type is identified according the values shown in Table 48-2.

Table 48-2   *Circuit Type Values for Hello Packets*

Value	Description
00	Reserved
01	Level 1
10	Level 2
11	Level 1 and 2

- **Source ID**—The length contained in the ID Length field. The source router's system ID.

- **Holding Timer**—16 bits.

- **PDU Length**—16 bits. The length includes the PDU header and the variable-length fields.

- **Reserved/Priority**—1 bit/7 bits. Determine the priority when electing the DIS on broadcast networks.

- **LAN ID**—System ID of the DIS plus 1 extra byte.

- **Variable-Length Fields**—TLVs are included here.

NOTE   The Point-to Point IS-IS hello PDU is very similar to the LAN hello. The octet containing the Priority field is omitted because there is no need to elect a DIS. The LAN ID field is replaced by a single octet local circuit ID.

IS-IS routers exchange routing information with their neighbors using LSPs. The actual advertised network addresses are stored as Type Length Values (TLVs) found at the end of the LSP.

Figure 48-4 *IS-IS Level 1 and Level 2 Hello Packet Fields*

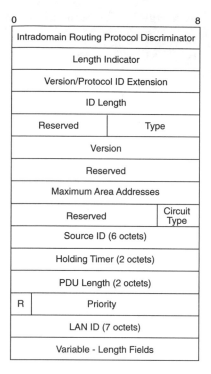

Figure 48-5 shows the fields in this packet.

Here are descriptions of the packet fields:

- **Intradomain Routing Protocol Discriminator**—8 bits. The network layer identifier for the IS-IS protocol (0x83).

- **Length Indicator**—8 bits. The header length in bytes.

- **Version/Protocol ID Extension**—8 bits. Set to 1.

- **ID Length**—8 bits. The length of the Source ID field. A value of 0 means a default ID Length field size of 6 bytes.

- **Reserved/PDU Type**—3 bits/5 bits. The first 3 bits are reserved. The last 5 bits define the type of PDU. Hello packets have the PDU type values shown in Table 48-3.

Table 48-3 *Hello Packet PDU Types*

Value	Description
18	Level 1 link state PDU
20	Level 2 link state PDU

- **Version**—8 bits. The current version is 1.

- **Maximum Area Addresses**—8 bits. The number of area addresses allowed within this area, from 1 to 254. A value of 0 implies three area addresses.

- **PDU Length**—16 bits. The length includes the PDU header and the variable-length fields.

- **Remaining Lifetime**—16 bits. The time in seconds before the LSP expires.

- **LSP ID**—The ID Length plus 16 bits. The ID is formed from the System ID plus the pseudonode ID and LSP fragmentation number.

- **Checksum**—32 bits. Calculated from the LSP ID to the end of the PDU.

- **P (Partition)**—1 bit. A value of 1 indicates that the originator supports partition repair.

- **ATT (Attached)**—4 bits. Indicates the type of routing metric: default, delay, expense, or error.

- **L bit**—1 bit. A value of 1 indicates that the originator is overloaded and should not be considered in shortest-path tree (SPT) calculations.

- **IS Type**—2 bits. Indicates the IS Level, as per Table 48-4.

Table 48-4 *IS Type*

Value	Description
01	Level 1
11	Level 2

- **Type Length Fields**—triple length value (TLV) are included here.

Figure 48-5 *IS-IS Level 1 and Level 2 LSP Packet Fields*

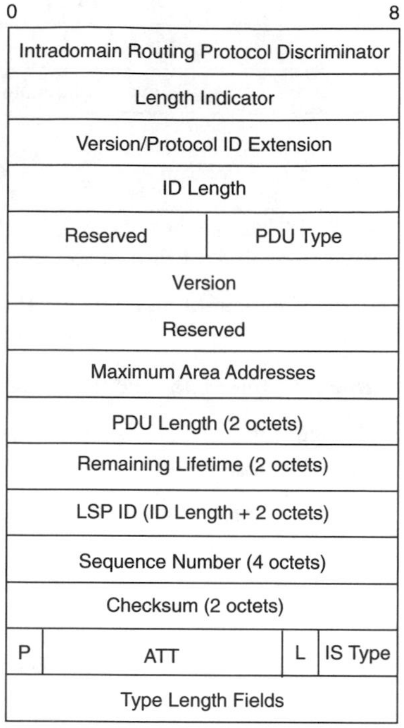

```
0                                                    8
┌─────────────────────────────────────────────────────┐
│     Intradomain Routing Protocol Discriminator        │
├─────────────────────────────────────────────────────┤
│                  Length Indicator                     │
├─────────────────────────────────────────────────────┤
│            Version/Protocol ID Extension              │
├─────────────────────────────────────────────────────┤
│                     ID Length                         │
├──────────────────────────┬────────────────────────────┤
│        Reserved          │        PDU Type            │
├──────────────────────────┴────────────────────────────┤
│                      Version                          │
├─────────────────────────────────────────────────────┤
│                      Reserved                         │
├─────────────────────────────────────────────────────┤
│                Maximum Area Addresses                 │
├─────────────────────────────────────────────────────┤
│                PDU Length (2 octets)                  │
├─────────────────────────────────────────────────────┤
│            Remaining Lifetime (2 octets)              │
├─────────────────────────────────────────────────────┤
│            LSP ID (ID Length + 2 octets)              │
├─────────────────────────────────────────────────────┤
│             Sequence Number (4 octets)                │
├─────────────────────────────────────────────────────┤
│                Checksum (2 octets)                    │
├───┬─────────────────────────────┬────┬────────────────┤
│ P │            ATT              │ L  │   IS Type      │
├───┴─────────────────────────────┴────┴────────────────┤
│                 Type Length Fields                    │
└─────────────────────────────────────────────────────┘
```

TLVS

The variable-length field at the end of the hello PDU and the Type Length field at the end of link state PDUs contain TLVs. This is where the actual network addresses are contained in an LSP. The generic fields for a TLV are shown in Table 48-5.

Table 48-5 *TLV Field Format*

Field	Length in Octets
Type	1
Length	1
Value	As defined by Length

Originally, ten TLV codes were defined for carrying information, such as CLNS addresses and neighbor and authentication information.

NOTE	RFC 1195, *Integrated IS-IS*, introduced a new set of TLV codes to support IPV4 addresses.

IS-IS is extensible by defining new TLVs. This is how IS-IS supports new features such as IPv6 or MPLS TE. Table 48-6 lists some of the common TLVs implemented in IOS.

Table 48-6   *Common TLVs*

Value	Description
1	Area addresses
2	IIS neighbors
8	Padding
10	Authentication
22	TE IIS neighbors
128	IP interior reachability
129	Protocols supported
130	IP exterior address
132	IP interior address
134	TE router ID
135	TE IP reachability
137	Dynamic host name
10 and 133	Authentication

Metrics Defined in IS-IS

Four metrics are defined in IS-IS: cost, delay, expense, and error. Of these, only cost is mandatory and is used in the Cisco IOS implementation.

The default cost is fixed at 10. The maximum interfaces cost is 63. The maximum path cost of 1023 limits the size of the network and places restrictions on routing design. IOS supports *wide metrics,* a 24-bit metric field, to address this issue. However, you must ensure that all IS-IS routers support this feature, or problems will occur when calculating the SPT.

IS-IS LSP Processing

As each router receives LSPs, it adds them to its LSDB if the LSP's sequence number is higher than the one already stored. The LSDB describes all the networks, metrics, and reachability information for each router to build its shortest-path tree using the Dijkstra algorithm. It then constructs its forwarding table from this.

When the router receives an LSP, it floods it to all its neighbors except the neighbor it was received from. IS-IS uses a reliable flooding mechanism and some additional PDU types: Complete Sequence Number PDU (CSNP) and Partial Sequence Number PDU (PSNP). Level 1 and Level 2 CSNP and PSNP PDU types exist.

The receiving router sends a PSNP (containing the LSP sequence number) back to the neighbor acknowledging receipt of the LSP. When the source router receives the acknowledgment, it stops sending the update LSP on that interface, but continues to do so on other interfaces where it has not yet received a PSNP.

On broadcast media, no PSNPs are sent as acknowledgments. The routers wait to receive a CSNP that contains a list of LSPs and their sequence number. The receiving routers can then determine if they missed any LSPs or if any are out of date and then request them via a PSNP.

IS-IS DIS Election

On broadcast media, one IS-IS router becomes the DIS and forms the pseudonode. This election is based on the priority configured on each router's interface. The pseudonode represents a LAN segment, and all routers (nonpseudonodes) form an adjacency with it.

Note that DIS election is preemptive. Adding a router with a higher priority causes it to displace the current DIS and become the DIS itself, creating a new pseudonode.

Every 3 seconds, the DIS sends out CSNPs listing all the LSPs. Any router can request missing or more-recent LSPs by sending a PSNP. Similarly, it can update the pseudonode by sending more-recent or missing LSPs to the DIS.

Avoiding Black Holes with IS-IS

The overload bit allows a router that is running low on critical resources to indicate to its neighbors that it should no longer be used as a path for transit traffic. However, the router still participates in the IS-IS router hierarchy. This overload bit is also used in RFC 3277, *Intermediate System–to–Intermediate System (IS-IS) Transient Blackhole Avoidance Feature*.

In an IS-IS/BGP IP network, when a core network router that is normally in the traffic path is rebooted, it might converge IS-IS more quickly than BGP. In this case, other routers send traffic to where the BGP next hop for that traffic can be reached via IS-IS. When that traffic arrives at that recently rebooted router, the router does not have a forwarding entry for that traffic's destination address, because BGP has not finished converging yet. The traffic is dropped into a black hole.

With RFC 3277, the rebooting router sets the overload bit in its LSPs until BGP is converged. This router still can be reached via IS-IS by other routers, but is not used for transit traffic. When BGP is fully up, it clears the overload bit and is used in the traffic path to reach the BGP next hops.

Route Leaking

As mentioned previously, careful route leaking from Level 2 to Level 1 can allow Level 1 routers to choose a more optimal path when an area has more than one Level 2 router. Normally, they choose the closest. Another application of route leaking is to support MPLS VPNs. MPLS VPNs use mBGP to exchange routing information between PE routers and must see the BGP next hop (a /32 host address) in their own routing table for the route to be valid.

MPLS Traffic Engineering

MPLS TE allows traffic to be forwarded based on decisions other than the next hop for an IP prefix. The MPLS router can set up tunnels based on the availability of resources in the network. These tunnels can have an explicit or dynamic Label-Switched Path. The setup of a dynamic LSP is governed by the available resources along the path, such as available bandwidth, link affinity, and MPLS-specific link cost. To obtain this additional "available resource" information about the network, new TLVs have been defined—TLV 22 and TLV 135. These describe neighbors and IP networks in the same way that TLVs 2, 128, and 130 do. However, these new TLVs also support sub-TLVs within the TLV to describe the additional characteristics of that neighbor or prefix, such as available bandwidth.

Refer to the "For More Information" section for further information on these and other IS-IS features and developments.

IDRP

IDRP is an OSI protocol that specifies how routers communicate with routers in different domains. IDRP is designed to operate seamlessly with CLNP, ES-IS, and IS-IS. IDRP is based on BGP, an interdomain routing protocol that originated in the IP community. IDRP features include the following:

- Support for CLNP quality of service (QoS)
- Loop suppression by keeping track of all routing domains (RDs) traversed by a route
- Reduction of route information and processing by using confederations, the compression of RD path information, and other means
- Reliability by using a built-in reliable transport
- Security by using cryptographic signatures on a per-packet basis
- Route servers

IDRP Terminology

IDRP introduces several environment-specific terms, including border intermediate system (BIS), routing domain (RD), routing domain identifier (RDI), routing information base (RIB), and confederation.

A *BIS* is an IS that participates in interdomain routing and, as such, uses IDRP. An *RD* is a group of ESs and ISs that operate under the same set of administrative rules and that share a common routing plan. An *RDI* is a unique RD identifier. An *RIB* is a routing database used by IDRP that is built by each BIS from information received from the RD and other BISs. An RIB contains the set of routes chosen for use by a particular BIS. A *confederation* is a group of RDs that appears to RDs outside the confederation as a single RD. The confederation's topology is invisible to RDs outside the confederation. Confederations must be nested within one another. They help reduce network traffic by acting as internetwork firewalls. Figure 48-6 illustrates the relationship between IDRP entities.

Figure 48-6 *Domains Communicate Via BISs*

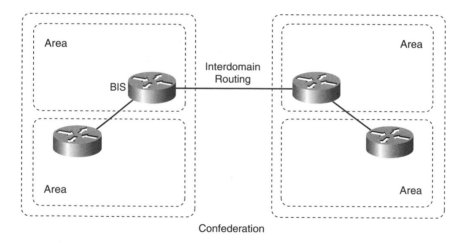

IDRP Routing

An IDRP route is a sequence of RDIs, some of which can be confederations. Each BIS is configured to know the RD and the confederations to which it belongs. It learns about other BISs, RDs, and confederations through information exchanges with each neighbor. As with distance-vector routing, routes to a particular destination accumulate outward from the destination. Only routes that satisfy a BIS's local policies and that have been selected for use are passed on to other BISs. Route recalculation is partial and occurs when one of three events occurs: an incremental routing update with new routes is received, a BIS neighbor goes down, or a BIS neighbor comes up.

Summary

IS-IS is based on work originally done at Digital Equipment Corporation (Digital). OSI routing protocols are summarized in several International Organization for Standardization (ISO) documents. The ISO developed a complete suite of routing protocols for use in the Open System Interconnection (OSI) protocol suite.

The world of OSI networking uses some specific terminology, such as end system (ES), which refers to any nonrouting network nodes, and intermediate system (IS), which refers to a router.

OSI routing begins when the ESs discover the nearest IS. When an ES wants to send a packet to another ES, it sends the packet to one of the ISs on its directly attached network.

End System–to–Intermediate System (ES-IS) is an OSI protocol that defines how end systems (hosts) and intermediate systems (routers) learn about each other.

Intermediate system–to–intermediate system (IS-IS) has been extended to also support routing of classless IP networks. This extended version is known as Integrated IS-IS.

Interdomain Routing Protocol (IDRP) is an OSI protocol that specifies how routers communicate with routers in different domains.

Review Questions

1 What two types of messages are sent between systems in an ES-IS?

2 What is the difference between a Level 1 router and a Level 2 IS-IS router?

3 Describe how IS-IS routers communicate with each other on broadcast networks.

4 What was the original purpose of the overload bit?

5 What is a TLV?

6 How is the IS-IS metric figured on each link?

For More Information

- ISO/IEC 10589:2002 Standard: Intermediate System–to–Intermediate System intra-domain routing information exchange protocol for use in conjunction with the protocol for providing the connectionless-mode network service (ISO 8473), www.iso.org.

- White paper: "Intermediate System–to–Intermediate System (IS-IS) TLVs," Cisco Systems, 2002, www.cisco.com.

- White paper: "Introduction to Intermediate System–to–Intermediate System Protocol," Cisco Systems, 2002, www.cisco.com.

- RFC 1195, *Use of OSI IS-IS for Routing in TCP/IP and Dual Environments,* Callon, R. (Digital Equipment Corporation), December 1990, www.ietf.org.

- RFC 3277, *Intermediate System–to–Intermediate System (IS-IS) Transient Blackhole Avoidance,* McPherson, D. (TCB), April 2002, www.ietf.org.

Objectives

- Name RIP's stability features.
- Explain the significance of RIP's timing mechanisms.
- Describe the differences between RIP and RIP 2.

CHAPTER 49

Routing Information Protocol

Background

The Routing Information Protocol, or RIP, as it is more commonly called, is one of the most enduring of all routing protocols. RIP is also one of the more easily confused protocols because a variety of RIP-like routing protocols proliferated, some of which even used the same name! RIP and the myriad RIP-like protocols were based on the same set of algorithms that use distance vectors to mathematically compare routes to identify the best path to any given destination address. These algorithms emerged from academic research that dates back to 1957.

Today's open standard version of RIP, sometimes referred to as IP RIP, is formally defined in two documents: Request For Comments (RFC) 1058 and Internet Standard (STD) 56. As IP-based networks became both more numerous and greater in size, it became apparent to the Internet Engineering Task Force (IETF) that RIP needed to be updated. Consequently, the IETF released RFC 1388 in January 1993, which was then superceded in November 1994 by RFC 1723, which describes RIP 2 (the second version of RIP). These RFCs described an extension of RIP's capabilities but did not attempt to obsolete the previous version of RIP. RIP 2 enabled RIP messages to carry more information, which permitted the use of a simple authentication mechanism to secure table updates. More importantly, RIP 2 supported subnet masks, a critical feature that was not available in RIP.

This chapter summarizes the basic capabilities and features associated with RIP. Topics include the routing update process, RIP routing metrics, routing stability, and routing timers.

Routing Updates

RIP sends routing-update messages at regular intervals and when the network topology changes. When a router receives a routing update that includes changes to an entry, it updates its routing table to reflect the new route. The metric value for the path is increased by 1, and the sender is indicated as the next hop. RIP routers maintain only the best route (the route with the lowest metric value) to a destination. After updating its routing table, the router immediately begins transmitting routing updates to inform other network routers of the change. These updates are sent independently of the regularly scheduled updates that RIP routers send.

RIP Routing Metric

RIP uses a single routing metric (hop count) to measure the distance between the source and a destination network. Each hop in a path from source to destination is assigned a hop count value, which is typically 1. When a router receives a routing update that contains a new or changed destination network entry, the router adds 1 to the metric value indicated in the update and enters the network in the routing table. The IP address of the sender is used as the next hop.

RIP Stability Features

RIP prevents routing loops from continuing indefinitely by implementing a limit on the number of hops allowed in a path from the source to a destination. The maximum number of hops in a path is 15. If a router receives a routing update that contains a new or changed entry, and if increasing the metric value by 1 causes the metric to be infinity (that is, 16), the network destination is considered unreachable. The downside of this stability feature is that it limits the maximum diameter of a RIP network to less than 16 hops.

RIP includes a number of other stability features that are common to many routing protocols. These features are designed to provide stability despite potentially rapid changes in a network's topology. For example, RIP implements the split horizon and holddown mechanisms to prevent incorrect routing information from being propagated.

RIP Timers

RIP uses numerous timers to regulate its performance. These include a routing-update timer, a route-timeout timer, and a route-flush timer. The routing-update timer clocks the interval between periodic routing updates. Generally, it is set to 30 seconds, with a small random amount of time added whenever the timer is reset. This is done to help prevent congestion, which could result from all routers simultaneously attempting to update their neighbors. Each routing table entry has a route-timeout timer associated with it. When the route-timeout timer expires, the route is marked invalid but is retained in the table until the route-flush timer expires.

Packet Formats

The following section focuses on the IP RIP and IP RIP 2 packet formats illustrated in Figures 44-1 and 44-2. Each illustration is followed by descriptions of the fields illustrated.

RIP Packet Format

Figure 49-1 illustrates the IP RIP packet format.

Figure 49-1 *An IP RIP Packet Consists of Nine Fields*

1-octet command field	1-octet version number field	2-octet zero field	2-octet AFI field	2-octet zero field	4-octet IP address field	4-octet zero field	4-octet zero field	4-octet metric field

The following descriptions summarize the IP RIP packet format fields illustrated in Figure 49-1:

- **Command**—Indicates whether the packet is a request or a response. The request asks that a router send all or part of its routing table. The response can be an unsolicited regular routing update or a reply to a request. Responses contain routing table entries. Multiple RIP packets are used to convey information from large routing tables.

- **Version number**—Specifies the RIP version used. This field can signal different potentially incompatible versions.

- **Zero**—This field is not actually used by RFC 1058 RIP; it was added solely to provide backward compatibility with prestandard varieties of RIP. Its name comes from its defaulted value: zero.

- **Address-family identifier (AFI)**—Specifies the address family used. RIP is designed to carry routing information for several different protocols. Each entry has an address-family identifier to indicate the type of address being specified. The AFI for IP is 2.

- **Address**—Specifies the IP address for the entry.

- **Metric**—Indicates how many internetwork hops (routers) have been traversed in the trip to the destination. This value is between 1 and 15 for a valid route, or 16 for an unreachable route.

NOTE   Up to 25 occurrences of the AFI, Address, and Metric fields are permitted in a single IP RIP packet. (Up to 25 destinations can be listed in a single RIP packet.)

RIP 2 Packet Format

The RIP 2 specification (described in RFC 1723) allows more information to be included in RIP packets and provides a simple authentication mechanism that is not supported by RIP. Figure 49-2 shows the IP RIP 2 packet format.

Figure 49-2 *An IP RIP 2 Packet Consists of Fields Similar to Those of an IP RIP Packet*

1-octet command field	1-octet version number field	2-octet unused field	2-octet AFI field	2-octet route tag field	4-octet network address field	4-octet subnet mask field	4-octet next hop field	4-octet metric field

The following descriptions summarize the IP RIP 2 packet format fields illustrated in Figure 49-2:

- **Command**—Indicates whether the packet is a request or a response. The request asks that a router send all or a part of its routing table. The response can be an unsolicited regular routing update or a reply to a request. Responses contain routing table entries. Multiple RIP packets are used to convey information from large routing tables.

- **Version**—Specifies the RIP version used. In a RIP packet implementing any of the RIP 2 fields or using authentication, this value is set to 2.

- **Unused**—Has a value set to zero.

- **Address-family identifier (AFI)**—Specifies the address family used. RIPv2's AFI field functions identically to RFC 1058 RIP's AFI field, with one exception: If the AFI for the first entry in the message is 0xFFFF, the remainder of the entry contains authentication information. Currently, the only authentication type is simple password.

- **Route tag**—Provides a method for distinguishing between internal routes (learned by RIP) and external routes (learned from other protocols).

- **IP address**—Specifies the IP address for the entry.

- **Subnet mask**—Contains the subnet mask for the entry. If this field is zero, no subnet mask has been specified for the entry.

- **Next hop**—Indicates the IP address of the next hop to which packets for the entry should be forwarded.

- **Metric**—Indicates how many internetwork hops (routers) have been traversed in the trip to the destination. This value is between 1 and 15 for a valid route, or 16 for an unreachable route.

NOTE	Up to 25 occurrences of the AFI, Address, and Metric fields are permitted in a single IP RIP packet. That is, up to 25 routing table entries can be listed in a single RIP packet. If the AFI specifies an authenticated message, only 24 routing table entries can be specified. Given that individual table entries aren't fragmented into multiple packets, RIP does not need a mechanism to resequence datagrams bearing routing table updates from neighboring routers.

Summary

Despite RIP's age and the emergence of more sophisticated routing protocols, it is far from obsolete. RIP is mature, stable, widely supported, and easy to configure. Its simplicity is well suited for use in stub networks and in small autonomous systems that do not have enough redundant paths to warrant the overheads of a more sophisticated protocol.

Review Questions

1 Name RIP's various stability features.

2 What is the purpose of the timeout timer?

3 What two capabilities are supported by RIP 2 but not RIP?

4 What is the maximum network diameter of a RIP network?

For More Information

- Sportack, Mark A. *IP Routing Fundamentals.* Indianapolis: Cisco Press, 1999.
- http://www.ietf.org/rfc/rfc1058.txt
- http://www.ietf.org/rfc/rfc1723.txt
- http://www.cisco.com/cpress/cc/td/cpress/fund/ith2nd/it2444.htm

Objectives

- Explain the difference between RSVP and routing protocols.
- Name the three traffic types supported by RSVP.
- Understand RSVP's different filter and style types.
- Explain the purpose of RSVP tunneling.

CHAPTER 50

Resource Reservation Protocol

Background

The *Resource Reservation Protocol (RSVP)* is a network-control protocol that enables Internet applications to obtain differing qualities of service (QoS) for their data flows. Such a capability recognizes that different applications have different network performance requirements. Some applications, including the more traditional interactive and batch applications, require reliable delivery of data but do not impose any stringent requirements for the timeliness of delivery. Newer application types, including videoconferencing, IP telephony, and other forms of multimedia communications require almost the exact opposite: Data delivery must be timely but not necessarily reliable. Thus, RSVP was intended to provide IP networks with the capability to support the divergent performance requirements of differing application types.

It is important to note that RSVP is not a routing protocol. RSVP works in conjunction with routing protocols and installs the equivalent of dynamic access lists along the routes that routing protocols calculate. Thus, implementing RSVP in an existing network does not require migration to a new routing protocol.

Researchers at the University of Southern California (USC) Information Sciences Institute (ISI) and Xerox's Palo Alto Research Center (PARC) originally conceived RSVP. The Internet Engineering Task Force (IETF) subsequently specified an open version of RSVP in its RFC 2205 based directly on the USC and PARC version. RSVP operational topics discussed in this chapter include data flows, quality of service, session startup, reservation style, and soft state implementation. Figure 50-1 illustrates an RSVP environment.

Figure 50-1 *In RSVP, Host Information Is Delivered to Receivers over Data Flows*

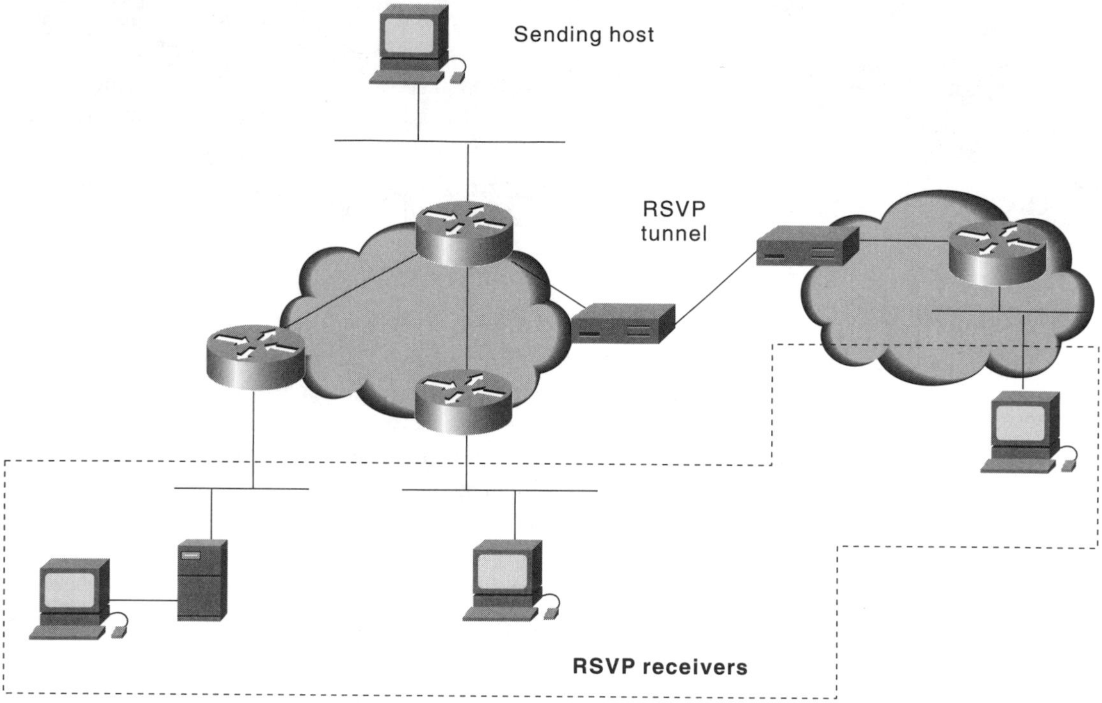

RSVP Data Flows

In RSVP, a data flow is a sequence of datagrams that have the same source, destination (regardless of whether that destination is one or more physical machines), and quality of service. QoS requirements are communicated through a network via a *flow specification*, which is a data structure used by internetwork hosts to request special services from the internetwork. A flow specification describes the level of service required for that data flow. This description takes the form of one of three traffic types. These traffic types are identified by their corresponding RSVP class of service:

1 Best-effort

2 Rate-sensitive

3 Delay-sensitive

Best-effort traffic is traditional IP traffic. Applications include file transfer (such as mail transmissions), disk mounts, interactive logins, and transaction traffic. These types of applications require reliable delivery of data regardless of the amount of time needed to achieve that delivery. Best-effort traffic types rely upon the native TCP mechanisms to resequence datagrams received out of order, as well as to request retransmissions of any datagrams lost or damaged in transit.

Rate-sensitive traffic requires a guaranteed transmission rate from its source to its destination. An example of such an application is H.323 videoconferencing, which is designed to run on ISDN (H.320) or ATM (H.310), but is also found on the Internet and many IP-based intranets. H.323 encoding is a constant (or nearly constant) rate, and it requires a constant transport rate such as is available in a circuit-switched network. By its very nature, IP is packet-switched. Thus, it lacks the mechanisms to support a constant bit rate of service for any given application's data flow. RSVP enables constant bit-rate service in packet-switched networks via its rate-sensitive level of service. This service is sometimes referred to as *guaranteed bit-rate service*.

Delay-sensitive traffic is traffic that requires timeliness of delivery and that varies its rate accordingly. MPEG-II video, for example, averages about 3 to 7 Mbps, depending on the amount of change in the picture. As an example, 3 Mbps might be a picture of a painted wall, although 7 Mbps would be required for a picture of waves on the ocean. MPEG-II video sources send key and delta frames. Typically, 1 or 2 key frames per second describe the whole picture, and 13 or 28 frames (known as delta frames) describe the change from the key frame. Delta frames are usually substantially smaller than key frames. As a result, rates vary quite a bit from frame to frame. A single frame, however, requires delivery within a specific time frame or the CODEC (code-decode) is incapable of doing its job. A specific priority must be negotiated for delta-frame traffic. RSVP services supporting delay-sensitive traffic are referred to as *controlled-delay service* (non-real-time service) and *predictive service* (real-time service).

RSVP Data Flows Process

Unlike routing protocols, RSVP is designed to manage flows of data rather than make decisions for each individual datagram. Data flows consist of discrete sessions between specific source and destination machines. A session is more specifically defined as a simplex flow of datagrams to a particular destination and transport layer protocol. Thus, sessions are identified by the following data: destination address, protocol ID, and destination port. RSVP supports both unicast and multicast simplex sessions.

NOTE   It is important to note that RSVP sessions are simplex. Thus, a bidirectional exchange of data between a pair of machines actually constitutes two separate RSVP simplex sessions.

A multicast session sends a copy of each datagram transmitted by a single sender to multiple destinations. A unicast session features a single source and destination machine. An RSVP source and destination address can correspond to a unique Internet host. A single host, however, can contain multiple logical senders and receivers distinguished by port numbers, with each port number corresponding to a different application. Given that RSVP tracks such application-specific information, it is possible for a unicast session to result in data being forwarded to multiple applications within the same destination host.

RSVP Quality of Service

In the context of RSVP, *quality of service (QoS)* is an attribute specified in flow specifications that are used to determine the way in which data interchanges are handled by participating entities (routers, receivers, and senders). RSVP is used to specify the QoS by both hosts and routers. Hosts use RSVP to request a QoS level from the network on behalf of an application data stream. Routers use RSVP to deliver QoS requests to other routers along the path(s) of the data stream. In doing so, RSVP maintains the router and host state to provide the requested service.

RSVP Session Startup

To initiate an RSVP multicast session, a receiver first joins the multicast group specified by an IP destination address by using the Internet Group Membership Protocol (IGMP). In the case of a unicast session, unicast routing serves the function that IGMP, coupled with protocol-independent multicast (PIM), serves in the multicast case. After the receiver joins a group, a potential sender starts sending RSVP path messages to the IP destination address. The receiver application receives a path message and starts sending appropriate reservation-request messages specifying the desired flow descriptors using RSVP. After the sender application receives a reservation-request message, the sender starts sending data packets.

RSVP Reservation Style

Reservation style refers to a set of control options that specify a number of supported parameters. RSVP supports two major classes of reservation: *distinct reservations* and *shared reservations*. Distinct reservations install a flow for each relevant sender in each session. A shared reservation is used by a set of senders that are known not to interfere with each other. Figure 50-2 illustrates distinct and shared RSVP reservation-style types in the context of their scope. Each supported reservation style/scope combination is described following the illustration.

Wildcard-Filter Style

The *wildcard-filter (WF) style* specifies a shared reservation with a wildcard scope. With a WF-style reservation, a single reservation is created into which flows from all upstream senders are mixed. Reservations can be thought of as a shared pipe whose size is the largest of the resource requests for that link from all receivers, independent of the number of senders. The reservation is propagated upstream toward all sender hosts and is automatically extended to new senders as they appear.

Figure 50-2 *RSVP Supports Both Distinct Reservations and Shared Reservations*

	Reservations	
Scope	Distinct	Shared
Explicit	Fixed-filter (FF) style	Shared-explicit (SE) style
Wildcard	None defined	Wildcard-Filter (WF) style

Fixed-Filter Style

The *fixed-filter (FF) style* specifies a distinct reservation with an explicit scope. With an FF-style reservation, a distinct reservation request is created for data packets from a particular sender. The reservation scope is determined by an explicit list of senders. The total reservation on a link for a given session is the total of the FF reservations for all requested senders. FF reservations that are requested by different receivers but that select the same sender must be merged to share a single reservation in a given node.

Shared-Explicit Style

The *shared-explicit (SE) style* reservation specifies a shared reservation environment with an explicit reservation scope. The SE style creates a single reservation into which flows from all upstream senders are mixed. As in the case of an FF reservation, the set of senders (and, therefore, the scope) is specified explicitly by the receiver making the reservation.

RSVP Reservation Style Implications

WF and SE are both shared reservations that are appropriate for multicast applications in which application-specific constraints make it unlikely that multiple data sources will transmit simultaneously. An example might be audioconferencing, in which a limited number of people talk at once. Each receiver might issue a WF or SE reservation request twice for one audio channel (to allow some overspeaking). The FF style creates independent reservations for the flows from different senders. The FF style is more appropriate for video signals. Unfortunately, it is not possible to merge shared reservations with distinct reservations.

RSVP Soft State Implementation

In the context of an RSVP-enabled network, a *soft state* refers to a state in routers and end nodes that can be updated by certain RSVP messages. The soft state characteristic permits an RSVP network to support dynamic group membership changes and adapt to changes in routing. In general, the soft state is maintained by an RSVP-based network to enable the network to change states without consultation with end points. This contrasts with a circuit-switch architecture, in which an endpoint places a call and, in the event of a failure, places a new call.

RSVP protocol mechanisms provide a general facility for creating and maintaining a distributed reservation state across a mesh of multicast and unicast delivery paths.

To maintain a reservation state, RSVP tracks a soft state in router and host nodes. The RSVP soft state is created and must be periodically refreshed by path and reservation-request messages. If no matching refresh messages arrive before the expiration of a cleanup timeout interval, the state is deleted. The soft state also can be deleted as the result of an explicit teardown message. RSVP periodically scans the soft state to build and forward path and reservation-request refresh messages to succeeding hops.

When a route changes, the next path message initializes the path state on the new route. Future reservation-request messages establish a reservation state. The state on the now-unused segment is timed out. (The RSVP specification requires initiation of new reservations through the network 2 seconds after a topology change.)

When state changes occur, RSVP propagates those changes from end to end within an RSVP network without delay. If the received state differs from the stored state, the stored state is updated. If the result modifies the refresh messages to be generated, refresh messages are generated and forwarded immediately.

RSVP Operational Model

Under RSVP, resources are reserved for simple data streams (that is, unidirectional data flows). Each sender is logically distinct from a receiver, but any application can act as a sender and a receiver. Receivers are responsible for requesting resource reservations. Figure 50-3 illustrates this general operational environment, while the subsequent section provides an outline of the specific sequence of events.

Figure 50-3 *The RSVP Operational Environment Reserves Resources for Unidirectional Data Flows*

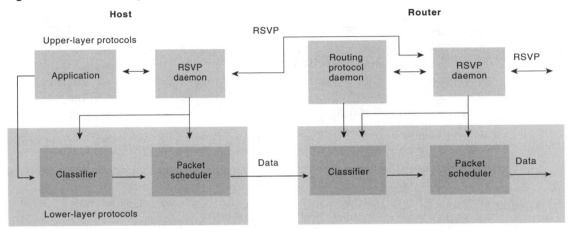

General RSVP Protocol Operation

The RSVP resource-reservation process initiation begins when an RSVP daemon consults the local routing protocol(s) to obtain routes. A host sends IGMP messages to join a multicast group and RSVP messages to reserve resources along the delivery path(s) from that group. Each router that is capable of participating in resource reservation passes incoming data packets to a packet classifier and then queues them as necessary in a packet scheduler. The RSVP packet classifier determines the route and QoS class for each packet. The RSVP scheduler allocates resources for transmission on the particular data link layer medium used by each interface. If the data link layer medium has its own QoS management capability, the packet scheduler is responsible for negotiation with the data link layer to obtain the QoS requested by RSVP.

The scheduler itself allocates packet-transmission capacity on a QoS-passive medium, such as a leased line, and also can allocate other system resources, such as CPU time or buffers. A QoS request, typically originating in a receiver host application, is passed to the local RSVP implementation as an RSVP daemon.

The RSVP protocol then is used to pass the request to all the nodes (routers and hosts) along the reverse data path(s) to the data source(s). At each node, the RSVP program applies a local decision procedure called admission control to determine whether it can supply the requested QoS. If admission control succeeds, the RSVP program sets the parameters of the packet classifier and scheduler to obtain the desired QoS. If admission control fails at any node, the RSVP program returns an error indication to the application that originated the request.

RSVP Tunneling

It is impossible to deploy RSVP or any new protocol at the same moment throughout the entire Internet. Indeed, RSVP might never be deployed everywhere. Therefore, RSVP must provide correct protocol operation even when two RSVP-capable routers are interconnected via an arbitrary cloud of non-RSVP routers. An intermediate cloud that does not support RSVP is incapable of performing resource reservation, so service guarantees cannot be made. However, if such a cloud has sufficient excess capacity, it can provide acceptable and useful real-time service.

To support connection of RSVP networks through non-RSVP networks, RSVP supports tunneling, which occurs automatically through non-RSVP clouds. Tunneling requires RSVP and non-RSVP routers to forward path messages toward the destination address by using a local routing table. When a path message traverses a non-RSVP cloud, the path message copies carry the IP address of the last RSVP-capable router. Reservation-request messages are forwarded to the next upstream RSVP-capable router.

Two arguments have been offered in defense of implementing tunneling in an RSVP environment. First, RSVP will be deployed sporadically rather than universally. Second, by implementing congestion control in situations in which congestion is a known problem, tunneling can be made more effective.

Sporadic, or piecemeal, deployment means that some parts of the network will actively implement RSVP before other parts. If RSVP is required end to end, no benefit is achievable without nearly universal deployment, which is unlikely unless early deployment shows substantial benefits.

Weighted Fair-Queuing Solution

Having the technology to enforce effective resource reservation (such as Cisco's weighted fair-queuing scheme) in a location that presents a bottleneck can have real positive effects. Tunneling presents a risk only when the bottleneck is within a non-RSVP domain and the bottleneck cannot be avoided. Figure 50-4 illustrates an RSVP environment featuring a tunnel between RSVP-based networks.

RSVP Messages

RSVP supports four basic message types: reservation-request messages, path messages, error and confirmation messages, and teardown messages. Each of these is described briefly in the sections that follow.

Figure 50-4 *An RSVP Environment Can Feature a Tunnel Between RSVP-Based Networks*

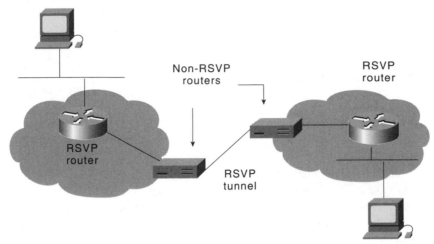

Reservation-Request Messages

A *reservation-request message* is sent by each receiver host toward the senders. This message follows in reverse the routes that the data packets use, all the way to the sender hosts. A reservation-request message must be delivered to the sender hosts so that the hosts can set up appropriate traffic-control parameters for the first hop. RSVP does not send any positive acknowledgment messages.

Path Messages

An *RSVP path message* is sent by each sender along the unicast or multicast routes provided by the routing protocol(s). A path message is used to store the path state in each node. The path state is used to route reservation request messages in the reverse direction.

Error and Confirmation Messages

Three error and confirmation message forms exist: path-error messages, reservation-request error messages, and reservation-request acknowledgment messages.

Path-error messages result from path messages and travel toward senders. Path-error messages are routed hop by hop using the path state. At each hop, the IP destination address is the unicast address of the previous hop.

Reservation-request error messages result from reservation-request messages and travel toward the receiver. Reservation-request error messages are routed hop by hop using the reservation state. At each hop, the IP destination address is the unicast address of the next-hop node. Information carried in error messages can include the following:

- Admission failure
- Bandwidth unavailable
- Service not supported
- Bad flow specification
- Ambiguous path

Reservation-request acknowledgment messages are sent as the result of the appearance of a reservation-confirmation object in a reservation-request message. This acknowledgment message contains a copy of the reservation confirmation. An acknowledgment message is sent to the unicast address of a receiver host, and the address is obtained from the reservation-confirmation object. A reservation-request acknowledgment message is forwarded to the receiver hop by hop (to accommodate the hop-by-hop integrity-check mechanism).

Teardown Messages

RSVP teardown messages remove the path and reservation state without waiting for the cleanup timeout period. Teardown messages can be initiated by an application in an end system (sender or receiver) or a router as the result of state timeout. RSVP supports two types of teardown messages: path-teardown and reservation-request teardown. *Path-teardown messages* delete the path state (which deletes the reservation state), travel toward all receivers downstream from the point of initiation, and are routed like path messages. *Reservation-request teardown messages* delete the reservation state, travel toward all matching senders upstream from the point of teardown initiation, and are routed like corresponding reservation-request messages.

RSVP Packet Format

Figure 50-5 illustrates the RSVP packet format. The summaries that follow outline the header and object fields illustrated in Figure 50-5.

Figure 50-5 *An RSVP Packet Format Consists of Message Headers and Object Fields*

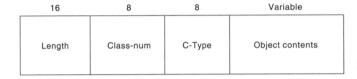

RSVP message header fields

Field length,
in bits

4	4	8	16	16	8	8	32	15	1	16
Version	Flags	Type	Checksum	Length	Reserved	Send TTL	Message ID	Reserved	MF	Fragment offset

RSVP object fields

Field length,
in bits

16	8	8	Variable
Length	Class-num	C-Type	Object contents

RSVP Message Header Fields

RSVP message header fields are comprised of the following:

- **Version**—A 4-bit field indicating the protocol version number (currently version 1).
- **Flags**—A 4-bit field with no flags currently defined.
- **Type**—An 8-bit field with six possible (integer) values, as shown in Table 50-1.

Table 50-1 *RSVP Message Type Field Values*

Value	Message Type
1	Path
2	Reservation-request
3	Path-error
4	Reservation-request error
5	Path-teardown
6	Reservation-teardown
7	Reservation-request acknowledgment

- **Checksum**—A 16-bit field representing a standard TCP/UDP checksum over the contents of the RSVP message, with the checksum field replaced by 0.

- **Length**—A 16-bit field representing the length of this RSVP packet in bytes, including the common header and the variable-length objects that follow. If the More Fragment (MF) flag is set or the Fragment Offset field is nonzero, this is the length of the current fragment of a larger message.

- **Send TTL**—An 8-bit field indicating the IP time-to-live (TTL) value with which the message was sent.

- **Message ID**—A 32-bit field providing a label shared by all fragments of one message from a given next/previous RSVP hop.

- **More fragments (MF) flag**—Low-order bit of a 1-byte word with the other 7 high-order bits specified as reserved. MF is set on for all but the last fragment of a message.

- **Fragment offset**—A 24-bit field representing the byte offset of the fragment in the message

RSVP Object Fields

RSVP object fields are comprised of the following:

- **Length**—Is a 16-bit field containing the total object length in bytes (must always be a multiple of 4 and must be at least 4).

- **Class-num**—Identifies the object class. Each object class has a name. An RSVP implementation must recognize the classes listed in Table 50-2.

The high-order bit of the Class-Num field determines what action a node should take if it does not recognize the Class-Num of an object.

- **C-type**—Object type, unique within Class-Num. The maximum object content length is 65528 bytes. The Class-Num and C-Type fields (together with the flag bit) can be used together as a 16-bit number to define a unique type for each object.

- **Object contents**—The Length, Class-Num, and C-Type fields specify the form of the object content. Refer to Table 50-2 for definitions of the classes of objects that can be included in the object contents.

Table 50-2   *RSVP Object Classes*

Object Class	Description
Null	Contains a Class-Num of 0, and its C-Type is ignored. Its length must be at least 4 but can be any multiple of 4. A null object can appear anywhere in a sequence of objects, and its contents will be ignored by the receiver.
Session	Contains the IP destination address and possibly a generalized destination port to define a specific session for the other objects that follow (required in every RSVP message).
RSVP Hop	Carries the IP address of the RSVP-capable node that sent this message.

Table 50-2   *RSVP Object Classes (Continued)*

Object Class	Description
Time Values	If present, contains values for the refresh period and the state TTL to override the default values.
Style	Defines the reservation style plus style-specific information that is not a flow-specification or filter-specification object (included in a reservation-request message).
Flow Specification	Defines a desired QoS (included in a reservation-request message).
Filter Specification	Defines a subset of session-data packets that should receive the desired QoS (specified by a flow-specification object within a reservation-request message).
Sender Template	Contains a sender IP address and perhaps some additional demultiplexing information to identify a sender (included in a path message).
Sender TSPEC	Defines the traffic characteristics of a sender's data stream (included in a path message).
Adspec	Carries advertising data in a path message.
Error Specification	Specifies an error (included in a path-error or reservation-request error message).
Policy Data	Carries information that will enable a local policy module to decide whether an associated reservation is administratively permitted (included in a path or reservation-request message).
Integrity	Contains cryptographic data to authenticate the originating node and perhaps to verify the contents of this reservation-request message.
Scope	Is an explicit specification of the scope for forwarding a reservation-request message.
Reservation Confirmation	Carries the IP address of a receiver that requested a confirmation. It appears in either a reservation-request or a reservation-request acknowledgment.

Summary

RSVP is a transport layer protocol that enables a network to provide differentiated levels of service to specific flows of data. Ostensibly, different application types have different performance requirements. RSVP acknowledges these differences and provides the mechanisms necessary to detect the levels of performance required by different applications and to modify network behaviors to accommodate those required levels. Over time, as time and latency-sensitive applications mature and proliferate, RSVP's capabilities will become increasingly important.

Review Questions

1 Is it necessary to migrate away from your existing routing protocol to support RSVP?

2 Identify the three RSVP levels of service, and explain the difference among them.

3 What are the two RSVP reservation classes, and how do they differ?

4 What are RSVP filters?

5 How can RSVP be used through network regions that do not support RSVP?

For More Information

- http://www.ietf.org/rfc/rfc2205.txt
- http://www.cisco.com/univercd/cc/td/doc/cisintwk/ito_doc/rsvp.htm

Objectives

- Describe background information about SMRP.

- Define the terms used in SMRP networking.

- Describe the functional characteristics of SMRP, including management, transaction, and packet format.

CHAPTER 51

Simple Multicast Routing Protocol

Introduction

The *Simple Multicast Routing Protocol (SMRP)* is a transport layer protocol developed to route multimedia data streams over AppleTalk networks. It supports Apple Computer's QuickTime Conferencing (QTC) technology. SMRP provides connectionless, best-effort delivery of multicast datagrams and relies on underlying network layer protocols for services. In particular, SMRP facilitates the transmission of data from a single source to multiple destinations. This chapter focuses on the functional elements and protocol operations of SMRP. Figure 51-1 illustrates a generalized SMRP environment.

In creating SMRP, Apple borrowed a number of strategies and concepts from other protocols and technologies. In doing so, many terms were adapted to have specific meanings in Apple's SMRP environment. Table 51-1 provides a summary of SMRP-specific terms and definitions. These terms are used throughout this chapter.

Table 51-1 *SMRP-Specific Terms and Definitions*

Term	Definition
adjacent endpoint	In relation to a node or an endpoint, an endpoint on the same local network, or a node connected through a tunnel.
adjacent node	In relation to a node or an endpoint, a node on the same local network.
child endpoint	An adjacent endpoint to which a node sends multicast data.
child node	In relation to a member node of a group, a neighbor node farther from the creator endpoint.
child port	In relation to a group, a port that is the interface to one or more child nodes.
creator endpoint	The endpoint that requested creation of the group, and the source of data forwarded to the group.
creator node	The primary node that created the group.
designated node	An SMRP router that has been designated as a primary or secondary node.
destination tree	The spanning tree rooted on a local network with paths directed toward the local group.
endpoint	A nonrouting source or destination of multicast packets.

continues

Table 51-1 *SMRP-Specific Terms and Definitions (Continued)*

Term	Definition
group	A set of recipient endpoints, or a multicast address.
join	Term for the process of becoming a member of a group.
joining path	A path on the destination tree for a local network used to reach a creator node, and constructed using the SMRP distance-vector algorithm.
leave	Term for the process of relinquishing membership in a group.
local net	A shared-access data link and its associated network layer protocol. A LAN might support more than one local net.
member endpoint	An endpoint that is a member of the group.
member node	A node that is on the distribution tree of a group.
neighbor node	In relation to a member node of a group, an adjacent node that is on the distribution tree for the group.
node	A router implementing SMRP.
parent port	In relation to a group, the port that is the interface to the parent node.
parent node	In relation to a member node of a group, the neighbor node closer to the creator endpoint.
port	A local network or tunnel interface on an SMRP router.
port parent	The address of the node that is responsible for handling group requests.
primary node	The node on a local network responsible for creating groups.
reverse path	The reverse of a joining path, a path on the source tree for a local net used to forward multicast data.
secondary node	The node ready to take over for a disappearing primary node.
source tree	The spanning tree rooted on a local network with paths directed away from the local network.
spanning tree	A connected set of paths using local networks between all nodes on an internetwork, with only one path between any two nodes.
tunnel	A point-to-point connection between nodes on nonadjacent networks through routers not implementing SMRP.

Figure 51-1 *A Generalized SMRP Environment Runs from a Multicast Group to an Endpoint*

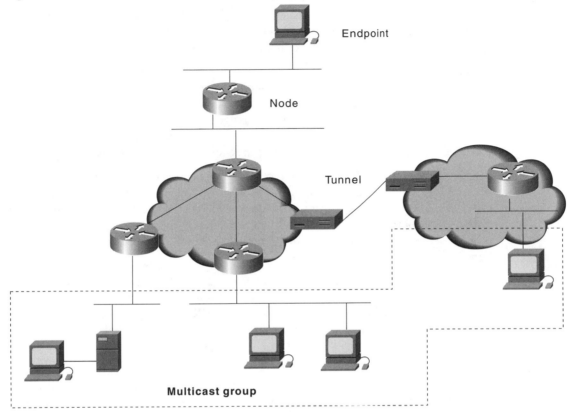

SMRP Multicast Transport Services

SMRP is designed to enable routers and end stations to exchange multicast packets over network layer protocols. SMRP provides the capability to manage multicast address assignment and enables a single source to send data addressed to a unique multicast group address. Receivers join this group if they are interested in receiving data for this group. In support of these functions, SMRP involves a number of services. The discussions that follow focus on the key processes and technologies that enable SMRP services, including address management, the Multicast Transaction Protocol (MTP), node management, multicast route management, data forwarding, and topology management.

SMRP Multicast Address Management

SMRP addressing is based on the local network of a creator endpoint. An SMRP address consists of two parts: a 3-byte network number and a 1-byte socket number. Each local network is configured with a range of unique network numbers.

In network number mapping, network numbers must be assigned to local nets for SMRP and must be unique throughout an entire internetwork. Each local net can be assigned any contiguous range of 3-byte network numbers. The number of multicast groups available for a local net is the number of network numbers assigned multiplied by 254. Network numbers can be configured or can be mapped from the network number of underlying network layer protocols. Unique network number ranges can be reserved for supported network protocols.

In the case of multicast address mapping, SMRP multicast addresses must be mapped to network layer multicast addresses, and these in turn are mapped to data link layer multicast addresses. For each network layer type, a block of multicast addresses must be obtained for SMRP. In the best case, these addresses will map directly. In most cases, a direct mapping is not possible, and more than one SMRP multicast address is mapped to a single network layer multicast address.

The manner in which multicast addresses are mapped to network layer addresses is network layer-dependent. When SMRP transport layer multicast addresses do not map directly to network layer multicast addresses, filtering of the SMRP multicast addresses is required. When network layer multicast addresses do not map directly to data link layer multicast addresses, the network layer is expected to filter out multicast addresses that have not been subscribed.

Network layer multicast addresses are preset for AllEndpoints, AllNodes, and AllEntities addresses. AllEndpoints messages sent to this multicast address are relayed to all endpoints on a network. AllNodes messages sent to this multicast address are relayed to all SMRP routing nodes on a network, and AllEntities messages sent to this multicast address are relayed to all endpoints and all SMRP routing nodes on a network.

SMRP Multicast Transaction Protocol

SMRP involves a multicast transaction protocol (MTP) that provides for three transaction types: node, endpoint, and simultaneous node/endpoint. Communications between adjacent nodes and between nodes and endpoints occurs through request/response transactions.

Responses always are unicast. MTP provides for the retransmission of requests or responses in case of network errors. Only hello and designated node-request packets are sent as multicast messages; all others are unicast. Endpoint-to-node requests are sent as multicasts, while node-to-endpoint requests are sent as either unicasts or multicasts.

The basic MTP design as implemented in SMRP routers uses two queues for all transactions: a request queue and a response queue. The request-queue entries are deleted after the router processes the response that it received. The response is processed, when matched with a request, using a callback specified in the entry.

After response processing, the request is discarded. If the request is unanswered, an internally generated reject response, with the error MCNoResponse, is sent to the callback. Requests can be sent to a unicast address or to the AllNodes or AllEndpoints multicast address, depending on the context. Unless explicitly redirected, requests are sent to the AllNodes multicast.

The response-queue entries are created upon receipt of a request packet. The entry is referenced during all processing of the request, and the processed entry remains in the queue until it expires and is deleted from the queue. If a duplicate request is received, it is ignored if the SMRP router is still processing the original request, or if a duplicate response is generated if processing is complete. Responses always are unicast to the requestor. Some received requests require an SMRP routing node to generate additional requests. In this case, the original request(s) will be processed by the callback handler of the routing node's request entry.

SMRP Node Management

SMRP relies on a number of node relationships, including designated nodes, adjacent nodes, and tunnel nodes, to permit transport of multicast datagrams.

Designated nodes are SMRP routers that have been specified as primary or secondary nodes. A designated primary node is responsible for allocating group addresses. A primary node is required for each local network with SMRP nodes. A designated secondary node is required if a local network has more than one node. The secondary is used to maintain a copy of the Group Creation table, and it becomes the primary node if the primary node for a network fails.

The basic process of primary and secondary node determination begins at startup, when a node first tries to become the designated secondary node on each local net. If successful, the node then tries to become the designated primary node. Transactions are initiated by either a primary-node request or a secondary-node request. No response to the request indicates that the negotiation succeeded, while a positive response indicates that the negotiation failed. If two nodes try to become the designated primary node or the designated secondary node at the same time, the node with the lower network layer unicast address becomes the designated node. A primary node then sends add-group entry packets and remove-group entry packets to the secondary node for a local network to maintain an identical group creation table.

In relation to a specific node or endpoint, an adjacent node exists on the same local network. Nodes periodically send out hello packets on each port. If a hello packet is not received from an adjacent node within a certain interval of time, the node's adjacency state is changed to not operational, and associated routes are marked unreachable. Notify packets are sent to each adjacent node whenever the state of a port in the node changes to a different operational state. Each node maintains an entry in the node table for each adjacent node. The table entry is allocated the first time that it receives a packet from adjacent node. Table entries include the time of the most recent hello packet and its state.

Tunnel nodes are point-to-point connections between nodes on nonadjacent networks through routers not implementing SMRP. Two distinct tunnel nodes are defined: tunnels between nodes, and tunnels between a node and an endpoint.

Tunnel nodes are maintained as entries in the adjacent node table in every node in the same way as for other adjacent nodes with respect to the use of hello packets and notify packets. Similarly, SMRP enables tunnel nodes to join and leave groups in the same manner as any other adjacent node.

NOTE   Cisco does not support tunnel nodes. However, SMRP can be enabled to run network layer tunnels between nonadjacent nodes.

SMRP Multicast Routes

SMRP relies on a spanning tree-based forwarding scheme to determine routing paths for multicast traffic. This route-determination process relies on the use of a distance-vector algorithm. A node sends distance-vector request packets to adjacent nodes at startup time and when routes change. The distance specified in the vector is the number of hops needed to reach a particular network number range. Nodes contain a vector for each entry in the network route table and send as many packets as necessary to send all the vectors. When routes change, each node sends distance-vector request packets to every adjacent node.

When a route is received on a port, the port-parent address must be set for the route for all ports. Because the group address is bound to the network address, the port-parent address also is used if a node is to handle a request for specified groups. When the port-parent address is the node's own address, the node is responsible for the request. Equal-path nodes decide which node is responsible for a request by determining which node has the highest network address.

When a distance-vector request with entries for unknown local networks is received by a node, network ranges for associated local networks are added to the network route table for the node, with a received distance incremented by 1. The adjacent node that sent the distance-vector packet then becomes the parent node for the local network. The table entry is updated if a distance-vector packet is received for known local networks, and if the distance-vector packet plus 1 is less than the entry in the node route table. A tie breaker is used if a distance-vector packet is received from an adjacent node with the same distance to a local network. The tie breaker is determined to be the adjacent node with a higher network layer unicast address. That node is identified as the parent node for the local network.

SMRP Multicast Group Management

In SMRP, multicast group participation is managed via a process involving negotiations among endpoints and nodes. An endpoint attempts to join a group by contacting a node on a local network. Any contacted node is responsible for joining the distribution tree for the group by activating paths to an existing distribution tree. Nodes leave a distribution tree for a group by deactivating paths whenever no more member endpoints for the group exist on those paths. Four basic processes are required to manage SMRP groups: creating, joining, leaving, and deleting.

An endpoint sends a create-group request to the designated primary node when it wants to start sending data to a group. The primary node then assigns an unused group address and allocates an entry in the group creation table. The primary node finally returns the group address to the creator endpoint and sends an add-group request to the secondary node, if it exists.

Endpoints send requests to initiate joining a multicast group. The parent node for a group on a local network responds to endpoint–join-group request packets. (A node determines whether it is the parent node by examining the network number in the group address.) When the parent node for a group gets a join-group request packet and that node is not yet a member of the group, the node forwards the join request toward the creator node of the group. Eventually the join-group request packet reaches a member node or the creator node for the group, and a join-group confirm packet is sent back along the reverse path. The member or creator node adds a child port to the group forwarding table if the join was received on that port. When data arrives in the reverse path, it is forwarded to all child ports. When the creator node receives the first join request for a group, it forwards the request to the creator endpoint to enable it to start sending data.

To leave a multicast group, endpoints send leave-group request packets on their local net. The parent node for the group on a local net returns a leave-group confirm packet to the endpoint and sends out a group-member request packet on the child port. If the parent node does not get a group-member confirm packet on the child port from a member node or endpoint, the parent node removes that port from the entry. If the parent node has no child ports left in the entry, it sets the state of the entry to leaving and sends a leave-group request packet up the distribution tree to its parent node. Each respective parent node removes the entry from its group forwarding table when it receives the leave-group confirm packet.

The endpoint sends a delete-group request when it wants to stop sending data to the group. Only the designated primary node responds to this request.

Forwarding Multicast Datagrams

SMRP data forwarding involves nodes forwarding multicast datagrams on active paths of the source tree for a particular group. An active path has member endpoints on it for the group, or it is a path needed as a transit path to reach other active paths. The subset of active paths for the source tree is the distribution tree for the group. Data forwarding under SMRP involves a series of negotiations among endpoints and nodes. In general, nodes receive multicast datagrams when endpoints send data to a group. The creator endpoint can send data packets with a network layer multicast address to its local network after it receives a join request from the creator node. Parent nodes on the local network receive this multicast and forward the packet to all child ports in the forwarding table for the group. A node multicasts a packet on a local network only if it is the parent node for the group on that local network and if the data was received on the parent port for the group. Nodes also forward data to adjacent tunnel nodes that are members of the group. In the case of an SMRP tunnel, multicast datagrams are encapsulated in a unicast network layer packet.

Handling SMRP Topology Changes

Topology maps are maintained by SMRP entities to manage path or membership changes within an SMRP environment. SMRP anticipates a number of typical topology changes and defines specific techniques for handling them.

Disappearing Member Endpoints

To detect disappearing member endpoints, nodes periodically send a group-member request packet to each active child port. Each member node and endpoint returns a group-member confirmation packet to the parent node. If no group-member confirmation packets are received by the parent node, the node sends a leave-group request packet to its parent node and then deletes the group entry.

Stranded Groups

To detect stranded groups, creator nodes periodically send a group-creator request packet to the creator endpoint. If after a number of retries no group-creator confirm packets are received by the creator node, the group is deleted. Network route tables are kept up-to-date by nodes sending distance-vector packets to their adjacent nodes when routes change. This allows nodes to change multicast group routing based on changes in topology.

SMRP Transaction Example

A typical SMRP-based transaction session involves a Macintosh workstation creating a group, other Macintosh workstations joining the group, and data being sent to the group members.

In a typical SMRP transaction session, a Macintosh (call this system Creator-Mac) first sends a create-group request to all nodes on a particular network. The primary router (Primary) for the local network assigns an unused group address and returns that address to the Creator-Mac. A Macintosh on a distant network (called Member-Mac) finds the Creator-Mac via the Name-Binding Protocol (NBP).

Creator-Mac then responds with the group address via an NBP response. The Member-Mac sends a join-group request to all nodes. A remote router (say, Router M) with a valid route to the group and a correct port parent sends a join-group request toward the Primary.

The Primary finally receives the join-group request and sends it to the Creator-Mac. It also adds the incoming port to the group in the forwarding table. The Creator-Mac confirms the join-group request and sends data to the group. The Primary receives the data and forwards it to the group's child ports.

Finally, the data is received by Router M, which looks up the group in the forwarding table and forwards the multicast data. The Member-Mac then receives data for the group.

SMRP Packet Format

Figure 51-2 illustrates the general SMRP packet format.

Figure 51-2 *A General SMRP Packet Consists of Five Fields*

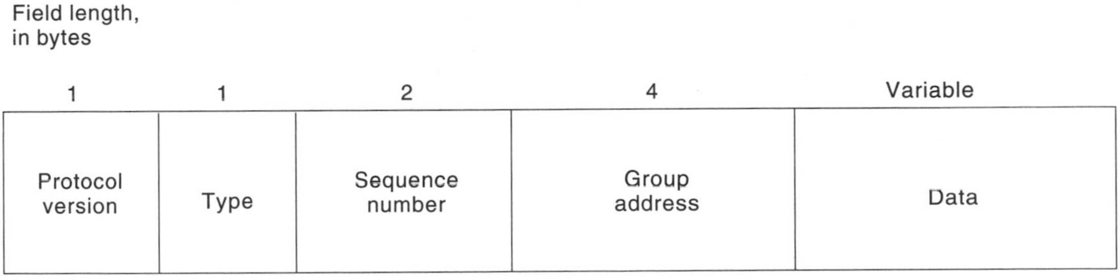

Field length,
in bytes

1	1	2	4	Variable
Protocol version	Type	Sequence number	Group address	Data

The following descriptions summarize the SMRP packet fields illustrated in Figure 51-2:

- **Protocol version**—Indicates the version of SMRP.

- **Type**—Consists of two subfields. The first 2 bits modify the packet type specified by the bottom 6 bits to identify whether a packet is a transaction packet and, if so, what type of transaction.

- **Sequence number**—Matches responses to requests in transactions to avoid duplicate requests and responses. All packet types are transaction packets and will have a nonzero sequence number (with the exception of multicast data packets and hello packets whose sequence numbers are set to zero).

- **Group address**—Serves as the designated primary node and assigns group addresses for all multicast sources on the local network. A particular local network can be assigned more than one network number, but multiple network numbers must be in a contiguous range. Nodes must configure network numbers that are unique to each local network and each primary node to prevent collisions of multicast addresses. When a primary node assigns a new group address, it arbitrarily assigns any unused group address for its network number.

- **Data**—Varies depending on SMRP packet type. Table 51-2 summarizes data characteristics based on packet type.

Table 51-2 *Data Characteristics Based on Packet Type*

Packet Type	Data Carried	Size
Multicast data	Data	Variable, depending on network layer datagram size
Hello	Port state	2 bytes
Notify	Port state	1 byte
Designated node	None	0 bytes
Distance vector	Multicast vector	8 bytes
Create group	None	0 bytes
Delete group	None	0 bytes
Join group	None	0 bytes
Add group entry	Network layer unicast address	Variable, depending on network layer address format
Remove group	None	0 bytes
Leave group	None	0 bytes
Creator request	None	0 bytes
Member request	None	0 bytes
Reject	Error indication	Short integer ranging from −7700 to −7710, depending on errors

Review Questions

1 Describe the SMRP address.

2 What type of message is sent when an endpoint-to-node request is made? What type of message is sent for a node-to-endpoint?

3 How does a node become the designated primary node on a network?

PART **VIII**

Network Management

Objectives

- Describe the need for network security.

- Identify and explain the security threats posed to networks.

- Discuss the importance of a security policy and its relationship to network security.

- Describe a defense-in-depth security solution.

- Describe how to mitigate the various threats against a network.

- Identify the tools used to improve network security.

CHAPTER 52

Security Technologies

The Internet has evolved from a network simply used to transfer files to a network that is used to purchase automobiles, fill prescriptions, apply for home loans, and pay bills. Companies have realized that to effectively use the network to conduct business, they must secure their networks. Governments have also recognized the need to protect individuals' privacy when their information is used by third parties, such as hospitals and financial institutions.

This chapter discusses the threats posed to networks and the principles of a defense-in-depth security solution when mitigating these threats.

Why Is Network Security Important?

Computer networks give companies and individuals different benefits and opportunities. An online book company relies on the availability of the Internet to allow customers from anywhere in the world to purchase a book anytime. A student in South America depends on an Australian e-learning company's servers to complete the courses required to obtain his technical product training. Ultimately, the importance of network security depends on the perspective of both the provider and end user.

This section focuses on the following factors that often dictate the need for network security:

- Growth of Internet applications
- Faster Internet access
- Government legislation

Internet applications have evolved from e-mail to streaming video and online banking. The introduction of these new applications has created new avenues for the hacking community to identify and exploit new vulnerabilities. These vulnerabilities include revealing passwords, causing a disruption of service, and obtaining unauthorized access to system resources.

With faster Internet access for home users with Digital Subscriber Line (DSL) and cable technologies, the Internet has expanded its boundaries. Now the average home user's PCs are more susceptible to attacks typically launched against corporate computers because they are "always on." In addition, faster Internet access has helped companies increase productivity by encouraging their employees to work from home. The worker's home network extends the company's network boundaries outside the company's walls. As a result, the company faces additional threats.

Governments have recognized the importance of network security and the role it plays in business and countries' infrastructure, such as transportation, water systems, emergency response systems, and the military. As a result, legislation has been introduced—and passed—requiring that appropriate network security measures be implemented. For example, in the U.S., the Health Information Privacy Protection Act (HIPPA) requires that health care providers protect a patient's health records. The European Union (EU) has enacted the EU Directive on Data Protection, which outlines how personal data is protected.

Security Threats

As networks evolve and new technologies emerge, so do the threats posed to networks. Entire books have been written on these various threats. This section discusses the most common:

- Unauthorized access
- Weak authentication
- Passwords
- Packet sniffers
- Application layer attacks
- Viruses, worms, and Trojan horses
- IP spoofing
- Denial of service (DoS)

Unauthorized Access

This broad threat encompasses the use of any system without the owner's consent. This act can range from a contractor who uses a company's network to run a multiuser online game server to a hacker accessing a home user's PC and retrieving personal files.

Weak Authentication

This threat includes a system that does not require authentication or that uses an authentication mechanism that provides little or no security benefit. An example of weak authentication is a web application that allows any user to add user accounts without first requiring authentication as a system administrator.

NOTE	Many systems have strong authentication mechanisms; however, they often are not implemented.

Passwords

Passwords are often a network's first line of defense. Passwords are used to authenticate and authorize users. Attackers often rely on the fact that users assign weak passwords and use the same password on multiple systems.

Systems generate password hashes based on an algorithm, such as MD5. A user enters a password that is hashed by the system. This is the password that hackers attempt to crack. Weak passwords can easily be cracked using password-cracking tools.

Password-cracking tools use two common methods to crack passwords: brute-force and dictionary. The brute-force method uses every combination of letters, numbers, and special characters to generate the password hash. The dictionary password-cracking method uses a list of words to generate the password hash. Both methods compare the password hash to the system-generated hash. If the hashes match, the password has been identified.

Packet Sniffers

Packet sniffers, also called *network sniffers*, are software applications that capture network packets off the wire.

NOTE	Packet sniffers capture traffic that exists on the same broadcast domain.

Network sniffers were generally used to perform traffic analysis to identify network bandwidth requirements and network problems. The hacker community developed packet sniffers to capture packets that had sensitive information, such as passwords, with the goal of using this information to gain unauthorized access to systems. These sniffers typically capture only packets with sessions associated with protocols and applications in which passwords are required (such as Telnet, FTP, HTTP, and POP).

Application Layer

Application layer attacks attempt to leverage weaknesses in the application's software implementation. The most common weaknesses associated with applications are buffer overflows. A buffer overflow is the result of trying to store more data in a buffer than has been allocated. Buffer overflows typically provide an attacker with a mechanism to execute malicious code with administrator- or root-level privileges.

NOTE   Aleph One's, *Smashing the Stack for Fun and Profit*, explains buffer overflows in technical detail.

Viruses, Worms, and Trojan Horses

A *virus* is a hidden, self-replicating section of computer software, usually malicious logic, that propagates by infecting (inserting a copy of itself into and becoming part of) another program. A virus cannot run by itself; it requires that its host program be run to make the virus active. Viruses are commonly spread through e-mail attachments, such as graphic images, word processing documents, and data spreadsheets. The virus is embedded in these attachments and infects the system when the user launches or executes the attachment. Examples of viruses include Melissa, BugBear, and Klez.

A *worm* is a computer program that can run independently or that can propagate a complete working version of itself onto other hosts on a network. It can consume computer resources destructively. Many consider a worm to be subset of a virus. Antivirus vendors, for example, include worms in their virus databases. Examples of worms include Nimda, CodeRed, Slapper, and Slammer.

A *Trojan horse* is a computer program that appears to have a useful function, but that also has a hidden and potentially malicious function that evades security mechanisms, sometimes by exploiting legitimate authorizations of a system entity that invokes the program.

IP Spoofing

An IP spoofing attack occurs when a hacker inside or outside a network pretends to be a trusted computer. The hacker can do this in one of two ways. He uses either an IP address that is within the range of trusted IP addresses for a network or an authorized, trusted external IP address to which access is provided to specified resources on a network. IP spoofing attacks are often a launch point for other attacks.

Denial of Service

Denial of service (DoS) attacks are perhaps most feared because downtime means lost revenue. The goal of a DoS attack is to disrupt or limit legitimate users' access to a resource. A simple form of a DoS attack can be caused by a brute-force password attack that causes users' accounts to be locked out. This can easily be accomplished from a single attacking host. DoS attacks typically involve sending a large number of unwanted packets to the target network from a spoofed IP address.

A new form of DoS attacks, distributed denial of service (DDoS), evolved in 2000. A DDoS attack uses resources from multiple systems using agent software that is controlled from a master system. This lets more packets be transmitted to the DoS's target.

Security Policy

A *security policy* defines and outlines a company's goals and objectives for securing its network. A security policy often includes the following sections:

- Acceptable use policy
- Password policy
- E-mail and Internet policy
- Incident-handling and response procedure
- Remote user access policy
- Extranet connection policy
- Allowed public services policy

An *acceptable use policy (AUP)* outlines what a user is allowed or not allowed to do on the network. It also defines the user's responsibilities as an authorized user. For instance, an AUP might state that the user must ensure that the antivirus software is run once a day.

A password *policy outlines* what constitutes a strong password, how often passwords are changed, how passwords are stored, and who has access to system passwords. For instance, the password policy might state that a router's enable password must be ten characters in length and must be changed every 90 days or whenever a system administrator leaves the group or company.

An *e-mail and Internet policy (EIP)* outlines which users have access to e-mail and the Internet. For example, an EIP might state that e-mail can be used only for business purposes and that Internet access is limited to sites deemed necessary for a user's job function.

An *incident-handling and response procedure* outlines how the network security staff deals with a security incident, such as a virus outbreak or an intrusion attempt. An intrusion response procedure for an intrusion attempt defines how to and who to contact when an intrusion attempt is detected.

A *remote user access policy (RAP)* outlines how employees access the corporate network from an untrusted network, such as an ISP network. A RAP, for example, can specify that each remote user must use Virtual Private Network (VPN) client software and one-time passwords (OTPs) to gain access to a corporate network or resource while telecommuting from home.

An *extranet connection policy (ECP)* outlines how business partners' connections are created. An ECP, for instance, can specify that partners are allowed to connect to the corporate site only by creating a site-to-site VPN tunnel using Triple Data Encryption Standard (3DES).

An *allowed public services policy (APP)* outlines which network services are made available to the Internet. Typically, public services include FTP, SMTP, HTTP, and DNS. An APP would specify that DNS services are made accessible only to root DNS servers.

Defense-in-Depth Security Solution

Traditional network security used to be considered a point solution or a single-device solution. The paradigm was, "Secure the network once or deploy a firewall, and you are protected." The network security community has learned that network security, much like any business process, is cyclical.

The security wheel, shown in Figure 52-1, depicts the recommended process of maintaining network security. The center of the wheel is the security policy. It has the following phases:

Step 1   Secure the network. Implement the security mechanisms outlined in the security policy. For instance, require authentication for all routers and switches deployed on the network.

Step 2   Monitor the network. Deploy software, such as an intrusion detection system (IDS), to monitor activity on the network. For instance, you could deploy a network IDS to monitor traffic allowed through the Internet firewall.

Step 3   Test the security. Periodically check the network's security to locate new vulnerabilities. This involves either hiring an outside consultant or using vulnerability scanner software to identify vulnerabilities and determine the effectiveness of the security mechanisms implemented in the secure phase. A popular networking-mapping tool is Nmap ("network mapper").

Step 4   Improve the security. Based on the findings in the test phase, enhance network security. For instance, if the testing phase identifies a vulnerability in the web server software, install the appropriate software patch in accordance with the vendor's recommendation.

Figure 52-1 *Security Wheel*

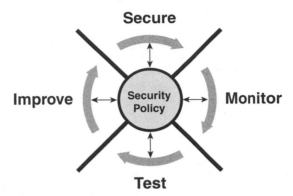

The defense-in-depth strategy is similar to wearing both a belt and suspenders. If the belt comes undone, the suspenders prevent your trousers from falling. In networks, the belt could be a filtering router, and the suspenders could be a firewall appliance. In other words, do not rely on only one line of defense. Each line of defense provides additional protection if one line of defense fails or is compromised. Figure 52-2 shows a defense-in-depth solution.

Figure 52-2 *Lines of Defense*

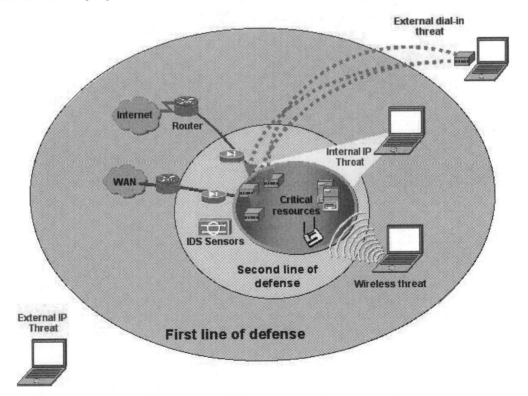

In Figure 52-2, the first line of defense in your network are the filtering firewall routers. Dedicated firewalls and IDS sensors are your second line of defense. Critical resources, such as servers, are further protected by host-based IDS, which is your final line of defense.

A defense-in-depth strategy is built on the premise that a network has multiple perimeters or zones. The security policy dictates the protection level implemented at each zone. Each zone protects devices that require different levels of protection and the complementary security technologies needed between zones. The zones can be divided into subzones if needed. Figure 52-3 shows a network divided into zones and subzones.

Figure 52-3 *Security Zones*

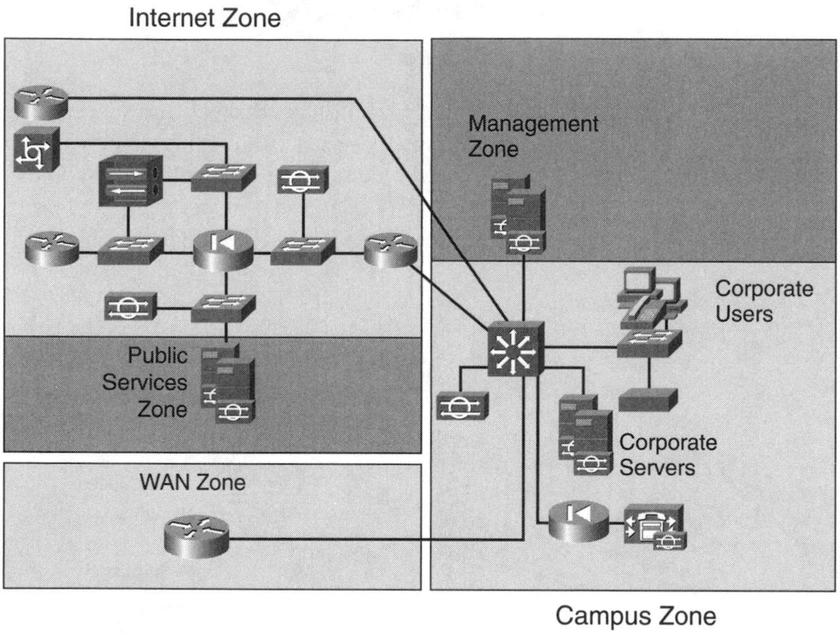

NOTE   The term *zone* is used instead of *perimeter* throughout this chapter.

The two primary zones in Figure 52-3 are Internet and Campus. The Internet zone is subdivided into smaller logical zones (subzones)—Public Services and WAN. The Internet zone has devices that provide connectivity to the Internet. The servers in the Public Services zone provide network services, such as HTTP and FTP, to Internet users. Security is implemented in the Internet zone using filtering routers, a firewall appliance, and an intrusion detection appliance. Host-based intrusion detection is used in the Public Services zone to complement that security mechanism implemented in the Internet zone.

Threat Mitigation

Not all security threats can be eliminated, which is why this section focuses on mitigating threats. Ultimately, a company must use its security policy to determine the acceptable risk and method to mitigate any given threat. The following are recommended methods of mitigating the stated security threats:

- **Unauthorized access**—Implement proper access controls that define which network traffic is allowed both into and out of a network.

- **Weak authentication**—Require the use of passwords on any network device. For environments in which strong authentication is required, implement authentication mechanisms, such as OTPs or biometrics.

- **Weak passwords**—Implement systems that enforce the creation of strong passwords. A strong password is one that has seven to 14 characters and does not include any dictionary words or common slang terms. Password aging and history should also be implemented to ensure that users are required to periodically change their passwords and that they do not reuse passwords. Most operating systems can enforce a strong password policy.

- **Packet sniffers**—Any data transmitted in clear text is susceptible to capture by packet sniffers. The following are common techniques used to mitigate this threat:

  - **Strong authentication**—The use of OTPs reduces the ability to use the captured password, because it is valid for only one use.

  - **Switching**—The use of switches reduces the direct threat that packet sniffing poses to a network where hubs are deployed.

  - **Cryptography**—Networks that require the most protection should implement cryptography through the use of IP Security (IPSec), for example.

- **Application layer**—Application layer attacks can never be completely eliminated. New vulnerabilities are discovered on a daily basis. The following are the common techniques used to mitigate this threat:

  - Stay informed of any vulnerabilities associated with your applications by subscribing to vendor security mailing lists.

  - Install security-related software patches.

  - Use host- and network-based IDSs to detect attacks launched against application servers.

- **Viruses, worms, and Trojan horses**—The use of antivirus software provides adequate protection for desktop systems. Personal firewalls can also be used on desktop systems. Host-based IDSs can be used on servers requiring additional protection.

- **IP spoofing**—Implement proper ingress and egress filtering as recommended in RFC 2827. Filtering RFC 1918 addresses is also encouraged.

- **Denial of service**—In addition to ingress and egress filtering, coordinate with your ISP to implement rate limiting on the ISP's router. Rate limiting can also be implemented on your edge router. Enable any anti-DoS features that can control the number of connections allowed to a specific host.

Security Tools

A key aspect of security is knowing what you want to protect. Many security issues arise because a vulnerable device was plugged into the network without the network administrator's knowledge. A complete network inventory must be taken to ensure that you know what exists on your network and what services are available.

A port-scanning tool is typically used to conduct the network inventory. The following explains the basic actions of a port scanner:

- It sends Internet Control Message Protocol (ICMP) echo packets to discover devices on the network. This is commonly referred to as *ping sweeping* the network.

- It sends Transport Control Protocol (TCP) connection request packets to devices to determine if common TCP services, such as HTTP, FTP, and Telnet, are available.

- It sends User Diagram Protocol (UDP) traffic to devices to determine if UDP services, such as DNS and SNMP, are available.

A network security scanner is used to determine if network services are vulnerable. This tool has a database of known security vulnerabilities and checks to see if the network service is vulnerable. The following explains some of the techniques this tool uses to determine if a service is vulnerable:

- It checks the operating system version. This is called *fingerprinting*.

- It checks the version of the software.

- It simulates the actual attack. For instance, if a server does not properly handle a long URL request, the scanner can send a long URL and check to see if the server returns a specific code.

Here are some other security tools that can be used to help secure your network:

- Nmap is an open-source utility for network exploration or security auditing. Nmap runs on most types of computers, and both console and graphical versions are available. A GTK+ front end for Nmap is available for users who prefer a graphical user interface tool instead of a command-line interface tool (see Figure 52-4). Visit the Nmap Web site at www.insecure.org for more information.

- Nessus is a free security-auditing tool that can identify the vulnerabilities that exist on your network. Visit the Nessus Web site at www.nessus.org for more information. A sample Nessus report is shown in Figure 52-5.

- SomarSoft has a suite of free Microsoft Windows utilities aimed at providing the system administrator information needed to secure a Windows system. The first is DumpSec, which is a security-auditing program for Windows NT and Windows 2000. The second is DumpEvt, which is a Windows NT program to dump the Event Log in a format suitable for importing into a database. The third is DumpReg, which is a program for Windows NT and Windows 95 that dumps the Registry, making it easy to find keys and values that contain a string. Visit the SomarSoft Web site at www.somarsoft.com for more information.

- John the Ripper is an open-source password-cracking tool that can identify weak passwords. Visit the John the Ripper Web site at www.openwall.com/john/ for more information.

Figure 52-4 *Nmap Front End*

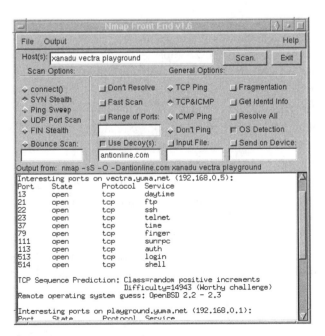

Figure 52-5 *Nessus Sample Report*

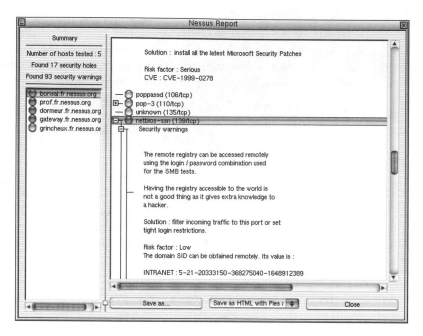

Summary

The Internet is no longer just a network used to transfer e-mail messages and files. It has changed our daily lives and how companies conduct business. Network security plays a key role in achieving goals for both individuals and companies. Individuals expect their information to be kept confidential when purchasing items online or registering for e-learning. The government is requiring companies to secure the data companies store on their networks.

The common threats posed to a network are unauthorized access, weak authentication, passwords, packet sniffers, application layer attacks, viruses, worms, Trojan horses, IP spoofing, and DoS attacks.

The network security policy is the document that explains and dictates the level of security a company implements on its network. A security policy outlines such things as how the company's users can use the network, how the company handles an incident, and how a company connects to partner networks.

A defense-in-depth security solution is based on the principle that multiple zones of defense are needed to protect the network. Each zone implements complementary defense mechanisms to ensure that if one zone's protection fails, the next zone can prevent the attack from succeeding.

The mitigation techniques used to protect a network depend on the threat posed. Password aging is used to mitigate attempts to protect against password attacks, not IP spoofing. The ingress and egress filtering techniques described in RFC 2827 are used to mitigate IP spoofing attacks.

System administrators can use port scanners, vulnerability scanners, and password-cracking tools to help improve network security. Port scanners help discover what network devices are on the network and what services are available. Vulnerability scanners identify weaknesses with devices on the network, such as routers, switches, servers, and desktop computers. Password-cracking tools help enforce password policies by identifying passwords that do not meet the requirements for a strong password.

Review Questions

1 What factors have influenced the importance of network security?

2 How have the growth of the Internet and emerging technologies affected network security?

3 How does a security policy affect a company's network?

4 Provide an example of a defense-in-depth security solution.

5 List common threats against networks.

6 Which network security threat attempts to flood a network with unwanted packets?

7 What type of attack involves sending e-mail attachments? How is this threat mitigated?

8 Describe how to mitigate IP spoofing attacks.

9 How does a switched infrastructure mitigate sniffer attacks?

10 What type of security tool discovers devices and network services available on a network?

11 What type of security tool identifies devices' vulnerabilities?

12 What type of security tool identifies weak passwords?

For More Information

Websites

- CERT, www.cert.org
- Cisco SAFE, www.cisco.com/go/safe

- Fact Sheet on EU Privacy Directive, www.dss.state.ct.us/digital/eupriv.html
- Health Privacy Project, www.healthprivacy.org/
- RFC 1918, *Address Allocation for Private Networks,* www.ietf.org/rfc/rfc1918.txt
- RFC 2196, *Site Security Handbook,* www.ietf.org/rfc/rfc2196.txt
- RFC 2827, *Network Address Ingress Filtering,* www.ietf.org/rfc/rfc2827.txt

Books

- Carter, Earl. *Cisco Secure Intrusion Detection,* Cisco Press: Indianapolis, 2001.
- Chapman, David, and Andy Fox. *Cisco Secure PIX Firewall,* Indianapolis: Cisco Press, 2001.
- Mason, Andrew. *Cisco Secure Virtual Private Networks,* Indianapolis: Cisco Press, 2001.
- Wenstrom, Michael. *Managing Cisco Network Security,* Indianapolis: Cisco Press, 2001.

Mailing Lists and Newsletters

- Bugtraq mailing list, www.securityfocus.com
- Cisco Security Consulting Security Bytes, www.cisco.com/en/US/netsol/ns110/ns129/ns131/ns267/networking_solutions_newsletters_list.html
- NTBugtraq mailing list, www.ntbugtraq.com

Glossary Terms

authentication. The process of verifying an identity claimed by or for a system entity.

Data Encryption Standard (DES). A U.S. government standard (FP046) that specifies the Data Encryption Algorithm and states the policy for using it to protect unclassified, sensitive data.

Internet Protocol Security (IPSec). A collective name for a security architecture and set of protocols that provide security services for Internet Protocol traffic. See www.ietf.org/rfc/rfc2401.txt.

intrusion detection. A security service that monitors and analyzes system events for the purpose of finding and providing real-time or near-real-time warnings about unauthorized attempts to access system resources.

one-time password (OTP). A simple authentication technique in which each password is used only once as authentication information that verifies an identity. This technique counters the threat of a replay attack, which uses passwords captured by wiretapping.

ping sweep. An attack that sends ICMP (RFC 792) echo requests (pings) to a range of IP addresses, with the goal of finding hosts that can be probed for vulnerabilities.

vulnerability. A flaw or weakness in a system's design, implementation, or operation and management that can be exploited to violate the system's security policy.

Objectives

- Provide a brief introduction to object-oriented information modeling.
- Provide a brief introduction to directories.
- Provide a brief overview of DEN.
- Show how DEN will be used in Cisco products.

CHAPTER **53**

Directory-Enabled Networking

Directory-enabled networking is not a product or even a technology. Rather, it is a *philosophy* that uses the Directory-Enabled Networks (DEN) specification to bind services available in the network to clients using the network. The DEN specification enables applications to leverage the capabilities of the network as well as better support the needs of the applications using it.

DEN is in reality two things:

1 A specification of an object-oriented information model that models network elements and services as part of a managed environment in a repository-independent fashion

2 A mapping of this information to a form that is suitable for implementation in a directory that uses LDAP or X.500 as its access protocol

More information on directory-enabled networking can be obtained from the book *Directory Enabled Networks*, by John Strassner.

Object-Oriented Information Modeling

An information model is fundamentally different than a data model or a schema (Figure 53-1). Here are definitions of each:

- **Data model**—A concrete representation of the characteristics of a set of related objects in terms appropriate to a specific data storage and access technology

- **Schema**—A set of data models that describe a set of related objects to be managed

- **Information model**—A *technology-independent* specification of the characteristics of a set of objects, and their relationships to other objects in a managed environment, with no reference to storage methods, access protocols, or specific type of repositories

Figure 53-1 *Information Models, Data Models, and Schemata*

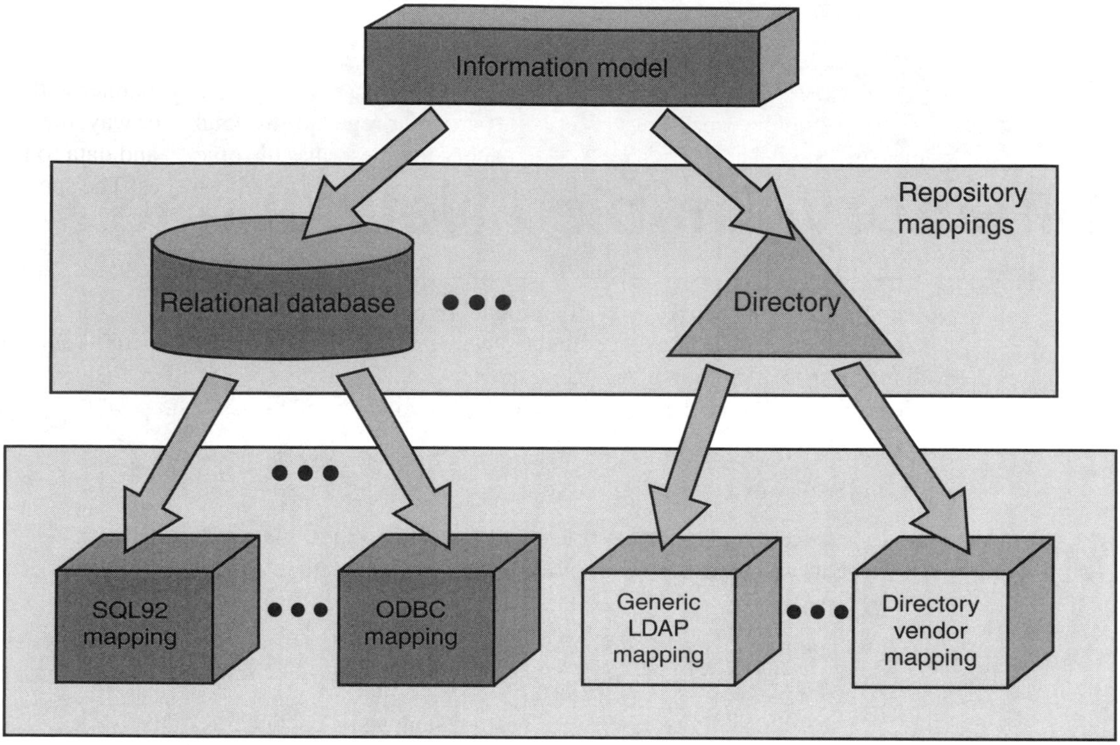

The primary purpose of the information model is to define a single universal representation of the data and objects to be managed that is independent of any specific storage technology and access protocol. The information model is used to define all appropriate objects in the environment that are to be managed and to show how they relate to each other.

Because the nature of the objects and the data describing these objects is different, it is therefore reasonable to expect that different data stores will be required to represent these objects and their interrelationships. For example, a policy might be written to change the type of queuing on a particular interface of an access router. This might be a function of the number of octets dropped and the number of users of specific service types (such as gold vs. silver vs. bronze service). Storing the results of an SNMP counter recording anything to do with the number of octets dropped is inappropriate for a directory because the counter data changes much too fast for the directory to keep up with. However, user service definitions, as well as the policy itself, are very appropriate to store in a directory because they can then take advantage of the replication mechanisms that directories have. As will be seen later in this chapter, directories are very well suited to serve as publication mechanisms; publishing data in a directory enables diverse applications to exchange and share data.

The advantage of the information model, then, is to be capable of representing how these different types of data and objects relate to each other in a single consistent manner without being biased by the capabilities of any one particular repository. Put another way, the information model specifies a *logical* repository that describes the objects and data to be managed. The logical repository maps into a set of *physical* data repositories. The specific set of data repositories to be used depends on the needs of the applications using the repositories. This enables the developer to choose the appropriate data store(s) and protocol(s) to use for a given application.

Applications have different needs, requiring different data stores. This isn't a problem— you simply build a set of mappings from the (single) information model to each type of data store that is being used. In general, these mappings will be different because each type of repository uses a specific type of storage technology that uses one or more particular access protocols. This makes one schema different from another. For example, a directory schema is fundamentally different than a relational database schema. However, all schemata so derived can be related to each other because they are all derived from a universal information model.

Data Models Are Bound to Specific Types of Repositories

A data model represents the fundamental characteristics of an object or a set of objects *in a way that is specific to a particular type of repository*. For example, there are fundamental differences between a router object and a user object. Furthermore, each object will have a different implementation in a directory than in a relational database, even though the same information is represented in both schemata.

The directory implementation will consist of a set of entries that have attributes defined according to the syntaxes (such as the data types and ways that you can search for and find information in a directory) supported in LDAP and X.500. In addition, it emphasizes containment. *Containment* describes the subordinate relationships between one object and other objects in the system. In our example, a user object is usually "contained" in, or scoped by, a higher-level object, such as a group or an organizational unit (a fancy X.500 word for "division").

The same user object implemented in a relational database will have a different structure than the same user object implemented in a directory. For example, data representing the user will be spread across one or more tables instead of existing within individual entries in a directory. Furthermore, the data will be structured slightly differently, to accommodate different data structures and access protocols that can be used in a database implementation compared to the directory implementation. Relationships to other objects, rather than containment of objects, is one of the main differences between a relational database implementation and a directory implementation.

An object-oriented information model uses object-oriented techniques to model information about a particular set of objects that exist in a managed environment. The key difference in an information model is that, in addition to describing the characteristics of entities, it also describes their behavior and interaction with each other. These latter two concepts may not be able to be captured in all repositories. Thus, the information model prescribes a means for relating different types of information, regardless of the type of data store that is being used. It is up to the developer to choose the right type of repository and other auxiliary tools to implement all facets of the information model if the repository itself is not capable of implementing the data and relationships in the information model.

An example may help to clarify this. Think of basing a decision to change the type of conditioning that a particular type of traffic is receiving on the network environment. This decision may depend on several factors:

- The number of dropped octets in a particular interface
- The service-level agreement assigned to a particular user or application
- Historical and other related information

These represent three fundamentally different types of information. Any one single data store is probably not optimal for storing this information because of the inherent differences in volume, frequency of update, types of queries, and data structures used to store and retrieve these data. The information model represents the relationships that each of these data structures have with each other and with other objects in the managed environment. This enables the developer to design optimized repositories to store each type of information and then recombine the data as appropriate. As another example, different data models could be used to model a router interface, users, and different types of services and application data that are provided on behalf of different users. However, the data model can't model the interaction between these objects. This is what the information model does. Therefore, we can see that different data models will be used to model different parts of the data described in the information model.

Thus, although directories are a very important type of repository for storing information about network elements and services, they are not the only type of data store that can be used. However, because directories usually contain the definitions of users, applications, and other network resources, they are often used in all applications to some extent. That is why this chapter concentrates on the mapping of DEN information to a form that enables DEN data to be stored and retrieved in a directory.

Realization of the Information Model

Currently, two important standard information models are being developed: the Common Information Model (CIM) and the Directory-Enabled Networks model, which is an extension of CIM. Both of these are currently governed by the DMTF.

The Common Information Model

CIM is an object-oriented information model that describes how a system and its components may be managed. It is defined by the Distributed Management Task Force (DMTF). Ongoing development of CIM is part of an industry-wide initiative for enabling enterprise management of devices and applications. A primary goal of CIM is the presentation of a consistent view of the managed environment, independent of the various protocols and data formats supported by those devices and applications. Many network infrastructure and management software providers have accepted CIM as an information model for enterprise management tools.

CIM is a layered information model, meaning that it consists of a set of submodels that build on and refine the knowledge present in outer, more generic layers. Specifically, a set of common abstractions and functions are defined in the core model (see Figure 53-2). These are then enhanced through the definition of submodels that are layered on, or use, the information in this core model. One of these layers is the network model, which came from DEN.

Figure 53-2 *The CIM Layered Information Model*

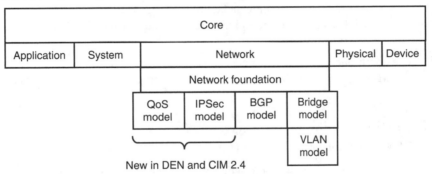

Version 2.2 of CIM consists of a core model, which is used to define concepts in the information model that apply to all areas of management. It is comprised of a set of classes, attributes, methods, and relationships that describe common concepts for managing systems and system components. The core model is the foundation for the class inheritance and relationship hierarchies, and is the basis for all common and extension models.

Common models are focused sets of classes, attributes, methods, and relationships that extend particular concepts in the core model. For example, the core model generically defines a service. The network model refines this concept to describe different types of services that are specific to networking, such as the forwarding and routing of traffic.

The best way to think of a common model is as a set of abstractions that frequently occur in a specific management domain. The seven common models are these:

- **System**—Defines key system components, such as computer system, operating system, file, and the relationships required to assemble them.

- **Device**—Defines how to realize physical devices in hardware and how to model connections between devices such as storage devices, media, sensors, printers, and power supplies.

- **Application**—Defines how to manage software installation within a system.

- **Network**—Defines refinement of the logical element class hierarchies to model network elements and services.

- **Physical**—Defines physical organization, containment structure, and compositions of devices and device interconnections.

- **User**—Models users, groups, and organizations, and shows how these objects interact with other components of a managed system.

- **Policy**—Builds on the original policy model proposed by DEN and provides a generic structure for representing and defining policy rules, conditions, and actions. It also specializes this to represent the specific requirement of QoS policy rules, conditions, and actions.

The combination of the core model and one or more common models provides the basis for a CIM- or DEN-compliant schema that can be bound to a specific application.

DEN, an Extension of CIM

DEN is two things:

- An extension of the information model defined in CIM that describes the physical and logical characteristics of network elements and services, as well as policies that control the provisioning and management of network elements and services

- A mapping of information to a format that can be stored in a directory that uses (L)DAP as its access protocol

The schemata for network integration defined in the DEN and CIM specifications are complementary. CIM is primarily concerned with the management of individual components in the context of an enterprise. DEN is primarily concerned with providing more detail about the networking components of a system, whether it is focused on the enterprise, the service provider, or both. This includes describing not just network elements and services, but also their provisioning and management through the use of policy objects.

The DEN schema, derived from the DEN information model, for mapping data in the DEN information model to a form suitable for implementation in a directory, incorporates concepts from both X.500 and CIM.

The utility of CIM is that it defines generic concepts of components to be managed in an environment. DEN extends CIM by adding information specific to networking that is more specialized than the information that CIM defines. The DEN mapping produces a directory schema that defines entries (along with other information) that can be added to an existing schema that represent network elements and services. It also defines entries that represent policy rules and related policy information.

The DEN information model and schema also incorporate information from the IETF Policy Framework working group (and possibly other working groups in the future) that has not yet been accepted by the DMTF.

A Brief Introduction to Directories

Today, the computing environment that must be managed includes not only the computers themselves, but also the network devices that connect them. Effective network management requires a variety of information from different sources, reflecting the different needs of the users of the network and the current state of the network. Furthermore, network management must be distributed throughout the various management points that are used to manage and control the network. Some of this information is appropriate for storing in directories, while other types are not. DEN prescribes a methodology to be used in modeling network elements and services so that information required for network provisioning and management may be implemented in whatever type of repository is appropriate. This usually involves directories, but it may also involve other types of repositories.

A directory service is a physically distributed, logically centralized repository of infrequently changing data that is used to manage the entire environment. Directories are commonly used to store information about users, applications, and network resources such as file servers and printers. DEN provides a schema that adds information to the directory. This schema in effect extends the directory, enabling it to contain information crucial for modeling network elements and services, as well as policies that control network elements and services. Better yet, DEN defines a schema that is independent of any particular directory vendor implementation.

Directories and Directory Services

This section provides a brief introduction to directories and directory services.

What Is a Directory?

A *directory* is used to record information about a particular group of objects. The directory is not intended to be a general-purpose data store. Rather, it is a special type of information repository whose primary purpose is to efficiently store and retrieve information about objects relevant to a particular application or set of applications.

Directory information is organized as shown in Figure 53-3. The groups of objects stored in a directory are organized in a hierarchical fashion. This is called the *directory information tree (DIT)*. The DIT consists of *directory objects*—each directory object corresponds to an entry in the DT. Each entry can have one or more attributes, and each attribute has at least one distinguished value (it may have more) and optionally additional nondistinguished values. This structure enables you to retrieve information either by specifying an exact set of criteria to be matched, or by specifying a more general set of criteria that describes the characteristics of the information that you are seeking.

Figure 53-3 *The Structure of Directory Information*

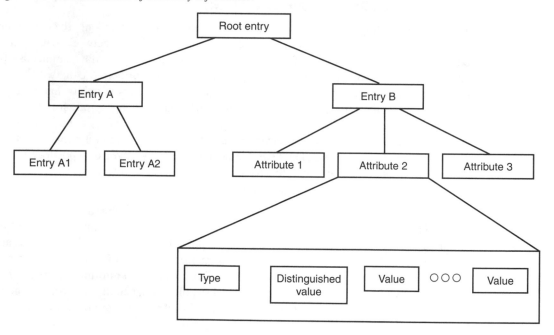

Distinguished values are used to compute relative distinguished names (RDNs) and fully qualified distinguished names (FQDNs). The FQDN for an entry is built by taking the FQDN of its parent entry and appending the RDN specified in the entry. Thus, the FQDN at any level is the set of RDNs that together specify a path from the root of the DIT to that particular directory entry. This is shown in Figure 53-4.

Figure 53-4 *Directory Entries, RDNs, and FQDNs*

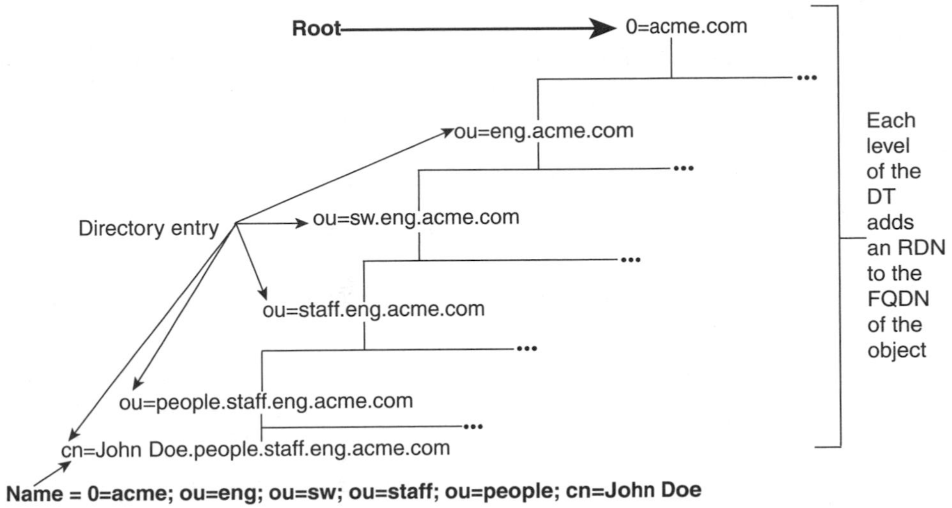
Root
0=acme.com
ou=eng.acme.com
Directory entry
ou=sw.eng.acme.com
ou=staff.eng.acme.com
ou=people.staff.eng.acme.com
cn=John Doe.people.staff.eng.acme.com
Name = 0=acme; ou=eng; ou=sw; ou=staff; ou=people; cn=John Doe
Each level of the DT adds an RDN to the FQDN of the object

An object in the real world can be modeled as one or more directory entries. Each directory entry is an object that has a set of characteristics describing the information carried by the object. These characteristics are implemented as attributes of the entry. For example, a User object might have attributes that define the first name, last name, employee ID, phone number, and other data associated with that user. Each of these attributes is common to all instances of the User class; however, the specific values of at least some of these attributes will be different so that different users can be identified.

The set of attributes that an entry has is determined by the *object class* of that entry. The object class defines which attributes must be included (for example, values must be specified for them) and which attributes may be included for a given entry (for example, they are defined in the schema but do not have to be instantiated). The complete set of object classes and attributes for a directory is defined as the *schema* of the directory.

Each attribute has a specific data type that may have restrictions qualifying the values of that data type (such as a string with alphanumeric characters only). This is called the *syntax* of the attribute. In addition, a predefined set of matching rules is defined for each entry to specify whether this attribute is considered a match for a search. (For example, given a string, ignore the case of each character in the string and see whether this attribute's value equals the value that is being searched for.) Attributes may also be multivalued, but they do not have to be. Finally, all attributes have object identifiers that uniquely define them. These are *ASN.1 identifiers*.

Characteristics of a Directory

Directories have five important characteristics:

- The storage of information is optimized so that it can be read much more frequently than it is written.

- Information is stored in a *hierarchical* fashion.

- Information in a directory is *attribute-based*.

- Directories provide a *unified namespace* for all resources for which they contain information.

- Directories can efficiently distribute information in a distributed system through replication.

The first point means that directories are very good at performing high-volume search operations (such as searching an address book), but not good at performing operations that require frequent writing (such as navigating an airline reservation system).

The second and third points are somewhat related. The second point means that the information infrastructure is based on parent-child relationships. Containment, not inheritance, is the driving factor of a good directory design. The third point refers to the fact that the directory is comprised of a set of objects. Each of the objects has a set of attributes that contain the information. Thus, the information is spread through the attributes of the objects that form the infrastructure of the directory.

The fourth point is very important. It means that common information can be located and shared by different directory clients because each application can use the same method of referencing an object. A unified namespace enables network elements and services to be seamlessly integrated with other types of information, such as users, applications, and servers.

The final point is critical for building an information infrastructure. The directory server has the capability to control what information gets distributed when and to what other nodes in the system.

What Is a Directory Service?

A *directory service* stores and retrieves information from the directory on behalf of one or more authorized users.

Directory services are built to provide certain types of application-specific information. However, multiple directory services can share the same directory. For example, think of two telephone books, a White Pages phone book and a Yellow Pages phone book. Both provide phone numbers, but in a different way. The White Pages phone book enables you to find the telephone number of a person, while the Yellow Pages phone book enables you to look up categories of information and retrieve multiple phone numbers.

A directory can be used to implement both of these services. In this example, the directory would contain the data model describing the different types of users and services that you are interested in. There are actually two different directory services, one for providing access to White Pages data and one for Yellow Pages data. However, they can use the same directory—the data model of the White Pages service is simply extended to suit the more complex needs of the Yellow Pages service.

This example also shows that directory services are usually restricted to operate in a particular way. For example, you can't give the telephone number of a user to a White Pages service and (easily) get the corresponding user.

Current Uses of the Directory

A traditional directory service provides a means for locating and identifying users and available resources in a distributed system. Directory services also provide the foundation for adding, modifying, removing, renaming, and managing system components without disrupting the services provided by other system components. Today's directory services are used to do the following:

- Store information about system components in a distributed manner. The directory is replicated among several servers so that a user or service needing access to the directory can query a local server for the information.

- Support common searching needs, such as by attribute (for example, "Find the phone number for James Smith") and by classification (for example, "Find all color printers on the third floor").

- Provide important information to enable single-user logon to services, resources, and applications.

- Enable a location-independent point of administration and management. Note that administrative tools do not have to be centrally located and managed.

- Replicate data to provide consistent access. Modifications made to any replica of the directory are propagated around the network so that any application accessing the directory anywhere sees consistent information after the change is propagated.

Motivation for DEN and Intelligent Networking

There are two major problems with pre-DEN directory servers and services that have prevented them from being used for intelligent networking. The first is the incapability for heterogeneous directory servers to replicate data with each other. The problem is that the LDAP protocol does not provide for this, and directory vendors have implemented their own proprietary replication mechanisms. Some directory service vendors use a form of synchronization, which is a tool that can read information from another vendor's directory server and translate that information into a format that can be used by the server performing the synchronization.

However, there are no synchronization standards (each works differently), and there are a variety of limitations with each implementation. It should be noted that this problem is currently being worked on in the IETF, in the LDAP Duplication and Update Protocol working group (LDUP). LDUP has defined an information model that has been used to guide the development of a replication protocol that is in the process of being standardized. This work should hopefully be finished by the end of 2000. More information about LDUP can be obtained at http://www.ietf.org/html.charters/ldup-charter.html.

The second problem is the lack of standardization in representing information. For example, there are many competing ways for representing generic user information. In addition, there is a tendency to design applications in a stovepipe fashion. This means that applications tend to represent data according to a set of naming conventions and structures that makes most sense to their use. Although this is beneficial for a single application, it makes it hard for different applications to share and reuse data. This problem is illustrated in Figure 53-5.

Figure 53-5   *Integration of Stovepipe Applications Is Very Difficult*

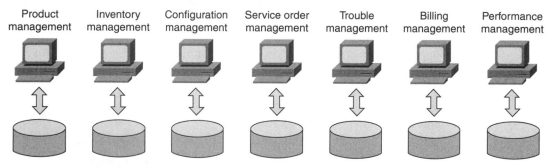

| Product management | Inventory management | Configuration management | Service order management | Trouble management | Billing management | Performance management |

- Architectural issues
  - Data redundancy
  - Synchronization problems
  - Application authorization issues
  - Vendor and application "lock in"

- Integration issues
  - Isolated data silos
  - Administrative nightmare
  - Integration/customization nightmare
  - Transition from legacy systems to a more flexible new operational architecture

As can be seen in Figure 53-5, the proliferation of disparate data stores, each built to support a particular application's needs, makes integration very difficult. The first problem is the continuing use of application-specific repositories. This is because each repository will define some of the same data using different storage and naming rules. This causes synchronization problems because now each copy of the data must be updated at the same time; because they are in different formats and representations, however, this is quite hard. Second, it results in different views of the same data. The final issue is integration. If all applications are using private versions of the same data model, how will they exchange data? Note that this also precludes the capability of applications to share and reuse the others' data.

Although this was a problem, a worse problem was that there was no standard at all for representing network elements and services before DEN. Therefore, DEN provides two important benefits:

- Network elements and services are represented in a standard way, enabling diverse applications to share and reuse the same data.
- All objects of a managed environment are represented as objects. This enables the different types of entities that make up a managed system to be treated in the same way. This provides a unified way of representing information about different types of entities.

As an example, think of the current way of providing unified network management. You might use HP/Openview for managing the different entities in an enterprise, and one or more Cisco-specific applications (assume for the sake of argument that they are running on Windows NT) for configuring and provisioning the Cisco devices in the enterprise network. This is a problem because these two types of applications need to share data. But this is very hard, if not impossible, because of these reasons:

- The applications have different ways of representing the same information (because they are built differently).
- The applications are running on different platforms.
- The applications are coded in different languages.
- Different user interfaces exist for each application.

Note that, in general, writing APIs doesn't work. This is not only because of the previously stated reasons, but also because a given API is usually a reflection of the internal functionality of the application. This requires the developer to have access to and be familiar with the operation of the application to be integrated. This clearly is not the usual case—and even if it were, each time that the applications being integrated change, the APIs would have to change.

DEN solves this by defining a standard way to represent information. By using techniques such as XML, developers can encode their data as represented in DEN and can ship it to another application on a different platform. That application can then decode the DEN data and use it directly in its own interface. Clearly, this is a very powerful concept:

- The administrator needs to learn only one application.
- APIs don't have to be built only to break with each change of each application.

- Data can be reused and shared between applications, which enables best-of-breed applications to work together seamlessly.

DEN therefore enables different vendors to build different network elements and applications that can communicate with each other. This enables various types of systems as well as network elements to be equal partners in implementing and reacting to decisions made throughout the networked environment.

Distributing Intelligence in Networked Applications

Rapid Internet growth over the past several years has created the need for more robust, scalable, and secure networking services. Residential customers desire rich multimedia services, such as data and video. Corporate customers are looking to telcos and service providers for powerful yet affordable services. Users want a reliable, easy-to-use, friendly service.

A fundamental shift toward bandwidth-intensive and isochronous network applications has occurred. Communication problems are no longer just a function of bandwidth. Rather, it is increasingly more important to understand the needs of different types of traffic flowing in the network and to design a network that can accommodate those needs. Furthermore, if resources become scarce, then an efficient way to allocate these resources according to the business rules of the company is required.

DEN plays a critical role in solving both of these problems. The information model is used to describe the function and needs of the different applications using the network. This translates into a set of traffic flows that will use the network. The DEN policy model can be used to translate from business terms to a form that is independent of any one particular device. This can then be used to map to device-specific protocols and mechanisms.

DEN Policy Model

The desire to allocate resources according to the business rules of the company is a critical requirement. The DEN policy model defined a continuum of policies, each optimized to represent different sets of information. For example, a business goal might be administrator-defined, which makes it device- and mechanism-independent. As an example, consider this business rule:

IF
   User is subscribed to gold service,
  THEN
    allow use of NetMeeting and
    provide premium data services
  ENDIF

This is a perfectly valid business rule, but it doesn't say how to configure the devices. It does, however, say what services should be allocated.

This business rule needs to be translated to device configuration rules so that the network can support the business policies of the organization. One such translation might be this:

```
IF
  SourceIPAddress = 172.3.128.0/15
THEN
  Mark Voice with EF and
  Mark Data with AF11
ENDIF
```

This rule starts mapping the services specified in the business rule to a form that can be applied to a device. This rule is device-independent in that it can apply to many different types of devices.

The next step is to map this to a form that can be implemented in a device. This means that we need to map the previous rule to a form that identifies the device mechanisms that must be controlled. There are several different forms of this, each appropriate for different actions:

- Configure component so that it can be used to condition forwarded traffic
- Configure component so that it can act on traffic directly
- Trigger action based on a network or system event (such as link failure)

This set of policy rules can now be translated into (for example) a set of device-specific CLI commands.

The advantage of this approach is that it can be used as a reusable template. That is, instead of trying to perform these mappings for each interface of each device in the network, a set of templates controlled by policy can be developed so that the device-independent rules can be separated from the device-dependent rules. The Policy Framework working group of the IETF is taking exactly this approach for the control and provisioning of QoS; see http://www.ietf.org/html.charters/policy-charter.html for more information.

Use of the Directory in Intelligent Networking

A directory service can be used to store and retrieve much of this information. This is because of the following four main reasons:

1 A directory is a natural publishing medium, capable of supporting a high number of reads as well as allowing arbitrary information to be stored and retrieved. Thus, there are no restrictions on the information itself; this provides inherent extensibility for accommodating additional as well as new information.

2 Directories are the *de facto* standard for containing user information and other types of information, and directory-enabled network applications require user, network, and other types of resource information to be integrated. The advantage is that information about network resources, elements, and services are not only colocated, but they are represented as equal objects that have a common representation. This enables the different applications that want to use and share this information to access a single repository. This greatly simplifies the design of the overall system.

3 Directories facilitate finding information without knowing the complete path or name of the object that has that information. A directory service is more than a naming service, such as DNS. A directory service enables both the searching and the retrieval of named information.

4 A directory can also be used to point to other systems that contain information; this provides a single place where applications can go to find information.

Challenges of Current Directory Services

Current directory services technology is not designed to meet the ever-increasing demands of today's public and private network applications. This is because current directory services were built mainly to accommodate administrative needs. Directories used in this fashion take the form of dumb warehouses, where they are simply used to store simple information. The directory must be transformed from a dumb warehouse to an authoritative, distributed, intelligent repository of information for services and applications. Viewed in this way, the directory is one of the foundations for an intelligent infrastructure.

Bandwidth-intensive and isochronous network applications require that the devices that lie on a path through the network between source and end devices be configured appropriately if they are to function properly. This configuration is often dynamic, taking place on demand when a particular user logs on to the network from any of a number of possible locations. Only when management information about the users, network devices, and services involved is available in a single, authoritative location is it possible to actually manage this new class of applications.

An Overview of DEN

This section defines the problem domains, information model, and usage for integrating networks with directory services. Directory-enabled networking is a design philosophy that uses the DEN specification to model components in a managed environment. These components include network devices, host systems, operating systems, management tools, and other components of a system to be managed. All these components use the directory service to do the following:

- Publish information about themselves
- Discover other resources
- Obtain information about other resources

DEN is two things:

1 An extension of CIM

2 A mapping of information to a format that can be stored in a directory that uses (L)DAP as its access protocol

The following sections provide an overview of building interoperable network-enabled solutions and the benefits that DEN can bring.

Networks and DEN

Administrative needs and the tools that service them have evolved as distributed systems have evolved. Today's directory services were designed to provide central management of security and contact information in a network with a relatively small number of relatively large computers. Network management has been the province of more specialized tools, each with its own information store. Application management has been addressed as an afterthought when it has been addressed at all.

Obtaining convergence on the structure and representation of information in any one type of repository (let alone across all the different information stores that are applicable to networking) has been very difficult. The result is an environment in which vertical management tools have proliferated. Lack of integration and the sheer complexity of the tools themselves has become a barrier to the deployment of new applications.

Administrators need a level of control over their networks that is currently unavailable. Streaming multimedia, use of public networks and the attendant security concerns, and rapidly growing user communities present a tremendous challenge.

Simply managing individual devices is no longer sufficient. Network administrators need to define and manage policies to control the network and its resources in a distributed yet logically centralized manner. In general terms, policies define what resources a given consumer can use in the context of a given application or service. The incapability to easily manage policies is a significant barrier to deployment of leading-edge distributed applications.

A consumer is a user, an application, a service, or another user of resources.

Defining and managing policies requires a common store of well-defined information about the network and its resources—users, applications, devices, protocols, and media—and the relationships among these elements. This is information about the network as well as the information traditionally viewed as defining the network (for example, routing tables). At issue is where to store policy and other information that needs to be applied across components in a way that makes it usable by a broad range of consumers.

A scalable, secure directory service that presents a logically centralized view of physically distributed information is the logical place to store the metainformation essential to creating and managing a next-generation network. The specification for the integration of directory services and network services defines the information model and schema to make this possible.

Two of the promises of DEN are these:

- To define a means of storing data in a common repository
- To provide a way for applications to be capable of taking advantage of data managed by other applications.

This represents a fundamentally new way of thinking about network management applications, along with applications that seek to leverage the power of the network. One example of this is to compare traditional network management with network management that uses DEN. In a traditional network management system, each device in the network is represented once. However, each device has detailed configuration information that is stored not in the network management system, but in either the application itself or another data store. The role of portraying the device in the network management system is to enable the user to launch a particular management application that is focused on one or more aspects of managing that device. Thus, the network management system provides a common place to represent the device, but not to store its information. This makes integrating applications and sharing information between different applications difficult, if not impossible.

This is very different than a directory-based approach that uses DEN. The fundamental purpose of DEN is to provide a common, unifying information repository that is used to store data and information about the data (such as metadata) for multiple applications to share and use. For example, consider a network management system using HP/Openview running on HP/UX. Suppose that it discovers a new router, one that it doesn't have any information on in its internal database. Before DEN, the only solution for the network administrator would be to purchase another management tool that supports the new router. Then, every time that router must be managed, the network administrator would have to get up and change consoles. Of course, this is only the beginning of the problems because the new management tool probably has its user interface and runs on a different platform.

With DEN, things have the potential to be seamless. I'll use an example from the 1999 N+I show in Atlanta, where HP and Cisco demonstrated this. Both HP and Cisco support DEN, which enables a set of common management information defined by the CIM and DEN standards to be exchanged (note that more detailed information can be exchanged by subclassing these standards and using them as the basis to represent Cisco-specific products and services). This was done by having the HP/Openview agent message the Cisco management agent, asking for the DEN description of the device. This information was encoded in XML and was shipped to HP/Openview over HTTP. The combination of XML and HTTP ensured that no platform- and language-specific problems got in the way.

However, the real bonus is that *the native Cisco router data is used to populate the HP/Openview screen*. This has the following implications:

- The administrator has to learn only one user interface.
- The system is inherently extensible. Because DEN is their common interface, it can dynamically accommodate new products as long as they are described in DEN.
- No complicated APIs must be built.
- Additional products that want to share data can do so.

Directory Service and Network Management

Network elements typically have a dynamic state and a persistent state. Dynamic state is well addressed by network management protocols. However, there is no standard way to describe and store persistent state. Moreover, existing tools and applications focus on managing individual network elements rather than the entire network. The DEN and CIM specifications define a standard schema for storing persistent state and an information model for describing the relationships among objects representing users, applications, network elements, and network services (see Figure 53-6). Network-management protocols (such as SNMP, CMIP, and HMMP) are used to talk to the network elements. The network schema extensions for the directory service are used to talk about network elements and services.

The integration of the network infrastructure with the directory service allows the applications and users to discover the existence of devices and relationships by querying the directory service rather than contacting the individual devices and aggregating the results. Exposing network elements in the directory enhances manageability and usability while reducing the load on the network. The end-user and administrator experience is enhanced because there is a single, authoritative place to obtain the information of interest.

The Extended Schema and Other Device Schemata

Schemata defined by SNMP (MIBs), DMTF CIM, and so on, are intended primarily to address the details of individual devices. The intent of the integrated, extended schema is to leverage the information exposed by existing schemata and management frameworks, not to replace them. Furthermore, the CIM and DEN information models are repository-independent. This means that the devices that are to be represented in and managed by a DEN schema do not themselves have to implement LDAP.

Figure 53-6 *Sampling of Important Base Classes of the DEN Schema*

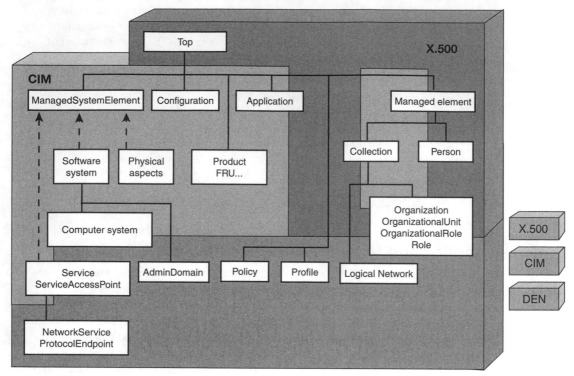

Network Applications Integrated with the Directory and Other Network Protocols

The schema and information model defined augments existing network services and associated protocols, such as Domain Name System (DNS), Dynamic Host Configuration Protocol (DHCP), and RADIUS.

The directory provides a common store for network information; the information model describes the relationships that can be represented in the directory. The usage model defines how existing network services and protocols work with the elements in the information model to accomplish specific goals, such as coordinating IP address allocation across multiple DHCP servers, establishing and propagating remote access login policy, and so on.

Benefits of Using DEN

DEN had three main use cases. The first was to help simplify device configuration. Device configuration has recently become increasingly complex, mainly because of two important factors. First, different types of users and applications are vying for limited network resources at the same time. The problem is *not* lack of bandwidth, but rather *traffic mix* (that is, how these different applications, all with their own specific needs, peacefully coexist in the same network). This has caused network device vendors to add more functionality in their devices. Thus, network devices are asked to do more, resulting in increasingly complex device configurations.

The second use case was to control the management and provisioning of network devices through the use of policies. The business community wanted a way to map service-level agreements and business rules to a common set of policies. These policies would *control the allocation of network resources* based on user, subnet, time-of-day, or other appropriate factors. Most importantly, they ensure that services are implemented in a hardware-independent way. Of course, this cannot be done without a standard information model.

The third use case is to define a means to make applications more network-aware and to make the network more application-aware. This is accomplished in the DEN information model by ensuring that network elements, services, and other components of a managed environment are all represented using objects. If all objects are equal and have equal capabilities, then they can all be represented equally well, and communication between them is assured.

Directory-Enabled Networks services benefit different constituencies in different ways.

For the end user, it helps enable single sign-on services. Single sign-on services enable the same set of access rights and privileges to be provided no matter where, when, or how the user logs on to the network (within the limits set by the policies of the system, of course). In addition, it enables individuals to be identified and provided services proportionate to their role in the company, service contract, and so on. It also helps companies enforce sophisticated policies. For example, a business rule may prohibit shipping code over the public Internet. Thus, even though a user successfully authenticates over a dialup line, the policy will correctly deny authorization to connect to a code server because the system recognizes that the user is connecting over the public Internet. The key technology used here is DEN's robust notions of services and policies, and the capability to link them to users as well as devices.

Service providers are interested in directory-enabled networking because they need a way to provide differentiated services. The $19.95 "all you can eat" philosophy doesn't even cover the cost of building out new networking infrastructure. In addition, they are interested in using directory-enabled networking to facilitate turning on new services through central management. The key advantage used here is the capability to define policy-based management of network elements and services, and to isolate the effect of turning on new services to a portion of the network.

Enterprise customers need a centralized way to protect mission-critical traffic and to better manage increasingly complex device configurations. DEN's capability to associate multiple traffic streams with a single application, along with its capability to define policy-based management of network elements and services, is critical here.

Application developers are provided a standard means of representing information describing network elements and services. This enables them to better leverage the power of the network. DEN's capability to describe applications, traffic that they generate, and how to manage these sets of traffic through policy is essential to implementing this goal.

How DEN Is Used in Cisco Products

Figure 53-7 shows the two layers of mapping that are inherent in DEN. The first is from the information model to a target repository. This mapping defines the type of repository to be used, which in turn defines the way data is stored, the set of data structures that can be used, the protocol(s) that will be used to store and retrieve the data, and other factors. The second mapping is sometimes required either to optimize the implementation to suit some application-specific needs, or because different vendors do not implement the same features in the same type of repository.

Figure 53-7 *DEN Mappings*

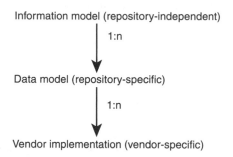

Information model (repository-independent)

1:n

Data model (repository-specific)

1:n

Vendor implementation (vendor-specific)

Cisco is using this philosophy to standardize its use of DEN. In fact, Cisco is building three models. The first is a standard mapping of the DEN information model into a set of implementations. A directory implementation of CIM 2.2 and the policy model will ship early in the second quarter of 2000.

The second is a set of common Cisco-specific extensions being developed by a cross-product group of Cisco engineers. This model extends the generic concepts of CIM and DEN to a device-independent intermediate layer. For example, the concept of a port is enhanced and linked to Cisco-specific network elements and services.

The third is a set of application-specific extensions that model Cisco devices and services. This set of models is derived from DEN and the Cisco extensions to DEN. It enables specific Cisco devices and services to be explicitly modeled to a very fine level of detail in the information model.

It should be noted that by basing the Cisco-specific extensions on DEN, Cisco proprietary network elements and services are modeled based on a standard. This is much better and more powerful than if Cisco had decided to base its work on either a competing standard or (worse) no standard at all. It guarantees a level of interoperability with the standard, and it opens the way in the future to exchange more detailed information with its partners. The same is true for the application-specific extensions that are based on the Cisco extensions.

The Directory-Enabled Networking Vision

The vision for enhancing networking through integration with the directory service is to provide network-enabled applications appropriate information from the directory. Eventually, intelligent network applications will transparently leverage the network on behalf of the user. The development of intelligent networks can be achieved through the following steps:

- Relying on a robust directory service
- Adding a standards-based schema for modeling network elements and services
- Adding protocols for accessing, managing, and manipulating directory information

The goals of work in developing directory-enabled networks are listed here:

- To provide support for applications that have the capability to leverage the network infrastructure transparently on behalf of the end user
- To provide a robust, extensible foundation for building network-centric applications
- To enable end-to-end network services on a per-user basis
- To enable network-wide service creation and provisioning
- To enable network-wide management

The focus is on providing management of the network as a system, not a set of disparate components or individual device interfaces. Using directory services to define the relationship among components allows the network manager to manage the network as a system. Vendors have adopted *de facto* open industry standards, such as DNS and DHCP, to tie these services into their enterprise management systems. DEN is the next such standard.

Summary

This chapter has provided a brief introduction to Directory-Enabled Networks. DEN is two very important things. First and foremost, it is an object-oriented information model that is used to describe entities to be managed in an environment. Although there are many such models, DEN is unique in that it is the only model to describe, in a repository-independent fashion, both networking elements and services as well as other objects that together constitute a managed environment. Second, DEN defines a mapping for the data specified in the DEN information model to a form that can be stored and retrieved in a directory (which uses either LDAP or X.500 as its access protocol).

A brief introduction to object-oriented information modeling, and the benefits of using such an approach, was described. This method enables any entity that needs to be managed to be modeled in a consistent manner in the managed environment. Directories are one important example of mapping this information. This is because directories already contain important information, such as users, printers, and other network resources. Conceptually, DEN extends the type of data that can be modeled in directories, and shows how that information is related to different types of data in other types of data stores.

DEN forms a cornerstone of building intelligent network services, as well as controlling systems through policies. DEN models the network as a provider of intelligent services, and models clients of the network as users of those services. This provides a methodology to make applications more aware of the network and to make the network more aware of the needs of various applications.

Finally, examples of how DEN is used within Cisco Systems to build a new set of intelligent products and solutions were provided.

Review Questions

1 What is DEN?

2 Does DEN require the use of a directory?

3 Is DEN just about modeling network devices and services?

4 What is an object-oriented information model?

5 Name some of the important benefits of DEN.

6 How does DEN model relationships between objects?

For More Information

DEN and Related Standards Work

The Desktop Management Task Force (DMTF) is the industry consortium chartered with development, support, and maintenance of management standards for PC systems and products, including CIM and DEN. More information can be obtained from http://www.dmtf.org.

Working Groups in the IETF

The charter of the Policy Framework Working Group of the IETF is available from http://www.ietf.org/html.charters/policy-charter.html.

The LDAPEXT (LDAP Extensions) Working Group of the IETF is chartered with continuing to develop an Internet directory service. The LDAPEXT Working Group defines and standardizes extensions to the LDAP Version 3 protocol, extensions to the use of LDAP on the Internet, and the API to LDAP. More information can be obtained from http://www.ietf.org/html.charters/ldapext-charter.html.

The LDUP (LDAP Duplication and Update Protocol) Working Group of the IETF is chartered with defining additions (protocol and schemata) to the LDAP protocol to enable different directory vendors to replicate with each other. More information can be obtained from http://www.ietf.org/html.charters/ldup-charter.html.

The RAP (RSVP Admission Policy) Working Group of the IETF is concerned with developing standards for enabling a scalable policy control model that can provide quality of service on the Internet using explicit signaling protocols such as RSVP. Common Open Policy Service (COPS) defines a protocol to transmit policy requests and responses. More information on both can be found at http://www.ietf.org/html.charters/rap-charter.html.

Simple Network Management Protocol (SNMP) is the de facto management standard for IP-based systems. Several IETF working groups actively work on the development of SNMP. Two to examine are these:

- http://www.ietf.org/html.charters/agentx-charter.html
- http://www.ietf.org/html.charters/snmpv3-charter.html

The goal of the first working group is to make the SNMP Agent more extensible. The goal of the SNMPv3 Working Group is to define the next generation of SNMP.

The Remote Network Monitoring Management Information Base is available in two versions. The following RFCs define it:

- http://info.internet.isi.edu/in-notes/rfc/files/rfc1757.txt
  ("Remote Network Monitoring Management Information Base")
- http://info.internet.isi.edu/in-notes/rfc/files/rfc2021.txt
  ("Remote Network Monitoring Management Information Base v2 Using SMI v2")
- http://info.internet.isi.edu/in-notes/rfc/files/rfc2074.txt
  ("Remote Network Monitoring MIB Protocol Identifiers")

RSVP is defined by several RFCs. The ones most relevant to this book are listed here. Also check the RAP Working Group. Go to the URL http://info.internet.isi.edu/in-notes/rfc/files/. Then pull the following files:

- rfc2205.txt—"RSVP Functional Specification"
- rfc2206.txt—"RSVP Management Information Base Using SMIv2"

- rfc2207.txt—"RSVP Extensions for IPSec Data Flows"
- rfc2208.txt—"RSVP Applicability Statement"
- rfc2209.txt—"RSVP Message Processing Rules"
- rfc2210.txt—"The Use of RSVP with IETF Integrated Services"

The Differentiated Services IETF Working Group is defining "relatively simple and coarse methods of providing differentiated classes of service for Internet traffic." Specifically, a small set of building blocks is defined that enables quality of service to be defined on a per-hop basis. This work is described in http://www.ietf.org/html.charters/diffserv-charter.html.

The Integrated Services Working Group of the IETF Recent Experiments demonstrates the capability of packet-switching protocols to support integrated services—the transport of audio, video, real-time, and classical data traffic within a single network infrastructure. More information can be obtained at http://www.ietf.org/html.charters/intserv-charter.html.

References on Directories

Probably the best source of information on directories is in the two IETF working groups LDAPEXT and LDUP, which were described previously. Two additional public URLs that contain some great information on directories are these:

- http://www.critical-angle.com/ldapworld/
- http://www.kingsmountain.com/ldapRoadmap.shtml

Strassner, John. *Directory Enabled Networks*. Indianapolis: Macmillan Technical Publishing, 1999.

Objectives

- Describe current network traffic overload issues.
- Describe how caching solves many of those issues.
- Describe how network caching works.
- Describe different caching technologies in use today.

CHAPTER 54

Network Caching Technologies

Introduction

Although the volume of Web traffic on the Internet is staggering, a large percentage of that traffic is redundant–multiple users at any given site request much of the same content. This means that a significant percentage of the WAN infrastructure carries the identical content (and identical requests for it) day after day. Eliminating a significant amount of recurring telecommunications charges offers an enormous savings opportunity for enterprise and service provider customers.

Web caching performs the local storage of Web content to serve these redundant user requests more quickly, without sending the requests and the resulting content over the WAN.

Network Caching

Network caching is the technique of keeping frequently accessed information in a location close to the requester. A *Web cache* stores Web pages and content on a storage device that is physically or logically closer to the user–closer and faster than a Web lookup. By reducing the amount of traffic on WAN links and on overburdened Web servers, caching provides significant benefits to ISPs, enterprise networks, and end users. There are two key benefits:

- **Cost savings due to WAN bandwidth reduction**–ISPs can place cache engines at strategic points on their networks to improve response times and lower the bandwidth demand on their backbones. ISPs can station cache engines at strategic WAN access points to serve Web requests from a local disk rather than from distant or overrun Web servers.

  In enterprise networks, the dramatic reduction in bandwidth usage due to Web caching allows a lower-bandwidth (lower-cost) WAN link to serve the same user base. Alternatively, the organization can add users or add more services that use the freed bandwidth on the existing WAN link.

- **Improved productivity for end users**—The response of a local Web cache is often three times faster than the download time for the same content over the WAN. End users see dramatic improvements in response times, and the implementation is completely transparent to them.

Other benefits include:

- **Secure access control and monitoring**—The cache engine provides network administrators with a simple, secure method to enforce a site-wide access policy through URL filtering.

- **Operational logging**—Network administrators can learn which URLs receive hits, how many requests per second the cache is serving, what percentage of URLs are served from the cache, and other related operational statistics.

How Web Caching Works

Web caching works as follows:

1 A user accesses a Web page.

2 The network analyzes the request, and based on certain parameters, transparently redirects it to a local network cache.

3 If the cache does not have the Web page, it will make its own Web request to the original Web server.

4 The original Web server delivers the content to the cache, which delivers the content to the client while saving the content in its local storage. That content is now cached.

5 Later, another user requests the same Web page, and the network analyzes this request, and based on certain parameters, transparently redirects it to the local network cache.

Instead of sending the request over the Internet and Intranet, the network cache locally fulfills the request. This process accelerates the delivery of content.

The important task of ensuring that data is up-to-date is addressed in a variety of ways, depending on the design of the system.

The Benefits of Localizing Traffic Patterns

Implementing caching technology localizes traffic patterns and addresses network traffic overload problems in the following ways:

- Content is delivered to users at accelerated rates.
- WAN bandwidth usage is optimized.
- Administrators can more easily monitor traffic.

Network-Integrated Caches

The first step in creating a network-integrated cache engine is to ensure that the network supports traffic localization, which can be achieved by enabling content routing technology at the system-level, and setting specific parameters to optimize network traffic. Cisco IOS ® Web Cache Communication Protocol (WCCP) is one example of content routing technology that can be set to support traffic localization.

Once the right network foundation is in place, network caches are added into strategic points within the existing network.

By pairing software and hardware, Cisco creates a network-integrated cache engine.

Network-integrated caches have at least the following three properties:

- Managed like networking equipment, resulting in minimized operational costs
- Designed like high-density networking hardware, resulting in better physical integration into the network infrastructure as network extensions and minimizing costs associated with leasing rack space
- Transparently inserted into the network, resulting in minimized deployment and operational costs and greater content availability

Existing Caching Solutions

The three most common types of caches on the market today are proxy servers, standalone caches, and browser-based caches.

Proxy Servers

Proxy servers are software applications that run on general-purpose hardware and operating systems. A proxy server is placed on hardware that is physically between a client application, such as a Web browser, and a Web server. The proxy acts as a gatekeeper that receives all packets destined for the Web server and examines each packet to determine if it can fulfill the requests itself; if not, it makes its own request to the Web server. Proxy servers can also be used to filter requests, for example, to prevent its employees from accessing a specific set of Web sites.

Unfortunately, proxy servers are not optimized for caching, and do not scale under heavy network loads. In addition, because the proxy is in the path of all user traffic, two problems arise: all traffic is slowed to allow the proxy to examine each packet, and failure of the proxy software or hardware causes all users to lose network access. Expensive hardware is required to compensate for the low software performance and the lack of scalability of proxy servers.

Proxies also require configuration of each user's browser—a costly and unscalable management task for service providers and large enterprises. In addition, proxy servers that are arranged in a hierarchical fashion form an additional overlay network, contradicting any plans to strategically converge disparate networks into a single, unified network.

Standalone Caches

In response to the shortcomings of proxy servers, some vendors have created *standalone caches*. These caching-focused software applications and appliances are designed to improve performance by enhancing the caching software and eliminating other slow aspects of proxy server implementations. While this is a step in the right direction, these standalone caches are not network integrated, resulting in higher costs of ownership and making them less desirable for wide-scale deployment.

Browser-Based Client Caching

Internet browser applications allow an individual user to cache Web pages (that is, images and HTML text) on his or her local hard disk. A user can configure the amount of disk space devoted to caching. Figure 54-1 shows the cache configuration window for Netscape Navigator.

Figure 54-1   *You Use the Cache Configuration Window to Configure the Amount of Disk Space Devoted to Caching in Netscape Navigator*

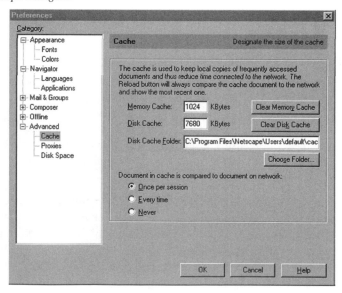

This setup is useful in cases where a user accesses a site more than once. The first time the user views a Web site, that content is saved as files in a subdirectory on that computer's hard disk. The next time the user points to this Web site, the browser gets the content from the cache without accessing the network. The user notices that the elements of the page-- especially larger Web graphics such as buttons, icons, and images appear much more quickly than they did the first time the page was opened.

This method serves this user well, but does not benefit other users on the same network who might access the same Web sites. In Figure 54-2, the fact that User A has cached a popular page has no effect on the download time of this page for Users B and C.

Figure 54-2 *This Figure Demonstrates the Benefits Gained by a Single Node Using Browser Caching*

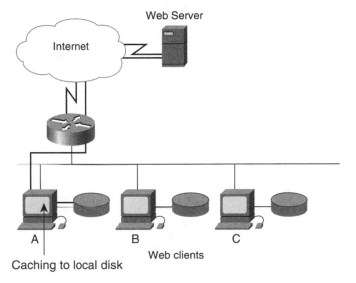

WCCP Network Caching

- In 1997, Cisco developed WCCP, a router-cache protocol that localizes network traffic and provides "network-intelligent" load distribution across multiple network caches for maximized download performance and content availability.

- The cache component of the Cisco caching solution comprises network-integrated caching solutions—the Cisco Cache Engine 500 Series. They are network-integrated because they:

- Provide network management capabilities already available on traditional Cisco networking gear (such as Cisco IOS CLI and RADIUS support), resulting in minimized management and operational costs.

- Are inherently designed and implemented as caching-specific networking hardware, rather than being standalone server platforms adapted as caches. Thus, the high-density Cisco Cache Engines physically integrate better into the network infrastructure as network extensions transparently insert into existing network infrastructures and adapt to unusual network conditions, resulting in minimized deployment and operational costs and greater content availability.

Network-Based Shared Caching

The cache engine was designed from the ground up as a loosely coupled, multinode network system optimized to provide robust shared network caching. The cache engine solution comprises the Web Cache Control Protocol (a standard feature of Cisco IOS software) and one or more Cisco cache engines that store the data in the local network.

The Web Cache Control Protocol defines the communication between the cache engine and the router. Using the Web Cache Control Protocol, the router directs only Web requests to the cache engine (rather than to the intended server). The router also determines cache engine availability, and redirects requests to new cache engines as they are added to an installation.

The Cisco cache engine is a single-purpose network appliance that stores and retrieves content using highly optimized caching and retrieval algorithms. (See Figure 54-3.)

Figure 54-3 *This Figure Shows a Cisco Cache Engine Connected to a Cisco IOS Router*

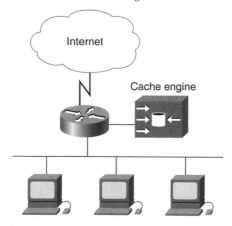

Transparent Network Caching

A cache engine transparently caches as follows (Figure 54-4):

1 A user requests a Web page from a browser.

2 The WCCP-enabled router analyzes the request, and based on TCP port number, determines if it should transparently redirect it to a cache engine.

3 If a cache engine does not have the requested content, it sets up a separate TCP connection to the end server to retrieve the content. The content returns to, and is stored on, the cache engine.

4 The cache engine sends the content to the client. Upon subsequent requests for the same content, the cache engine transparently fulfills the requests from its local storage.

Figure 54-4 *Transparent Network Caching*

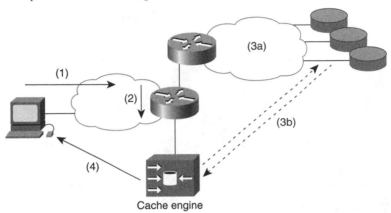

Cache engine

Because the WCCP router redirects packets destined for Web servers to a cache engine, the cache engine operates transparently to clients. Clients do not need to configure their browsers to point to a specific proxy server. This is a compelling feature for ISPs and large enterprises, for whom uniform browser configuration is expensive and difficult to manage. In addition, the cache engine operation is transparent to the network—the router operates entirely in its normal role for nonredirected traffic.

Hierarchical Deployment

Because a Cisco Cache Engine is transparent to the client and to network operation, customers can easily place cache engines in several network locations in a hierarchical fashion. For example, if an ISP deploys a Cache Engine 590 at its main point of access to the Internet, all of its points of presence (POPs) benefit (Figure 54-5). Client requests hit the Cisco Cache Engine 590 and are fulfilled from its storage. To further improve service to clients, ISPs can deploy the Cache Engine 590 or 570 at each POP. Then, when a client accesses the Internet, the request is first redirected to the POP cache. If the POP cache is unable to fulfill the request from local storage, it makes a normal Web request to the end server. Upstream, this request is redirected to the Cisco Cache Engine 590 at the main Internet access point. If the request is fulfilled by the Cisco Cache Engine 590, traffic on the main Internet access link is avoided, the origin Web servers experience lower demand, and the client experiences better network response times. Enterprise networks can apply this hierarchical-transparent architecture to benefit in the same way (Figure 54-6).

Figure 54-5 *Hierarchical Implementation of Cache Engines (ISP)*

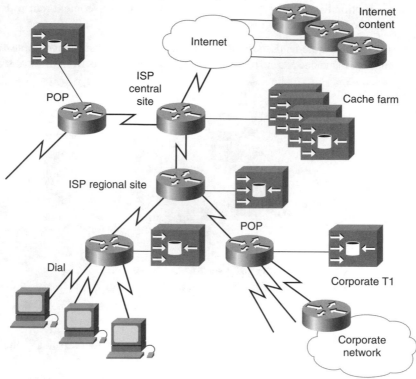

Figure 54-6 *Hierarchical Implementation of Cache Engines (Enterprise)*

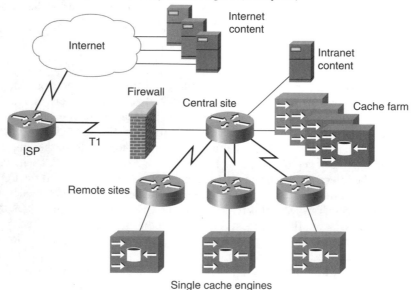

Scalable Clustering

The Cisco caching solution was designed to enable network administrators to easily cluster cache engines to scale high traffic loads. This design approach allows customers to linearly scale performance and cache storage as cache engines are added. For example, a single Cisco Cache Engine 590 can support a 45-Mbps WAN link and 144 GB of cache storage; adding a second Cisco Cache Engine 590 provides support for a 90-Mbps WAN link and 288 GB of cache storage. Up to 32 cache engines can be clustered together.

This linear scalability is achieved because of the manner in which WCCP-enabled routers redirect traffic to cache engines. WCCP-enabled routers perform a hashing function on the incoming request's destination IP address, mapping the request into one of 256 discrete buckets. Statistically, this hashing function distributes incoming requests evenly across all buckets. In addition, these buckets are evenly allocated among all cache engines in a cluster. WCCP-enabled routers ensure that a certain cache engine deterministically fulfills requests for a certain destination IP address on the Internet. Empirically, this distribution algorithm has consistently demonstrated even load distribution across a cache engine cluster. Most of the popular Web sites have multiple IP addresses, thus preventing uneven load distribution.

When the customer adds a new cache engine to the cluster, the WCCP-enabled router detects the presence of the new cache engine and reallocates the 256 buckets to accommodate the additional cache engine. For example, the simplest installation using one router and one cache engine assigns all 256 buckets to the single cache engine. If a customer adds another cache engine, the WCCP-enabled router redirects packets to the two cache engines evenly — 128 buckets are allocated to each cache engine. If the customer adds a third cache engine, the WCCP-enabled router assigns 85 or 86 buckets to each of the three cache engines.

Customers can hot-insert cache engines into a fully operating cache cluster. In this situation, the WCCP-enabled router automatically reallocates the buckets evenly among all cache cluster members, including the new cache engine. Because a new cache engine will not have any content, it will incur frequent cache misses until enough content has been populated in its local storage. To alleviate this cold startup problem, the new cache engine, for an initial period, sends a message to the other cache cluster members to see if they have the requested content. If they have the content, they will send it to the new cache engine. Once the new cache engine determines it has retrieved enough content from its peers (based on configurable numbers), it will handle cache misses by directly requesting the content from the end server rather than from its peers.

Fault Tolerance and Fail Safety

If any cache engine in a cache cluster fails, the cluster automatically heals itself. The WCCP-enabled router redistributes the failed cache engine's load evenly among the remaining cache engines. The cache cluster continues operation using one less cache engine, but operation is otherwise unaffected.

The Cisco network caching solution enables an WCCP-enabled, Multigroup Hot-Standby Router Protocol (MHSRP) router pair to share a cache engine cluster, creating a fully redundant caching system. This is referred to as *WCCP multihoming*. If the WCCP-enabled router fails, existing Cisco IOS fault tolerance and fail-safe mechanisms are applied. For example, a hot-standby router could dynamically take over operations, redirecting Web requests to the cache cluster.

If an entire cache cluster fails, the WCCP-enabled router automatically stops redirecting traffic to the cache cluster, sending clients' Web requests to the actual destination Web site in the traditional fashion. This loss of the entire cache cluster can appear to users as an increase in download time for Web content, but has no other significant effect. This designed-in, failsafe response is made possible because the cache cluster is not directly in line with clients' other network traffic.

WCCP Multihome Router Support

As previously mentioned, the Cisco network caching solution enables a cache engine cluster to home to multiple WCCP-enabled routers for added redundancy. Thus, Web traffic from all of the WCCP home routers will be redirected to the cache cluster. For example, a cache engine cluster that is homing to both routers in a MHSRP router pair creates a fully redundant caching system, eliminating any single points of failure (Figure 54-7).

Figure 54-7   *Fully Redundant Cache Engine Cluster Configuration*

Overload Bypass

With a sudden Web traffic surge, a cache engine cluster could become overloaded. To gracefully handle this overload situation, each cache engine detects when it is overloaded, refuses additional requests, and forwards them to the origin Web servers. The origin Web servers respond directly to the clients because the bypassed requests were not handled by a cache engine (Figure 54-8).

Figure 54-8 *Overload Bypass*

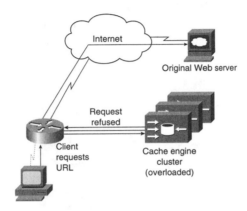

The overloaded cache engine will resume accepting requests when it determines that it has the resources to do so without retriggering overload bypass in the near future. The overload bypass on/off triggers are automatically determined by CPU and file system load. In the extreme situation that the cache engine becomes so overloaded that it is unable to respond to the basic WCCP status check messages from its home router, the WCCP home router will remove the cache engine from the cluster and reallocate its buckets.

Thus, overload bypass ensures that a cache engine cluster does not introduce abnormal latencies and maintains network availability even under unusually high traffic conditions.

Dynamic Client Bypass

Some Web sites require clients to be authenticated using the client's IP address. However, when a network cache is inserted between a client and a Web server, the Web server only sees the cache's IP address and not the client's IP address.

To overcome this issue and similar situations, the Cisco Cache Engine has a dynamic client bypass feature that effectively allows clients, under certain conditions, to bypass cache engines and directly connect to origin Web servers. The result is that a Cisco Cache Engine can preserve existing source IP authentication models and pass through server error messages to clients. Because the cache engine dynamically adapts to these situations, less management is required to ensure cache transparency.

Dynamic Client Bypass Function

In Figure 54-9, a client issues a Web request, which is redirected to a cache engine. If the cache engine does not have the content, it will try to fetch the content from the origin Web server.

Figure 54-9 *Dynamic Client Bypass*

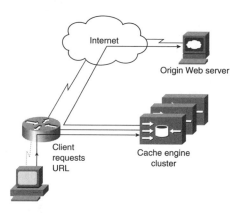

In Figure 54-10, if the server responds to the cache engine with certain HTTP error return codes (such as 401-Unauthorized request, 403-Forbidden, or 503-Service Unavailable), the cache engine will invoke the dynamic client bypass feature. The cache engine will dynamically store a client IP-destination IP address bypass pair, so that future packets with this IP address pair will bypass the cache engine. The cache engine sends an automatic HTTP retry message to the client's browser.

Figure 54-10 *Dynamic Client Bypass*

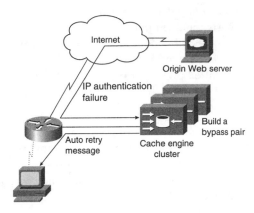

In Figure 54-11, when the client's browser automatically issues a reload, the request will be redirected to the cache engine. However, when the bypass table is checked and the request matches one of the table entries, the cache engine will refuse the request and send it directly to the origin Web server. Thus, the origin Web server will see the client's IP address, authenticate the client, and respond directly to the client.

Figure 54-11 *Dynamic Client Bypass*

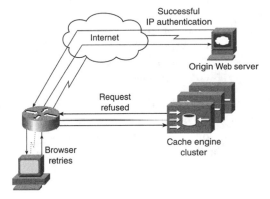

Reverse Proxy Caching

Cache engines are frequently deployed nearby clients to ensure faster network response time and minimal WAN bandwidth usage. Thus, the caches are caching the clients' most frequently accessed content. In addition, cache engines can also be deployed in front of Web server farms to increase the server farm capacity and improve Web site performance. This configuration is called reverse proxy caching because the cache engines are only caching content from the servers for whom they are acting as a front-end.

This feature is particularly important when cache engines are acting as a front-end for server farms in which certain content is dramatically more popular than other content on the servers. Using reverse-proxy caching allows administrators to prevent a small number high-demand URLs from impacting overall server performance. Better yet, this means the high-demand URLs do not have to be identified, manually replicated, or independently managed from the bulk of the URLs on the servers.

Reverse Proxy Caching Function

In Figure 54-12, each cache engine homes to WCCP-enabled routers/switches that are supporting server farms. When an incoming Web request reaches an WCCP-enabled router, the router performs a hashing function on the incoming request's source IP address and port number, mapping the request into one of 256 discrete buckets. Statistically, this hashing function distributes incoming requests evenly across all buckets. In addition, these buckets are evenly allocated among all cache engines in a cluster.

Because the hashing function is based on source IP address and port number instead of destination IP address, a given Web object could be stored in multiple cache engines in a cluster. By spreading popular content across a cache cluster, reverse proxy caching allows multiple cache engines to service requests for very popular content. Thus, additional cache engines can be added to a cluster to incrementally scale the performance of a popular site and decrease content download latency.

Note that hashing on a destination IP address could also do the reverse-proxy caching. But in this case, all requests would have the same destination IP address and would be redirected to one cache engine. If you do not need to scale beyond one cache engine act as a front-end to a server farm, then this method is sufficient.

Figure 54-12 *Reverse Proxy Caching*

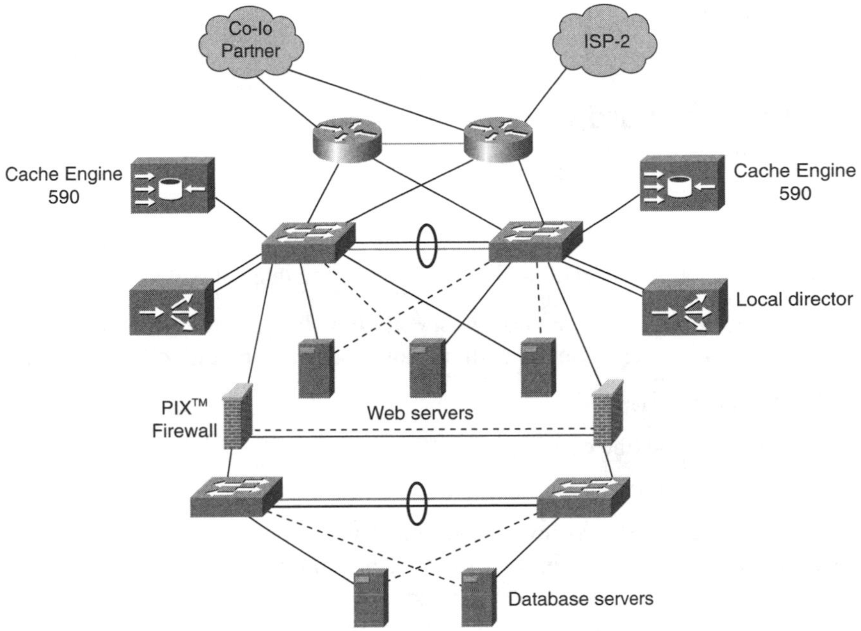

Ensuring Fresh Content

A requirement for any caching system is the ability to ensure that users see the same content from a network cache as they would from the Web. Every Web page comprises several Web objects and each Web object has its own caching parameters, determined by content authors and HTTP standards (see the "HTTP Caching Standards" section). Thus, even a Web page with real-time objects typically has many other objects that are cacheable. Rotating ad banners and Common Gateway Interface (CGI)-generated responses are examples of objects that are typically noncacheable. Toolbars, navigation bars, GIFs, and JPEGs are examples of objects that are typically cacheable. Thus, for a given Web page, only a few dynamic objects need to be retrieved from the end server, while static objects can be fulfilled locally.

Cisco Cache Engine products deliver fresh content by obeying the HTTP caching standards and by enabling cache administrators to have control over when content should be refreshed from origin Web servers.

HTTP Caching Standards

HTTP 1.0 and 1.1 are caching standards, which specify caching parameters for each object on a Web page.

HTTP 1.0 allows content authors to enable a "Pragma: no cache" header field for any object that should not be cached and allows authors to enable content to be cached indefinitely.

HTTP 1.1 allows content authors to specify how long content is to be cached. For each object on a Web page, content authors can choose among the following caching attributes:

- Noncacheable
- OK to cache (the default setting)
- Explicit expiration date

HTTP 1.1 has a freshness revalidation mechanism called If-Modified-Since (IMS) to ensure that cached data is up to date. A cache engine will send a lightweight IMS request to the end Web server when the cache engine receives requests for cached content that has expired or IMS requests from clients where the cached content is more than a configured percentage of its maximum age. If the object has not been modified on the end server since the object was cached, the end server will return a lightweight message indicating that the cache engine can deliver its cached copy to clients. If the object has been modified on the end server since the object was cached, the end server will return this information to the cache engine. If the case of the client issuing an IMS request, and the content is less than a configured percentage of its maximum age, the cache will serve the content without checking if it is fresh.

Cache Engine Content Freshness Controls

Administrators can control the freshness of Web objects in a cache engine by configuring a parameter called the *freshness factor*, which determines how fast or slow content expires. When an object is stored in the cache, its time-to-live (TTL) value is calculated using the following formula:

TTL value = (Current date - last modified date) * Configurable freshness factor

When an object expires, based on its TTL value, the cache engine will issue an IMS request the next time the object is requested (see "HTTP Caching Standards" section for a description of the IMS process).

If an administrator wants to adopt a conservative freshness policy, he or she can set the freshness factor to a small value (such as 0.05), so that objects expire more quickly. But the disadvantage to this approach is that IMS requests will be issued more frequently, consuming extra bandwidth. If an administrator wants to adopt a liberal freshness policy, the fresh factor can be set to a larger value, so that objects will expire more slowly and the IMS bandwidth overhead will be smaller.

Browser Freshness Controls

Finally, clients can always explicitly refresh content at any time by using the browser's reload/refresh button.

The **reload/refresh** command is a browser-triggered command to request a data refresh. A **reload/refresh** will issue a series of IMS requests asking for only data that has changed.

The **shift+reload/shift+refresh** command is an extension of the **reload/refresh** command. In correctly implemented browsers, this command always triggers a "pragma: no cache" rather than an IMS request. As a result, cache engines are bypassed and the end server directly fulfills all content.

Summary

Much of the traffic on the Web is redundant, meaning that users in the same location often access the same content over and over. Eliminating a significant portion of recurring telecommunications offers huge savings to enterprise and service providers.

Caching is the technique of keeping frequently accessed information in a location close to the requester. The two key benefits are:

- Cost
- Improved usability

Implementing caching technology in a network accelerates content delivery, optimizes WAN bandwidth, and enables content monitoring.

Cisco has created a network-integrated cache engine by pairing system-level software and hardware.

Review Questions

1 On what concept is network caching based?

2 What are two secondary benefits of implementing caching technology?

3 Provide a brief description of network-integrated caching technology.

4 How do Cisco cache engines ensure that web pages are kept up to date?

5 Name an object that can be saved in cache memory, and one that cannot.

Objectives

- Become familiar with storage networking and its purpose.

- Become familiar with the components of a storage network.

- Become familiar with the Fibre Channel protocol.

- Become familiar with the iSCSI protocol.

CHAPTER 55

Storage Networking

In today's world of automation, IT organizations continue to seek new methods, leveraging technology to optimize business processes and reduce overall costs. Gone are the days of visiting a bank teller and having your transactions recorded in a ledger. Instead, more and more business processes and services are being migrated to computer applications, offering faster service, greater access, better availability, and less-expensive operation. Today, you can execute bank transactions from an ATM, a web browser, a telephone, and even a PDA. However, the continual development and deployment of computer applications, especially Internet-facing applications, results in exorbitant amounts of data being created at a rapid pace. In addition, the availability and mobility requirements of such data continue to grow. Faced with the challenge of deploying and managing large amounts of stored data, IT organizations are changing the way in which storage is deployed, accessed, and maintained.

In the past, most deployed storage was directly attached (in the direct-attached storage [DAS] model) to the application servers requiring it. This attachment was commonly made over a parallel SCSI connection, although some relatively newer installations might have used direct (point-to-point) Fibre Channel loop connectivity. However, the DAS model presented inefficiencies in terms of performance, provisioning flexibility, and cost. By its nature, DAS was dedicated to the sole use of the application server to which it was attached. This made it difficult to add new capacity or redeploy unused capacity.

In addition to these inefficiencies, a DAS model posed additional costs because of the required management of numerous, and often heterogeneous, storage devices deployed throughout the data center. Finally, the directly connected channel bandwidth offered by a parallel SCSI or Fibre Channel loop connection was shared among all devices on the bus or loop. The shared-bandwidth model limited the number of storage devices that could be accessed and the overall available bandwidth.

To address the imminent storage challenge, many IT organizations continue to migrate away from the DAS model to a storage area network (SAN) model. By openly networking block storage devices with application servers, several advantages are realized. The SAN brings capabilities to storage, including a more granular provisioning and migration model. This allows quicker deployment and redeployment and a more efficient use of storage. The SAN also represents a centralized point at which consolidated storage resources, including disk and tape, can be managed more efficiently. Figure 55-1 shows the components and layout of a typical storage network. As you can see, a storage network can consist of a local data center and remote connectivity over metro-area networks (MANs) or wide-area networks (WANs).

Figure 55-1 *Storage Networking Model*

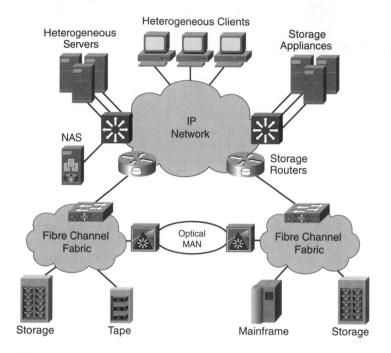

What Is a SAN?

A *SAN* is a communication network used to connect computing devices, such as application hosts, to storage devices, such as disk and tape arrays. In a common storage networking terminology derived from the SCSI protocol, the users of storage are called *initiators,* and the block storage devices are called *targets*.

The two primary communication protocols used to build a SAN are Fibre Channel and SCSI over TCP/IP, or iSCSI. Fibre Channel is predominantly the protocol of choice, because it has been in existence for some time. However, iSCSI, now a ratified IETF standard, lets you build a SAN using a less-costly Ethernet infrastructure. Figure 55-2 shows the *initiator-target* communication model as it relates to both Fibre Channel and iSCSI SANs. In the case of iSCSI, most common implementations include a gateway function that bridges an iSCSI Ethernet infrastructure into a Fibre Channel infrastructure. This hybrid SAN infrastructure results from the current lack of target devices that natively support iSCSI. The primary focus of this chapter is Fibre Channel, although an introduction to iSCSI is presented.

Figure 55-2 *SCSI Communication Model*

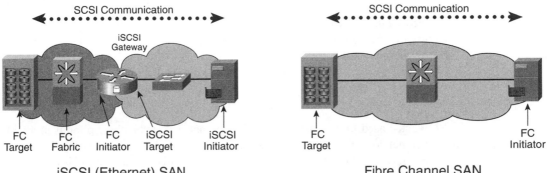

A SAN is built from a series of Fibre Channel or Ethernet switches, networked in different topologies to build larger networks with higher port densities. In Fibre Channel, an individual switch is called a *fabric,* and a connected group of switches is also called a *fabric*. The term *Ethernet fabric* is often used to refer to an Ethernet network used to build an iSCSI SAN. This chapter uses the term *fabric* to refer to a connected group of switches in a SAN.

The purpose of a SAN is to provide a flexible and centralized means of connectivity, such that large numbers of initiators can gain access to large numbers of targets. This networking model resembles a client/server model of networking rather than a peer-to-peer model.

A SAN is much like any other data communication network, including an IP network, in that it possesses the following characteristics:

- **Multiple protocol options**—Although the predominantly used communication protocol is Fibre Channel, other storage networking protocols exist including IBM's ESCON, FICON, and SSA. iSCSI is a newcomer to storage networking that offers lots of benefits in terms of infrastructure cost and manageability.

- **Multiple connectivity options**—A storage network possesses multiple connectivity options that depend on such factors as shared or dedicated bandwidth, speed of connection, length of connection, and connection media. For example, with Fibre Channel, you can connect using the arbitrated-loop method (shared), the fabric connect method (dedicated), copper or fiber media, or at speeds of 1 Gbps or 2 Gbps.

- **Hierarchical addressing scheme**—Storage networks, regardless of whether they use Fibre Channel or iSCSI, leverage a hierarchical, assigned address scheme to route data frames between end nodes. In addition, SANs possess a dynamic routing protocol, such as Fabric Shortest Path First (FSPF) in Fibre Channel. Such protocols dynamically build preferred paths within a SAN and provide alternative routing if a link in the network fails.

- **Integrated network security**—Storage networks, like other communication networks, incorporate features to selectively restrict visibility and communication between pairs of devices within a common physical network. In Fibre Channel storage networking, the concept of *zoning* is used to restrict visibility and communication to only nodes that are assigned to the same zone. Within an iSCSI SAN, mechanisms used to secure IP networks, such as access control lists, can also be used to secure iSCSI devices.

- **Network-based flow control**—As with any network, oversubscription is part of all storage network designs. It is always present because it is too costly to eliminate it from a network. Also, because of the premise that all communication is between initiators and targets, it is very unlikely that the targets can sustain the amount of I/O that can be generated by all initiators at their peak rate. Therefore, storage networks are designed with oversubscription, usually inherited from the chosen core-edge design model. However, there are cases in which congestion can occur at points of consolidation, such as uplinks from core to edge. Storage networks using Fibre Channel, like other networks, possess flow-control capabilities using a buffer credit mechanism that can throttle end devices to help eliminate points of congestion.

- **Network-based preferential service**—There are times within networks that you might want to provide preferential treatment of traffic through the network. Such treatment is often applied to give preference to certain applications and/or hosts during times of congestion. As with IP networks, storage networks built with Fibre Channel offer quality of service (QoS) capabilities, which allow preferential scheduling of frames based on a tagged frame identity, thereby minimizing the effects of congestion on application traffic generated from chosen hosts.

- **Hybrid communication model**—Two primary communication models are used in data networking. One common model is the *datagram* model, whereby data frames are simply forwarded into the network without any assurance that frames will make it to their destination or that adequate resources exist within the network to handle the injected data frames. Independent forwarding decisions are made at each hop along the path from source to destination. The second model is the *channel* communication model, whereby a dedicated channel is established from source to destination to reserve resources along a chosen path for the intended communication. Many network protocols actually use a hybrid of the two models. Fibre Channel, like TCP/IP, represents a hybrid communication model in that a channel is created from source to destination using a login procedure; however, no resources are generally dedicated along the chosen path. Each hop within a Fibre Channel storage network, like a TCP/IP network, makes independent forwarding decisions.

However, many differences between a storage network and a traditional IP data network must be recognized:

- **Sensitivity to latency**—The transactions that generally travel over storage networks are sensitive to excessive amounts of latency. These transactions, primarily consisting of SCSI commands, such as **read** and **write**, are synchronous transactions that are sequenced and that often depend on the previous command to complete before the next command is generated. Because of the high rates of I/O that can occur within a storage network, any excessive incurred latency can significantly affect an application's performance. Therefore, the goal within SANs is to minimize latency by reducing the number of hops between the source and destination and giving preferential treatment to high-priority data frames at points of congestion. This can be accomplished in both Fibre Channel- and TCP/IP-based storage networks through proper design and tuning.

- **In-order delivery requirement**—It is a general requirement to ensure that frames are delivered in order from source to destination within a storage network wherever possible. Although frames are sequenced with frame numbering, some devices within a storage network might not be able to reorder frames, or they might potentially suffer a fault condition should frames be received out of order. In all cases, additional latency is incurred if frames have to be reordered. Therefore, in designing storage networks and the load balancing of frames across equal paths or bundled links, it is important to try to keep frames associated with the same SCSI exchange traveling down the same path.

- **Log in to fabric**—Before exchanges can be sent between initiators and targets, all devices must log in to the network. Within Fibre Channel, this login occurs in two places. Devices must first log in to the network, and then they log in to each other before data exchanges may occur.

- **Permission-based flow control**—A unique characteristic of a Fibre Channel storage network is its permission-based flow control. Before devices can transmit frames, they must receive permission or *credit* from their neighbor, whether it be another device or the network itself. This credit is in the form of a *buffer credit,* otherwise known as a *receiver-ready (R_RDY) ordered set* received from the fabric. The *buffer credit* mechanism allows data flow to be throttled as necessary in a graceful fashion if congestion occurs within the fabric.

The following two sections provide a detailed account of the Fibre Channel and iSCSI protocols.

Fibre Channel Protocol

Development began on the Fibre Channel standards as early as 1988. The first American National Standards Institute (ANSI) standard was approved in 1994 and was named the FC-PH standard (ANSI X3.230:1994). Fibre Channel as a transport protocol was primarily developed to overcome the shortcomings of the current Small Computer System Interface (SCSI) parallel infrastructure, because it represented a higher speed and more-scalable transport. Although Fibre Channel can also transport other upper-layer protocols, including Intelligent Peripheral Interface (IPI), High-Performance Parallel Interface (HIPPI), IP, and IEEE 802.2, it is primarily used today to transport SCSI command sets and data.

Fibre Channel is defined by the ANSI T11 standards organization as using a layered services model. The ANSI *FC-PH Physical and Signaling Interface* specification defines the Fibre Channel layered services model shown in Figure 55-3.

Figure 55-3 *Layered Services Model*

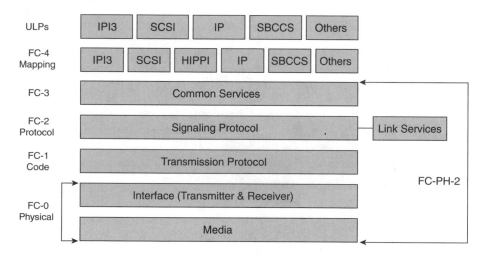

Each layer of this model provides a set of services, each relying on the layer below and serving the layer above. As you can also see, Fibre Channel was developed to support multiple upper-layer protocols. However, it is primarily used today to provide transport for SCSI-3 communication.

The following list describes each layer shown in Figure 55-3:

- **FC-0**—The FC-0 layer defines the physical interface specifications for a variety of media and associated receivers and transmitters. Media types may include various forms of copper and fiber, along with supported line speeds. Connectors, cable types, carrier signaling levels, and rates are also defined at the FC-0 layer.

- **FC-1**—This layer provides three primary functions. The first is encoding and decoding data streams. The 8B/10B encoding scheme is defined at the FC-1 layer, which intertwines the data characters with synchronization bits. The second function of the FC-1 layer is managing ordered sets. Ordered sets are unique transmission words that support link synchronization and control protocols. Frame delimiters are an example of ordered sets managed by the FC-1 layer. The third function of the FC-1 layer is managing link-level protocols and states, such as active, offline, link failure, and link recovery.

- **FC-2**—The FC-2 layer is responsible for the functions associated with the establishment of and communication between two ports. These functions include port login, the exchange (a communication construct through a Fibre Channel SAN) and associated frame sequences, flow control, and error detection and recovery. Each of these topics is covered later in more detail. The FC-2 layer also defines the Fibre Channel frame formats associated with all data and control frames.

- **FC-3**—The FC-3 (Common Services) layer is generally a placeholder for future advanced services, which are common across multiple ports of a node. Such FC-3 common services (some of which have been implemented but are not heavily used) include multicast services, compression services, and stacked connection request services.

- **FC-4**—The FC-4 layer defines how different protocols are mapped to use Fibre Channel. Such upper-layer protocols include SCSI-3, IP, virtual interface (VI), and several others. Each of these protocols' commands, data, and status are mapped to information units that are then carried by Fibre Channel.

These layers can roughly be mapped to the common OSI networking model and are meant to provide structure to the protocol for its understanding and implementation.

The following section explores the Fibre Channel protocol in more detail.

Fibre Channel Topologies

A Fibre Channel SAN can consist of multiple connection topologies, including switched-fabric, arbitrated-loop, and point-to-point. Each topology dictates associated Fibre Channel port modes that must be supported by the participating devices.

Point-to-Point Topology

Point-to-point topology is used primarily to connect a host directly to a disk or tape device. It offers higher bandwidth than a parallel SCSI implementation, but is restricted to communication between two devices. Point-to-point topology is giving way to a more network-oriented topology, such that more devices can be interconnected as one larger network or fabric.

Arbitrated-Loop Topology

A widely deployed yet older connection topology is the arbitrated-loop topology. An *arbitrated loop* is a logical loop consisting of up to 126 Fibre Channel devices that arbitrate for permission to transmit data. The loop is generally implemented using a Fibre Channel hub for cable management, thereby creating a star physical topology. All devices on the loop share the available loop bandwidth. For example, Fibre Channel disk drives are commonly arranged in smaller arbitrated loops within larger disk subsystems. The benefit of the arbitrated loop is that it can interconnect multiple devices.

Private Loops

Older loop topologies are generally called *private-loop topologies*, because the devices on the loop understand only an 8-bit private logical address of other devices on the local loop. This addressing scheme restricts loop devices from addressing devices on other loops. A more recent public-loop implementation supports a full 24-bit hierarchical address, allowing communication beyond the local loop to devices on other loops. Therefore, using a public-loop implementation, multiple arbitrated loops can be interconnected using a switched fabric.

Switched-Fabric Topology

The preferred Fibre Channel topology today is the *switched-fabric topology*. It offers the best of both worlds in terms of connection counts and available bandwidth. The switched-fabric topology represents a capability similar to that of Ethernet/IP switched networks.

Fibre Channel switches are arranged in a fabric and use a hierarchical 24-bit Fibre Channel ID (FC_ID) to route frames around the fabric from switch to switch. A Fibre Channel fabric may consist of a maximum of 239 switches, each with up to potentially 64 KB ports. Each port on a Fibre Channel switch provides a dedicated 1 Gbps or 2 Gbps of bandwidth to each connected device. A switched fabric also consists of a series of distributed services, including fabric-routing services, name services, and security services.

Figure 55-4 shows three of the four topologies.

Fibre Channel Port Types

Fibre Channel is a connection-oriented protocol in that *nodes* must establish a channel via a login before communicating. Communication is established between *logical elements,* otherwise known as *ports,* existing within physical devices. A port can be one of several types, depending on the type of physical device and the connection topology.

Port types autonegotiate depending on what device or topology they are directly connected to. However, you can restrict the port modes that can be negotiated.

Figure 55-4 *Fibre Channel Topologies*

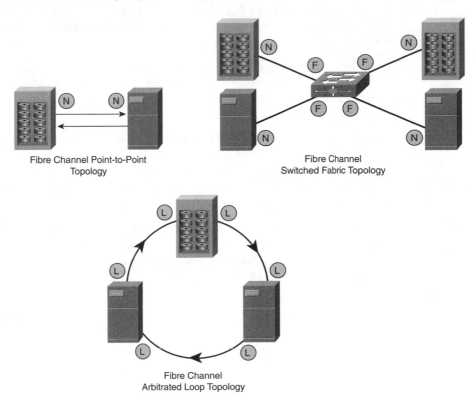

Fibre Channel Point-to-Point
Topology

Fibre Channel
Switched Fabric Topology

Fibre Channel
Arbitrated Loop Topology

The following list describes all the standard and some of the nonstandard common port types that are used in Fibre Channel SANs:

- **N_Port**—The most basic port type is the N_Port, or node port. All communication in a Fibre Channel network takes place between N_Ports or NL_Ports. An N_Port exists in an end device that is connected to a point-to-point or switched-fabric topology. Multiple N_Ports can exist within a single physical device.

- **NL_Port**—Node ports that are within end devices attached to an arbitrated loop are called node-loop ports or NL_Ports.

- **F_Port**—Within a switched fabric, switch ports that are connected directly to end devices (N_Ports) are called fabric ports or F_Ports.

- **FL_Port**—Ports within a fabric switch that are connected to a public arbitrated loop are called fabric-loop ports or FL_Ports. Using an FL_Port, public arbitrated loops can be connected over a switched-fabric topology. FL_Ports are connected to a loop of NL_Ports.

- **E_Port**—When two Fibre Channel switches are connected, the resulting port mode becomes an expansion port, or E_Port. The resulting link formed between two switches is called an Inter-Switch Link (ISL). E_Ports are connected only to other E_Ports.

- **B_Port**—The bridge port, or B_Port, is not a common port mode. A B_Port extends a Fibre Channel ISL over a non-Fibre Channel port. B_Ports connect only to E_Ports and participate only in a basic set of link services. Channel extenders over IP typically use a B_Port interface to extend a Fibre Channel ISL over the IP network.

- **TE_Port**—A special port mode negotiated between two Cisco MDS 9000 multilayer switches is a trunking-expansion port, or TE_Port. A TE_Port is a superset of an E_Port in that a special tagging mechanism supports the virtual SAN capability of building numerous logical fabrics on top of a common physical fabric. TE_Ports can be connected only to other TE_Ports.

- **TL_Port**—A translative-loop port, or TL_Port, connects private loops to public loops or switched fabrics. A TL_Port acts as an address proxy for the private devices on the arbitrated loop. A translative-loop function is useful for older Fibre Channel devices that do not support public addressing.

- **GL_Port**—A generic-loop port, or GL_Port, is not an actual negotiated mode, but rather refers to the port's capability. A port that can negotiate an F_Port, FL_Port, and E_Port is called a GL_Port.

Figure 55-5 illustrates the connection modes and possibilities.

Fibre Channel Communication Model

Fibre Channel uses a connection methodology that requires the setup of a channel between two devices before any exchange of data. However, several steps must occur to establish a channel. After the channel has been established, communication between two end devices occurs according to a hierarchical model.

The following is a list of the major steps required to establish communication between two devices using different Fibre Channel topologies. Several minor steps have been omitted for simplicity.

Figure 55-5 *Fibre Channel Connection Modes*

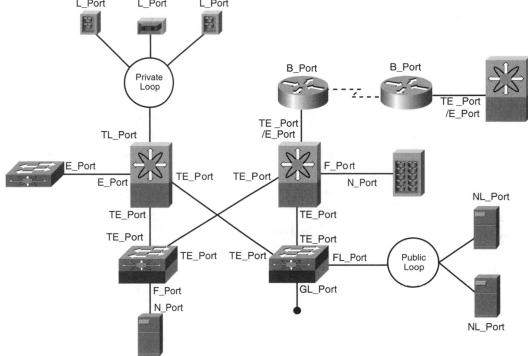

For point-to-point:

Step 1 Devices connected in a point-to-point configuration behave as two
devices on a private arbitrated loop. Devices connected point-to-point
must first perform a loop initialization procedure (LIP) to determine that
they are in a point-to-point configuration rather than an arbitrated loop.

Step 2 One NL_Port opens a channel to the other NL_Port.

Step 3 Ports can exchange data between themselves.

For arbitrated loop:

Step 1 Devices connected to an arbitrated loop must perform a LIP to acquire
an Arbitrated Loop Physical Address (AL_PA), an 8-bit address used to
communicate with other devices on the network. During this process, the
NL_Port determines whether an FL_Port is present on the loop, making
it a public loop. If no FL_Port is present, the loop is a private loop.

Step 2 One NL_Port arbitrates for access to the loop to communicate with another NL_Port.

Step 3 After arbitration has been won, the NL_Port opens a connection to the other NL_Port (or FL_Port if communicating with a device on the switched fabric).

Step 4 Ports can exchange data between themselves.

For switched fabric:

Step 1 Devices connected to the switched fabric must perform a fabric login procedure (FLOGI) to acquire a Fibre Channel address (FC_ID), a 24-bit address used to communicate with other devices on the switched network.

Step 2 One N_Port must log in to the other N_Port or NL_Port it will communicate with. It performs a port login procedure (PLOGI) to establish a channel with the targeted device.

Step 3 Ports can exchange data between themselves.

As soon as a communication channel has been established between two devices, Fibre Channel follows a strict communication model that consists of a hierarchy of data structures. At the top of the hierarchy is the exchange. A Fibre Channel exchange is typically mapped to an upper-layer protocol command such as a SCSI-3 **read** command. Each exchange consists of a series of unidirectional sequences. Each sequence consists of a series of numbered frames that travel from source to destination. Multiple exchanges may be open between two devices, each with its own set of originator exchange IDs (OX_IDs) and responder exchange IDs (RX_IDs). Figure 55-6 illustrates this hierarchical relationship and provides a simple SCSI-3 exchange example.

Figure 55-6 *Fibre Channel SCSI Exchange Example*

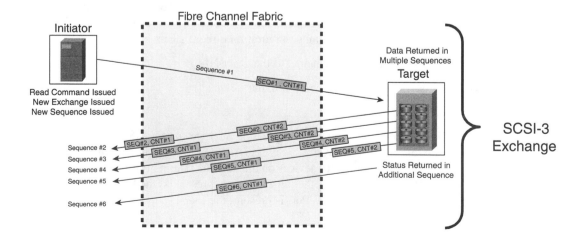

Fibre Channel Addressing

Fibre Channel has two types of addresses that are used to identify a device or switch port. The first is a globally unique assigned address called the *worldwide name* (WWN). The WWN is assigned by the manufacturer and is guaranteed to be globally unique. This concept is very similar to the MAC address in an Ethernet device.

The second type of address used in Fibre Channel is a dynamically assigned hierarchical address that lets frames be intelligently routed from one device to another. This address is called the Fibre Channel ID (FC_ID). In a Fibre Channel network, the FC_ID is mapped to the WWN such that initiators can use the WWN to contact a device, and it will be translated to an FC_ID for communication.

The FC_ID addresses assigned to devices depend on the type of topology:

- **Point-to-point**—Point-to-point connections are actually implemented as a private loop with two devices. Because the devices are in a private loop, they use only an 8-bit AL_PA. The address is in the range of 0x000001h to 0x0000EFh.

- **Arbitrated loop**—Arbitrated loops can be implemented as private or public loops that determine the type of addresses assigned. In a private-loop topology, a standard AL_PA is assigned in a similar fashion to a point-to-point topology. Each device on a private loop is assigned an address in the range of 0x000001h to 0x0000EFh (however only 126 devices may exist in a given arbitrated loop).

- **Public loop**—A public loop contains one or more FL_Ports that act as gateways to a switched fabric. As such, the addresses assigned to devices on a public loop contain a full 24-bit address. The first octet is the Domain_ID that is assigned to the switch. The second octet identifies the particular loop on the switch. The third octet is used for the AL_PA assigned to the devices on the loop. The FL_Port always has an AL_PA of 0x00h. Therefore, the valid FC_ID address range for devices on a public arbitrated loop are 0x*ddllaa*, where *dd* is the Domain_ID of the attached switch in the range of 0x01h to 0xEFh (1 to 239), *ll* is the loop identifier in the range of 0x00h to 0xFF, and *aa* is the AL_PA in the range of 0x01h to 0xEFh, where 0x00h is reserved for the FL_Port.

- **Switched fabric**—A switched-fabric address is based on FC_IDs that use the entire 24-bit address. Each switch within a switched fabric is assigned one or more Domain_IDs. This Domain_ID can be thought of as a routing prefix that the switch uses to route frames to devices connected to other switches. The first octet of a switched-fabric FC_ID is the Domain_ID. It is in the range of 0x01h to 0xEFh. The second and third octets of a switched fabric FC_ID are called the Area_ID and Port_ID, respectively. These components of the FC_ID must be locally unique on each switch. However, they are used in different ways by different switch vendors to identify end-fabric devices. Some vendors allocate these components based on the physical port to which an end device is connected. Other vendors allocate these on a first-come, first-served basis. The standard does not dictate any rules for how these address components must be allocated. However, the valid range for these components is 0x0000h to 0xFFFFh.

Table 55-1 summarizes the different FC_ID models and their addressing ranges and limits.

Table 55-1   *FC_ID Models and Limits*

	8 bits	**8 bits**	**8 bits**
Switch topology model	Domain (01-EF)	Area (00-FF)	Device (00-FF)
Private-loop device address model	00	00	Arbitrated loop Physical address (AL_PA) (01-EF)
Public-loop device address model	Domain (01-EF)	Area (00-FF)	Arbitrated loop Physical address (AL_PA) (00-EF)

Fibre Channel Frame Format

A Fibre Channel frame has the standard structure shown in Figure 55-7.

Figure 55-7   *Fibre Channel Frame Format*

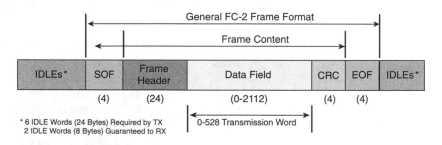

A Fibre Channel frame can range in size from 36 bytes to 2148 bytes, depending on the amount of data payload. The following is a description of the major components of a Fibre Channel frame:

- **IDLEs**—IDLEs are used for synchronization and word alignment between transmitter and receiver. IDLEs indicate the readiness to transmit and are constantly transmitted when no other data is presented to send. An IDLE is actually a 4-byte *ordered set* that is transmitted from one device to another. According to the Fibre Channel standards, every transmitted frame must have six ordered sets, which often include IDLEs, inserted afterward. Each received frame must be spaced by a minimum of two ordered sets.

- **SOF**—The Start of Frame is a 4-byte *ordered set* that immediately precedes the frame content. The SOF also indicates the class of the Fibre Channel frame to be received.

- **Frame header**—The frame header is a 24-byte header consisting of multiple control fields. The frame header includes fields such as the source FC_ID, destination FC_ID, exchange IDs, routing control, and several other parameters. The total structure of the Fibre Channel header is shown in Figure 55-8.

- **Data field**—The data field consists of the actual upper-layer protocol data. It can range from 0 to 2112 bytes.

- **CRC**—The Cyclical Redundancy Check is a 4-byte field used to verify the frame's integrity. The CRC is only calculated using the frame header and the Data field.

- **EOF**—The End of Frame is a 4-byte ordered set that immediately precedes the frame content. The EOF also indicates the class of the Fibre Channel frame.

Figure 55-8 *Fibre Channel Frame Header Format*

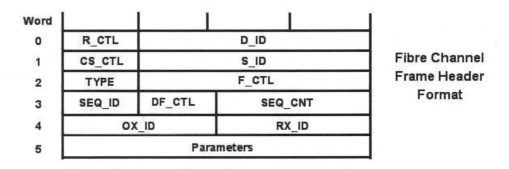

The following is a brief description of each field in the Fibre Channel header:

- **R_CTL**—Routing Control (1 byte) contains two 4-bit subfields, routing type, and information. Routing bits differentiate frames based on function or service, such as data frames versus link control frames containing commands or status.

- **D_ID**—Fibre Channel destination Fibre Channel ID (FC_ID) (3 bytes).

- **CS_CTL**—Class-Specific Control (1 byte) is used only in Class 1 or Class 4. The Fibre Channel classes are discussed in more detail in the next section.

- **S_ID**—Fibre Channel source FC_ID (3 bytes).

- **Type**—The Type field (1 byte) indicates the upper-level protocol carried in the frame payload.

- **F_CTL**—Frame Control (3 bytes) contains a number of flags that control the flow of the sequence.

- **SEQ_ID**—The Sequence Identifier (1 byte) uniquely identifies a given sequence within the context of an exchange. Each frame is identified within an exchange by a SEQ_ID.

- **DF_CTL**—Data Field Control (1 byte) specifies the presence of optional headers at the beginning of the Data field for Device_Data or Video_Data frames. DF_CTL bits are not meaningful on Link_Control or Basic Link Service frames.

- **SEQ_CNT**—Sequence Count (2 bytes) identifies the order of the transmission of frames within a sequence. It is used by a sequence recipient to account for all transmitted frames.

- **OX_ID**—Originator Exchange ID (2 bytes) identifies an individual exchange. This identity is set by the originator of the exchange.

- **RX_ID**—Responder Exchange ID (2 bytes) identifies an individual exchange. This identity is set by the responder to the exchange.

- **Parameters**—The Parameters field (4 bytes) is dependent on the specific frame type, as identified in the R_CTL field.

Fibre Channel Classes of Service

Fibre Channel defines several classes of service, although in practice only two classes are predominantly used. Each class of service is differentiated by its use of acknowledgment, flow control, and channel reservation:

- Class 1 is a connection-oriented service with confirmation of delivery or notification of nondelivery. A channel must be established from source to destination before the connection is granted.

- Class 2 is a connectionless service between ports with confirmation of delivery or notification of nondelivery.

- Class 3 is a connectionless service between ports with no confirmation of delivery or notification of nondelivery. This is the most widely used class of service in practice today.

- Class 4 is a connection-oriented service that provides a virtual circuit between N_Ports with confirmation of delivery or notification of nondelivery and guaranteed bandwidth.

- Class 6 is a multicast variant of Class 1 providing one-to-many service with confirmation of delivery or notification of nondelivery.

Table 55-2 provides an overview of the characteristics of each class of service. In SANs today, Class 3 is the most widely used. Most fabrics also support Class 2. Any other class is not commonly used today.

Table 55-2   *Fibre Channel Class of Service*

Attribute	Class 1	Class 2	Class 3	Class 4	Class 6
Connection-oriented	Yes	No	No	Yes	Yes
Bandwidth reserved	100%	No	No	Fractional	100%
Guaranteed latency	Yes	No	No	Yes (QoS)	Yes
Guaranteed delivery order	Yes	No	No	Yes	Yes
Delivery confirmation—ACK	Yes	Yes	No	Yes	Yes
Frame multiplexing with ports	No	Yes	Yes	No	No
End-to-end flow control	Yes	Yes	No	Yes	Yes
Link-level flow control	SOFc1	Yes	Yes	Yes	SOFc1

Fibre Channel Fabric Routing

In a switched-fabric topology, a dynamic routing protocol is used to route frames through the connected fabric. This routing protocol is called Fabric Shortest Path First (FSPF).

FSPF is loosely based on a subset of the IP routing protocol Open Shortest Path First (OSPF). FSPF is a link-state protocol that requires all switches to exchange link-state information, including the operational state and routing metric for each direct ISL. Using this information stored in a local database, each switch performs the well-known Dykstra algorithm to compute the shortest path to every other Domain_ID.

In the case where multiple equal-cost paths to the same domain exist, a load-balancing function is performed between the paths. Should changes to link-state status occur, such as a modified metric or failed link, link-state updates (LSUs) are advertised, and routes are recomputed based on the newly acquired information. By tuning link metrics, you can engineer traffic flows and recovery paths in a Fibre Channel network.

Fibre Channel Flow Control

One of the most effective mechanisms within Fibre Channel is the flow-control capability. Fibre Channel flow control is based on a permission system whereby a device or port cannot transmit a frame unless it has a credit. Fibre Channel has two flow-control mechanisms— *end-to-end* and *buffer-to-buffer*.

End-to-end flow control is used to pace traffic between two end devices and is not used very often. Buffer-to-buffer flow control takes place between every adjacent pair of ports along any given path in a Fibre Channel network or between two devices on an arbitrated loop.

Buffer credits relate to the number of input buffers that exist on the adjacent connected port. During a fabric login procedure, the number of buffer credits available to adjacent devices is exchanged. Buffer credits are replenished to the neighboring device when an input buffer is emptied. When an input buffer is emptied, a device generates a 4-byte R_RDY command and sends it to the neighboring device, thereby replenishing the credit.

Buffer-to-buffer flow control becomes increasingly important as distance is introduced between adjacent ports. As distance increases, transit delay or latency also increases. The added latency increases the time required to receive an R_RDY back from the remote end. If not enough credits are available, neighboring devices might not be able to sustain wire-rate use of the link between them because of the throttling nature of buffer credits.

This scenario is the basis of a planning exercise when extending a Fibre Channel SAN across an optical or SONET/SDH network for the purposes of remote data replication for disaster recovery. The rule of thumb is that one BB_Credit is required for every 2 km of distance to sustain 1 Gbps of utilization. For example, to sustain a 1-Gbps line rate over an optical 100 km link, 50 credits must be supported on either end. Any additional latency introduced through actions such as protocol conversion, compression, or encryption further increases the need for more buffer credits.

Figure 55-9 shows the Fibre Channel buffer-to-buffer flow-control model as it relates to communication between a host and a disk in a fabric.

Figure 55-9 *Fibre Channel Buffer-to-Buffer Flow Control*

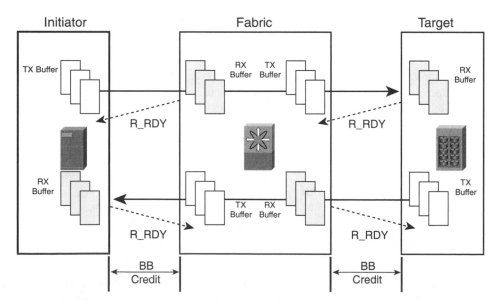

Fibre Channel Distributed Fabric Services

A Fibre Channel switched fabric provides a series of distributed services that aid in the management, configuration, and security of a Fibre Channel fabric. Some of the more common services are described in this section.

Directory Services

A Fibre Channel fabric supports a distributed directory service often called the *name server*. Because the FC_ID addressing assigned in a Fibre Channel fabric is dynamic, the directory service helps map a device's static WWN to its routeable FC_ID. When a device logs in to the fabric, it automatically registers itself with the *name server* along with some of its attributes. This information can then be queried by any end devices to locate a specific device or devices with specific capabilities.

Zone Services

To provide some degree of security within a Fibre Channel fabric, *zone services* restrict communication between attached devices. A Fibre Channel *zone* is a logical grouping of devices that are permitted to communicate. Because these devices may be attached to different switches, the zoning configuration is distributed between all switches in the fabric.

Zones can be built using a variety of identifiers, including FC_IDs, physical switch port indexes, or the most common WWN. There are two zone enforcement methods — *hard zoning* and *soft zoning*. Hard zoning involves filtering frames in hardware to enforce the zoning configuration. It is the most secure implementation. Soft zoning simply involves filtering directory service inquiries to allow only certain devices to be visible. Soft zoning is not fully secure, because an end device must know another end device's FC_ID to bypass the zone and communicate with the end device.

Management Services

Another very useful distributed service, based on the ANSI T11 Generic Services Standard (FC-GS and FC-GS-3), is the distributed management service. It lets device attributes and configuration information be retrieved within the fabric. This information may include such attributes as software version, hardware versions, device capabilities, logical device names, and device management IP addresses. In addition, information can be gathered about connected ports and neighbor devices. Although this information is very useful for management purposes, many vendors have been slow to adopt the capability. However, more and more vendors are planning support for the next revision, named FC-GS-4, which will let even more configuration information be retrieved from the fabric.

State Change Notification Services

In most traditional data networks, information about faults in the network was relayed to other network elements, such as switches and routers. However, Fibre Channel extends this service to end devices. Using the State Change Notification Service and, more recently, the Registered State Change Notification (RSCN) Service, end devices can register to receive notification of events in the fabric. When events occur in the network, either accidentally or intentionally, RSCNs are generated to notify other devices of the event occurrence. Using the RSCN facility, devices can react much more quickly to failure events rather than waiting for timers to expire.

The iSCSI Protocol

The iSCSI protocol enables a SAN solution whereby SCSI is transported over the top of TCP/IP. iSCSI can leverage any IP-capable transport, but is primarily targeted toward Ethernet-based SANs. Using iSCSI, SAN designers can build more cost-effective SANs, especially for the connection of midrange servers and storage.

iSCSI Communication Model

iSCSI uses TCP/IP to establish sessions similar to that of Fibre Channel. However, unlike Fibre Channel, iSCSI nodes do not need to log in to the Ethernet fabric to establish communication. Sessions are established between iSCSI initiators (hosts) and iSCSI targets and may consist of multiple TCP/IP connections. However, any given SCSI exchange (command) must be conducted on one TCP connection. ISCSI uses the well-known TCP port number TCP/3260 for all iSCSI connections. An iSCSI target can be either an iSCSI/Fibre Channel gateway or an actual iSCSI-enabled disk or tape array.

Figure 55-10 illustrates the iSCSI communication model.

Figure 55-10 *iSCSI Communication Model*

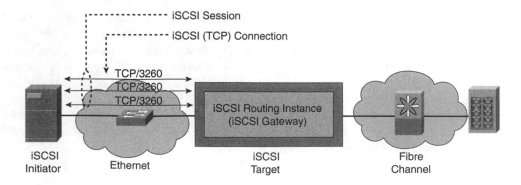

Before transmitting any SCSI commands, an iSCSI initiator must log in to an iSCSI target. During this login phase, the iSCSI targets are discovered and are mapped to block devices within the host. Figure 55-11 illustrates the login procedure.

Figure 55-11 *iSCSI Login Procedure*

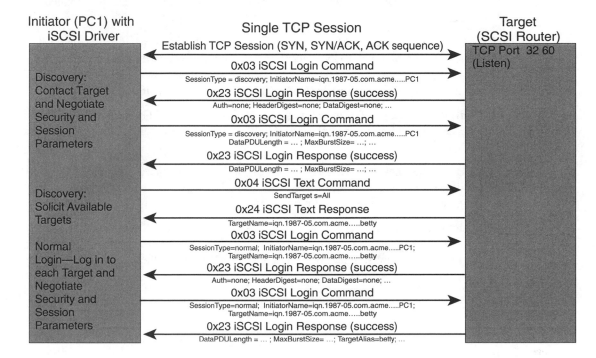

iSCSI Frame Format

iSCSI uses TCP for its transport. However, a specific iSCSI header is used for session control. Figure 55-12 outlines the iSCSI header and its various components. The following list provides the details.

- **Opcode**—The Opcode (1 byte) indicates the type of iSCSI PDU the header encapsulates. There are two types of opcodes: initiator and target. Initiator opcodes are in PDUs sent by the initiators (request PDUs), and target opcodes are in PDUs sent by the target (response PDUs). An iSCSI login and a SCSI command are two different examples of opcodes.

- **Opcode-specific fields**—This field (3 bytes) has different meanings depending on the type of opcode. For example, an iSCSI login opcode uses this area to store iSCSI version numbers and login control flags.

- **AHS Len**—This is the total length of all additional header segments (AHS) in 4-byte words, including padding, if any. The TotalAHSLength (1 byte) is used only in PDUs that have an AHS. It is 0 in all other PDUs.

- **Data field length**—This is the data segment payload length in bytes (excluding padding). The DataSegmentLength (3 bytes) is 0 whenever the PDU has no data segment.

- **LUN or opcode-specific fields**—Some opcodes operate on a specific logical unit. The Logical Unit Number (LUN) field (8 bytes) identifies which logical unit should be operated on. If the opcode does not relate to a logical unit, this field is either ignored or may be used in a unique method, as mandated by the specific opcode.

- **Initiator task tag**—The initiator assigns a task tag to each iSCSI task it issues. While a task exists, this tag must uniquely identify the task session-wide. This component is 4-bytes long.

- **AHS**—The Additional Header Segment is optional and is used only when an additional command header is required. The AHS is a miniheader consisting of its own length, type code, and command info.

- **Data field**—This area is where the actual data is transferred. This could be SCSI data from a **read** command or login credentials within a **login** command. The length of this field varies, but must abide by the maximum MTU of the Ethernet frame.

Figure 55-12 *iSCSI Frame Format*

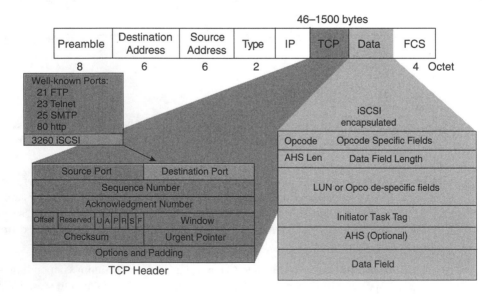

iSCSI Services

This section outlines a series of iSCSI network services that are part of an overall iSCSI SAN solution.

Directory Services

iSCSI initiators can use several methods to locate iSCSI targets. Most implementations today simply use a static mapping to the IP address of the iSCSI server hosting a series of targets. However, two mechanisms can automatically locate an iSCSI target. They are defined as IETF drafts.

The first mechanism is using the Service Location Protocol (SLP). SLP requires iSCSI servers to register each of their targets using a set of service URLs, one for each address on which the target may be accessed. Initiators discover these targets using SLP service requests, which are generally multicast requests. iSCSI servers that hear the SLP requests respond with a list of available targets. A centralized directory agent (DA) may also be used for iSCSI servers to register targets and for iSCSI initiators to acquire information about targets.

The second mechanism for an iSCSI initiator to locate targets is through a protocol called Internet Storage Name Service (iSNS). Using iSNS, iSCSI initiators and targets can locate each other through a directory server.

The iSNS protocol facilitates configuration and management of iSCSI devices in an IP network by providing a set of directory services comparable to that available in Fibre Channel networks. Using the iSNS protocol, iSCSI devices automatically register their attributes with an iSNS server. The iSNS server thereby serves as the consolidated configuration point through which management stations can configure and manage the entire iSCSI storage network. In addition, the iSNS server can send notifications about iSCSI devices or network events to interested or affected devices.

Authentication Services

One nice benefit of iSCSI is its inclusion of authentication services in the login process. When an iSCSI node logs into an iSCSI target, usually an iSCSI gateway, authentication can be performed against the iSCSI initiator before access is granted to the target. Although several protocols can be used for this authentication, two primary methods are used to perform a secure connection from iSCSI host to iSCSI target.

The first method is to use Challenge Handshake Authentication Protocol (CHAP), which is mandated by the iSCSI standard and is a common mechanism used in IP dialup connections. Using CHAP, targets can challenge iSCSI initiators, and vice versa. A convenient implementation method is to use a centralized RADIUS server to provide a centralized authentication engine for iSCSI gateways. RADIUS is a standard protocol used for such purposes.

The second method used for authentication is the Secure Remote Password (SRP) protocol. SRP is a password-based authentication and key-exchange protocol, providing authentication (optionally mutual authentication) and the negotiation of a session key. The SRP protocol can also be used to open a secure and authenticated connection between iSCSI initiators and targets.

iSCSI Boot Services

Many diskless clients are configured to boot from remote SCSI devices. This capability also exists for diskless clients bootstrapping off Fibre Channel devices. Such diskless entities are lightweight, space-efficient, and power-conserving and are increasingly popular in various environments. Using these remote-boot services, new CPUs can be quickly inserted to either add capacity or replace failed units. These new devices replace the existing devices and simply boot and run the same image.

The IETF IP storage working group has devised a proposal to support remote iSCSI boot capabilities called draft-ietf-ips-iscsi-boot. This proposal describes a mechanism that lets clients bootstrap themselves using the iSCSI protocol. The goal of this standard is to let iSCSI boot clients obtain the information to open an iSCSI session with an iSCSI boot server.

Summary

This chapter provided a brief introduction to storage area networking. SANs are rapidly becoming critical infrastructure components of today's enterprise environments. With the continual growth of storage requirements, the challenges associated with storage are rapidly becoming networking challenges.

A brief overview of the drivers leading to the development of SAN technologies and solutions was presented. SANs primarily focus on optimizing both usage and access to enterprise storage resources. SANs also help solve many of the provisioning challenges associated with storage by enabling more-flexible and less-disruptive storage deployment.

A typical SAN architecture was presented that outlined the various components of a SAN, including hosts, disks, tapes, and various networking devices. In addition, a functional model was presented that related nodes of a SAN as either initiators or targets. These roles are directly derived from the SCSI protocol. The SCSI protocol is the primary protocol transported over SANs.

A more in-depth exploration of Fibre Channel was presented that included many of the protocol's structural attributes, such as addressing schemes, routing protocols, flow control, connection types, network topologies, and distributed services.

Finally, a brief introduction to iSCSI was presented. iSCSI is a protocol that is drawing tremendous interest from enterprise IT organizations, because it represents a way to leverage existing Ethernet infrastructures for SAN deployment. An overview of iSCSI was presented, describing it as an alternative transport for SCSI communication. iSCSI architectural components, such as its communication model, frame format, and associated network services, were also presented in detail.

Review Questions

1 What is a storage area network (SAN)?

2 What two primary transport protocols are used within a SAN?

3 What primary upper-layer communication protocol is transported over a SAN?

4 What two primary roles are assumed by SCSI devices?

5 Name three upper-layer protocols besides SCSI that were adapted to the Fibre Channel transport.

6 What governing body presides over the Fibre Channel protocols standards and drafts?

7 When was the first Fibre Channel standard approved, and what was it called?

8 What layer of the Fibre Channel protocol model is responsible for establishing communication between two ports in a SAN?

9 Name the three common Fibre Channel network topologies.

10 How many devices can an arbitrated loop support?

11 What is the difference between a private arbitrated loop and a public arbitrated loop?

12 What is a B_Port?

13 What is the name of the primary Fibre Channel routing protocol, and what part of an FC_ID does it use to make routing decisions?

14 What is a Fibre Channel IDLE, and what is it used for?

15 What Fibre Channel class of service does not provide delivery confirmation of frames?

16 What is the rule of thumb in determining how many buffer credits are required to sustain wire rate capability across a 1-Gbps Fibre Channel link?

17 What is soft zoning?

18 True or false: An individual iSCSI exchange can be conducted over multiple TCP connections.

19 What standard TCP port number is used for iSCSI?

20 Name two mechanisms for performing iSCSI initiator authentication.

For More Information

Books

- Kembel, Robert W. *Fibre Channel: A Comprehensive Introduction*. Tucson: Northwest Learning Associates, Inc., 2000.

URLs

- www.fibrealliance.org
- www.ietf.org/html.charters/ips-charter.html
- www.searchstorage.com
- www.snia.org
- www.t11.org

Objectives

- Discuss configuration management.
- Discuss performance and accountant management.
- Discuss problem management.
- Discuss operations management.
- Discuss change management.

IBM Network Management

Background

IBM network management refers to any architecture used to manage IBM Systems Network Architecture (SNA) networks or Advanced Peer-to-Peer Networking (APPN) networks. IBM network management is part of the IBM Open-Network Architecture (ONA) and is performed centrally by using management platforms such as NetView and others. It is divided into five functions that are similar to the network management functions specified under the Open System Interconnection (OSI) model. This chapter summarizes the IBM network management functional areas, ONA network management architecture, and management platforms. Figure 56-1 illustrates a basic managed IBM network.

Figure 56-1 *IBM Network Management Handles SNA or APPN Networks*

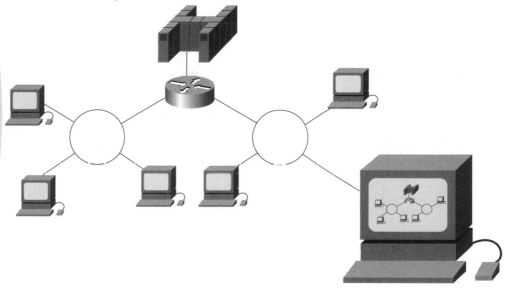

IBM Network-Management Functional Areas

IBM divides network management into the following five user-based functions: configuration management, performance and accountant management, problem management, operations management, and change management.

IBM Configuration Management

IBM configuration management controls information describing the physical and logical characteristics of network resources, as well as the relationships between those resources. A central management system stores data in configuration management databases and might include information such as system software or microcode version numbers; serial numbers of hardware or software; physical locations of network devices; and names, addresses, and telephone numbers of contacts. As might be expected, IBM configuration management corresponds closely to OSI configuration management.

Configuration-management facilities aid in maintaining an inventory of network resources and in ensuring that network configuration changes are reflected in the configuration-management database. Configuration management also provides information that is used by problem-management and change-management systems. Problem-management systems use this information to compare version differences and to locate, identify, and check the characteristics of network resources. Change-management systems use the information to analyze the effect of changes and to schedule changes at times of minimal network impact.

IBM Performance and Accounting Management

IBM performance and accounting management provides information about the performance of network resources. The functions of the performance- and accounting-management facilities include monitoring response times of systems; measuring availability of resources; measuring the use of resources; and tuning, tracking, and controlling network performance. The information gathered by the performance- and accounting-management functions is useful for determining whether network performance goals are being met and whether problem-determination procedures should be initiated based on performance. IBM performance and accounting management performs functions similar to those handled by OSI performance management and OSI accounting management.

IBM Problem Management

IBM problem management is similar to OSI fault management in that it handles error conditions that cause users to lose the full functionality of a network resource. Problem management is performed in five steps: problem determination, problem diagnosis, problem bypass and recovery, problem resolution, and problem tracking and control.

Problem determination consists of detecting a problem and completing the steps necessary for beginning problem diagnosis, such as isolating the problem to a particular subsystem. Problem diagnosis consists of determining the precise cause of the problem and the action required to solve it. Problem bypass and recovery consists of attempts to bypass the problem, either partially or completely. It provides only a temporary solution and relies on problem resolution to solve the problem permanently. Problem resolution consists of efforts to eliminate the problem. It usually begins after problem diagnosis is complete and often involves corrective action, such as the replacement of failed hardware or software. Problem tracking and control consists of tracking each problem until final resolution is reached. Vital information describing the problem is recorded in a problem database.

IBM Operations Management

IBM operations management consists of managing distributed network resources from a central site, using two sets of functions: operations-management services and common-operations services. Operations-management services provide the capability to control remote resources centrally using the following functions: resource activation and deactivation, command cancellation, and clock setting. Operations-management services can be initiated automatically in response to certain system problem notifications.

Common-operations services allow for the management of resources not explicitly addressed by other management areas, using specialized communication through new, more capable applications. Common-operations services offer two important services, the **execute** command and the resource-management service. The **execute** command provides a standardized means of executing remote commands. The resource-management service provides a way to transport information in a context-independent manner.

IBM Change Management

IBM change management tracks network changes and maintains change files at remote nodes. Network changes occur primarily for two reasons: changing user requirements and problem circumvention. Changing user requirements include hardware and software upgrades, new applications and services, and other factors that constantly change the needs of network users. Problem circumvention is needed to deal with unexpected changes resulting from the failure of hardware, software, or other network components. Change management attempts to minimize problems by promoting orderly network changes and managing change files, which log network changes. IBM change management is similar in some respects to OSI accounting management.

IBM Network-Management Architectures

Two of the most well-known IBM network-management architectures are the Open-Network Architecture (ONA) and SystemView.

Open-Network Architecture

The *Open-Network Architecture (ONA)* is a generalized network-management architecture that defines four key management entities: the focal point, collection point, entry point, and service point.

The focal point is a management entity that provides support for centralized network-management operations. It responds to end-station alerts, maintains management databases, and provides a user interface for the network-management operator. Three kinds of focal points exist: primary, secondary, and nested. The primary focal points performs all focal point functions. The secondary focal point acts as a backup for primary focal points and is used when primary focal points fail. The nested focal point provides distributed management support in large networks. Nested focal points are responsible for forwarding critical information to more global focal points.

Collection points relay information from self-contained SNA subnetworks to focal points. They are commonly used to forward data from IBM peer-to-peer networks into the ONA hierarchy.

An entry point is an SNA device that can implement ONA for itself and other devices. Most standard SNA devices are capable of being entry points.

A service point is a system that provides access into ONA for non-SNA devices and is essentially a gateway into ONA. Service points are capable of sending management information about non-SNA systems to focal points, receiving commands from focal points, translating commands into a format acceptable to non-SNA devices, and forwarding commands to non-SNA devices for execution.

Figure 56-2 illustrates the relationships between the different ONA management entities.

SystemView

SystemView is a blueprint for creating management applications that are capable of managing multivendor information systems. SystemView describes how applications that manage heterogeneous networks operate with other management systems. It is the official systems management strategy of the IBM Systems Application Architecture.

Figure 56-2 *The Four Types of Focal Points Link to One Another Within the ONA Environment*

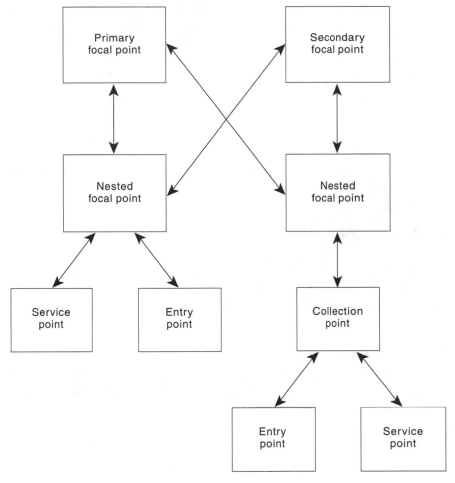

IBM Network-Management Platforms

IBM network management is implemented on several platforms, including NetView, LAN Network Manager (LNM), and Simple Network Management Protocol (SNMP).

NetView

NetView is a comprehensive IBM enterprise network-management platform that provides centralized SNA network-management services. It is used on IBM mainframes and is part of the ONA. NetView consists of the command-control facility, hardware monitor, session monitor, help function, status monitor, performance monitor, and distribution monitor.

The command-control facility provides network control by issuing basic operator and file-access commands to Virtual Telecommunications Access Method (VTAM) applications, controllers, operating systems, and NetView/PC (an interface between NetView and non-SNA devices). The hardware monitor function monitors the network and automatically alerts the network operator when hardware errors occur. The session monitor acts as a VTAM performance monitor and provides software-problem determination and configuration management. The help function provides help for NetView users and includes a browse facility, a help desk facility, and a library of commonly encountered network operation situations. The status monitor summarizes and presents network status information. The performance monitor function monitors the performance of front-end processors (FEPs), the Network Control Program (NCP), and other attached resources. The distribution manager plans, schedules, and tracks the distribution of data, software, and microcode in SNA environments.

LAN Network Manager

The *LAN Network Manager (LNM)* is an IBM network-management application that controls Token Ring LANs from a central support site. LNM is an OS/2 Extended Edition-based product that interoperates with IBM NetView (which is aware of such LNM activities as alarms) and other IBM management software.

Simple Network Management Protocol

IBM network management can be implemented by using SNMP. Refer to Chapter 58, "Simple Network Management Protocol," for details about SNMP implementation.

Review Questions

1 What are the five steps of problem management?

2 How does the command-control facility of the NetView program operate?

3 To perform resource activation and deactivation, command cancellation, and clock setting on a remote system, you would need to use what?

Objectives

- Describe the background of Remote Monitoring.
- Describe the nine RMON groups of monitoring.

CHAPTER 57

Remote Monitoring

Background

Remote Monitoring (RMON) is a standard monitoring specification that enables various network monitors and console systems to exchange network-monitoring data. RMON provides network administrators with more freedom in selecting network-monitoring probes and consoles with features that meet their particular networking needs. This chapter provides a brief overview of the RMON specification, focusing on RMON groups.

The RMON specification defines a set of statistics and functions that can be exchanged between RMON-compliant console managers and network probes. As such, RMON provides network administrators with comprehensive network-fault diagnosis, planning, and performance-tuning information.

RMON was defined by the user community with the help of the Internet Engineering Task Force (IETF). It became a proposed standard in 1992 as RFC 1271 (for Ethernet). RMON then became a draft standard in 1995 as RFC 1757, effectively obsoleting RFC 1271.

Figure 57-1 illustrates an RMON probe capable of monitoring an Ethernet segment and transmitting statistical information back to an RMON-compliant console.

Figure 57-1 *An RMON Probe Can Send Statistical Information to an RMON Console*

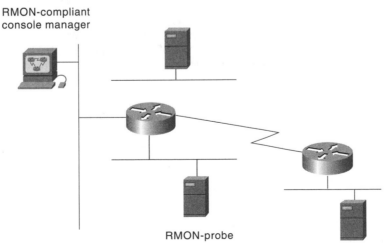

RMON-compliant console manager

RMON-probe

RMON Groups

RMON delivers information in nine RMON groups of monitoring elements, each providing specific sets of data to meet common network-monitoring requirements. Each group is optional so that vendors do not need to support all the groups within the Management Information Base (MIB). Some RMON groups require support of other RMON groups to function properly. Table 57-1 summarizes the nine monitoring groups specified in the RFC 1757 Ethernet RMON MIB.

Table 57-1   *RMON Monitoring Groups*

RMON Group	Function	Elements
Statistics	Contains statistics measured by the probe for each monitored interface on this device.	Packets dropped, packets sent, bytes sent (octets), broadcast packets, multicast packets, CRC errors, runts, giants, fragments, jabbers, collisions, and counters for packets ranging from 64 to 128, 128 to 256, 256 to 512, 512 to 1024, and 1024 to 1518 bytes.
History	Records periodic statistical samples from a network and stores them for later retrieval.	Sample period, number of samples, items sampled.
Alarm	Periodically takes statistical samples from variables in the probe and compares them with previously configured thresholds. If the monitored variable crosses a threshold, an event is generated.	Includes the alarm table and requires the implementation of the event group. Alarm type, interval, starting threshold, stop threshold.
Host	Contains statistics associated with each host discovered on the network.	Host address, packets, and bytes received and transmitted, as well as broadcast, multicast, and error packets.
HostTopN	Prepares tables that describe the hosts that top a list ordered by one of their base statistics over an interval specified by the management station. Thus, these statistics are rate-based.	Statistics, host(s), sample start and stop periods, rate base, duration.
Matrix	Stores statistics for conversations between sets of two addresses. As the device detects a new conversation, it creates a new entry in its table.	Source and destination address pairs and packets, bytes, and errors for each pair.

Table 57-1   *RMON Monitoring Groups (Continued)*

RMON Group	Function	Elements
Filters	Enables packets to be matched by a filter equation. These matched packets form a data stream that might be captured or that might generate events.	Bit-filter type (mask or not mask), filter expression (bit level), conditional expression (and, or not) to other filters.
Packet Capture	Enables packets to be captured after they flow through a channel.	Size of buffer for captured packets, full status (alarm), number of captured packets.
Events	Controls the generation and notification of events from this device.	Event type, description, last time event sent.

Review Questions

1 What is the function of the RMON group Matrix?

2 What is RMON?

3 Multicast packets, CRC errors, runts, giants, fragments, and jabbers are elements of what RMON group?

Objectives

- Discuss the SNMP Management Information Base.

- Describe SNMP versions 1, 2, and 3.

CHAPTER 58

Simple Network Management Protocol

Simple Network Management Protocol (SNMP) is an application layer protocol that facilitates the exchange of management information between network devices. It is part of the TCP/IP protocol suite. SNMP is defined in several RFCs that are part of Internet Engineering Task Force (IETF) standards. SNMP lets network administrators monitor, configure, and troubleshoot the network and plan for network growth.

The RFC documents that define SNMP makes very clear the intention to keep SNMP as simple as possible and to make it relatively inexpensive to deploy a minimal conforming implementation. Therefore, SNMP does not have a complex database structure or very sophisticated operations.

Several versions of SNMP have been developed. Some of them have become industry standards, such as SNMP version 1 (SNMPv1), SNMP version 2 community-based (SNMPv2c), and SNMP version 3 (SNMPv3). These versions have a number of features in common, but the newer versions offer enhancements, such as additional protocol operations, versatility, and security.

SNMPv2c is the most used today, but SNMPv1 is still supported on most platforms. The most recent version of SNMPv3 was published at the end of 2002 in a set of IETF documents (RFC 3410 to RFC 3418). It has been implemented by a growing number of vendors and will gradually replace SNMPv2c. This chapter describes the SNMPv1, SNMPv2c, and SNMPv3 protocol operations. Figure 58-1 illustrates a basic network managed by SNMP.

Figure 58-1 *SNMP Facilitates the Exchange of Network Information Between Devices*

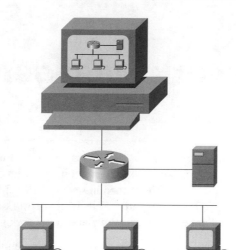

SNMP Basic Components

An SNMP-managed network consists of three key components: managed devices, agents, and network management systems (NMSs or managers).

A *managed device* is a network node that contains an SNMP agent and that resides on a managed network. Managed devices collect statistics, store management information, and make this information available to NMSs using SNMP. Managed devices, sometimes called network elements, are devices such as routers, switches, bridges, hubs, printers, computers, servers, hosts, and firewalls.

An *agent* is a network-management software module that resides in a managed device. An agent has local knowledge of the management information and translates that information into a form compatible with SNMP.

An *NMS (manager)* executes applications that monitor and control managed devices. NMSs provide the bulk of the processing and memory resources required for network management. One or more NMSs must exist on any managed network to manage large numbers of devices. The NMS collect or receive information from the network devices via SNMP and store this information, generate statistics, and display it to network administrators.

Figure 58-2 illustrates the relationships of these three components.

Figure 58-2 *An SNMP-Managed Network Consists of Managed Devices, Agents, and NMSs*

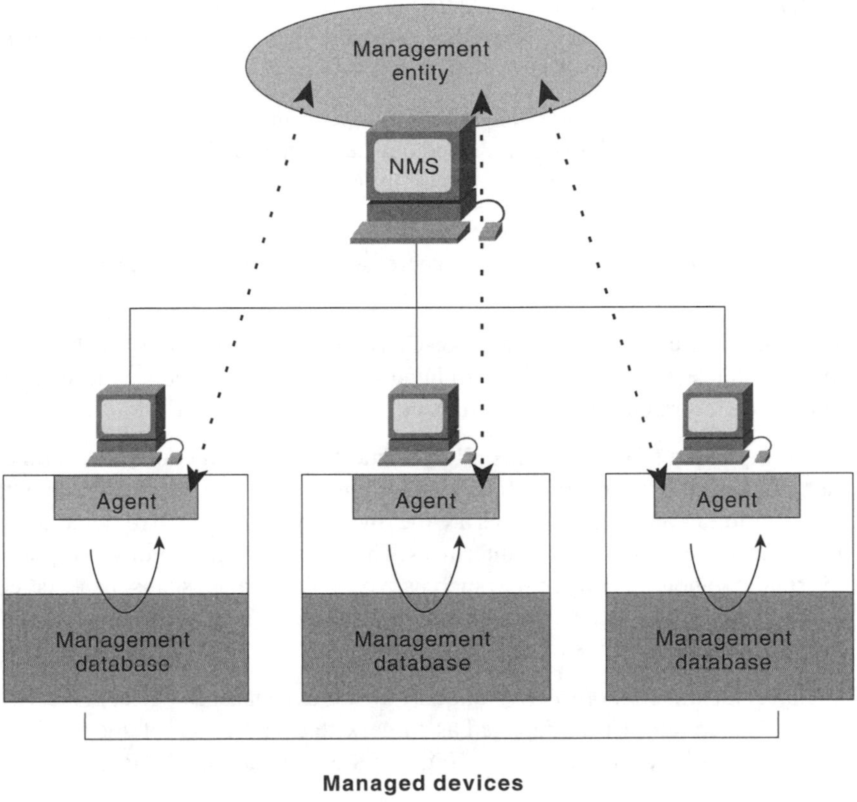

Managed devices

Basic SNMP Commands

Managed devices are monitored and controlled using four basic SNMP commands: **read**, **write**, **trap**, and traversal operations.

An NMS uses the **read** command to monitor managed devices. The NMS examines different variables that are maintained by managed devices.

An NMS uses the **write** command to control managed devices. The NMS changes the values of variables stored in managed devices.

Managed devices use the **trap** command to asynchronously report events to the NMS. When certain types of events occur, a managed device sends a trap to the NMS.

An NMS uses traversal operations to determine which variables a managed device supports and to sequentially gather information in variable tables, such as a routing table.

SNMP Management Information Base

A *Management Information Base (MIB)* is a collection of information that is organized hierarchically. A MIB is accessed using a network-management protocol, such as SNMP. It is composed of managed objects and is identified by object identifiers.

A *managed object* (sometimes called a *MIB object*, an *object*, or a *MIB*) is one of a number of specific characteristics of a managed device. Managed objects are composed of one or more object instances, which are essentially variables.

Two types of managed objects exist: scalar and tabular. *Scalar objects* define a single object instance. *Tabular objects* define multiple, related object instances that are grouped in MIB tables.

An example of a managed object is sysUpTime. It is a scalar object that contains a single object instance, which is the time (in hundredths of a second) since the system's network management portion was last reinitialized.

An example of a tabular object is ifTable (interface table). It contains several objects, and each object can have several instances. You can think of it as a table in which the objects are the columns and their instances are the rows. If you consider a router as an example, the ifTable is related to the router's interfaces. The table's objects (columns) represent different information about each interface, such as type, speed, name, status, packets received, and packets transmitted. Each object has several instances (rows of the table), one for each interface that exists in the router.

An *object identifier* (or *object ID*) uniquely identifies a managed object in the MIB hierarchy. The MIB hierarchy can be depicted as a tree with a nameless root, the levels of which are assigned by different organizations. Figure 58-3 illustrates the MIB tree.

The top-level MIB object IDs belong to different standards organizations, and lower-level object IDs are allocated by associated organizations.

Vendors can define private branches that include managed objects for their own products. With private MIBs, you can define very specific objects to allow more-complete management of different devices. MIBs that have not been standardized typically are positioned in the experimental branch.

The managed object atInput can be uniquely identified either by its object name—iso.identified-organization.dod.internet.private.enterprise.cisco.temporary variables.AppleTalk.atInput—or by its equivalent object descriptor, 1.3.6.1.4.1.9.3.3.1.

Figure 58-3 *MIB Tree Illustrates the Various Hierarchies Assigned by Different Organizations*

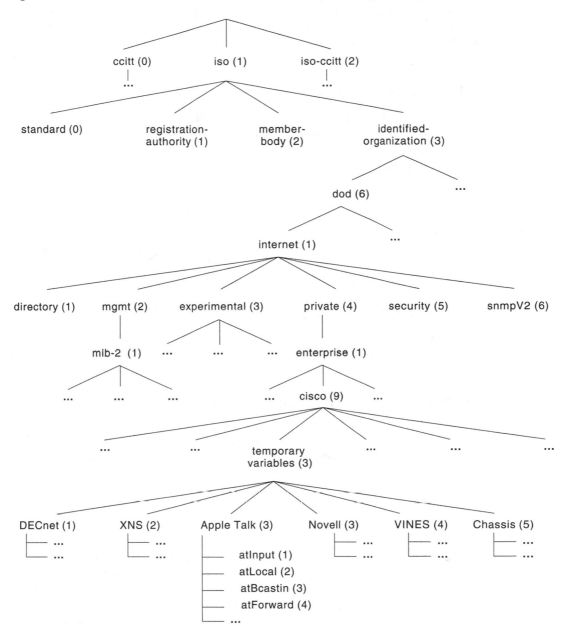

One of the tasks of a network administrator, when deploying or configuring SNMP to manage the network, is to find the correct objects to be used by the NMS station. To accomplish this, you must go over the several private and public MIBs and find which MIB branch, table, or object has the information to be monitored or updated.

SNMP and Data Representation

SNMP must account for and adjust to incompatibilities between managed devices. Different computers use different data representation techniques, which can compromise SNMP's capability to exchange information between managed devices. SNMP uses a subset of Abstract Syntax Notation 1 (ASN.1) to accommodate communication between diverse systems.

SNMP Version 1

SNMP version 1 (SNMPv1) is the initial implementation of SNMP. It is described in RFC 1157 and functions within the specifications of the Structure of Management Information (SMI). SNMPv1 operates over protocols such as User Datagram Protocol (UDP), Internet Protocol (IP), OSI Connectionless Network Service (CLNS), AppleTalk Datagram-Delivery Protocol (DDP), and Novell Internetwork Packet Exchange (IPX). SNMPv1 is widely used and is the de facto network-management protocol in the Internet community. For TCP/IP, SNMP uses ports UDP 161 (read and write) and UDP 162 (trap).

SNMPv1 and the Structure of Management Information

SMI defines the rules for describing management information using Abstract Syntax Notation 1 (ASN.1). The SNMPv1 SMI is defined in RFC 1155. The SMI makes three key specifications: ASN.1 data types, SMI-specific data types, and SNMP MIB tables.

SNMPv1 and ASN.1 Data Types

The SNMPv1 SMI specifies that all managed objects have a certain subset of ASN.1 data types associated with them. Three ASN.1 data types are required: name, syntax, and encoding. The name serves as the object identifier (object ID). The syntax defines the object's data type (such as integer or string). The SMI uses a subset of the ASN.1 syntax definitions. The encoding data describes how information associated with a managed object is formatted as a series of data items for transmission over the network.

SNMPv1 and SMI-Specific Data Types

The SNMPv1 SMI specifies the use of a number of SMI-specific data types. They are divided into two categories: simple data types and application-wide data types.

Three simple data types are defined in the SNMPv1 SMI, all of which are unique values: integers, octet strings, and object IDs. The integer data type is a signed integer in the range of −2,147,483,648 to 2,147,483,647. Octet strings are ordered sequences of 0 to 65,535 octets. Object IDs come from the set of all object identifiers allocated according to the rules specified in ASN.1.

Seven application-wide data types exist in the SNMPv1 SMI:

- A network address represents an address from a particular protocol family. SNMPv1 supports only 32-bit IP addresses.

- A counter is a nonnegative integer that increases until it reaches a maximum value and then returns to 0. In SNMPv1, a 32-bit counter size is specified.

- A gauge is a nonnegative integer that can increase or decrease, but that retains the maximum value reached.

- A time tick represents a hundredth of a second since some event.

- An opaque represents an arbitrary encoding that is used to pass arbitrary information strings that do not conform to the strict data typing used by the SMI.

- An integer represents signed integer-valued information. This data type redefines the integer data type, which has arbitrary precision in ASN.1, but bounded precision in the SMI.

- An unsigned integer represents unsigned integer-valued information and is useful when values are always nonnegative. This data type redefines the integer data type, which has arbitrary precision in ASN.1, but bounded precision in the SMI.

SNMP MIB Tables

The SNMPv1 SMI defines highly structured tables that are used to group the instances of a tabular object (that is, an object that contains multiple variables). Tables are composed of zero or more rows, which are indexed in a way that allows SNMP to retrieve or alter an entire row with a single Get, GetNext, or Set command.

SNMPv1 Protocol Operations

SNMP is a simple request/response protocol. The network-management system issues a request, and managed devices return responses. This behavior is implemented using one of four protocol operations: Get, GetNext, Set, or Trap. The NMS uses the Get operation to retrieve the value of one or more object instances from an agent. If the agent responding to the Get operation cannot provide values for all the object instances in a list, it does not provide any values. The NMS uses the GetNext operation to retrieve the value of the next object instance in a table or a list within an agent. The NMS uses the Set operation to set the values of object instances within an agent. Agents use the Trap operation to asynchronously inform the NMS of a significant event.

SNMP Version 2

SNMP version 2 (SNMPv2) is an evolution of the initial version of SNMP, SNMPv1. Originally, SNMPv2 was published as a set of proposed Internet standards in 1993; currently, it is a draft standard. As with SNMPv1, SNMPv2 functions within the specifications of the SMI.

In theory, SNMPv2 offers a number of improvements to SNMPv1, including additional protocol operations and security. Because there was no consensus about the security specification of SNMPv2, a new version was proposed in 1996, SNMP version 2 community-based (SNMPv2c). SNMPv2c dropped the security features of SNMPv2 and used the same community concept as SNMPv1. The concept of communities is explained later in this chapter. When we talk about SNMPv2, we are referring to the updated version (SNMPv2c).

SNMPv2 and the Structure of Management Information

SMI defines the rules for describing management information using ASN.1.

The SNMPv2 SMI is described in RFC 1902. It makes certain additions and enhancements to the SNMPv1 SMI-specific data types, such as including bit strings, network addresses, and counters. Bit strings are defined only in SNMPv2 and comprise 0 or more named bits that specify a value. Network addresses represent an address from a particular protocol family. SNMPv1 supports only 32-bit IP addresses, but SNMPv2 can support other types of addresses as well. Counters are nonnegative integers that increase until they reach a maximum value and then return to 0. In SNMPv1, a 32-bit counter size is specified. In SNMPv2, 32-bit and 64-bit counters are defined.

SMI Information Modules

The SNMPv2 SMI also specifies information modules, which specify a group of related definitions. Three types of SMI information modules exist:

- MIB modules contain definitions of interrelated managed objects.

- Compliance statements provide a systematic way to describe a group of managed objects that must be implemented for conformance to a standard.

- Capability statements indicate the precise level of support that an agent claims with respect to a MIB group.

An NMS can adjust its behavior toward agents according to the capabilities statements associated with each agent.

SNMPv2 Protocol Operations

The Get, GetNext, and Set operations used in SNMPv1 are exactly the same as those used in SNMPv2. However, SNMPv2 adds and enhances some protocol operations. The SNMPv2 Trap operation, for example, serves the same function as that used in SNMPv1, but it uses a different message format and is designed to replace the SNMPv1 Trap.

SNMPv2 also defines two new protocol operations: GetBulk and Inform. The NMS uses the GetBulk operation to efficiently retrieve large blocks of data, such as multiple rows in a table. GetBulk fills a response message with as much of the requested data as will fit. The Inform operation allows one NMS to send trap information to another NMS and to then receive a response.

In SNMPv2, if the agent responding to GetBulk operations cannot provide values for all the variables in a list, it provides partial results. It is important to notice the direction of each operation, as shown in Figure 58-4. Get, GetNext, and Set operations generate packets (UDP port 161) sent from the NMS station (manager) to the managed device (agent). The agent then sends a response back to the NMS station. The Trap operation generates packets (UDP port 162) sent by the managed device to the NMS station. There is no response or confirmation for a trap.

Security Considerations

Because SNMPv2 and SNMPv1 do not implement authentication, many vendors do not implement Set operations, thereby reducing SNMP to a monitoring facility.

To reduce the security risks when working with SNMPv1/SNMPv2, it is recommended that you restrict the range of addresses that have access to the SNMP agent to a few management stations. In the case of routers, for instance, this can be done with access lists. It is also recommended that you use SNMP views that restrict the number of MIBs and objects accessible. Nevertheless, this does not totally prevent unauthorized access if SNMPv1/SNMPv2 is enabled for an agent.

Figure 58-4 *SNMP Messages*

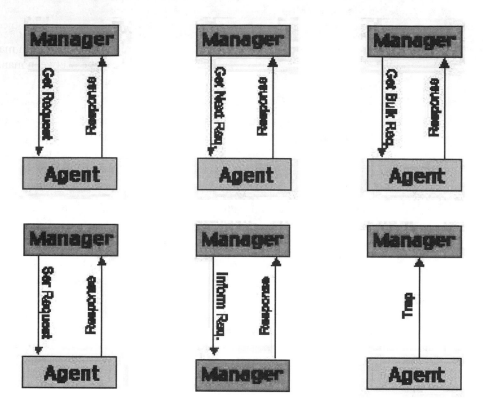

SNMP Version 3

SNMP version 3 (SNMPv3) was proposed as an Internet standard in January 1998 to correct the security deficiencies of SNMPv1 and SNMPv2. These initial versions of SNMP could not provide encryption or authenticate the SNMP messages. A second and third set of documents were proposed as Internet standards for SNMPv3 in April 1999 and December 2002. This last one is the current standard for SNMPv3.

Security Threads

The lack of any authentication capabilities in SNMPv1/SNMPv2 resulted in vulnerability to a variety of security threats. Known threats that are part of the security requirements for the SNMPv3 architecture include masquerading occurrences, modification of information, disclosure, and message stream modification:

- Masquerading occurs when an unauthorized entity attempts to perform management operations by assuming the identity of an authorized management entity.

- Modification of information involves an unauthorized entity attempting to alter in-transit SNMP messages generated on behalf of an authorized entity in such a way as to effect unauthorized management operations, including falsifying an object's value.

- Disclosure results when an unauthorized entity extracts values stored in managed objects or learns of notifiable events by monitoring exchanges between managers and agents.

- Message stream modifications occur when an unauthorized entity reorders, delays, or copies and later replays a message generated by an authorized entity.

Two other types of threats, denial of service and traffic analysis, are considered less important and are not necessarily protected by the SNMPv3 architecture. They are not discussed in this chapter.

Modular Architecture

The SNMPv3 architecture is designed to be modular, as shown in Figure 58-5. The modular architecture allows the evolution of SNMP standards over time. An SNMP entity contains an SNMP engine that has a dispatcher, a message processing subsystem, a security subsystem, and an access control subsystem. It also has possible multiple SNMP applications to provide specific functional processing of management data.

Figure 58-5 *SNMP Entity Components*

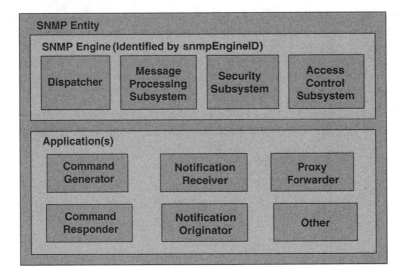

Each type of SNMP entity has an SNMP engine and different application modules. An SNMP manager, for instance, should contain an entity with command-generator applications and/or a notification receiver. An SNMP agent should contain command responders and/or notification originator applications.

An SNMP entity has one SNMP engine that provides services for sending, receiving, and processing messages, authenticating and encrypting messages, and controlling access to managed objects. These services are provided by the following:

- The dispatcher allows for concurrent support of multiple versions of SNMP messages in the SNMP engine. It sends and receives SNMP messages and dispatches SNMP protocol data units (PDUs) to SNMP applications. When an SNMP message needs to be prepared or when data needs to be extracted from an SNMP message, the dispatcher delegates these tasks to a message version-specific message processing model within the message processing subsystem.

- The message processing subsystem is the part of an SNMP engine that interacts with the dispatcher to handle the version-specific SNMP messages. It potentially contains multiple message processing models for SNMPv3, SNMPv2, SNMPv1, and others.

- The security subsystem provides security services, such as authentication and privacy.

- The access control subsystem provides authorization services that let entities work with different levels of access to managed objects.

The application modules are as follows:

- The command generator monitors and manipulates management data. It generates and processes the response of the Get, GetNext, GetBulk, and Set PDUs.

- The command responder provides access to management data. It receives the PDU types just mentioned (generated by the command responder), generates a response message, and sends it back to the originator of the request.

- The notification originator initiates asynchronous messages. It monitors the system. Then, depending on what it is configured for, it generates Trap or Inform messages and sends them to predefined destination entities.

- The notification receiver processes asynchronous messages. It listens to the network for notification messages, traps, and informs. When the message received is an inform, it sends a response to the originator.

- The proxy forwarder forwards SNMP messages between entities. The implementation of a proxy forwarder application is optional.

Security Architecture

The RFC documents that define SNMPv3 characterize security in two different stages: the transmission/receipt of messages and the processing of the messages' contents. The SNMPv3 RFCs refer to "security" as message-level security and to "access control" as the security applied to protocol operations.

Authentication, encryption, and timeliness checking are common functions of message-level security. Access control might be required during the processing of a message. It controls access to managed objects for operations. The Access Control Model defines mechanisms to determine whether access to a managed object should be allowed.

To deliver the security and access control services, SNMP created the concept of a *principal*. A principal is the entity on whose behalf services are provided or processing takes place. A principal can be, among other things, an individual performing a particular role; a set of individuals, each performing a particular role; an application or a set of applications; and combinations thereof. The identity of the principal is used to identify the security features (authentication, privacy, and access control) that will be used in the communication with the agent. The SNMPv3 architecture recognizes three levels of security: no authentication and no privacy, authentication and no privacy, and authentication and privacy.

User-Based Security Model (USM)

The SNMP security model provides services to support: data integrity, origin authentication, confidentiality, timeliness, and limited replay protection. To achieve this, SNMPv3 uses the concept of the authoritative SNMP engine—one of the parts of the transmission of a message. There are two rules to determine who is the authoritative engine:

- If the message payload needs confirmation or a response (confirmed class PDU: Get, GetNext, GetBulk, Set, or Inform), the receiver is the authoritative engine.

- If the message payload does not require a response (unconfirmed class PDU: Response, Report, or Trap), the sender is the authoritative engine.

When an SNMP message is sent, the sender engine includes a set of time-line indicators, and the receiver evaluates them to determine if a received message is recent. A message's timeliness is determined based on a clock maintained by the authoritative engine. Each message also includes an identifier unique to the authoritative SNMP engine associated with the message's sender or intended recipient.

For every message sent, the USM includes in the header several security parameters that are evaluated by the USM process on the receiver side. These parameters have information about the user, authorization protocol, authorization key, authoritative engine, privacy protocol, and time. For this security model, the SNMP engines must have previous knowledge of any user who has authorization for management operations.

RFC 3414, *User-based Security Model for SNMPv3*, specifies the following:

- HMAC-MD5-96 must be supported as an authentication protocol.

- HMAC-SHA-96 should be supported as an authentication protocol, and additional or replacement authentication protocols may be supported in the future.

Note that HMAC-MD5-96 uses MD5 (see RFC 1321, Message Digest 5) as a hash function for Hash-based Message Authentication Code (HMAC) mode. MD5-96 truncates the output to 96 bits. HMAC-SHA-96 is the same, but uses the SHA (SHA-NIST) hash function instead. HMAC (see RFC 2104) is a mechanism for message authentication, and MD5 and SHA are cryptographic hash functions.

For privacy protocol, CBC-DES symmetric encryption is defined to be used with the user-based security model. In the future, additional or replacement privacy protocols might be defined as well. CBC-DES is the cipher-block-chaining mode of Data Encryption Standard (DES), which when requested, USM uses to encrypt the messages sent and avoids third parties to read the content.

View-Based Access Control Model (VACM)

As specified in RFC 3415, VACM for the SNMP, the access control subsystem of an SNMP engine checks whether a specific type of access (read, write, notify) to a particular object (instance) is allowed. When an SNMP engine processes retrieval (Get, GetNext, GetBulk) or a modification request (Set), it should apply access control. For example, a command responder application applies access control when processing requests it receives from a command generator application. Before sending an SNMP notification message (originated by the notification originator application), the SNMP entity should also apply access control.

The access control is configured by groups of users; each group can contain several users. The security policy should be preconfigured on the SNMP entities performing the access control. To create the access policy, the administrator first defines the type of operation a group can use (read, write, or notify). Then the administrator defines the access rights for that operation. For instance, an agent can be configured to give only read access to one MIB (or a portion of a MIB) to a group of users. It can also be configured to give write access to a few MIB objects to another group of users.

SNMP Management

SNMP is a distributed-management protocol. A system can operate exclusively as either an NMS or an agent, or it can perform the functions of both. When a system operates as both an NMS and an agent, another NMS might require that the system query manage devices and provide a summary of the information learned, or that it report locally stored management information.

SNMP Reference: SNMP Message Formats

SNMP messages contain two parts, a message header and a PDU, as shown in Figure 58-6.

Figure 58-6 *An SNMP Message Consists of a Header and a PDU*

Message header	PDU

The following sections describe in more detail the parts of an SNMP message and the two types of SNMP PDUs.

SNMP Message Header

SNMP message headers contain two fields: Version Number and Community Name:

- Version Number specifies the version of SNMP used.

- Community Name defines an access environment for a group of NMSs. NMSs within the community are said to exist within the same administrative domain. For SNMPv1 and SNMPv2, community names serve as a weak form of authentication, because devices that do not know the proper community name are precluded from SNMP operations.

SNMP PDU

SNMP specifies two PDU formats, depending on the SNMP operation. SNMP PDU fields are variable in length, as prescribed by ASN.1.

Figure 58-7 illustrates the fields of the SNMP Get, GetNext, Inform, Response, Set, and Trap PDUs.

Figure 58-7 *SNMPv2 Get, GetNext, Inform, Response, Set, and Trap PDUs Contain the Same Fields*

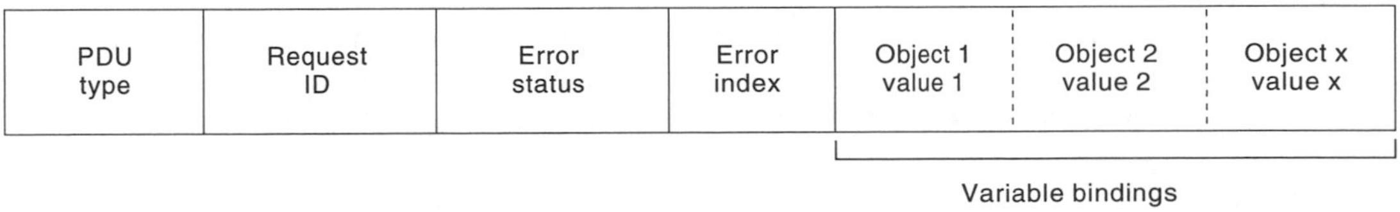

PDU type	Request ID	Error status	Error index	Object 1 value 1	Object 2 value 2	Object x value x

Variable bindings

The following descriptions summarize the fields shown in Figure 58-7:

- PDU Type identifies the type of PDU transmitted (Get, GetNext, Inform, Response, Set, or Trap).

- Request ID associates SNMP requests with responses.

- Error Status indicates one of a number of errors and error types. Only the response operation sets this field. Other operations set this field to 0.

- Error Index associates an error with a particular object instance. Only the response operation sets this field. Other operations set this field to 0.

- Variable Bindings serves as the data field of the SNMP PDU. Each variable binding associates a particular object instance with its current value (with the exception of Get and GetNext requests, for which the value is ignored).

GetBulk PDU Format

Figure 58-8 illustrates the fields of the SNMP GetBulk PDU.

Figure 58-8   *SNMP GetBulk PDU Fields*

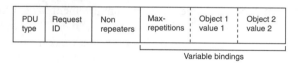

The following descriptions summarize the fields shown in Figure 58-8:

- PDU Type identifies the PDU as a GetBulk operation.

- Request ID associates SNMP requests with responses.

- Nonrepeaters specifies the number of object instances in the Variable Bindings field that should be retrieved no more than once from the beginning of the request. This field is used when some of the instances are scalar objects with only one variable.

- Max Repetitions defines the maximum number of times that other variables beyond those specified by the Nonrepeaters field should be retrieved.

- Variable Bindings serves as the data field of the SNMP PDU. Each variable binding associates a particular object instance with its current value (with the exception of Get and GetNext requests, for which the value is ignored).

Trap PDU Format

Figure 58-9 illustrates the fields of the SNMP Trap PDU.

Figure 58-9 *SNMP Trap PDU Fields*

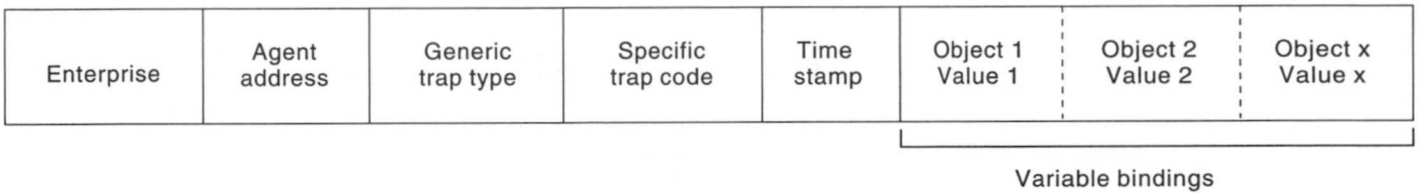

Enterprise	Agent address	Generic trap type	Specific trap code	Time stamp	Object 1 Value 1	Object 2 Value 2	Object x Value x

Variable bindings

The following descriptions summarize the fields shown in Figure 58-9:

- Enterprise identifies the type of managed object generating the trap.

- Agent Address provides the address of the managed object generating the trap.

- Generic Trap Type indicates one of a number of generic trap types.

- Specific Trap Code indicates one of a number of specific trap codes.

- Time Stamp provides the amount of time that has elapsed between the last network reinitialization and generation of the trap.

- Variable Bindings is the data field of the SNMP Trap PDU. Each variable binding associates a particular object instance with its current value.

Summary

SNMP is an application layer protocol part of the TCP/IP suite. It was created to standardize an architecture for network management. SNMP uses the concept of network management stations (managers), which monitor and control managed devices. The manager also works as an interface to the network administrator. A managed device has agent software that interacts with the manager through a set of protocol operations, such as Get, Set, Get-Next, GetBulk, and Trap. These operations manipulate a collection of hierarchically organized variables called the MIB, which is maintained by the agent software at the managed devices.

During the past several years, several versions of SNMP have been defined to expand its capabilities. The most recent version (SNMPv3) addresses the security limitations of the previous versions, employing authentication, encryption, and access control.

Review Questions

1 What is an SNMP agent?

2 What is a MIB, and how is it accessed?

3 Name some protocol operations available in SNMPv2.

4 What is the major deficiency of SNMPv1 and SNMPv2 that is addressed in SNMPv3?

Objectives

- Introduce QoS concepts.
- Define QoS tools.
- Discuss QoS tool capabilities.
- Discuss examples of QoS tool usage.

CHAPTER 59

Quality of Service Networking

Introduction

Quality of Service (QoS) refers to the capability of a network to provide better service to selected network traffic over various technologies, including Frame Relay, Asynchronous Transfer Mode (ATM), Ethernet and 802.1 networks, SONET, and IP-routed networks that may use any or all of these underlying technologies. The primary goal of QoS is to provide priority including dedicated bandwidth, controlled jitter and latency (required by some real-time and interactive traffic), and improved loss characteristics. Also important is making sure that providing priority for one or more flows does not make other flows fail. QoS technologies provide the elemental building blocks that will be used for future business applications in campus, WAN, and service provider networks. This chapter outlines the features and benefits of the QoS provided by the Cisco IOS QoS.

NOTE A flow can be defined in a number of ways. One common way refers to a combination of source and destination addresses, source and destination socket numbers, and the session identifier. It can also be defined more broadly as any packet from a certain application or from an incoming interface. Recent identification tools have allowed the definition of a flow to be performed more precisely (for instance, to the URL or MIME type inside an HTTP packet). Within this chapter, references to a *flow* could be any one of these definitions.

The Cisco IOS QoS software enables complex networks to control and predictably service a variety of networked applications and traffic types. Almost any network can take advantage of QoS for optimum efficiency, whether it is a small corporate network, an Internet service provider, or an enterprise network. The Cisco IOS QoS software provides these benefits:

- **Control over resources**—You have control over which resources (bandwidth, equipment, wide-area facilities, and so on) are being used. For example, you can limit the bandwidth consumed over a backbone link by FTP transfers or give priority to an important database access.

- **More efficient use of network resources**—Using Cisco's network analysis management and accounting tools, you will know what your network is being used for and that you are servicing the most important traffic to your business.

- **Tailored services**—The control and visibility provided by QoS enables Internet service providers to offer carefully tailored grades of service differentiation to their customers.

- **Coexistence of mission-critical applications**—Cisco's QoS technologies make certain that your WAN is used efficiently by mission-critical applications that are most important to your business, that bandwidth and minimum delays required by time-sensitive multimedia and voice applications are available, and that other applications using the link get their fair service without interfering with mission-critical traffic.

- **Foundation for a fully integrated network in the future**—Implementing Cisco QoS technologies in your network now is a good first step toward the fully integrated multimedia network needed in the near future.

QoS Concepts

Fundamentally, QoS enables you to provide better service to certain flows. This is done by either raising the priority of a flow or limiting the priority of another flow. When using congestion-management tools, you try to raise the priority of a flow by queuing and servicing queues in different ways. The queue management tool used for congestion avoidance raises priority by dropping lower-priority flows before higher-priority flows. Policing and shaping provide priority to a flow by limiting the throughput of other flows. Link efficiency tools limit large flows to show a preference for small flows.

Cisco IOS QoS is a tool box, and many tools can accomplish the same result. A simple analogy comes from the need to tighten a bolt: You can tighten a bolt with pliers or with a wrench. Both are equally effective, but these are different tools. This is the same with QoS tools. You will find that results can be accomplished using different QoS tools. Which one to use depends on the traffic. You wouldn't pick a tool without knowing what you were trying to do, would you? If the job is to drive a nail, you do not bring a screwdriver.

QoS tools can help alleviate most congestion problems. However, many times there is just too much traffic for the bandwidth supplied. In such cases, QoS is merely a bandage. A simple analogy comes from pouring syrup into a bottle. Syrup can be poured from one container into another container at or below the size of the spout. If the amount poured is greater than the size of the spout, syrup is wasted. However, you can use a funnel to catch syrup pouring at a rate greater than the size of the spout. This allows you to pour more than what the spout can take, while still not wasting the syrup. However, consistent overpouring will eventually fill and overflow the funnel.

Basic QoS Architecture

The basic architecture introduces the three fundamental pieces for QoS implementation (see Figure 59-1):

- QoS identification and marking techniques for coordinating QoS from end to end between network elements

- QoS within a single network element (for example, queuing, scheduling, and traffic-shaping tools)

- QoS policy, management, and accounting functions to control and administer end-to-end traffic across a network

Figure 59-1 *A Basic QoS Implementation Has Three Main Components*

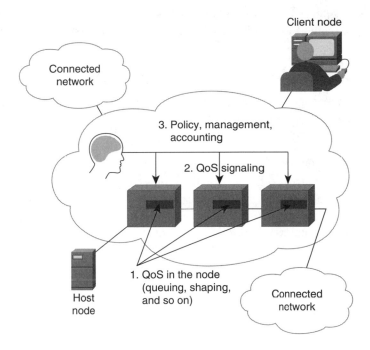

QoS Identification and Marking

Identification and marking is accomplished through classification and reservation.

Classification

To provide preferential service to a type of traffic, it must first be identified. Second, the packet may or may not be marked. These two tasks make up classification. When the packet is identified but not marked, classification is said to be on a per-hop basis. This is when the classification pertains only to the device that it is on, not passed to the next router. This happens with priority queuing (PQ) and custom queuing (CQ). When packets are marked for network-wide use, IP precedence bits can be set (see the section "IP Precedence: Signaling Differentiated QoS").

Common methods of identifying flows include access control lists (ACLs), policy-based routing, committed access rate (CAR), and network-based application recognition (NBAR).

QoS Within a Single Network Element

Congestion management, queue management, link efficiency, and shaping/policing tools provide QoS within a single network element.

Congestion Management

Because of the bursty nature of voice/video/data traffic, sometimes the amount of traffic exceeds the speed of a link. At this point, what will the router do? Will it buffer traffic in a single queue and let the first packet in be the first packet out? Or, will it put packets into different queues and service certain queues more often? Congestion-management tools address these questions. Tools include PQ, CQ, weighted fair queuing (WFQ), and class-based weighted fair queuing (CBWFQ).

Queue Management

Because queues are not of infinite size, they can fill and overflow. When a queue is full, any additional packets cannot get into the queue and will be dropped. This is a tail drop. The issue with tail drops is that the router cannot prevent this packet from being dropped (even if it is a high-priority packet). So, a mechanism is necessary to do two things:

1 Try to make sure that the queue does not fill up, so that there is room for high-priority packets

2 Allow some sort of criteria for dropping packets that are of lower priority before dropping higher-priority packets

Weighted random early detect (WRED) provides both of these mechanisms.

Link Efficiency

Many times low-speed links present an issue for smaller packets. For example, the serialization delay of a 1500-byte packet on a 56-Kbps link is 214 milliseconds. If a voice packet were to get behind this big packet, the delay budget for voice would be exceeded even before the packet left the router! Link fragmentation and interleave allow this large packet to be segmented into smaller packets interleaving the voice packet. Interleaving is as important as the fragmentation. There is no reason to fragment the packet and have the voice packet go behind all the fragmented packets.

NOTE Serialization delay is the time that it takes to put a packet on the link. For the example just given, these mathematics apply:

Packet size: 1500-byte packet · 8 bits/byte = 12,000 bits

Line rate: 56,000 bps

Result: 12,000 bits/56,000 bps = .214 sec or 214 msec

Another efficiency is the elimination of too many overhead bits. For example, RTP headers have a 40-byte header. With a payload of as little as 20 bytes, the overhead can be twice that of the payload in some cases. RTP header compression (also known as Compressed Real-Time Protocol header) reduces the header to a more manageable size.

Traffic Shaping and Policing

Shaping is used to create a traffic flow that limits the full bandwidth potential of the flow(s). This is used many times to prevent the overflow problem mentioned in the introduction. For instance, many network topologies use Frame Relay in a hub-and-spoke design. In this case, the central site normally has a high-bandwidth link (say, T1), while remote sites have a low-bandwidth link in comparison (say, 384 Kbps). In this case, it is possible for traffic from the central site to overflow the low bandwidth link at the other end. Shaping is a perfect way to pace traffic closer to 384 Kbps to avoid the overflow of the remote link. Traffic above the configured rate is buffered for transmission later to maintain the rate configured.

Policing is similar to shaping, but it differs in one very important way: Traffic that exceeds the configured rate is not buffered (and normally is discarded).

NOTE Cisco's implementation of policing CAR allows a number of actions besides discard to be performed. However, policing normally refers to the discard of traffic above a configured rate.

QoS Management

QoS management helps to set and evaluate QoS policies and goals. A common methodology entails the following steps:

Step 1   Baseline the network with devices such as RMON probes. This helps in determining the traffic characteristics of the network. Also, applications targeted for QoS should be baselined (usually in terms of response time).

Step 2   Deploy QoS techniques when the traffic characteristics have been obtained and an application(s) has been targeted for increased QoS.

Step 3   Evaluate the results by testing the response of the targeted applications to see whether the QoS goals have been reached.

For ease of deployment, you can use Cisco's Quality of Service Policy Manager (QPM) and Quality of Service Device Manager (QDM). For verification of service levels, you can use Cisco's Internetwork Performance Monitor (IPM).

You must consider that in an ever-changing network environment, QoS is not a one-time deployment, but an ongoing, essential part of network design.

End-to-End QoS Levels

Service levels refer to the actual end-to-end QoS capabilities, meaning the capability of a network to deliver service needed by specific network traffic from end to end or edge to edge. The services differ in their level of *QoS strictness*, which describes how tightly the service can be bound by specific bandwidth, delay, jitter, and loss characteristics.

Three basic levels of end-to-end QoS can be provided across a heterogeneous network, as shown in Figure 59-2:

- **Best-effort service**—Also known as lack of QoS, best-effort service is basic connectivity with no guarantees. This is best characterized by First-In, First-Out (FIFO) queues, which have no differentiation between flows.

- **Differentiated service (also called soft QoS)**—Some traffic is treated better than the rest (faster handling, more average bandwidth, and lower average loss rate). This is a statistical preference, not a hard and fast guarantee. This is provided by classification of traffic and the use of QoS tools such as PQ, CQ, WFQ, and WRED (all discussed later in this chapter).

- **Guaranteed service (also called hard QoS)**—This is an absolute reservation of network resources for specific traffic. This is provided through QoS tools Resource Reservation Protocol (RSVP) and CBWFQ (discussed later in this chapter).

Deciding which type of service is appropriate to deploy in the network depends on several factors:

- The application or problem that the customer is trying to solve. Each of the three types of service is appropriate for certain applications. This does not imply that a customer must migrate to differentiated and then to guaranteed service (although many probably eventually will). A differentiated service—or even a best-effort service— may be appropriate, depending on the customer application requirements.

- The rate at which customers can realistically upgrade their infrastructures. There is a natural upgrade path from the technology needed to provide differentiated services to that needed to provide guaranteed services, which is a superset of that needed for differentiated services.

- The cost of implementing and deploying guaranteed service is likely to be more than that for a differentiated service.

Figure 59-2 *The Three Levels of End-to-End QoS Are Best-Effort Service, Differentiated Service, and Guaranteed Service*

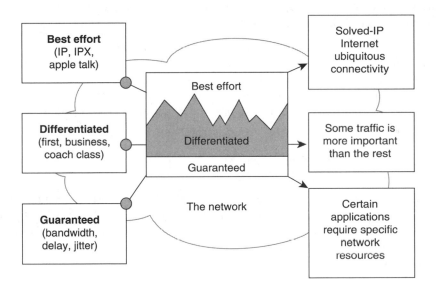

Modular QoS Command-Line Interface (MQC)

Cisco's Modular QoS Command-Line Interface (CLI) defines a new modular CLI-based QoS configuration on a router. This new framework for defining QoS policies groups the QoS configuration into three distinguished modules: traffic class definition, policy definition, and policy application.

In the modular QoS CLI model, QoS policies can be configured in a router in three steps, a step for each module in the new CLI model:

1 Traffic class definition: configuring the traffic classification policy. This is achieved by using a **class map** configuration command.

2 Policy definition: configuring policies on the various traffic classes defined. This is achieved by using a **policy map** configuration command.

3 Policy application: enabling the policy to an interface. This is achieved by using the **service policy** configuration command.

QoS Architectures

To facilitate end-to-end QoS on an IP network, the Internet Engineering Task Force (IETF) has defined two models: Integrated Services (IntServ) and Differentiated Services (DiffServ or DS). IntServ follows the signaled QoS model, in which the end hosts signal their QoS need to the network. DiffServ works on the provisioned QoS model, in which network elements are set up to service multiple classes of traffic, with varying QoS requirements. Cisco IOS software supports both the IntServ and DiffServ QoS models.

IntServ provides a rich end-to-end QoS solution by way of end-to-end signaling, state maintenance (for each RSVP flow and reservation), and admission control at each network element. DiffServ, on the other hand, addresses the clear need for relatively simple and coarse methods of categorizing traffic into different classes (or CoS) and applying QoS parameters to those classes. To accomplish this, packets are first divided into classes by marking the type-of-service (ToS) byte in the IP header.

Integrated Services Architecture

The IntServ model relies on the RSVP to signal and reserve the desired QoS for each flow in the network. In a network, packets are normally identified on a flow basis by the five flow fields in the IP header—source IP address, destination IP address, IP protocol field, and source and destination ports. An individual flow is made up of packets going from an application on a source machine to an application on a destination machine. Packets that belong to a flow carry the same values for the five IP header flow fields. Two ToS can be requested via RSVP (assuming that all network devices support RSVP along the path from the source to the destination). The first type is a very strict guaranteed service that provides firm boundaries on end-to-end delay and assured bandwidth for traffic that conforms to the reserved specifications. The second type is a controlled-load service in which the network guarantees that the reserved flow will reach its destination with a minimum of interference from the best-effort traffic.

Differentiated Services Architecture

The DiffServ model supports various types of application traffic by grouping traffic into multiple classes of service.

The differentiated services architecture proposes the use of a well-defined set of building blocks from which a variety of services may be built. In this architecture, each packet carries information in the packet header that is used by each hop to give it a particular forwarding treatment.

The DiffServ architecture standardizes the layout of the DiffServ byte and assigns a specific forwarding treatment, called per-hop behavior, to a certain number of patterns of the DS byte. Best-effort treatment, which is provided by the Internet today, is one of the many possible forwarding treatments.

The DiffServ architecture provides a framework within which service providers can offer their customers a range of network services, each differentiated based on performance. A customer can choose the level of performance needed on a packet-by-packet basis by simply marking the packet's Differentiated Services Code Point (DSCP) field to a specific value.

Differentiated Services Byte

IP precedence uses the 3 precedence bits in the IPv4 header's ToS field to specify a class of service for each packet.

The IETF Differentiated Services group standardized the use of 6 bits of the ToS byte in the IP header with DSCP. The lowest-order 2 bits are currently unused (CU). DSCP is an extension to the 3 bits used by IP precedence.

Similar to IP precedence, DSCP can provide differential treatment to packets marked appropriately. The ToS byte is renamed the DS byte with the standardization of the DSCP field. A 6-bit pattern (the DSCP) in the DS byte is defined by RFC 2474, as shown in Figure 59-3.

Figure 59-3 *RFC 2474 DSCP*

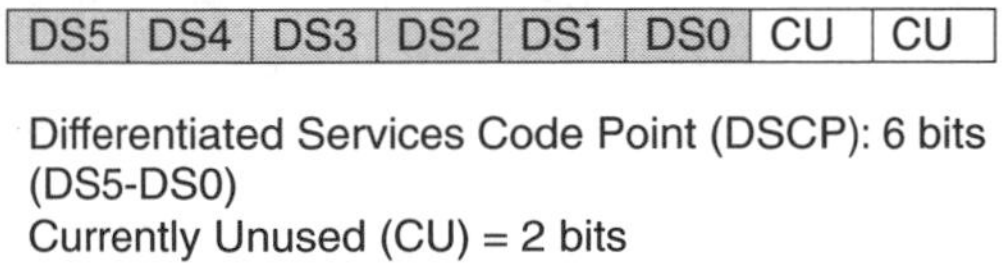

| DS5 | DS4 | DS3 | DS2 | DS1 | DS0 | CU | CU |

Differentiated Services Code Point (DSCP): 6 bits
(DS5-DS0)
Currently Unused (CU) = 2 bits

Classification—Identifying Flows

To provide priority to certain flows, the flow must first be identified and (if desired) marked. These two tasks are commonly referred to as just *classification*.

Historically, identification was done using access control lists (ACLs). ACLs identify traffic for congestion-management tools, such as PQ and CQ. Because PQ and CQ are placed on routers on a hop-by-hop basis (that is, priority settings for QoS pertain only to that router and are not passed to subsequent router hops in the network), identification of the packet is used only within a single router. In some instances, CBWFQ classification is for only a single router. This is contrasted by setting IP precedence bits.

Features such as policy-based routing and CAR can be used to set precedence based on extended access list classification. This allows considerable flexibility for precedence assignment, including assignment by application or user, by destination and source subnet, and so on. Typically this functionality is deployed as close to the edge of the network (or administrative domain) as possible so that each subsequent network element can provide service based on the determined policy.

Network-based application recognition (NBAR) is used to identify traffic more granularly. For example, URLs in an HTTP packet can be identified. Once the packet has been identified, it can be marked with a precedence setting.

QoS Policy Setting with Policy-Based Routing

Cisco IOS Policy-Based Routing (PBR) enables you to classify traffic based on extended access list criteria, set IP precedence bits, and even route to specific traffic-engineered paths that may be required to allow a specific QoS through the network. By setting precedence levels on incoming traffic and using them in combination with the queuing tools described earlier in this chapter, you can create differentiated service. These tools provide powerful, simple, and flexible options for implementing QoS policies in your network.

Using policy-based routing, route maps are made to match on certain flow criteria and then set precedence bits when ACLs are matched.

The capability to set IP precedence bits should not be confused with PBR's primary capability: routing packets based on configured policies. Some applications or traffic can benefit from QoS-specific routing—transferring stock records to a corporate office on a higher-bandwidth, higher-cost link for a short time, while transmitting routine application data, such as e-mail, over a lower-bandwidth, lower-cost link. PBR can be used to direct packets to take different paths than the path derived from the routing protocols. It provides a more flexible mechanism for routing packets, complementing the existing mechanisms provided by routing protocols.

Also available using route maps is the capability to identify packets based on Border Gateway Protocol (BGP) attributes, such as community lists and AS paths. This is known as *QoS policy propagation via Border Gateway Protocol.*

CAR: Setting IP Precedence

Similar in some ways to PBR, the CAR feature enables you to classify traffic on an incoming interface. It also allows specification of policies for handling traffic that exceeds a certain bandwidth allocation. CAR looks at traffic received on an interface, or a subset of that traffic selected by access list criteria, compares its rate to that of a configured token bucket, and then takes action based on the result (for example, drop or rewrite IP precedence).

There is some confusion with using CAR to set IP precedence bits. An attempt to clear up any confusion follows. As described later in this chapter, CAR (as its name describes) is used to police traffic flows to a *committed access rate*. CAR does this with a token bucket. A token bucket is a bucket with tokens in it that represent bytes (1 token = 1 byte). The bucket is filled with tokens at a user-configured rate. As packets arrive to be delivered, the system checks the bucket for tokens. If there are enough tokens in the bucket to match the size of the packet, those tokens are removed and the packet is passed (this packet *conforms*). If there aren't enough tokens, the packet is dropped (this packet *exceeds*).

When using Cisco IOS's CAR implementation, you have more options than just pass or drop. One option is to set the IP precedence bits. When the conform and exceed actions both say to set precedence bits to the same setting, then it is no longer a policing feature, but merely a method of setting IP precedence bits.

Figure 59-4 shows a committed rate that is decided upon. Any packet that is below the rate conforms. Packets above the rate exceed. In this example, the action for both conditions is to set prec = 5. In this case, what the rate is does not matter and CAR is simply being used to set precedence bits.

Figure 59-4 *Committed Rate That Is Decided Upon*

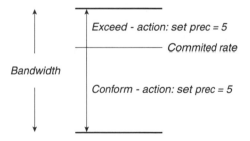

When IP precedence is set in the host or network client, this setting can be used optionally; however, this can be overridden by policy within the network. IP precedence enables service classes to be established using existing network queuing mechanisms (for example, WFQ or WRED), with no changes to existing applications or complicated network requirements. Note that this same approach is easily extended to IPv6 using its Priority field.

Cisco IOS software takes advantage of the end-to-end nature of IP to meet this challenge by overlaying Layer 2 technology-specific QoS signaling solutions with the Layer 3 IP QoS signaling methods of RSVP and IP precedence.

7500 Platform

Cisco IOS software also provides distributed committed access rate (D-CAR) on the 7500 Versatile Interface Processors (VIPs). D-CAR can be used to set IP precedence bits just like CAR. It also can place packets in QoS groups that are used in class-based D-WFQ and for policing in D-CAR.

NBAR: Dynamic Identification of Flows

Cisco's newest method of classification is Network-Based Application Recognition (NBAR). For clarity, NBAR is actually only an identification tool, but it will be referred to here as a classification tool. As with any classification tool, the hard part is identifying the traffic. Marking the packet later is relatively easy. NBAR takes the identification portion of classification to another level. Looking deeper into the packet, identification can be performed, for example, to the URL or MIME type of an HTTP packet. This becomes essential as more applications become web-based. You would need to differentiate between an order being placed and casual web browsing. In addition, NBAR can identify various applications that use ephemeral ports. NBAR does this by looking at control packets to determine which ports the application decides to pass data on.

NBAR adds a couple of interesting features that make it extremely valuable. One feature is a protocol discovery capability. This allows NBAR to baseline the protocols on an interface. NBAR lists the protocols that it can identify and provides statistics on each one. Another feature is the Packet Description Language Module (PDLM), which allows additional protocols to be easily added to NBAR's list of identifiable protocols. These modules are created and loaded into Flash memory, which then is uploaded into RAM. Using PDLMs, additional protocols can be added to the list without upgrading the IOS level or rebooting the router.

NOTE Although NBAR only identifies packets, these packets may also be marked with an IP precedence setting.

Congestion-Management Tools

One way network elements handle an overflow of arriving traffic is to use a queuing algorithm to sort the traffic, and then determine some method of prioritizing it onto an output link. Cisco IOS software includes the following queuing tools:

- First-in, first-out (FIFO) queuing

- Priority queuing (PQ)

- Custom queuing (CQ)

- Flow-based weighted fair queuing (WFQ)

- Class-based weighted fair queuing (CBWFQ)

Each queuing algorithm was designed to solve a specific network traffic problem and has a particular effect on network performance, as described in the following sections.

NOTE   Queuing algorithms take effect when congestion is experienced. By definition, if the link is not congested, then there is no need to queue packets. In the absence of congestion, all packets are delivered directly to the interface.

FIFO: Basic Store-and-Forward Capability

In its simplest form, *FIFO* queuing involves storing packets when the network is congested and forwarding them in order of arrival when the network is no longer congested. FIFO is the default queuing algorithm in some instances, thus requiring no configuration, but it has several shortcomings. Most importantly, FIFO queuing makes no decision about packet priority; the order of arrival determines bandwidth, promptness, and buffer allocation. Nor does it provide protection against ill-behaved applications (sources). Bursty sources can cause long delays in delivering time-sensitive application traffic, and, potentially, to delivering network control and signaling messages. FIFO queuing was a necessary first step in controlling network traffic, but today's intelligent networks need more sophisticated algorithms. In addition, a full queue causes tail drops. This is undesirable because the packet dropped could have been a high-priority packet. The router couldn't prevent this packet from being dropped because there was no room in the queue for it (in addition to the fact that FIFO cannot tell a high-priority packet from a low-priority packet). Cisco IOS software implements queuing algorithms that avoid the shortcomings of FIFO queuing.

PQ: Prioritizing Traffic

PQ ensures that important traffic gets the fastest handling at each point where it is used. It was designed to give strict priority to important traffic. Priority queuing can flexibly prioritize according to network protocol (for example, IP, IPX, or AppleTalk), incoming interface, packet size, source/destination address, and so on. In PQ, each packet is placed in one of four queues—high, medium, normal, or low—based on an assigned priority. Packets that are not classified by this priority list mechanism fall into the normal queue (see Figure 59-5). During transmission, the algorithm gives higher-priority queues absolute preferential treatment over low-priority queues.

Figure 59-5 *Priority Queuing Places Data into Four Levels of Queues: High, Medium, Normal, and Low*

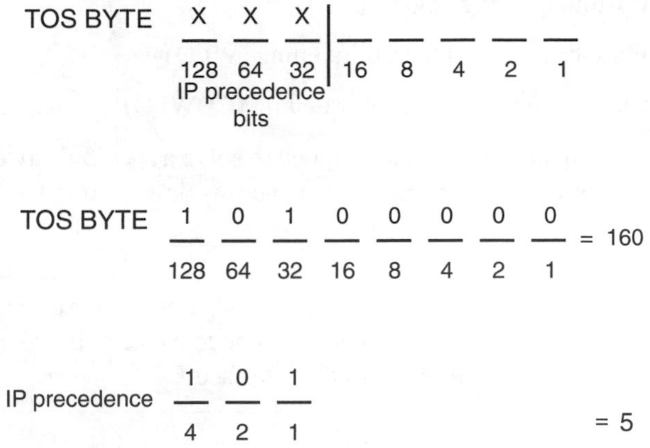

TOS BYTE

$$\underset{\substack{128 \quad 64 \quad 32 \\ \text{IP precedence} \\ \text{bits}}}{\text{X} \quad \text{X} \quad \text{X}} \bigg| \underset{16 \quad 8 \quad 4 \quad 2 \quad 1}{\text{—} \quad \text{—} \quad \text{—} \quad \text{—} \quad \text{—}}$$

TOS BYTE

$$\underset{128 \quad 64 \quad 32 \quad 16 \quad 8 \quad 4 \quad 2 \quad 1}{1 \quad 0 \quad 1 \quad 0 \quad 0 \quad 0 \quad 0 \quad 0} = 160$$

IP precedence

$$\underset{4 \quad 2 \quad 1}{1 \quad 0 \quad 1} \qquad = 5$$

PQ is useful for making sure that mission-critical traffic traversing various WAN links gets priority treatment. For example, Cisco uses PQ to ensure that important Oracle-based sales reporting data gets to its destination ahead of other, less-critical traffic. PQ currently uses static configuration and, thus, does not automatically adapt to changing network requirements.

CQ: Guaranteeing Bandwidth

CQ was designed to allow various applications or organizations to share the network among applications with specific minimum bandwidth or latency requirements. In these environments, bandwidth must be shared proportionally between applications and users. You can use the Cisco CQ feature to provide guaranteed bandwidth at a potential congestion point, ensuring the specified traffic a fixed portion of available bandwidth and leaving the remaining bandwidth to other traffic. Custom queuing handles traffic by assigning a specified amount of queue space to each class of packets and then servicing the queues in a round-robin fashion (see Figure 59-6).

As an example, encapsulated Systems Network Architecture (SNA) requires a guaranteed minimum level of service. You could reserve half of available bandwidth for SNA data and allow the remaining half to be used by other protocols, such as IP and Internetwork Packet Exchange (IPX).

Figure 59-6 *Custom Queuing Handles Traffic by Assigning a Specified Amount of Queue Space to Each Class of Packets and Then Servicing up to 17 Queues in a Round-Robin Fashion*

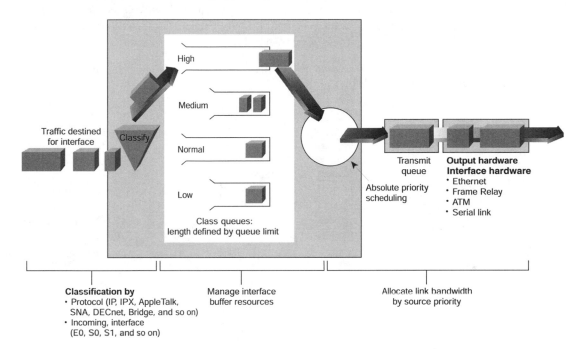

The queuing algorithm places the messages in one of 17 queues (queue 0 holds system messages, such as keepalives and signaling) and is emptied with weighted priority. The router services queues 1 through 16 in round-robin order, dequeuing a configured byte count from each queue in each cycle. This feature ensures that no application (or specified group of applications) achieves more than a predetermined proportion of overall capacity when the line is under stress. Like PQ, CQ is statically configured and does not automatically adapt to changing network conditions.

Flow-Based WFQ: Creating Fairness Among Flows

For situations in which it is desirable to provide consistent response time to heavy and light network users alike without adding excessive bandwidth, the solution is flow-based WFQ (commonly referred to as just WFQ). WFQ is one of Cisco's premier queuing techniques. It is a flow-based queuing algorithm that creates bit-wise fairness by allowing each queue to be serviced fairly in terms of byte count. For example, if queue 1 has 100-byte packets and queue 2 has 50-byte packets, the WFQ algorithm will take two packets from queue 2 for every one packet from queue 1. This makes service fair for each queue: 100 bytes each time the queue is serviced.

WFQ ensures that queues do not starve for bandwidth and that traffic gets predictable service. Low-volume traffic streams—which comprise the majority of traffic—receive increased service, transmitting the same number of bytes as high-volume streams. This behavior results in what appears to be preferential treatment for low-volume traffic, when in actuality it is creating fairness, as shown in Figure 59-7.

Figure 59-7 *With WFQ, If High-Volume Conversations Are Active, Their Transfer Rates and Interarrival Periods Are Made Much More Predictable*

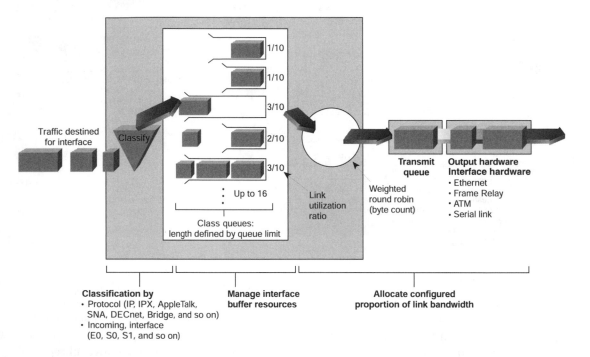

WFQ is designed to minimize configuration effort, and it automatically adapts to changing network traffic conditions. In fact, WFQ does such a good job for most applications that it has been made the default queuing mode on most serial interfaces configured to run at or below E1 speeds (2.048 Mbps).

Flow-based WFQ creates *flows* based on a number of characteristics in a packet. Each flow (also referred to as a *conversation*) is given its own queue for buffering if congestion is experienced. The following descriptions use flow, conversation, and queue interchangeably.

NOTE	Characteristics defining a flow include source and destination addresses, socket numbers, and session identifiers. These are general characteristics. Review the Cisco Systems technical documents (www.cisco.com) to see the exact criteria for the definition of a flow. For different protocols, a different criterion is used.

The weighted portion of WFQ comes from the use of IP precedence bits to provide greater service for certain queues. Using settings 0 to 5 (6 and 7 are reserved), WFQ uses its algorithm to determine how much more service to provide to a queue. See the next section "Cooperation Between WFQ and QoS Signaling Technologies," for more details.

WFQ is efficient in that it uses whatever bandwidth is available to forward traffic from lower-priority flows if no traffic from higher-priority flows is present. This is different from strict time-division multiplexing (TDM), which simply carves up the bandwidth and lets it go unused if no traffic is present for a particular traffic type. WFQ works with both—IP precedence and RSVP, described later in this chapter—to help provide differentiated QoS as well as guaranteed services.

The WFQ algorithm also addresses the problem of round-trip delay variability. If multiple high-volume conversations are active, their transfer rates and interarrival periods are made much more predictable. This is created by the bit-wise fairness. If conversations are serviced in a consistent manner with every round-robin approach, delay variation (or jitter) stabilizes. WFQ greatly enhances algorithms such as SNA Logical Link Control (LLC) and the Transmission Control Protocol (TCP) congestion control and slow-start features. The result is more predictable throughput and response time for each active flow, as shown in Figure 59-8.

Cooperation Between WFQ and QoS Signaling Technologies

As mentioned previously, WFQ is IP precedence–aware; that is, it is capable of detecting higher-priority packets marked with precedence by the IP forwarder and can schedule them faster, providing superior response time for this traffic. This is the weighted portion of WFQ. The IP Precedence field has values between 0 (the default) and 7 (6 and 7 are reserved and normally are not set by network administrators). As the precedence value increases, the algorithm allocates more bandwidth to that conversation to make sure that it is served more quickly when congestion occurs. WFQ assigns a weight to each flow, which determines the transmit order for queued packets. In this scheme, lower weights are provided more service. IP precedence serves as a divisor to this weighting factor. For instance, traffic with an IP Precedence field value of 7 gets a lower weight than traffic with an IP Precedence field value of 3, and thus, has priority in the transmit order.

Figure 59-8 *This Diagram Shows an Example of Interactive Traffic Delay (128-Kbps Frame Relay WAN Link)*

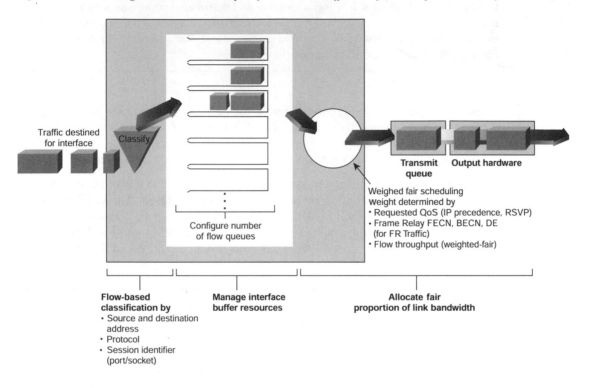

NOTE A *weight* is a number calculated from the IP precedence setting for a packet in flow. This weight is used in WFQ's algorithm to determine when the packet will be serviced.

Weight = (4096 / (IP precedence + 1)

Weight = (32384 / (IP precedence + 1)

The numerator of the equation changed from 4096 to 32384 in a v12.0 maintenance release.

Weight settings can be viewed using the **show queue <interface>** command.

Effect of IP Precedence Settings

The effect of IP precedence settings is described here:

If you have one flow at each precedence level on an interface, each flow will get precedence + 1 part of the link, as follows:

1 + 2 + 3 + 4 + 5 + 6 + 7 + 8 = 36

The flows will get 8/36, 7/36, 6/36, and 5/36 of the link, and so on. However, if you have 18 precedence—1 flow and 1 of each of the others—the formula looks like this:

$$1 + 18 \cdot 2 + 3 + 4 + 5 + 6 + 7 + 8 = 36 - 2 + 18 \cdot 2 = 70$$

The flows will get 8/70, 7/70, 6/70, 5/70, 4/70, 3/70, 2/70, and 1/70 of the link, and 18 of the flows will each get approximately 2/70 of the link.

WFQ is also RSVP-aware; RSVP uses WFQ to allocate buffer space and schedule packets, and it guarantees bandwidth for reserved flows. Additionally, in a Frame Relay network, the presence of congestion is flagged by the forward explicit congestion notification (FECN) and backward explicit congestion notification (BECN) bits. WFQ weights are affected by Frame Relay discard eligible (DE), FECN, and BECN bits when the traffic is switched by the Frame Relay switching module. When congestion is flagged, the weights used by the algorithm are altered so that the conversation encountering the congestion transmits less frequently.

7500 Platform

Cisco IOS software also provides distributed weighted fair queuing (D-WFQ), a high-speed version of WFQ that runs on VIP-distributed processors. The D-WFQ algorithm provides two types of WFQ: flow-based fair queuing and class-based fair queuing. The flow-based implementation of D-WFQ differs from WFQ by not recognizing IP precedence bits—thus, there is no weighting to flows.

Class-Based WFQ: Ensuring Network Bandwidth

Class-based WFQ (CBWFQ) is one of Cisco's newest congestion-management tools for providing greater flexibility. When you want to provide a minimum amount of bandwidth, use CBWFQ. This is in comparison to a desire to provide a maximum amount of bandwidth. CAR and traffic shaping are used in that case.

CBWFQ allows a network administrator to create minimum-guaranteed bandwidth classes. Instead of providing a queue for each individual flow, a class is defined that consists of one or more flows. Each class can be guaranteed a minimum amount of bandwidth.

One example in which CBWFQ can be used is in preventing multiple low-priority flows from swamping out a single high-priority flow. For example, a video stream that needs half the bandwidth of T1 will be provided that by WFQ if there are two flows. As more flows are added, the video stream gets less of the bandwidth because WFQ's mechanism creates fairness. If there are 10 flows, the video stream will get only 1/10th of the bandwidth, which is not enough. Even setting the IP precedence bit = 5 does not solve this problem.

$$1 \cdot 9 + 6 = 15$$

Video gets 6/15 of the bandwidth, which is less than the bandwidth video needs. A mechanism must be invoked to provide the half of the bandwidth that video needs. CBWFQ provides this. The network administrator defines a class, places the video stream in the class, and tells the router to provide 768 Kbps (half of a T1) service for the class. Video is now given the bandwidth that it needs. A default class is used for the rest of flows. This class is serviced using flow-based WFQ schemes allocating the remainder of the bandwidth (half of the T1, in this example)

NOTE   This is *not* to discount the use of WFQ. For most implementations, WFQ is an excellent congestion-management tool (that's why it's the default on interfaces E1 and below). The previous example was meant to show a situation in which CBWFQ is very effective.

In addition, a low-latency queue (LLQ) may be designated, which essentially is a priority queue. Note that this feature is also referred to as priority queue class-based weighted fair queuing (PQCBWFQ).

Low-latency queuing allows a class to be serviced as a strict-priority queue. Traffic in this class will be serviced before any of the other classes. A reservation for an amount of bandwidth is made. Any traffic above this reservation is discarded. Outside of CBWFQ, you can use IP RTP priority (also known as PQWFQ) or IP RTP reserve to provide similar service for RTP traffic only.

NOTE   With CBWFQ, a minimum amount of bandwidth can be reserved for a certain class. If more bandwidth is available, that class is welcome to use it. The key is that it is guaranteed a minimum amount of bandwidth. Also, if a class is not using its guaranteed bandwidth, other applications may use the bandwidth.

7500 Platform

Cisco IOS software also provides distributed class–based weighted fair queuing (still referred to as D-WFQ), a high-speed version of WFQ that runs on VIP-distributed processors. Class-based WFQ in D-WFQ differs from CBWFQ by using different syntax, but it essentially provides the same service. In addition to providing the capability to guarantee bandwidth, class-based WFQ in D-WFQ has an option to recognize IP precedence bits not recognized in flow-based (this is called ToS-based).

Queue Management (Congestion-Avoidance Tools)

Congestion avoidance is a form of queue management. *Congestion-avoidance techniques* monitor network traffic loads in an effort to anticipate and avoid congestion at common network bottlenecks, as opposed to congestion-management techniques that operate to control congestion after it occurs. The primary Cisco IOS congestion avoidance tool is weighted random early detection (WRED).

WRED: Avoiding Congestion

The *random early detection (RED)* algorithms are designed to avoid congestion in internetworks before it becomes a problem. RED works by monitoring traffic load at points in the network and stochastically discarding packets if the congestion begins to increase. The result of the drop is that the source detects the dropped traffic and slows its transmission. RED is primarily designed to work with TCP in IP internetwork environments.

WRED Cooperation with QoS Signaling Technologies

WRED combines the capabilities of the RED algorithm with IP precedence. This combination provides for preferential traffic handling for higher-priority packets. It can selectively discard lower-priority traffic when the interface starts to get congested and can provide differentiated performance characteristics for different classes of service (see Figure 59-9). WRED is also RSVP-aware and can provide an integrated services controlled-load QoS.

Figure 59-9 *WRED Provides a Method That Stochastically Discards Packets If the Congestion Begins to Increase*

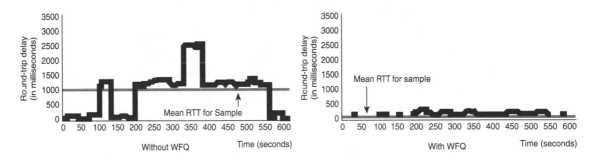

Within each queue, a finite number of packets can be housed. A full queue causes tail drops. This is undesirable because the packet discarded may have been a high-priority packet and the router did not have a chance to queue it. If the queue is not full, the router can look at the priority of all arriving packets and drop the lower-priority packets, allowing high-priority packets into the queue. Through managing the depth of the queue (the number of packets in the queue) by dropping various packets, the router can do its best to make sure that the queue does not fill and that tail drops are not experienced. This allows the router to make the decision on which packets get dropped when the queue depth increases. WRED also helps prevent overall congestion in an internetwork. WRED uses a minimum threshold for each IP precedence level to determine when a packet can be dropped. (The minimum threshold must be exceeded for WRED to consider a packet as a candidate for being dropped.)

Take a look at this WRED example:

> Depth of the queue: 21 packets
>
> Minimum drop threshold for IP precedence = 0: 20
>
> Minimum drop threshold for IP precedence = 1: 22

Because the minimum drop threshold for IP precedence = 0 has been exceeded, packets with an IP precedence = 0 can be dropped. However, the minimum drop threshold for IP precedence = 1 has not been exceeded, so those packets will not be dropped. If the queue depth deepens and exceeds 22, then packets with IP precedence = 1 can be dropped as well. WRED uses an algorithm that raises the probability that a packet can be dropped as the queue depth rises from the minimum drop threshold to the maximum drop threshold. Above the maximum drop threshold, all packets are dropped.

Flow RED: RED for Non-TCP-Compliant Flows

WRED is primarily used for TCP flows that will scale back transmission if a packet is dropped. There are non-TCP-compliant flows that do not scale back when packets are dropped. Flow RED is used to deal with such flows. The approach is to increase the probability of dropping a flow if it exceeds a threshold.

Flow-based WRED relies on these two main approaches to remedy the problem of linear packet dumping:

- It classifies incoming traffic into flows based on parameters, such as destination and source addresses and ports.

- It maintains state about active flows, which are flows that have packets in the output queues.

Flow-based WRED uses this classification and state information to ensure that each flow does not consume more than its permitted share of the output buffer resources. Flow-based WRED determines which flows monopolize resources, and it more heavily penalizes these flows.

This is how flow-based WRED ensures fairness among flows: It maintains a count of the number of active flows that exist through an output interface. Given the number of active flows and the output queue size, flow-based WRED determines the number of buffers available per flow.

To allow for some burstiness, flow-based WRED scales the number of buffers available per flow by a configured factor and allows each active flow to have a certain number of packets in the output queue. This scaling factor is common to all flows. The outcome of the scaled number of buffers becomes the per-flow limit. When a flow exceeds the per-flow limit, the probability that a packet from that flow will be dropped increases.

7500 Platform

Cisco IOS software also provides distributed weighted random early detection (D-WRED), a high-speed version of WRED that runs on VIP-distributed processors. The D-WRED algorithm provides the same functionality that WRED provides, such as minimum and maximum queue depth thresholds and drop capabilities for each class of service.

WARNING Although IOS allows the configuration of the minimum and maximum queue depth thresholds and drop capabilities, it is recommended that you use the defaults. Consult Cisco Technical Support before changing any of these defaults.

Traffic-Shaping and Policing Tools

Cisco's QoS software solutions include two traffic-shaping tools—generic traffic shaping (GTS) and Frame-Relay traffic shaping (FRTS)—to manage traffic and congestion on the network. Cisco's IOS policing tool is CAR. This was briefly described in the "Classification" section, earlier in this chapter, as it pertains to classification. Here it will be described for its policing function.

CAR: Managing Access Bandwidth Policy and Performing Policing

As described earlier, fundamentally, QoS provides priority either by raising the priority of one flow or by limiting the priority of another. CAR is used to limit the bandwidth of a flow in order to favor another flow.

In the earlier "Classification" section, a generic token bucket was described. In that description, packets that conform are passed and packets that exceed are dropped.

With Cisco's IOS implementation of CAR, a number of actions can be performed. These actions consist of transmitting, dropping, setting IP precedence bits, and continuing (this refers to cascading CAR statements). This flexibility allows for a number of ways to act upon traffic. Here are some scenarios:

- Conforming traffic can be classified with an IP precedence of 5, and exceeding traffic can be dropped.

- Conforming traffic can be transmitted with an IP precedence setting of 5, while exceeding traffic can also be transmitted, but with an IP precedence setting of 1.

- Conforming traffic can be transmitted, and exceeding traffic can be reclassified to a lower IP precedence setting and then sent to the next CAR statement for additional conditions.

Cisco IOS's CAR implementation also provides an excess burst bucket not found in a generic token bucket. In this bucket are additional tokens above the original (or normal) burst bucket. When these tokens are used, the packet has the possibility of being dropped (even if the action is to transmit). A RED-like algorithm is used that says, "The more tokens you use from this bucket, the higher probability that the next packet will be dropped." This allows the flow to be scaled back slowly as in WRED, while still getting the opportunity to send above the normal bucket.

GTS: Controlling Outbound Traffic Flow

GTS provides a mechanism to control the traffic flow on a particular interface. It reduces outbound traffic flow to avoid congestion by constraining specified traffic to a particular bit rate (it also uses a token bucket approach) while queuing bursts of the specified traffic. So, any traffic above the configured rate is queued. This differs from CAR, in which packets are not queued. Thus, traffic adhering to a particular profile can be shaped to meet downstream requirements, eliminating bottlenecks in topologies with data-rate mismatches. Figure 59-10 illustrates GTS.

Figure 59-10 *Generic Traffic Shaping Is Applied on a Per-Interface Basis*

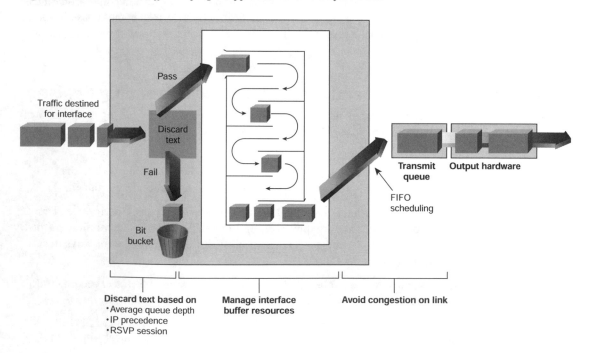

GTS applies on a per-interface basis, can use access lists to select the traffic to shape, and works with a variety of Layer 2 technologies, including Frame Relay, ATM, Switched Multimegabit Data Service (SMDS), and Ethernet.

On a Frame-Relay subinterface, GTS can be set up to adapt dynamically to available bandwidth by integrating BECN signals, or it can be set up simply to shape to a prespecified rate. GTS can also be configured on an ATM Interface Processor (ATM/AIP) interface card to respond to RSVP signaled over statically configured ATM permanent virtual circuits (PVCs).

FRTS: Managing Frame-Relay Traffic

FRTS provides parameters that are useful for managing network traffic congestion. These include committed information rate (CIR), FECN and BECN, and the DE bit. For some time, Cisco has provided support for FECN for DECnet, BECN for SNA traffic using direct LLC2 encapsulation via RFC 1490, and DE bit support. The FRTS feature builds on this Frame-Relay support with additional capabilities that improve the scalability and performance of a Frame-Relay network, increasing the density of virtual circuits and improving response time.

For example, you can configure rate enforcement—a peak rate configured to limit outbound traffic—to either the CIR or some other defined value, such as the excess information rate (EIR), on a per-virtual-circuit (VC) basis.

You can also define priority and custom queuing at the VC or subinterface level. This allows for finer granularity in the prioritization and queuing of traffic, and provides more control over the traffic flow on an individual VC. If you combine CQ with the per-VC queuing and rate enforcement capabilities, you enable Frame-Relay VCs to carry multiple traffic types, such as IP, SNA, and IPX, with bandwidth guaranteed for each traffic type.

FRTS can eliminate bottlenecks in Frame-Relay networks with high-speed connections at the central site and low-speed connections at the branch sites. You can configure rate enforcement to limit the rate at which data is sent on the VC at the central site. You can also use rate enforcement with the existing data-link connection identifier (DLCI) prioritization feature to further improve performance in this situation. FRTS applies only to Frame-Relay PVCs and switched virtual circuits (SVCs).

Using information contained in BECN-tagged packets received from the network, FRTS can also dynamically throttle traffic. With BECN-based throttling, packets are held in the router's buffers to reduce the data flow from the router into the Frame-Relay network. The throttling is done on a per-VC basis, and the transmission rate is adjusted based on the number of BECN-tagged packets received.

FRTS also provides a mechanism for sharing media by multiple VCs. Rate enforcement allows the transmission speed used by the router to be controlled by criteria other than line speed, such as the CIR or EIR. The rate-enforcement feature can also be used to preallocate bandwidth to each VC, creating a virtual TDM network. Finally, with Cisco's FRTS feature, you can integrate StrataCom ATM Foresight closed-loop congestion control to actively adapt to downstream congestion conditions.

Link Efficiency Mechanisms

Currently, Cisco IOS software offers two link efficiency mechanisms—link fragmentation and interleaving (LFI) and real-time protocol header compression (RTP-HC)—that work with queuing and traffic shaping to improve the efficiency and predictability of the application service levels.

LFI: Fragmenting and Interleaving IP Traffic

Interactive traffic (Telnet, Voice over IP, and the like) is susceptible to increased latency and jitter when the network processes large packets (for example, LAN-to-LAN FTP transfers traversing a WAN link), especially as they are queued on slower links. The Cisco IOS LFI feature reduces delay and jitter on slower-speed links by breaking up large datagrams and interleaving low-delay traffic packets with the resulting smaller packets (see Figure 59-11).

Figure 59-11 *By Dividing Large Datagrams with the LFI Feature, Delay Is Reduced on Slower-Speed Links*

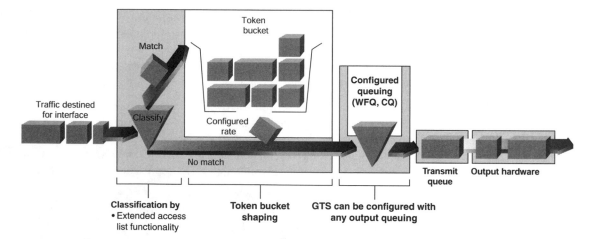

LFI was designed especially for lower-speed links in which serialization delay is significant. LFI requires that multilink Point-to-Point Protocol (PPP) be configured on the interface with interleaving turned on. A related IETF draft, called "Multiclass Extensions to Multilink PPP (MCML)," implements almost the same function as LFI.

Note that for implementation of fragmentation over Frame Relay, you should use the FRF.12 feature, which provides the same results.

RTP Header Compression: Increasing Efficiency of Real-Time Traffic

RTP is a host-to-host protocol used for carrying newer multimedia application traffic, including packetized audio and video, over an IP network. RTP provides end-to-end network transport functions intended for applications transmitting real-time requirements, such as audio, video, or simulation data over multicast or unicast network services. RTP header compression increases efficiency for many of the newer VoIP or multimedia applications that take advantage of RTP, especially on slow links. Figure 59-12 illustrates RTP header compression.

Figure 59-12 *This Diagram Illustrates RTP Header Compression*

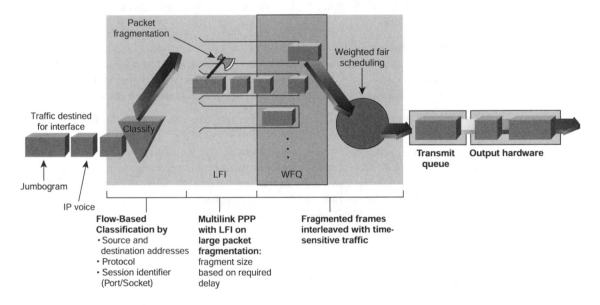

For compressed-payload audio applications, the RTP packet has a 40-byte header and typically a 20- to 150-byte payload. Given the size of the IP/UDP/RTP header combination, it is inefficient to transmit an uncompressed header. RTP header compression helps RTP run more efficiently—especially over lower-speed links—by compressing the RTP/UDP/IP header from 40 bytes to 2–5 bytes. This is especially beneficial for smaller packets (such as IP voice traffic) on slower links (385 Kbps and below), where RTP header compression can reduce overhead and transmission delay significantly. RTP header compression reduces line overhead for multimedia RTP traffic with a corresponding reduction in delay, especially for traffic that uses short packets relative to header length.

RTP header compression is supported on serial lines using Frame Relay, High-Level Data Link Control (HDLC), or PPP encapsulation. It is also supported over ISDN interfaces. A related IETF draft, called "Compressed RTP (CRTP)," defines essentially the same functionality.

RSVP: Guaranteeing QoS

RSVP is an IETF Internet standard (RFC 2205) protocol for allowing an application to dynamically reserve network bandwidth. RSVP enables applications to request a specific QoS for a data flow, as shown in Figure 59-13. Cisco's implementation also allows RSVP to be initiated within the network, using configured proxy RSVP. Network managers can thereby take advantage of the benefits of RSVP in the network, even for non-RSVP-enabled applications and hosts.

Hosts and routers use RSVP to deliver QoS requests to the routers along the paths of the data stream and to maintain router and host state to provide the requested service, usually bandwidth and latency. RSVP uses a mean data rate, the largest amount of data that the router will keep in queue, and minimum QoS to determine bandwidth reservation.

WFQ or WRED acts as the workhorse for RSVP, setting up the packet classification and scheduling required for the reserved flows. Using WFQ, RSVP can deliver an integrated services guaranteed service. Using WRED, it can deliver a controlled load service. WFQ continues to provide its advantageous handling of nonreserved traffic by expediting interactive traffic and fairly sharing the remaining bandwidth between high-bandwidth flows; WRED provides its commensurate advantages for non-RSVP flow traffic. RSVP can be deployed in existing networks with a software upgrade.

Figure 59-13 *This Figure Shows RSVP Implemented in a Cisco-Based Router Network*

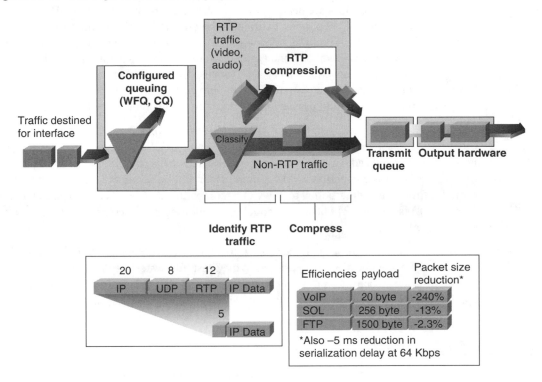

QoS Management

The introduction discussed a common method (and by no means the only method) for QoS management.

For baselining a network, you can use Remote Monitoring (RMON) probes and an application (such as Traffic Director) to develop a good understanding of traffic characteristics. The discovery feature in NBAR (discussed earlier in this chapter) provides a brief look at utilization on an interface basis, but RMON probes provide more complete information. In addition, targeted applications should be baselined (this is commonly measured by response time). This information helps to validate any QoS deployment. From this data, QoS policy is set and deployed.

Once deployed, it is important to evaluate the QoS policies and deployment and to decide whether additional services are needed. Internetwork Performance Monitor (IPM) can assist in determining if QoS policies continue to be effective by measuring response times within the internetwork. Comparing new baseline data for specific applications with the original baseline data will validate the QoS policies deployed. In addition, RMON probes should still continue to monitor the network because the traffic characteristics likely will change. A constant look at network traffic will help with changing trends and allow a network administrator to address new network requirements more expeditiously.

For the network-wide configuration of QoS in a Cisco network, Cisco's QoS Policy Manager (QPM) provides a graphical user interface for managing QoS in a network. Rules or policies are created and then downloaded to the devices. This simplifies QoS configuration of devices. QPM is compatible with Common Open Policy Server (COPS), a standard protocol for downloading policy to any COPs-compatible devices. The proposed standard (RFC 2748) is a simple client/server model for supporting policy control over QoS signaling protocols.

For device management of QoS, there is Cisco's QoS Device Manager (QDM). QDM is a web-based Java application that is stored in the Flash file system of the router. The client browser makes a connection to the embedded web server of the router where the QDM application is stored and can configure that device for the QDM.

QoS on Ethernet

In the Catalyst line of multilayer switches, is the capability to provide QoS at Layer 2. At Layer 2, the frame uses CoS in 802.1p and Interlink Switch Link (ISL). CoS uses 3 bits, just like IP precedence, and maps well from Layer 2 to Layer 3, and vice versa.

The switches have the capability to differentiate frames based on CoS settings. If multiple queues are present, frames can be placed in different queues and serviced via weighted round-robin (WRR). This allows each queue to have different service levels. Within the queue, WRED thresholds are set. These thresholds are similar to the minimum thresholds set in WRED at Layer 3. They act as the starting point for the probability that a packet will be dropped.

Figure 59-14 explains the use of WRR with WRED using two queues with two thresholds each. This is referred to as *2Q2T*. In this instance, settings 4 to 7 are put in queue 1. Settings 0 to 3 are put in queue 2. Queue 1 is set to get service 70 percent of the time, and queue 2 gets service 30 percent of the time. In queue 1, when the queue is 30-percent full, settings 4 and 5 can be dropped. Not until the queue is 85-percent full are settings 6 and 7 dropped. In queue 2, when the queue is 20-percent full, settings 0 and 1 can be dropped. Not until the queue is 60-percent full can settings 2 and 3 be dropped.

Many implementations provided mapping of ToS (or IP precedence) to CoS. In this instance, an Ethernet frame CoS setting can be mapped to the ToS byte of the IP packet, and vice versa. This provides end-to-end priority for the traffic flow.

Figure 59-14 *WRR with WRED Using Two Queues with Two Thresholds Each*

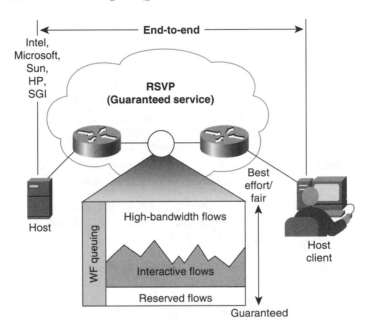

Multiprotocol Label Switching (MPLS): Allowing Flexible Traffic Engineering

Cisco's MPLS (also know as *tag switching*) feature contains the mechanisms to interoperate with and take advantage of both RSVP and IP precedence signaling. The tag-switching header contains a 3-bit field that can be used as a traffic prioritization signal. It can also be used to map particular flows and classes of traffic along engineered tag-switching paths to obtain the required QoS through the tag-switching portion of a network.

QoS Policy Control

The QoS policy control architecture is being developed as a key initial piece of the CiscoAssure policy networking initiative. This initiative leverages standards-based QoS policy control protocols and mechanisms to implement QoS policy from a single console interface.

At the infrastructure level, packet classification is a key capability for each policy technique that allows the appropriate packets traversing a network element or particular interface to be selected for QoS. These packets can then be marked for the appropriate IP precedence in some cases, or can be identified as an RSVP. Policy control also requires integration with underlying data-link layer network technologies or non-IP protocols.

SNA ToS

SNA ToS, in conjunction with data-link switching plus (DLSw+), allows mapping of traditional SNA CoS into IP-differentiated service. This feature takes advantage of both QoS signaling and pieces of the architecture. DLSW+ opens four TCP sessions and maps each SNA ToS traffic into a different session. Each session is marked by IP precedence. Cisco's congestion control technologies (CQ, PQ, and WFQ) act on these sessions to provide a bandwidth guarantee or other improved handling across an intranet, as shown in Figure 59-15. This provides a migration path for traditional SNA customers onto an IP-based intranet, while preserving the performance characteristics expected of SNA.

Thus, traditional mainframe-based, mission-critical applications can take advantage of evolving IP intranets and extranets without sacrificing the QoS capabilities historically provided by SNA networking.

Figure 59-15 *SNA ToS, in Conjunction with DLSw, Allows Mapping of SNA CoS into IP Differentiated Services*

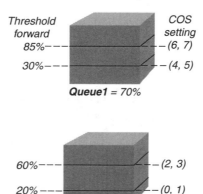

QoS for Packetized Voice

One of the most promising uses for IP networks is to allow sharing of voice traffic with the traditional data and LAN-to-LAN traffic. Typically, this can help reduce transmission costs by reducing the number of network connections sharing existing connections and infrastructure, and so on.

Cisco has a wide range of voice networking products and technologies, including a number of VoIP solutions. To provide the required voice quality, however, QoS capability must be added to the traditional data-only network. Cisco IOS software QoS features give VoIP traffic the service that it needs, while providing the traditional data traffic with the service that it needs as well.

Figure 59-16 shows a business that has chosen to reduce some of its voice costs by combining voice traffic onto its existing IP network. Voice traffic at each office is digitized on voice modules on 3600 processors. This traffic is then routed via H.323 Gatekeeper, which also requests specific QoS for the voice traffic. In this case, IP precedence is set to high for the voice traffic. WFQ is enabled on all the router interfaces for this network. WFQ automatically expedites the forwarding of high-precedence voice traffic out each interface, reducing delay and jitter for this traffic.

Because the IP network was originally handling LAN-to-LAN traffic, many datagrams traversing the network are large, 1500-byte packets. On slow links (below T1/E1 speeds), voice packets may be forced to wait behind one of these large packets, adding tens or even hundreds of milliseconds to the delay. LFI is used in conjunction with WFQ to break up these jumbograms and interleave the voice traffic to reduce this delay as well as jitter.

Figure 59-16 *This Diagram Provides an Overview of a QoS VoIP Solution*

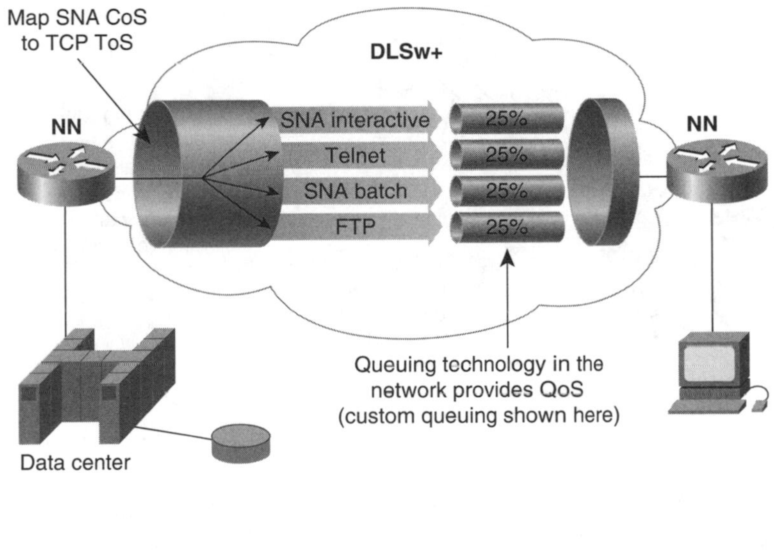

QoS for Streaming Video

One of the most significant challenges for IP-based networks, which have traditionally provided only best-effort service, has been to provide some type of service guarantees for different types of traffic. This has been a particular challenge for streaming video applications, which often require a significant amount of reserved bandwidth to be useful.

In the network shown in Figure 59-17, RSVP is used in conjunction with ATM PVCs to provide guaranteed bandwidth to a mesh of locations. RSVP is configured from within Cisco IOS to provide paths from the router networks, at the edges, and through the ATM core. Simulation traffic then uses these guaranteed paths to meet the constraints of geographically distributed real-time simulation. Video-enabled machines at the various sites also use this network to do live videoconferencing.

Figure 59-17 *The Network Diagram Shows the Use of RSVP in a Meshed ATM Environment*

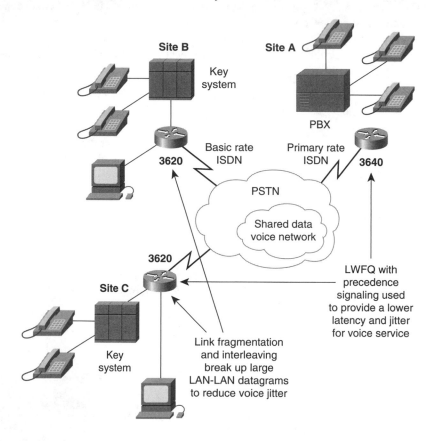

In this instance, OC-3 ATM links are configured with multiple 3-Mbps PVCs connecting to various remote sites. RSVP ensures that QoS from this PVC is extended to the appropriate application across the local routed network. In the future, Cisco IOS will extend this RSVP capability to dynamically set up ATM SVCs. This will reduce configuration complexity and add a great degree of automatic configuration.

Automated QoS

Automated QoS (AutoQoS) simplifies QoS configuration and deployment. Mission-critical applications are making QoS more important than ever to the success of both businesses and service providers. However, QoS can be a very demanding networking task. Multiple applications have divergent QoS needs. Finding an appropriate QoS configuration for each application has been a deployment and management challenge. As a result, companies and service providers have not been able to take full advantage of new and innovative IP applications. Cisco AutoQoS addresses this issue by greatly lowering the total cost and time to deploy QoS.

Cisco AutoQoS is an initiative that integrates QoS functions in Cisco IOS software and automates them for particular network and traffic situations. Currently, Cisco AutoQoS provides automation of QoS configuration for VoIP deployments. Future phases will include support for enterprise data applications, video, and other multimedia applications, as well as more-advanced management features, such as detailed traffic reporting.

Summary

Cisco IOS QoS provides a set of tools to provide a flow(s) with the necessary network services to work successfully.

QoS provides differentiated services, which provide higher priority to flows, or guaranteed services that provide an assured service level. Both of these are contrasted by best-effort services, which are provided by what is generally considered a lack of QoS. FIFO provides best-effort service. Here, flows are not differentiated and are serviced on a first-come, first-served basis.

Using classification tools (PBR, CAR, and NBAR), flows are identified and, optionally, are marked for use by other QoS tools throughout the internetwork. Congestion-management tools (PQ, CQ, WFQ, and CBWFQ) all manage the delivery of packets when there is more bandwidth than the link can handle. Queue management (WRED) is used for congestion avoidance within individual queues, as well as to prevent congestion in the internetwork. Using the behavior of TCP, WRED can throttle the speed of flows by dropping certain flows. It can also provide priority by dropping low-priority flows before high-priority flows. Link-efficiency tools (LFI and RTP header compression) provide relief for time-sensitive, low-bandwidth flows. LFI does this by fragmenting large packets. RTP header compression does this by reducing the overhead for RTP packets.

Guaranteed services are generally provided by RSVP, although CBWFQ could be considered a form of guaranteed services. RSVP is a signaling protocol that signals the network to provide guaranteed services for the entire path of the packet. CBWFQ differs in that it guarantees service onto an interface.

QoS Looking Forward

In a continued evolution toward end-to-end services, Cisco is expanding QoS interworking to operate more seamlessly across heterogeneous link layer technologies, and working closely with host platform partners to ensure interoperation between networks and end systems.

QoS is on the forefront of networking technology. The future brings us the notion of user-based QoS in which QoS policies are based on a user as well as application. Capabilities such as NBAR and its ability to read deeper into the packet provides a robust implementation for identifying flows. Cisco's end-to-end QoS solutions (from desktop to desktop) make a Cisco network the premier provider of end-to-end quality of service.

Review Questions

1   What is the main goal of QoS?

2   What are the types of QoS tools?

3   What is signaling?

4   What is IP precedence?

5   What is Differentiated Services Code Point (DSCP)

6   What is Modular QoS CLI (MQC)?

7   How does flow-based WFQ (WFQ) differ from class-based WFQ (CBWFQ)?

8   What is used for queue management to provide congestion avoidance? How does it avoid congestion?

9   What are the two primary uses for CAR?

10   What QoS tool would you use to guarantee a minimum amount of bandwidth?

11   What QoS tool would you use to limit a flow to a maximum amount of bandwidth?

12   What does NBAR do? What are two unique features of it?

13   What is a common use for traffic shaping?

14   What tool is used for Integrated QoS?

For More Information

- Cisco Systems. *Cisco IOS 12.0 Quality of Service*. Indianapolis: Cisco Press, 1999.

- Ferguson, Paul, and Geoff Huston. *Quality of Service: Delivering QoS on the Internet and in Corporate Networks*. New York: John Wiley & Sons, 1998.

- Lee, Donn. *Enhanced IP Services*. Indianapolis: Cisco Press, 1999.
- Vegesna, Srinivas. *IP Quality of Service*. Indianapolis: Cisco Press, 2000.
- Cisco IOS QoS (www.cisco.com/warp/public/732/Tech/quality.shtml).
- RFC 2386, "A Framework for QoS-Based Routing in the Internet."

PART **IX**

Appendix

Answers to Review Questions

Chapter 1

1 What are the layers of the OSI model?

Answer: Application, presentation, session, transport, network, data link, physical. Remember the sentence "All people seem to need data processing."

2 Which layer determines path selection in an internetwork?

Answer: Layer 3, the network layer.

3 What types of things are defined at the physical layer?

Answer: Voltage levels, time of voltage changes, physical data rates, maximum transmission distances, physical connectors, and type of media.

4 What is one method of mapping network addresses to MAC addresses?

Answer: ARP, Hello, predictable.

5 Which includes more overhead, connection-oriented or connectionless services?

Answer: Connection-oriented.

Chapter 2

1 Describe the type of media access used by Ethernet.

Answer: Ethernet uses carrier sense multiple access collision detect (CSMA/CD). Each network station listens before and after transmitting data. If a collision is detected, both stations wait a random time before trying to resend.

2 Describe the type of media access used by Token Ring.

Answer: Token Ring passes a special type of packet called a token around the network. If a network device has data to send, it must wait until it has the token to send it. After the data has been sent, the token is released back on the network.

3   Describe unicast, multicast, and broadcast transmissions.

Answer: A unicast is a transmission from one source to one destination. A multicast is a transmission from one source to many stations that register to receive the traffic. A broadcast is a transmission from one source to every station on the local network segment.

Chapter 3

1   What are some types of WAN circuits?

Answer: Point-to-point, packet-switched, and circuit-switched.

2   What is DDR, and how is it different from dial backup?

Answer: DDR is dial-on-demand routing. DDR dials up the remote site when traffic needs to be transmitted. Dial backup uses the same type of services, but for backup to a primary circuit. When the primary circuit fails, the dial backup line is initiated until the primary circuit is restored.

3   What is a CSU/DSU used for?

Answer: A CSU/DSU interfaces a router with a digital line such as a T1.

4   What is the difference between a modem and an ISDN terminal adapter?

Answer: A modem converts digital signals into analog for transmission over a telephone line. Because ISDN circuits are digital, the conversion from digital to analog is not required.

Chapter 4

1   What are the four main memory types in a router?

Answer: ROM, Flash, RAM, and NVRAM

2   What are the three Cisco IOS command modes?

Answer: User, privileged, and configuration

3   What is the process of restarting a Cisco IOS system called?

Answer: Reloading

Chapter 5

1 What layer of the OSI reference model to bridges and switches operate.

Answer: Bridges and switches are data communications devices that operate principally at Layer 2 of the OSI reference model. As such, they are widely referred to as data link-layer devices.

2 What is controlled at the link layer?

Answer: Bridging and switching occur at the link layer, which controls data flow, handles transmission errors, provides physical (as opposed to logical) addressing, and manages access to the physical medium.

3 Under one popular classification scheme what are bridges classified as?

Answer: Local or Remote: *Local* **bridges provide a direct connection between multiple LAN segments in the same area.** *Remote* **bridges connect multiple LAN segments in different areas, usually over telecommunications lines.**

4 What is a switch?

Answer: *Switches* **are data link-layer devices that, like bridges, enable multiple physical LAN segments to be interconnected into a single larger network.**

Chapter 6

1 Describe the process of routing packets.

Answer: Routing is the act of moving information across an internetwork from a source to a destination.

2 What are some routing algorithm types?

Answer: Static, dynamic, flat, hierarchical, host-intelligent, router-intelligent, intradomain, interdomain, link-state, and distance vector.

3 Describe the difference between static and dynamic routing.

Answer: Static routing is configured by the network administrator and is not capable of adjusting to changes in the network without network administrator intervention. Dynamic routing adjusts to changing network circumstances by analyzing incoming routing update messages without administrator intervention.

4 What are some of the metrics used by routing protocols?

Answer: Path length, reliability, delay, bandwidth, load, and communication cost.

Chapter 7

1 Name the different areas of network management.

Answer: Configuration, accounting, fault, security, and performance.

2 What are the goals of performance management?

Answer: Measure and make available various aspects of network performance so that internetwork performance can be maintained at an acceptable level.

3 What are the goals of configuration management?

Answer: Monitor network and system configuration information so that the effects on network operation of various versions of hardware and software elements can be tracked and managed.

4 What are the goals of accounting management?

Answer: Measure network utilization parameters so that individual or group uses on the network can be regulated appropriately.

5 What are the goals of fault management?

Answer: Detect, log, notify users of, and automatically fix network problems to keep the network running effectively.

6 What are the goals of security management?

Answer: Control access to network resources according to local guidelines so that the network cannot be sabotaged and so that sensitive information cannot be accessed by those without appropriate authorization.

Chapter 8

1 Shouldn't all 10Base-T networks just be upgraded to 100 Mbps? Why or why not?

Answer: Not necessarily—if the current 10Base-T network is repeater-based, replacing the repeaters with 10/100 nonsaturating switches would result in an automatic *n* times increase in the average available bandwidth for each end station.

2 Which 100Base version(s) are recommended? Why?

Answer: 100Base-TX is recommended if the horizontal wiring is Category5 or better UTP. If the horizontal cabling is Category 3, 100BaseT4 can be used, but it may be difficult to acquire (some reports indicate that because 100Base-TX was available more than a year before T4, it captured as much as 95 percent of the market). 100Base-T2 is not available.

3 Which 1000Base version(s) are recommended? Where would they be used?

Answer: 1000Base-T, is recommended if the horizontal cabling is Category 5 or better UTP. 1000Base-SX can be used if the horizontal cabling is multimode optical fiber, as well as for some multimode backbones. 1000Base-LX can be used for either single-mode or multimode optical fiber (see Table 8-5). 1000Base-CX can be used for short-haul equipment-room jumpers up to 25 meters.

4 What cable types should be used for new networks? For upgrading existing networks? Why?

Answer: New or replacement UTP links may be Category 5E or better to allow for data rate growth to 1000 Mbps. Multimode fiber may be used as indicated in Table 8-5 for 1000Base-SX, or as noted in the paragraph following Table 8-5 for 1000Base-LX. (These fibers will also provide future support for shorter distances [between 100 and 300 meters, depending on the wavelength] at 10,000 Mbps.) To be truly future-proof and to ensure that you will be able to operate longer-distance backbones, choose single-mode fiber.

5 How do you know when a network needs to be upgraded? Where do you start?

Answer: There are several ways:

- **Your users will tell you (but often only after they have crossed the frustration threshold).**

- **Your network management system should be capable of indicating the load characteristics for each DCE port.**

- **Your organization is considering adding new applications (such as multimedia) that will require more communication bandwidth.**

- **Your organization is growing, and there are not sufficient DCE ports in the right locations to accommodate the additional users.**

After you have determined the need, you can consider the options. Remember that the network elements with the longest useful life (the link media, followed by the network servers and network switches) can also be the most expensive to replace. Choose with an eye to future growth, and consider reusing these elements wherever possible.

Chapter 9

1 What are the benefits of using FDDI instead of CDDI?

Answer: Longer distance, no RFI, no EFI.

   2 What role does the DAC play in the FDDI network?

   Answer: The concentrator is a dual-attachment station device and ensures that when single-attachment station devices—such as PCs—are turned off, they do not interrupt the network ring.

Chapter 10

   1 What kind of technology is Frame Relay?

   Answer: Packet-switched technology.

   2 Name the two kinds of packet-switching techniques discussed in this chapter, and briefly describe each.

   Answer: 1. In variable-length switching, variable-length packets are switched between various network segments to best use network resources until the final destination is reached. 2. Statistical multiplexing techniques essentially use network resources in a more efficient way,

   3 Describe the difference between SVCs and PVCs.

   Answer: A SVC, switched virtual circuit, is created for each data transfer and is terminated when the data transfer is complete. PVC, permanent virtual circuit, is a permanent network connection that does not terminate when the transfer of data is complete. Previously not widely supported by Frame Relay equipment, SVCs are now used in many of today's networks.

   4 What is the data-link connection identifier (DLCI)?

   Answer: The DLCI is a value assigned to each virtual circuit and DTE device connection point in the Frame Relay WAN. Two different connections can be assigned the same value within the same Frame Relay WAN—one on each side of the virtual connection.

   5 Describe how LMI Frame Relay differs from basic Frame Relay.

   Answer: LMI Frame Relay adds a set of enhancements, referred to as extensions, to basic Frame Relay. Key LMI extensions provide the following functionality: global addressing, virtual circuit status messages, and multicasting.

Chapter 11

   1 Name at least three benefits of implementing HSSI technology in a network.

   Answer: Benefits include these:

   HSSI provides high-speed data communication over WAN and LAN links.

HSSI uses differential emitter-coupled logic (ECL), which provides high-speed data transfer with low noise levels.

HSSI uses a subminiature FCC-approved 50-pin connector that is smaller than its V.35 competitor.

The HSSI cable uses the same number of pins and wires as the Small Computer Systems Interface 2 (SCSI-2) cable, but the HSSI electrical specification is more concise.

HSSI makes bandwidth resources easy to allocate, making T3 and other broadband services available and affordable.

HSSI requires the presence of only two control signals ("DTE available" and "DCE available"), making it highly reliable because there are fewer circuits that can fail.

HSSI performs four loopback tests for reliability.

2   Name the four loopback tests that HSSI performs.

Answer: Cable test, DCE test, Telco line test, DTE test.

Chapter 12

1   Which reference point for ISDN logical devices is relevant only in North America?

Answer: U, the reference point between NT1 devices and line-termination equipment in the carrier network.

2   What are the two speeds of ISDN PRI services?

Answer: In North America and Japan, 23 B channels (1.472 Mbps) plus 1 D channel (64 kbps); in Europe and Australia, 31 B channels (1.984 Mbps) plus 1 D channel (64 kbps).

3   Of the 48 bits in the ISDN physical layer frame formats, how many bits represent data?

Answer: 36.

Chapter 13

1   What are the main components of PPP?

Answer: Encapsulation of datagrams, LCP, and NCP.

2   What is the only absolute physical layer requirement imposed by PPP?

Answer: The provision of a duplex circuit, either dedicated or switched, that can operate in either an asynchronous or synchronous bit-serial mode, transparent to PPP link layer frames.

3   How many fields make up the PPP frame, and what are they?

Answer: Six: Flag, Address, Control, Protocol, Data, and Frame Check Sequence.

4   How many phases does the PPP LCP go through, and what are they?

Answer: Four: Link establishment, link quality determination, network layer protocol configuration negotiation, and link termination.

Chapter 14

1   Where does the SNI interface exist?

Answer: Between the CPE and the carrier equipment—where the customer network ends and the carrier network begins.

2   What does SIP stand for?

Answer: SMDS Interface Protocol.

3   At which layers of the OSI reference model do each of the three SIP levels operate?

Answer: SIP Level 3 and Level 2 operate at the MAC sublayer of the data link layer; SIP Level 1 operates at the physical layer.

4   How do multiple devices reconcile usage of a DQDB?

Answer: By using a distributed queuing algorithm, which makes implementing a multi-CPE configuration much more complicated than implementing a single-CPE configuration.

5   A credit-management scheme is sometimes used to implement SMDS access classes on which SMDS interfaces only?

Answer: DS-3 rate SMDS interfaces.

Chapter 15

1   How many years did it take the telephone to reach 90 percent of the homes in the United States?

Answer: The telephone was invented in 1875, and in 1970, 90 percent of American homes had a phone—it took 95 years.

2 Which V series recommendations pertain to bits per second?

Answer: V.21, V.23, V.27ter, V.29, V.32bis, V.34, and V.90.

3 How many DS 0s are in a BRI, T1, and E1m respectively?

Answer: Two in a BRI (although the D channel might be considered a third); 24 in a T1; and 32 in an E1.

4 What is the flow of data going through a modem from the RJ 11 to the DTE?

Answer: The data flows in the RJ 11 jack to the analog-to-digital converter. The DSP then gets the data and forwards it on to the packetizer, which sends the data to the data compressor. The decompressed data is then sent to the UART, which gets the data to the DTE device.

5 What are the three phases of PPP negotiation? Why is the order significant?

Answer: LCP, authentication, and NCP. LCP must complete first because it determines whether the link is viable and negotiates the link properties between the two peers. LCP also finds out whether authentication is needed. Authentication happens before network protocols are negotiated so that the network protocol negotiation will be capable of identifying the incoming user or host and assigning the appropriate network attributes.

6 How does interesting traffic relate to the idle timer?

Answer: Interesting traffic determines whether the link will remain up or time out. Interesting traffic resets the idle timer to zero.

7 Is a BRI interface a dialer? How would an async interface become a dialer?

Answer: A BRI interface is a dialer. An async interface could become a dialer by having the dialer in-band configuration command entered into it.

8 When is dialup connectivity appropriate to use? When isn't it appropriate?

Answer: Dialup connectivity is adaptable but expensive. For intermittent connections or connections in which the endpoints move around, dialup is a convenient and sensible use. For permanent connectivity or links that stay up most of the time, it is not appropriate.

Chapter 16

1 Name two of the link types that SDLC supports.

Answer: Point-to-point links, multipoint links, bounded media, unbounded media, half-duplex transmission facilities, full-duplex transmission facilities, circuit-switched networks, and packet-switched networks.

2 Name the four basic SDLC connection configurations.

Answer: Point-to-point, which involves only two nodes, one primary and one secondary; multipoint, which involves one primary and multiple secondary nodes; loop, which involves a loop topology with the primary connected to the first and last secondaries, and intermediate secondaries in between; and hub go-ahead, which involves an inbound and an outbound channel—the primary uses the outbound channel to communicate with the secondaries, and the secondaries use the inbound channel to communicate with the primary.

3 How many fields does the SDLC frame have, and what are they?

Answer: Six: Flag, Address, Control, Data, FCS, Flag.

4 List the derivative protocols of SDLC, and describe their primary difference(s) from SDLC.

Answer: HDLC, which supports three transfer modes, while SDLC supports only one; LAPB, which is restricted to the ABM transfer mode and is appropriate only for combined stations; IEEE 802.2, which is often referred to as LLC and has three types; and QLLC, which provides the data-link control capabilities that are required to transport SNA data across X.25 networks.

Chapter 17

1 In what kind of networks does X.25 generally operate?

Answer: It is typically used in packet-switched networks of common carriers, such as the telephone companies.

2 Name the three general categories into which X.25 devices fall.

Answer: DTEs, DCEs, and PSEs.

3 What are the three main functions of the PAD?

Answer: Buffering, packet assembly, and packet disassembly.

4 Name the X.25 protocol suite and the layers in the OSI reference model to which they map.

Answer: PLP: network layer; LAPB: data link layer; X.21bis, EIA/TIA-232, EIA/TIA-449, EIA-530, and G.703: physical layer.

Chapter 18

1 What is a VPN?

Answer: VPN is a generic term that describes any combination of technologies that can be used to secure a connection through an otherwise unsecured or untrusted network.

2 What key security services does IPSec provide?

Answer: Confidentiality, data integrity, and data origin authentication.

3 What is the function of the IKE protocol?

Answer: To derive authenticated key material and negotiate IPSec security associations in a secure manner.

4 IKE is a two-phase protocol. What does each phase accomplish?

Answer: The phase I exchange, using either main mode or aggressive mode, establishes a secure, authenticated communication channel between two IPSec peers. The phase II exchange, using quick mode, negotiates security associations on behalf of IPSec under the protection of the security association established in the phase I exchange.

5 What are L2TP's operation modes?

Answer: Compulsory tunneling and voluntary tunneling

6 How does MPLS support hierarchical routing in BGP/MPLS VPN?

Answer: In BGP/MPLS VPN, the data packets carry two labels organized as a label stack. The provider routers use the outer labels to forward packets from one PE router to the other PE router within the MPLS core. The PE router uses the inner label to help forward the packet to the corresponding VPN customer.

Chapter 19

1 What are the three main packet voice technologies?

Answer: Voice over Frame Relay, Voice over ATM, and Voice over IP are the three main packet voice technologies.

2 How are packet voice technologies used to provide toll bypass cost savings?

Answer: Voice traffic between locations can be routed over a wide-area network with data instead of using long-distance carriers. Depending on distance and toll charges, cost savings can be substantial.

3 What are the primary voice-signaling protocols?

Answer: These are H.323, Session Initiation Protocol (SIP), and Media Gateway Control Protocol (MGCP).

4 Describe how peer-to-peer voice signaling protocols are different from client/server protocols.

Answer: Client/server signaling protocols depend upon a central call control entity to maintain the state of the endpoints. This model makes it easier to support advanced call features. Peer-to-peer protocols utilize smarter endpoints and do not require a central call control entity, so they scale better.

Chapter 20

1 What are the main components of a wireless system?

Answer:

- **Information source**
- **Transceiver-receiver/transmitter**
- **Modulator/demodulator**
- **Local oscillator**
- **Upconverter/outdoor unit**
- **Cables, control, and coaxial**
- **Duplexer**

2 What is the wavelength of an 850 MHz carrier?

Answer: 0.35 meters

3 What are some considerations when choosing a transmission line?

Answer:

- **RF attenuation**
- **Impedance**
- **DC loss**
- **Physical characteristics such as weight, bend radius, and diameter**
- **Cost**

4 What are the two basic antenna types?

Answer: Directional and omnidirectional

5 What does the acronym EIRP stand for?

Answer: Effective Isotropic Radiated Power

6 What is a Fresnel zone?

Answer: A Fresnel zone is a zone of radiated energy. In theory, there are an infinite number of them. In practice, however, we concern ourselves only with the first Fresnel zone. These zones are ellipsoid in shape and exist around the direct LOS path. The energy as it radiates from the antenna looks like a football.

7 What are multipath signals?

Answer: Multipath signals are the product of the same transmit signals that arrive at a receiver separated in the time domain because they took different transmission paths.

8 What are the five basic building blocks of an 802.11 reference architecture?

Answer:

- **Basic Service Set (BSS)**
- **Independent BSS**
- **Infrastructure BSS**
- **Distribution system**
- **Extended service set**

9 What five services does the distribution service offer?

Answer:

- **Association**
- **Disassociation**
- **Reassociation**
- **Distribution**
- **Integration**

10 What are four main benefits of using wireless technologies?

Answer:

- **They complete the access technology portfolio, along with Digital Subscriber Line, cable, leased line, and other access network technologies.**

- They go where other technologies may not, such as hilly terrain where deploying other technologies is cost-prohibitive or difficult.

- They are rapidly deployable, especially when facilities exist and unlicensed frequencies are used.

- They can be used to bypass more-expensive fixed transmission technologies such as fiber and cable.

Chapter 21

1 Name the current versions of DSL technology.

Answer: ADSL, SDSL, HDSL, HDSL-2, G.SHDL, IDSL, and VDSL.

2 What are the two-line coding methods used for ADSL?

Answer: DMT and CAP.

3 Which versions of DSL offer symmetrical service?

Answer: SDSL, HDSL, and HDSL-2.

4 What symmetrical version of DSL offers multirate service over a single pair of wire?

Answer: G.SHDSL

5 How far of a reach can IDSL achieve from the CO?

Answer: 26,000 feet.

6 What downstream and upstream rates are proposed for VDSL?

Answer: The maximum downstream rate under consideration is between 51 and 55 Mbps over lines up to 1000 feet (300 m) in length. Downstream speeds as low as 13 Mbps over lengths beyond 4000 feet (1500 m) are also common. Upstream rates in early models will be asymmetric, just like ADSL, at speeds from 1.6 to 2.3 Mbps.

Chapter 22

1 Describe the advantages or benefits offered by an HFC network.

Answer: HFC networks provide increased bandwidth, increased reliability, ready support for two-way operation, improved noise immunity, and reduced operation and maintenance costs.

2 Identify the process of providing two-way operation of an HFC cable plant.

Answer: Two-way operation can be established on an HFC cable plant by installing the narrow- band upstream amplifiers in the amplifier housings, adding a narrow-band return laser at the optical node, providing an optical return path, and placing an optical receiver at the head end or hub location. Proper alignment procedure of the return path is also required.

3 Describe the upstream and downstream bandwidths associated with the DOCSIS standard.

Answer: The DOCSIS bandwidth limitations are 5 to 42 MHz for the upstream direction, and 54 to 860 MHz for the downstream direction.

4 Summarize the DOCSIS availability criteria.

Answer: A DOCSIS system must provide greater than 99 percent availability when forwarding 1500-byte packets at a rate of 100 packets per second when the cable plant meets the published DOCSIS system specifications.

5 Identify the DOCSIS-defined networking layers.

Answer: The DOCSIS-defined layers consist of the IP network Layer, the data link layer, and the physical (PHY) layer.

6 Identify the DOCSIS 1.0 servers, and describe their respective purposes in the network.

Answer: DOCSIS servers include the DHCP server (RFC 2181), which provides IP addresses to both the CM and PC devices; the TFTP server (RFC 1350), which registers and downloads CM configuration files; and the TOD server (RFC 868), which provides a time stamp to operational system events.

7 What are the facilities in which an MSO might deploy the universal broadband router?

Answer: The universal broadband router can be deployed as needed in both the head end and hub locations.

8 Define Telco return and tell when this application might be considered.

Answer: Telco return describes a data service that provides high-speed downstream connectivity over the coax plant, and low-speed connectivity over the PSTN. This application is typically used in rural networks, where the upgrade cost is prohibitive, or as an interim networking solution permitting the MSO to offer service while the cable plant is being upgraded for two-way service.

9 List a few of the properties and future applications associated with DOCSIS 1.1.

Answer: DOCSIS 1.1 will support VoIP, enhanced security, packet concatenation and fragmentation, as well as QoS. Service applications include telephony and video.

Chapter 23

1 What are the LSR's interfaces?

Answer: Packet Switch-Capable (PSC), Layer 2 Switch-Capable (L2SC), Time-Division Multiplexing- (TDM) Capable, Lambda Switch-Capable (LSC), and Fiber Switch-Capable (FSC).

2 What three planes are used in G.8080 to perform signaling and connection services?

Answer: The control plane, management plane, and transport plane

3 What is the purpose of domains used in G.ASON?

Answer: Domains allow subdivision of the control planes. By subdividing control planes, service providers can administer these domains.

4 When you use PONs, which traffic, upstream or downstream, requires more bandwidth? Why?

Answer: Downstream traffic uses more bandwidth than upstream traffic. Asymmetrical sharing of downstream traffic to multiple destinations is the primary reason for bandwidth. For this reason, customers require significantly more bandwidth upstream than downstream (for signaling and so on). Cable service providers use PONs to transport video and other services.

5 What two domains are used for administration in the OTN for the overlay model?

Answer: One is used for the IP layer, and the other is for the optical layer.

6 What type of optical network allows customers to directly plug optical signals regardless of optical line rate or framing?

Answer: Transparent optical network

7 In G.ASON, what is used as the reference point between domains?

Answer: E-NNI

8 Which protocol is used to provide link and neighboring node knowledge? Why?

Answer: Link Management Protocol (LMP) is used. GMPLS has separate control and data planes that require LMP to provide knowledge for discovery.

Chapter 24

1 What is an H.323 gatekeeper?

Answer: An H.323 gatekeeper is an optional component that allows H.323 networks to scale and centrally manage H.323 calls and endpoints. It stores a dynamically populated table of H.323 or E.164 alias-to-number matchings that allow it to identify the destination for call requests.

2 What is the purpose of SDP?

Answer: SDP negotiates the capabilities between SIP endpoints involved in SIP session setup. Items such as audio CODECs and RTP mappings are exchanged.

3 What is the main reason that companies deploy H.323 and/or SIP networks?

Answer: Argue if you like, but when it comes down to it, money is all that matters. H.323 and SIP allow companies to save on an array of network charges and let them deploy network services for a fraction of the cost. VoIP is particularly useful to smaller service providers, which need to be able to compete with the larger service providers while earning money.

4 What protocol are the messages in H.225 based on—Q.921, Q.931, Q.932, or Q.703?

Answer: H.225 is based on ISDN's Q.931.

5 Which device is responsible for processing voice streams and performing complex CODEC algorithms?

Answer: Digital Signal Processor (DSP)

6 What message must follow a 200 OK message when it is received?

Answer: ACK

Chapter 25

1 How does DPT/SRP differ from other ring technologies such as Token Ring and FDDI?

Answer: No token is required for a node to transmit on an SRP ring, and packets are destination-stripped rather than source-stripped. Both rings are in use in DPT, unlike the idle ring in FDDI.

2 How does DPT/SRP implement packet priority?

Answer: The SRP MAC protocol supports eight levels of precedence in the packet format copied from the IP Precedence field. These are then mapped to one of two SRP physical queues—low- or high-priority. There are two queues for transmit traffic and two queues for transit traffic.

3 What mechanism determines which ring a node should send a data packet to reach another node?

Answer: The sending node issues an ARP on either of the two rings. The target responds via the ring with the shortest number of node hops back to the source as determined by the auto-topology discovery process.

4 How does DPT/SRP recover from a fiber break?

Answer: The nodes detecting the break perform a ring wrap. One node loops packets from the inner ring onto the outer ring. The opposite happens at the other node.

Chapter 26

1 What field of an EAP packet identifies whether the message is a request, response, success, or failure?

Answer: The Code field

2 What is the primary benefit of using EAP as an authentication mechanism?

Answer: The NAS is not required to support the authentication method being used to authenticate the client.

3 What two RADIUS attributes are used in EAP authentication?

Answer: EAP-Message and Message-Authenticator

4 Does EAP support server-side certificates, client-side certificates, or both?

Answer: EAP supports both server-side and client-side certificates. With EAP-TLS, both server and client certificates are used. With PEAP, only server-side certificates are used, and the client is still required to enter authentication credentials.

Chapter 27

1 What three frame types does a transparent bridge flood?

Answer: Transparent bridges flood unknown unicast frames (where the bridge has no entry in its table for the destination MAC address), broadcast frames, and mulitcast frames.

2 How does a bridge learn the relative location of a workstation?

Answer: A bridge learns about the direction to send frames to reach a station by building a bridge table. The bridge builds the table by observing the source MAC address of each frame that it receives and associating that address with the received port.

3 What two bridge PDUs does a transparent bridge generate, and what are they used for?

Answer: Transparent bridges create either a configuration PDU or a topology-change PDU. Configuration PDUs help bridges learn about the network topology so that loops may be eliminated. Topology-change PDUs enable bridges to relearn the network topology whenever a significant change occurs when a segment may no longer have connectivity or when a new loop is created.

4 What is the difference between forwarding and flooding?

Answer: Bridges forward frames out a *single* interface whenever the bridge knows that the destination is on a different port than the source. On the other hand, bridges flood whenever the bridge does not know where the destination is located.

5 After bridges determine the spanning-tree topology, they will take on various roles and configure ports into various modes. Specifically, the roles are root and designated bridges, and the modes are designated ports and root ports. If there are 10 bridges and 11 segments, how many of each are there in the broadcast domain?

Answer: There is one and only one root bridge in a broadcast domain, and all other bridges are designated bridges. Therefore, there is one root bridge and nine designated bridges. There must be one designated port for each segment, so there are ten. Each bridge, except the root, must have one and only one root port. Therefore there are nine root ports.

Chapter 28

1 Translational bridging addresses several issues when interconnecting different media types such as Ethernet and Token Ring. List and describe four of the methods described in the chapter.

Answer: Answer is in the text and does not need to be restated.

2 One of the challenges of translational bridging is the reordering of bits whenever a frame moves from an Ethernet to a Token Ring segment. If an Ethernet station targets a Token Ring station with a destination MAC address of 00-00-0C-11-22-33 (canonical format), what would the MAC address look like on Token Ring (noncanonical format)?

Answer: To convert the address between canonical and noncanonical format, invert each byte of the address. For example, the third octet (0x0C) looks in binary like 00001100. Reversing the bit order produces 00110000. This translates to a hex value of 0x30. Doing this for each byte of the address produces a noncanonical address of 00-00-30-88-44-CC.

3 Can a translational bridge work for all Ethernet and Token Ring networks and protocols?

Answer: Not necessarily. For a translational bridge to correctly translate all pertinent fields in the frame, the bridge must understand the protocol format. Therefore, if the bridge does not understand the protocol, it will not make all changes, breaking the protocol.

4 What is the difference between a source-route bridge and a source-route transparent bridge?

Answer: A source-route transparent bridge understands both source-route frames and transparently bridged frames. Therefore, it bridges frames both with and without a RIF field. A pure source-route bridge, on the other hand, can forward frames only if the frame contains a RIF.

Chapter 29

1 Describe a basic difference between transparent bridges and source-route bridges relative to the forwarding processes.

Answer: In a transparent bridged environment, bridges determine whether a frame needs to be forwarded, and through what path based upon local bridge tables. In an SRB network, the source device prescribes the route to the destination and indicates the desired path in the RIF.

2 Recall that the SRB standards do not specify how a source selects a path to the destination whenever multiple choices exist. The chapter listed four methods that a source could use to make the decision and said that the first received frame (path) was the most commonly used method. What assumptions might the source make about the network when using this method?

Answer: The source may assume that the frame arrived first because of more bandwidth on the links, less congestion in the system, and less latency in the bridge equipment. Therefore, this may be a preferred route over the other choices.

3 How do stations and bridges know if there is a source route defined in the frame?

Answer: By the value of the RII bit. The RII is set if there is a RIF included in the frame.

4 What problems might you anticipate in a large SRB network with many alternate paths?

Answer: With this network topology, many explorer frames may propagate throughout the network. Because explorers are broadcast frames, they consume bandwidth throughout the entire broadcast domain and consume CPU cycles within end stations.

5 Because only 4 bits are used to define bridge numbers, does this mean that there can be only 16 bridges (2^4=16)? Why or why not?

Answer: No. This means only that there can be no more than 16 bridges in parallel between the same two adjacent rings.

6 Can you have a large number of bridges attached to a central ring, all with the same bridge value?

Answer: Yes, as long as none of the bridges directly interconnects the same two rings.

7 A 12-bit value defines ring numbers. Can you have more than 4096 rings in the network (2^{12}=4096)? Why or why not?

Answer: No, you cannot, because this value defines the total number of rings. Each ring number must be unique in the network.

Chapter 30

1 A multilayer switch mimics the actions of a router when an initial frame passes through a router. What things does the multilayer switch do to the Layer 2 and Layer 3 headers to thoroughly imitate the router?

Answer: The switch must modify the source and destination MAC addresses in the Layer 2 header so that the frame appears to come from/to the router/workstation. Furthermore, the switch must change things in the Layer 3 header such as the IP time-to-live value.

2 A LAN switch most closely resembles what type of internetworking device?

Answer: A LAN switch behaves like a multiport bridge.

3 Two trunk protocols were described. For what situation would you use the IEEE 802.1Q mode?

Answer: Whenever you deploy a hybrid of switches from multiple vendors and need to trunk between them. All other trunk protocols work within specific vendor equipment environments.

4 Which switching method protects network segment bandwidth from errored frames?

Answer: Store-and-forward transmits frames only if the frame's integrity is assured. If the switch receives an errored frame, then the switch discards it.

5 How does a store-and-forward switch know if a frame is errored?

Answer: The switch uses the CRC to determine whether any changes occurred to the frame since the source generated it. The switch calculates CRC for the received frame and compares it with the CRC transmitted with the frame. If they differ, the frame changed during transit and will be discarded in a store-and-forward switch.

6 Do VLAN borders cross routers?

Answer: No. VLANs are broadcast domains and describe the extent that broadcast frames transit the network. Routers do not pass broadcasts. Therefore, the same VLAN cannot exist on two ports of a router.

7 How does a trunk link differ from an access link?

Answer: An access link carries traffic for a single VLAN. The traffic on an access link looks like any other Ethernet frame. A trunk link transports traffic for multiple VLANs across a single physical link. Trunks encapsulate Ethernet frames with other information to support the multiplexing technology employed.

8 Before switches and VLANs, administrators assigned users to a network based not on the user's needs, but on something else. What determined the user network assignment?

Answer: Administrators previously assigned users to a network based upon the user's physical proximity to a network device or cable.

Chapter 31

1 Name the four components of LANE.

Answer: LAN Emulation client (LEC), LANE Configuration Server (LECS), LAN Emulation Server (LES), Broadcast and Unknown Server (BUS).

2 Which LANE component maintains an ATM ARP table?

Answer: The LAN Emulation Server (LES) keeps a database of LEC MAC and NSAP addresses.

3 Which LANE component maintains policy for ELAN membership?

Answer: The LANE Configuration Server (LECS) acts as a membership policy device.

4 List two functions of PNNI.

Answer: ATM topology discovery and switched circuit establishment.

5 Which field in the ATM header checks the header integrity?

Answer: The HEC field checks for header errors and can correct a single header bit error.

6 What is the primary difference between the UNI header and the NNI header?

Answer: The UNI header has an 8-bit VPI field and a 4-bit GFC, while the NNI header absorbs the GFC field and expands the VPI field to 12 bits.

7 Which adaptation mode is most appropriate to interconnect T1 signals from PBXs over ATM?

Answer: AAL1 is most suitable for constant bit rate traffic such as a T1 source.

8 Which adaptation mode is most frequently implemented for data transport over ATM?

Answer: AAL5 provides an appropriate adaptation method for data traffic such as that produced by routers and ATM-attached workstations.

9 What VCI value is reserved for call setup requests from an ATM edge device?

Answer: VCI = 5 is reserved for ATM edge devices to send a signaling request to the ingress ATM switch requesting a connection to another device.

10 What ATM protocol simplifies the ATM administrator's life by automatically ensuring that certain ATM parameters are compatible between two devices connected to the same link?

Answer: ILMI enables two devices to communicate with each other and share ATM parameters that facilitate the link functionality.

11 What ATM protocol communicates exclusively between ATM switches?

Answer: PNNI, the ATM routing protocol, occurs only between ATM switches.

12 Describe the difference between PVC and SVC.

Answer: A PVC (permanent virtual circuit) must be manually provisioned. Every piece of equipment supporting the circuit between the source and destination must be configured. PVC does not provide any resiliency for media or equipment failures. SVC (switched virtual circuit) automatically establishes a connection between the source and the destination. The source indicates that it desires a connection, and the network builds the circuit.

13 What is the purpose of the adaptation layer?

Answer: The adaptation layer converts user data into cell payloads. Some adaptation modes use all 48 bytes of the payload, while others use extra bits from the payload for functional purposes resulting in lower than 48 bit user data/ payload size.

14 What advantage is there to implementing MPOA?

Answer: MPOA provides two advantages. First, it reduces the workload for routers because the routers will not need to support continuous flows of data. Second, MPOA can reduce the number of times that data must cross the ATM network. Without MPOA, the data must cross all necessary ELANs to get to the destination. With MPOA, a single circuit is built, allowing the data to traverse the network once.

Chapter 32

1 In downstream-on-demand distribution, how does the upstream LSR know it needs a label?

Answer: The unicast routing protocols distribute the presence of a network. When the upstream LSR needs to forward a frame to the new network, it can request a label from the downstream LSR.

2 How does FIB differ from LFIB?

Answer: FIB tables are developed from routing protocols such as OSPF, BGP, and IS-IS. LSRs reference these tables whenever they need to perform an IP lookup. LFIBs are used to perform label switching.

3 What are the two LDP modes?

Answer: One mode is downstream unsolicited distribution, in which an LSR announces a binding without a request from a neighbor LSR. The other mode is downstream-on-demand, in which an LSR requests a binding.

4 It is highly recommended that neighbor LSRs operate in the same LDP mode. What might happen if an upstream LSR operates in downstream unsolicited distribution mode and the downstream LSR runs in downstream-on-demand mode?

Answer: This is a case in which labels would never get distributed. The upstream LSR assumes that it never needs to ask for a binding, and the downstream unit assumes that it should never create one unless explicitly requested. Neither LSR triggers a label distribution.

5 If a vendor's router already uses high-speed switching and caching techniques to forward frames, performance might not be a valid motivation for using MPLS. Is there any other reason that might merit deployment of MPLS in such a network?

Answer: Traffic engineering could further enhance the network by letting an administrator select a path between locations based on policy. The policy may take into consideration parameters such as network loading, security, and several other elements. Otherwise, the administrator leaves the path selection to the destination-based routing protocols.

Chapter 33

1 DLSw provides link layer acknowledgments. What is meant by link layer acknowledgments? Why is this advantageous?

Answer: Link-layer acknowledgments (acks) refer to a process within the *broadcast domain* of the end device. The acks are between the end device and the local DLSw switch (router). Without link layer acks, the ack must reach all the way to the other end device. The ack may need to cross several LAN segments and a wide-area network. While crossing the WAN, significant propagation delay may be introduced, causing the protocol to time out and fail.

2 DLSw SSP uses what transport protocol? What are the advantages and disadvantages of this selection?

Answer: SSP uses TCP. This has the normal advantages of a reliable transport protocol, in which the data flow is monitored and retransmitted if any data is lost (sequence numbers and acks). However, TCP may not scale well when there are many DLSw switches that need to establish a peer-to-peer relationship.

3 List and describe the three operational phases of DLSw.

Answer: In phase one, DLSw peers establish two TCP connections. In phase two, the peers exchange capabilities with each other. This helps to ensure that the peers use the same options. It is particularly necessary to do this in an environment in which DLSw components come from multiple vendors. In phase three, the circuit establishment phase, end devices establish a connection to their intended end-device target. This involves a local connection between the end device and the DLSw switch, and for the DLSw switches to discover what DLSw peer to send the data to.

4 What protocols does DLSw support?

Answer: SNA and NetBIOS. Both of these depend upon link layer acknowledgments.

5 What is the normal Layer 2 process employed without DLSw?

Answer: Before DLSw, systems used source-route bridging (SRB). However, SRB doesn't scale well in a WAN environment because of the hop-count limitation (7) and the inefficient handling of broadcast traffic.

6 DLSw defines two message types. What are they, which has the larger header, and is there anything in common between them?

Answer: The two messages are for control and information flow. The control frame has a 72-byte header, and the information message supports a 16-byte header. Therefore, the control frame has a larger header. The first 16 bytes of both headers have the same format.

Chapter 34

1 What are the two routing protocols specified in the OSI suite?

Answer: End System-to-Intermediate System (ES-IS) and Intermediate System-to-Intermediate System (IS-IS).

2 Describe the OSI connectionless network protocol.

Answer: OSI connectionless network service is implemented by using the Connectionless Network Protocol (CLNP) and Connectionless Network Service (CLNS). CLNP and CLNS are described in the ISO 8473 standard.

3 Describe the OSI connection-oriented network protocol.

Answer: OSI connection-oriented network service is implemented by using the Connection-Oriented Network Protocol (CONP) and Connection-Mode Network Service (CMNS).

4 How are requests to services at the session layer made within OSI protocols?

Answer: Requests are made at session-service access points (SSAPs), and SS-users are uniquely identified by using an SSAP address.

5 Describe common-application service elements (CASEs).

Answer: Common-application service elements (CASEs) are ASEs that provide services used by a wide variety of application processes. In many cases, multiple CASEs are used by a single application entity.

6 Name some of the media types that the OSI protocol suite supports.

Answer: IEEE 802.2 LLC, IEEE 802.3, Token Ring/IEEE 802.5, Fiber Distributed Data Interface (FDDI), and X.25.

7 Why was the OSI protocol suite created?

Answer: The OSI specifications were conceived and implemented by two international standards organizations: the International Organization for Standardization (ISO) and the International Telecommunication Union–Telecommunications Standards Sector (ITU-T).

8 Describe the session layer protocols within the OSI protocol suite.

Answer: The session layer implementation of the OSI protocol suite consists of a session protocol and a session service. The session protocol enables session-service users (SS-users) to communicate with the session service. An SS-user is an entity that requests the services of the session layer. Such requests are made at session-service access points (SSAPs), and SS-users are uniquely identified by using an SSAP address.

9   Describe the presentation layer protocols of the OSI protocol suite.

Answer: The presentation layer implementation of the OSI protocol suite consists of a presentation protocol and a presentation service. The presentation protocol enables presentation-service users (PS-users) to communicate with the presentation service.

10   What are the two types of ASEs?

Answer: ASEs fall into one of the two following classifications: common-application service elements (CASEs) and specific-application service elements (SASEs). Both of these might be present in a single application entity.

Chapter 35

1   How are Internet protocols documented?

Answer: In Request For Comments (RFCs).

2   What are the two primary responsibilities of IP?

Answer: Providing best-effort delivery of datagrams through an internetwork, and providing fragmentation and reassembly of datagrams to support data links with different maximum transmission unit (MTU) sizes.

3   Which field in the IP packet keeps packets from looping endlessly in a malconfigured network?

Answer: The Time-to-Live (TTL) counter gradually decrements down to zero as a packet travels through routers. When the TTL reaches zero, the packet is discarded.

4   How is an IP address generally represented?

Answer: The 32-bit IP address is grouped 8 bits at a time, separated by dots, and represented in decimal format (known as dotted decimal notation). Each bit in the octet has a binary weight (128, 64, 32, 16, 8, 4, 2, 1). The minimum value for an octet is 0, and the maximum value for an octet is 255.

5   How is the class of an IP address determined?

Answer: By the first octet in the address.

6   What is the purpose of the subnet mask in an IP address?

Answer: The subnet mask defines which part of the address defines the network and which part defines the host.

7   What is the purpose of Address Resolution Protocol (ARP)?

Answer: ARP is used to map Layer 3 IP addresses to Layer 2 MAC addresses.

8 What is the function of Internet Control Message Protocol (ICMP)?

Answer: ICMP is used to report errors and other information regarding IP packet processing.

9 What type of data delivery does TCP provide?

Answer: TCP provides reliable transmission of data in an IP environment using a connection-oriented session.

10 How does User Datagram Protocol (UDP) differ from Transmission Control Protocol (TCP)?

Answer: UDP is a connectionless transport layer protocol that does not guarantee delivery of data. TCP is a connection-oriented protocol that guarantees delivery of data.

Chapter 36

1 What is the current standard?

Answer: IPv4.

2 What is the main reason for IPv6 being developed?

Answer: The main issue surrounding IPv6 is addressing, or the lack of addressing. Many people believe that we are nearly out of the four billion addresses available in IPv4. IPv6 could be the solution to many problems, but IPv6 is still not fully developed and is not yet a standard.

3 How many bits does the new expanded addressing provide?

Answer: The expanded addressing moves us from 32-bit address to a 128-bit addressing method.

4 What other benefits does expanded addressing provide?

Answer: It provides newer unicast and broadcasting methods. Expanded addressing also injects hexadecimal into the IP address and moves from using "." to using ":" as delimiters.

5 What are the new broadcast methods included in IPv6?

Answer: Unicast, multicast, and anycast.

6 What is unicast?

Answer: Unicast is a communication between a single host and a single receiver.

7 What is multicast?

Answer: Multicast is communication between a single host and multiple receivers.

8 What is anycast?

Answer: Anycast is a communication between a single sender and a list of addresses.

Chapter 37

1 What are the two types of routing protocols used by IPX?

Answer: Routing Information Protocol (RIP) and NetWare Link-State Protocol (NLSP).

2 What information is used by IPX RIP to determine a path for network traffic?

Answer: IPX RIP uses ticks to determine a network path. If a tie exists, the number of hops is used to break the tie.

3 What are the two parts of an IPX address?

Answer: Network and node.

4 How do Novell stations discover services available on the network?

Answer: Through the Service Advertisement Protocol (SAP).

5 What protocol is used at the transport layer?

Answer: Sequenced Packet Exchange (SPX) protocol is the most common NetWare transport protocol.

6 How do IPX stations map the MAC address to an IPX address?

Answer: The MAC address is used as the node address in IPX networks, so no mapping is required.

7 What enhancement in NetWare 4.0 reduces the need for SAPs?

Answer: NetWare Directory Services (NDS).

8 What services are provided by NetWare Core Protocol?

Answer: NetWare Core Protocol (NCP) is a series of server routines designed to satisfy application requests coming from, for example, the NetWare shell. The services provided by NCP include file access, printer access, name management, accounting, security, and file synchronization.

9 Describe NetWare's support of NetBIOS.

Answer: NetWare also supports the Network Basic Input/Output System (NetBIOS) session layer interface specification from IBM and Microsoft. NetWare's NetBIOS emulation software allows programs written to the industry-standard NetBIOS interface to run within the NetWare system.

10 Would you want to filter SAPs?

Answer: SAPs don't need to traverse slow WAN links, so filtering can reduce the amount of traffic that IPX generates across these types of links.

Chapter 38

1 Describe an AppleTalk Zone.

Answer: An AppleTalk zone is a logical group of nodes or networks that is defined when the network administrator configures the network. The nodes or networks need not be physically contiguous to belong to the same AppleTalk zone.

2 What are the four main media-access implementations for the AppleTalk protocol?

Answer: EtherTalk, LocalTalk, TokenTalk, and FDDITalk.

3 How are node addresses assigned to workstations?

Answer: When a node starts up, LLAP assigns the node a randomly chosen node identifier (node ID). The uniqueness of this node ID is determined by the transmission of a special packet that is addressed to the randomly chosen node ID. If the node receives a reply to this packet, the node ID is not unique. The node therefore is assigned another randomly chosen node ID and sends out another packet addressed to that node until no reply returns.

4 What is the primary network layer routing protocol used by AppleTalk?

Answer: The Datagram Delivery Protocol (DDP) is the primary network layer routing protocol in the AppleTalk protocol suite that provides a best-effort connectionless datagram service between AppleTalk sockets.

5 Name the five key transport layer protocols in AppleTalk.

Answer: RTMP, NBP, AURP, ATP, and AEP.

Chapter 39

1 What did IBM create to accommodate peer-based networking?

Answer: Advanced Peer-to-Peer Networking (APPN) and Advanced Program-to-Program Computing (APPC).

2 What are the types of physical entities that IBM SNA supports?

Answer: Hosts, communications controllers, establishment controllers, and terminals.

3 What are the three types of network addressable units in SNA?

Answer: Logical units, physical units, and control points.

4 What is the function of an LU?

Answer: Logical units function as end-user access ports into an SNA network.

5 What is the function of a PU?

Answer: Physical units are used to monitor and control attached network links and other network resources associated with a particular node.

6 What is the function of a CP?

Answer: Control points manage SNA nodes and their resources.

7 Under APPN, what are the well-defined node types?

Answer: Low-entry nodes (LENs), end nodes (ENs), and network nodes (NNs).

8 What are the four basic service categories for APPN?

Answer: Configuration, directories, topology, and routing and session services.

9 In APPN, what service helps network devices locate service providers?

Answer: Directory services.

10 For what is the network topology database used?

Answer: Calculating routes with a particular class of service (CoS).

Chapter 40

1 How do DECnet hosts use the manufacturer-assigned Media Access Control (MAC) address?

Answer: They do not use the MAC address. Instead, network level addresses are embedded in the MAC-layer address according to an algorithm that multiplies the area number by 1,024 and adds the node number to the product. The resulting 16-bit decimal address is converted to a hexadecimal number and is appended to the address AA00.0400 in byte-swapped order, with the least-significant byte first.

2 What protocol in DECnet Phase IV is responsible for routing?

Answer: DECnet Phase IV routing is implemented by the DECnet Routing Protocol (DRP), which is a relatively simple and efficient protocol whose primary function is to provide optimal path determination through a DECnet Phase IV network.

3 What functions does Network-Services Protocol (NSP) provide?

Answer: The Network-Services Protocol (NSP) is a proprietary, connection-oriented, end communications protocol developed by Digital that is responsible for creating and terminating connections between nodes, performing message fragmentation and reassembly, and managing error control.

4 What functions does the Session Control Protocol (SCP) provide?

Answer: The Session Control Protocol (SCP) is the DECnet Phase IV session control-layer protocol that performs a number of functions. In particular, SCP requests a logical link from an end device, receives logical-link requests from end devices, accepts or rejects logical-link requests, translates names to addresses, and terminates logical links.

5 The user layer provides what types of functions in DECnet?

Answer: The DNA user layer supports user services and programs that interact with user applications. The end user interacts directly with these applications, and the applications use the services and programs provided by the user layer.

Chapter 41

1 Can IBGP be used in place of an IGP (RIP, IGRP, EIGRP, OSPF, or ISIS)?

Answer: Yes and no. Remember that the next-hop information from EBGP is carried into IBGP. If IBGP does not have a route to reach the next hop, then the route will be discarded. Typically an IGP needs to be used to exchange routes to the next hop, but this can be achieved by using static routes on all the routers running IBGP. So, the answer is yes if you want to use and maintain static routes. Otherwise, the answer is no.

2 Assume that a BGP router is learning the same route from two different EBGP peers. The AS_path information from peer 1 is {2345,86,51}, and the AS_path information from peer 2 is {2346,51}. What BGP attributes could be adjusted to force the router to prefer the route advertised by peer 1?

Answer: Weight and local preference. Both have a higher preference than AS_path length.

3 Can BGP be used only by Internet service providers?

Answer: No. BGP can be used to scale large enterprise networks. A large network can be divided into segments, with each segment running an IGP. Routing information between segments could then be exchanged using BGP.

4 If a directly connected interface is redistributed into BGP, what value will the origin attribute have for this route?

Answer: Any redistributed route will have an origin of incomplete.

Chapter 42

1 Name the four key technologies that are used by EIGRP.

Answer: EIGRP employs four key technologies, including neighbor discover/ recovery, Reliable Transport Protocol (RTP), Diffusing Update ALgorithm (DUAL) finite-state machine, and a modular architecture that enables support for new protocols to be easily added to an existing network.

2 Explain why EIGRP is more efficient in operation than IGRP.

Answer: Unlike most other distance vector routing protocols, EIGRP does not mandate a periodic update of routing tables between neighboring routers. Instead, it employs a neighbor discovery/recovery mechanism to ensure that neighbors remain aware of each other's accessibility. As long as a router receives periodic hello packets from its neighbors, it can assume that those neighbors remain functional. More importantly, it can assume that all of its routes that rely upon passage through those neighbors remain usable. Thus, EIGRP is much more efficient than conventional distance vector routing protocols because it imposes much less overhead on routers and transmission facilities during normal operation.

3 How does RTP enable improved convergence times?

Answer: RTP is responsible for providing guaranteed delivery of EIGRP packets between neighboring routers. However, not all of the EIGRP packets that neighbors exchange must be sent reliably. Some packets, such as hello packets, can be sent unreliably. More importantly, they can be multicast rather than

having separate datagrams with essentially the same payload being discretely addressed and sent to individual routers. This helps an EIGRP network converge quickly, even when its links are of varying speeds.

4 Why does EIGRP tag certain routes?

Answer: EIGRP supports both internal and external routes. Routes that are internal to an AS are completely contained within that AS. External routes are those that are learned from neighbors that lie outside the AS. External routes are tagged with information that identifies their origin. This enables a network administrator to develop customized interdomain routing policies.

Chapter 43

1 What are SNA session connectors used for?

Answer: IBM SNA session connectors are used to bridge address spaces when sessions traverse multiple address spaces. Three types of session connectors exist: boundary functions, SNA network interconnection (SNI) gateways, and APPN intermediate routing functions.

2 What is created when a network node determines via the LOCATE request that the two end nodes are attached to the same medium?

Answer: A network node (NN) then is used to locate the destination specified in the LOCATE request. If the NN sees that the two ENs (source and destination) are attached to the same transport medium (such as Token Ring), a virtual node (VN) is used to connect the two endpoints and form a connection network.

3 True or false: All NAUs within a subarea have the same element address.

Answer: False. All NAUs within a given subarea share the same subarea address but have different element addresses.

Chapter 44

1 Name the benefits of using IGRP instead of RIP.

Answer: Despite its enduring success as an Interior Gateway Routing Protocol, RIP suffers from fundamental limitations that are not easily avoided. For example, it (and the subsequent RIPv2) is limited to a maximum of 16 hops per route. This tends to limit the size and complexity of a network that can be effectively routed with RIP. Other RIP limitations include its support for only equal-cost load balancing and its single, simple routing metric (hop count). IGRP was specifically designed to offer an alternative to RIP that was as easy to implement and administer as RIP, yet that did not suffer from these fundamental limitations.

2 How can an administrator influence route selection?

Answer: A network administrator can accept IGRP's default settings or can fine-tune network performance by manipulating any of IGRP's four routing metrics or their constant weights. These mathematical components of IGRP's composite routing metric offer remarkable latitude to network administrators by enabling them to emphasize or de-emphasize delay, link speed, historical reliability, or load levels in the selection of optimal routes.

3 What is variance, and how does it affect multipath routing?

Answer: Variance is another value that can be established and modified by a network administrator to fine-tune an IGRP network. In essence, variance enables a range of routing costs to be used to select multiple redundant paths of unequal cost to any given destination. Thus, variance is the mechanism by which IGRP supports unequal-cost load balancing.

4 Identify and explain IGRP's stability features.

Answer: IGRP uses holddowns, split horizons, and poison-reverse updates to improve operational stability. Holddowns prevent IGRP's interval updates from wrongly reinstating an invalid route. Split horizons help prevent routing loops by preventing a router from updating neighbors of any routing changes that it originally learned from those neighbors. Poison-reverse updates function similarly but are not limited to use between adjacent routers. Thus, they prevent large routing loops from occurring between nonadjacent routers.

5 What timers are used by IGRP, and what is their function?

Answer: IGRP features several functionally distinct timers, including an update timer, an invalid timer, a hold-time period, and a flush timer. The *update* timer specifies how frequently routing update messages should be sent. The *invalid* timer specifies how long a router should wait in the absence of routing-update messages about a specific route before declaring that route invalid. The *hold-time variable* specifies the holddown period. Finally, the *flush* timer indicates how much time should pass before a route should be flushed from the routing table.

Chapter 45

1 What is the range of available IP multicast addresses?

Answer: 224.0.0.0 to 239.255.255.255.

2 What is the purpose of IGMP?

Answer: IGMP is used between the hosts and their local multicast router to join and leave multicast groups.

3 What is an advantage of IGMPv2 over IGMPv1?

Answer: IGMPv2 has a leave group message that can greatly reduce the latency of unwanted traffic on a LAN.

4 What is a potential disadvantage of IGMP snooping over CGMP on a low-end Layer 2 switch?

Answer: IGMP snooping requires the switch to examine every multicast packet for an IGMP control message. On a low-end switch, this might have a severe performance impact.

5 What is an advantage of shortest path (or source) trees compared to shared trees?

Answer: Source trees guarantee an optimal path between each source and each receiver, which will minimize network latency.

6 What is an advantage of using shared trees?

Answer: Shared trees require very little state to be kept in the routers, which requires less memory.

7 What information does the router use to do an RPF check?

Answer: The unicast routing table.

8 Why is protocol-independent multicast called "independent"?

Answer: PIM works with any underlying IP unicast routing protocol—RIP, EIGRP, OSPF, BGP or static routes.

9 What is the main advantage of MBGP?

Answer: Providers can have noncongruent unicast and multicast routing topologies.

10 How do RPs learn about sources from other RPs with MSDP?

Answer: RPs are configured to be MSDP peers with other RPs. Each RP forwards source active (SA) messages to each other.

11 What is the purpose of the anycast RP?

Answer: Load balancing and fault tolerance.

Chapter 46

1 What is the purpose of a Layer 2 router within the NLSP hierarchical routing scheme?

Answer: The Layer 2 router connects network segments within a given routing area. A Level 2 router connects areas and also acts as a Level 1 router within its own area.

2 How long are hello packets sent after a router is initialized and reaches a fully functional state?

Answer: Hello packets are continuously sent out an active interface. This allows the adjacent router to know that the interface or connection is still active and usable. If a router does not receive a hello packet from a neighbor after a set period of time, it assumes that the interface or connection is no longer available and deletes it from its database.

3 What type of LSPs are sent over a WAN—directed or multicast?

Answer: When LSPs are sent via a WAN link, they are sent as directed packets, meaning that they contain the IP address of the neighbor. On a LAN, a multicast packet is sent.

Chapter 47

1 When using OSPF, can you have two areas attached to each other where only one AS has an interface in Area 0?

Answer: Yes, you can. This describes the use of a virtual path. One area has an interface in Area 0 (legal), and the other AS is brought up and attached off an ABR in Area 1, so we'll call it Area 2. Area 2 has no interface in Area 0, so it must have a virtual path to Area 0 through Area 1. When this is in place, Area 2 looks like it is directly connected to Area 0. When Area 1 wants to send packets to Area 2, it must send them to Area 0, which in turn redirects them back through Area 1 using the virtual path to Area 2.

2 Area 0 contains five routers (A, B, C, D, and E), and Area 1 contains three routers (R, S, and T). What routers does Router T know exists? Router S is the ABR.

Answer: Router T knows about routers R and S only. Likewise, Router S only knows about R and T, as well as routers to the ABR in Area 0. The AS's separate the areas so that router updates contain only information needed for that AS.

Chapter 48

1 What two types of messages are sent between systems in an ES-IS?

Answer: Between ES and IS systems, IS hellos and ES hellos are sent at regular intervals to maintain the connections and to exchange subnetwork and network layer addresses.

2 What is the difference between a Level 1 router and a Level 2 IS-IS router?

Answer: A Level 1 router can see only routes within the area. A Level 2 router connects to at least one Level 2 router in another area and exchanges interarea routes.

3 Describe how IS-IS routers communicate with each other on broadcast networks.

Answer: By sending multicast hellos, the IS-IS router with the highest priority becomes the DIS and advertises the pseudonode. All other IS-IS routers only send and receive LSPs from the DIS. The DIS election process is preemptive.

4 What was the original purpose of the overload bit?

Answer: It is a mechanism for a router that is running low on system resources to notify its neighbors that it should no longer be considered a possible path for transit traffic.

5 What is a TLV?

Answer: TLV stands for Type Length Value. It is the generic format for information carried in the variable-length data field of hello and LSP PDUs. The types of TLVs are defined by the original ISO specification and the many RFC extensions to IS-IS for the field, such as CLNS and IPv4 addresses.

6 How is the IS-IS metric figured on each link?

Answer: IS-IS uses a single required default metric with a maximum path value of 1024. The metric is arbitrary and typically is assigned by a network administrator. Any single link can have a maximum value of 64, and path links are calculated by summing link values.

Chapter 49

1 Name RIP's various stability features.

Answer: RIP has numerous stability features, the most obvious of which is RIP's maximum hop count. By placing a finite limit on the number of hops that a route can take, routing loops are discouraged, if not completely eliminated. Other stability features include its various timing mechanisms that help ensure that the routing table contains only valid routes, as well as split horizon and holddown mechanisms that prevent incorrect routing information from being disseminated throughout the network.

2 What is the purpose of the timeout timer?

Answer: The timeout timer is used to help purge invalid routes from a RIP node. Routes that aren't refreshed for a given period of time are likely invalid because of some change in the network. Thus, RIP maintains a timeout timer for each known route. When a route's timeout timer expires, the route is marked invalid but is retained in the table until the route-flush timer expires.

3 What two capabilities are supported by RIP 2 but not RIP?

Answer: RIP 2 enables the use of a simple authentication mechanism to secure table updates. More importantly, RIP 2 supports subnet masks, a critical feature that is not available in RIP.

4 What is the maximum network diameter of a RIP network?

Answer: A RIP network's maximum diameter is 15 hops. RIP can count to 16, but that value is considered an error condition rather than a valid hop count.

Chapter 50

1 Is it necessary to migrate away from your existing routing protocol to support RSVP?

Answer: RSVP is *not* a routing protocol. Instead, it was designed to work in conjunction with existing routing protocols. Thus, it is not necessary to migrate to a new routing protocol to support RSVP.

2 Identify the three RSVP levels of service, and explain the difference among them.

Answer: RSVP's three levels of service include best-effort, rate-sensitive, and delay-sensitive service. Best-effort service is used for applications that require reliable delivery rather than a timely delivery. Rate-sensitive service is used for any traffic that is sensitive to variation in the amount of bandwidth available. Such applications include H.323 videoconferencing, which was designed to run at a nearly constant rate. RSVP's third level of service is delay-sensitive service. Delay-sensitive traffic requires timely but not reliable delivery of data.

3 What are the two RSVP reservation classes, and how do they differ?

Answer: A reservation style is a set of control options that defines how a reservation operates. RSVP supports two primary types of reservation styles: distinct reservations and shared reservations. A distinct reservation establishes a flow for each sending device in a session. Shared reservations aggregate communications flows for a set of senders. Each of these two reservation styles is defined by a series of filters.

   4 What are RSVP filters?

   Answer: A filter in RSVP is a specific set of control options that specifies operational parameters for a reservation. RSVP's styles include wildcard-filter (WF), fixed-filter (FF), and shared-explicit (SE) filters.

   5 How can RSVP be used through network regions that do not support RSVP?

   Answer: RSVP supports tunneling through network regions that do not support RSVP. This capability was developed to enable a phased-in implementation of RSVP.

Chapter 51

   1 Describe the SMRP address.

   Answer: SMRP addressing is based on the local network of a creator endpoint. An SMRP address consists of two parts: a 3-byte network number and a 1-byte socket number. Each local network is configured with a range of unique network numbers.

   2 What type of message is sent when an endpoint-to-node request is made? What type of message is sent for a node-to-endpoint?

   Answer: Endpoint-to-node requests are sent as multicasts, while node-to-endpoint requests are sent as either unicasts or multicasts.

   3 How does a node become the designated primary node on a network?

   Answer: The basic process of primary and secondary node determination begins at startup, when a node first tries to become the designated secondary node on each local net. If successful, the node then tries to become the designated primary node. Transactions are initiated by either a primary-node request or a secondary-node request. No response to the request indicates that the negotiation succeeded, while a positive response indicates that the negotiation failed.

Chapter 52

   1 What factors have influenced the importance of network security?

   Answer: The growth of Internet applications, faster access to the Internet, government legislation

   2 How have the growth of the Internet and emerging technologies affected network security?

   Answer: The Internet has grown to provide new applications such as streaming video and IP phones. With the use of these applications and technologies come new vulnerabilities that introduce new security risks to the network.

3 How does a security policy affect a company's network?

Answer: A security policy defines how the company's network staff designs and implements security throughout the network.

4 Provide an example of a defense-in-depth security solution.

Answer: A defense-in-depth security solution is one in which a company deploys complementary security technologies throughout the network to protect against failures at different points in the network. One possible solution is for a company to deploy a firewall and install host-based IDS software on its web servers. The firewall protects the web server from unwanted traffic, and the software protects against the allowed traffic to the server.

5 List common threats against networks.

Answer: Unauthorized access, weak authentication, passwords, packet sniffers, application layer attacks, viruses, worms, Trojan horses, IP spoofing, and denial of service (DoS)

6 Which network security threat attempts to flood a network with unwanted packets?

Answer: DoS attacks are launched to disrupt network services by exhausting available bandwidth.

7 What type of attack involves sending e-mail attachments? How is this threat mitigated?

Answer: A virus or Trojan horse can be embedded in an e-mail attachment. Antivirus software is recommended to mitigate this threat.

8 Describe how to mitigate IP spoofing attacks.

Answer: IP spoofing is mitigated by filtering RFC 1918 addresses and implementing ingress and egress filtering as recommended in RFC 2827.

9 How does a switched infrastructure mitigate sniffer attacks?

Answer: Sniffers capture traffic on the same broadcast domain. Switched networks create separate broadcast domains for each port.

10 What type of security tool discovers devices and network services available on a network?

Answer: A port scanner, such as Nmap, is used to discover devices and network services using ICMP packets and TCP SYN packets. Nmap also uses advanced methods to discover both devices and network services.

11   What type of security tool identifies devices' vulnerabilities?

Answer: A network security scanner or security audit tool, such as Nessus, identifies vulnerabilities that exist on a network.

12   What type of security tool identifies weak passwords?

Answer: A password cracker, such as John the Ripper, can identify weak passwords.

Chapter 53

1   What is DEN?

Answer: DEN stands for Directory-Enabled Networks, a specification that defines different entities in a managed system using an object-oriented information model that is independent of repository and access protocol. DEN also defines a mapping of the data in the information model to a form that can be stored and retrieved from a directory that uses (L)DAP as its access protocol

2   Does DEN require the use of a directory?

Answer: No. DEN is, first and foremost, an object-oriented information model that is *independent* of repository and access protocol. Data can be mapped to a directory, but also to other types of data stores (such as a relational or object database).

3   Is DEN just about modeling network devices and services?

Answer: No. Although DEN concentrates on building a robust and extensible infrastructure that can model different network elements and services, one of its primary benefits is that it treats all types of entities in the managed environment as equal objects.

4   What is an object-oriented information model?

Answer: An object-oriented information model is a means of using object-oriented techniques to design a set of classes and relationships to represent the different objects in a managed environment.

5   Name some of the important benefits of DEN.

Answer: First and foremost, DEN is an object-oriented information model that describes different components of a managed environment in a common way. This enables a close relationship to be established between classes that define network elements, and services and classes that define other objects. This is the primary mechanism used to define which network services a client needs.

Second, DEN is object-oriented, so it is inherently extensible. This means that concepts not yet defined in DEN can be easily modeled and added to the DEN standard.

Third, DEN enables the application developer as well as the network designer to think of the network as a provider of intelligent services. This enables application developers to describe the functions and treatment that the traffic of their applications requires in terms that the network can represent directly. Thus, if a certain application has specific jitter and latency requirements, DEN can be used to define the set of services that together meet these requirements.

Fourth, and closely related, DEN enables businesses to prioritize the treatment of different applications that are vying for network resources. This enables a business administrator to write a policy that says that SAP and PeopleSoft applications should get preferential treatment over FTP traffic. This enables the network to be designed to treat the applications that a business runs according to the business rules of that organization.

A final example benefit of DEN (although there are more) is that DEN is a standard. This means that it can be used by network vendors, system integrators, and others to define a common framework to describe, define, share, and reuse data.

6 How does DEN model relationships between objects?

Answer: This is one of the crucial advantages of the DEN approach. DEN is not just a set of data models describing the characteristics of managed objects. DEN also defines a set of relationships between these objects. Without such a set of relationships, you could not relate the specific set of services that must be used to provision different applications for different users. In addition, DEN implements these relationships as classes. This enables all the benefits of object-orientation (such as subclassing, putting properties and methods on the relationship itself, and so on) to be applied to the relationship. Note that DEN is unique in this respect among the different modeling approaches that exist.

Chapter 54

1 On what concept is network caching based?

Answer: Based on the assumption that users access the same content over and over.

2 What are two secondary benefits of implementing caching technology?

Answer: 1. Secure access and control. 2. Operational logging—administrators can log how many hits sites receive.

3 Provide a brief description of network-integrated caching technology.

Answer: Network-integrated caching technology combines system-level software and hardware. Network-integrated caches must be managed like network equipment, designed like high-density hardware, and transparently inserted into the network.

4 How do Cisco cache engines ensure that web pages are kept up to date?

Answer: By obeying HTTP caching standards that dictate which elements on a page can be cached and which cannot. Those that are not are retrieved from the source every time they are accessed.

5 Name an object that can be saved in cache memory, and one that cannot.

Answer: Saved in cache: rotating banners, GIFs and JPEGs, toolbars, navigation bars. Noncacheable: CGI-generated responses.

Chapter 55

1 What is a storage area network (SAN)?

Answer: A SAN is a communication network used to connect devices such as application hosts to storage devices such as disk and tape arrays.

2 What two primary transport protocols are used within a SAN?

Answer: The first, and most predominant, protocol used is Fibre Channel. The second transport protocol is iSCSI, which leverages TCP/IP and Ethernet.

3 What primary upper-layer communication protocol is transported over a SAN?

Answer: SCSI

4 What two primary roles are assumed by SCSI devices?

Answer: Initiator and target. An initiator is a node responsible for generating SCSI commands, and a target is a node responsible for responding to such commands.

5 Name three upper-layer protocols besides SCSI that were adapted to the Fibre Channel transport.

Answer: IP, IPI-3 (used to map HIPPI to Fibre Channel), and SBCCS (Single-Byte Command Code Set, used to support FICON in SANs)

6 What governing body presides over the Fibre Channel protocols standards and drafts?

Answer: The ANSI T11 working group

7 When was the first Fibre Channel standard approved, and what was it called?

Answer: The first standard was approved in 1994 as the FC-PH standard (ANSI X3.230:1994).

8 What layer of the Fibre Channel protocol model is responsible for establishing communication between two ports in a SAN?

Answer: The FC-2 layer

9 Name the three common Fibre Channel network topologies.

Answer: Point-to-point, arbitrated-loop, and switched-fabric

10 How many devices can an arbitrated loop support?

Answer: 126

11 What is the difference between a private arbitrated loop and a public arbitrated loop?

Answer: A private arbitrated loop supports only an 8-bit addressing scheme, and connected devices cannot communicate outside the local loop. A public arbitrated loop supports a full 24-bit hierarchical addressing schedule that allows for communication external to the local loop.

12 What is a B_Port?

Answer: A bridge port, or B_Port, extends a Fibre Channel ISL over a non-Fibre Channel network. B_Ports connect only to E_Ports and participate in only a basic set of link services.

13 What is the name of the primary Fibre Channel routing protocol, and what part of an FC_ID does it use to make routing decisions?

Answer: The primary Fibre Channel routing protocol is Fabric Shortest Path First (FSPF). It uses the Domain_ID (8 bits) to build routing tables and make routing decisions within the fabric.

14 What is a Fibre Channel IDLE, and what is it used for?

Answer: Fibre Channel IDLEs are 4-byte commands or ordered sets transmitted from one device to another. They are used for synchronization and word alignment between transmitter and receiver. IDLEs indicate readiness to transmit and are constantly transmitted when no other data is presented to send.

15 What Fibre Channel class of service does not provide delivery confirmation of frames?

Answer: Class 3, which is the only traffic class widely used, does not provide delivery confirmation.

16 What is the rule of thumb in determining how many buffer credits are required to sustain wire rate capability across a 1 Gbps Fibre Channel link?

Answer: The rule of thumb is that 1 BB_Credit is required for every 2 km of distance between transmitter and receiver.

17 What is soft zoning?

Answer: Soft zoning involves filtering directory service inquiries to allow only certain devices to be visible as a means of isolating traffic between Fibre Channel end nodes. Soft zoning is not fully secure, because an end device must know the FC_ID of another end device to bypass the zone and communicate with the end device.

18 True or false: An individual iSCSI exchange can be conducted over multiple TCP connections.

Answer: False. Although an iSCSI initiator can conduct multiple exchanges across multiple TCP connections, each exchange can use only one TCP connection.

19 What standard TCP port number is used for iSCSI?

Answer: TCP/3260

20 Name two mechanisms for performing iSCSI initiator authentication.

Answer: The first primary method is to use CHAP, which is mandated by the iSCSI standard and is a common mechanism used in IP dialup connections. The second primary method is the SRP protocol.

Chapter 56

1 What are the five steps of problem management?

Answer: Problem management is performed in five steps: problem determination, problem diagnosis, problem bypass and recovery, problem resolution, and problem tracking and control.

2 How does the command-control facility of the NetView program operate?

Answer: The command-control facility provides network control by issuing basic operator and file-access commands to Virtual Telecommunications Access Method (VTAM) applications, controllers, operating systems, and NetView/PC (an interface between NetView and non-SNA devices).

3 To perform resource activation and deactivation, command cancellation, and clock setting on a remote system, you would need to use what?

Answer: IBM operations management consists of managing distributed network resources from a central site, using two sets of functions: operations-management services and common-operations services. Operations-management services provide the capability to control remote resources centrally using the following functions: resource activation and deactivation, command cancellation, and clock setting.

Chapter 57

1 What is the function of the RMON group Matrix?

Answer: This group stores statistics for conversations between sets of two addresses. As the device detects a new conversation, it creates a new entry in its table.

2 What is RMON?

Answer: Remote Monitoring (RMON) is a standard monitoring specification that enables various network monitors and console systems to exchange network-monitoring data.

3 Multicast packets, CRC errors, runts, giants, fragments, and jabbers are elements of what RMON group?

Answer: Statistics.

Chapter 58

1 What is an SNMP agent?

Answer: An agent is a software module that resides in a managed device. An agent has local knowledge of the management information and translates that information into a form that is compatible with SNMP.

2 What is a MIB, and how is it accessed?

Answer: A Management Information Base (MIB) is a collection of information that is organized hierarchically. MIBs are accessed using a network-management protocol such as SNMP. They are comprised of managed objects and are identified by object identifiers.

3 Name some protocol operations available in SNMPv2.

Answer: SNMPv2 has the Get, GetNext, Set, and Trap operations. These are available in SNMPv1 as well. SNMPv2 also introduced two new protocol operations: GetBulk and Inform.

4 What is the major deficiency of SNMPv1 and SNMPv2 that is addressed in SNMPv3?

Answer: Security. The initial versions of SNMP could not provide encryption or authentication for the SNMP messages.

Chapter 59

1 What is the main goal of QoS?

Answer: QoS provides preferential treatment to an identified flow(s). You must also provide enough service for other flows to successfully pass traffic. Providing priority to a certain flow(s) by breaking other applications is not desirable.

2 What are the types of QoS tools?

- **Classification—These tools identify and (if desired) mark flows.**

- **Congestion management—These tools queue and service flows in different ways to provide preferential treatment to a certain flow(s).**

- **Congestion avoidance—This tool prevents a queue from filling, to allow high-priority traffic to enter the queue. This tool also provides for overall congestion avoidance in an Internet/intranet.**

- **Shaping/policing—These tools limit the bandwidth that a flow(s) uses.**

- **Link efficiency—These tools provide a method of mitigating delay experienced on lower-speed links.**

3 What is signaling?

Answer: Signaling notifies the network in regard to the priority of a flow(s). Most commonly, this is accomplished through the setting of IP precedence bits in the ToS byte, setting Class of Service bits (for Ethernet), and RSVP for end-to-end reservation.

4 What is IP precedence?

Answer: IP precedence consists of the 3 most significant bits of the ToS byte in the IP header. It is used to mark a packet to notify the network in regard to the importance of the packet. The 3 bits allow settings from 0 to 7 (6 and 7 are reserved and should not be set by a network administrator).

5 What is Differentiated Services Code Point (DSCP)

Answer: It is a modification to the type of service byte where the six most significant bits of this byte are being reallocated for use as the DSCP field, where each DSCP specifies a particular per-hop behavior that is applied to a packet.

6 What is Modular Qos CLI (MQC)?

Answer: MQC is a modular configuration framework for QoS functionality which seperates the classification, policy definition and policy application definitions on a cisco router. Eventually, all cisco QoS functionality should be configurabale using MQC.

7 How does flow-based WFQ (WFQ) differ from class-based WFQ (CBWFQ)?

Answer:

- **WFQ provides a queue for each flow. CBWFQ provides classes that can consist of more than one flow.**
- **WFQ creates fairness among all flows (given equal IP precedence settings). CBWFQ has classes of flows that are provided a user-determined minimum amount of bandwidth.**
- **CBWFQ supports WRED.**

8 What is used for queue management to provide congestion avoidance? How does it avoid congestion?

Answer: Weighted random early detection avoids congestion by the following actions:

- **Trying to make sure that the queue does not fill up, so there is room for high priority packets**
- **Providing an algorithm that drops packets that are of lower priority before dropping higher-priority packets**

9 What are the two primary uses for CAR?

Answer:

- **Classifying packets using IP precedence bits or QoS groups (for D-WFQ)**
- **Limiting the amount of traffic (or policing) that a flow(s) can pass**

10 What QoS tool would you use to guarantee a minimum amount of bandwidth?

Answer: CBWFQ.

11 What QoS tool would you use to limit a flow to a maximum amount of bandwidth?

Answer: CAR or GTS/FRTS.

12 What does NBAR do? What are two unique features of it?

Answer: NBAR provides for greater granularity of identification of a flow. By looking deeper into the packet, NBAR can identify flows such as URL (instead of merely by HTTP port 80).

Two unique features are:

- **Protocol discovery, in which the router can identify protocols and provide statistical data on each protocol**
- **PDLMs, which provide easy upgrade of the protocols that NBAR can identify**

13 What is a common use for traffic shaping?

Answer: One common use is in a hub-and-spoke topology, where a single high-speed link at the central site terminates a number of lower-speed remote links. With such a topology, many will traffic shape at the central site, so the slower remote site links are not overrun, causing packets to drop.

14 What tool is used for Integrated QoS?

Answer: RSVP.

Early Technologies

This appendix discusses three early technologies: Token Ring/IEEE 802.5, Xerox Network Systems, and Banyan VINES.

Token Ring/IEEE 802.5

The Token Ring network was originally developed by IBM in the 1970s. It is still IBM's primary local-area network (LAN) technology. The related IEEE 802.5 specification is almost identical to and completely compatible with IBM's Token Ring network. In fact, the IEEE 802.5 specification was modeled after IBM Token Ring, and it continues to shadow IBM's Token Ring development. The term *Token Ring* generally is used to refer to both IBM's Token Ring network and IEEE 802.5 networks. This chapter addresses both Token Ring and IEEE 802.5.

Token Ring and IEEE 802.5 networks are basically compatible, although the specifications differ in minor ways. IBM's Token Ring network specifies a star, with all end stations attached to a device called a multistation access unit (MSAU). In contrast, IEEE 802.5 does not specify a topology, although virtually all IEEE 802.5 implementations are based on a star. Other differences exist, including media type (IEEE 802.5 does not specify a media type, although IBM Token Ring networks use twisted-pair wire) and routing information field size. Figure B-1 summarizes IBM Token Ring network and IEEE 802.5 specifications.

Figure B-1   *Although Dissimilar in Some Respects, IBM's Token Ring Network and IEEE 802.5 Are Generally*
Compatible

	IBM Token Ring network	IEEE 802.5
Data rates	4.16 Mbps	4.16 Mbps
Stations/segment	260 (shielded twisted pair) 72 (unshielded twisted pair)	250
Topology	Star	Not specified
Media	Twisted pair	Not specified
Signaling	Baseband	Baseband
Access method	Token passing	Token passing
Encoding	Differential manchester	Differential manchester

Physical Connections

IBM Token Ring network stations are directly connected to MSAUs, which can be wired
together to form one large ring (see Figure B-2). Patch cables connect MSAUs to adjacent
MSAUs, while lobe cables connect MSAUs to stations. MSAUs include bypass relays for
removing stations from the ring.

Figure B-2   *MSAUs Can Be Wired Together to Form One Large Ring in an IBM Token Ring Network*

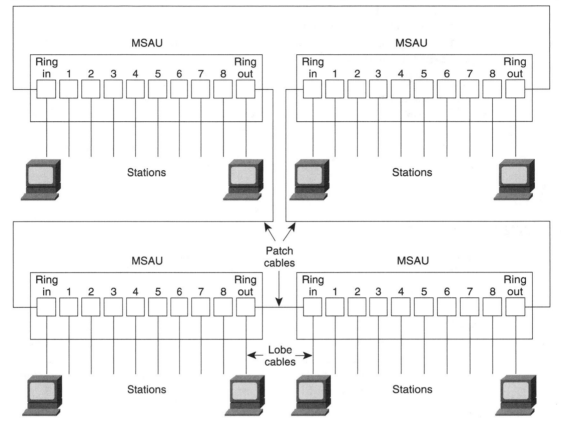

Token Ring Operation

Token Ring and IEEE 802.5 are two principal examples of token-passing networks (FDDI is the other). *Token-passing networks* move a small frame, called a token, around the network. Possession of the token grants the right to transmit. If a node receiving the token has no information to send, it passes the token to the next end station. Each station can hold the token for a maximum period of time.

If a station possessing the token does have information to transmit, it seizes the token, alters 1 bit of the token (which turns the token into a start-of-frame sequence), appends the information that it wants to transmit, and sends this information to the next station on the ring. While the information frame is circling the ring, no token is on the network (unless the ring supports early token release), which means that other stations wanting to transmit must wait. Therefore, collisions cannot occur in Token Ring networks. If early token release is supported, a new token can be released when frame transmission is complete.

The information frame circulates the ring until it reaches the intended destination station, which copies the information for further processing. The information frame continues to circle the ring and is finally removed when it reaches the sending station. The sending station can check the returning frame to see whether the frame was seen and subsequently copied by the destination.

Unlike CSMA/CD networks (such as Ethernet), token-passing networks are *deterministic*, which means that it is possible to calculate the maximum time that will pass before any end station will be capable of transmitting. This feature and several reliability features, which are discussed in the section "Fault-Management Mechanisms," later in this chapter, make Token Ring networks ideal for applications in which delay must be predictable and robust network operation is important. Factory automation environments are examples of such applications.

Priority System

Token Ring networks use a sophisticated priority system that permits certain user-designated, high-priority stations to use the network more frequently. Token Ring frames have two fields that control priority: the priority field and the reservation field.

Only stations with a priority equal to or higher than the priority value contained in a token can seize that token. After the token is seized and changed to an information frame, only stations with a priority value higher than that of the transmitting station can reserve the token for the next pass around the network. When the next token is generated, it includes the higher priority of the reserving station. Stations that raise a token's priority level must reinstate the previous priority after their transmission is complete.

Fault-Management Mechanisms

Token Ring networks employ several mechanisms for detecting and compensating for network faults. For example, one station in the Token Ring network is selected to be the *active monitor*. This station, which potentially can be any station on the network, acts as a centralized source of timing information for other ring stations and performs a variety of ring-maintenance functions. One of these functions is the removal of continuously circulating frames from the ring. When a sending device fails, its frame may continue to circle the ring. This can prevent other stations from transmitting their own frames and essentially can lock up the network. The active monitor can detect such frames, remove them from the ring, and generate a new token.

The IBM Token Ring network's star topology also contributes to overall network reliability. Because all information in a Token Ring network is seen by active MSAUs, these devices can be programmed to check for problems and selectively remove stations from the ring, if necessary.

A Token Ring algorithm called *beaconing* detects and tries to repair certain network faults. Whenever a station detects a serious problem with the network (such as a cable break), it sends a beacon frame, which defines a failure domain. This domain includes the station reporting the failure, its nearest active upstream neighbor (NAUN), and everything in between. Beaconing initiates a process called *autoreconfiguration*, in which nodes within the failure domain automatically perform diagnostics in an attempt to reconfigure the network around the failed areas. Physically, the MSAU can accomplish this through electrical reconfiguration.

Frame Format

Token Ring and IEEE 802.5 support two basic frame types: tokens and data/command frames. Tokens are 3 bytes in length and consist of a start delimiter, an access control byte, and an end delimiter. Data/command frames vary in size, depending on the size of the Information field. Data frames carry information for upper-layer protocols, while command frames contain control information and have no data for upper-layer protocols. Both formats are shown in Figure B-3.

Figure B-3   *IEEE 802.5 and Token Ring Specify Tokens and Data/Command Frames*

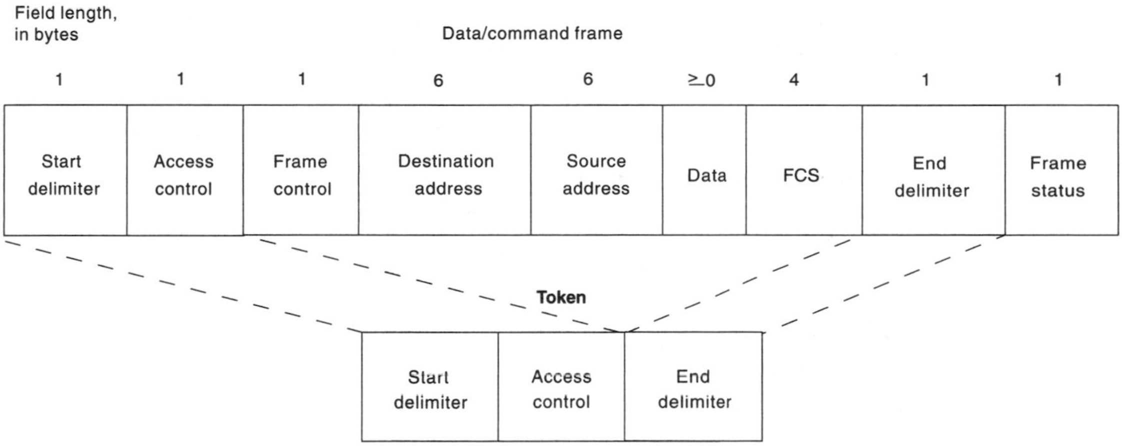

Token Frame Fields

The three token frame fields illustrated in Figure B-3 are summarized in the descriptions that follow:

- **Start delimiter**—Alerts each station of the arrival of a token (or data/command frame). This field includes signals that distinguish the byte from the rest of the frame by violating the encoding scheme used elsewhere in the frame.

- **Access-control byte**—Contains the Priority field (the most significant 3 bits) and the Reservation field (the least significant 3 bits), as well as a token bit (used to differentiate a token from a data/command frame) and a monitor bit (used by the active monitor to determine whether a frame is circling the ring endlessly).

- **End delimiter**—Signals the end of the token or data/command frame. This field also contains bits to indicate a damaged frame and identify the frame that is the last in a logical sequence.

Data/Command Frame Fields

Data/command frames have the same three fields as Token Frames, plus several others. The Data/command frame fields illustrated in Figure B-3 are described in the following summaries:

- **Start delimiter**—Alerts each station of the arrival of a token (or data/command frame). This field includes signals that distinguish the byte from the rest of the frame by violating the encoding scheme used elsewhere in the frame.

- **Access-control byte**—Contains the Priority field (the most significant 3 bits) and the Reservation field (the least significant 3 bits), as well as a token bit (used to differentiate a token from a data/command frame) and a monitor bit (used by the active monitor to determine whether a frame is circling the ring endlessly).

- **Frame-control bytes**—Indicates whether the frame contains data or control information. In control frames, this byte specifies the type of control information.

- **Destination and source addresses**—Consists of two 6-byte address fields that identify the destination and source station addresses.

- **Data**—Indicates that the length of field is limited by the ring token holding time, which defines the maximum time a station can hold the token.

- **Frame-check sequence (FCS)**—Is filed by the source station with a calculated value dependent on the frame contents. The destination station recalculates the value to determine whether the frame was damaged in transit. If so, the frame is discarded.

- **End Delimiter**—Signals the end of the token or data/command frame. The end delimiter also contains bits to indicate a damaged frame and identify the frame that is the last in a logical sequence.

- **Frame Status**—Is a 1-byte field terminating a command/data frame. The Frame Status field includes the address-recognized indicator and frame-copied indicator.

Summary

Token Ring technology was developed in the 1970s by IBM. Token-passing networks move a small frame, called a token, around the network. Possession of the token grants the right to transmit. If a node receiving the token has no information to send, it passes the token to the next end station. Each station can hold the token for a maximum period of time.

If a station possessing the token does have information to transmit, it seizes the token, alters 1 bit of the token (which turns the token into a start-of-frame sequence), appends the information that it wants to transmit, and sends this information to the next station on the ring.

Xerox Network Systems

Background

The Xerox Network Systems (XNS) protocols were created by the Xerox Corporation in the late 1970s and early 1980s. They were designed to be used across a variety of communication media, processors, and office applications. Several XNS protocols resemble the Internet Protocol (IP) and Transmission Control Protocol (TCP) entities developed by the Defense Advanced Research Projects Agency (DARPA) for the U.S. Department of Defense (DoD).

Because of its availability and early entry into the market, XNS was adopted by most of the early LAN companies, including Novell, Inc.; Ungermann-Bass, Inc. (now a part of Tandem Computers); and 3Com Corporation. Each of these companies has since made various changes to the XNS protocols. Novell added the Service Advertisement Protocol (SAP) to permit resource advertisement and modified the OSI Layer 3 protocols (which Novell renamed IPX, for Internetwork Packet Exchange) to run on IEEE 802.3 rather than Ethernet networks. Ungermann-Bass modified RIP to support delay as well as hop count, and made other small changes. Over time, the XNS implementations for PC networking have become more popular than XNS as it was designed by Xerox. This chapter presents a summary of the XNS protocol stack in the context of the OSI reference model.

XNS Hierarchy Overview

Although the XNS design objectives are the same as those for the OSI reference model, the XNS concept of a protocol hierarchy is somewhat different from that provided by the OSI reference model, as Figure B-4 illustrates.

Figure B-4   *Xerox Adopted a Five-Layer Model of Packet Communication*

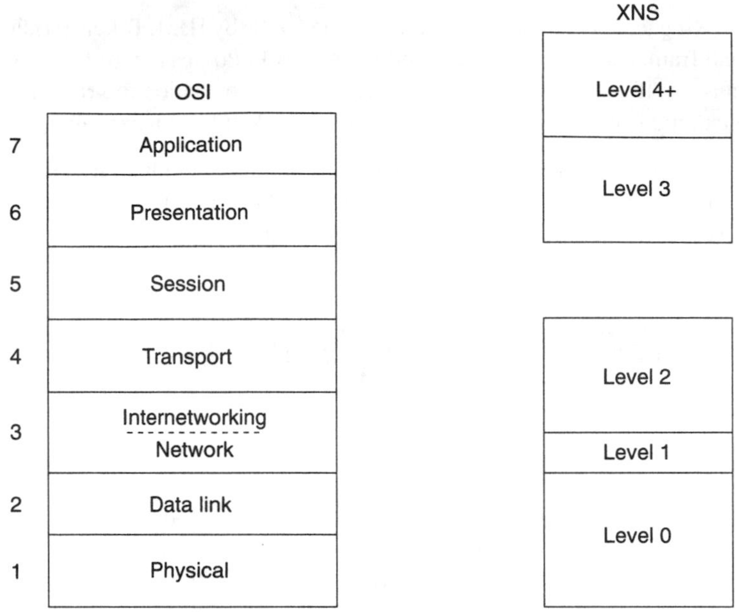

As illustrated in Figure B-4, Xerox provided a five-level model of packet communications. Level 0 corresponds roughly to OSI Layers 1 and 2, handling link access and bit-stream manipulation. Level 1 corresponds roughly to the portion of OSI Layer 3 that pertains to network traffic. Level 2 corresponds to the portion of OSI Layer 3 that pertains to internetwork routing, and to OSI Layer 4, which handles interprocess communication. Levels 3 and 4 correspond roughly to the upper two layers of the OSI model, handling data structuring, process-to-process interaction, and applications. XNS has no protocol corresponding to OSI Layer 5 (the session layer).

Media Access

Although XNS documentation mentions X.25, Ethernet, and High-Level Data Link Control (HDLC), XNS does not expressly define what it refers to as a Level 0 protocol. As with many other protocol suites, XNS leaves media access an open issue, implicitly allowing any such protocol to host the transport of XNS packets over a physical medium.

Network Layer

The XNS network layer protocol is called the Internet Datagram Protocol (IDP). IDP performs standard Layer 3 functions, including logical addressing and end-to-end datagram delivery across an internetwork. Figure B-5 illustrates the format of an IDP packet.

The following descriptions summarize the IDP packet fields illustrated in Figure B-5:

- **Checksum**—A 16-bit field that helps gauge the integrity of the packet after it traverses the internetwork.

- **Length**—A 16-bit field that carries the complete length (including the checksum) of the current datagram.

- **Transport control**—An 8-bit field that contains the hop count and Maximum Packet Lifetime (MPL) subfields. The Hop Count subfield is initialized to 0 by the source and is incremented by 1 as the datagram passes through a router. When the Hop Count field reaches 16, the datagram is discarded on the assumption that a routing loop is occurring. The MPL subfield provides the maximum amount of time, in seconds, that a packet can remain on the internetwork.

Figure B-5   *Eleven Fields Comprise an IDP Packet*

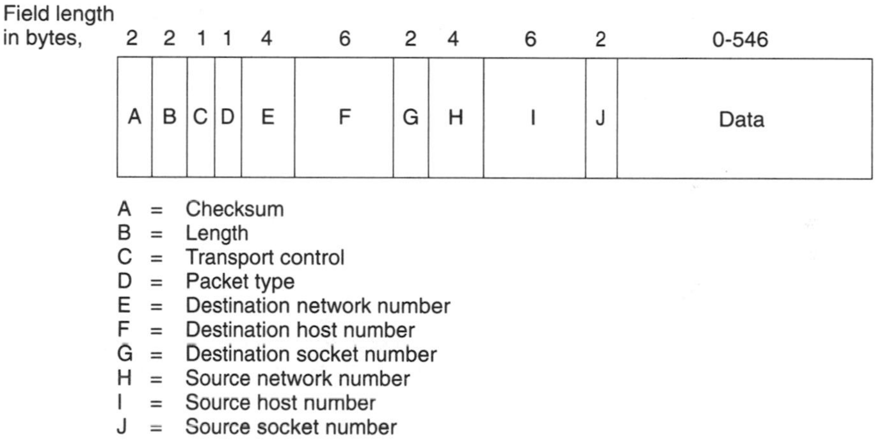

A = Checksum
B = Length
C = Transport control
D = Packet type
E = Destination network number
F = Destination host number
G = Destination socket number
H = Source network number
I = Source host number
J = Source socket number

- **Packet type**—An 8-bit field that specifies the format of the data field.

- **Destination network number**—A 32-bit field that uniquely identifies the destination network in an internetwork.

- **Destination host number**—A 48-bit field that uniquely identifies the destination host.

- **Destination socket number**—A 16-bit field that uniquely identifies a socket (process) within the destination host.

- **Source network number**—A 32-bit field that uniquely identifies the source network in an internetwork.

- **Source host number**—A 48-bit field that uniquely identifies the source host.

- **Source socket number**—A 16-bit field that uniquely identifies a socket (process) within the source host.

IEEE 802 addresses are equivalent to host numbers, so hosts that are connected to more than one IEEE 802 network have the same address on each segment. This makes network numbers redundant but nevertheless useful for routing. Certain socket numbers are well known, which means that the service performed by the software using them is statically defined. All other socket numbers are reusable.

XNS supports Ethernet Version 2.0 encapsulation for Ethernet, and three types of encapsulation for Token Ring: 3Com, SubNet Access Protocol (SNAP), and Ungermann-Bass.

XNS supports unicast (point-to-point), multicast, and broadcast packets. Multicast and broadcast addresses are further divided into directed and global types. Directed multicasts deliver packets to members of the multicast group on the network specified in the destination multicast network address. Directed broadcasts deliver packets to all members of a specified network. Global multicasts deliver packets to all members of the group within the entire internetwork, whereas global broadcasts deliver packets to all internetwork addresses. One bit in the host number indicates a single versus a multicast address. Conversely, all ones in the host field indicate a broadcast address.

To route packets in an internetwork, XNS uses the RIP dynamic routing scheme. Today, RIP is the most commonly used Interior Gateway Protocol (IGP) in the Internet community. For more information about RIP, see Chapter 47, "Routing Information Protocol (RIP)."

Transport Layer

OSI transport layer functions are implemented by several protocols. Each of the following protocols is described in the XNS specification as a Level 2 protocol.

The Sequenced Packet Protocol (SPP) provides reliable, connection-based, flow-controlled packet transmission on behalf of client processes. It is similar in function to the Internet Protocol suite's Transmission Control Protocol (TCP) and the OSI protocol suite's Transport Protocol 4 (TP4). For more information about TCP, see Chapter 35, "Internet Protocols." For more information about TP4, see Chapter 34, "Open System Interconnection Protocols."

Each SPP packet includes a sequence number, which is used to order packets and to determine whether any have been duplicated or missed. SPP packets also contain two 16-bit connection identifiers. One connection identifier is specified by each end of the connection; together, the two connection identifiers uniquely identify a logical connection between client processes.

SPP packets cannot be longer than 576 bytes. Client processes can negotiate use of a different packet size during connection establishment, but SPP does not define the nature of this negotiation.

The Packet Exchange Protocol (PEP) is a request-response protocol designed to have greater reliability than simple datagram service (as provided by IDP, for example) but less reliability than SPP. PEP is functionally similar to the Internet Protocol suite's User Datagram Protocol (UDP). (For more information about UDP, see Chapter 35.) PEP is single packet-based, providing retransmissions but no duplicate packet detection. As such, it is useful in applications where request-response transactions can be repeated without damaging data, or where reliable transfer is executed at another layer.

The Error Protocol (EP) can be used by any client process to notify another client process that a network error has occurred. This protocol is used, for example, in situations in which an SPP implementation has identified a duplicate packet.

Upper-Layer Protocols

XNS offers several upper-layer protocols. The Printing Protocol provides print services, the Filing Protocol provides file access services, and the Clearinghouse Protocol provides name services. Each of these three protocols runs on top of the Courier Protocol, which provides conventions for data structuring and process interaction.

XNS also defines Level 4 protocols, which are application protocols. However, because they have little to do with actual communication functions, the XNS specification does not include any pertinent definitions.

The Level 2 Echo Protocol is used to test the reachability of XNS network nodes and to support functions such as that provided by the **ping** command found in UNIX and other environments.

Summary

XNS is used as a protocol today only in networks by vendors that adopted some of the standards that XNS provides. These number are shrinking still, and very few new networks are being based upon XNS.

Banyan VINES

Background

Banyan Virtual Integrated Network Service (VINES) implements a distributed network operating system based on a proprietary protocol family derived from the Xerox Corporation's Xerox Network Systems (XNS) protocols. VINES uses a client/server architecture in which clients request certain services, such as file and printer access, from servers. This chapter provides a summary of VINES communications protocols. The VINES protocol stack is illustrated in Figure B-6.

Figure B-6   *The VINES Protocol Stack Consists of Five Separate Levels*

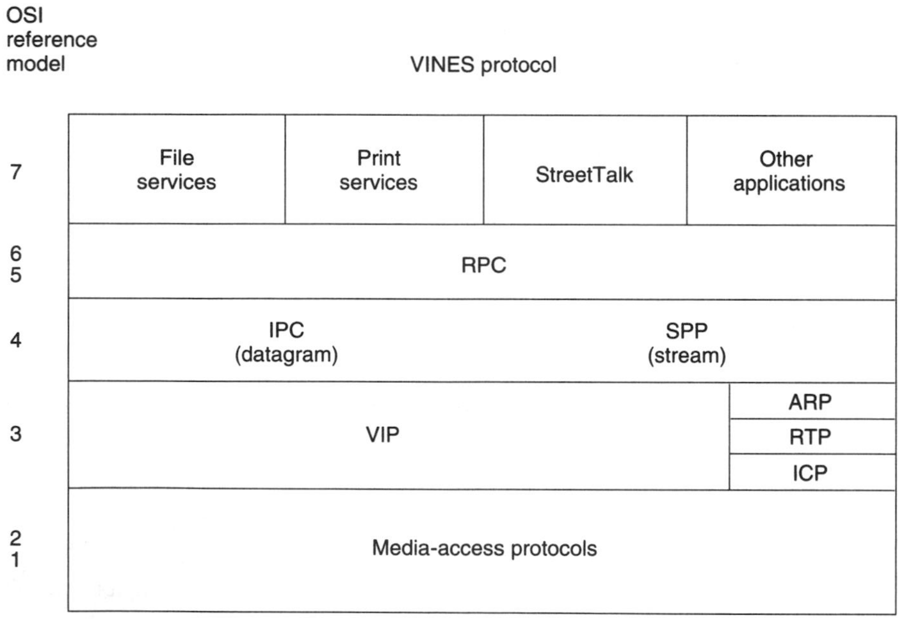

OSI reference model	VINES protocol			
7	File services	Print services	StreetTalk	Other applications
6 5	RPC			
4	IPC (datagram)		SPP (stream)	
3	VIP			ARP / RTP / ICP
2 1	Media-access protocols			

Media Access

The lower two layers of the VINES stack are implemented with a variety of well-known media-access mechanisms, including High-Level Data Link Control (HDLC), X.25, Ethernet, and Token Ring.

Network Layer

VINES uses the VINES Internetwork Protocol (VIP) to perform Layer 3 activities (including internetwork routing). VINES also supports its own Address Resolution Protocol (ARP), its own version of the Routing Information Protocol (RIP)—called the Routing Table Protocol (RTP)—and the Internet Control Protocol (ICP), which provides exception handling and special routing cost information. ARP, ICP, and RTP packets are encapsulated in a VIP header.

VINES Internetwork Protocol

VINES network layer addresses are 48-bit entities subdivided into network (32 bits) and subnetwork (16 bits) portions. The network number is better described as a server number because it is derived directly from the server's key (a hardware module that identifies a unique number and the software options for that server). The subnetwork portion of a VINES address is better described as a host number because it is used to identify hosts on VINES networks. Figure B-7 illustrates the VINES address format.

Figure B-7   *A VINES Address Consists of a Network Number and a Subnet Number*

The network number identifies a VINES logical network, which is represented as a two-level tree with the root at a service node. Service nodes, which are usually servers, provide address resolution and routing services to clients, which represent the leaves of the tree. The service node assigns Vines Internetwork Protocol (VIP) addresses to clients.

When a client is powered on, it broadcasts a request for servers, and all servers that hear the request respond. The client chooses the first response and requests a subnetwork (host) address from that server. The server responds with an address consisting of its own network address (derived from its key) concatenated with a subnetwork (host) address of its own choosing. Client subnetwork addresses typically are assigned sequentially, starting with 8001H. Server subnetwork addresses are always 1. Figure B-8 illustrates the VINES address-selection process.

Dynamic address assignment is not unique in the industry (AppleTalk also uses this process), but it certainly is not as common as static address assignment. Because addresses are chosen exclusively by a particular server (whose address is unique as a result of the hardware key), very little chance exists for duplicating an address. This is fortunate because duplicate addresses could cause potentially devastating problems for Internet Protocol (IP) and other networks.

Figure B-8 *VINES Moves Through Four Steps in Selecting an Address*

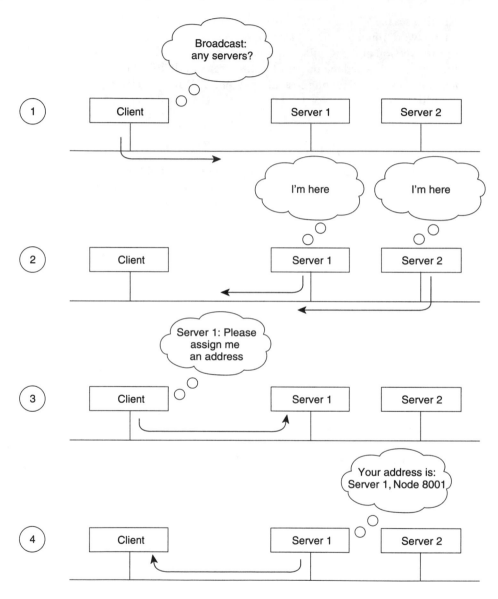

In the VINES network scheme, all servers with multiple interfaces are essentially routers. Clients always choose their own server as a first-hop router, even if another server on the same cable provides a better route to the ultimate destination. Clients can learn about other routers by receiving redirect messages from their own server. Because clients rely on their servers for first-hop routing, VINES servers maintain routing tables to help them find remote nodes.

VINES routing tables consist of host/cost pairs, where the host corresponds to a network node that can be reached, and cost corresponds to a delay (expressed in milliseconds) to get to that node. RTP helps VINES servers find neighboring clients, servers, and routers.

Periodically, all clients advertise both their network layer and MAC-layer addresses with the equivalent of a hello packet, which indicates that the client is still operating and network-ready. The servers themselves send routing updates to other servers periodically to alert other routers to changes in node addresses and network topology.

When a VINES server receives a packet, it checks to see whether the packet is destined for another server or whether it is a broadcast. If the current server is the destination, the server handles the request appropriately. If another server is the destination, the current server either forwards the packet directly (if the server is a neighbor) or routes it to the next server in line. If the packet is a broadcast, the current server checks to see whether the packet came from the least-cost path. If not, the packet is discarded. If so, the packet is forwarded on all interfaces except the one on which it was received. This approach helps diminish the number of broadcast storms, a common problem in other network environments. Figure B-9 illustrates the VINES routing algorithm.

Figure B-10 illustrates the VIP packet format.

The fields of a VIP packet include information on the checksum, packet length, transport control, protocol type, destination network number, destination subnetwork number, source network number, and source subnetwork number.

The Checksum field is used to detect packet corruption. The Packet Length field indicates the length of the entire VIP packet.

The Transport Control field consists of several subfields. If the packet is a broadcast packet, two subfields are provided: Class (bits 1 through 3) and Hop Count (bits 4 through 7). If the packet is not a broadcast packet, four subfields are provided: Error, Metric, Redirect, and Hop Count. The Class subfield specifies the type of node that should receive the broadcast. For this purpose, nodes are broken into various categories according to the type of node and the type of link on which the node is found. By specifying the type of nodes to receive broadcasts, the Class subfield reduces the disruption caused by broadcasts. The Hop Count subfield represents the number of hops (router traversals) the packet has been through. The Error subfield specifies whether the ICP protocol should send an exception-notification packet to the packet's source if a packet turns out to be unroutable. The Metric subfield is set to 1 by a transport entity when it must learn the routing cost of moving packets between a service node and a neighbor. The Redirect subfield specifies whether the router should generate a redirect, when appropriate.

Figure B-9   *The VINES Routing Algorithm Determines the Appropriate Path to a Destination*

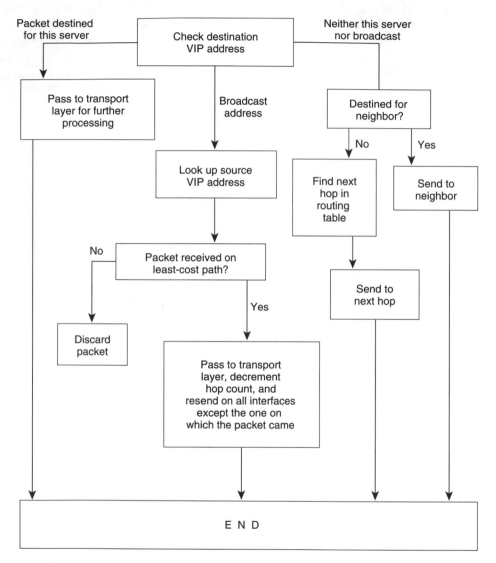

Figure B-10   *A VIP Packet Consists of Nine Individual Fields*

Field length,
in bytes

2	2	1	1	4	2	4	2	Variable
Check-sum	Packet length	Trans-port control	Protocol type	Destination network number	Destination subnetwork number	Source network number	Source subnetwork number	Data

The Protocol Type field indicates the network layer or transport layer protocol for which the metric or exception-notification packet is destined.

Finally, the Destination Network Number, Destination Subnetwork Number, Source Network Number, and Source Subnetwork Number fields all provide VIP address information.

Routing Table Protocol

Routing Table Protocol (RTP) distributes network topology information. Routing update packets are broadcast periodically by both client and service nodes. These packets inform neighbors of a node's existence and also indicate whether the node is a client or a service node. In each routing update packet, service nodes include a list of all known networks and the cost factors associated with reaching those networks.

Two routing tables are maintained: a table of all known networks and a table of neighbors. For service nodes, the table of all known networks contains an entry for each known network except the service node's own network. Each entry contains a network number, a routing metric, and a pointer to the entry for the next hop to the network in the table of neighbors. The table of neighbors contains an entry for each neighbor service node and client node. Entries include a network number, a subnetwork number, the media-access protocol (for example, Ethernet) used to reach that node, a local-area network (LAN) address (if the medium connecting the neighbor is a LAN), and a neighbor metric.

RTP specifies four packet types: routing update, routing request, routing response, and routing redirect. A routing update is issued periodically to notify neighbors of an entity's existence. Routing requests are exchanged by entities when they must learn the network's topology quickly. Routing responses contain topological information and are used by service nodes to respond to routing-request packets. A routing-redirect packet provides better path information to nodes using inefficient paths.

RTP packets have a 4-byte header that consists of the following 1-byte fields: Operation Type, which indicates the packet type; Node Type, which indicates whether the packet came from a service node or a nonservice node; Controller Type, which indicates whether the controller in the node transmitting the RTP packet has a multibuffer controller; and Machine Type, which indicates whether the processor in the RTP sender is fast or slow.

Both the Controller Type and the Machine Type fields are used for pacing.

Address Resolution Protocol

Address Resolution Protocol (ARP) entities are classified as either address-resolution clients or address-resolution services. Address-resolution clients usually are implemented in client nodes, whereas address-resolution services typically are provided by service nodes.

ARP packets have an 8-byte header that consists of a 2-byte packet type, a 4-byte network number, and a 2-byte subnetwork number. Four packet types exist: a query request, which is a request for an ARP service; a service response, which is a response to a query request; an assignment request, which is sent to an ARP service to request a VINES internetwork address; and an assignment response, which is sent by the ARP service as a response to the assignment request. The Network Number and Subnet Number fields have meaning only in an assignment-response packet.

ARP clients and services implement the following algorithm when a client starts up. First, the client broadcasts query-request packets. Then, each service that is a neighbor of the client responds with a service-response packet. The client then issues an assignment-request packet to the first service that responded to its query-request packet. The service responds with an assignment-response packet that contains the assigned internetwork address.

Internet Control Protocol

The *Internet Control Protocol (ICP)* defines exception-notification and metric-notification packets. Exception-notification packets provide information about network layer exceptions; metric-notification packets contain information about the final transmission used to reach a client node.

Exception notifications are sent when a VIP packet cannot be routed properly, and the Error subfield in the VIP header's Transport Control field is enabled. These packets also contain a field identifying the particular exception by its error code.

ICP entities in service nodes generate metric-notification messages when the Metric subfield in the VIP header's Transport Control field is enabled, and the destination address in the service node's packet specifies one of the service node's neighbors.

Transport Layer

VINES provides three transport layer services: unreliable datagram service, reliable message service, and data-stream service.

Unreliable datagram service sends packets that are routed on a best-effort basis but not acknowledged at the destination.

Reliable message service is a virtual circuit service that provides reliable sequenced and acknowledged delivery of messages between network nodes. A reliable message can be transmitted in a maximum of four VIP packets.

Data-stream service supports the controlled flow of data between two processes. The data-stream service is an acknowledged virtual circuit service that supports the transmission of messages of unlimited size.

Upper-Layer Protocols

As a distributed network, VINES uses the remote procedure call (RPC) model for communication between clients and servers. RPC is the foundation of distributed-service environments. The NetRPC protocol (Layers 5 and 6) provides a high-level programming language that allows access to remote services in a manner transparent to both the user and the application.

At Layer 7, VINES offers file-service and print-service applications, as well as StreetTalk, which provides a globally consistent name service for an entire internetwork.

VINES also provides an integrated applications-development environment under several operating systems, including DOS and UNIX. This development environment enables third parties to develop both clients and services that run in the VINES environment.

Summary

This may be the last book that talks about VINES as a protocol. The user community has almost completely disappeared, the server OS and VINES software are not sold anymore, and migration to TCP/IP is no longer provided.

For More Information

http://products.banyan.com/

INDEX

Numerics

A

G

O

P

Q

S